A First Course in Database Systems

Second Edition

Jeffrey D. Ullman
and
Jennifer Widom

Department of Computer Science
Stanford University

An Alan R. Apt Book

Prentice Hall

Prentice Hall
Upper Saddle River, New Jersey 07458

Library of Congress Cataloging-in-Publication Data

Ullman, Jeffrey D.
    A first course in database systems / Jeffrey D.
    Ullman and Jennifer Widom—2nd Edition
    p.cm.
    Includes bibliographical references and index.
    ISBN 0-13-035300-0
    1. Database management. I. Widom, Jennifer.
    II. Title.
    CIP Data available.

Vice President and Editorial Director, ECS: *Marcia J. Horton*
Publisher: *Alan R. Apt*
Associate Editor: *Toni Holm*
Editorial Assistant: *Patrick Lindner*
Vice President and Director of Production and Manufacturing, ESM: *David W. Riccardi*
Executive Managing Editor: *Vince O'Brien*
Managing Editor: *David A. George*
Production Editor: *Irwin Zucker*
Director of Creative Services: *Paul Belfanti*
Creative Director: *Carole Anson*
Art Director: *Heather Scott*
Cover Art and Design: *Tamara L. Newnam*
Manufacturing Manager: *Trudy Pisciotti*
Manufacturing Buyer: *Lisa McDowell*
Senior Marketing Manager: *Jennie Burger*
Marketing Assistant: *Barrie Reinhold*

 © 2002, 1997 by Prentice Hall
Prentice-Hall, Inc.
Upper Saddle River, New Jersey 07458

The author and publisher of this book have used their best efforts in preparing this book. These efforts include the development, research, and testing of the theories and programs to determine their effectiveness. The author and publisher make no warranty of any kind, expressed or implied, with regard to these programs or the documentation contained in this book. The author and publisher shall not be liable in any event for incidental or consequential damages in connection with, or arising out of, the furnishing, performance, or use of these programs.

Printed in the United States of America

10 9 8 7 6 5 4 3 2 1

ISBN 0-13-035300-0

Pearson Education Ltd., *London*
Pearson Education Australia Pty. Ltd., *Sydney*
Pearson Education Singapore, Pte. Ltd.
Pearson Education North Asia Ltd., *Hong Kong*
Pearson Education Canada, Inc., *Toronto*
Pearson Educacíon de Mexico, S.A. de C.V.
Pearson Education—Japan, *Tokyo*
Pearson Education Malaysia, Pte. Ltd.

Preface

At Stanford, we are on the quarter system, and as a result, our introductory database instruction is divided into two courses. The first, CS145, is designed for students who will use database systems but not necessarily take a job implementing a DBMS. It is a prerequisite for CS245, which is the introduction to DBMS implementation. Students wishing to go further in the database field then take CS345 (theory), CS346 (DBMS implementation project), and CS347 (transaction processing and distributed databases).

Starting in 1997, we published a pair of books. *A First Course in Database Systems* was designed for CS145, and *Database System Implementation* was for CS245 and parts of CS346. Because many schools are on the semester system or combine the two kinds of database instruction into one introductory course, we felt that there was a need to produce the two books as a single volume, which we call *Database Systems: The Complete Book*.

However, because many more students need to know how to use database systems than to implement them, we have continued to package the material originally in *A First Course in Database Systems* as the present book, giving it the new material on modeling and programming in the first ten chapters of *Database Systems: The Complete Book*. This new material includes object-relational data, SQL/PSM (stored programs), SQL/CLI (the emerging standard for the C/SQL interface), and JDBC (the same for Java/SQL). At the same time, we have reorganized the material, separating the treatment of object-oriented models from coverage of the entity-relationship model, and separating the discussion of logical queries from that of relational algebra. The latter has been expanded to include operators not in the traditional relational algebra but necessary to reflect the semantics of SQL.

- Warning: because this book is the first part of a larger book, it contains certain cross-references to chapters not present in this volume. If you are uninterested in DBMS implementation, the lack of the referenced sections will not impede your understanding of the modeling and programming issues considered here. However, if you are considering buying this book, and anticipate a later study of implementation, you should consider buying *Database Systems: The Complete Book* instead.

Use of the Book

There is adequate material in this volume for a one-semester course on database modeling and programming. For a one-quarter course, you will probably have to omit some of the topics. We regard Chapters 2–7 as the core of the course. The remaining three chapters contain material from which it is safe to select at will, although we believe that every student should get some exposure to the issues of embedding SQL in standard host languages from one of the sections in Chapter 8.

If, as we do in CS145, you give students a substantial database-application design and implementation project, then you may have to reorder the material somewhat, so that SQL instruction occurs earlier in the book. You may wish to defer material such as dependencies, although students need normalization for design.

Prerequisites

We have used the book at the "mezzanine" level, in a course taken both by undergraduates and beginning graduate students. The formal prerequisites for the course are Sophomore-level treatments of: (1) Data structures, algorithms, and discrete math, and (2) Software systems, software engineering, and programming languages. Of this material, it is important that students have at least a rudimentary understanding of such topics as: algebraic expressions and laws, logic, basic data structures, object-oriented programming concepts, and programming environments. However, we believe that adequate background is acquired by the Junior year of a typical computer science program.

Exercises

The book contains extensive exercises, with some for almost every section. We indicate harder exercises or parts of exercises with an exclamation point. The hardest exercises have a double exclamation point.

Some of the exercises or parts are marked with a star. For these exercises, we shall endeavor to maintain solutions accessible through the book's web page. These solutions are publicly available and should be used for self-testing. Note that in a few cases, one exercise B asks for modification or adaptation of your solution to another exercise A. If certain parts of A have solutions, then you should expect the corresponding parts of B to have solutions as well.

Support on the World Wide Web

The book's home page is

```
http://www-db.stanford.edu/~ullman/fcdb.html
```

There are solutions to starred exercises, errata as we learn of them, and backup materials. We are making available the notes for each offering of CS145 as we teach it, including homeworks, projects and exams.

Acknowledgements

A large number of people have helped us, either with the initial vetting of the text for this book and its predecessors, or by contacting us with errata in the books and/or other Web-based materials. It is our pleasure to acknowledge them all here.

Marc Abromowitz, Joseph H. Adamski, Brad Adelberg, Gleb Ashimov, Donald Aingworth, Jonathan Becker, Margaret Benitez, Larry Bonham, Phillip Bonnet, David Brokaw, Ed Burns, Karen Butler, Christopher Chan, Sudarshan Chawathe, Per Christensen, Ed Chang, Surajit Chaudhuri, Ken Chen, Rada Chirkova, Nitin Chopra, Bobbie Cochrane, Arturo Crespo, Linda DeMichiel, Tom Dienstbier, Pearl D'Souza, Oliver Duschka.

Also Xavier Faz, Greg Fichtenholtz, Bart Fisher, Jarl Friis, John Fry, Chiping Fu, Tracy Fujieda, Manish Godara, Meredith Goldsmith, Luis Gravano, Gerard Guillemette, Rafael Hernandez, Antti Hjelt, Ben Holtzman, Steve Huntsberry, Leonard Jacobson, Thulasiraman Jeyaraman, Dwight Joe, Seth Katz, Yeong-Ping Koh, Gyorgy Kovacs, Phillip Koza, Brian Kulman, Sang Ho Lee, Olivier Lobry, Lu Chao-Jun, Arun Marathe, Le-Wei Mo, Fabian Modoux, Peter Mork, Mark Mortensen.

Also Ramprakash Narayanaswami, Hankyung Na, Marie Nilsson, Torbjorn Norbye, Chang-Min Oh, Mehul Patel, Bert Porter, Limbek Reka, Prahash Ramanan, Ken Ross, Tim Roughgarten, Mema Roussopoulos, Richard Scherl, Catherine Tornabene, Anders Uhl, Jonathan Ullman, Mayank Upadhyay, Vassilis Vassalos, Qiang Wang, Kristian Widjaja, Janet Wu, Sundar Yamunachari, Takeshi Yokukawa, Min-Sig Yun, Torben Zahle, Sandy Zhang. The remaining errors are ours, of course.

J. D. U.
J. W.
Stanford, CA
July, 2001

Table of Contents

Chapter 1

The Worlds of Database Systems

Databases today are essential to every business. They are used to maintain internal records, to present data to customers and clients on the World-Wide-Web, and to support many other commercial processes. Databases are likewise found at the core of many scientific investigations. They represent the data gathered by astronomers, by investigators of the human genome, and by biochemists exploring the medicinal properties of proteins, along with many other scientists.

The power of databases comes from a body of knowledge and technology that has developed over several decades and is embodied in specialized software called a *database management system*, or *DBMS*, or more colloquially a "database system." A DBMS is a powerful tool for creating and managing large amounts of data efficiently and allowing it to persist over long periods of time, safely. These systems are among the most complex types of software available. The capabilities that a DBMS provides the user are:

1. *Persistent storage.* Like a file system, a DBMS supports the storage of very large amounts of data that exists independently of any processes that are using the data. However, the DBMS goes far beyond the file system in providing flexibility, such as data structures that support efficient access to very large amounts of data.

2. *Programming interface.* A DBMS allows the user or an application program to access and modify data through a powerful query language. Again, the advantage of a DBMS over a file system is the flexibility to manipulate stored data in much more complex ways than the reading and writing of files.

3. *Transaction management.* A DBMS supports concurrent access to data, i.e., simultaneous access by many distinct processes (called "transac-

tions") at once. To avoid some of the undersirable consequences of simultaneous access, the DBMS supports *isolation*, the appearance that
transactions execute one-at-a-time, and *atomicity*, the requirement that
transactions execute either completely or not at all. A DBMS also supports *durability*, the ability to recover from failures or errors of many
types.

1.1 The Evolution of Database Systems

What is a database? In essence a database is nothing more than a collection of
information that exists over a long period of time, often many years. In common
parlance, the term *database* refers to a collection of data that is managed by a
DBMS. The DBMS is expected to:

1. Allow users to create new databases and specify their *schema* (logical
   structure of the data), using a specialized language called a *data-definition
   language*.

2. Give users the ability to *query* the data (a "query" is database lingo for
   a question about the data) and modify the data, using an appropriate
   language, often called a *query language* or *data-manipulation language*.

3. Support the storage of very large amounts of data — many gigabytes or
   more — over a long period of time, keeping it secure from accident or
   unauthorized use and allowing efficient access to the data for queries and
   database modifications.

4. Control access to data from many users at once, without allowing the
   actions of one user to affect other users and without allowing simultaneous
   accesses to corrupt the data accidentally.

1.1.1 Early Database Management Systems

The first commercial database management systems appeared in the late 1960's.
These systems evolved from file systems, which provide some of item (3) above;
file systems store data over a long period of time, and they allow the storage of
large amounts of data. However, file systems do not generally guarantee that
data cannot be lost if it is not backed up, and they don't support efficient access
to data items whose location in a particular file is not known.

Further, file systems do not directly support item (2), a query language for
the data in files. Their support for (1) — a schema for the data — is limited to
the creation of directory structures for files. Finally, file systems do not satisfy
(4). When they allow concurrent access to files by several users or processes,
a file system generally will not prevent situations such as two users modifying
the same file at about the same time, so the changes made by one user fail to
appear in the file.

The first important applications of DBMS's were ones where data was composed of many small items, and many queries or modifications were made. Here are some of these applications.

Airline Reservations Systems

In this type of system, the items of data include:

1. Reservations by a single customer on a single flight, including such information as assigned seat or meal preference.

2. Information about flights — the airports they fly from and to, their departure and arrival times, or the aircraft flown, for example.

3. Information about ticket prices, requirements, and availability.

Typical queries ask for flights leaving around a certain time from one given city to another, what seats are available, and at what prices. Typical data modifications include the booking of a flight for a customer, assigning a seat, or indicating a meal preference. Many agents will be accessing parts of the data at any given time. The DBMS must allow such concurrent accesses, prevent problems such as two agents assigning the same seat simultaneously, and protect against loss of records if the system suddenly fails.

Banking Systems

Data items include names and addresses of customers, accounts, loans, and their balances, and the connection between customers and their accounts and loans, e.g., who has signature authority over which accounts. Queries for account balances are common, but far more common are modifications representing a single payment from, or deposit to, an account.

As with the airline reservation system, we expect that many tellers and customers (through ATM machines or the Web) will be querying and modifying the bank's data at once. It is vital that simultaneous accesses to an account not cause the effect of a transaction to be lost. Failures cannot be tolerated. For example, once the money has been ejected from an ATM machine, the bank must record the debit, even if the power immediately fails. On the other hand, it is not permissible for the bank to record the debit and then not deliver the money if the power fails. The proper way to handle this operation is far from obvious and can be regarded as one of the significant achievements in DBMS architecture.

Corporate Records

Many early applications concerned corporate records, such as a record of each sale, information about accounts payable and receivable, or information about employees — their names, addresses, salary, benefit options, tax status, and so on. Queries include the printing of reports such as accounts receivable or employees' weekly paychecks. Each sale, purchase, bill, receipt, employee hired, fired, or promoted, and so on, results in a modification to the database.

The early DBMS's, evolving from file systems, encouraged the user to visualize data much as it was stored. These database systems used several different data models for describing the structure of the information in a database, chief among them the "hierarchical" or tree-based model and the graph-based "network" model. The latter was standardized in the late 1960's through a report of CODASYL (Committee on Data Systems and Languages).[1]

A problem with these early models and systems was that they did not support high-level query languages. For example, the CODASYL query language had statements that allowed the user to jump from data element to data element, through a graph of pointers among these elements. There was considerable effort needed to write such programs, even for very simple queries.

1.1.2   Relational Database Systems

Following a famous paper written by Ted Codd in 1970,[2] database systems changed significantly. Codd proposed that database systems should present the user with a view of data organized as tables called *relations*. Behind the scenes, there might be a complex data structure that allowed rapid response to a variety of queries. But, unlike the user of earlier database systems, the user of a relational system would not be concerned with the storage structure. Queries could be expressed in a very high-level language, which greatly increased the efficiency of database programmers.

We shall cover the relational model of database systems throughout most of this book, starting with the basic relational concepts in Chapter 3. SQL ("Structured Query Language"), the most important query language based on the relational model, will be covered starting in Chapter 6. However, a brief introduction to relations will give the reader a hint of the simplicity of the model, and an SQL sample will suggest how the relational model promotes queries written at a very high level, avoiding details of "navigation" through the database.

Example 1.1: Relations are tables. Their columns are headed by *attributes*, which describe the entries in the column. For instance, a relation named `Accounts`, recording bank accounts, their balance, and type might look like:

accountNo	*balance*	*type*
12345	1000.00	savings
67890	2846.92	checking
...	...	...

---

[1] *CODASYL Data Base Task Group April 1971 Report*, ACM, New York.

[2] Codd, E. F., "A relational model for large shared data banks," *Comm. ACM*, **13**:6, pp. 377–387.

Heading the columns are the three attributes: `accountNo`, `balance`, and `type`. Below the attributes are the rows, or *tuples*. Here we show two tuples of the relation explicitly, and the dots below them suggest that there would be many more tuples, one for each account at the bank. The first tuple says that account number 12345 has a balance of one thousand dollars, and it is a savings account. The second tuple says that account 67890 is a checking account with \$2846.92.

Suppose we wanted to know the balance of account 67890. We could ask this query in SQL as follows:

```
SELECT balance
FROM Accounts
WHERE accountNo = 67890;
```

For another example, we could ask for the savings accounts with negative balances by:

```
SELECT accountNo
FROM Accounts
WHERE type = 'savings' AND balance < 0;
```

We do not expect that these two examples are enough to make the reader an expert SQL programmer, but they should convey the high-level nature of the SQL "select-from-where" statement. In principle, they ask the DBMS to

1. Examine all the tuples of the relation `Accounts` mentioned in the `FROM` clause,

2. Pick out those tuples that satisfy some criterion indicated in the `WHERE` clause, and

3. Produce as an answer certain attributes of those tuples, as indicated in the `SELECT` clause.

In practice, the system must "optimize" the query and find an efficient way to answer the query, even though the relations involved in the query may be very large. □

By 1990, relational database systems were the norm. Yet the database field continues to evolve, and new issues and approaches to the management of data surface regularly. In the balance of this section, we shall consider some of the modern trends in database systems.

1.1.3   Smaller and Smaller Systems

Originally, DBMS's were large, expensive software systems running on large computers. The size was necessary, because to store a gigabyte of data required a large computer system. Today, many gigabytes fit on a single disk, and it is quite feasible to run a DBMS on a personal computer. Thus, database systems based on the relational model have become available for even very small machines, and they are beginning to appear as a common tool for computer applications, much as spreadsheets and word processors did before them.

1.1.4 Bigger and Bigger Systems

On the other hand, a gigabyte isn't much data. Corporate databases often occupy hundreds of gigabytes. Further, as storage becomes cheaper people find new reasons to store greater amounts of data. For example, retail chains often store *terabytes* (a terabyte is 1000 gigabytes, or 10^{12} bytes) of information recording the history of every sale made over a long period of time (for planning inventory; we shall have more to say about this matter in Section 1.1.7).

Further, databases no longer focus on storing simple data items such as integers or short character strings. They can store images, audio, video, and many other kinds of data that take comparatively huge amounts of space. For instance, an hour of video consumes about a gigabyte. Databases storing images from satellites can involve *petabytes* (1000 terabytes, or 10^{15} bytes) of data.

Handling such large databases required several technological advances. For example, databases of modest size are today stored on arrays of disks, which are called *secondary storage devices* (compared to main memory, which is "primary" storage). One could even argue that what distinguishes database systems from other software is, more than anything else, the fact that database systems routinely assume data is too big to fit in main memory and must be located primarily on disk at all times. The following two trends allow database systems to deal with larger amounts of data, faster.

Tertiary Storage

The largest databases today require more than disks. Several kinds of *tertiary storage devices* have been developed. Tertiary devices, perhaps storing a terabyte each, require much more time to access a given item than does a disk. While typical disks can access any item in 10-20 milliseconds, a tertiary device may take several seconds. Tertiary storage devices involve transporting an object, upon which the desired data item is stored, to a reading device. This movement is performed by a robotic conveyance of some sort.

For example, compact disks (CD's) or digital versatile disks (DVD's) may be the storage medium in a tertiary device. An arm mounted on a track goes to a particular disk, picks it up, carries it to a reader, and loads the disk into the reader.

Parallel Computing

The ability to store enormous volumes of data is important, but it would be of little use if we could not access large amounts of that data quickly. Thus, very large databases also require speed enhancers. One important speedup is through index structures, which we shall mention in Section 1.2.2 and cover extensively in Chapter 13. Another way to process more data in a given time is to use parallelism. This parallelism manifests itself in various ways.

For example, since the rate at which data can be read from a given disk is fairly low, a few megabytes per second, we can speed processing if we use many disks and read them in parallel (even if the data originates on tertiary storage, it is "cached" on disks before being accessed by the DBMS). These disks may be part of an organized parallel machine, or they may be components of a distributed system, in which many machines, each responsible for a part of the database, communicate over a high-speed network when needed.

Of course, the ability to move data quickly, like the ability to store large amounts of data, does not by itself guarantee that queries can be answered quickly. We still need to use algorithms that break queries up in ways that allow parallel computers or networks of distributed computers to make effective use of all the resources. Thus, parallel and distributed management of very large databases remains an active area of research and development; we consider some of its important ideas in Section 15.9.

1.1.5 Client-Server and Multi-Tier Architectures

Many varieties of modern software use a *client-server* architecture, in which requests by one process (the *client*) are sent to another process (the *server*) for execution. Database systems are no exception, and it has become increasingly common to divide the work of a DBMS into a server process and one or more client processes.

In the simplest client/server architecture, the entire DBMS is a server, except for the query interfaces that interact with the user and send queries or other commands across to the server. For example, relational systems generally use the SQL language for representing requests from the client to the server. The database server then sends the answer, in the form of a table or relation, back to the client. The relationship between client and server can get more complex, especially when answers are extremely large. We shall have more to say about this matter in Section 1.1.6.

There is also a trend to put more work in the client, since the server will be a bottleneck if there are many simultaneous database users. In the recent proliferation of system architectures in which databases are used to provide dynamically-generated content for Web sites, the two-tier (client-server) architecture gives way to three (or even more) tiers. The DBMS continues to act as a server, but its client is typically an *application server*, which manages connections to the database, transactions, authorization, and other aspects. Application servers in turn have clients such as Web servers, which support end-users or other applications.

1.1.6   Multimedia Data

Another important trend in database systems is the inclusion of multimedia data. By "multimedia" we mean information that represents a signal of some sort. Common forms of multimedia data include video, audio, radar signals, satellite images, and documents or pictures in various encodings. These forms have in common that they are much larger than the earlier forms of data — integers, character strings of fixed length, and so on — and of vastly varying sizes.

The storage of multimedia data has forced DBMS's to expand in several ways. For example, the operations that one performs on multimedia data are not the simple ones suitable for traditional data forms. Thus, while one might search a bank database for accounts that have a negative balance, comparing each balance with the real number 0.0, it is not feasible to search a database of pictures for those that show a face that "looks like" a particular image.

To allow users to create and use complex data operations such as image-processing, DBMS's have had to incorporate the ability of users to introduce functions of their own choosing. Often, the object-oriented approach is used for such extensions, even in relational systems, which are then dubbed "object-relational." We shall take up object-oriented database programming in various places, including Chapters 4 and 9.

The size of multimedia objects also forces the DBMS to modify the storage manager so that objects or tuples of a gigabyte or more can be accommodated. Among the many problems that such large elements present is the delivery of answers to queries. In a conventional, relational database, an answer is a set of tuples. These tuples would be delivered to the client by the database server as a whole.

However, suppose the answer to a query is a video clip a gigabyte long. It is not feasible for the server to deliver the gigabyte to the client as a whole. For one reason it takes too long and will prevent the server from handling other requests. For another, the client may want only a small part of the film clip, but doesn't have a way to ask for exactly what it wants without seeing the initial portion of the clip. For a third reason, even if the client wants the whole clip, perhaps in order to play it on a screen, it is sufficient to deliver the clip at a fixed rate over the course of an hour (the amount of time it takes to play a gigabyte of compressed video). Thus, the storage system of a DBMS supporting multimedia data has to be prepared to deliver answers in an interactive mode, passing a piece of the answer to the client on request or at a fixed rate.

1.1.7   Information Integration

As information becomes ever more essential in our work and play, we find that existing information resources are being used in many new ways. For instance, consider a company that wants to provide on-line catalogs for all its products, so that people can use the World Wide Web to browse its products and place on-line orders. A large company has many divisions. Each division may have built its own database of products independently of other divisions. These divisions may use different DBMS's, different structures for information, perhaps even different terms to mean the same thing or the same term to mean different things.

Example 1.2: Imagine a company with several divisions that manufacture disks. One division's catalog might represent rotation rate in revolutions per second, another in revolutions per minute. Another might have neglected to represent rotation speed at all. A division manufacturing floppy disks might refer to them as "disks," while a division manufacturing hard disks might call *them* "disks" as well. The number of tracks on a disk might be referred to as "tracks" in one division, but "cylinders" in another.   □

Central control is not always the answer. Divisions may have invested large amounts of money in their database long before information integration across divisions was recognized as a problem. A division may have been an independent company, recently acquired. For these or other reasons, these so-called *legacy databases* cannot be replaced easily. Thus, the company must build some structure on top of the legacy databases to present to customers a unified view of products across the company.

One popular approach is the creation of *data warehouses*, where information from many legacy databases is copied, with the appropriate translation, to a central database. As the legacy databases change, the warehouse is updated, but not necessarily instantaneously updated. A common scheme is for the warehouse to be reconstructed each night, when the legacy databases are likely to be less busy.

The legacy databases are thus able to continue serving the purposes for which they were created. New functions, such as providing an on-line catalog service through the Web, are done at the data warehouse. We also see data warehouses serving needs for planning and analysis. For example, company analysts may run queries against the warehouse looking for sales trends, in order to better plan inventory and production. *Data mining*, the search for interesting and unusual patterns in data, has also been enabled by the construction of data warehouses, and there are claims of enhanced sales through exploitation of patterns discovered in this way. These and other issues of information integration are discussed in Chapter 20.

1.2 Overview of a Database Management System

In Fig. 1.1 we see an outline of a complete DBMS. Single boxes represent system components, while double boxes represent in-memory data structures. The solid lines indicate control and data flow, while dashed lines indicate data flow only.

Since the diagram is complicated, we shall consider the details in several stages. First, at the top, we suggest that there are two distinct sources of commands to the DBMS:

1. Conventional users and application programs that ask for data or modify data.

2. A *database administrator*: a person or persons responsible for the structure or *schema* of the database.

1.2.1 Data-Definition Language Commands

The second kind of command is the simpler to process, and we show its trail beginning at the upper right side of Fig. 1.1. For example, the database administrator, or *DBA*, for a university registrar's database might decide that there should be a table or relation with columns for a student, a course the student has taken, and a grade for that student in that course. The DBA might also decide that the only allowable grades are A, B, C, D, and F. This structure and constraint information is all part of the schema of the database. It is shown in Fig. 1.1 as entered by the DBA, who needs special authority to execute schema-altering commands, since these can have profound effects on the database. These schema-altering *DDL commands* ("DDL" stands for "data-definition language") are parsed by a DDL processor and passed to the execution engine, which then goes through the index/file/record manager to alter the *metadata*, that is, the schema information for the database.

1.2.2 Overview of Query Processing

The great majority of interactions with the DBMS follow the path on the left side of Fig. 1.1. A user or an application program initiates some action that does not affect the schema of the database, but may affect the content of the database (if the action is a modification command) or will extract data from the database (if the action is a query). Remember from Section 1.1 that the language in which these commands are expressed is called a data-manipulation language (*DML*) or somewhat colloquially a query language. There are many data-manipulation languages available, but SQL, which was mentioned in Example 1.1, is by far the most commonly used. DML statements are handled by two separate subsystems, as follows.

Answering the query

The query is parsed and optimized by a *query compiler*. The resulting *query plan*, or sequence of actions the DBMS will perform to answer the query, is passed to the *execution engine*. The execution engine issues a sequence of requests for small pieces of data, typically records or tuples of a relation, to a resource manager that knows about *data files* (holding relations), the format

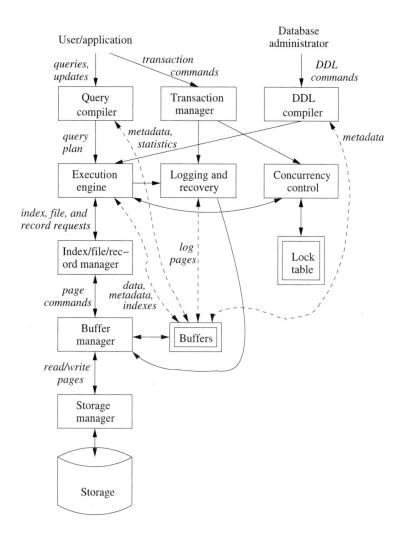

Figure 1.1: Database management system components

and size of records in those files, and *index files*, which help find elements of data files quickly.

The requests for data are translated into pages and these requests are passed to the *buffer manager*. We shall discuss the role of the buffer manager in Section 1.2.3, but briefly, its task is to bring appropriate portions of the data from secondary storage (disk, normally) where it is kept permanently, to main-memory buffers. Normally, the page or "disk block" is the unit of transfer between buffers and disk.

The buffer manager communicates with a storage manager to get data from disk. The storage manager might involve operating-system commands, but more typically, the DBMS issues commands directly to the disk controller.

Transaction processing

Queries and other DML actions are grouped into *transactions*, which are units that must be executed atomically and in isolation from one another. Often each query or modification action is a transaction by itself. In addition, the execution of transactions must be *durable*, meaning that the effect of any completed transaction must be preserved even if the system fails in some way right after completion of the transaction. We divide the transaction processor into two major parts:

1. A *concurrency-control manager*, or *scheduler*, responsible for assuring atomicity and isolation of transactions, and

2. A *logging and recovery manager*, responsible for the durability of transactions.

We shall consider these components further in Section 1.2.4.

1.2.3   Storage and Buffer Management

The data of a database normally resides in secondary storage; in today's computer systems "secondary storage" generally means magnetic disk. However, to perform any useful operation on data, that data must be in main memory. It is the job of the *storage manager* to control the placement of data on disk and its movement between disk and main memory.

In a simple database system, the storage manager might be nothing more than the file system of the underlying operating system. However, for efficiency purposes, DBMS's normally control storage on the disk directly, at least under some circumstances. The *storage manager* keeps track of the location of files on the disk and obtains the block or blocks containing a file on request from the buffer manager. Recall that disks are generally divided into *disk blocks*, which are regions of contiguous storage containing a large number of bytes, perhaps 2^{12} or 2^{14} (about 4000 to 16,000 bytes).

The *buffer manager* is responsible for partitioning the available main memory into *buffers*, which are page-sized regions into which disk blocks can be transferred. Thus, all DBMS components that need information from the disk will interact with the buffers and the buffer manager, either directly or through the execution engine. The kinds of information that various components may need include:

1. *Data*: the contents of the database itself.

2. *Metadata*: the database schema that describes the structure of, and constraints on, the database.

3. *Statistics*: information gathered and stored by the DBMS about data properties such as the sizes of, and values in, various relations or other components of the database.

4. *Indexes*: data structures that support efficient access to the data.

A more complete discussion of the buffer manager and its role appears in Section 15.7.

1.2.4 Transaction Processing

It is normal to group one or more database operations into a *transaction*, which is a unit of work that must be executed atomically and in apparent isolation from other transactions. In addition, a DBMS offers the guarantee of durability: that the work of a completed transaction will never be lost. The *transaction manager* therefore accepts *transaction commands* from an application, which tell the transaction manager when transactions begin and end, as well as information about the expectations of the application (some may not wish to require atomicity, for example). The transaction processor performs the following tasks:

1. *Logging*: In order to assure durability, every change in the database is logged separately on disk. The *log manager* follows one of several policies designed to assure that no matter when a system failure or "crash" occurs, a *recovery manager* will be able to examine the log of changes and restore the database to some consistent state. The log manager initially writes the log in buffers and negotiates with the buffer manager to make sure that buffers are written to disk (where data can survive a crash) at appropriate times.

2. *Concurrency control*: Transactions must appear to execute in isolation. But in most systems, there will in truth be many transactions executing at once. Thus, the scheduler (concurrency-control manager) must assure that the individual actions of multiple transactions are executed in such an order that the net effect is the same as if the transactions had in fact executed in their entirety, one-at-a-time. A typical scheduler does its work by maintaining *locks* on certain pieces of the database. These locks prevent two transactions from accessing the same piece of data in

---

The ACID Properties of Transactions

Properly implemented transactions are commonly said to meet the "ACID test," where:

- "A" stands for "atomicity," the all-or-nothing execution of transactions.

- "I" stands for "isolation," the fact that each transaction must appear to be executed as if no other transaction is executing at the same time.

- "D" stands for "durability," the condition that the effect on the database of a transaction must never be lost, once the transaction has completed.

The remaining letter, "C," stands for "consistency." That is, all databases have consistency constraints, or expectations about relationships among data elements (e.g., account balances may not be negative). Transactions are expected to preserve the consistency of the database. We discuss the expression of consistency constraints in a database schema in Chapter 7, while Section 18.1 begins a discussion of how consistency is maintained by the DBMS.

---

ways that interact badly. Locks are generally stored in a main-memory *lock table*, as suggested by Fig. 1.1. The scheduler affects the execution of queries and other database operations by forbidding the execution engine from accessing locked parts of the database.

3. *Deadlock resolution*: As transactions compete for resources through the locks that the scheduler grants, they can get into a situation where none can proceed because each needs something another transaction has. The transaction manager has the responsibility to intervene and cancel ("rollback" or "abort") one or more transactions to let the others proceed.

1.2.5   The Query Processor

The portion of the DBMS that most affects the performance that the user sees is the *query processor*. In Fig. 1.1 the query processor is represented by two components:

1. The *query compiler*, which translates the query into an internal form called a *query plan*. The latter is a sequence of operations to be performed on the data. Often the operations in a query plan are implementations of

"relational algebra" operations, which are discussed in Section 5.2. The query compiler consists of three major units:

(a) A *query parser*, which builds a tree structure from the textual form of the query.

(b) A *query preprocessor*, which performs semantic checks on the query (e.g., making sure all relations mentioned by the query actually exist), and performing some tree transformations to turn the parse tree into a tree of algebraic operators representing the initial query plan.

(c) A *query optimizer*, which transforms the initial query plan into the best available sequence of operations on the actual data.

The query compiler uses metadata and statistics about the data to decide which sequence of operations is likely to be the fastest. For example, the existence of an *index*, which is a specialized data structure that facilitates access to data, given values for one or more components of that data, can make one plan much faster than another.

2. The *execution engine*, which has the responsibility for executing each of the steps in the chosen query plan. The execution engine interacts with most of the other components of the DBMS, either directly or through the buffers. It must get the data from the database into buffers in order to manipulate that data. It needs to interact with the scheduler to avoid accessing data that is locked, and with the log manager to make sure that all database changes are properly logged.

1.3 Outline of Database-System Studies

Ideas related to database systems can be divided into three broad categories:

1. *Design of databases.* How does one develop a useful database? What kinds of information go into the database? How is the information structured? What assumptions are made about types or values of data items? How do data items connect?

2. *Database programming.* How does one express queries and other operations on the database? How does one use other capabilities of a DBMS, such as transactions or constraints, in an application? How is database programming combined with conventional programming?

3. *Database system implementation.* How does one build a DBMS, including such matters as query processing, transaction processing and organizing storage for efficient access?

How Indexes Are Implemented

The reader may have learned in a course on data structures that a hash table is a very efficient way to build an index. Early DBMS's did use hash tables extensively. Today, the most common data structure is called a *B-tree*; the "B" stands for "balanced." A B-tree is a generalization of a balanced binary search tree. However, while each node of a binary tree has up to two children, the B-tree nodes have a large number of children. Given that B-trees normally reside on disk rather than in main memory, the B-tree is designed so that each node occupies a full disk block. Since typical systems use disk blocks on the order of 2^{12} bytes (4096 bytes), there can be hundreds of pointers to children in a single block of a B-tree. Thus, search of a B-tree rarely involves more than a few levels.

The true cost of disk operations generally is proportional to the number of disk blocks accessed. Thus, searches of a B-tree, which typically examine only a few disk blocks, are much more efficient than would be a binary-tree search, which typically visits nodes found on many different disk blocks. This distinction, between B-trees and binary search trees, is but one of many examples where the most appropriate data structure for data stored on disk is different from the data structures used for algorithms that run in main memory.

1.3.1 Database Design

Chapter 2 begins with a high-level notation for expressing database designs, called the *entity-relationship model*. We introduce in Chapter 3 the relational model, which is the model used by the most widely adopted DBMS's, and which we touched upon briefly in Section 1.1.2. We show how to translate entity-relationship designs into relational designs, or "relational database schemas." Later, in Section 6.6, we show how to render relational database schemas formally in the data-definition portion of the SQL language.

Chapter 3 also introduces the reader to the notion of "dependencies," which are formally stated assumptions about relationships among tuples in a relation. Dependencies allow us to improve relational database designs, through a process known as "normalization" of relations.

In Chapter 4 we look at object-oriented approaches to database design. There, we cover the language ODL, which allows one to describe databases in a high-level, object-oriented fashion. We also look at ways in which object-oriented design has been combined with relational modeling, to yield the so-called "object-relational" model. Finally, Chapter 4 also introduces "semistructured data" as an especially flexible database model, and we see its modern embodiment in the document language XML.

1.3.2 Database Programming

Chapters 5 through 10 cover database programming. We start in Chapter 5 with an abstract treatment of queries in the relational model, introducing the family of operators on relations that form "relational algebra."

Chapters 6 through 8 are devoted to SQL programming. As we mentioned, SQL is the dominant query language of the day. Chapter 6 introduces basic ideas regarding queries in SQL and the expression of database schemas in SQL. Chapter 7 covers aspects of SQL concerning constraints and triggers on the data.

Chapter 8 covers certain advanced aspects of SQL programming. First, while the simplest model of SQL programming is a stand-alone, generic query interface, in practice most SQL programming is embedded in a larger program that is written in a conventional language, such as C. In Chapter 8 we learn how to connect SQL statements with a surrounding program and to pass data from the database to the program's variables and vice versa. This chapter also covers how one uses SQL features that specify transactions, connect clients to servers, and authorize access to databases by nonowners.

In Chapter 9 we turn our attention to standards for object-oriented database programming. Here, we consider two directions. The first, OQL (Object Query Language), can be seen as an attempt to make C++, or other object-oriented programming languages, compatible with the demands of high-level database programming. The second, which is the object-oriented features recently adopted in the SQL standard, can be viewed as an attempt to make relational databases and SQL compatible with object-oriented programming.

Finally, in Chapter 10, we return to the study of abstract query languages that we began in Chapter 5. Here, we study logic-based languages and see how they have been used to extend the capabilities of modern SQL.

1.3.3 Database System Implementation

The third part of the book concerns how one can implement a DBMS. The subject of database system implementation in turn can be divided roughly into three parts:

1. *Storage management*: how secondary storage is used effectively to hold data and allow it to be accessed quickly.

2. *Query processing*: how queries expressed in a very high-level language such as SQL can be executed efficiently.

3. *Transaction management*: how to support transactions with the ACID properties discussed in Section 1.2.4.

Each of these topics is covered by several chapters of the book.

Storage-Management Overview

Chapter 11 introduces the memory hierarchy. However, since secondary storage, especially disk, is so central to the way a DBMS manages data, we examine in the greatest detail the way data is stored and accessed on disk. The "block model" for disk-based data is introduced; it influences the way almost everything is done in a database system.

Chapter 12 relates the storage of data elements — relations, tuples, attribute-values, and their equivalents in other data models — to the requirements of the block model of data. Then we look at the important data structures that are used for the construction of indexes. Recall that an index is a data structure that supports efficient access to data. Chapter 13 covers the important one-dimensional index structures — indexed-sequential files, B-trees, and hash tables. These indexes are commonly used in a DBMS to support queries in which a value for an attribute is given and the tuples with that value are desired. B-trees also are used for access to a relation sorted by a given attribute. Chapter 14 discusses multidimensional indexes, which are data structures for specialized applications such as geographic databases, where queries typically ask for the contents of some region. These index structures can also support complex SQL queries that limit the values of two or more attributes, and some of these structures are beginning to appear in commercial DBMS's.

Query-Processing Overview

Chapter 15 covers the basics of query execution. We learn a number of algorithms for efficient implementation of the operations of relational algebra. These algorithms are designed to be efficient when data is stored on disk and are in some cases rather different from analogous main-memory algorithms.

In Chapter 16 we consider the architecture of the query compiler and optimizer. We begin with the parsing of queries and their semantic checking. Next, we consider the conversion of queries from SQL to relational algebra and the selection of a *logical query plan*, that is, an algebraic expression that represents the particular operations to be performed on data and the necessary constraints regarding order of operations. Finally, we explore the selection of a *physical query plan*, in which the particular order of operations and the algorithm used to implement each operation have been specified.

Transaction-Processing Overview

In Chapter 17 we see how a DBMS supports durability of transactions. The central idea is that a log of all changes to the database is made. Anything that is in main-memory but not on disk can be lost in a crash (say, if the power supply is interrupted). Therefore we have to be careful to move from buffer to disk, in the proper order, both the database changes themselves and the log of what changes were made. There are several log strategies available, but each limits our freedom of action in some ways.

Then, we take up the matter of concurrency control — assuring atomicity and isolation — in Chapter 18. We view transactions as sequences of operations that read or write database elements. The major topic of the chapter is how to manage locks on database elements: the different types of locks that may be used, and the ways that transactions may be allowed to acquire locks and release their locks on elements. Also studied are a number of ways to assure atomicity and isolation without using locks.

Chapter 19 concludes our study of transaction processing. We consider the interaction between the requirements of logging, as discussed in Chapter 17, and the requirements of concurrency that were discussed in Chapter 18. Handling of deadlocks, another important function of the transaction manager, is covered here as well. The extension of concurrency control to a distributed environment is also considered in Chapter 19. Finally, we introduce the possibility that transactions are "long," taking hours or days rather than milliseconds. A long transaction cannot lock data without causing chaos among other potential users of that data, which forces us to rethink concurrency control for applications that involve long transactions.

1.3.4 Information Integration Overview

Much of the recent evolution of database systems has been toward capabilities that allow different *data sources*, which may be databases and/or information resources that are not managed by a DBMS, to work together in a larger whole. We introduced you to these issues briefly, in Section 1.1.7. Thus, in the final Chapter 20, we study important aspects of information integration. We discuss the principal modes of integration, including translated and integrated copies of sources called a "data warehouse," and virtual "views" of a collection of sources, through what is called a "mediator."

1.4 Summary of Chapter 1

✦ *Database Management Systems*: A DBMS is characterized by the ability to support efficient access to large amounts of data, which persists over time. It is also characterized by support for powerful query languages and for durable transactions that can execute concurrently in a manner that appears atomic and independent of other transactions.

✦ *Comparison With File Systems*: Conventional file systems are inadequate as database systems, because they fail to support efficient search, efficient modifications to small pieces of data, complex queries, controlled buffering of useful data in main memory, or atomic and independent execution of transactions.

✦ *Relational Database Systems*: Today, most database systems are based on the relational model of data, which organizes information into tables. SQL is the language most often used in these systems.

✦ *Secondary and Tertiary Storage*: Large databases are stored on secondary storage devices, usually disks. The largest databases require tertiary storage devices, which are several orders of magnitude more capacious than disks, but also several orders of magnitude slower.

✦ *Client-Server Systems*: Database management systems usually support a client-server architecture, with major database components at the server and the client used to interface with the user.

✦ *Future Systems*: Major trends in database systems include support for very large "multimedia" objects such as videos or images and the integration of information from many separate information sources into a single database.

✦ *Database Languages*: There are languages or language components for defining the structure of data (data-definition languages) and for querying and modification of the data (data-manipulation languages).

✦ *Components of a DBMS*: The major components of a database management system are the storage manager, the query processor, and the transaction manager.

✦ *The Storage Manager*: This component is responsible for storing data, metadata (information about the schema or structure of the data), indexes (data structures to speed the access to data), and logs (records of changes to the database). This material is kept on disk. An important storage-management component is the buffer manager, which keeps portions of the disk contents in main memory.

✦ *The Query Processor*: This component parses queries, optimizes them by selecting a query plan, and executes the plan on the stored data.

✦ *The Transaction Manager*: This component is responsible for logging database changes to support recovery after a system crashes. It also supports concurrent execution of transactions in a way that assures atomicity (a transaction is performed either completely or not at all), and isolation (transactions are executed as if there were no other concurrently executing transactions).

1.5 References for Chapter 1

Today, on-line searchable bibliographies cover essentially all recent papers concerning database systems. Thus, in this book, we shall not try to be exhaustive in our citations, but rather shall mention only the papers of historical importance and major secondary sources or useful surveys. One searchable index of database research papers has been constructed by Michael Ley [5]. Alf-Christian Achilles maintains a searchable directory of many indexes relevant to the database field [1].

While many prototype implementations of database systems contributed to the technology of the field, two of the most widely known are the System R project at IBM Almaden Research Center [3] and the INGRES project at Berkeley [7]. Each was an early relational system and helped establish this type of system as the dominant database technology. Many of the research papers that shaped the database field are found in [6].

The 1998 "Asilomar report" [4] is the most recent in a series of reports on database-system research and directions. It also has references to earlier reports of this type.

You can find more about the theory of database systems than is covered here from [2], [8], and [9].

1. `http://liinwww.ira.uka.de/bibliography/Database` .

2. Abiteboul, S., R. Hull, and V. Vianu, *Foundations of Databases*, Addison-Wesley, Reading, MA, 1995.

3. M. M. Astrahan et al., "System R: a relational approach to database management," *ACM Trans. on Database Systems* **1**:2 (1976), pp. 97–137.

4. P. A. Bernstein et al., "The Asilomar report on database research," `http://s2k-ftp.cs.berkeley.edu:8000/postgres/papers/Asilomar_Final.htm` .

5. `http://www.informatik.uni-trier.de/~ley/db/index.html` . A mirror site is found at `http://www.acm.org/sigmod/dblp/db/index.html` .

6. Stonebraker, M. and J. M. Hellerstein (eds.), *Readings in Database Systems*, Morgan-Kaufmann, San Francisco, 1998.

7. M. Stonebraker, E. Wong, P. Kreps, and G. Held, "The design and implementation of INGRES," *ACM Trans. on Database Systems* **1**:3 (1976), pp. 189–222.

8. Ullman, J. D., *Principles of Database and Knowledge-Base Systems, Volume I*, Computer Science Press, New York, 1988.

9. Ullman, J. D., *Principles of Database and Knowledge-Base Systems, Volume II*, Computer Science Press, New York, 1989.

Chapter 2

The Entity-Relationship Data Model

The process of designing a database begins with an analysis of what information the database must hold and what are the relationships among components of that information. Often, the structure of the database, called the *database schema*, is specified in one of several languages or notations suitable for expressing designs. After due consideration, the design is committed to a form in which it can be input to a DBMS, and the database takes on physical existence.

In this book, we shall use several design notations. We begin in this chapter with a traditional and popular approach called the "entity-relationship" (E/R) model. This model is graphical in nature, with boxes and arrows representing the essential data elements and their connections.

In Chapter 3 we turn our attention to the relational model, where the world is represented by a collection of tables. The relational model is somewhat restricted in the structures it can represent. However, the model is extremely simple and useful, and it is the model on which the major commercial DBMS's depend today. Often, database designers begin by developing a schema using the E/R or an object-based model, then translate the schema to the relational model for implementation.

Other models are covered in Chapter 4. In Section 4.2, we shall introduce ODL (Object Definition Language), the standard for object-oriented databases. Next, we see how object-oriented ideas have affected relational DBMS's, yielding a model often called "object-relational."

Section 4.6 introduces another modeling approach, called "semistructured data." This model has an unusual amount of flexibility in the structures that the data may form. We also discuss, in Section 4.7, the XML standard for modeling data as a hierarchically structured document, using "tags" (like HTML tags) to indicate the role played by text elements. XML is an important embodiment of the semistructured data model.

Figure 2.1 suggests how the E/R model is used in database design. We

Figure 2.1: The database modeling and implementation process

start with ideas about the information we want to model and render them in the E/R model. The abstract E/R design is then converted to a schema in the data-specification language of some DBMS. Most commonly, this DBMS uses the relational model. If so, then by a fairly mechanical process that we shall discuss in Section 3.2, the abstract design is converted to a concrete, relational design, called a "relational database schema."

It is worth noting that, while DBMS's sometimes use a model other than relational or object-relational, there are no DBMS's that use the E/R model directly. The reason is that this model is not a sufficiently good match for the efficient data structures that must underlie the database.

2.1   Elements of the E/R Model

The most common model for abstract representation of the structure of a database is the *entity-relationship model* (or *E/R model*). In the E/R model, the structure of data is represented graphically, as an "entity-relationship diagram," using three principal element types:

1. Entity sets,

2. Attributes, and

3. Relationships.

We shall cover each in turn.

2.1.1   Entity Sets

An *entity* is an abstract object of some sort, and a collection of similar entities forms an *entity set*. There is some similarity between the entity and an "object" in the sense of object-oriented programming. Likewise, an entity set bears some resemblance to a class of objects. However, the E/R model is a static concept, involving the structure of data and not the operations on data. Thus, one would not expect to find methods associated with an entity set as one would with a class.

Example 2.1 : We shall use as a running example a database about movies, their stars, the studios that produce them, and other aspects of movies. Each movie is an entity, and the set of all movies constitutes an entity set. Likewise, the stars are entities, and the set of stars is an entity set. A studio is another

---

E/R Model Variations

In some versions of the E/R model, the type of an attribute can be either:

1. Atomic, as in the version presented here.

2. A "struct," as in C, or tuple with a fixed number of atomic components.

3. A set of values of one type: either atomic or a "struct" type.

For example, the type of an attribute in such a model could be a set of pairs, each pair consisting of an integer and a string.

---

kind of entity, and the set of studios is a third entity set that will appear in our examples. □

2.1.2 Attributes

Entity sets have associated *attributes*, which are properties of the entities in that set. For instance, the entity set *Movies* might be given attributes such as *title* (the name of the movie) or *length*, the number of minutes the movie runs. In our version of the E/R model, we shall assume that attributes are atomic values, such as strings, integers, or reals. There are other variations of this model in which attributes can have some limited structure; see the box on "E/R Model Variations."

2.1.3 Relationships

Relationships are connections among two or more entity sets. For instance, if *Movies* and *Stars* are two entity sets, we could have a relationship *Stars-in* that connects movies and stars. The intent is that a movie entity m is related to a star entity s by the relationship *Stars-in* if s appears in movie m. While binary relationships, those between two entity sets, are by far the most common type of relationship, the E/R model allows relationships to involve any number of entity sets. We shall defer discussion of these multiway relationships until Section 2.1.7.

2.1.4 Entity-Relationship Diagrams

An *E/R diagram* is a graph representing entity sets, attributes, and relationships. Elements of each of these kinds are represented by nodes of the graph, and we use a special shape of node to indicate the kind, as follows:

- Entity sets are represented by rectangles.

- Attributes are represented by ovals.

- Relationships are represented by diamonds.

Edges connect an entity set to its attributes and also connect a relationship to its entity sets.

Example 2.2 : In Fig. 2.2 is an E/R diagram that represents a simple database about movies. The entity sets are *Movies, Stars*, and *Studios*.

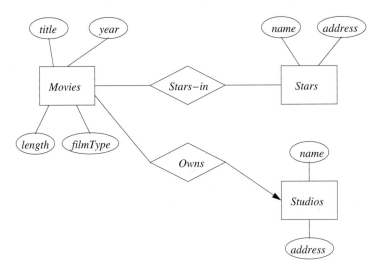

Figure 2.2: An entity-relationship diagram for the movie database

The *Movies* entity set has four attributes: *title, year* (in which the movie was made), *length*, and *filmType* (either "color" or "blackAndWhite"). The other two entity sets *Stars* and *Studios* happen to have the same two attributes: *name* and *address*, each with an obvious meaning. We also see two relationships in the diagram:

1. *Stars-in* is a relationship connecting each movie to the stars of that movie. This relationship consequently also connects stars to the movies in which they appeared.

2. *Owns* connects each movie to the studio that owns the movie. The arrow pointing to entity set *Studios* in Fig. 2.2 indicates that each movie is owned by a unique studio. We shall discuss uniqueness constraints such as this one in Section 2.1.6.

☐

2.1.5 Instances of an E/R Diagram

E/R diagrams are a notation for describing the *schema* of databases, that is, their structure. A database described by an E/R diagram will contain particular data, which we call the database *instance*. Specifically, for each entity set, the database instance will have a particular finite set of entities. Each of these entities has particular values for each attribute. Remember, this data is abstract only; we do not store E/R data directly in a database. Rather, imagining this data exists helps us to think about our design, before we convert to relations and the data takes on physical existence.

The database instance also includes specific choices for the relationships of the diagram. A relationship R that connects n entity sets $E_1, E_2, \ldots, E_n$ has an instance that consists of a finite set of lists $(e_1, e_2, \ldots, e_n)$, where each e_i is chosen from the entities that are in the current instance of entity set E_i. We regard each of these lists of n entities as "connected" by relationship R.

This set of lists is called the *relationship set* for the current instance of R. It is often helpful to visualize a relationship set as a table. The columns of the table are headed by the names of the entity sets involved in the relationship, and each list of connected entities occupies one row of the table.

Example 2.3: An instance of the *Stars-in* relationship could be visualized as a table with pairs such as:

Movies	*Stars*
Basic Instinct	Sharon Stone
Total Recall	Arnold Schwarzenegger
Total Recall	Sharon Stone

The members of the relationship set are the rows of the table. For instance,

(Basic Instinct, Sharon Stone)

is a tuple in the relationship set for the current instance of relationship *Stars-in*. □

2.1.6 Multiplicity of Binary E/R Relationships

In general, a binary relationship can connect any member of one of its entity sets to any number of members of the other entity set. However, it is common for there to be a restriction on the "multiplicity" of a relationship. Suppose R is a relationship connecting entity sets E and F. Then:

- If each member of E can be connected by R to at most one member of F, then we say that R is *many-one* from E to F. Note that in a many-one relationship from E to F, each entity in F can be connected to many members of E. Similarly, if instead a member of F can be connected by R to at most one member of E, then we say R is many-one from F to E (or equivalently, one-many from E to F).

- If R is both many-one from E to F and many-one from F to E, then we say that R is *one-one*. In a one-one relationship an entity of either entity set can be connected to at most one entity of the other set.

- If R is neither many-one from E to F or from F to E, then we say R is *many-many*.

As we mentioned in Example 2.2, arrows can be used to indicate the multiplicity of a relationship in an E/R diagram. If a relationship is many-one from entity set E to entity set F, then we place an arrow entering F. The arrow indicates that each entity in set E is related to at most one entity in set F. Unless there is also an arrow on the edge to E, an entity in F may be related to many entities in E.

Example 2.4: Following this principle, a one-one relationship between entity sets E and F is represented by arrows pointing to both E and F. For instance, Fig. 2.3 shows two entity sets, *Studios* and *Presidents*, and the relationship *Runs* between them (attributes are omitted). We assume that a president can run only one studio and a studio has only one president, so this relationship is one-one, as indicated by the two arrows, one entering each entity set.

Figure 2.3: A one-one relationship

Remember that the arrow means "at most one"; it does not guarantee existence of an entity of the set pointed to. Thus, in Fig. 2.3, we would expect that a "president" is surely associated with some studio; how could they be a "president" otherwise? However, a studio might not have a president at some particular time, so the arrow from *Runs* to *Presidents* truly means "at most one" and not "exactly one." We shall discuss the distinction further in Section 2.3.6. □

2.1.7 Multiway Relationships

The E/R model makes it convenient to define relationships involving more than two entity sets. In practice, ternary (three-way) or higher-degree relationships are rare, but they are occasionally necessary to reflect the true state of affairs. A multiway relationship in an E/R diagram is represented by lines from the relationship diamond to each of the involved entity sets.

Example 2.5: In Fig. 2.4 is a relationship *Contracts* that involves a studio, a star, and a movie. This relationship represents that a studio has contracted with a particular star to act in a particular movie. In general, the value of an E/R relationship can be thought of as a relationship set of tuples whose

---

Implications Among Relationship Types

We should be aware that a many-one relationship is a special case of a many-many relationship, and a one-one relationship is a special case of a many-one relationship. That is, any useful property of many-many relationships applies to many-one relationships as well, and a useful property of many-one relationships holds for one-one relationships too. For example, a data structure for representing many-one relationships will work for one-one relationships, although it might not work for many-many relationships.

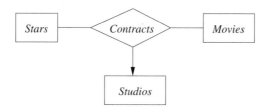

Figure 2.4: A three-way relationship

components are the entities participating in the relationship, as we discussed in Section 2.1.5. Thus, relationship *Contracts* can be described by triples of the form

$$\text{(studio, star, movie)}$$

In multiway relationships, an arrow pointing to an entity set E means that if we select one entity from each of the other entity sets in the relationship, those entities are related to at most one entity in E. (Note that this rule generalizes the notation used for many-one, binary relationships.) In Fig. 2.4 we have an arrow pointing to entity set *Studios*, indicating that for a particular star and movie, there is only one studio with which the star has contracted for that movie. However, there are no arrows pointing to entity sets *Stars* or *Movies*. A studio may contract with several stars for a movie, and a star may contract with one studio for more than one movie. □

2.1.8 Roles in Relationships

It is possible that one entity set appears two or more times in a single relationship. If so, we draw as many lines from the relationship to the entity set as the entity set appears in the relationship. Each line to the entity set represents a different *role* that the entity set plays in the relationship. We therefore label the edges between the entity set and relationship by names, which we call "roles."

Limits on Arrow Notation in Multiway Relationships

There are not enough choices of arrow or no-arrow on the lines attached to a relationship with three or more participants. Thus, we cannot describe every possible situation with arrows. For instance, in Fig. 2.4, the studio is really a function of the movie alone, not the star and movie jointly, since only one studio produces a movie. However, our notation does not distinguish this situation from the case of a three-way relationship where the entity set pointed to by the arrow is truly a function of both other entity sets. In Section 3.4 we shall take up a formal notation — functional dependencies — that has the capability to describe all possibilities regarding how one entity set can be determined uniquely by others.

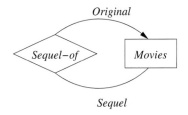

Figure 2.5: A relationship with roles

Example 2.6: In Fig. 2.5 is a relationship *Sequel-of* between the entity set *Movies* and itself. Each relationship is between two movies, one of which is the sequel of the other. To differentiate the two movies in a relationship, one line is labeled by the role *Original* and one by the role *Sequel*, indicating the original movie and its sequel, respectively. We assume that a movie may have many sequels, but for each sequel there is only one original movie. Thus, the relationship is many-one from *Sequel* movies to *Original* movies, as indicated by the arrow in the E/R diagram of Fig. 2.5. □

Example 2.7: As a final example that includes both a multiway relationship and an entity set with multiple roles, in Fig. 2.6 is a more complex version of the *Contracts* relationship introduced earlier in Example 2.5. Now, relationship *Contracts* involves two studios, a star, and a movie. The intent is that one studio, having a certain star under contract (in general, not for a particular movie), may further contract with a second studio to allow that star to act in a particular movie. Thus, the relationship is described by 4-tuples of the form

$$(studio1, studio2, star, movie),$$

meaning that studio2 contracts with studio1 for the use of studio1's star by studio2 for the movie.

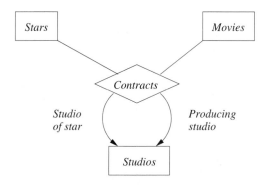

Figure 2.6: A four-way relationship

We see in Fig. 2.6 arrows pointing to *Studios* in both of its roles, as "owner" of the star and as producer of the movie. However, there are not arrows pointing to *Stars* or *Movies*. The rationale is as follows. Given a star, a movie, and a studio producing the movie, there can be only one studio that "owns" the star. (We assume a star is under contract to exactly one studio.) Similarly, only one studio produces a given movie, so given a star, a movie, and the star's studio, we can determine a unique producing studio. Note that in both cases we actually needed only one of the other entities to determine the unique entity—for example, we need only know the movie to determine the unique producing studio—but this fact does not change the multiplicity specification for the multiway relationship.

There are no arrows pointing to *Stars* or *Movies*. Given a star, the star's studio, and a producing studio, there could be several different contracts allowing the star to act in several movies. Thus, the other three components in a relationship 4-tuple do not necessarily determine a unique movie. Similarly, a producing studio might contract with some other studio to use more than one of their stars in one movie. Thus, a star is not determined by the three other components of the relationship. □

2.1.9 Attributes on Relationships

Sometimes it is convenient, or even essential, to associate attributes with a relationship, rather than with any one of the entity sets that the relationship connects. For example, consider the relationship of Fig. 2.4, which represents contracts between a star and studio for a movie.[1] We might wish to record the salary associated with this contract. However, we cannot associate it with the star; a star might get different salaries for different movies. Similarly, it does not make sense to associate the salary with a studio (they may pay different

---

[1] Here, we have reverted to the earlier notion of three-way contracts in Example 2.5, not the four-way relationship of Example 2.7.

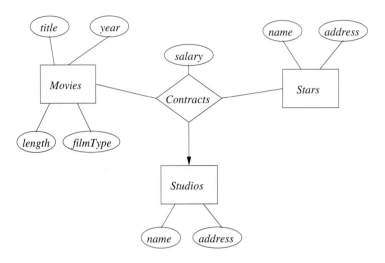

Figure 2.7: A relationship with an attribute

salaries to different stars) or with a movie (different stars in a movie may receive different salaries).

However, it is appropriate to associate a salary with the

$$(\text{star, movie, studio})$$

triple in the relationship set for the *Contracts* relationship. In Fig. 2.7 we see Fig. 2.4 fleshed out with attributes. The relationship has attribute *salary*, while the entity sets have the same attributes that we showed for them in Fig. 2.2.

It is never necessary to place attributes on relationships. We can instead invent a new entity set, whose entities have the attributes ascribed to the relationship. If we then include this entity set in the relationship, we can omit the attributes on the relationship itself. However, attributes on a relationship are a useful convention, which we shall continue to use where appropriate.

Example 2.8: Let us revise the E/R diagram of Fig. 2.7, which has the salary attribute on the *Contracts* relationship. Instead, we create an entity set *Salaries*, with attribute *salary*. *Salaries* becomes the fourth entity set of relationship *Contracts*. The whole diagram is shown in Fig. 2.8.   □

2.1.10   Converting Multiway Relationships to Binary

There are some data models, such as ODL (Object Definition Language), which we introduce in Section 4.2, that limit relationships to be binary. Thus, while the E/R model does not require binary relationships, it is useful to observe that any relationship connecting more than two entity sets can be converted to a collection of binary, many-one relationships. We can introduce a new entity set

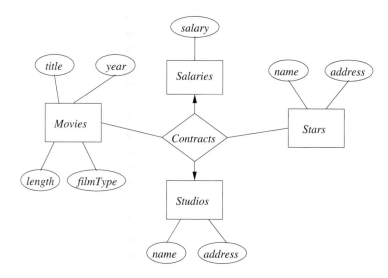

Figure 2.8: Moving the attribute to an entity set

whose entities we may think of as tuples of the relationship set for the multiway relationship. We call this entity set a *connecting* entity set. We then introduce many-one relationships from the connecting entity set to each of the entity sets that provide components of tuples in the original, multiway relationship. If an entity set plays more than one role, then it is the target of one relationship for each role.

Example 2.9: The four-way *Contracts* relationship in Fig. 2.6 can be replaced by an entity set that we may also call *Contracts*. As seen in Fig. 2.9, it participates in four relationships. If the relationship set for the relationship *Contracts* has a 4-tuple

(studio1, studio2, star, movie)

then the entity set *Contracts* has an entity *e*. This entity is linked by relationship *Star-of* to the entity *star* in entity set *Stars*. It is linked by relationship *Movie-of* to the entity *movie* in *Movies*. It is linked to entities *studio1* and *studio2* of *Studios* by relationships *Studio-of-star* and *Producing-studio*, respectively.

Note that we have assumed there are no attributes of entity set *Contracts*, although the other entity sets in Fig. 2.9 have unseen attributes. However, it is possible to add attributes, such as the date of signing, to entity set *Contracts*. □

2.1.11   Subclasses in the E/R Model

Often, an entity set contains certain entities that have special properties not associated with all members of the set. If so, we find it useful to define certain

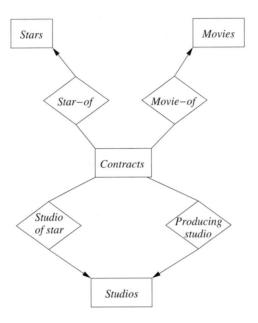

Figure 2.9: Replacing a multiway relationship by an entity set and binary relationships

special-case entity sets, or *subclasses*, each with its own special attributes and/or relationships. We connect an entity set to its subclasses using a relationship called *isa* (i.e., "an *A* is a *B*" expresses an "isa" relationship from entity set *A* to entity set *B*).

An isa relationship is a special kind of relationship, and to emphasize that it is unlike other relationships, we use for it a special notation. Each isa relationship is represented by a triangle. One side of the triangle is attached to the subclass, and the opposite point is connected to the superclass. Every isa relationship is one-one, although we shall not draw the two arrows that are associated with other one-one relationships.

Example 2.10 : Among the kinds of movies we might store in our example database are cartoons, murder mysteries, adventures, comedies, and many other special types of movies. For each of these movie types, we could define a subclass of the entity set *Movies*. For instance, let us postulate two subclasses: *Cartoons* and *Murder-Mysteries*. A cartoon has, in addition to the attributes and relationships of *Movies* an additional relationship called *Voices* that gives us a set of stars who speak, but do not appear in the movie. Movies that are not cartoons do not have such stars. Murder-mysteries have an additional attribute *weapon*. The connections among the three entity sets *Movies*, *Cartoons*, and *Murder-Mysteries* is shown in Fig. 2.10.   □

While, in principle, a collection of entity sets connected by *isa* relationships

---

Parallel Relationships Can Be Different

Figure 2.9 illustrates a subtle point about relationships. There are two different relationships, *Studio-of-Star* and *Producing-Studio*, that each connect entity sets *Contracts* and *Studios*. We should not presume that these relationships therefore have the same relationship sets. In fact, in this case, it is unlikely that both relationships would ever relate the same contract to the same studios, since a studio would then be contracting with itself.

More generally, there is nothing wrong with an E/R diagram having several relationships that connect the same entity sets. In the database, the instances of these relationships will normally be different, reflecting the different meanings of the relationships. In fact, if the relationship sets for two relationships are expected to be the same, then they are really the same relationship and should not be given distinct names.

---

could have any structure, we shall limit isa-structures to trees, in which there is one *root* entity set (e.g., *Movies* in Fig. 2.10) that is the most general, with progressively more specialized entity sets extending below the root in a tree.

Suppose we have a tree of entity sets, connected by *isa* relationships. A single entity consists of *components* from one or more of these entity sets, as long as those components are in a subtree including the root. That is, if an entity e has a component c in entity set E, and the parent of E in the tree is F, then entity e also has a component d in F. Further, c and d must be paired in the relationship set for the *isa* relationship from E to F. The entity e has whatever attributes any of its components has, and it participates in whatever relationships any of its components participate in.

Example 2.11 : The typical movie, being neither a cartoon nor a murder-mystery, will have a component only in the root entity set *Movies* in Fig. 2.10. These entities have only the four attributes of *Movies* (and the two relationships of *Movies* — *Stars-in* and *Owns* — that are not shown in Fig. 2.10).

A cartoon that is not a murder-mystery will have two components, one in *Movies* and one in *Cartoons*. Its entity will therefore have not only the four attributes of *Movies*, but the relationship *Voices*. Likewise, a murder-mystery will have two components for its entity, one in *Movies* and one in *Murder-Mysteries* and thus will have five attributes, including *weapon*.

Finally, a movie like *Roger Rabbit*, which is both a cartoon and a murder-mystery, will have components in all three of the entity sets *Movies*, *Cartoons*, and *Murder-Mysteries*. The three components are connected into one entity by the *isa* relationships. Together, these components give the *Roger Rabbit* entity all four attributes of *Movies* plus the attribute *weapon* of entity set *Murder-Mysteries* and the relationship *Voices* of entity set *Cartoons*. □

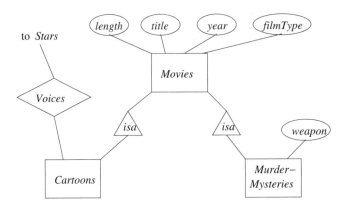

Figure 2.10: Isa relationships in an E/R diagram

2.1.12   Exercises for Section 2.1

* **Exercise 2.1.1:** Let us design a database for a bank, including information about customers and their accounts. Information about a customer includes their name, address, phone, and Social Security number. Accounts have numbers, types (e.g., savings, checking) and balances. We also need to record the customer(s) who own an account. Draw the E/R diagram for this database. Be sure to include arrows where appropriate, to indicate the multiplicity of a relationship.

Exercise 2.1.2: Modify your solution to Exercise 2.1.1 as follows:

a) Change your diagram so an account can have only one customer.

b) Further change your diagram so a customer can have only one account.

! c) Change your original diagram of Exercise 2.1.1 so that a customer can have a set of addresses (which are street-city-state triples) and a set of phones. Remember that we do not allow attributes to have nonatomic types, such as sets, in the E/R model.

! d) Further modify your diagram so that customers can have a set of addresses, and at each address there is a set of phones.

Exercise 2.1.3: Give an E/R diagram for a database recording information about teams, players, and their fans, including:

1. For each team, its name, its players, its team captain (one of its players), and the colors of its uniform.

2. For each player, his/her name.

3. For each fan, his/her name, favorite teams, favorite players, and favorite color.

Subclasses in Object-Oriented Systems

There is a significant resemblance between "isa" in the E/R model and subclasses in object-oriented languages. In a sense, "isa" relates a subclass to its superclass. However, there is also a fundamental difference between the conventional E/R view and the object-oriented approach: entities are allowed to have representatives in a tree of entity sets, while objects are assumed to exist in exactly one class or subclass.

The difference becomes apparent when we consider how the movie *Roger Rabbit* was handled in Example 2.11. In an object-oriented approach, we would need for this movie a fourth entity set, "cartoon-murder-mystery," which inherited all the attributes and relationships of *Movies*, *Cartoons*, and *Murder-Mysteries*. However, in the E/R model, the effect of this fourth subclass is obtained by putting components of the movie *Roger Rabbit* in both the *Cartoons* and *Murder-Mysteries* entity sets.

Remember that a set of colors is not a suitable attribute type for teams. How can you get around this restriction?

Exercise 2.1.4: Suppose we wish to add to the schema of Exercise 2.1.3 a relationship *Led-by* among two players and a team. The intention is that this relationship set consists of triples

$$(player1, player2, team)$$

such that player 1 played on the team at a time when some other player 2 was the team captain.

   a) Draw the modification to the E/R diagram.

   b) Replace your ternary relationship with a new entity set and binary relationships.

   ! c) Are your new binary relationships the same as any of the previously existing relationships? Note that we assume the two players are different, i.e., the team captain is not self-led.

Exercise 2.1.5: Modify Exercise 2.1.3 to record for each player the history of teams on which they have played, including the start date and ending date (if they were traded) for each such team.

! **Exercise 2.1.6:** Suppose we wish to keep a genealogy. We shall have one entity set, *Person*. The information we wish to record about persons includes their name (an attribute) and the following relationships: mother, father, and children. Give an E/R diagram involving the *Person* entity set and all the relationships in which it is involved. Include relationships for mother, father, and children. Do not forget to indicate roles when an entity set is used more than once in a relationship.

! Exercise 2.1.7: Modify your "people" database design of Exercise 2.1.6 to include the following special types of people:

1. Females.

2. Males.

3. People who are parents.

You may wish to distinguish certain other kinds of people as well, so relationships connect appropriate subclasses of people.

Exercise 2.1.8: An alternative way to represent the information of Exercise 2.1.6 is to have a ternary relationship *Family* with the intent that a triple in the relationship set for *Family*

(person, mother, father)

is a person, their mother, and their father; all three are in the *People* entity set, of course.

* a) Draw this diagram, placing arrows on edges where appropriate.

   b) Replace the ternary relationship *Family* by an entity set and binary relationships. Again place arrows to indicate the multiplicity of relationships.

Exercise 2.1.9: Design a database suitable for a university registrar. This database should include information about students, departments, professors, courses, which students are enrolled in which courses, which professors are teaching which courses, student grades, TA's for a course (TA's are students), which courses a department offers, and any other information you deem appropriate. Note that this question is more free-form than the questions above, and you need to make some decisions about multiplicities of relationships, appropriate types, and even what information needs to be represented.

! Exercise 2.1.10: Informally, we can say that two E/R diagrams "have the same information" if, given a real-world situation, the instances of these two diagrams that reflect this situation can be computed from one another. Consider the E/R diagram of Fig. 2.6. This four-way relationship can be decomposed into a three-way relationship and a binary relationship by taking advantage of the fact that for each movie, there is a unique studio that produces that movie. Give an E/R diagram without a four-way relationship that has the same information as Fig. 2.6.

2.2 Design Principles

We have yet to learn many of the details of the E/R model, but we have enough to begin study of the crucial issue of what constitutes a good design and what should be avoided. In this section, we offer some useful design principles.

2.2.1 Faithfulness

First and foremost, the design should be faithful to the specifications of the application. That is, entity sets and their attributes should reflect reality. You can't attach an attribute *number-of-cylinders* to *Stars*, although that attribute would make sense for an entity set *Automobiles*. Whatever relationships are asserted should make sense given what we know about the part of the real world being modeled.

Example 2.12: If we define a relationship *Stars-in* between *Stars* and *Movies*, it should be a many-many relationship. The reason is that an observation of the real world tells us that stars can appear in more than one movie, and movies can have more than one star. It is incorrect to declare the relationship `Stars-in` to be many-one in either direction or to be one-one. □

Example 2.13: On the other hand, sometimes it is less obvious what the real world requires us to do in our E/R model. Consider, for instance, entity sets *Courses* and *Instructors*, with a relationship *Teaches* between them. Is *Teaches* many-one from *Courses* to *Instructors*? The answer lies in the policy and intentions of the organization creating the database. It is possible that the school has a policy that there can be only one instructor for any course. Even if several instructors may "team-teach" a course, the school may require that exactly one of them be listed in the database as the instructor responsible for the course. In either of these cases, we would make *Teaches* a many-one relationship from *Courses* to *Instructors*.

Alternatively, the school may use teams of instructors regularly and wish its database to allow several instructors to be associated with a course. Or, the intent of the *Teaches* relationship may not be to reflect the current teacher of a course, but rather those who have ever taught the course, or those who are capable of teaching the course; we cannot tell simply from the name of the relationship. In either of these cases, it would be proper to make *Teaches* be many-many. □

2.2.2 Avoiding Redundancy

We should be careful to say everything once only. For instance, we have used a relationship *Owns* between movies and studios. We might also choose to have an attribute *studioName* of entity set *Movies*. While there is nothing illegal about doing so, it is dangerous for several reasons.

1. The two representations of the same owning-studio fact take more space, when the data is stored, than either representation alone.

2. If a movie were sold, we might change the owning studio to which it is related by relationship *Owns* but forget to change the value of its *studioName* attribute, or vice versa. Of course one could argue that one should never do such careless things, but in practice, errors are frequent, and by trying to say the same thing in two different ways, we are inviting trouble.

These problems will be described more formally in Section 3.6, and we shall also learn there some tools for redesigning database schemas so the redundancy and its attendant problems go away.

2.2.3   Simplicity Counts

Avoid introducing more elements into your design than is absolutely necessary.

Example 2.14 : Suppose that instead of a relationship between *Movies* and *Studios* we postulated the existence of "movie-holdings," the ownership of a single movie. We might then create another entity set *Holdings*. A one-one relationship *Represents* could be established between each movie and the unique holding that represents the movie. A many-one relationship from *Holdings* to *Studios* completes the picture shown in Fig. 2.11.

Figure 2.11: A poor design with an unnecessary entity set

Technically, the structure of Fig. 2.11 truly represents the real world, since it is possible to go from a movie to its unique owning studio via *Holdings*. However, *Holdings* serves no useful purpose, and we are better off without it. It makes programs that use the movie-studio relationship more complicated, wastes space, and encourages errors.   □

2.2.4   Choosing the Right Relationships

Entity sets can be connected in various ways by relationships. However, adding to our design every possible relationship is not often a good idea. First, it can lead to redundancy, where the connected pairs or sets of entities for one relationship can be deduced from one or more other relationships. Second, the resulting database could require much more space to store redundant elements, and modifying the database could become too complex, because one change in the data could require many changes to the stored relationships. The problems are essentially the same as those discussed in Section 2.2.2, although the cause of the problem is different from the problems we discussed there.

We shall illustrate the problem and what to do about it with two examples. In the first example, several relationships could represent the same information; in the second, one relationship could be deduced from several others.

Example 2.15 : Let us review Fig. 2.7, where we connected movies, stars, and studios with a three-way relationship *Contracts*. We omitted from that figure the two binary relationships *Stars-in* and *Owns* from Fig. 2.2. Do we also need these relationships, between *Movies* and *Stars*, and between *Movies* and *Studios*, respectively? The answer is: "we don't know; it depends on our assumptions regarding the three relationships in question."

It might be possible to deduce the relationship *Stars-in* from *Contracts*. If a star can appear in a movie only if there is a contract involving that star, that movie, and the owning studio for the movie, then there truly is no need for relationship *Stars-in*. We could figure out all the star-movie pairs by looking at the star-movie-studio triples in the relationship set for *Contracts* and taking only the star and movie components. However, if a star can work on a movie without there being a contract — or what is more likely, without there being a contract that we know about in our database — then there could be star-movie pairs in *Stars-in* that are not part of star-movie-studio triples in *Contracts*. In that case, we need to retain the *Stars-in* relationship.

A similar observation applies to relationship *Owns*. If for every movie, there is at least one contract involving that movie, its owning studio, and some star for that movie, then we can dispense with *Owns*. However, if there is the possibility that a studio owns a movie, yet has no stars under contract for that movie, or no such contract is known to our database, then we must retain *Owns*.

In summary, we cannot tell you whether a given relationship will be redundant. You must find out from those who wish the database created what to expect. Only then can you make a rational decision about whether or not to include relationships such as *Stars-in* or *Owns*. □

Example 2.16 : Now, consider Fig. 2.2 again. In this diagram, there is no relationship between stars and studios. Yet we can use the two relationships *Stars-in* and *Owns* to build a connection by the process of composing those two relationships. That is, a star is connected to some movies by *Stars-in*, and those movies are connected to studios by *Owns*. Thus, we could say that a star is connected to the studios that own movies in which the star has appeared.

Would it make sense to have a relationship *Works-for*, as suggested in Fig. 2.12, between *Stars* and *Studios* too? Again, we cannot tell without knowing more. First, what would the meaning of this relationship be? If it is to mean "the star appeared in at least one movie of this studio," then probably there is no good reason to include it in the diagram. We could deduce this information from *Stars-in* and *Owns* instead.

However, it is conceivable that we have other information about stars working for studios that is not entailed by the connection through a movie. In that

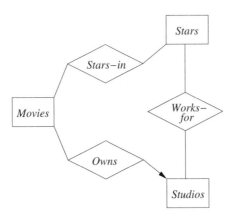

Figure 2.12: Adding a relationship between *Stars* and *Studios*

case, a relationship connecting stars directly to studios might be useful and would not be redundant. Alternatively, we might use a relationship between stars and studios to mean something entirely different. For example, it might represent the fact that the star is under contract to the studio, in a manner unrelated to any movie. As we suggested in Example 2.7, it is possible for a star to be under contract to one studio and yet work on a movie owned by another studio. In this case, the information found in the new *Works-for* relation would be independent of the *Stars-in* and *Owns* relationships, and would surely be nonredundant.   □

2.2.5   Picking the Right Kind of Element

Sometimes we have options regarding the type of design element used to represent a real-world concept. Many of these choices are between using attributes and using entity set/relationship combinations. In general, an attribute is simpler to implement than either an entity set or a relationship. However, making everything an attribute will usually get us into trouble.

Example 2.17 : Let us consider a specific problem. In Fig. 2.2, were we wise to make studios an entity set? Should we instead have made the name and address of the studio be attributes of movies and eliminated the *Studio* entity set? One problem with doing so is that we repeat the address of the studio for each movie. This situation is another instance of redundancy, similar to those seen in Sections 2.2.2 and 2.2.4. In addition to the disadvantages of redundancy discussed there, we also face the risk that, should we not have any movies owned by a given studio, we lose the studio's address.

On the other hand, if we did not record addresses of studios, then there is no harm in making the studio name an attribute of movies. We do not have redundancy due to repeating addresses. The fact that we have to say the name of a studio like `Disney` for each movie owned by Disney is not true redundancy, since we must represent the owner of each movie somehow, and saying the name is a reasonable way to do so. □

We can abstract what we have observed in Example 2.17 to give the conditions under which we prefer to use an attribute instead of an entity set. Suppose E is an entity set. Here are conditions that E must obey, in order for us to replace E by an attribute or attributes of several other entity sets.

1. All relationships in which E is involved must have arrows entering E. That is, E must be the "one" in many-one relationships, or its generalization for the case of multiway relationships.

2. The attributes for E must collectively identify an entity. Typically, there will be only one attribute, in which case this condition is surely met. However, if there are several attributes, then no attribute must depend on the other attributes, the way *address* depends on *name* for *Studios*.

3. No relationship involves E more than once.

If these conditions are met, then we can replace entity set E as follows:

a) If there is a many-one relationship R from some entity set F to E, then remove R and make the attributes of E be attributes of F, suitably renamed if they conflict with attribute names for F. In effect, each F-entity takes, as attributes, the name of the unique, related E-entity,[2] as movie objects could take their studio name as an attribute, should we dispense with studio addresses.

b) If there is a multiway relationship R with an arrow to E, make the attributes of E be attributes of R and delete the arc from R to E. An example of transformation is replacing Fig. 2.8, where we had introduced a new entity set *Salaries*, with a number as its lone attribute, by its original diagram, in Fig. 2.7.

Example 2.18 : Let us consider a point where there is a tradeoff between using a multiway relationship and using a connecting entity set with several binary relationships. We saw a four-way relationship *Contracts* among a star, a movie, and two studios in Fig. 2.6. In Fig. 2.9, we mechanically converted it to an entity set *Contracts*. Does it matter which we choose?

As the problem was stated, either is appropriate. However, should we change the problem just slightly, then we are almost forced to choose a connecting entity set. Let us suppose that contracts involve one star, one movie, but any set of studios. This situation is more complex than the one in Fig. 2.6, where we had two studios playing two roles. In this case, we can have any number of

---

[2]In a situation where an F-entity is not related to any E-entity, the new attributes of F would be given special "null" values to indicate the absence of a related E-entity. A similar arrangement would be used for the new attributes of R in case (b).

studios involved, perhaps one to do production, one for special effects, one for distribution, and so on. Thus, we cannot assign roles for studios.

It appears that a relationship set for the relationship *Contracts* must contain triples of the form

$$\text{(star, movie, set-of-studios)}$$

and the relationship *Contracts* itself involves not only the usual *Stars* and *Movies* entity sets, but a new entity set whose entities are *sets of* studios. While this approach is unpreventable, it seems unnatural to think of sets of studios as basic entities, and we do not recommend it.

A better approach is to think of contracts as an entity set. As in Fig. 2.9, a contract entity connects a star, a movie and a set of studios, but now there must be no limit on the number of studios. Thus, the relationship between contracts and studios is many-many, rather than many-one as it would be if contracts were a true "connecting" entity set. Figure 2.13 sketches the E/R diagram. Note that a contract is associated with a single star and a single movie, but any number of studios.   □

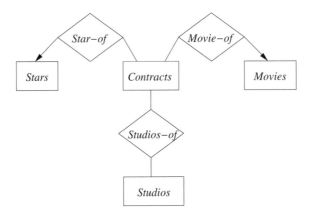

Figure 2.13: Contracts connecting a star, a movie, and a set of studios

2.2.6   Exercises for Section 2.2

* **Exercise 2.2.1 :** In Fig. 2.14 is an E/R diagram for a bank database involving customers and accounts. Since customers may have several accounts, and accounts may be held jointly by several customers, we associate with each customer an "account set," and accounts are members of one or more account sets. Assuming the meaning of the various relationships and attributes are as expected given their names, criticize the design. What design rules are violated? Why? What modifications would you suggest?

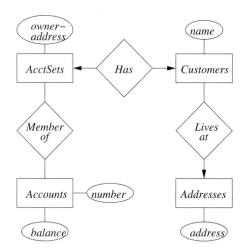

Figure 2.14: A poor design for a bank database

* **Exercise 2.2.2:** Under what circumstances (regarding the unseen attributes of *Studios* and *Presidents* would you recommend combining the two entity sets and relationship in Fig. 2.3 into a single entity set and attributes?

Exercise 2.2.3: Suppose we delete the attribute *address* from *Studios* in Fig. 2.7. Show how we could then replace an entity set by an attribute. Where would that attribute appear?

Exercise 2.2.4: Give choices of attributes for the following entity sets in Fig. 2.13 that will allow the entity set to be replaced by an attribute:

   a) *Stars.*

   b) *Movies.*

 ! c) *Studios.*

!! **Exercise 2.2.5:** In this and following exercises we shall consider two design options in the E/R model for describing births. At a birth, there is one baby (twins would be represented by two births), one mother, any number of nurses, and any number of doctors. Suppose, therefore, that we have entity sets *Babies*, *Mothers*, *Nurses*, and *Doctors*. Suppose we also use a relationship *Births*, which connects these four entity sets, as suggested in Fig. 2.15. Note that a tuple of the relationship set for *Births* has the form

(baby, mother, nurse, doctor)

If there is more than one nurse and/or doctor attending a birth, then there will be several tuples with the same baby and mother, one for each combination of nurse and doctor.

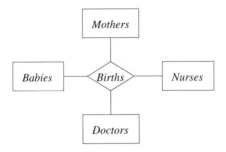

Figure 2.15: Representing births by a multiway relationship

There are certain assumptions that we might wish to incorporate into our design. For each, tell how to add arrows or other elements to the E/R diagram in order to express the assumption.

a) For every baby, there is a unique mother.

b) For every combination of a baby, nurse, and doctor, there is a unique mother.

c) For every combination of a baby and a mother there is a unique doctor.

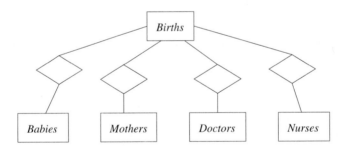

Figure 2.16: Representing births by an entity set

! **Exercise 2.2.6:** Another approach to the problem of Exercise 2.2.5 is to connect the four entity sets *Babies*, *Mothers*, *Nurses*, and *Doctors* by an entity set *Births*, with four relationships, one between *Births* and each of the other entity sets, as suggested in Fig. 2.16. Use arrows (indicating that certain of these relationships are many-one) to represent the following conditions:

a) Every baby is the result of a unique birth, and every birth is of a unique baby.

b) In addition to (a), every baby has a unique mother.

c) In addition to (a) and (b), for every birth there is a unique doctor.

In each case, what design flaws do you see?

!! **Exercise 2.2.7:** Suppose we change our viewpoint to allow a birth to involve more than one baby born to one mother. How would you represent the fact that every baby still has a unique mother using the approaches of Exercises 2.2.5 and 2.2.6?

2.3 The Modeling of Constraints

We have seen so far how to model a slice of the real world using entity sets and relationships. However, there are some other important aspects of the real world that we cannot model with the tools seen so far. This additional information often takes the form of *constraints* on the data that go beyond the structural and type constraints imposed by the definitions of entity sets, attributes, and relationships.

2.3.1 Classification of Constraints

The following is a rough classification of commonly used constraints. We shall not cover all of these constraint types here. Additional material on constraints is found in Section 5.5 in the context of relational algebra and in Chapter 7 in the context of SQL programming.

1. *Keys* are attributes or sets of attributes that uniquely identify an entity within its entity set. No two entities may agree in their values for all of the attributes that constitute a key. It *is* permissible, however, for two entities to agree on some, but not all, of the key attributes.

2. *Single-value constraints* are requirements that the value in a certain context be unique. Keys are a major source of single-value constraints, since they require that each entity in an entity set has unique value(s) for the key attribute(s). However, there are other sources of single-value constraints, such as many-one relationships.

3. *Referential integrity constraints* are requirements that a value referred to by some object actually exists in the database. Referential integrity is analogous to a prohibition against dangling pointers, or other kinds of dangling references, in conventional programs.

4. *Domain constraints* require that the value of an attribute must be drawn from a specific set of values or lie within a specific range.

5. *General constraints* are arbitrary assertions that are required to hold in the database. For example, we might wish to require that no more than ten stars be listed for any one movie. We shall see general constraint-expression languages in Sections 5.5 and 7.4.

There are several ways these constraints are important. They tell us something about the structure of those aspects of the real world that we are modeling. For example, keys allow the user to identify entities without confusion. If we know that attribute *name* is a key for entity set *Studios*, then when we refer to a studio entity by its name we know we are referring to a unique entity. In addition, knowing a unique value exists saves space and time, since storing a single value is easier than storing a set, even when that set has exactly one member.[3] Referential integrity and keys also support certain storage structures that allow faster access to data, as we shall discuss in Chapter 13.

2.3.2   Keys in the E/R Model

A *key* for an entity set E is a set K of one or more attributes such that, given any two distinct entities e_1 and e_2 in E, e_1 and e_2 cannot have identical values for each of the attributes in the key K. If K consists of more than one attribute, then it is possible for e_1 and e_2 to agree in some of these attributes, but never in all attributes. Three useful points to remember are:

- A key can consist of more than one attribute; an illustration appears in Example 2.19.

- There can also be more than one possible key for an entity set, as we shall see in Example 2.20. However, it is customary to pick one key as the "primary key," and to act as if that were the only key.

- When an entity set is involved in an isa-hierarchy, we require that the root entity set have all the attributes needed for a key, and that the key for each entity is found from its component in the root entity set, regardless of how many entity sets in the hierarchy have components for the entity in question.

Example 2.19 : Let us consider the entity set *Movies* from Example 2.1. One might first assume that the attribute *title* by itself is a key. However, there are several titles that have been used for two or even more movies, for example, *King Kong*. Thus, it would be unwise to declare that *title* by itself is a key. If we did so, then we would not be able to include information about both *King Kong* movies in our database.

A better choice would be to take the set of two attributes *title* and *year* as a key. We still run the risk that there are two movies made in the same year with the same title (and thus both could not be stored in our database), but that is unlikely.

For the other two entity sets, *Stars* and *Studios*, introduced in Example 2.1, we must again think carefully about what can serve as a key. For studios, it is reasonable to assume that there would not be two movie studios with the same

---

[3]In analogy, note that in a C program it is simpler to represent an integer than it is to represent a linked list of integers, even when that list contains only one integer.

Constraints Are Part of the Schema

We could look at the database as it exists at a certain time and decide erroneously that an attribute forms a key because no two entities have identical values for this attribute. For example, as we create our movie database we might not enter two movies with the same title for some time. Thus, it might look as if *title* were a key for entity set *Movies*. However, if we decided on the basis of this preliminary evidence that *title* is a key, and we designed a storage structure for our database that assumed *title* is a key, then we might find ourselves unable to enter a second *King Kong* movie into the database.

Thus, key constraints, and constraints in general, are part of the database schema. They are declared by the database designer along with the structural design (e.g., entities and relationships). Once a constraint is declared, insertions or modifications to the database that violate the constraint are disallowed.

Hence, although a particular instance of the database may satisfy certain constraints, the only "true" constraints are those identified by the designer as holding for all instances of the database that correctly model the real-world. These are the constraints that may be assumed by users and by the structures used to store the database.

---

name, so we shall take *name* to be a key for entity set *Studios*. However, it is less clear that stars are uniquely identified by their name. Surely name does not distinguish among people in general. However, since stars have traditionally chosen "stage names" at will, we might hope to find that *name* serves as a key for *Stars* too. If not, we might choose the pair of attributes *name* and *address* as a key, which would be satisfactory unless there were two stars with the same name living at the same address. □

Example 2.20: Our experience in Example 2.19 might lead us to believe that it is difficult to find keys or to be sure that a set of attributes forms a key. In practice the matter is usually much simpler. In the real-world situations commonly modeled by databases, people often go out of their way to create keys for entity sets. For example, companies generally assign employee ID's to all employees, and these ID's are carefully chosen to be unique numbers. One purpose of these ID's is to make sure that in the company database each employee can be distinguished from all others, even if there are several employees with the same name. Thus, the employee-ID attribute can serve as a key for employees in the database.

In US corporations, it is normal for every employee to also have a Social Security number. If the database has an attribute that is the Social Security number, then this attribute can also serve as a key for employees. Note that there is nothing wrong with there being several choices of key for an entity set, as there would be for employees having both employee ID's and Social Security numbers.

The idea of creating an attribute whose purpose is to serve as a key is quite widespread. In addition to employee ID's, we find student ID's to distinguish students in a university. We find drivers' license numbers and automobile registration numbers to distinguish drivers and automobiles, respectively, in the Department of Motor Vehicles. The reader can undoubtedly find more examples of attributes created for the primary purpose of serving as keys. □

2.3.3   Representing Keys in the E/R Model

In our E/R diagram notation, we underline the attributes belonging to a key for an entity set. For example, Fig. 2.17 reproduces our E/R diagram for movies, stars, and studios from Fig. 2.2, but with key attributes underlined. Attribute *name* is the key for *Stars*. Likewise, *Studios* has a key consisting of only its own attribute *name*. These choices are consistent with the discussion in Example 2.19.

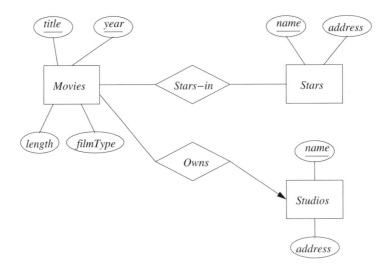

Figure 2.17: E/R diagram; keys are indicated by underlines

The attributes *title* and *year* together form the key for *Movies*, as we discussed in Example 2.19. Note that when several attributes are underlined, as in Fig. 2.17, then they are each members of the key. There is no notation for representing the situation where there are several keys for an entity set; we underline only the primary key. You should also be aware that in some unusual situations, the attributes forming the key for an entity set do not all belong to the entity set itself. We shall defer this matter, called "weak entity sets," until Section 2.4.

2.3.4 Single-Value Constraints

Often, an important property of a database design is that there is at most one value playing a particular role. For example, we assume that a movie entity has a unique title, year, length, and film type, and that a movie is owned by a unique studio.

There are several ways in which single-value constraints are expressed in the E/R model.

1. Each attribute of an entity set has a single value. Sometimes it is permissible for an attribute's value to be missing for some entities, in which case we have to invent a "null value" to serve as the value of that attribute. For example, we might suppose that there are some movies in our database for which the length is not known. We could use a value such as -1 for the length of a movie whose true length is unknown. On the other hand, we would not want the key attributes *title* or *year* to be null for any movie entity. A requirement that a certain attribute not have a null value does not have any special representation in the E/R model. We could place a notation beside the attribute stating this requirement if we wished.

2. A relationship R that is many-one from entity set E to entity set F implies a single-value constraint. That is, for each entity e in E, there is at most one associated entity f in F. More generally, if R is a multiway relationship, then each arrow out of R indicates a single value constraint. Specifically, if there is an arrow from R to entity set E, then there is at most one entity of set E associated with a choice of entities from each of the other related entity sets.

2.3.5 Referential Integrity

While single-value constraints assert that at most one value exists in a given role, a *referential integrity constraint* asserts that exactly one value exists in that role. We could see a constraint that an attribute have a non-null, single value as a kind of referential integrity requirement, but "referential integrity" is more commonly used to refer to relationships among entity sets.

Let us consider the many-one relationship *Owns* from *Movies* to *Studios* in Fig. 2.2. The many-one requirement simply says that no movie can be owned by more than one studio. It does *not* say that a movie must surely be owned by a studio, or that, even if it is owned by some studio, that the studio must be present in the *Studios* entity set, as stored in our database.

A referential integrity constraint on relationship *Owns* would require that for each movie, the owning studio (the entity "referenced" by the relationship for this movie) must exist in our database. There are several ways this constraint could be enforced.

1. We could forbid the deletion of a referenced entity (a studio in our example). That is, we could not delete a studio from the database unless it did not own any movies.

2. We could require that if a referenced entity is deleted, then all entities that reference it are deleted as well. In our example, this approach would require that if we delete a studio, we also delete from the database all movies owned by that studio.

In addition to one of these policies about deletion, we require that when a movie entity is inserted into the database, it is given an existing studio entity to which it is connected by relationship *Owns*. Further, if the value of that relationship changes, then the new value must also be an existing *Studios* entity. Enforcing these policies to assure referential integrity of a relationship is a matter for the implementation of the database, and we shall not discuss the details here.

2.3.6   Referential Integrity in E/R Diagrams

We can extend the arrow notation in E/R diagrams to indicate whether a relationship is expected to support referential integrity in one or more directions. Suppose R is a relationship from entity set E to entity set F. We shall use a rounded arrowhead pointing to F to indicate not only that the relationship is many-one or one-one from E to F, but that the entity of set F related to a given entity of set E is required to exist. The same idea applies when R is a relationship among more than two entity sets.

Example 2.21 : Figure 2.18 shows some appropriate referential integrity constraints among the entity sets *Movies*, *Studios*, and *Presidents*. These entity sets and relationships were first introduced in Figs. 2.2 and 2.3. We see a rounded arrow entering *Studios* from relationship *Owns*. That arrow expresses the referential integrity constraint that every movie must be owned by one studio, and this studio is present in the *Studios* entity set.

Figure 2.18: E/R diagram showing referential integrity constraints

Similarly, we see a rounded arrow entering *Studios* from *Runs*. That arrow expresses the referential integrity constraint that every president runs a studio that exists in the *Studios* entity set.

Note that the arrow to *Presidents* from *Runs* remains a pointed arrow. That choice reflects a reasonable assumption about the relationship between studios and their presidents. If a studio ceases to exist, its president can no longer be called a (studio) president, so we would expect the president of the studio to be deleted from the entity set *Presidents*. Hence there is a rounded arrow to *Studios*. On the other hand, if a president were deleted from the database, the studio would continue to exist. Thus, we place an ordinary, pointed arrow to *Presidents*, indicating that each studio has at most one president, but might have no president at some time. □

2.3.7 Other Kinds of Constraints

As mentioned at the beginning of this section, there are other kinds of constraints one could wish to enforce in a database. We shall only touch briefly on these here, with the meat of the subject appearing in Chapter 7.

Domain constraints restrict the value of an attribute to be in a limited set. A simple example would be declaring the type of an attribute. A stronger domain constraint would be to declare an enumerated type for an attribute or a range of values, e.g., the *length* attribute for a movie must be an integer in the range 0 to 240. There is no specific notation for domain constraints in the E/R model, but you may place a notation stating a desired constraint next to the attribute, if you wish.

There are also more general kinds of constraints that do not fall into any of the categories mentioned in this section. For example, we could choose to place a constraint on the degree of a relationship, such as that a movie entity cannot be connected by relationship `stars` to more than 10 star entities. In the E/R model, we can attach a bounding number to the edges that connect a relationship to an entity set, indicating limits on the number of entities that can be connected to any one entity of the related entity set.

Figure 2.19: Representing a constraint on the number of stars per movie

Example 2.22: Figure 2.19 shows how we can represent the constraint that no movie has more than 10 stars in the E/R model. As another example, we can think of the arrow as a synonym for the constraint "≤ 1," and we can think of the rounded arrow of Fig. 2.18 as standing for the constraint "$= 1$." □

2.3.8 Exercises for Section 2.3

Exercise 2.3.1: For your E/R diagrams of:

* a) Exercise 2.1.1.

  b) Exercise 2.1.3.

   c) Exercise 2.1.6.

(*i*) Select and specify keys, and (*ii*) Indicate appropriate referential integrity constraints.

! **Exercise 2.3.2:** We may think of relationships in the E/R model as having keys, just as entity sets do. Let R be a relationship among the entity sets $E_1, E_2, \ldots, E_n$. Then a *key* for R is a set K of attributes chosen from the attributes of $E_1, E_2, \ldots, E_n$ such that if $(e_1, e_2, \ldots, e_n)$ and $(f_1, f_2, \ldots, f_n)$ are two different tuples in the relationship set for R, then it is not possible that these tuples agree in all the attributes of K. Now, suppose $n = 2$; that is, R is a binary relationship. Also, for each i, let K_i be a set of attributes that is a key for entity set E_i. In terms of E_1 and E_2, give a smallest possible key for R under the assumption that:

   a) R is many-many.

 * b) R is many-one from E_1 to E_2.

   c) R is many-one from E_2 to E_1.

   d) R is one-one.

!! **Exercise 2.3.3:** Consider again the problem of Exercise 2.3.2, but with n allowed to be any number, not just 2. Using only the information about which arcs from R to the E_i's have arrows, show how to find a smallest possible key K for R in terms of the K_i's.

 ! **Exercise 2.3.4:** Give examples (other than those of Example 2.20) from real life of attributes created for the primary purpose of being keys.

2.4   Weak Entity Sets

There is an occasional condition in which an entity set's key is composed of attributes some or all of which belong to another entity set. Such an entity set is called a *weak entity set*.

2.4.1   Causes of Weak Entity Sets

There are two principal sources of weak entity sets. First, sometimes entity sets fall into a hierarchy based on classifications unrelated to the "isa hierarchy" of Section 2.1.11. If entities of set E are subunits of entities in set F, then it is possible that the names of E entities are not unique until we take into account the name of the F entity to which the E entity is subordinate. Several examples will illustrate the problem.

Example 2.23: A movie studio might have several film crews. The crews might be designated by a given studio as crew 1, crew 2, and so on. However, other studios might use the same designations for crews, so the attribute *number* is not a key for crews. Rather, to name a crew uniquely, we need to give both the name of the studio to which it belongs and the number of the crew. The situation is suggested by Fig. 2.20. The key for weak entity set *Crews* is its own *number* attribute and the *name* attribute of the unique studio to which the crew is related by the many-one *Unit-of* relationship.[4] □

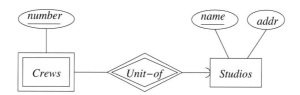

Figure 2.20: A weak entity set for crews, and its connections

Example 2.24: A species is designated by its genus and species names. For example, humans are of the species *Homo sapiens*; *Homo* is the genus name and *sapiens* the species name. In general, a genus consists of several species, each of which has a name beginning with the genus name and continuing with the species name. Unfortunately, species names, by themselves, are not unique. Two or more genera may have species with the same species name. Thus, to designate a species uniquely we need both the species name and the name of the genus to which the species is related by the *Belongs-to* relationship, as suggested in Fig. 2.21. *Species* is a weak entity set whose key comes partially from its genus. □

Figure 2.21: Another weak entity set, for species

The second common source of weak entity sets is the connecting entity sets that we introduced in Section 2.1.10 as a way to eliminate a multiway relationship.[5] These entity sets often have no attributes of their own. Their

---

[4]The double diamond and double rectangle will be explained in Section 2.4.3.

[5]Remember that there is no particular requirement in the E/R model that multiway relationships be eliminated, although this requirement exists in some other database design models.

key is formed from the attributes that are the key attributes for the entity sets they connect.

Example 2.25 : In Fig. 2.22 we see a connecting entity set *Contracts* that replaces the ternary relationship *Contracts* of Example 2.5. *Contracts* has an attribute *salary*, but this attribute does not contribute to the key. Rather, the key for a contract consists of the name of the studio and the star involved, plus the title and year of the movie involved. □

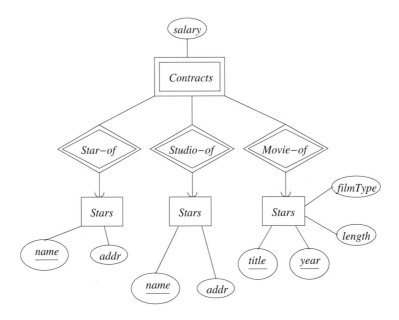

Figure 2.22: Connecting entity sets are weak

2.4.2 Requirements for Weak Entity Sets

We cannot obtain key attributes for a weak entity set indiscriminately. Rather, if E is a weak entity set then its key consists of:

1. Zero or more of its own attributes, and

2. Key attributes from entity sets that are reached by certain many-one relationships from E to other entity sets. These many-one relationships are called *supporting relationships* for E.

In order for R, a many-one relationship from E to some entity set F, to be a supporting relationship for E, the following conditions must be obeyed:

a) R must be a binary, many-one relationship[6] from E to F.

---

[6]Remember that a one-one relationship is a special case of a many-one relationship. When we say a relationship must be many-one, we always include one-one relationships as well.

b) R must have referential integrity from E to F. That is, for every E-entity, the F-entity related to it by R must actually exist in the database. Put another way, a rounded arrow from R to F must be justified.

c) The attributes that F supplies for the key of E must be key attributes of F.

d) However, if F is itself weak, then some or all of the key attributes of F supplied to E will be key attributes of one or more entity sets G to which F is connected by a supporting relationship. Recursively, if G is weak, some key attributes of G will be supplied from elsewhere, and so on.

e) If there are several different supporting relationships from E to F, then each relationship is used to supply a copy of the key attributes of F to help form the key of E. Note that an entity e from E may be related to different entities in F through different supporting relationships from E. Thus, the keys of several different entities from F may appear in the key values identifying a particular entity e from E.

The intuitive reason why these conditions are needed is as follows. Consider an entity in a weak entity set, say a crew in Example 2.23. Each crew is unique, abstractly. In principle we can tell one crew from another, even if they have the same number but belong to different studios. It is only the data about crews that makes it hard to distinguish crews, because the number alone is not sufficient. The only way we can associate additional information with a crew is if there is some deterministic process leading to additional values that make the designation of a crew unique. But the only unique values associated with an abstract crew entity are:

1. Values of attributes of the *Crews* entity set, and

2. Values obtained by following a relationship from a crew entity to a unique entity of some other entity set, where that other entity has a unique associated value of some kind. That is, the relationship followed must be many-one (or one-one as a special case) to the other entity set F, and the associated value must be part of a key for F.

2.4.3 Weak Entity Set Notation

We shall adopt the following conventions to indicate that an entity set is weak and to declare its key attributes.

1. If an entity set is weak, it will be shown as a rectangle with a double border. Examples of this convention are *Crews* in Fig. 2.20 and *Contracts* in Fig. 2.22.

2. Its supporting many-one relationships will be shown as diamonds with a double border. Examples of this convention are *Unit-of* in Fig. 2.20 and all three relationships in Fig. 2.22.

3. If an entity set supplies any attributes for its own key, then those attributes will be underlined. An example is in Fig. 2.20, where the number of a crew participates in its own key, although it is not the complete key for *Crews*.

We can summarize these conventions with the following rule:

- Whenever we use an entity set E with a double border, it is weak. E's attributes that are underlined, if any, plus the key attributes of those entity sets to which E is connected by many-one relationships with a double border, must be unique for the entities of E.

We should remember that the double-diamond is used only for supporting relationships. It is possible for there to be many-one relationships from a weak entity set that are not supporting relationships, and therefore do not get a double diamond.

Example 2.26: In Fig. 2.22, the relationship *Studio-of* need not be a supporting relationship for *Contracts*. The reason is that each movie has a unique owning studio, determined by the (not shown) many-one relationship from *Movies* to *Studios*. Thus, if we are told the name of a star and a movie, there is at most one contract with any studio for the work of that star in that movie. In terms of our notation, it would be appropriate to use an ordinary single diamond, rather than the double diamond, for *Studio-of* in Fig. 2.22. □

2.4.4 Exercises for Section 2.4

* **Exercise 2.4.1:** One way to represent students and the grades they get in courses is to use entity sets corresponding to students, to courses, and to "enrollments." Enrollment entities form a "connecting" entity set between students and courses and can be used to represent not only the fact that a student is taking a certain course, but the grade of the student in the course. Draw an E/R diagram for this situation, indicating weak entity sets and the keys for the entity sets. Is the grade part of the key for enrollments?

Exercise 2.4.2: Modify your solution to Exercise 2.4.1 so that we can record grades of the student for each of several assignments within a course. Again, indicate weak entity sets and keys.

Exercise 2.4.3: For your E/R diagrams of Exercise 2.2.6(a)–(c), indicate weak entity sets, supporting relationships, and keys.

Exercise 2.4.4: Draw E/R diagrams for the following situations involving weak entity sets. In each case indicate keys for entity sets.

a) Entity sets *Courses* and *Departments*. A course is given by a unique department, but its only attribute is its number. Different departments can offer courses with the same number. Each department has a unique name.

*! b) Entity sets *Leagues*, *Teams*, and *Players*. League names are unique. No league has two teams with the same name. No team has two players with the same number. However, there can be players with the same number on different teams, and there can be teams with the same name in different leagues.

2.5 Summary of Chapter 2

✦ *The Entity/Relationship Model*: In the E/R model we describe entity sets, relationships among entity sets, and attributes of entity sets and relationships. Members of entity sets are called entities.

✦ *Entity/Relationship Diagrams*: We use rectangles, diamonds, and ovals to draw entity sets, relationships, and attributes, respectively.

✦ *Multiplicity of Relationships*: Binary relationships can be one-one, many-one, or many-many. In a one-one relationship, an entity of either set can be associated with at most one entity of the other set. In a many-one relationship, each entity of the "many" side is associated with at most one entity of the other side. Many-many relationships place no restriction on multiplicity.

✦ *Keys*: A set of attributes that uniquely determines an entity in a given entity set is a key for that entity set.

✦ *Good Design*: Designing databases effectively requires that we represent the real world faithfully, that we select appropriate elements (e.g., relationships, attributes), and that we avoid redundancy — saying the same thing twice or saying something in an indirect or overly complex manner.

✦ *Referential Integrity*: A requirement that an entity be connected, through a given relationship, to an entity of some other entity set, and that the latter entity exists in the database, is called a referential integrity constraint.

✦ *Subclasses*: The E/R model uses a special relationship *isa* to represent the fact that one entity set is a special case of another. Entity sets may be connected in a hierarchy with each child node a special case of its parent. Entities may have components belonging to any subtree of the hierarchy, as long as the subtree includes the root.

✦ *Weak Entity Sets*: An occasional complication that arises in the E/R model is a weak entity set that requires attributes of some related entity set(s) to identify its own entities. A special notation involving diamonds and rectangles with double borders is used to distinguish weak entity sets.

2.6   References for Chapter 2

The original paper on the Entity/Relationship model is [2]. Two modern books on the subject of E/R design are [1] and [3].

1. Batini, Carlo., S. Ceri, and S. B. Navathe, and Carol Batini, *Conceptual Database Design: an Entity/Relationship Approach*, Addison-Wesley, Reading MA, 1991.

2. Chen, P. P., "The entity-relationship model: toward a unified view of data," *ACM Trans. on Database Systems* **1**:1, pp. 9–36, 1976.

3. Thalheim, B., "Fundamentals of Entity-Relationship Modeling," Spring-er-Verlag, Berlin, 2000.

Chapter 3

The Relational Data Model

While the entity-relationship approach to data modeling that we discussed in Chapter 2 is a simple and appropriate way to describe the structure of data, today's database implementations are almost always based on another approach, called the *relational model*. The relational model is extremely useful because it has but a single data-modeling concept: the "relation," a two-dimensional table in which data is arranged. We shall see in Chapter 6 how the relational model supports a very high-level programming language called SQL (structured query language). SQL lets us write simple programs that manipulate in powerful ways the data stored in relations. In contrast, the E/R model generally is not considered suitable as the basis of a data manipulation language.

On the other hand, it is often easier to design databases using the E/R notation. Thus, our first goal is to see how to translate designs from E/R notation into relations. We shall then find that the relational model has a design theory of its own. This theory, often called "normalization" of relations, is based primarily on "functional dependencies," which embody and expand the concept of "key" discussed informally in Section 2.3.2. Using normalization theory, we often improve our choice of relations with which to represent a particular database design.

3.1 Basics of the Relational Model

The relational model gives us a single way to represent data: as a two-dimensional table called a *relation*. Figure 3.1 is an example of a relation. The name of the relation is Movies, and it is intended to hold information about the entities in the entity set *Movies* of our running design example. Each row corresponds to one movie entity, and each column corresponds to one of the attributes of the entity set. However, relations can do much more than represent entity sets, as we shall see.

title	year	length	filmType
Star Wars	1977	124	color
Mighty Ducks	1991	104	color
Wayne's World	1992	95	color

Figure 3.1: The relation Movies

3.1.1 Attributes

Across the top of a relation we see *attributes*; in Fig. 3.1 the attributes are title, year, length, and filmType. Attributes of a relation serve as names for the columns of the relation. Usually, an attribute describes the meaning of entries in the column below. For instance, the column with attribute length holds the length in minutes of each movie.

Notice that the attributes of the relation Movies in Fig. 3.1 are the same as the attributes of the entity set *Movies*. We shall see that turning one entity set into a relation with the same set of attributes is a common step. However, in general there is no requirement that attributes of a relation correspond to any particular components of an E/R description of data.

3.1.2 Schemas

The name of a relation and the set of attributes for a relation is called the *schema* for that relation. We show the schema for the relation with the relation name followed by a parenthesized list of its attributes. Thus, the schema for relation Movies of Fig. 3.1 is

$$\text{Movies(title, year, length, filmType)}$$

The attributes in a relation schema are a set, not a list. However, in order to talk about relations we often must specify a "standard" order for the attributes. Thus, whenever we introduce a relation schema with a list of attributes, as above, we shall take this ordering to be the standard order whenever we display the relation or any of its rows.

In the relational model, a design consists of one or more relation schemas. The set of schemas for the relations in a design is called a *relational database schema*, or just a *database schema*.

3.1.3 Tuples

The rows of a relation, other than the header row containing the attribute names, are called *tuples*. A tuple has one *component* for each attribute of the relation. For instance, the first of the three tuples in Fig. 3.1 has the four components Star Wars, 1977, 124, and color for attributes title, year, `length`, and `filmType`, respectively. When we wish to write a tuple in isolation, not as part of a relation, we normally use commas to separate components, and we use parentheses to surround the tuple. For example,

$$(\text{Star Wars}, 1977, 124, \text{color})$$

is the first tuple of Fig. 3.1. Notice that when a tuple appears in isolation, the attributes do not appear, so some indication of the relation to which the tuple belongs must be given. We shall always use the order in which the attributes were listed in the relation schema.

3.1.4 Domains

The relational model requires that each component of each tuple be atomic; that is, it must be of some elementary type such as integer or string. It is not permitted for a value to be a record structure, set, list, array, or any other type that can reasonably have its values broken into smaller components.

It is further assumed that associated with each attribute of a relation is a *domain*, that is, a particular elementary type. The components of any tuple of the relation must have, in each component, a value that belongs to the domain of the corresponding column. For example, tuples of the `Movies` relation of Fig. 3.1 must have a first component that is a string, second and third components that are integers, and a fourth component whose value is one of the constants `color` and `blackAndWhite`. Domains are part of a relation's schema, although we shall not develop a notation for specifying domains until we reach Section 6.6.2.

3.1.5 Equivalent Representations of a Relation

Relations are sets of tuples, not lists of tuples. Thus the order in which the tuples of a relation are presented is immaterial. For example, we can list the three tuples of Fig. 3.1 in any of their six possible orders, and the relation is "the same" as Fig. 3.1.

Moreover, we can reorder the attributes of the relation as we choose, without changing the relation. However, when we reorder the relation schema, we must be careful to remember that the attributes are column headers. Thus, when we change the order of the attributes, we also change the order of their columns. When the columns move, the components of tuples change their order as well. The result is that each tuple has its components permuted in the same way as the attributes are permuted.

For example, Fig. 3.2 shows one of the many relations that could be obtained from Fig. 3.1 by permuting rows and columns. These two relations are considered "the same." More precisely, these two tables are different presentations of the same relation.

year	title	filmType	length
1991	Mighty Ducks	color	104
1992	Wayne's World	color	95
1977	Star Wars	color	124

Figure 3.2: Another presentation of the relation `Movies`

3.1.6 Relation Instances

A relation about movies is not static; rather, relations change over time. We expect that these changes involve the tuples of the relation, such as insertion of new tuples as movies are added to the database, changes to existing tuples if we get revised or corrected information about a movie, and perhaps deletion of tuples for movies that are expelled from the database for some reason.

It is less common for the schema of a relation to change. However, there are situations where we might want to add or delete attributes. Schema changes, while possible in commercial database systems, are very expensive, because each of perhaps millions of tuples needs to be rewritten to add or delete components. If we add an attribute, it may be difficult or even impossible to find the correct values for the new component in the existing tuples.

We shall call a set of tuples for a given relation an *instance* of that relation. For example, the three tuples shown in Fig. 3.1 form an instance of relation `Movies`. Presumably, the relation `Movies` has changed over time and will continue to change over time. For instance, in 1980, `Movies` did not contain the tuples for `Mighty Ducks` or `Wayne's World`. However, a conventional database system maintains only one version of any relation: the set of tuples that are in the relation "now." This instance of the relation is called the *current instance*.

3.1.7 Exercises for Section 3.1

Exercise 3.1.1: In Fig. 3.3 are instances of two relations that might constitute part of a banking database. Indicate the following:

a) The attributes of each relation.

b) The tuples of each relation.

c) The components of one tuple from each relation.

d) The relation schema for each relation.

e) The database schema.

f) A suitable domain for each attribute.

g) Another equivalent way to present each relation.

acctNo	type	balance
12345	savings	12000
23456	checking	1000
34567	savings	25

The relation Accounts

firstName	lastName	idNo	account
Robbie	Banks	901-222	12345
Lena	Hand	805-333	12345
Lena	Hand	805-333	23456

The relation Customers

Figure 3.3: Two relations of a banking database

!! **Exercise 3.1.2:** How many different ways (considering orders of tuples and attributes) are there to represent a relation instance if that instance has:

* a) Three attributes and three tuples, like the relation Accounts of Fig. 3.3?

 b) Four attributes and five tuples?

 c) n attributes and m tuples?

3.2 From E/R Diagrams to Relational Designs

Let us consider the process whereby a new database, such as our movie database, is created. We begin with a design phase, in which we address and answer questions about what information will be stored, how information elements will be related to one another, what constraints such as keys or referential integrity may be assumed, and so on. This phase may last for a long time, while options are evaluated and opinions are reconciled.

The design phase is followed by an implementation phase using a real database system. Since the great majority of commercial database systems use the relational model, we might suppose that the design phase should use this model too, rather than the E/R model or another model oriented toward design.

However, in practice it is often easier to start with a model like E/R, make our design, and then convert it to the relational model. The primary reason for doing so is that the relational model, having only one concept — the relation —

Schemas and Instances

Let us not forget the important distinction between the schema of a relation and an instance of that relation. The schema is the name and attributes for the relation and is relatively immutable. An instance is a set of tuples for that relation, and the instance may change frequently.

The schema/instance distinction is common in data modeling. For instance, entity set and relationship descriptions are the E/R model's way of describing a schema, while sets of entities and relationship sets form an instance of an E/R schema. Remember, however, that when designing a database, a database instance is not part of the design. We only imagine what typical instances would look like, as we develop our design.

---

rather than several complementary concepts (e.g., entity sets and relationships in the E/R model) has certain inflexibilities that are best handled after a design has been selected.

To a first approximation, converting an E/R design to a relational database schema is straightforward:

- Turn each entity set into a relation with the same set of attributes, and

- Replace a relationship by a relation whose attributes are the keys for the connected entity sets.

While these two rules cover much of the ground, there are also several special situations that we need to deal with, including:

1. Weak entity sets cannot be translated straightforwardly to relations.

2. "Isa" relationships and subclasses require careful treatment.

3. Sometimes, we do well to combine two relations, especially the relation for an entity set E and the relation that comes from a many-one relationship from E to some other entity set.

3.2.1   From Entity Sets to Relations

Let us first consider entity sets that are not weak. We shall take up the modifications needed to accommodate weak entity sets in Section 3.2.4. For each non-weak entity set, we shall create a relation of the same name and with the same set of attributes. This relation will not have any indication of the relationships in which the entity set participates; we'll handle relationships with separate relations, as discussed in Section 3.2.2.

Example 3.1 : Consider the three entity sets Movies, Stars and Studios from
Fig. 2.17, which we reproduce here as Fig. 3.4. The attributes for the Movies
entity set are title, year, length, and filmType. As a result, the relation
Movies looks just like the relation Movies of Fig. 3.1 with which we began
Section 3.1.

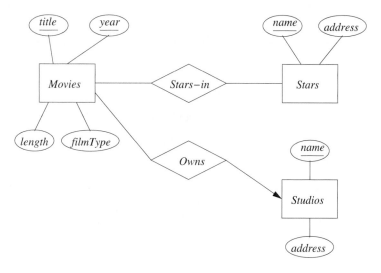

Figure 3.4: E/R diagram for the movie database

Next, consider the entity set *Stars* from Fig. 3.4. There are two attributes,
name and *address*. Thus, we would expect the corresponding Stars relation to
have schema Star(name, address) and for a typical instance of the relation
to look like:

name	address
Carrie Fisher	123 Maple St., Hollywood
Mark Hamill	456 Oak Rd., Brentwood
Harrison Ford	789 Palm Dr., Beverly Hills

□

3.2.2 From E/R Relationships to Relations

Relationships in the E/R model are also represented by relations. The relation
for a given relationship R has the following attributes:

1. For each entity set involved in relationship R, we take its key attribute
   or attributes as part of the schema of the relation for R.

2. If the relationship has attributes, then these are also attributes of relation
   R.

A Note About Data Quality :-)

While we have endeavored to make example data as accurate as possible, we have used bogus values for addresses and other personal information about movie stars, in order to protect the privacy of members of the acting profession, many of whom are shy individuals who shun publicity.

If one entity set is involved several times in a relationship, in different roles, then its key attributes each appear as many times as there are roles. We must rename the attributes to avoid name duplication. More generally, should the same attribute name appear twice or more among the attributes of R itself and the keys of the entity sets involved in relationship R, then we need to rename to avoid duplication.

Example 3.2: Consider the relationship *Owns* of Fig. 3.4. This relationship connects entity sets *Movies* and *Studios*. Thus, for the schema of relation `Owns` we use the key for `Movies`, which is `title` and `year`, and the key of `Studios`, which is `name`. That is, the schema is:

$$\texttt{Owns(title, year, studioName)}$$

A sample instance of this relation is:

title	year	studioName
Star Wars	1977	Fox
Mighty Ducks	1991	Disney
Wayne's World	1992	Paramount

We have chosen the attribute `studioName` for clarity; it corresponds to the attribute `name` of `Studios`. □

Example 3.3: Similarly, the relationship `Stars-In` of Fig. 3.4 can be transformed into a relation with the attributes `title` and `year` (the key for *Movies*) and attribute `starName`, which is the key for entity set *Stars*. Figure 3.5 shows a sample relation `Stars-In`.

Because these movie titles are unique, it seems that the year is redundant in Fig. 3.5. However, had there been several movies of the same title, like "King Kong," we would see that the year was essential to sort out which stars appear in which version of the movie. □

Example 3.4: Multiway relationships are also easy to convert to relations. Consider the four-way relationship *Contracts* of Fig. 2.6, reproduced here as Fig. 3.6, involving a star, a movie, and two studios — the first holding the

title	year	starName
Star Wars	1977	Carrie Fisher
Star Wars	1977	Mark Hamill
Star Wars	1977	Harrison Ford
Mighty Ducks	1991	Emilio Estevez
Wayne's World	1992	Dana Carvey
Wayne's World	1992	Mike Meyers

Figure 3.5: A relation for relationship `Stars-In`

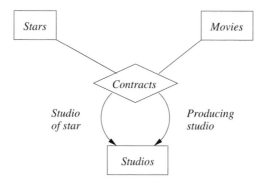

Figure 3.6: The relationship *Contracts*

star's contract and the second contracting for that star's services in that movie. We represent this relationship by a relation `Contracts` whose schema consists of the attributes from the keys of the following four entity sets:

1. The key `starName` for the star.

2. The key consisting of attributes `title` and `year` for the movie.

3. The key `studioOfStar` indicating the name of the first studio; recall we assume the studio name is a key for the entity set `Studios`.

4. The key `producingStudio` indicating the name of the studio that will produce the movie using that star.

That is, the schema is:

```
Contracts(starName, title, year, studioOfStar, producingStudio)
```

Notice that we have been inventive in choosing attribute names for our relation schema, avoiding "name" for any attribute, since it would be unobvious whether that referred to a star's name or studio's name, and in the latter case, which studio. Also, were there attributes attached to entity set *Contracts*, such as *salary*, these attributes would be added to the schema of relation `Contracts`. □

3.2.3 Combining Relations

Sometimes, the relations that we get from converting entity sets and relationships to relations are not the best possible choice of relations for the given data. One common situation occurs when there is an entity set E with a many-one relationship R from E to F. The relations from E and R will each have the key for E in their relation schema. In addition, the relation for E will have in its schema the attributes of E that are not in the key, and the relation for R will have the key attributes of F and any attributes of R itself. Because R is many-one, all these attributes have values that are determined uniquely by the key for E, and we can combine them into one relation with a schema consisting of:

1. All attributes of E.

2. The key attributes of F.

3. Any attributes belonging to relationship R.

For an entity e of E that is not related to any entity of F, the attributes of types (2) and (3) will have null values in the tuple for e. Null values were introduced informally in Section 2.3.4, in order to represent a situation where a value is missing or unknown. Nulls are not a formal part of the relational model, but a null value, denoted `NULL`, is available in SQL, and we shall use it where needed in our discussions of representing E/R designs as relational database schemas.

Example 3.5: In our running movie example, *Owns* is a many-one relation from *Movies* to *Studios*, which we converted to a relation in Example 3.2. The relation obtained from entity set *Movies* was discussed in Example 3.1. We can combine these relations by taking all their attributes and forming one relation schema. If we do, the relation looks like that in Fig. 3.7.   □

title	year	length	filmType	studioName
Star Wars	1977	124	color	Fox
Mighty Ducks	1991	104	color	Disney
Wayne's World	1992	95	color	Paramount

Figure 3.7: Combining relation `Movies` with relation `Owns`

Whether or not we choose to combine relations in this manner is a matter of judgement. However, there are some advantages to having all the attributes that are dependent on the key of entity set E together in one relation, even if there are a number of many-one relationships from E to other entity sets. For example, it is often more efficient to answer queries involving attributes of one relation than to answer queries involving attributes of several relations. In fact, some design systems based on the E/R model combine these relations automatically for the user.

On the other hand, one might wonder if it made sense to combine the relation for E with the relation of a relationship R that involved E but was not many-one from E to some other entity set. Doing so is risky, because it often leads to redundancy, an issue we shall take up in Section 3.6.

Example 3.6 : To get a sense of what can go wrong, suppose we combined the relation of Fig. 3.7 with the relation that we get for the many-many relationship *Stars-in*; recall this relation was suggested by Fig. 3.5. Then the combined relation would look like Fig. 3.8.

title	year	length	filmType	studioName	starName
Star Wars	1977	124	color	Fox	Carrie Fisher
Star Wars	1977	124	color	Fox	Mark Hamill
Star Wars	1977	124	color	Fox	Harrison Ford
Mighty Ducks	1991	104	color	Disney	Emilio Estevez
Wayne's World	1992	95	color	Paramount	Dana Carvey
Wayne's World	1992	95	color	Paramount	Mike Meyers

Figure 3.8: The relation `Movies` with star information

Because a movie can have several stars, we are forced to repeat all the information about a movie, once for each star. For instance, we see in Fig. 3.8 that the length of *Star Wars* is repeated three times — once for each star — as is the fact that the movie is owned by Fox. This redundancy is undesirable, and the purpose of the relational-database design theory of Section 3.6 is to split relations such as that of Fig. 3.8 and thereby remove the redundancy. □

3.2.4 Handling Weak Entity Sets

When a weak entity set appears in an E/R diagram, we need to do three things differently.

1. The relation for the weak entity set W itself must include not only the attributes of W but also the key attributes of the other entity sets that help form the key of W. These helping entity sets are easily recognized because they are reached by supporting (double-diamond) relationships from W.

2. The relation for any relationship in which the weak entity set W appears must use as a key for W all of its key attributes, including those of other entity sets that contribute to W's key.

3. However, a supporting relationship R, from the weak entity set W to another entity set that helps provide the key for W, need not be converted to a relation at all. The justification is that, as discussed in Section 3.2.3, the attributes of many-one relationship R's relation will either *be* attributes of the relation for W, or (in the case of attributes on R) can be combined with the schema for W's relation.

Of course, when introducing additional attributes to build the key of a weak entity set, we must be careful not to use the same name twice. If necessary, we rename some or all of these attributes.

Example 3.7: Let us consider the weak entity set *Crews* from Fig. 2.20, which we reproduce here as Fig. 3.9. From this diagram we get three relations, whose schemas are:

```
Studios(name, addr)
Crews(number, studioName)
Unit-of(number, studioName, name)
```

The first relation, `Studios`, is constructed in a straightforward manner from the entity set of the same name. The second, `Crews`, comes from the weak entity set *Crews*. The attributes of this relation are the key attributes of *Crews*; if there were any nonkey attributes for *Crews*, they would be included in the relation schema as well. We have chosen `studioName` as the attribute in relation `Crews` that corresponds to the attribute `name` in the entity set *Studios*.

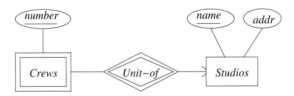

Figure 3.9: The crews example of a weak entity set

The third relation, `Unit-of`, comes from the relationship of the same name. As always, we represent an E/R relationship in the relational model by a relation whose schema has the key attributes of the related entity sets. In this case, `Unit-of` has attributes `number` and `studioName`, the key for weak entity set *Crews*, and attribute `name`, the key for entity set *Studios*. However, notice that since *Unit-of* is a many-one relationship, the studio `studioName` is surely the same as the studio `name`.

For instance, suppose Disney crew #3 is one of the crews of the Disney studio. Then the relationship set for E/R relationship *Unit-of* includes the pair

---

Relations With Subset Schemas

You might imagine from Example 3.7 that whenever one relation R has a set of attributes that is a subset of the attributes of another relation S, we can eliminate R. That is not exactly true. R might hold information that doesn't appear in S because the additional attributes of S do not allow us to extend a tuple from R to S.

For instance, the Internal Revenue Service tries to maintain a relation People(name, ss#) of potential taxpayers and their social-security numbers, even if the person had no income and did not file a tax return. They might also maintain a relation TaxPayers(name, ss#, amount) indicating the amount of tax paid by each person who filed a return in the current year. The schema of People is a subset of the schema of TaxPayers, yet there may be value in remembering the social-security number of those who are mentioned in People but not in Taxpayers.

In fact, even identical sets of attributes may have different semantics, so it is not possible to merge their tuples. An example would be two relations Stars(name, addr) and Studios(name, addr). Although the schemas look alike, we cannot turn star tuples into studio tuples, or vice-versa.

On the other hand, when the two relations come from the weak-entity-set construction, then there can be no such additional value to the relation with the smaller set of attributes. The reason is that the tuples of the relation that comes from the supporting relationship correspond one-for-one with the tuples of the relation that comes from the weak entity set. Thus, we routinely eliminate the former relation.

(Disney-crew-#3, Disney)

This pair gives rise to the tuple

(3, Disney, Disney)

for the relation Unit-of.

Notice that, as must be the case, the components of this tuple for attributes studioName and name are identical. As a consequence, we can "merge" the attributes studioName and name of Unit-of, giving us the simpler schema:

Unit-of(number, name)

However, now we can dispense with the relation Unit-of altogether, since it is now identical to the relation Crews. □

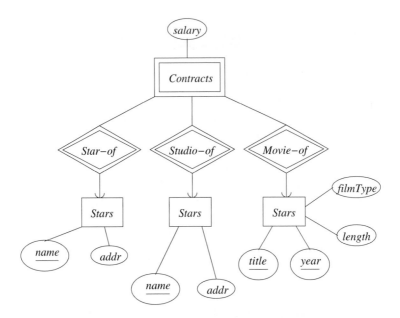

Figure 3.10: The weak entity set *Contracts*

Example 3.8 : Now consider the weak entity set *Contracts* from Example 2.25 and Fig. 2.22 in Section 2.4.1. We reproduce this diagram as Fig. 3.10. The schema for relation `Contracts` is

`Contracts(starName, studioName, title, year, salary)`

These attributes are the key for *Stars*, suitably renamed, the key for *Studios*, suitably renamed, the two attributes that form the key for *Movies*, and the lone attribute, *salary*, belonging to the entity set *Contracts* itself. There are no relations constructed for the relationships *Star-of*, *Studio-of*, or *Movie-of*. Each would have a schema that is a proper subset of that for `Contracts` above.

Incidentally, notice that the relation we obtain is exactly the same as what we would obtain had we started from the E/R diagram of Fig. 2.7. Recall that figure treats contracts as a three-way relationship among stars, movies, and studios, with a salary attribute attached to *Contracts*.   □

The phenomenon observed in Examples 3.7 and 3.8 — that a supporting relationship needs no relation — is universal for weak entity sets. The following is a modified rule for converting to relations entity sets that are weak.

- If W is a weak entity set, construct for W a relation whose schema consists of:

    1. All attributes of W.

    2. All attributes of supporting relationships for W.

3. For each supporting relationship for W, say a many-one relationship from W to entity set E, all the *key* attributes of E.

Rename attributes, if necessary, to avoid name conflicts.

- Do *not* construct a relation for any supporting relationship for W.

3.2.5 Exercises for Section 3.2

* **Exercise 3.2.1:** Convert the E/R diagram of Fig. 3.11 to a relational database schema.

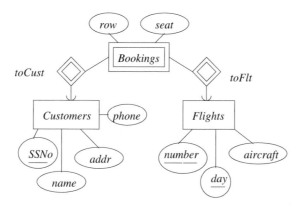

Figure 3.11: An E/R diagram about airlines

! **Exercise 3.2.2:** There is another E/R diagram that could describe the weak entity set *Bookings* in Fig. 3.11. Notice that a booking can be identified uniquely by the flight number, day of the flight, the row, and the seat; the customer is not then necessary to help identify the booking.

a) Revise the diagram of Fig. 3.11 to reflect this new viewpoint.

b) Convert your diagram from (a) into relations. Do you get the same database schema as in Exercise 3.2.1?

* **Exercise 3.2.3:** The E/R diagram of Fig. 3.12 represents ships. Ships are said to be *sisters* if they were designed from the same plans. Convert this diagram to a relational database schema.

Exercise 3.2.4: Convert the following E/R diagrams to relational database schemas.

a) Figure 2.22.

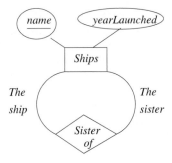

Figure 3.12: An E/R diagram about sister ships

b) Your answer to Exercise 2.4.1.

c) Your answer to Exercise 2.4.4(a).

d) Your answer to Exercise 2.4.4(b).

3.3   Converting Subclass Structures to Relations

When we have an isa-hierarchy of entity sets, we are presented with several choices of strategy for conversion to relations. Recall we assume that:

- There is a root entity set for the hierarchy,

- This entity set has a key that serves to identify every entity represented by the hierarchy, and

- A given entity may have *components* that belong to the entity sets of any subtree of the hierarchy, as long as that subtree includes the root.

The principal conversion strategies are:

1. *Follow the E/R viewpoint.* For each entity set E in the hierarchy, create a relation that includes the key attributes from the root and any attributes belonging to E.

2. *Treat entities as objects belonging to a single class.* For each possible subtree including the root, create one relation, whose schema includes all the attributes of all the entity sets in the subtree.

3. *Use null values.* Create one relation with all the attributes of all the entity sets in the hierarchy. Each entity is represented by one tuple, and that tuple has a null value for whatever attributes the entity does not have.

We shall consider each approach in turn.

3.3.1 E/R-Style Conversion

Our first approach is to create a relation for each entity set, as usual. If the entity set E is not the root of the hierarchy, then the relation for E will include the key attributes at the root, to identify the entity represented by each tuple, plus all the attributes of E. In addition, if E is involved in a relationship, then we use these key attributes to identify entities of E in the relation corresponding to that relationship.

Note, however, that although we spoke of "isa" as a relationship, it is unlike other relationships, in that it connects components of a single entity, not distinct entities. Thus, we do not create a relation for "isa."

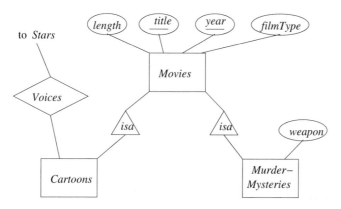

Figure 3.13: The movie hierarchy

Example 3.9: Consider the hierarchy of Fig. 2.10, which we reproduce here as Fig. 3.13. The relations needed to represent the four different kinds of entities in this hierarchy are:

1. `Movies(title, year, length, filmType)`. This relation was discussed in Example 3.1, and every movie is represented by a tuple here.

2. `MurderMysteries(title, year, weapon)`. The first two attributes are the key for all movies, and the last is the lone attribute for the corresponding entity set. Those movies that are murder mysteries have a tuple here as well as in `Movies`.

3. `Cartoons(title, year)`. This relation is the set of cartoons. It has no attributes other than the key for movies, since the extra information about cartoons is contained in the relationship *Voices*. Movies that are cartoons have a tuple here as well as in `Movies`.

Note that the fourth kind of movie — those that are both cartoons and murder mysteries — have tuples in all three relations.

In addition, we shall need the relation `Voices(title, year, starName)` that corresponds to the relationship *Voices* between *Stars* and *Cartoons*. The last attribute is the key for *Stars* and the first two form the key for *Cartoons*.

For instance, the movie *Roger Rabbit* would have tuples in all four relations. Its basic information would be in `Movies`, the murder weapon would appear in `MurderMysteries`, and the stars that provided voices for the movie would appear in `Voices`.

Notice that the relation `Cartoons` has a schema that is a subset of the schema for the relation `Voices`. In many situations, we would be content to eliminate a relation such as `Cartoons`, since it appears not to contain any information beyond what is in `Voices`. However, there may be silent cartoons in our database. Those cartoons would have no voices, and we would therefore lose the fact that these movies were cartoons.   □

3.3.2   An Object-Oriented Approach

An alternative strategy for converting isa-hierarchies to relations is to enumerate all the possible subtrees of the hierarchy. For each, create one relation that represents entities that have components in exactly those subtrees; the schema for this relation has all the attributes of any entity set in the subtree. We refer to this approach as "object-oriented," since it is motivated by the assumption that entities are "objects" that belong to one and only one class.

Example 3.10: Consider the hierarchy of Fig. 3.13. There are four possible subtrees including the root:

1. *Movies* alone.

2. *Movies* and *Cartoons* only.

3. *Movies* and *Murder-Mysteries* only.

4. All three entity sets.

We must construct relations for all four "classes." Since only Murder-Mysteries contributes an attribute that is unique to its entities, there is actually some repetition, and these four relations are:

```
Movies(title, year, length, filmType)
MoviesC(title, year, length, filmType)
MoviesMM(title, year, length, filmType, weapon)
MoviesCMM(title, year, length, filmType, weapon)
```

Had *Cartoons* had attributes unique to that entity set, then all four relations would have different sets of attributes. As that is not the case here, we could combine `Movies` with `MoviesC` (i.e., create one relation for non-murder-mysteries) and combine `MoviesMM` with `MoviesCMM` (i.e., create one relation for all murder mysteries), although doing so loses some information — which movies are cartoons.

We also need to consider how to handle the relationship *Voices* from *Cartoons* to *Stars*. If *Voices* were many-one from *Cartoons*, then we could add a `voice` attribute to `MoviesC` and `MoviesCMM`, which would represent the *Voices* relationship and would have the side-effect of making all four relations different. However, *Voices* is many-many, so we need to create a separate relation for this relationship. As always, its schema has the key attributes from the entity sets connected; in this case

```
Voices(title, year, starName)
```

would be an appropriate schema.

One might consider whether it was necessary to create two such relations, one connecting cartoons that are not murder mysteries to their voices, and the other for cartoons that *are* murder mysteries. However, there does not appear to be any benefit to doing so in this case. □

3.3.3 Using Null Values to Combine Relations

There is one more approach to representing information about a hierarchy of entity sets. If we are allowed to use NULL (the null value as in SQL) as a value in tuples, we can handle a hierarchy of entity sets with a single relation. This relation has all the attributes belonging to any entity set of the hierarchy. An entity is then represented by a single tuple. This tuple has NULL in each attribute that is not defined for that entity.

Example 3.11: If we applied this approach to the diagram of Fig. 3.13, we would create a single relation whose schema is:

```
Movie(title, year, length, filmType, weapon)
```

Those movies that are not murder mysteries would have NULL in the `weapon` component of their tuple. It would also be necessary to have a relation `Voices` to connect those movies that are cartoons to the stars performing the voices, as in Example 3.10. □

3.3.4 Comparison of Approaches

Each of the three approaches, which we shall refer to as "straight-E/R," "object-oriented," and "nulls," respectively, have advantages and disadvantages. Here is a list of the principal issues.

1. It is expensive to answer queries involving several relations, so we would prefer to find all the attributes we needed to answer a query in one relation. The nulls approach uses only one relation for all the attributes, so it has an advantage in this regard. The other two approaches have advantages for different kinds of queries. For instance:

(a) A query like "what films of 1999 were longer than 150 minutes?" can be answered directly from the relation `Movies` in the straight-E/R approach of Example 3.9. However, in the object-oriented approach of Example 3.10, we need to examine `Movies`, `MoviesC`, `MoviesMM`, and `MoviesCMM`, since a long movie may be in any of these four relations.[1]

(b) On the other hand, a query like "what weapons were used in cartoons of over 150 minutes in length?" gives us trouble in the straight-E/R approach. We must access `Movies` to find those movies of over 150 minutes. We must access `Cartoons` to verify that a movie is a cartoon, and we must access `MurderMysteries` to find the murder weapon. In the object-oriented approach, we have only to access the relation `MoviesCMM`, where all the information we need will be found.

2. We would like not to use too many relations. Here again, the nulls method shines, since it requires only one relation. However, there is a difference between the other two methods, since in the straight-E/R approach, we use only one relation per entity set in the hierarchy. In the object-oriented approach, if we have a root and n children ($n + 1$ entity sets in all), then there are 2^n different classes of entities, and we need that many relations.

3. We would like to minimize space and avoid repeating information. Since the object-oriented method uses only one tuple per entity, and that tuple has components for only those attributes that make sense for the entity, this approach offers the minimum possible space usage. The nulls approach also has only one tuple per entity, but these tuples are "long"; i.e., they have components for all attributes, whether or not they are appropriate for a given entity. If there are many entity sets in the hierarchy, and there are many attributes among those entity sets, then a large fraction of the space could wind up not being used in the nulls approach. The straight-E/R method has several tuples for each entity, but only the key attributes are repeated. Thus, this method could use either more or less space than the nulls method.

3.3.5   Exercises for Section 3.3

* **Exercise 3.3.1:** Convert the E/R diagram of Fig. 3.14 to a relational database schema, using each of the following approaches:

a) The straight-E/R method.

b) The object-oriented method.

c) The nulls method.

---

[1]Even if we combine the four relations into two, we must still access both relations to answer the query.

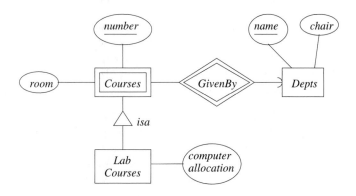

Figure 3.14: E/R diagram for Exercise 3.3.1

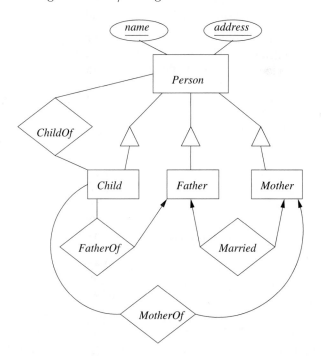

Figure 3.15: E/R diagram for Exercise 3.3.2

! Exercise 3.3.2 : Convert the E/R diagram of Fig. 3.15 to a relational database schema, using:

    a) The straight-E/R method.

    b) The object-oriented method.

    c) The nulls method.

Exercise 3.3.3 : Convert your E/R design from Exercise 2.1.7 to a relational database schema, using:

    a) The straight-E/R method.

    b) The object-oriented method.

    c) The nulls method.

! Exercise 3.3.4 : Suppose that we have an isa-hierarchy involving e entity sets. Each entity set has a attributes, and k of those at the root form the key for all these entity sets. Give formulas for (i) the minimum and maximum number of relations used, and (ii) the minimum and maximum number of components that the tuple(s) for a single entity have all together, when the method of conversion to relations is:

    * a) The straight-E/R method.

    b) The object-oriented method.

    c) The nulls method.

3.4   Functional Dependencies

Sections 3.2 and 3.3 showed us how to convert E/R designs into relational schemas. It is also possible for database designers to produce relational schemas directly from application requirements, although doing so can be difficult. Regardless of how relational designs are produced, we shall see that frequently it is possible to improve designs systematically based on certain types of constraints. The most important type of constraint we use for relational schema design is a unique-value constraint called a "functional dependency" (often abbreviated FD). Knowledge of this type of constraint is vital for the redesign of database schemas to eliminate redundancy, as we shall see in Section 3.6. There are also some other kinds of constraints that help us design good databases schemas. For instance, multivalued dependencies are covered in Section 3.7, and referential-integrity constraints are mentioned in Section 5.5.

3.4.1 Definition of Functional Dependency

A *functional dependency* (FD) on a relation R is a statement of the form "If two tuples of R agree on attributes $A_1, A_2, \ldots, A_n$ (i.e., the tuples have the same values in their respective components for each of these attributes), then they must also agree on another attribute, B." We write this FD formally as $A_1 A_2 \cdots A_n \rightarrow B$ and say that "$A_1, A_2, \ldots, A_n$ functionally determine B."

If a set of attributes $A_1, A_2, \ldots, A_n$ functionally determines more than one attribute, say

$$A_1 A_2 \cdots A_n \rightarrow B_1$$
$$A_1 A_2 \cdots A_n \rightarrow B_2$$
$$\cdots$$
$$A_1 A_2 \cdots A_n \rightarrow B_m$$

then we can, as a shorthand, write this set of FD's as

$$A_1 A_2 \cdots A_n \rightarrow B_1 B_2 \cdots B_m$$

Figure 3.16 suggests what this FD tells us about any two tuples t and u in the relation R.

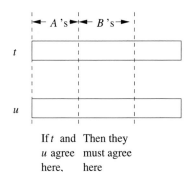

Figure 3.16: The effect of a functional dependency on two tuples.

Example 3.12 : Let us consider the relation

```
Movies(title, year, length, filmType, studioName, starName)
```

from Fig. 3.8, an instance of which we reproduce here as Fig. 3.17. There are several FD's that we can reasonably assert about the Movies relation. For instance, we can assert the three FD's:

$$\text{title year} \rightarrow \text{length}$$
$$\text{title year} \rightarrow \text{filmType}$$
$$\text{title year} \rightarrow \text{studioName}$$

title	year	length	filmType	studioName	starName
Star Wars	1977	124	color	Fox	Carrie Fisher
Star Wars	1977	124	color	Fox	Mark Hamill
Star Wars	1977	124	color	Fox	Harrison Ford
Mighty Ducks	1991	104	color	Disney	Emilio Estevez
Wayne's World	1992	95	color	Paramount	Dana Carvey
Wayne's World	1992	95	color	Paramount	Mike Meyers

Figure 3.17: An instance of the relation `Movies(title, year, length, filmType, studioName, starName)`

Since the three FD's each have the same left side, `title` and `year`, we can summarize them in one line by the shorthand

$$\texttt{title year} \rightarrow \texttt{length filmType studioName}$$

Informally, this set of FD's says that if two tuples have the same value in their `title` components, and they also have the same value in their `year` components, then these two tuples must have the same values in their `length` components, the same values in their `filmType` components, and the same values in their `studioName` components. This assertion makes sense if we remember the original design from which this relation schema was developed. Attributes `title` and `year` form a key for the *Movies* entity set. Thus, we expect that given a title and year, there is a unique movie. Therefore, there is a unique length for the movie and a unique film type. Further, there is a many-one relationship from *Movies* to *Studios*. Consequently, we expect that given a movie, there is only one owning studio.

On the other hand, we observe that the statement

$$\texttt{title year} \rightarrow \texttt{starName}$$

is false; it is not a functional dependency. Given a movie, it is entirely possible that there is more than one star for the movie listed in our database. □

3.4.2 Keys of Relations

We say a set of one or more attributes $\{A_1, A_2, \ldots, A_n\}$ is a *key* for a relation R if:

1. Those attributes functionally determine all other attributes of the relation. That is, because relations are sets, it is impossible for two distinct tuples of R to agree on all of $A_1, A_2, \ldots, A_n$.

Functional Dependencies Tell Us About the Schema

Remember that a FD, like any constraint, is an assertion about the schema of a relation, not about a particular instance. If we look at an instance, we cannot tell for certain that a FD holds. For example, looking at Fig. 3.17 we might suppose that a FD like `title` → `filmType` holds, because for every tuple in this particular instance of the relation `Movies` it happens that any two tuples agreeing on `title` also agree on `filmType`.

However, we cannot claim this FD for the relation `Movies`. Were our instance to include, for example, tuples for the two versions of *King Kong*, one of which was in color and the other in black-and-white, then the proposed FD would not hold.

---

2. No proper subset of $\{A_1, A_2, \ldots, A_n\}$ functionally determines all other attributes of R; i.e., a key must be *minimal*.

When a key consists of a single attribute A, we often say that A (rather than $\{A\}$) is a key.

Example 3.13 : Attributes {title, year, starName} form a key for the relation `Movies` of Fig. 3.17. First, we must show that they functionally determine all the other attributes. That is, suppose two tuples agree on these three attributes: `title`, `year`, and `starName`. Because they agree on `title` and `year`, they must agree on the other attributes — `length`, `filmType`, and `studioName` — as we discussed in Example 3.12. Thus, two different tuples cannot agree on all of `title`, `year`, and `starName`; they would in fact be the same tuple.

Now, we must argue that no proper subset of {title, year, starName} functionally determines all other attributes. To see why, begin by observing that `title` and `year` do not determine `starName`, because many movies have more than one star. Thus, {title, year} is not a key.

{year, starName} is not a key because we could have a star in two movies in the same year; therefore

year starName → title

is not a FD. Also, we claim that {title, starName} is not a key, because two movies with the same title, made in different years, occasionally have a star in common.[2]   □

---

[2]Since we asserted in an earlier book that there were no known examples of this phenomenon, several people have shown us we were wrong. It's an interesting challenge to discover stars that appeared in two versions of the same movie.

Minimality of Keys

The requirement that a key be minimal was not present in the E/R model, although in the relational model, we *do* require keys to be minimal. While we suppose designers using the E/R model would not add unnecessary attributes to the keys they declare, we have no way of knowing whether an E/R key is minimal or not. Only when we have a formal representation such as FD's can we even ask the question whether a set of attributes is a minimal set that can serve as a key for some relation.

Incidentally, remember the difference between "minimal" — you can't throw anything out — and "minimum" — smallest of all possible. A minimal key may not have the minimum number of attributes of any key for the given relation. For example, we might find that ABC and DE are both keys (i.e., minimal), while only DE is of the minimum possible size for any key.

Sometimes a relation has more than one key. If so, it is common to designate one of the keys as the *primary key*. In commercial database systems, the choice of primary key can influence some implementation issues such as how the relation is stored on disk. A useful convention we shall follow is:

- Underline the attributes of the primary key when displaying its relation schema.

3.4.3 Superkeys

A set of attributes that contains a key is called a *superkey*, short for "superset of a key." Thus, every key is a superkey. However, some superkeys are not (minimal) keys. Note that every superkey satisfies the first condition of a key: it functionally determines all other attributes of the relation. However, a superkey need not satisfy the second condition: minimality.

Example 3.14: In the relation of Example 3.13, there are many superkeys. Not only is the key

$$\{\texttt{title, year, starName}\}$$

a superkey, but any superset of this set of attributes, such as

$$\{\texttt{title, year, starName, length, studioName}\}$$

is a superkey.   □

What Is "Functional" About Functional Dependencies?

$A_1 A_2 \cdots A_n \rightarrow B$ is called a "functional" dependency because in principle there is a function that takes a list of values, one for each of attributes $A_1, A_2, \ldots, A_n$ and produces a unique value (or no value at all) for B. For example, in the Movies relation, we can imagine a function that takes a string like "Star Wars" and an integer like 1977 and produces the unique value of length, namely 124, that appears in the relation Movies. However, this function is not the usual sort of function that we meet in mathematics, because there is no way to compute it from first principles. That is, we cannot perform some operations on strings like "Star Wars" and integers like 1977 and come up with the correct length. Rather, the function is only computed by lookup in the relation. We look for a tuple with the given title and year values and see what value that tuple has for length.

3.4.4 Discovering Keys for Relations

When a relation schema was developed by converting an E/R design to relations, we can often predict the key of the relation. Our first rule about inferring keys is:

- If the relation comes from an entity set then the key for the relation is the key attributes of this entity set.

Example 3.15: In Example 3.1 we described how the entity sets *Movies* and *Stars* could be converted to relations. The keys for these entity sets were {*title, year*} and {*name*}, respectively. Thus, these are the keys for the corresponding relations, and

$$\text{Movies}(\underline{\text{title}}, \underline{\text{year}}, \text{length}, \text{filmType})$$
$$\text{Stars}(\underline{\text{name}}, \text{address})$$

are the schemas of the relations, with keys indicated by underline. □

Our second rule concerns binary relationships. If a relation R is constructed from a relationship, then the multiplicity of the relationship affects the key for R. There are three cases:

- If the relationship is many-many, then the keys of both connected entity sets are the key attributes for R.

- If the relationship is many-one from entity set E_1 to entity set E_2, then the key attributes of E_1 are key attributes of R, but those of E_2 are not.

Other Key Terminology

In some books and articles one finds different terminology regarding keys. One can find the term "key" used the way we have used the term "superkey," that is, a set of attributes that functionally determine all the attributes, with no requirement of minimality. These sources typically use the term "candidate key" for a key that is minimal — that is, a "key" in the sense we use the term.

- If the relationship is one-one, then the key attributes for either of the connected entity sets are key attributes of R. Thus, there is not a unique key for R.

Example 3.16: Example 3.2 discussed the relationship *Owns*, which is many-one from entity set *Movies* to entity set *Studios*. Thus, the key for the relation Owns is the key attributes `title` and `year`, which come from the key for *Movies*. The schema for Owns, with key attributes underlined, is thus

$$\text{Owns}(\underline{\texttt{title}}, \underline{\texttt{year}}, \texttt{studioName})$$

In contrast, Example 3.3 discussed the many-many relationship *Stars-in* between *Movies* and *Stars*. Now, all attributes of the resulting relation

$$\text{Stars-in}(\underline{\texttt{title}}, \underline{\texttt{year}}, \underline{\texttt{starName}})$$

are key attributes. In fact, the only way the relation from a many-many relationship could not have all its attributes be part of the key is if the relationship itself has an attribute. Those attributes are omitted from the key. □

Finally, let us consider multiway relationships. Since we cannot describe all possible dependencies by the arrows coming out of the relationship, there are situations where the key or keys will not be obvious without thinking in detail about which sets of entity sets functionally determine which other entity sets. One guarantee we can make, however, is

- If a multiway relationship R has an arrow to entity set E, then there is at least one key for the corresponding relation that excludes the key of E.

3.4.5 Exercises for Section 3.4

Exercise 3.4.1: Consider a relation about people in the United States, including their name, Social Security number, street address, city, state, ZIP code, area code, and phone number (7 digits). What FD's would you expect to hold? What are the keys for the relation? To answer this question, you need to know

> # Other Notions of Functional Dependencies
>
> We take the position that a FD can have several attributes on the left but only a single attribute on the right. Moreover, the attribute on the right may not appear also on the left. However, we allow several FD's with a common left side to be combined as a shorthand, giving us a set of attributes on the right. We shall also find it occasionally convenient to allow a "trivial" FD whose right side is one of the attributes on the left.
>
> Other works on the subject often start from the point of view that both left and right side are arbitrary sets of attributes, and attributes may appear on both left and right. There is no important difference between the two approaches, but we shall maintain the position that, unless stated otherwise, there is no attribute on both left and right of a FD.

something about the way these numbers are assigned. For instance, can an area code straddle two states? Can a ZIP code straddle two area codes? Can two people have the same Social Security number? Can they have the same address or phone number?

* **Exercise 3.4.2:** Consider a relation representing the present position of molecules in a closed container. The attributes are an ID for the molecule, the x, y, and z coordinates of the molecule, and its velocity in the x, y, and z dimensions. What FD's would you expect to hold? What are the keys?

! **Exercise 3.4.3:** In Exercise 2.2.5 we discussed three different assumptions about the relationship *Births*. For each of these, indicate the key or keys of the relation constructed from this relationship.

* **Exercise 3.4.4:** In your database schema constructed for Exercise 3.2.1, indicate the keys you would expect for each relation.

Exercise 3.4.5: For each of the four parts of Exercise 3.2.4, indicate the expected keys of your relations.

!! **Exercise 3.4.6:** Suppose R is a relation with attributes $A_1, A_2, \ldots, A_n$. As a function of n, tell how many superkeys R has, if:

* a) The only key is A_1.

  b) The only keys are A_1 and A_2.

  c) The only keys are $\{A_1, A_2\}$ and $\{A_3, A_4\}$.

  d) The only keys are $\{A_1, A_2\}$ and $\{A_1, A_3\}$.

3.5   Rules About Functional Dependencies

In this section, we shall learn how to *reason* about FD's. That is, suppose we are told of a set of FD's that a relation satisfies. Often, we can deduce that the relation must satisfy certain other FD's. This ability to discover additional FD's is essential when we discuss the design of good relation schemas in Section 3.6.

Example 3.17 : If we are told that a relation R with attributes A, B, and C, satisfies the FD's $A \to B$ and $B \to C$, then we can deduce that R also satisfies the FD $A \to C$. How does that reasoning go? To prove that $A \to C$, we must consider two tuples of R that agree on A and prove they also agree on C.

Let the tuples agreeing on attribute A be (a, b_1, c_1) and (a, b_2, c_2). We assume the order of attributes in tuples is A, B, C. Since R satisfies $A \to B$, and these tuples agree on A, they must also agree on B. That is, $b_1 = b_2$, and the tuples are really (a, b, c_1) and (a, b, c_2), where b is both b_1 and b_2. Similarly, since R satisfies $B \to C$, and the tuples agree on B, they agree on C. Thus, $c_1 = c_2$; i.e., the tuples *do* agree on C. We have proved that any two tuples of R that agree on A also agree on C, and that is the FD $A \to C$.   □

FD's often can be presented in several different ways, without changing the set of legal instances of the relation. We say:

- Two sets of FD's S and T are *equivalent* if the set of relation instances satisfying S is exactly the same as the set of relation instances satisfying T.

- More generally, a set of FD's S *follows* from a set of FD's T if every relation instance that satisfies all the FD's in T also satisfies all the FD's in S.

Note then that two sets of FD's S and T are equivalent if and only if S follows from T, and T follows from S.

In this section we shall see several useful rules about FD's. In general, these rules let us replace one set of FD's by an equivalent set, or to add to a set of FD's others that follow from the original set. An example is the *transitive rule* that lets us follow chains of FD's, as in Example 3.17. We shall also give an algorithm for answering the general question of whether one FD follows from one or more other FD's.

3.5.1   The Splitting/Combining Rule

Recall that in Section 3.4.1 we defined the FD:

$$A_1 A_2 \cdots A_n \ \to \ B_1 B_2 \cdots B_m$$

to be a shorthand for the set of FD's:

$$A_1 A_2 \cdots A_n \rightarrow B_1$$
$$A_1 A_2 \cdots A_n \rightarrow B_2$$
$$\cdots$$
$$A_1 A_2 \cdots A_n \rightarrow B_m$$

That is, we may split attributes on the right side so that only one attribute appears on the right of each FD. Likewise, we can replace a collection of FD's with a common left side by a single FD with the same left side and all the right sides combined into one set of attributes. In either event, the new set of FD's is equivalent to the old. The equivalence noted above can be used in two ways.

- We can replace a FD $A_1 A_2 \cdots A_n \rightarrow B_1 B_2 \cdots B_m$ by a set of FD's $A_1 A_2 \cdots A_n \rightarrow B_i$ for $i = 1, 2, \ldots, m$. This transformation we call the *splitting rule*.

- We can replace a set of FD's $A_1 A_2 \cdots A_n \rightarrow B_i$ for $i = 1, 2, \ldots, m$ by the single FD $A_1 A_2 \cdots A_n \rightarrow B_1 B_2 \cdots B_m$. We call this transformation the *combining rule*.

For instance, we mentioned in Example 3.12 how the set of FD's:

$$\text{title year} \rightarrow \text{length}$$
$$\text{title year} \rightarrow \text{filmType}$$
$$\text{title year} \rightarrow \text{studioName}$$

is equivalent to the single FD:

$$\text{title year} \rightarrow \text{length filmType studioName}$$

One might imagine that splitting could be applied to the left sides of FD's as well as to right sides. However, there is no splitting rule for left sides, as the following example shows.

Example 3.18 : Consider one of the FD's such as:

$$\text{title year} \rightarrow \text{length}$$

for the relation Movies in Example 3.12. If we try to split the left side into

$$\text{title} \rightarrow \text{length}$$
$$\text{year} \rightarrow \text{length}$$

then we get two false FD's. That is, title does not functionally determine length, since there can be two movies with the same title (e.g., *King Kong*) but of different lengths. Similarly, year does not functionally determine length, because there are certainly movies of different lengths made in any one year. □

3.5.2 Trivial Functional Dependencies

A FD $A_1 A_2 \cdots A_n \rightarrow B$ is said to be *trivial* if B is one of the A's. For example,

$$\text{title year} \rightarrow \text{title}$$

is a trivial FD.

Every trivial FD holds in every relation, since it says that "two tuples that agree in all of $A_1, A_2, \ldots, A_n$ agree in one of them." Thus, we may assume any trivial FD, without having to justify it on the basis of what FD's are asserted for the relation.

In our original definition of FD's, we did not allow a FD to be trivial. However, there is no harm in including them, since they are always true, and they sometimes simplify the statement of rules.

When we allow trivial FD's, then we also allow (as shorthands) FD's in which some of the attributes on the right are also on the left. We say that a FD $A_1 A_2 \cdots A_n \rightarrow B_1 B_2 \cdots B_m$ is

- *Trivial* if the B's are a subset of the A's.

- *Nontrivial* if at least one of the B's is not among the A's.

- *Completely nontrivial* if none of the B's is also one of the A's.

Thus

$$\text{title year} \rightarrow \text{year length}$$

is nontrivial, but not completely nontrivial. By eliminating year from the right side we would get a completely nontrivial FD.

We can always remove from the right side of a FD those attributes that appear on the left. That is:

- The FD $A_1 A_2 \cdots A_n \rightarrow B_1 B_2 \cdots B_m$ is equivalent to

$$A_1 A_2 \cdots A_n \rightarrow C_1 C_2 \cdots C_k$$

where the C's are all those B's that are not also A's.

We call this rule, illustrated in Fig. 3.18, the *trivial-dependency rule*.

3.5.3 Computing the Closure of Attributes

Before proceeding to other rules, we shall give a general principle from which all rules follow. Suppose $\{A_1, A_2, \ldots, A_n\}$ is a set of attributes and S is a set of FD's. The *closure* of $\{A_1, A_2, \ldots, A_n\}$ under the FD's in S is the set of attributes B such that every relation that satisfies all the FD's in set S also satisfies $A_1 A_2 \cdots A_n \rightarrow B$. That is, $A_1 A_2 \cdots A_n \rightarrow B$ follows from the FD's of S. We denote the closure of a set of attributes $A_1 A_2 \cdots A_n$ by

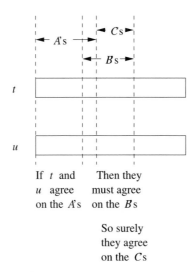

Figure 3.18: The trivial-dependency rule

$\{A_1, A_2, \ldots, A_n\}^+$. To simplify the discussion of computing closures, we shall allow trivial FD's, so $A_1, A_2, \ldots, A_n$ are always in $\{A_1, A_2, \ldots, A_n\}^+$.

Figure 3.19 illustrates the closure process. Starting with the given set of attributes, we repeatedly expand the set by adding the right sides of FD's as soon as we have included their left sides. Eventually, we cannot expand the set any more, and the resulting set is the closure. The following steps are a more detailed rendition of the algorithm for computing the closure of a set of attributes $\{A_1, A_2, \ldots, A_n\}$ with respect to a set of FD's.

1. Let X be a set of attributes that eventually will become the closure. First, we initialize X to be $\{A_1, A_2, \ldots, A_n\}$.

2. Now, we repeatedly search for some FD $B_1 B_2 \cdots B_m \rightarrow C$ such that all of $B_1, B_2, \ldots, B_m$ are in the set of attributes X, but C is not. We then add C to the set X.

3. Repeat step 2 as many times as necessary until no more attributes can be added to X. Since X can only grow, and the number of attributes of any relation schema must be finite, eventually nothing more can be added to X.

4. The set X, after no more attributes can be added to it, is the correct value of $\{A_1, A_2, \ldots, A_n\}^+$.

Example 3.19: Let us consider a relation with attributes A, B, C, D, E, and F. Suppose that this relation has the FD's $AB \rightarrow C$, $BC \rightarrow AD$, $D \rightarrow E$, and $CF \rightarrow B$. What is the closure of $\{A, B\}$, that is, $\{A, B\}^+$?

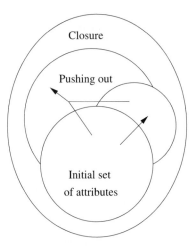

Figure 3.19: Computing the closure of a set of attributes

We start with $X = \{A, B\}$. First, notice that both attributes on the left side of FD $AB \rightarrow C$ are in X, so we may add the attribute C, which is on the right side of that FD. Thus, after one iteration of step 2, X becomes $\{A, B, C\}$.

Next, we see that the left side of $BC \rightarrow AD$ is now contained in X, so we may add to X the attributes A and D.[3] A is already there, but D is not, so X next becomes $\{A, B, C, D\}$. At this point, we may use the FD $D \rightarrow E$ to add E to X, which is now $\{A, B, C, D, E\}$. No more changes to X are possible. In particular, the FD $CF \rightarrow B$ can not be used, because its left side never becomes contained in X. Thus, $\{A, B\}^+ = \{A, B, C, D, E\}$. □

If we know how to compute the closure of any set of attributes, then we can test whether any given FD $A_1 A_2 \cdots A_n \rightarrow B$ follows from a set of FD's S. First compute $\{A_1, A_2, \ldots, A_n\}^+$ using the set of FD's S. If B is in $\{A_1, A_2, \ldots, A_n\}^+$, then $A_1 A_2 \cdots A_n \rightarrow B$ does follow from S, and if B is not in $\{A_1, A_2, \ldots, A_n\}^+$, then this FD does not follow from S. More generally, a FD with a set of attributes on the right can be tested if we remember that this FD is a shorthand for a set of FD's. Thus, $A_1 A_2 \cdots A_n \rightarrow B_1 B_2 \cdots B_m$ follows from set of FD's S if and only if all of $B_1, B_2, \ldots, B_m$ are in $\{A_1, A_2, \ldots, A_n\}^+$.

Example 3.20 : Consider the relation and FD's of Example 3.19. Suppose we wish to test whether $AB \rightarrow D$ follows from these FD's. We compute $\{A, B\}^+$, which is $\{A, B, C, D, E\}$, as we saw in that example. Since D is a member of the closure, we conclude that $AB \rightarrow D$ does follow.

On the other hand, consider the FD $D \rightarrow A$. To test whether this FD follows from the given FD's, first compute $\{D\}^+$. To do so, we start with $X = \{D\}$. We can use the FD $D \rightarrow E$ to add E to the set X. However,

---

[3]Recall that $BC \rightarrow AD$ is shorthand for the pair of FD's $BC \rightarrow A$ and $BC \rightarrow D$. We could treat each of these FD's separately if we wished.

then we are stuck. We cannot find any other FD whose left side is contained in $X = \{D, E\}$, so $\{D\}^+ = \{D, E\}$. Since A is not a member of $\{D, E\}$, we conclude that $D \rightarrow A$ does not follow. □

3.5.4 Why the Closure Algorithm Works

In this section, we shall show why the closure algorithm correctly decides whether or not a FD $A_1 A_2 \cdots A_n \rightarrow B$ follows from a given set of FD's S. There are two parts to the proof:

1. We must prove that the closure algorithm does not claim too much. That is, we must show that if $A_1 A_2 \cdots A_n \rightarrow B$ is asserted by the closure test (i.e., B is in $\{A_1, A_2, \ldots, A_n\}^+$), then $A_1 A_2 \cdots A_n \rightarrow B$ holds in any relation that satisfies all the FD's in S.

2. We must prove that the closure algorithm does not fail to discover a FD that truly follows from the set of FD's S.

Why the Closure Algorithm Claims only True FD's

We can prove by induction on the number of times that we apply the growing operation of step 2 that for every attribute D in X, the FD $A_1 A_2 \cdots A_n \rightarrow D$ holds (in the special case where D is among the A's, this FD is trivial). That is, every relation R satisfying all of the FD's in S also satisfies $A_1 A_2 \cdots A_n \rightarrow D$.

BASIS: The basis case is when there are zero steps. Then D must be one of $A_1, A_2, \ldots, A_n$, and surely $A_1 A_2 \cdots A_n \rightarrow D$ holds in any relation, because it is a trivial FD.

INDUCTION: For the induction, suppose D was added when we used the FD $B_1 B_2 \cdots B_m \rightarrow D$. We know by the inductive hypothesis that R satisfies $A_1 A_2 \cdots A_n \rightarrow B_i$ for all $i = 1, 2, \ldots, m$. Put another way, any two tuples of R that agree on all of $A_1, A_2, \ldots, A_n$ also agree on all of $B_1, B_2, \ldots, B_m$. Since R satisfies $B_1 B_2 \cdots B_m \rightarrow D$, we also know that these two tuples agree on D. Thus, R satisfies $A_1 A_2 \cdots A_n \rightarrow D$.

Why the Closure Algorithm Discovers All True FD's

Suppose $A_1 A_2 \cdots A_n \rightarrow B$ were a FD that the closure algorithm says does not follow from set S. That is, the closure of $\{A_1, A_2, \ldots, A_n\}$ using set of FD's S does not include B. We must show that FD $A_1 A_2 \cdots A_n \rightarrow B$ really doesn't follow from S. That is, we must show that there is at least one relation instance that satisfies all the FD's in S, and yet does not satisfy $A_1 A_2 \cdots A_n \rightarrow B$.

This instance I is actually quite simple to construct; it is shown in Fig. 3.20. I has only two tuples t and s. The two tuples agree in all the attributes of $\{A_1, A_2, \ldots, A_n\}^+$, and they disagree in all the other attributes. We must show first that I satisfies all the FD's of S, and then that it does not satisfy $A_1 A_2 \cdots A_n \rightarrow B$.

	$\{A_1, A_2, \ldots, A_n\}^+$	Other Attributes
t:	1 1 1 $\cdots$ 1 1	0 0 0 $\cdots$ 0 0
s:	1 1 1 $\cdots$ 1 1	1 1 1 $\cdots$ 1 1

Figure 3.20: An instance I satisfying S but not $A_1 A_2 \cdots A_n \to B$

Suppose there were some FD $C_1 C_2 \cdots C_k \to D$ in set S that instance I does not satisfy. Since I has only two tuples, t and s, those must be the two tuples that violate $C_1 C_2 \cdots C_k \to D$. That is, t and s agree in all the attributes of $\{C_1, C_2, \ldots, C_k\}$, yet disagree on D. If we examine Fig. 3.20 we see that all of $C_1, C_2, \ldots, C_k$ must be among the attributes of $\{A_1, A_2, \ldots, A_n\}^+$, because those are the only attributes on which t and s agree. Likewise, D must be among the other attributes, because only on those attributes do t and s disagree.

But then we did not compute the closure correctly. $C_1 C_2 \cdots C_k \to D$ should have been applied when X was $\{A_1, A_2, \ldots, A_n\}$ to add D to X. We conclude that $C_1 C_2 \cdots C_k \to D$ cannot exist; i.e., instance I satisfies S.

Second, we must show that I does not satisfy $A_1 A_2 \cdots A_n \to B$. However, this part is easy. Surely, $A_1, A_2, \ldots, A_n$ are among the attributes on which t and s agree. Also, we know that B is not in $\{A_1, A_2, \ldots, A_n\}^+$, so B is one of the attributes on which t and s disagree. Thus, I does not satisfy $A_1 A_2 \cdots A_n \to B$. We conclude that the closure algorithm asserts neither too few nor too many FD's; it asserts exactly those FD's that do follow from S.

3.5.5 The Transitive Rule

The transitive rule lets us cascade two FD's.

- If $A_1 A_2 \cdots A_n \to B_1 B_2 \cdots B_m$ and $B_1 B_2 \cdots B_m \to C_1 C_2 \cdots C_k$ hold in relation R, then $A_1 A_2 \cdots A_n \to C_1 C_2 \cdots C_k$ also holds in R.

If some of the C's are among the A's, we may eliminate them from the right side by the trivial-dependencies rule.

To see why the transitive rule holds, apply the test of Section 3.5.3. To test whether $A_1 A_2 \cdots A_n \to C_1 C_2 \cdots C_k$ holds, we need to compute the closure $\{A_1, A_2, \ldots, A_n\}^+$ with respect to the two given FD's.

The FD $A_1 A_2 \cdots A_n \to B_1 B_2 \cdots B_m$ tells us that all of $B_1, B_2, \ldots, B_m$ are in $\{A_1, A_2, \ldots, A_n\}^+$. Then, we can use the FD $B_1 B_2 \cdots B_m \to C_1 C_2 \cdots C_k$ to add $C_1, C_2, \ldots, C_k$ to $\{A_1, A_2, \ldots, A_n\}^+$. Since all the C's are in

$$\{A_1, A_2, \ldots, A_n\}^+$$

we conclude that $A_1 A_2 \cdots A_n \to C_1 C_2 \cdots C_k$ holds for any relation that satisfies both $A_1 A_2 \cdots A_n \to B_1 B_2 \cdots B_m$ and $B_1 B_2 \cdots B_m \to C_1 C_2 \cdots C_k$.

Closures and Keys

Notice that $\{A_1, A_2, \ldots, A_n\}^+$ is the set of all attributes of a relation if and only if $A_1, A_2, \ldots, A_n$ is a superkey for the relation. For only then does $A_1, A_2, \ldots, A_n$ functionally determine all the other attributes. We can test if $A_1, A_2, \ldots, A_n$ is a key for a relation by checking first that $\{A_1, A_2, \ldots, A_n\}^+$ is all attributes, and then checking that, for no set X formed by removing one attribute from $\{A_1, A_2, \ldots, A_n\}$, is X^+ the set of all attributes.

Example 3.21: Let us begin with the relation `Movies` of Fig. 3.7 that was constructed in Example 3.5 to represent the four attributes of entity set *Movies*, plus its relationship *Owns* with *Studios*. The relation and some sample data is:

title	year	length	filmType	studioName
Star Wars	1977	124	color	Fox
Mighty Ducks	1991	104	color	Disney
Wayne's World	1992	95	color	Paramount

Suppose we decided to represent some data about the owning studio in this same relation. For simplicity, we shall add only a city for the studio, representing its address. The relation might then look like

title	year	length	filmType	studioName	studioAddr
Star Wars	1977	124	color	Fox	Hollywood
Mighty Ducks	1991	104	color	Disney	Buena Vista
Wayne's World	1992	95	color	Paramount	Hollywood

Two of the FD's that we might reasonably claim to hold are:

$$\text{title year} \rightarrow \text{studioName}$$
$$\text{studioName} \rightarrow \text{studioAddr}$$

The first is justified because the *Owns* relationship is many-one. The second is justified because the address is an attribute of *Studios*, and the name of the studio is the key of *Studios*.

The transitive rule allows us to combine the two FD's above to get a new FD:

$$\text{title year} \rightarrow \text{studioAddr}$$

This FD says that a title and year (i.e., a movie) determines an address — the address of the studio owning the movie. □

3.5.6   Closing Sets of Functional Dependencies

As we have seen, given a set of FD's, we can often infer some other FD's, including both trivial and nontrivial FD's. We shall, in later sections, want to distinguish between *given* FD's that are stated initially for a relation and *derived* FD's that are inferred using one of the rules of this section or by using the algorithm for closing a set of attributes.

Moreover, we sometimes have a choice of which FD's we use to represent the full set of FD's for a relation. Any set of given FD's from which we can infer all the FD's for a relation will be called a *basis* for that relation. If no proper subset of the FD's in a basis can also derive the complete set of FD's, then we say the basis is *minimal*.

Example 3.22: Consider a relation $R(A, B, C)$ such that each attribute functionally determines the other two attributes. The full set of derived FD's thus includes six FD's with one attribute on the left and one on the right; $A \rightarrow B$, $A \rightarrow C$, $B \rightarrow A$, $B \rightarrow C$, $C \rightarrow A$, and $C \rightarrow B$. It also includes the three nontrivial FD's with two attributes on the left: $AB \rightarrow C$, $AC \rightarrow B$, and $BC \rightarrow A$. There are also the shorthands for pairs of FD's such as $A \rightarrow BC$, and we might also include the trivial FD's such as $A \rightarrow A$ or FD's like $AB \rightarrow BC$ that are not completely nontrivial (although in our strict definition of what is a FD we are not required to list trivial or partially trivial FD's, or dependencies that have several attributes on the right).

This relation and its FD's have several minimal bases. One is

$$\{A \rightarrow B,\ B \rightarrow A,\ B \rightarrow C,\ C \rightarrow B\}$$

Another is

$$\{A \rightarrow B,\ B \rightarrow C,\ C \rightarrow A\}$$

There are many other bases, even minimal bases, for this example relation, and we leave their discovery as an exercise. □

3.5.7   Projecting Functional Dependencies

When we study design of relation schemas, we shall also have need to answer the following question about FD's. Suppose we have a relation R with some FD's F, and we "project" R by eliminating certain attributes from the schema. Suppose S is the relation that results from R if we eliminate the components corresponding to the dropped attributes, in all R's tuples. Since S is a set, duplicate tuples are replaced by one copy. What FD's hold in S?

The answer is obtained in principle by computing all FD's that:

a) Follow from F, and

b) Involve only attributes of S.

A Complete Set of Inference Rules

If we want to know whether one FD follows from some given FD's, the closure computation of Section 3.5.3 will always serve. However, it is interesting to know that there is a set of rules, called *Armstrong's axioms*, from which it is possible to derive any FD that follows from a given set. These axioms are:

1. *Reflexivity.* If $\{B_1, B_2, \ldots, B_m\} \subseteq \{A_1, A_2, \ldots, A_n\}$, then $A_1 A_2 \cdots A_n \rightarrow B_1 B_2 \cdots B_m$. These are what we have called trivial FD's.

2. *Augmentation.* If $A_1 A_2 \cdots A_n \rightarrow B_1 B_2 \cdots B_m$, then

$$A_1 A_2 \cdots A_n C_1 C_2 \cdots C_k \rightarrow B_1 B_2 \cdots B_m C_1 C_2 \cdots C_k$$

for any set of attributes $C_1, C_2, \ldots, C_k$.

3. *Transitivity.* If

$$A_1 A_2 \cdots A_n \rightarrow B_1 B_2 \cdots B_m \text{ and } B_1 B_2 \cdots B_m \rightarrow C_1 C_2 \cdots C_k$$

then $A_1 A_2 \cdots A_n \rightarrow C_1 C_2 \cdots C_k$.

Since there may be a large number of such FD's, and many of them may be redundant (i.e., they follow from other such FD's), we are free to simplify that set of FD's if we wish. However, in general, the calculation of the FD's for S is in the worst case exponential in the number of attributes of S.

Example 3.23: Suppose $R(A, B, C, D)$ has FD's $A \rightarrow B$, $B \rightarrow C$, and $C \rightarrow D$. Suppose also that we wish to project out the attribute B, leaving a relation $S(A, C, D)$. In principle, to find the FD's for S, we need to take the closure of all eight subsets of $\{A, C, D\}$, using the full set of FD's, including those involving B. However, there are some obvious simplifications we can make.

- Closing the empty set and the set of all attributes cannot yield a nontrivial FD.

- If we already know that the closure of some set X is all attributes, then we cannot discover any new FD's by closing supersets of X.

Thus, we may start with the closures of the singleton sets, and then move on to the doubleton sets if necessary. For each closure of a set X, we add the

FD $X \rightarrow E$ for each attribute E that is in X^+ and in the schema of S, but not in X.

First, $\{A\}^+ = \{A, B, C, D\}$. Thus, $A \rightarrow C$ and $A \rightarrow D$ hold in S. Note that $A \rightarrow B$ is true in R, but makes no sense in S because B is not an attribute of S.

Next, we consider $\{C\}^+ = \{C, D\}$, from which we get the additional FD $C \rightarrow D$ for S. Since $\{D\}^+ = \{D\}$, we can add no more FD's, and are done with the singletons.

Since $\{A\}^+$ includes all attributes of S, there is no point in considering any superset of $\{A\}$. The reason is that whatever FD we could discover, for instance $AC \rightarrow D$, follows by the augmentation rule (as described in the box on "A Complete Set of Inference Rules") from one of the FD's we already discovered for S by considering A alone as the left side. Thus, the only doubleton whose closure we need to take is $\{C, D\}^+ = \{C, D\}$. This observation allows us to add nothing. We are done with the closures, and the FD's we have discovered are $A \rightarrow C$, $A \rightarrow D$, and $C \rightarrow D$.

If we wish, we can observe that $A \rightarrow D$ follows from the other two by transitivity. Therefore a simpler, equivalent set of FD's for S is $A \rightarrow C$ and $C \rightarrow D$. □

3.5.8 Exercises for Section 3.5

* **Exercise 3.5.1:** Consider a relation with schema $R(A, B, C, D)$ and FD's $AB \rightarrow C$, $C \rightarrow D$, and $D \rightarrow A$.

   a) What are all the nontrivial FD's that follow from the given FD's? You should restrict yourself to FD's with single attributes on the right side.

   b) What are all the keys of R?

   c) What are all the superkeys for R that are not keys?

Exercise 3.5.2: Repeat Exercise 3.5.1 for the following schemas and sets of FD's:

   i) $S(A, B, C, D)$ with FD's $A \rightarrow B$, $B \rightarrow C$, and $B \rightarrow D$.

   ii) $T(A, B, C, D)$ with FD's $AB \rightarrow C$, $BC \rightarrow D$, $CD \rightarrow A$, and $AD \rightarrow B$.

   iii) $U(A, B, C, D)$ with FD's $A \rightarrow B$, $B \rightarrow C$, $C \rightarrow D$, and $D \rightarrow A$.

Exercise 3.5.3: Show that the following rules hold, by using the closure test of Section 3.5.3.

* a) *Augmenting left sides.* If $A_1 A_2 \cdots A_n \rightarrow B$ is a FD, and C is another attribute, then $A_1 A_2 \cdots A_n C \rightarrow B$ follows.

b) *Full augmentation.* If $A_1 A_2 \cdots A_n \rightarrow B$ is a FD, and C is another attribute, then $A_1 A_2 \cdots A_n C \rightarrow BC$ follows. Note: from this rule, the "augmentation" rule mentioned in the box of Section 3.5.6 on "A Complete Set of Inference Rules" can easily be proved.

c) *Pseudotransitivity.* Suppose FD's $A_1 A_2 \cdots A_n \rightarrow B_1 B_2 \cdots B_m$ and $C_1 C_2 \cdots C_k \rightarrow D$ hold, and the B's are each among the C's. Then $A_1 A_2 \cdots A_n E_1 E_2 \cdots E_j \rightarrow D$ holds, where the E's are all those of the C's that are not found among the B's.

d) *Addition.* If FD's $A_1 A_2 \cdots A_n \rightarrow B_1 B_2 \cdots B_m$ and

$$C_1 C_2 \cdots C_k \rightarrow D_1 D_2 \cdots D_j$$

hold, then FD $A_1 A_2 \cdots A_n C_1 C_2 \cdots C_k \rightarrow B_1 B_2 \cdots B_m D_1 D_2 \cdots D_j$ also holds. In the above, we should remove one copy of any attribute that appears among both the A's and C's or among both the B's and D's.

! **Exercise 3.5.4 :** Show that each of the following are *not* valid rules about FD's by giving example relations that satisfy the given FD's (following the "if") but not the FD that allegedly follows (after the "then").

* a) If $A \rightarrow B$ then $B \rightarrow A$.

b) If $AB \rightarrow C$ and $A \rightarrow C$, then $B \rightarrow C$.

c) If $AB \rightarrow C$, then $A \rightarrow C$ or $B \rightarrow C$.

! **Exercise 3.5.5 :** Show that if a relation has no attribute that is functionally determined by all the other attributes, then the relation has no nontrivial FD's at all.

! **Exercise 3.5.6 :** Let X and Y be sets of attributes. Show that if $X \subseteq Y$, then $X^+ \subseteq Y^+$, where the closures are taken with respect to the same set of FD's.

! **Exercise 3.5.7 :** Prove that $(X^+)^+ = X^+$.

!! **Exercise 3.5.8 :** We say a set of attributes X is *closed* (with respect to a given set of FD's) if $X^+ = X$. Consider a relation with schema $R(A, B, C, D)$ and an unknown set of FD's. If we are told which sets of attributes are closed, we can discover the FD's. What are the FD's if:

* a) All sets of the four attributes are closed.

b) The only closed sets are $\emptyset$ and $\{A, B, C, D\}$.

c) The closed sets are $\emptyset$, $\{A,B\}$, and $\{A, B, C, D\}$.

! **Exercise 3.5.9 :** Find all the minimal bases for the FD's and relation of Example 3.22.

! **Exercise 3.5.10 :** Suppose we have relation $R(A, B, C, D, E)$, with some set of FD's, and we wish to project those FD's onto relation $S(A, B, C)$. Give the FD's that hold in S if the FD's for R are:

* a) $AB \rightarrow DE$, $C \rightarrow E$, $D \rightarrow C$, and $E \rightarrow A$.

   b) $A \rightarrow D$, $BD \rightarrow E$, $AC \rightarrow E$, and $DE \rightarrow B$.

   c) $AB \rightarrow D$, $AC \rightarrow E$, $BC \rightarrow D$, $D \rightarrow A$, and $E \rightarrow B$.

   d) $A \rightarrow B$, $B \rightarrow C$, $C \rightarrow D$, $D \rightarrow E$, and $E \rightarrow A$.

In each case, it is sufficient to give a minimal basis for the full set of FD's of S.

!! **Exercise 3.5.11 :** Show that if a FD F follows from some given FD's, then we can prove F from the given FD's using Armstrong's axioms (defined in the box "A Complete Set of Inference Rules" in Section 3.5.6). *Hint*: Examine the algorithm for computing the closure of a set of attributes and show how each step of that algorithm can be mimicked by inferring some FD's by Armstrong's axioms.

3.6   Design of Relational Database Schemas

Careless selection of a relational database schema can lead to problems. For instance, Example 3.6 showed what happens if we try to combine the relation for a many-many relationship with the relation for one of its entity sets. The principal problem we identified is redundancy, where a fact is repeated in more than one tuple. This problem is seen in Fig. 3.17, which we reproduce here as Fig. 3.21; the length and film-type for *Star Wars* and *Wayne's World* are each repeated, once for each star of the movie.

   In this section, we shall tackle the problem of design of good relation schemas in the following stages:

1. We first explore in more detail the problems that arise when our schema is flawed.

2. Then, we introduce the idea of "decomposition," breaking a relation schema (set of attributes) into two smaller schemas.

3. Next, we introduce "Boyce-Codd normal form," or "BCNF," a condition on a relation schema that eliminates these problems.

4. These points are tied together when we explain how to assure the BCNF condition by decomposing relation schemas.

title	*year*	*length*	*filmType*	*studioName*	*starName*
Star Wars	1977	124	color	Fox	Carrie Fisher
Star Wars	1977	124	color	Fox	Mark Hamill
Star Wars	1977	124	color	Fox	Harrison Ford
Mighty Ducks	1991	104	color	Disney	Emilio Estevez
Wayne's World	1992	95	color	Paramount	Dana Carvey
Wayne's World	1992	95	color	Paramount	Mike Meyers

Figure 3.21: The relation `Movies` exhibiting anomalies

3.6.1 Anomalies

Problems such as redundancy that occur when we try to cram too much into a single relation are called *anomalies*. The principal kinds of anomalies that we encounter are:

1. *Redundancy.* Information may be repeated unnecessarily in several tuples. Examples are the length and film type for movies as in Fig. 3.21.

2. *Update Anomalies.* We may change information in one tuple but leave the same information unchanged in another. For example, if we found that *Star Wars* was really 125 minutes long, we might carelessly change the length in the first tuple of Fig. 3.21 but not in the second or third tuples. True, we might argue that one should never be so careless. But we shall see that it is possible to redesign relation `Movies` so that the risk of such mistakes does not exist.

3. *Deletion Anomalies.* If a set of values becomes empty, we may lose other information as a side effect. For example, should we delete Emilio Estevez from the set of stars of *Mighty Ducks*, then we have no more stars for that movie in the database. The last tuple for *Mighty Ducks* in the relation `Movies` would disappear, and with it information that it is 104 minutes long and in color.

3.6.2 Decomposing Relations

The accepted way to eliminate these anomalies is to *decompose* relations. Decomposition of R involves splitting the attributes of R to make the schemas of two new relations. Our decomposition rule also involves a way of populating those relations with tuples by "projecting" the tuples of R. After describing the decomposition process, we shall show how to pick a decomposition that eliminates anomalies.

Given a relation R with schema $\{A_1, A_2, \ldots, A_n\}$, we may *decompose* R into two relations S and T with schemas $\{B_1, B_2, \ldots, B_m\}$ and $\{C_1, C_2, \ldots, C_k\}$, respectively, such that

1. $\{A_1, A_2, \ldots, A_n\} = \{B_1, B_2, \ldots, B_m\} \cup \{C_1, C_2, \ldots, C_k\}$.

2. The tuples in relation S are the *projections* onto $\{B_1, B_2, \ldots, B_m\}$ of all the tuples in R. That is, for each tuple t in the current instance of R, take the components of t in the attributes $B_1, B_2, \ldots, B_m$. These components form a tuple, and this tuple belongs in the current instance of S. However, relations are sets, and the same tuple of S could result from projecting two different tuples of R. If so, we put into the current instance of S only one copy of each tuple.

3. Similarly, the tuples in relation T are the projections, onto set of attributes $\{C_1, C_2, \ldots, C_k\}$, of the tuples in the current instance of R.

Example 3.24: Let us decompose the `Movies` relation of Fig. 3.21. First, we shall decompose the schema. Our choice, whose merit will be seen in Section 3.6.3, is to use

1. A relation called `Movies1`, whose schema is all the attributes except for `starName`.

2. A relation called `Movies2`, whose schema consists of the attributes `title`, `year`, and `starName`.

Now, let us illustrate the process of decomposing relation instances by decomposing the sample data of Fig. 3.21. First, let us construct the projection onto the `Movies1` schema:

$$\{\texttt{title}, \texttt{year}, \texttt{length}, \texttt{filmType}, \texttt{studioName}\}$$

The first three tuples of Fig. 3.21 each have the same components in these five attributes:

$$(\texttt{Star Wars}, 1977, 124, \texttt{color}, \texttt{Fox})$$

The fourth tuple yields a different tuple for the first five components, and the fifth and sixth tuple each yield the same five-component tuple. The resulting relation for `Movies1` is shown in Fig. 3.22.

title	year	length	*filmType*	*studioName*
Star Wars	1977	124	color	Fox
Mighty Ducks	1991	104	color	Disney
Wayne's World	1992	95	color	Paramount

Figure 3.22: The relation `Movies1`

Next, consider the projection of Fig. 3.21 onto the schema of `Movies2`. Each of the six tuples of that figure differ in at least one of the attributes `title`, `year`, and `starName`, so the result is the relation shown in Fig. 3.23.   □

title	year	starName
Star Wars	1977	Carrie Fisher
Star Wars	1977	Mark Hamill
Star Wars	1977	Harrison Ford
Mighty Ducks	1991	Emilio Estevez
Wayne's World	1992	Dana Carvey
Wayne's World	1992	Mike Meyers

Figure 3.23: The relation Movies2

Notice how this decomposition eliminates the anomalies we mentioned in Section 3.6.1. The redundancy has been eliminated; for example, the length of each film appears only once, in relation Movies1. The risk of an update anomaly is gone. For instance, since we only have to change the length of *Star Wars* in one tuple of Movies1, we cannot wind up with two different lengths for that movie.

Finally, the risk of a deletion anomaly is gone. If we delete all the stars for *Mighty Ducks*, say, that deletion makes the movie disappear from Movies2. But all the other information about the movie can still be found in Movies1.

It might appear that Movies2 still has redundancy, since the title and year of a movie can appear several times. However, these two attributes form a key for movies, and there is no more succinct way to represent a movie. Moreover, Movies2 does not offer an opportunity for an update anomaly. For instance, one might suppose that if we changed to 2003 the year in the Carrie Fisher tuple, but not the other two tuples for *Star Wars*, then there would be an update anomaly. However, there is nothing in our assumed FD's that prevents there being a different movie named *Star Wars* in 2003, and Carrie Fisher may star in that one as well. Thus, we do not want to prevent changing the year in one *Star Wars* tuple, nor is such a change necessarily incorrect.

3.6.3 Boyce-Codd Normal Form

The goal of decomposition is to replace a relation by several that do not exhibit anomalies. There is, it turns out, a simple condition under which the anomalies discussed above can be guaranteed not to exist. This condition is called *Boyce-Codd normal form*, or *BCNF*.

- A relation R is in BCNF if and only if: whenever there is a nontrivial FD $A_1 A_2 \cdots A_n \rightarrow B$ for R, it is the case that $\{A_1, A_2, \ldots, A_n\}$ is a superkey for R.

That is, the left side of every nontrivial FD must be a superkey. Recall that a superkey need not be minimal. Thus, an equivalent statement of the BCNF condition is that the left side of every nontrivial FD must contain a key.

When we find a BCNF-violating FD, we sometimes wind up with a simpler complete decomposition into BCNF relations if we augment the right side of the FD to include the right sides of all the other FD's that have the same left side, whether or not they are BCNF violations. The following is an alternative definition of BCNF in which we look for a set of FD's with common left side, at least one of which is nontrivial and violates the BCNF condition.

- Relation R is in BCNF if and only if: whenever there is a nontrivial FD $A_1 A_2 \cdots A_n \rightarrow B_1 B_2 \cdots B_m$ for R, it is the case that $\{A_1, A_2, \ldots, A_n\}$ is a superkey for R.

This requirement is equivalent to the original BCNF condition. Recall that the FD $A_1 A_2 \cdots A_n \rightarrow B_1 B_2 \cdots B_m$ is shorthand for the set of FD's $A_1 A_2 \cdots A_n \rightarrow B_i$ for $i = 1, 2, \ldots, m$. Since there must be at least one B_i that is not among the A's (or else $A_1 A_2 \cdots A_n \rightarrow B_1 B_2 \cdots B_m$ would be trivial), $A_1 A_2 \cdots A_n \rightarrow B_i$ is a BCNF violation according to our original definition.

Example 3.25 : Relation Movies, as in Fig. 3.21, is not in BCNF. To see why, we first need to determine what sets of attributes are keys. We argued in Example 3.13 why {title, year, starName} is a key. Thus, any set of attributes containing these three is a superkey. The same arguments we followed in Example 3.13 can be used to explain why no set of attributes that does not include all three of title, year, and starName could be a superkey. Thus, we assert that {title, year, starName} is the only key for Movies.

However, consider the FD

$$\texttt{title year} \rightarrow \texttt{length filmType studioName}$$

which holds in Movies according to our discussion in Example 3.13.

Unfortunately, the left side of the above FD is not a superkey. In particular, we know that title and year do not functionally determine the sixth attribute, starName. Thus, the existence of this FD violates the BCNF condition and tells us Movies is not in BCNF. Moreover, according to the original definition of BCNF, where a single attribute on the right side was required, we can offer any of the three FD's, such as title year $\rightarrow$ length, as a BCNF violation. □

Example 3.26 : On the other hand, Movies1 of Fig. 3.22 is in BCNF. Since

$$\texttt{title year} \rightarrow \texttt{length filmType studioName}$$

holds in this relation, and we have argued that neither title nor year by itself functionally determines any of the other attributes, the only key for Movies1 is {title, year}. Moreover, the only nontrivial FD's must have at least title and year on the left side, and therefore their left sides must be superkeys. Thus, Movies1 is in BCNF. □

Example 3.27: We claim that any two-attribute relation is in BCNF. We need to examine the possible nontrivial FD's with a single attribute on the right. There are not too many cases to consider, so let us consider them in turn. In what follows, suppose that the attributes are A and B.

1. There are no nontrivial FD's. Then surely the BCNF condition must hold, because only a nontrivial FD can violate this condition. Incidentally, note that $\{A, B\}$ is the only key in this case.

2. $A \rightarrow B$ holds, but $B \rightarrow A$ does not hold. In this case, A is the only key, and each nontrivial FD contains A on the left (in fact the left can only be A). Thus there is no violation of the BCNF condition.

3. $B \rightarrow A$ holds, but $A \rightarrow B$ does not hold. This case is symmetric to case (2).

4. Both $A \rightarrow B$ and $B \rightarrow A$ hold. Then both A and B are keys. Surely any FD has at least one of these on the left, so there can be no BCNF violation.

It is worth noticing from case (4) above that there may be more than one key for a relation. Further, the BCNF condition only requires that *some* key be contained in the left side of any nontrivial FD, not that all keys are contained in the left side. Also observe that a relation with two attributes, each functionally determining the other, is not completely implausible. For example, a company may assign its employees unique employee ID's and also record their Social Security numbers. A relation with attributes `empID` and `ssNo` would have each attribute functionally determining the other. Put another way, each attribute is a key, since we don't expect to find two tuples that agree on either attribute. □

3.6.4 Decomposition into BCNF

By repeatedly choosing suitable decompositions, we can break any relation schema into a collection of subsets of its attributes with the following important properties:

1. These subsets are the schemas of relations in BCNF.

2. The data in the original relation is represented faithfully by the data in the relations that are the result of the decomposition, in a sense to be made precise in Section 3.6.5. Roughly, we need to be able to reconstruct the original relation instance exactly from the decomposed relation instances.

Example 3.27 suggests that perhaps all we have to do is break a relation schema into two-attribute subsets, and the result is surely in BCNF. However, such an arbitrary decomposition will not satisfy condition (2), as we shall see in

Section 3.6.5. In fact, we must be more careful and use the violating FD's to guide our decomposition.

The decomposition strategy we shall follow is to look for a nontrivial FD $A_1 A_2 \cdots A_n \rightarrow B_1 B_2 \cdots B_m$ that violates BCNF; i.e., $\{A_1, A_2, \ldots, A_n\}$ is not a superkey. As a heuristic, we shall generally add to the right side as many attributes as are functionally determined by $\{A_1, A_2, \ldots, A_n\}$. Figure 3.24 illustrates how the attributes are broken into two overlapping relation schemas. One is all the attributes involved in the violating FD, and the other is the left side of the FD plus all the attributes *not* involved in the FD, i.e., all the attributes except those B's that are not A's.

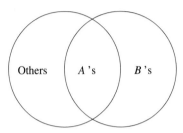

Figure 3.24: Relation schema decomposition based on a BCNF violation

Example 3.28: Consider our running example, the `Movies` relation of Fig. 3.21. We saw in Example 3.25 that

$$\texttt{title year} \rightarrow \texttt{length filmType studioName}$$

is a BCNF violation. In this case, the right side already includes all the attributes functionally determined by `title` and `year`, so we shall use this BCNF violation to decompose `Movies` into:

1. The schema with all the attributes of the FD, that is:

    $$\{\texttt{title, year, length, filmType, studioName}\}$$

2. The schema with all attributes of `Movies` except the three that appear on the right of the FD. Thus, we remove `length`, `filmType`, and `studioName`, leaving the second schema:

    $$\{\texttt{title, year, starName}\}$$

Notice that these schemas are the ones selected for relations `Movies1` and `Movies2` in Example 3.24. We observed that these are each in BCNF in Example 3.26. □

title	year	length	filmType	studioName	studioAddr
Star Wars	1977	124	color	Fox	Hollywood
Mighty Ducks	1991	104	color	Disney	Buena Vista
Wayne's World	1992	95	color	Paramount	Hollywood
Addams Family	1991	102	color	Paramount	Hollywood

Figure 3.25: The relation `MovieStudio`

Example 3.29 : Let us consider the relation that was introduced in Example 3.21. This relation, which we shall call `MovieStudio`, stores information about movies, their owning studios, and the addresses of those studios. The schema and some typical tuples for this relation are shown in Fig. 3.25.

Note that `MovieStudio` contains redundant information. Because we added to our usual sample data a second movie owned by Paramount, the address of Paramount is stated twice. However, the source of this problem is not the same as in Example 3.28. In the latter example, the problem was that a many-many relationship (the stars of a given movie) was being stored with other information about the movie. Here, everything is single-valued: the attribute `length` for a movie, the relationship `ownedBy` that relates a movie to its unique owning studio, and the attribute `address` for studios.

In this case, the problem is that there is a "transitive dependency." That is, as mentioned in Example 3.21, relation `MovieStudio` has the FD's:

$$\text{title year} \rightarrow \text{studioName}$$
$$\text{studioName} \rightarrow \text{studioAddr}$$

We may apply the transitive rule to these to get a new FD:

$$\text{title year} \rightarrow \text{studioAddr}$$

That is, a title and year (i.e., the key for movies) functionally determine a studio address — the address of the studio that owns the movie. Since

$$\text{title year} \rightarrow \text{length filmType}$$

is another obvious functional dependency, we conclude that {`title`, `year`} is a key for `MovieStudio`; in fact it is the only key.

On the other hand, FD:

$$\text{studioName} \rightarrow \text{studioAddr}$$

which is one of those used in the application of the transitive rule above, is non-trivial but its left side is not a superkey. This observation tells us `MovieStudio` is not in BCNF. We can fix the problem by following the decomposition rule, using the above FD. The first schema of the decomposition is the attributes of the FD itself, that is: {studioName, studioAddr}. The second schema is all the attributes of MovieStudio except for studioAddr, because the latter attribute is on the right of the FD used in the decomposition. Thus, the other schema is:

{title, year, length, filmType, studioName}

The projection of Fig. 3.25 onto these schemas gives us the two relations MovieStudio1 and MovieStudio2 shown in Figs. 3.26 and 3.27. Each of these is in BCNF. Recall from Section 3.5.7 that for each of the relations in the decomposition, we need to compute its FD's by computing the closure of each subset of its attributes, using the full set of given FD's. In general, the process is exponential in the number of attributes of the decomposed relations, but we also saw in Section 3.5.7 that there were some simplifications possible.

In our case, it is easy to determine that a basis for the FD's of MovieStudio1 is

title year → length filmType studioname

and for MovieStudio2 the only nontrivial FD is

studioName → studioAddr

Thus, the sole key for MovieStudio1 is {title, year}, and the sole key for MovieStudio2 is {studioName}. In each case, there are no nontrivial FD's that do not contain these keys on the left. □

title	*year*	*length*	*filmType*	*studioName*
Star Wars	1977	124	color	Fox
Mighty Ducks	1991	104	color	Disney
Wayne's World	1992	95	color	Paramount
Addams Family	1991	102	color	Paramount

Figure 3.26: The relation MovieStudio1

studioName	*studioAddr*
Fox	Hollywood
Disney	Buena Vista
Paramount	Hollywood

Figure 3.27: The relation MovieStudio2

In each of the previous examples, one judicious application of the decomposition rule is enough to produce a collection of relations that are in BCNF. In general, that is not the case.

Example 3.30: We could generalize Example 3.29 to have a chain of FD's longer than two. Consider a relation with schema

$$\{\texttt{title, year, studioName, president, presAddr}\}$$

That is, each tuple of this relation tells about a movie, its studio, the president of the studio, and the address of the president of the studio. Three FD's that we would assume in this relation are

$$\texttt{title year} \rightarrow \texttt{studioName}$$
$$\texttt{studioName} \rightarrow \texttt{president}$$
$$\texttt{president} \rightarrow \texttt{presAddr}$$

The sole key for this relation is {`title, year`}. Thus the last two FD's above violate BCNF. Suppose we choose to decompose starting with

$$\texttt{studioName} \rightarrow \texttt{president}$$

First, we should add to the right side of this functional dependency any other attributes in the closure of `studioName`. By the transitive rule applied to `studioName` $\rightarrow$ `president` and `president` $\rightarrow$ `presAddr`, we know

$$\texttt{studioName} \rightarrow \texttt{presAddr}$$

Combining the two FD's with `studioName` on the left, we get:

$$\texttt{studioName} \rightarrow \texttt{president presAddr}$$

This FD has a maximally expanded right side, so we shall now decompose into the following two relation schemas.

$$\{\texttt{title, year, studioName}\}$$
$$\{\texttt{studioName, president, presAddr}\}$$

If we follow the projection algorithm of Section 3.5.7, we determine that the FD's for the first relation has a basis:

$$\texttt{title year} \rightarrow \texttt{studioName}$$

while the second has

$$\texttt{studioName} \rightarrow \texttt{president}$$
$$\texttt{president} \rightarrow \texttt{presAddr}$$

Thus, the sole key for the first relation is {`title, year`}, and it is therefore in BCNF. However, the second has {`studioName`} for its only key but also has the FD:

$$\texttt{president} \rightarrow \texttt{presAddr}$$

which is a BCNF violation. Thus, we must decompose again, this time using the above FD. The resulting three relation schemas, all in BCNF, are:

> {title, year, studioName}
> {studioName, president}
> {president, presAddr}

□

In general, we must keep applying the decomposition rule as many times as needed, until all our relations are in BCNF. We can be sure of ultimate success, because every time we apply the decomposition rule to a relation R, the two resulting schemas each have fewer attributes than that of R. As we saw in Example 3.27, when we get down to two attributes, the relation is sure to be in BCNF; often relations with larger sets of attributes are also in BCNF.

3.6.5 Recovering Information from a Decomposition

Let us now turn our attention to the question of why the decomposition algorithm of Section 3.6.4 preserves the information that was contained in the original relation. The idea is that if we follow this algorithm, then the projections of the original tuples can be "joined" again to produce all and only the original tuples.

To simplify the situation, let us consider a relation $R(A, B, C)$ and a FD $B \to C$, which we suppose is a BCNF violation. It is possible, for example, that as in Example 3.29, there is a transitive dependency chain, with another FD $A \to B$. In that case, $\{A\}$ is the only key, and the left side of $B \to C$ clearly is not a superkey. Another possibility is that $B \to C$ is the only nontrivial FD, in which case the only key is $\{A, B\}$. Again, the left side of $B \to C$ is not a superkey. In either case, the required decomposition based on the FD $B \to C$ separates the attributes into schemas $\{A, B\}$ and $\{B, C\}$.

Let t be a tuple of R. We may write $t = (a, b, c)$, where a, b, and c are the components of t for attributes A, B, and C, respectively. Tuple t projects as (a, b) for the relation with schema $\{A, B\}$ and as (b, c) for the relation with schema $\{B, C\}$.

It is possible to *join* a tuple from $\{A, B\}$ with a tuple from $\{B, C\}$, provided they agree in the B component. In particular, (a, b) joins with (b, c) to give us the original tuple $t = (a, b, c)$ back again. That is, regardless of what tuple t we started with, we can always join its projections to get t back.

However, getting back those tuples we started with is not enough to assure that the original relation R is truly represented by the decomposition. What might happen if there were two tuples of R, say $t = (a, b, c)$ and $v = (d, b, e)$? When we project t onto $\{A, B\}$ we get $u = (a, b)$, and when we project v onto $\{B, C\}$ we get $w = (b, e)$, as suggested by Fig. 3.28.

Tuples u and w join, since they agree on their B components. The resulting tuple is $x = (a, b, e)$. Is it possible that x is a bogus tuple? That is, could (a, b, e) not be a tuple of R?

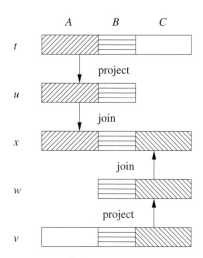

Figure 3.28: Joining two tuples from projected relations

Since we assume the FD $B \rightarrow C$ for relation R, the answer is "no." Recall that this FD says any two tuples of R that agree in their B components must also agree in their C components. Since t and v agree in their B components (they both have b there), they also agree on their C components. That means $c = e$; i.e., the two values we supposed were different are really the same. Thus, (a, b, e) is really (a, b, c); that is, $x = t$.

Since t is in R, it must be that x is in R. Put another way, as long as FD $B \rightarrow C$ holds, the joining of two projected tuples cannot produce a bogus tuple. Rather, every tuple produced by joining is guaranteed to be a tuple of R.

This argument works in general. We assumed A, B, and C were each single attributes, but the same argument would apply if they were any sets of attributes. That is, we take any BCNF-violating FD, let B be the attributes on the left side, let C be the attributes on the right but not the left, and let A be the attributes on neither side. We may conclude:

- If we decompose a relation according to the method of Section 3.6.4, then the original relation can be recovered exactly by joining the tuples of the new relations in all possible ways.

If we decompose relations in a way that is not based on a FD, then we might not be able to recover the original relation. Here is an example.

Example 3.31 : Suppose we have the relation $R(A, B, C)$ as above, but that the FD $B \rightarrow C$ does not hold. Then R might consist of the two tuples

A	B	C
1	2	3
4	2	5

The projections of R onto the relations with schemas $\{A, B\}$ and $\{B, C\}$ are

A	B
1	2
4	2

and

B	C
2	3
2	5

respectively. Since all four tuples share the same B-value, 2, each tuple of one relation joins with both tuples of the other relation. Thus, when we try to reconstruct R by joining, we get

A	B	C
1	2	3
1	2	5
4	2	3
4	2	5

That is, we get "too much"; we get two bogus tuples, $(1, 2, 5)$ and $(4, 2, 3)$ that were not in the original relation R.   □

3.6.6   Third Normal Form

Occasionally, one encounters a relation schema and its FD's that are not in BCNF but that one doesn't want to decompose further. The following example is typical.

Example 3.32: Suppose we have a relation `Bookings` with attributes:

1. `title`, the name of a movie.

2. `theater`, the name of a theater where the movie is being shown.

3. `city`, the city where the theater is located.

The intent behind a tuple (m, t, c) is that the movie with title m is currently being shown at theater t in city c.

We might reasonably assert the following FD's:

$$\text{theater} \rightarrow \text{city}$$
$$\text{title city} \rightarrow \text{theater}$$

The first says that a theater is located in one city. The second is not obvious but is based on the assumed practice of not booking a movie into two theaters in the same city. We shall assert this FD if only for the sake of the example.

Let us first find the keys. No single attribute is a key. For example, `title` is not a key because a movie can play in several theaters at once and in several cities at once.[4] Also, `theater` is not a key, because although `theater` functionally determines `city`, there are multiscreen theaters that show many movies at once. Thus, `theater` does not determine `title`. Finally, `city` is not a key because cities usually have more than one theater and more than one movie playing.

On the other hand, two of the three sets of two attributes are keys. Clearly {`title, city`} is a key because of the given FD that says these attributes functionally determine `theater`.

It is also true that {`theater, title`} is a key. To see why, start with the given FD `theater` $\rightarrow$ `city`. By the augmentation rule of Exercise 3.5.3(a), `theater title` $\rightarrow$ `city` follows. Intuitively, if `theater` alone functionally determines `city`, then surely `theatre` and `title` together will do so.

The remaining pair of attributes, `city` and `theater`, do not functionally determine `title`, and are therefore not a key. We conclude that the only two keys are

$$\{\texttt{title, city}\}$$
$$\{\texttt{theater, title}\}$$

Now we immediately see a BCNF violation. We were given functional dependency `theater` $\rightarrow$ `city`, but its left side, `theater`, is not a superkey. We are therefore tempted to decompose, using this BCNF-violating FD, into the two relation schemas:

$$\{\texttt{theater, city}\}$$
$$\{\texttt{theater, title}\}$$

There is a problem with this decomposition, concerning the FD

$$\texttt{title city} \;\rightarrow\; \texttt{theater}$$

There could be current relations for the decomposed schemas that satisfy the FD `theater` $\rightarrow$ `city` (which can be checked in the relation {`theater, city`}) but that, when joined, yield a relation not satisfying `title city` $\rightarrow$ `theater`. For instance, the two relations

theater	*city*
Guild	Menlo Park
Park	Menlo Park

---

[4]In this example we assume that there are not two "current" movies with the same title, even though we have previously recognized that there could be two movies with the same title made in different years.

Other Normal Forms

If there is a "third normal form," what happened to the first two "normal forms"? They indeed were defined, but today there is little use for them. *First normal form* is simply the condition that every component of every tuple is an atomic value. *Second normal form* is less restrictive than 3NF. It permits transitive FD's in a relation but forbids a nontrivial FD with a left side that is a proper subset of a key. There is also a "fourth normal form" that we shall meet in Section 3.7.

---

and

theater	title
Guild	The Net
Park	The Net

are permissible according to the FD's that apply to each of the above relations, but when we join them we get two tuples

theater	city	title
Guild	Menlo Park	The Net
Park	Menlo Park	The Net

that violate the FD `title city` → `theater`.   □

The solution to the above problem is to relax our BCNF requirement slightly, in order to allow the occasional relation schema, like that of Example 3.32, which cannot be decomposed into BCNF relations without our losing the ability to check each FD within one relation. This relaxed condition is called the *third normal form* condition:

- A relation R is in *third normal form* (3NF) if: whenever $A_1 A_2 \cdots A_n \rightarrow B$ is a nontrivial FD, either $\{A_1, A_2, \ldots, A_n\}$ is a superkey, or B is a member of some key.

An attribute that is a member of some key is often said to be *prime*. Thus, the 3NF condition can be stated as "for each nontrivial FD, either the left side is a superkey, or the right side is prime."

Note that the difference between this 3NF condition and the BCNF condition is the clause "or B is a member of some key (i.e., prime)." This clause "excuses" a FD like `theater` → `city` in Example 3.32, because the right side, `city`, is prime.

It is beyond the scope of this book to prove that 3NF is in fact adequate for its purposes. That is, we can always decompose a relation schema in a way that does not lose information, into schemas that are in 3NF and allow all FD's to be checked. When these relations are not in BCNF, there will be some redundancy left in the schema, however.

3.6.7 Exercises for Section 3.6

Exercise 3.6.1: For each of the following relation schemas and sets of FD's:

* a) $R(A, B, C, D)$ with FD's $AB \to C, C \to D$, and $D \to A$.

* b) $R(A, B, C, D)$ with FD's $B \to C$, and $B \to D$.

  c) $R(A, B, C, D)$ with FD's $AB \to C, BC \to D, CD \to A$, and $AD \to B$.

  d) $R(A, B, C, D)$ with FD's $A \to B, B \to C, C \to D$, and $D \to A$.

  e) $R(A, B, C, D, E)$ with FD's $AB \to C, DE \to C$, and $B \to D$.

  f) $R(A, B, C, D, E)$ with FD's $AB \to C, C \to D, D \to B$, and $D \to E$.

do the following:

  i) Indicate all the BCNF violations. Do not forget to consider FD's that are not in the given set, but follow from them. However, it is not necessary to give violations that have more than one attribute on the right side.

  ii) Decompose the relations, as necessary, into collections of relations that are in BCNF.

  iii) Indicate all the 3NF violations.

  iv) Decompose the relations, as necessary, into collections of relations that are in 3NF.

Exercise 3.6.2: We mentioned in Section 3.6.4 that we should expand the right side of a FD that is a BCNF violation if possible. However, it was deemed an optional step. Consider a relation R whose schema is the set of attributes $\{A, B, C, D\}$ with FD's $A \to B$ and $A \to C$. Either is a BCNF violation, because the only key for R is $\{A, D\}$. Suppose we begin by decomposing R according to $A \to B$. Do we ultimately get the same result as if we first expand the BCNF violation to $A \to BC$? Why or why not?

! **Exercise 3.6.3:** Let R be as in Exercise 3.6.2, but let the FD's be $A \to B$ and $B \to C$. Again compare decomposing using $A \to B$ first against decomposing by $A \to BC$ first.

! **Exercise 3.6.4:** Suppose we have a relation schema $R(A, B, C)$ with FD $A \to B$. Suppose also that we decide to decompose this schema into $S(A, B)$ and $T(B, C)$. Give an example of an instance of relation R whose projection onto S and T and subsequent rejoining as in Section 3.6.5 does not yield the same relation instance.

3.7 Multivalued Dependencies

A "multivalued dependency" is an assertion that two attributes or sets of attributes are independent of one another. This condition is, as we shall see, a generalization of the notion of a functional dependency, in the sense that every FD implies a corresponding multivalued dependency. However, there are some situations involving independence of attribute sets that cannot be explained as FD's. In this section we shall explore the cause of multivalued dependencies and see how they can be used in database schema design.

3.7.1 Attribute Independence and Its Consequent Redundancy

There are occasional situations where we design a relation schema and find it is in BCNF, yet the relation has a kind of redundancy that is not related to FD's. The most common source of redundancy in BCNF schemas is an attempt to put two or more many-many relationships in a single relation.

Example 3.33: In this example, we shall suppose that stars may have several addresses. We shall also break addresses of stars into street and city components. Along with star names and their addresses, we shall include in a single relation the usual *Stars-in* information about the titles and years of movies in which the star appeared. Then Fig. 3.29 is a typical instance of this relation.

name	street	city	title	year
C. Fisher	123 Maple St.	Hollywood	Star Wars	1977
C. Fisher	5 Locust Ln.	Malibu	Star Wars	1977
C. Fisher	123 Maple St.	Hollywood	Empire Strikes Back	1980
C. Fisher	5 Locust Ln.	Malibu	Empire Strikes Back	1980
C. Fisher	123 Maple St.	Hollywood	Return of the Jedi	1983
C. Fisher	5 Locust Ln.	Malibu	Return of the Jedi	1983

Figure 3.29: Sets of addresses independent from movies

We focus in Fig. 3.29 on Carrie Fisher's two hypothetical addresses and three best-known movies. There is no reason to associate an address with one movie and not another. Thus, the only way to express the fact that addresses and movies are independent properties of stars is to have each address appear with each movie. But when we repeat address and movie facts in all combinations, there is obvious redundancy. For instance, Fig. 3.29 repeats each of Carrie Fisher's addresses three times (once for each of her movies) and each movie twice (once for each address).

Yet there is no BCNF violation in the relation suggested by Fig. 3.29. There are, in fact, no nontrivial FD's at all. For example, attribute `city` is not functionally determined by the other four attributes. There might be a star with two homes that had the same street address in different cities. Then there would be two tuples that agreed in all attributes but `city` and disagreed in `city`. Thus,

$$\text{name street title year} \rightarrow \text{city}$$

is not a FD for our relation. We leave it to the reader to check that none of the five attributes is functionally determined by the other four. Since there are no nontrivial FD's, it follows that all five attributes form the only key and that there are no BCNF violations. □

3.7.2 Definition of Multivalued Dependencies

A *multivalued dependency* (often abbreviated MVD) is a statement about some relation R that when you fix the values for one set of attributes, then the values in certain other attributes are independent of the values of all the other attributes in the relation. More precisely, we say the MVD

$$A_1 A_2 \cdots A_n \twoheadrightarrow B_1 B_2 \cdots B_m$$

holds for a relation R if when we restrict ourselves to the tuples of R that have particular values for each of the attributes among the A's, then the set of values we find among the B's is independent of the set of values we find among the attributes of R that are not among the A's or B's. Still more precisely, we say this MVD holds if

> For each pair of tuples t and u of relation R that agree on all the A's, we can find in R some tuple v that agrees:
>
> 1. With both t and u on the A's,
> 2. With t on the B's, and
> 3. With u on all attributes of R that are not among the A's or B's.

Note that we can use this rule with t and u interchanged, to infer the existence of a fourth tuple w that agrees with u on the B's and with t on the other attributes. As a consequence, for any fixed values of the A's, the associated values of the B's and the other attributes appear in all possible combinations in different tuples. Figure 3.30 suggests how v relates to t and u when a MVD holds.

In general, we may assume that the A's and B's (left side and right side) of a MVD are disjoint. However, as with FD's, it is permissible to add some of the A's to the right side if we wish. Also note that unlike FD's, where we started with single attributes on the right and allowed sets of attributes on the right as a shorthand, with MVD's, we must consider sets of attributes on the right immediately. As we shall see in Example 3.35, it is not always possible to break the right sides of MVD's into single attributes.

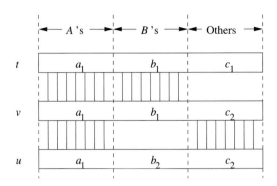

Figure 3.30: A multivalued dependency guarantees that v exists

Example 3.34: In Example 3.33 we encountered a MVD that in our notation is expressed:

$$\text{name} \twoheadrightarrow \text{street city}$$

That is, for each star's name, the set of addresses appears in conjunction with each of the star's movies. For an example of how the formal definition of this MVD applies, consider the first and fourth tuples from Fig. 3.29:

name	street	city	title	year
C. Fisher	123 Maple St.	Hollywood	Star Wars	1977
C. Fisher	5 Locust Ln.	Malibu	Empire Strikes Back	1980

If we let the first tuple be t and the second be u, then the MVD asserts that we must also find in R the tuple that has name C. Fisher, a street and city that agree with the first tuple, and other attributes (title and year) that agree with the second tuple. There is indeed such a tuple; it is the third tuple of Fig. 3.29.

Similarly, we could let t be the second tuple above and u be the first. Then the MVD tells us that there is a tuple of R that agrees with the second in attributes name, street, and city and with the first in name, title, and year. This tuple also exists; it is the second tuple of Fig. 3.29.   □

3.7.3   Reasoning About Multivalued Dependencies

There are a number of rules about MVD's that are similar to the rules we learned for FD's in Section 3.5. For example, MVD's obey

- The *trivial dependencies rule*, which says that if MVD

$$A_1 A_2 \cdots A_n \twoheadrightarrow B_1 B_2 \cdots B_m$$

holds for some relation, then so does $A_1 A_2 \cdots A_n \twoheadrightarrow C_1 C_2 \cdots C_k$, where the C's are the B's plus one or more of the A's. Conversely, we can also remove attributes from the B's if they are among the A's and infer the MVD $A_1 A_2 \cdots A_n \twoheadrightarrow D_1 D_2 \cdots D_r$ if the D's are those B's that are not among the A's.

- The *transitive rule*, which says that if $A_1 A_2 \cdots A_n \twoheadrightarrow B_1 B_2 \cdots B_m$ and $B_1 B_2 \cdots B_m \twoheadrightarrow C_1 C_2 \cdots C_k$ hold for some relation, then so does

$$A_1 A_2 \cdots A_n \twoheadrightarrow C_1 C_2 \cdots C_k$$

However, any C's that are also B's must be deleted from the right side.

On the other hand, MVD's do not obey the splitting part of the splitting/combining rule, as the following example shows.

Example 3.35 : Consider again Fig. 3.29, where we observed the MVD:

$$\texttt{name} \twoheadrightarrow \texttt{street city}$$

If the splitting rule applied to MVD's, we would expect

$$\texttt{name} \twoheadrightarrow \texttt{street}$$

also to be true. This MVD says that each star's street addresses are independent of the other attributes, including `city`. However, that statement is false. Consider, for instance, the first two tuples of Fig. 3.29. The hypothetical MVD would allow us to infer that the tuples with the streets interchanged:

name	street	city	title	year
C. Fisher	5 Locust Ln.	Hollywood	Star Wars	1977
C. Fisher	123 Maple St.	Malibu	Star Wars	1977

were in the relation. But these are not true tuples, because, for instance, the home on 5 Locust Ln. is in Malibu, not Hollywood. □

However, there are several new rules dealing with MVD's that we can learn. First,

- Every FD is a MVD. That is, if $A_1 A_2 \cdots A_n \rightarrow B_1 B_2 \cdots B_m$, then $A_1 A_2 \cdots A_n \twoheadrightarrow B_1 B_2 \cdots B_m$.

To see why, suppose R is some relation for which the FD

$$A_1 A_2 \cdots A_n \rightarrow B_1 B_2 \cdots B_m$$

holds, and suppose t and u are tuples of R that agree on the A's. To show that the MVD $A_1 A_2 \cdots A_n \twoheadrightarrow B_1 B_2 \cdots B_m$ holds, we have to show that R

also contains a tuple v that agrees with t and u on the A's, with t on the B's, and with u on all other attributes. But v can be u. Surely u agrees with t and u on the A's, because we started by assuming that these two tuples agree on the A's. The FD $A_1 A_2 \cdots A_n \rightarrow B_1 B_2 \cdots B_m$ assures us that u agrees with t on the B's. And of course u agrees with itself on the other attributes. Thus, whenever a FD holds, the corresponding MVD holds.

Another rule that has no counterpart in the world of FD's is the *complementation rule*:

- If $A_1 A_2 \cdots A_n \twoheadrightarrow B_1 B_2 \cdots B_m$ is a MVD for relation R, then R also satisfies $A_1 A_2 \cdots A_n \twoheadrightarrow C_1 C_2 \cdots C_k$, where the C's are all attributes of R not among the A's and B's.

Example 3.36 : Again consider the relation of Fig. 3.29, for which we asserted the MVD:

$$\text{name} \twoheadrightarrow \text{street city}$$

The complementation rule says that

$$\text{name} \twoheadrightarrow \text{title year}$$

must also hold in this relation, because `title` and `year` are the attributes not mentioned in the first MVD. The second MVD intuitively means that each star has a set of movies starred in, which are independent of the star's addresses. □

3.7.4 Fourth Normal Form

The redundancy that we found in Section 3.7.1 to be caused by MVD's can be eliminated if we use these dependencies in a new decomposition algorithm for relations. In this section we shall introduce a new normal form, called "fourth normal form." In this normal form, all "nontrivial" (in a sense to be defined below) MVD's are eliminated, as are all FD's that violate BCNF. As a result, the decomposed relations have neither the redundancy from FD's that we discussed in Section 3.6.1 nor the redundancy from MVD's that we discussed in Section 3.7.1.

A MVD $A_1 A_2 \cdots A_n \twoheadrightarrow B_1 B_2 \cdots B_m$ for a relation R is *nontrivial* if:

1. None of the B's is among the A's.

2. Not all the attributes of R are among the A's and B's.

The "fourth normal form" condition is essentially the BCNF condition, but applied to MVD's instead of FD's. Formally:

- A relation R is in *fourth normal form* (4NF) if whenever

$$A_1 A_2 \cdots A_n \twoheadrightarrow B_1 B_2 \cdots B_m$$

is a nontrivial MVD, $\{A_1, A_2, \ldots, A_n\}$ is a superkey.

That is, if a relation is in 4NF, then every nontrivial MVD is really a FD with a superkey on the left. Note that the notions of keys and superkeys depend on FD's only; adding MVD's does not change the definition of "key."

Example 3.37: The relation of Fig. 3.29 violates the 4NF condition. For example,

> name $\twoheadrightarrow$ street city

is a nontrivial MVD, yet `name` by itself is not a superkey. In fact, the only key for this relation is all the attributes. $\square$

Fourth normal form is truly a generalization of BCNF. Recall from Section 3.7.3 that every FD is also a MVD. Thus, every BCNF violation is also a 4NF violation. Put another way, every relation that is in 4NF is therefore in BCNF.

However, there are some relations that are in BCNF but not 4NF. Figure 3.29 is a good example. The only key for this relation is all five attributes, and there are no nontrivial FD's. Thus it is surely in BCNF. However, as we observed in Example 3.37, it is not in 4NF.

3.7.5 Decomposition into Fourth Normal Form

The 4NF decomposition algorithm is quite analogous to the BCNF decomposition algorithm. We find a 4NF violation, say $A_1 A_2 \cdots A_n \twoheadrightarrow B_1 B_2 \cdots B_m$, where $\{A_1, A_2, \ldots, A_n\}$ is not a superkey. Note this MVD could be a true MVD, or it could be derived from the corresponding FD $A_1 A_2 \cdots A_n \to B_1 B_2 \cdots B_m$, since every FD is a MVD. Then we break the schema for the relation R that has the 4NF violation into two schemas:

1. The A's and the B's.

2. The A's and all attributes of R that are not among the A's or B's.

Example 3.38: Let us continue Example 3.37. We observed that

> name $\twoheadrightarrow$ street city

was a 4NF violation. The decomposition rule above tells us to replace the five-attribute schema by one schema that has only the three attributes in the above MVD and another schema that consists of the left side, `name`, plus the attributes that do not appear in the MVD. These attributes are `title` and `year`, so the following two schemas

---

Projecting Multivalued Dependencies

When we decompose into fourth normal form, we need to find the MVD's that hold in the relations that are the result of the decomposition. We wish it were easier to find these MVD's. However, there is no simple test analogous to computing the closure of a set of attributes (as in Section 3.5.3) for FD's. In fact, even a complete set of rules for reasoning about collections of functional and multivalued dependencies is quite complex and beyond the scope of this book. Section 3.9 mentions some places where the subject is treated.

Fortunately, we can often obtain the relevant MVD's for one of the products of a decomposition by using the transitive rule, the complementation rule, and the intersection rule [Exercise 3.7.7(b)]. We recommend that the reader try these in examples and exercises.

$$\{name, street, city\}$$
$$\{name, title, year\}$$

are the result of the decomposition. In each schema there are no nontrivial multivalued (or functional) dependencies, so they are in 4NF. Note that in the relation with schema {name, street, city}, the MVD:

$$name \twoheadrightarrow street\ city$$

is trivial since it involves all attributes. Likewise, in the relation with schema {name, title, year}, the MVD:

$$name \twoheadrightarrow title\ year$$

is trivial. Should one or both schemas of the decomposition not be in 4NF, we would have had to decompose the non-4NF schema(s).   □

As for the BCNF decomposition, each decomposition step leaves us with schemas that have strictly fewer attributes than we started with, so eventually we get to schemas that need not be decomposed further; that is, they are in 4NF. Moreover, the argument justifying the decomposition that we gave in Section 3.6.5 carries over to MVD's as well. When we decompose a relation because of a MVD $A_1 A_2 \cdots A_n \twoheadrightarrow B_1 B_2 \cdots B_m$, this dependency is enough to justify the claim that we can reconstruct the original relation from the relations of the decomposition.

3.7.6   Relationships Among Normal Forms

As we have mentioned, 4NF implies BCNF, which in turn implies 3NF. Thus, the sets of relation schemas (including dependencies) satisfying the three normal forms are related as in Fig. 3.31. That is, if a relation with certain dependencies is in 4NF, it is also in BCNF and 3NF. Also, if a relation with certain dependencies is in BCNF, then it is in 3NF.

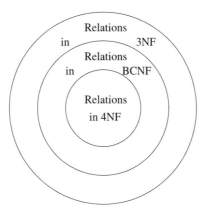

Figure 3.31: 4NF implies BCNF implies 3NF

Another way to compare the normal forms is by the guarantees they make about the set of relations that result from a decomposition into that normal form. These observations are summarized in the table of Fig. 3.32. That is, BCNF (and therefore 4NF) eliminates the redundancy and other anomalies that are caused by FD's, while only 4NF eliminates the additional redundancy that is caused by the presence of nontrivial MVD's that are not FD's. Often, 3NF is enough to eliminate this redundancy, but there are examples where it is not. A decomposition into 3NF can always be chosen so that the FD's are preserved; that is, they are enforced in the decomposed relations (although we have not discussed the algorithm to do so in this book). BCNF does not guarantee preservation of FD's, and none of the normal forms guarantee preservation of MVD's, although in typical cases the dependencies are preserved.

Property	3NF	BCNF	4NF
Eliminates redundancy due to FD's	Most	Yes	Yes
Eliminates redundancy due to MVD's	No	No	Yes
Preserves FD's	Yes	Maybe	Maybe
Preserves MVD's	Maybe	Maybe	Maybe

Figure 3.32: Properties of normal forms and their decompositions

3.7.7   Exercises for Section 3.7

* **Exercise 3.7.1 :** Suppose we have a relation $R(A, B, C)$ with a MVD $A \twoheadrightarrow B$. If we know that the tuples (a, b_1, c_1), (a, b_2, c_2), and (a, b_3, c_3) are in the current instance of R, what other tuples do we know must also be in R?

* **Exercise 3.7.2 :** Suppose we have a relation in which we want to record for each person their name, Social Security number, and birthdate. Also, for each child of the person, the name, Social Security number, and birthdate of the child, and for each automobile the person owns, its serial number and make. To be more precise, this relation has all tuples

$$(n, s, b, cn, cs, cb, as, am)$$

such that

1. n is the name of the person with Social Security number s.

2. b is n's birthdate.

3. cn is the name of one of n's children.

4. cs is cn's Social Security number.

5. cb is cn's birthdate.

6. as is the serial number of one of n's automobiles.

7. am is the make of the automobile with serial number as.

For this relation:

a) Tell the functional and multivalued dependencies we would expect to hold.

b) Suggest a decomposition of the relation into 4NF.

Exercise 3.7.3 : For each of the following relation schemas and dependencies

* a) $R(A, B, C, D)$ with MVD's $A \twoheadrightarrow B$ and $A \twoheadrightarrow C$.

b) $R(A, B, C, D)$ with MVD's $A \twoheadrightarrow B$ and $B \twoheadrightarrow CD$.

c) $R(A, B, C, D)$ with MVD $AB \twoheadrightarrow C$ and FD $B \rightarrow D$.

d) $R(A, B, C, D, E)$ with MVD's $A \twoheadrightarrow B$ and $AB \twoheadrightarrow C$ and FD's $A \rightarrow D$ and $AB \rightarrow E$.

do the following:

i) Find all the 4NF violations.

ii) Decompose the relations into a collection of relation schemas in 4NF.

! **Exercise 3.7.4:** In Exercise 2.2.5 we discussed four different assumptions about the relationship *Births*. For each of these, indicate the MVD's (other than FD's) that would be expected to hold in the resulting relation.

Exercise 3.7.5: Give informal arguments why we would not expect any of the five attributes in Example 3.33 to be functionally determined by the other four.

! **Exercise 3.7.6:** Using the definition of MVD, show why the complementation rule holds.

! **Exercise 3.7.7:** Show the following rules for MVD's:

* a) The *union rule*. If X, Y, and Z are sets of attributes, $X \twoheadrightarrow Y$, and $X \twoheadrightarrow Z$, then $X \twoheadrightarrow (Y \cup Z)$.

  b) The *intersection rule*. If X, Y, and Z are sets of attributes, $X \twoheadrightarrow Y$, and $X \twoheadrightarrow Z$, then $X \twoheadrightarrow (Y \cap Z)$.

  c) The *difference rule*. If X, Y, and Z are sets of attributes, $X \twoheadrightarrow Y$, and $X \twoheadrightarrow Z$, then $X \twoheadrightarrow (Y - Z)$.

  d) *Trivial MVD's*. If $Y \subseteq X$, then $X \twoheadrightarrow Y$ holds in any relation.

  e) *Another source of trivial MVD's*. If $X \cup Y$ is all the attributes of relation R, then $X \twoheadrightarrow Y$ holds in R.

  f) *Removing attributes shared by left and right side*. If $X \twoheadrightarrow Y$ holds, then $X \twoheadrightarrow (Y - X)$ holds.

! **Exercise 3.7.8:** Give counterexample relations to show why the following rules for MVD's do *not* hold.

* a) If $A \twoheadrightarrow BC$, then $A \twoheadrightarrow B$.

  b) If $A \twoheadrightarrow B$, then $A \to B$.

  c) If $AB \twoheadrightarrow C$, then $A \twoheadrightarrow C$.

3.8 Summary of Chapter 3

✦ *Relational Model*: Relations are tables representing information. Columns are headed by attributes; each attribute has an associated domain, or data type. Rows are called tuples, and a tuple has one component for each attribute of the relation.

✦ *Schemas*: A relation name, together with the attributes of that relation, form the relation schema. A collection of relation schemas forms a database schema. Particular data for a relation or collection of relations is called an instance of that relation schema or database schema.

✦ *Converting Entity Sets to Relations*: The relation for an entity set has one attribute for each attribute of the entity set. An exception is a weak entity set E, whose relation must also have attributes for the key attributes of those other entity sets that help identify entities of E.

✦ *Converting Relationships to Relations*: The relation for an E/R relationship has attributes corresponding to the key attributes of each entity set that participates in the relationship. However, if a relationship is a supporting relationship for some weak entity set, it is not necessary to produce a relation for that relationship.

✦ *Converting Isa Hierarchies to Relations*: One approach is to partition entities among the various entity sets of the hierarchy and create a relation, with all necessary attributes, for each such entity set. A second approach is to create a relation for each possible subset of the entity sets in the hierarchy, and create for each entity one tuple; that tuple is in the relation for exactly the set of entity sets to which the entity belongs. A third approach is to create only one relation and to use null values for those attributes that do not apply to the entity represented by a given tuple.

✦ *Functional Dependencies*: A functional dependency is a statement that two tuples of a relation which agree on some particular set of attributes must also agree on some other particular attribute.

✦ *Keys of a Relation*: A superkey for a relation is a set of attributes that functionally determines all the attributes of the relation. A key is a superkey, no proper subset of which functionally determines all the attributes.

✦ *Reasoning About Functional Dependencies*: There are many rules that let us infer that one FD $X \to A$ holds in any relation instance that satisfies some other given set of FD's. The simplest approach to verifying that $X \to A$ holds usually is to compute the closure of X, using the given FD's to expand X until it includes A.

✦ *Decomposing Relations*: We can decompose one relation schema into two without losing information as long as the attributes that are common to both schemas form a superkey for at least one of the decomposed relations.

✦ *Boyce-Codd Normal Form*: A relation is in BCNF if the only nontrivial FD's say that some superkey functionally determines one of the other attributes. It is possible to decompose any relation into a collection of BCNF relations without losing information. A major benefit of BCNF is that it eliminates redundancy caused by the existence of FD's.

✦ *Third Normal Form*: Sometimes decomposition into BCNF can hinder us in checking certain FD's. A relaxed form of BCNF, called 3NF, allows a FD $X \to A$ even if X is not a superkey, provided A is a member of some key. 3NF does not guarantee to eliminate all redundancy due to FD's, but often does so.

✦ *Multivalued Dependencies*: A multivalued dependency is a statement that two sets of attributes in a relation have sets of values that appear in all possible combinations.

✦ *Fourth Normal Form*: MVD's can also cause redundancy in a relation. 4NF is like BCNF, but also forbids nontrivial MVD's (unless they are actually FD's that are allowed by BCNF). It is possible to decompose a relation into 4NF without losing information.

3.9 References for Chapter 3

The classic paper by Codd on the relational model is [4]. This paper introduces the idea of functional dependencies, as well as the basic relational concept. Third normal form was also described there, while Boyce-Codd normal form is described by Codd in a later paper [5].

Multivalued dependencies and fourth normal form were defined by Fagin in [7]. However, the idea of multivalued dependencies also appears independently in [6] and [9].

Armstrong was the first to study rules for inferring FD's [1]. The rules for FD's that we have covered here (including what we call "Armstrong's axioms") and rules for inferring MVD's as well, come from [2]. The technique for testing a FD by computing the closure for a set of attributes is from [3].

There are a number of algorithms and/or proofs that algorithms work which have not been given in this book, including how one infers multivalued dependencies, how one projects multivalued dependencies onto decomposed relations, and how one decomposes into 3NF without losing the ability to check functional dependencies. These and other matters concerned with dependencies are explained in [8].

1. Armstrong, W. W., "Dependency structures of database relationships," *Proceedings of the 1974 IFIP Congress*, pp. 580–583.

2. Beeri, C., R. Fagin, and J. H. Howard, "A complete axiomatization for functional and multivalued dependencies," *ACM SIGMOD International Conference on Management of Data*, pp. 47–61, 1977.

3. Bernstein, P. A., "Synthesizing third normal form relations from functional dependencies," *ACM Transactions on Database Systems* **1**:4, pp. 277–298, 1976.

4. Codd, E. F., "A relational model for large shared data banks," *Comm. ACM* **13**:6, pp. 377–387, 1970.

5. Codd, E. F., "Further normalization of the data base relational model," in *Database Systems* (R. Rustin, ed.), Prentice-Hall, Englewood Cliffs, NJ, 1972.

6. Delobel, C., "Normalization and hierarchical dependencies in the relational data model," *ACM Transactions on Database Systems* **3**:3, pp. 201–222, 1978.

7. Fagin, R., "Multivalued dependencies and a new normal form for relational databases," *ACM Transactions on Database Systems* **2**:3, pp. 262–278, 1977.

8. Ullman, J. D., *Principles of Database and Knowledge-Base Systems, Volume I*, Computer Science Press, New York, 1988.

9. Zaniolo, C. and M. A. Melkanoff, "On the design of relational database schemata," *ACM Transactions on Database Systems* **6**:1, pp. 1–47, 1981.

Chapter 4

Other Data Models

The entity-relationship and relational models are just two of the models that have importance in database systems today. In this chapter we shall introduce you to several other models of rising importance.

We begin with a discussion of object-oriented data models. One approach to object-orientation for a database system is to extend the concepts of object-oriented programming languages such as C++ or Java to include persistence. That is, the presumption in ordinary programming is that objects go away after the program finishes, while an essential requirement of a DBMS is that the objects are preserved indefinitely, unless changed by the user, as in a file system. We shall study a "pure" object-oriented data model, called ODL (object definition language), which has been standardized by the ODMG (object data management group).

Next, we consider a model called object-relational. This model, part of the most recent SQL standard, called SQL-99 (or SQL:1999, or SQL3), is an attempt to extend the relational model, as introduced in Chapter 3, to include many of the common object-oriented concepts. This standard forms the basis for object-relational DBMS's that are now available from essentially all the major vendors, although these vendors differ considerably in the details of how the concepts are implemented and made available to users. Chapter 9 includes a discussion of the object-relational model of SQL-99.

Then, we take up the "semistructured" data model. This recent innovation is an attempt to deal with a number of database problems, including the need to combine databases and other data sources, such as Web pages, that have different schemas. While an essential of object-oriented or object-relational systems is their insistence on a fixed schema for every class or every relation, semistructured data is allowed much more flexibility in what components are present. For instance, we could think of movie objects, some of which have a director listed, some of which might have several different lengths for several different versions, some of which may include textual reviews, and so on.

The most prominent implementation of semistructured data is XML (extensible markup language). Essentially, XML is a specification for "documents," which are really collections of nested data elements, each with a role indicated by a tag. We believe that XML data will serve as an essential component in systems that mediate among data sources or that transmit data among sources. XML may even become an important approach to flexible storage of data in databases.

4.1 Review of Object-Oriented Concepts

Before introducing object-oriented database models, let us review the major object-oriented concepts themselves. Object-oriented programming has been widely regarded as a tool for better program organization and, ultimately, more reliable software implementation. First popularized in the language Smalltalk, object-oriented programming received a big boost with the development of C++ and the migration to C++ of much software development that was formerly done in C. More recently, the language Java, suitable for sharing programs across the World Wide Web, has also focused attention on object-oriented programming.

The database world has likewise been attracted to the object-oriented paradigm, particularly for database design and for extending relational DBMS's with new features. In this section we shall review the ideas behind object orientation:

1. A powerful type system.

2. *Classes*, which are types associated with an *extent*, or set of *objects* belonging to the class. An essential feature of classes, as opposed to conventional data types is that classes may include *methods*, which are procedures that are applicable to objects belonging to the class.

3. *Object Identity*, the idea that each object has a unique identity, independent of its value.

4. *Inheritance*, which is the organization of classes into hierarchies, where each class inherits the properties of the classes above it.

4.1.1 The Type System

An object-oriented programming language offers the user a rich collection of types. Starting with *atomic types*, such as integers, real numbers, booleans, and character strings, one may build new types by using *type constructors*. Typically, the type constructors let us build:

1. *Record structures*. Given a list of types $T_1, T_2, \ldots, T_n$ and a corresponding list of *field names* (called *instance variables* in Smalltalk) $f_1, f_2, \ldots, f_n$, one can construct a record type consisting of n components. The ith

component has type T_i and is referred to by its field name f_i. Record structures are exactly what C or C++ calls "structs," and we shall frequently use that term in what follows.

2. *Collection types.* Given a type T, one can construct new types by applying a *collection operator* to type T. Different languages use different collection operators, but there are several common ones, including arrays, lists, and sets. Thus, if T were the atomic type integer, we might build the collection types "array of integers," "list of integers," or "set of integers."

3. *Reference types.* A reference to a type T is a type whose values are suitable for locating a value of the type T. In C or C++, a reference is a "pointer" to a value, that is, the virtual-memory address of the value pointed to.

Of course, record-structure and collection operators can be applied repeatedly to build ever more complex types. For instance, a bank might define a type that is a record structure with a first component named `customer` of type string and whose second component is of type set-of-integers and is named `accounts`. Such a type is suitable for associating bank customers with the set of their accounts.

4.1.2 Classes and Objects

A *class* consists of a type and possibly one or more functions or procedures (called *methods*; see below) that can be executed on objects of that class. The objects of a class are either values of that type (called *immutable objects*) or variables whose value is of that type (called *mutable objects*). For example, if we define a class C whose type is "set of integers," then $\{2, 5, 7\}$ is an immutable object of class C, while variable s could be declared to be a mutable object of class C and assigned a value such as $\{2, 5, 7\}$.

4.1.3 Object Identity

Objects are assumed to have an *object identity* (OID). No two objects can have the same OID, and no object has two different OID's. Object identity has some interesting effects on how we model data. For instance, it is essential that an entity set have a key formed from values of attributes possessed by it or a related entity set (in the case of weak entity sets). However, within a class, we assume we can distinguish two objects whose attributes all have identical values, because the OID's of the two objects are guaranteed to be different.

4.1.4 Methods

Associated with a class there are usually certain functions, often called *methods*. A method for a class C has at least one argument that is an object of class C; it may have other arguments of any class, including C. For example, associated with a class whose type is "set of integers," we might have methods to sum the elements of a given set, to take the union of two sets, or to return a boolean indicating whether or not the set is empty.

In some situations, classes are referred to as "abstract data types," meaning that they *encapsulate*, or restrict access to objects of the class so that only the methods defined for the class can modify objects of the class directly. This restriction assures that the objects of the class cannot be changed in ways that were not anticipated by the designer of the class. Encapsulation is regarded as one of the key tools for reliable software development.

4.1.5 Class Hierarchies

It is possible to declare one class C to be a *subclass* of another class D. If so, then class C *inherits* all the properties of class D, including the type of D and any functions defined for class D. However, C may also have additional properties. For example, new methods may be defined for objects of class C, and these methods may be either in addition to or in place of methods of D. It may even be possible to extend the type of D in certain ways. In particular, if the type of D is a record-structure type, then we can add new fields to this type that are present only in objects of type C.

Example 4.1 : Consider a class of bank account objects. We might describe the type for this class informally as:

```
CLASS Account = {accountNo: integer;
                 balance: real;
                 owner: REF Customer;
                }
```

That is, the type for the `Account` class is a record structure with three fields: an integer account number, a real-number balance, and an owner that is a reference to an object of class `Customer` (another class that we'd need for a banking database, but whose type we have not introduced here).

We could also define some methods for the class. For example, we might have a method

```
deposit(a: Account, m: real)
```

that increases the `balance` for `Account` object a by amount m.

Finally, we might wish to have several subclasses of the `Account` subclass. For instance, a time-deposit account could have an additional field `dueDate`, the date at which the account balance may be withdrawn by the owner. There might also be an additional method for the subclass `TimeDeposit`

```
penalty(a: TimeDeposit)
```

that takes an account a belonging to the subclass `TimeDeposit` and calculates the penalty for early withdrawal, as a function of the `dueDate` field in object a and the current date; the latter would be obtainable from the system on which the method is run. □

4.2 Introduction to ODL

ODL (Object Definition Language) is a standardized language for specifying the structure of databases in object-oriented terms. It is an extension of IDL (Interface Description Language), a component of CORBA (Common Object Request Broker Architecture). The latter is a standard for distributed, object-oriented computing.

4.2.1 Object-Oriented Design

In an object-oriented design, the world to be modeled is thought of as composed of *objects*, which are observable entities of some sort. For example, people may be thought of as objects; so may bank accounts, airline flights, courses at a college, buildings, and so on. Objects are assumed to have a unique *object identity* (OID) that distinguishes them from any other object, as we discussed in Section 4.1.3.

To organize information, we usually want to group objects into *classes* of objects with similar properties. However, when speaking of ODL object-oriented designs, we should think of "similar properties" of the objects in a class in two different ways:

- The real-world concepts represented by the objects of a class should be similar. For instance, it makes sense to group all customers of a bank into one class and all accounts at the bank into another class. It would not make sense to group customers and accounts together in one class, because they have little or nothing in common and play essentially different roles in the world of banking.

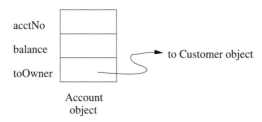

Figure 4.1: An object representing an account

- The properties of objects in a class must be the same. When programming in an object-oriented language, we often think of objects as records, like that suggested by Fig. 4.1. Objects have fields or slots in which values are placed. These values may be of common types such as integers, strings, or arrays, or they may be references to other objects.

When specifying the design of ODL classes, we describe properties of three kinds:

1. *Attributes*, which are values associated with the object. We discuss the legal types of ODL attributes in Section 4.2.8.

2. *Relationships*, which are connections between the object at hand and another object or objects.

3. *Methods*, which are functions that may be applied to objects of the class.

Attributes, relationships, and methods are collectively referred to as *properties*.

4.2.2 Class Declarations

A declaration of a class in ODL, in its simplest form, consists of:

1. The keyword `class`,

2. The name of the class, and

3. A bracketed list of properties of the class. These properties can be attributes, relationships, or methods, mixed in any order.

That is, the simple form of a class declaration is

`class <name> {`
  `<list of properties>`
`}`

4.2.3 Attributes in ODL

The simplest kind of property is the *attribute*. These properties describe some aspect of an object by associating a value of a fixed type with that object. For example, person objects might each have an attribute `name` whose type is string and whose value is the name of that person. Person objects might also have an attribute `birthdate` that is a triple of integers (i.e., a record structure) representing the year, month, and day of their birth.

In ODL, unlike the E/R model, attributes need not be of simple types, such as integers and strings. We just mentioned `birthdate` as an example of an attribute with a structured type. For another example, an attribute such as `phones` might have a set of strings as its type, and even more complex types are possible. We summarize the type system of ODL in Section 4.2.8.

Example 4.2 : In Fig. 4.2 is an ODL declaration of the class of movies. It is not a complete declaration; we shall add more to it later. Line (1) declares `Movie` to be a class. Following line (1) are the declarations of four attributes that all `Movie` objects will have.

```
1)   class Movie {
2)       attribute string title;
3)       attribute integer year;
4)       attribute integer length;
5)       attribute enum Film {color,blackAndWhite} filmType;
     };
```

Figure 4.2: An ODL declaration of the class `Movie`

The first attribute, on line (2), is named `title`. Its type is `string`—a character string of unknown length. We expect the value of the `title` attribute in any `Movie` object to be the name of the movie. The next two attributes, `year` and `length` declared on lines (3) and (4), have integer type and represent the year in which the movie was made and its length in minutes, respectively. On line (5) is another attribute `filmType`, which tells whether the movie was filmed in color or black-and-white. Its type is an *enumeration*, and the name of the enumeration is `Film`. Values of enumeration attributes are chosen from a list of *literals*, `color` and `blackAndWhite` in this example.

An object in the class `Movie` as we have defined it so far can be thought of as a record or tuple with four components, one for each of the four attributes. For example,

```
("Gone With the Wind", 1939, 231, color)
```

is a `Movie` object. □

Example 4.3 : In Example 4.2, all the attributes have atomic types. Here is an example with a nonatomic type. We can define the class `Star` by

```
1)   class Star {
2)       attribute string name;
3)       attribute Struct Addr
             {string street, string city} address;
     };
```

Line (2) specifies an attribute `name` (of the star) that is a string. Line (3) specifies another attribute `address`. This attribute has a type that is a *record structure*. The name of this structure is `Addr`, and the type consists of two fields: `street` and `city`. Both fields are strings. In general, one can define record structure types in ODL by the keyword `Struct` and curly braces around

---

Why Name Enumerations and Structures?

The name `Film` for the enumeration on line 5 of Fig. 4.2 doesn't seem to be necessary. However, by giving it a name, we can refer to it outside the scope of the declaration for class `Movie`. We do so by referring to it by the *scoped name* `Movie::Film`. For instance, in a declaration of a class of cameras, we could have a line:

`attribute Movie::Film uses;`

This line declares attribute `uses` to be of the same enumerated type with the values `color` and `blackAndWhite`.

   Another reason for giving names to enumerated types (and structures as well, which are declared in a manner similar to enumerations) is that we can declare them in a "module" outside the declaration of any particular class, and have that type available to all the classes in the module.

---

the list of field names and their types. Like enumerations, structure types must have a name, which can be used elsewhere to refer to the same structure type.
□

4.2.4   Relationships in ODL

While we can learn much about an object by examining its attributes, sometimes a critical fact about an object is the way it connects to other objects in the same or another class.

Example 4.4 : Now, suppose we want to add to the declaration of the `Movie` class from Example 4.2 a property that is a set of stars. More precisely, we want each `Movie` object to connect the set of `Star` objects that are its stars. The best way to represent this connection between the `Movie` and `Star` classes is with a *relationship*. We may represent this relationship in `Movie` by a line:

```
relationship Set<Star> stars;
```

in the declaration of class `Movie`. This line may appear in Fig. 4.2 after any of the lines numbered (1) through (5). It says that in each object of class `Movie` there is a set of references to `Star` objects. The set of references is called `stars`. The keyword `relationship` specifies that `stars` contains references to other objects, while the keyword `Set` preceding `<Star>` indicates that `stars` references a set of `Star` objects, rather than a single object. In general, a type that is a set of elements of some other type T is defined in ODL by the keyword `Set` and angle brackets around the type T.   □

4.2.5 Inverse Relationships

Just as we might like to access the stars of a given movie, we might like to know the movies in which a given star acted. To get this information into `Star` objects, we can add the line

```
relationship Set<Movie> starredIn;
```

to the declaration of class `Star` in Example 4.3. However, this line and a similar declaration for `Movie` omits a very important aspect of the relationship between movies and stars. We expect that if a star S is in the `stars` set for movie M, then movie M is in the `starredIn` set for star S. We indicate this connection between the relationships `stars` and `starredIn` by placing in each of their declarations the keyword **inverse** and the name of the other relationship. If the other relationship is in some other class, as it usually is, then we refer to that relationship by the name of its class, followed by a double colon (`::`) and the name of the relationship.

Example 4.5: To define the relationship `starredIn` of class `Star` to be the inverse of the relationship `stars` in class `Movie`, we revise the declarations of these classes, as shown in Fig. 4.3 (which also contains a definition of class `Studio` to be discussed later). Line (6) shows the declaration of relationship `stars` of movies, and says that its inverse is `Star::starredIn`. Since relationship `starredIn` is defined in another class, the relationship name is preceded by the name of that class (`Star`) and a double colon. Recall the double colon is used whenever we refer to something defined in another class, such as a property or type name.

Similarly, relationship `starredIn` is declared in line (11). Its inverse is declared by that line to be `stars` of class `Movie`, as it must be, because inverses always are linked in pairs. □

As a general rule, if a relationship R for class C associates with object x of class C with objects $y_1, y_2, \ldots, y_n$ of class D, then the inverse relationship of R associates with each of the y_i's the object x (perhaps along with other objects). Sometimes, it helps to visualize a relationship R from class C to class D as a list of pairs, or tuples, of a relation. The idea is the same as the "relationship set" we used to describe E/R relationships in Section 2.1.5. Each pair consists of an object x from class C and an associated object y of class D, as:

C	D
x_1	y_1
x_2	y_2
$\ldots$	$\ldots$

Then the inverse relationship for R is the set of pairs with the components reversed, as:

```
1)   class Movie {
2)      attribute string title;
3)      attribute integer year;
4)      attribute integer length;
5)      attribute enum Film {color,blackAndWhite} filmType;
6)      relationship Set<Star> stars
                    inverse Star::starredIn;
7)      relationship Studio ownedBy
                    inverse Studio::owns;
     };

8)   class Star {
9)      attribute string name;
10)     attribute Struct Addr
            {string street, string city} address;
11)     relationship Set<Movie> starredIn
                    inverse Movie::stars;
     };

12)  class Studio {
13)     attribute string name;
14)     attribute string address;
15)     relationship Set<Movie> owns
                    inverse Movie::ownedBy;
     };
```

Figure 4.3: Some ODL classes and their relationships

D	C
y_1	x_1
y_2	x_2
...	...

Notice that this rule works even if C and D are the same class. There are some relationships that logically run from a class to itself, such as "child of" from the class "Persons" to itself.

4.2.6   Multiplicity of Relationships

Like the binary relationships of the E/R model, a pair of inverse relationships in ODL can be classified as either many-many, many-one in either direction, or one-one. The type declarations for the pair of relationships tells us which.

1. If we have a many-many relationship between classes C and D, then in class C the type of the relationship is Set<D>, and in class D the type is Set<C>.[1]

2. If the relationship is many-one from C to D, then the type of the relationship in C is just D, while the type of the relationship in D is Set<C>.

3. If the relationship is many-one from D to C, then the roles of C and D are reversed in (2) above.

4. If the relationship is one-one, then the type of the relationship in C is just D, and in D it is just C.

Note, that as in the E/R model, we allow a many-one or one-one relationship to include the case where for some objects the "one" is actually "none." For instance, a many-one relationship from C to D might have a missing or "null" value of the relationship in some of the C objects. Of course, since a D object could be associated with any set of C objects, it is also permissible for that set to be empty for some D objects.

Example 4.6: In Fig. 4.3 we have the declaration of three classes, Movie, Star, and Studio. The first two of these have already been introduced in Examples 4.2 and 4.3. We also discussed the relationship pair stars and starredIn. Since each of their types uses Set, we see that this pair represents a many-many relationship between Star and Movie.

Studio objects have attributes name and address; these appear in lines (13) and (14). Notice that the type of addresses here is a string, rather than a structure as was used for the address attribute of class Star on line (10). There is nothing wrong with using attributes of the same name but different types in different classes.

In line (7) we see a relationship ownedBy from movies to studios. Since the type of the relationship is Studio, and not Set<Studio>, we are declaring that for each movie there is one studio that owns it. The inverse of this relationship is found on line (15). There we see the relationship owns from studios to movies. The type of this relationship is Set<Movie>, indicating that each studio owns a set of movies—perhaps 0, perhaps 1, or perhaps a large number of movies. □

4.2.7 Methods in ODL

The third kind of property of ODL classes is the method. As in other object-oriented languages, a method is a piece of executable code that may be applied to the objects of the class.

In ODL, we can declare the names of the methods associated with a class and the input/output types of those methods. These declarations, called *signatures*,

---

[1] Actually, the Set could be replaced by another "collection type," such as list or bag, as discussed in Section 4.2.8. We shall assume all collections are sets in our exposition of relationships, however.

Why Signatures?

The value of providing signatures is that when we implement the schema in a real programming language, we can check automatically that the implementation matches the design as was expressed in the schema. We cannot check that the implementation correctly implements the "meaning" of the operations, but we can at least check that the input and output parameters are of the correct number and of the correct type.

---

are like function declarations in C or C++ (as opposed to function *definitions*, which are the code to implement the function). The code for a method would be written in the host language; this code is not part of ODL.

Declarations of methods appear along with the attributes and relationships in a class declaration. As is normal for object-oriented languages, each method is associated with a class, and methods are invoked on an object of that class. Thus, the object is a "hidden" argument of the method. This style allows the same method name to be used for several different classes, because the object upon which the operation is performed determines the particular method meant. Such a method name is said to be *overloaded*.

The syntax of method declarations is similar to that of function declarations in C, with two important additions:

1. Method parameters are specified to be **in**, **out**, or **inout**, meaning that they are used as input parameters, output parameters, or both, respectively. The last two types of parameters can be modified by the method; **in** parameters cannot be modified. In effect, **out** and **inout** parameters are passed by reference, while **in** parameters may be passed by value. Note that a method may also have a return value, which is a way that a result can be produced by a method other than by assigning a value to an **out** or **inout** parameter.

2. Methods may raise *exceptions*, which are special responses that are outside the normal parameter-passing and return-value mechanisms by which methods communicate. An exception usually indicates an abnormal or unexpected condition that will be "handled" by some method that called it (perhaps indirectly through a sequence of calls). Division by zero is an example of a condition that might be treated as an exception. In ODL, a method declaration can be followed by the keyword **raises**, followed by a parenthesized list of one or more exceptions that the method can raise.

Example 4.7: In Fig. 4.4 we see an evolution of the definition for class `Movie`, last seen in Fig. 4.3. The methods included with the class declaration are as follows.

Line (8) declares a method `lengthInHours`. We might imagine that it produces as a return value the length of the movie object to which it is applied, but converted from minutes (as in the attribute `length`) to a floating-point number that is the equivalent in hours. Note that this method takes no parameters. The `Movie` object to which the method is applied is the "hidden" argument, and it is from this object that a possible implementation of `lengthInHours` would obtain the length of the movie in minutes.[2]

Method `lengthInHours` may raise an exception called `noLengthFound`. Presumably this exception would be raised if the `length` attribute of the object to which the method `lengthInHours` was applied had an undefined value or a value that could not represent a valid length (e.g., a negative number).

```
1)   class Movie {
2)       attribute string title;
3)       attribute integer year;
4)       attribute integer length;
5)       attribute enumeration(color,blackAndWhite) filmType;
6)       relationship Set<Star> stars
                     inverse Star::starredIn;
7)       relationship Studio ownedBy
                     inverse Studio::owns;
8)       float lengthInHours() raises(noLengthFound);
9)       void starNames(out Set<String>);
10)      void otherMovies(in Star, out Set<Movie>)
                     raises(noSuchStar);
     };
```

Figure 4.4: Adding method signatures to the `Movie` class

In line (9) we see another method signature, for a method called `starNames`. This method has no return value but has an output parameter whose type is a set of strings. We presume that the value of the output parameter is computed by `starNames` to be the set of strings that are the values of the attribute `name` for the stars of the movie to which the method is applied. However, as always there is no guarantee that the method definition behaves in this particular way.

Finally, at line (10) is a third method, `otherMovies`. This method has an input parameter of type `Star`. A possible implementation of this method is as follows. We may suppose that `otherMovies` expects this star to be one of the stars of the movie; if it is not, then the exception `noSuchStar` is raised. If it is one of the stars of the movie to which the method is applied, then the output parameter, whose type is a set of movies, is given as its value the set of all the

---

[2]In the actual definition of the method `lengthInHours` a special term such as `self` would be used to refer to the object to which the method is applied. This matter is of no concern as far as declarations of method signatures is concerned.

other movies of this star.   □

4.2.8   Types in ODL

ODL offers the database designer a type system similar to that found in C or other conventional programming languages. A type system is built from a basis of types that are defined by themselves and certain recursive rules whereby complex types are built from simpler types. In ODL, the basis consists of:

1. *Atomic types*: integer, float, character, character string, boolean, and *enumerations*. The latter are lists of names declared to be abstract values. We saw an example of an enumeration in line (5) of Fig. 4.3, where the names are `color` and `blackAndWhite`.

2. *Class names*, such as `Movie`, or `Star`, which represent types that are actually structures, with components for each of the attributes and relationships of that class.

These basic types are combined into structured types using the following *type constructors*:

1. *Set*. If T is any type, then `Set<T>` denotes the type whose values are finite sets of elements of type T. Examples using the set type-constructor occur in lines (6), (11), and (15) of Fig. 4.3.

2. *Bag*. If T is any type, then `Bag<T>` denotes the type whose values are finite bags or *multisets* of elements of type T. A bag allows an element to appear more than once. For example, $\{1, 2, 1\}$ is a bag but not a set, because 1 appears more than once.

3. *List*. If T is any type, then `List<T>` denotes the type whose values are finite lists of zero or more elements of type T. As a special case, the type `string` is a shorthand for the type `List<char>`.

4. *Array*. If T is a type and i is an integer, then `Array<T,i>` denotes the type whose elements are arrays of i elements of type T. For example, `Array<char,10>` denotes character strings of length 10.

5. *Dictionary*. If T and S are types, then `Dictionary<T,S>` denotes a type whose values are finite sets of pairs. Each pair consists of a value of the *key type* T and a value of the *range type* S. The dictionary may not contain two pairs with the same key value. Presumably, the dictionary is implemented in a way that makes it very efficient, given a value t of the key type T, to find the associated value of the range type S.

6. *Structures*. If $T_1, T_2, \ldots, T_n$ are types, and $F_1, F_2, \ldots, F_n$ are names of fields, then

---

Sets, Bags, and Lists

To understand the distinction between sets, bags, and lists, remember that a set has unordered elements, and only one occurrence of each element. A bag allows more than one occurrence of an element, but the elements and their occurrences are unordered. A list allows more than one occurrence of an element, but the occurrences are ordered. Thus, $\{1, 2, 1\}$ and $\{2, 1, 1\}$ are the same bag, but $(1, 2, 1)$ and $(2, 1, 1)$ are not the same list.

$$\texttt{Struct N \{T}_1 \texttt{ F}_1\texttt{, T}_2 \texttt{ F}_2\texttt{,..., T}_n \texttt{ F}_n\texttt{\}}$$

denotes the type named N whose elements are structures with n fields. The ith field is named F_i and has type T_i. For example, line (10) of Fig. 4.3 showed a structure type named `Addr`, with two fields. Both fields are of type `string` and have names `street` and `city`, respectively.

The first five types — set, bag, list, array, and dictionary — are called *collection types*. There are different rules about which types may be associated with attributes and which with relationships.

- The type of a relationship is either a class type or a (single use of a) collection type constructor applied to a class type.

- The type of an attribute is built starting with an atomic type or types. Class types may also be used, but typically these will be classes that are used as "structures," much as the `Addr` structure was used in Example 4.3. We generally prefer to connect classes with relationships, because relationships are two-way, which makes queries about the database easier to express. In contrast, we can go from an object to its attributes, but not vice-versa. After beginning with atomic or class types, we may then apply the structure and collection type constructors as we wish, as many times as we wish.

Example 4.8 : Some of the possible types of attributes are:

1. `integer`.

2. `Struct N {string field1, integer field2}`.

3. `List<real>`.

4. `Array<Struct N {string field1, integer field2}, 10>`.

Example (1) is an atomic type; (2) is a structure of atomic types, (3) a collection of an atomic type, and (4) a collection of structures built from atomic types.

Now, suppose the class names `Movie` and `Star` are available basic types. Then we may construct relationship types such as `Movie` or `Bag<Star>`. However, the following are illegal as relationship types:

1. `Struct N {Movie field1, Star field2}`. Relationship types cannot involve structures.

2. `Set<integer>`. Relationship types cannot involve atomic types.

3. `Set<Array<Star, 10>>`. Relationship types cannot involve two applications of collection types.

□

4.2.9   Exercises for Section 4.2

* **Exercise 4.2.1:** In Exercises 2.1.1 was the informal description of a bank database. Render this design in ODL.

Exercise 4.2.2: Modify your design of Exercise 4.2.1 in the ways enumerated in Exercise 2.1.2. Describe the changes; do not write a complete, new schema.

Exercise 4.2.3: Render the teams-players-fans database of Exercise 2.1.3 in ODL. Why does the complication about sets of team colors, which was mentioned in the original exercise, not present a problem in ODL?

*! **Exercise 4.2.4:** Suppose we wish to keep a genealogy. We shall have one class, `Person`. The information we wish to record about persons includes their name (an attribute) and the following relationships: mother, father, and children. Give an ODL design for the `Person` class. Be sure to indicate the inverses of the relationships that, like `mother`, `father`, and `children`, are also relationships from `Person` to itself. Is the inverse of the `mother` relationship the `children` relationship? Why or why not? Describe each of the relationships and their inverses as sets of pairs.

! **Exercise 4.2.5:** Let us add to the design of Exercise 4.2.4 the attribute `education`. The value of this attribute is intended to be a collection of the degrees obtained by each person, including the name of the degree (e.g., B.S.), the school, and the date. This collection of structs could be a set, bag, list, or array. Describe the consequences of each of these four choices. What information could be gained or lost by making each choice? Is the information lost likely to be important in practice?

Exercise 4.2.6: In Fig. 4.5 is an ODL definition for the classes `Ship` and `TG` (*task group*, a collection of ships). We would like to make some modifications to this definition. Each modification can be described by mentioning a line or lines to be changed and giving the replacement, or by inserting one or more new lines after one of the numbered lines. Describe the following modifications:

a) The type of the attribute `commander` is changed to be a pair of strings, the first of which is the rank and the second of which is the name.

b) A ship is allowed to be assigned to more than one task group.

c) *Sister ships* are identical ships made from the same plans. We wish to represent, for each ship, the set of its sister ships (other than itself). You may assume that each ship's sister ships are `Ship` objects.

```
1)  class Ship {
2)      attribute string name;
3)      attribute integer yearLaunched;
4)      relationship TG assignedTo inverse TG::unitsOf;
    };

5)  class TG {
6)      attribute real number;
7)      attribute string commander;
8)      relationship Set<Ship> unitsOf
            inverse Ship::assignedTo;
    };
```

Figure 4.5: An ODL description of ships and task groups

*!! Exercise 4.2.7 : Under what circumstances is a relationship its own inverse? *Hint*: Think about the relationship as a set of pairs, as discussed in Section 4.2.5.

4.3 Additional ODL Concepts

There are a number of other features of ODL that we must learn if we are to express in ODL the things that we can express in the E/R or relational models. In this section, we shall cover:

1. Representing multiway relationships. Notice that all ODL relationships are binary, and we have to go to some lengths to represent 3-way or higher arity relationships that are simple to represent in E/R diagrams or relations.

2. Subclasses and inheritance.

3. Keys, which are optional in ODL.

4. Extents, the set of objects of a given class that exist in a database. These are the ODL equivalent of entity sets or relations, and must not be confused with the class itself, which is a schema.

4.3.1   Multiway Relationships in ODL

ODL supports only binary relationships. There is a trick, which we introduced in Section 2.1.7, to replace a multiway relationship by several binary, many-one relationships. Suppose we have a multiway relationship R among classes or entity sets $C_1, C_2, \ldots, C_n$. We may replace R by a class C and n many-one binary relationships from C to each of the C_i's. Each object of class C may be thought of as a tuple t in the relationship set for R. Object t is related, by the n many-one relationships, to the objects of the classes C_i that participate in the relationship-set tuple t.

Example 4.9 : Let us consider how we would represent in ODL the 3-way relationship contracts, whose E/R diagram was given in Fig. 2.7. We may start with the class definitions for `Movie`, `Star`, and `Studio`, the three classes that are related by *Contracts*, that we saw in Fig. 4.3.

We must create a class `Contract` that corresponds to the 3-way relationship *Contracts*. The three many-one relationships from `Contract` to the other three classes we shall call `theMovie`, `theStar`, and `theStudio`. Figure 4.6 shows the definition of the class `Contract`.

```
1)      class Contract {
2)          attribute integer salary;
3)          relationship Movie theMovie
                inverse ... ;
4)          relationship Star theStar
                inverse ... ;
5)          relationship Studio theStudio
                inverse ... ;
        };
```

Figure 4.6: A class `Contract` to represent the 3-way relationship *Contracts*

There is one attribute of the class `Contract`, the salary, since that quantity is associated with the contract itself, not with any of the three participants. Recall that in Fig. 2.7 we made an analogous decision to place the attribute *salary* on the relationship *Contracts*, rather than on one of the participating entity sets. The other properties of `Contract` objects are the three relationships mentioned.

Note that we have not named the inverses of these relationships. We need to modify the declarations of `Movie`, `Star`, and `Studio` to include relationships from each of these to `Contract`. For instance, the inverse of `theMovie` might be named `contractsFor`. We would then replace line (3) of Fig. 4.6 by

```
3)  relationship Movie theMovie
        inverse Movie::contractsFor;
```

and add to the declaration of `Movie` the statement:

```
relationship Set<Contract> contractsFor
    inverse Contract::theMovie;
```

Notice that in `Movie`, the relationship `contractsFor` gives us a set of contracts, since there may be several contracts associated with one movie. Each contract in the set is essentially a triple consisting of that movie, a star, and a studio, plus the salary that is paid to the star by the studio for acting in that movie. □

4.3.2 Subclasses in ODL

Let us recall the discussion of subclasses in the E/R model from Section 2.1.11. There is a similar capability in ODL to declare one class C to be a subclass of another class D. We follow the name C in its declaration with the keyword `extends` and the name D.

Example 4.10: Recall Example 2.10, where we declared cartoons to be a subclass of movies, with the additional property of a relationship from a cartoon to a set of stars that are its "voices." We can create a subclass `Cartoon` for Môvie with the ODL declaration:

```
class Cartoon extends Movie {
    relationship Set<Star> voices;
};
```

We have not indicated the name of the inverse of relationship `voices`, although technically we must do so.

A subclass *inherits* all the properties of its superclass. Thus, each cartoon object has attributes `title`, `year`, `length`, and `filmType` inherited from `Movie` (recall Fig. 4.3), and it inherits relationships `stars` and `ownedBy` from `Movie`, in addition to its own relationship `voices`.

Also in that example, we defined a class of murder mysteries with additional attribute `weapon`.

```
class MurderMystery extends Movie {
    attribute string weapon;
};
```

is a suitable declaration of this subclass. Again, all the properties of movies are inherited by `MurderMystery`. □

4.3.3 Multiple Inheritance in ODL

Sometimes, as in the case of a movie like "Roger Rabbit," we need a class that is a subclass of two or more other classes at the same time. In the E/R model, we were able to imagine that "Roger Rabbit" was represented by components in all three of the *Movies*, *Cartoons*, and *MurderMysteries* entity sets, which were connected in an isa-hierarchy. However, a principle of object-oriented systems is that objects belong to one and only one class. Thus, to represent movies that are both cartoons and murder mysteries, we need a fourth class for these movies.

The class `CartoonMurderMystery` must inherit properties from both `Cartoon` and `MurderMystery`, as suggested by Fig. 4.7. That is, a `CartoonMurderMystery` object has all the properties of a `Movie` object, plus the relationship `voices` and the attribute `weapon`.

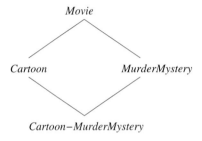

Movie

Cartoon   *MurderMystery*

Cartoon–MurderMystery

Figure 4.7: Diagram showing multiple inheritance

In ODL, we may follow the keyword `extends` by several classes, separated by colons.[3] Thus, we may declare the fourth class by:

```
class CartoonMurderMystery
    extends MurderMystery : Cartoon;
```

When a class C inherits from several classes, there is the potential for *conflicts* among property names. Two or more of the superclasses of C may have a property of the same name, and the types of these properties may differ. Class `CartoonMurderMystery` did not present such a problem, since the only properties in common between `Cartoon` and `MurderMystery` are the properties of `Movie`, which are the same property in both superclasses of `CartoonMurderMystery`. Here is an example where we are not so lucky.

Example 4.11 : Suppose we have subclasses of `Movie` called `Romance` and `Courtroom`. Further suppose that each of these subclasses has an attribute called `ending`. In class `Romance`, attribute `ending` draws its values from the

---

[3]Technically, the second and subsequent names must be "interfaces," rather than classes. Roughly, an *interface* in ODL is a class definition without an associated set of objects, or "extent." We discuss the distinction further in Section 4.3.4.

enumeration {happy, sad}, while in class Courtroom, attribute ending draws its values from the enumeration {guilty, notGuilty}. If we create a further subclass, Courtroom-Romance, that has as superclasses both Romance and Courtroom, then the type for inherited attribute ending in class Courtroom-Romance is unclear. □

The ODL standard does not dictate how such conflicts are to be resolved. Some possible approaches to handling conflicts that arise from multiple inheritance are:

1. Disallow multiple inheritance altogether. This approach is generally regarded as too limiting.

2. Indicate which of the candidate definitions of the property applies to the subclass. For instance, in Example 4.11 we may decide that in a courtroom romance we are more interested in whether the movie has a happy or sad ending than we are in the verdict of the courtroom trial. In this case, we would specify that class Courtroom-Romance inherits attribute ending from superclass Romance, and not from superclass Courtroom.

3. Give a new name in the subclass for one of the identically named properties in the superclasses. For instance, in Example 4.11, if Courtroom-Romance inherits attribute ending from superclass Romance, then we may specify that class Courtroom-Romance has an additional attribute called verdict, which is a renaming of the attribute ending inherited from class Courtroom.

4.3.4 Extents

When an ODL class is part of the database being defined, we need to distinguish the class definition itself from the set of objects of that class that exist at a given time. The distinction is the same as that between a relation schema and a relation instance, even though both can be referred to by the name of the relation, depending on context. Likewise, in the E/R model we need to distinguish between the definition of an entity set and the set of existing entities of that kind.

In ODL, the distinction is made explicit by giving the class and its *extent*, or set of existing objects, different names. Thus, the class name is a schema for the class, while the extent is the name of the current set of objects of that class. We provide a name for the extent of a class by following the class name by a parenthesized expression consisting of the keyword extent and the name chosen for the extent.

Example 4.12 : In general, we find it a useful convention to name classes by a singular noun and name the corresponding extent by the same noun in plural. Following this convention, we could call the extent for class Movie by the name

---

Interfaces

ODL provides for the definition of *interfaces*, which are essentially class definitions with no associated extent (and therefore, with no associated objects). We first mentioned interfaces in Section 4.3.3, where we pointed out that they could support inheritance by one class from several classes. Interfaces also are useful if we have several classes that have different extents, but the same properties; the situation is analogous to several relations that have the same schema but different sets of tuples.

If we define an interface I, we can then define several classes that inherit their properties from I. Each of those classes has a distinct extent, so we can maintain in our database several sets of objects that have the same type, yet belong to distinct classes.

Movies. To declare this name for the extent, we would begin the declaration of class Movie by:

```
class Movie (extent Movies) {
    attribute string title;
        ...
```

As we shall see when we study the query language OQL that is designed for querying ODL data, we refer to the extent Movies, not to the class Movie, when we want to examine the movies currently stored in our database. Remember that the choice of a name for the extent of a class is entirely arbitrary, although we shall follow the "make it plural" convention in this book.   □

4.3.5   Declaring Keys in ODL

ODL differs from the other models studied so far in that the declaration and use of keys is optional. That is, in the E/R model, entity sets need keys to distinguish members of the entity set from one another. In the relational model, where relations are sets, all attributes together form a key unless some proper subset of the attributes for a given relation can serve as a key. Either way, there must be at least one key for a relation.

However, objects have a unique object identity, as we discussed in Section 4.1.3. Consequently, in ODL, the declaration of a key or keys is optional. It is entirely appropriate for there to be several objects of a class that are indistinguishable by any properties we can observe; the system still keeps them distinct by their internal object identity.

In ODL we may declare one or more attributes to be a key for a class by using the keyword key or keys (it doesn't matter which) followed by the attribute or attributes forming keys. If there is more than one attribute in a key, the list of attributes must be surrounded by parentheses. The key declaration itself appears, along with the extent declaration, inside parentheses that may follow the name of the class itself in the first line of its declaration.

Example 4.13: To declare that the set of two attributes `title` and `year` form a key for class `Movie`, we could begin its declaration:

```
class Movie
    (extent Movies key (title, year))
{
    attribute string title;
        ...
```

We could have used `keys` in place of `key`, even though only one key is declared. Similarly, if `name` is a key for class `Star`, then we could begin its declaration:

```
class Star
    (extent Stars key name)
{
    attribute string name;
        ...
```

□

It is possible that several sets of attributes are keys. If so, then following the word `key(s)` we may place several keys separated by commas. As usual, a key that consists of more than one attribute must have parentheses around the list of its attributes, so we can disambiguate a key of several attributes from several keys of one attribute each.

Example 4.14: As an example of a situation where it is appropriate to have more than one key, consider a class `Employee`, whose complete set of attributes and relationships we shall not describe here. However, suppose that two of its attributes are `empID`, the employee ID, and `ssNo`, the Social Security number. Then we can declare each of these attributes to be a key by itself with

```
class Employee
    (extent Employees key empID, ssNo)
        ...
```

Because there are no parentheses around the list of attributes, ODL interprets the above as saying that each of the two attributes is a key by itself. If we put parentheses around the list (`empID`, `ssNo`), then ODL would interpret the two attributes together as forming one key. That is, the implication of writing

```
class Employee
    (extent Employees key (empID, ssNo))
        ...
```

is that no two employees could have both the same employee ID and the same Social Security number, although two employees might agree on one of these attributes. □

The ODL standard also allows properties other than attributes to appear in keys. There is no fundamental problem with a method or relationship being declared a key or part of a key, since keys are advisory statements that the DBMS can take advantage of or not, as it wishes. For instance, one could declare a method to be a key, meaning that on distinct objects of the class the method is guaranteed to return distinct values.

When we allow many-one relationships to appear in key declarations, we can get an effect similar to that of weak entity sets in the E/R model. We can declare that the object O_1 referred to by an object O_2 on the "many" side of the relationship, perhaps together with other properties of O_2 that are included in the key, is unique for different objects O_2. However, we should remember that there is no requirement that classes have keys; we are never obliged to handle, in some special way, classes that lack attributes of their own to form a key, as we did for weak entity sets.

Example 4.15: Let us review the example of a weak entity set *Crews* in Fig. 2.20. Recall that we hypothesized that crews were identified by their number, and the studio for which they worked, although two studios might have crews with the same number. We might declare the class `Crew` as in Fig. 4.8. Note that we need to modify the declaration of `Studio` to include the relationship `crewsOf` that is an inverse to the relationship `partOf` in `Crew`; we omit this change.

```
    class Crew
        (extent Crews key (number, partOf))
    {
        attribute integer number;
        relationship Studio partOf
            inverse Studio::crewsOf;
    }
```

Figure 4.8: A ODL declaration for crews

What this key declaration asserts is that there cannot be two crews that both have the same value for the `number` attribute and are related to the same studio by `partOf`. Notice how this assertion resembles the implication of the E/R diagram in Fig. 2.20, which is that the number of a crew and the name of the related studio (i.e., the key for studios) uniquely determine a crew entity. □

4.3.6 Exercises for Section 4.3

* **Exercise 4.3.1:** Add suitable extents and keys to your ODL schema from Exercise 4.2.1.

Exercise 4.3.2: Add suitable extents and keys to your ODL schema from Exercise 4.2.3.

! **Exercise 4.3.3:** Suppose we wish to modify the ODL declarations of Exercise 4.2.4, where we had a class of people with relationships mother-of, father-of, and child-of, to include certain subclasses of people: (1) Males (2) Females (3) People who are parents. In addition, we want the relationships mother-of, father-of, and child-of to run between the smallest classes for which all possible instances of the relationship appear. You may therefore wish to define other subclasses as well. Write these declarations, including multiple inheritances when appropriate.

Exercise 4.3.4: Is there a suitable key for the class `Contract` declared in Fig. 4.6? If so, what is it?

Exercise 4.3.5: In Exercise 2.4.4 we saw two examples of situations where weak entity sets were essential. Render these databases in ODL, including declarations for extents and suitable keys.

Exercise 4.3.6: Give an ODL design for the registrar's database described in Exercise 2.1.9.

4.4 From ODL Designs to Relational Designs

While the E/R model is intended to be converted into a model such as the relational model when we implement the design as an actual database, ODL was originally intended to be used as the specification language for real, object-oriented DBMS's. However ODL, like all object-oriented design systems, can also be used for preliminary design and converted to relations prior to implementation. In this section we shall consider how to convert ODL designs into relational designs. The process is similar in many ways to what we introduced in Section 3.2 for converting E/R diagrams to relational database schemas. Yet some new problems arise for ODL, including:

1. Entity sets must have keys, but there is no such guarantee for ODL classes. Therefore, in some situations we must invent a new attribute to serve as a key when we construct a relation for the class.

2. While we have required E/R attributes and relational attributes to be atomic, there is no such constraint for ODL attributes. The conversion of attributes that have collection types to relations is tricky and ad-hoc, often resulting in unnormalized relations that must be redesigned by the techniques of Section 3.6.

3. ODL allows us to specify methods as part of a design, but there is no simple way to convert methods directly into a relational schema. We shall visit the issue of methods in relational schemas in Section 4.5.5 and again in Chapter 9 covering the SQL-99 standard. For now, let us assume that any ODL design we wish to convert into a relational design does not include methods.

4.4.1 From ODL Attributes to Relational Attributes

As a starting point, let us assume that our goal is to have one relation for each class and for that relation to have one attribute for each property. We shall see many ways in which this approach must be modified, but for the moment, let us consider the simplest possible case, where we can indeed convert classes to relations and properties to attributes. The restrictions we assume are:

1. All properties of the class are attributes (not relationships or methods).

2. The types of the attributes are atomic (not structures or sets).

Example 4.16: Figure 4.9 is an example of such a class. There are four attributes and no other properties. These attributes each have an atomic type; title is a string, year and length are integers, and filmType is an enumeration of two values.

```
class Movie (extent Movies) {
    attribute string title;
    attribute integer year;
    attribute integer length;
    attribute enum Film {color,blackAndWhite} filmType;
};
```

Figure 4.9: Attributes of the class Movie

We create a relation with the same name as the extent of the class, Movies in this case. The relation has four attributes, one for each attribute of the class. The names of the relational attributes can be the same as the names of the corresponding class attributes. Thus, the schema for this relation is

```
Movies(title, year, length, filmType)
```

For each object in the extent Movies, there is one tuple in the relation Movies. This tuple has a component for each of the four attributes, and the value of each component is the same as the value of the corresponding attribute of the object. □

4.4.2 Nonatomic Attributes in Classes

Unfortunately, even when a class' properties are all attributes we may have some difficulty converting the class to a relation. The reason is that attributes in ODL can have complex types such as structures, sets, bags, or lists. On the other hand, a fundamental principle of the relational model is that a relation's attributes have an atomic type, such as numbers and strings. Thus, we must find some way of representing nonatomic attribute types as relations.

Record structures whose fields are themselves atomic are the easiest to handle. We simply expand the structure definition, making one attribute of the relation for each field of the structure. The only possible problem is that two structures could have fields of the same name, in which case we have to invent new attribute names to distinguish them in the relation.

```
class Star (extent Stars) {
    attribute string name;
    attribute Struct Addr
        {string street, string city} address;
};
```

Figure 4.10: Class with a structured attribute

Example 4.17 : In Fig. 4.10 is a declaration for class **Star**, with only attributes as properties. The attribute **name** is atomic, but attribute **address** is a structure with two fields, **street** and **city**. Thus, we can represent this class by a relation with three attributes. The first attribute, **name**, corresponds to the ODL attribute of the same name. The second and third attributes we shall call **street** and **city**; they correspond to the two fields of the **address** structure and together represent an address. Thus, the schema for our relation is

```
Stars(name, street, city)
```

Figure 4.11 shows some typical tuples of this relation. □

name	street	city
Carrie Fisher	123 Maple St.	Hollywood
Mark Hamill	456 Oak Rd.	Brentwood
Harrison Ford	789 Palm Dr.	Beverly Hills

Figure 4.11: A relation representing stars

4.4.3   Representing Set-Valued Attributes

However, record structures are not the most complex kind of attribute that can appear in ODL class definitions. Values can also be built using type constructors `Set`, `Bag`, `List`, `Array`, and `Dictionary` from Section 4.2.8. Each presents its own problems when migrating to the relational model. We shall only discuss the `Set` constructor, which is the most common, in detail.

One approach to representing a set of values for an attribute A is to make one tuple for each value. That tuple includes the appropriate values for all the other attributes besides A. Let us first see an example where this approach works well, and then we shall see a pitfall.

```
class Star (extent Stars) {
    attribute string name;
    attribute Set<
            Struct Addr {string street, string city}
        > address;
};
```

Figure 4.12: Stars with a set of addresses

Example 4.18 : Suppose that class `Star` were defined so that for each star we could record a set of addresses, as in Fig. 4.12. Suppose next that Carrie Fisher also has a beach home, but the other two stars mentioned in Fig. 4.11 each have only one home. Then we may create two tuples with `name` attribute equal to `"Carrie Fisher"`, as shown in Fig. 4.13. Other tuples remain as they were in Fig. 4.11.   □

name	street	city
Carrie Fisher	123 Maple St.	Hollywood
Carrie Fisher	5 Locust Ln.	Malibu
Mark Hamill	456 Oak Rd.	Brentwood
Harrison Ford	789 Palm Dr.	Beverly Hills

Figure 4.13: Allowing a set of addresses

Unfortunately, this technique of replacing objects with one or more set-valued attributes by collections of tuples, one for each combination of values for these attributes, can lead to unnormalized relations, of the type discussed in Section 3.6. In fact, even one set-valued attribute can lead to a BCNF violation, as the next example shows.

Atomic Values: Bug or Feature?

It seems that the relational model puts obstacles in our way, while ODL is more flexible in allowing structured values as properties. One might be tempted to dismiss the relational model altogether or regard it as a primitive concept that has been superseded by more elegant "object-oriented" approaches such as ODL. However, the reality is that database systems based on the relational model are dominant in the marketplace. One of the reasons is that the simplicity of the model makes possible powerful programming languages for querying databases, especially SQL (see Chapter 6), the standard language used in most of today's database systems.

```
class Star (extent Stars) {
    attribute string name;
    attribute Set<
            Struct Addr {string street, string city}
        > address;
    attribute Date birthdate;
};
```

Figure 4.14: Stars with a set of addresses and a birthdate

Example 4.19: Suppose that we add `birthdate` as an attribute in the definition of the `Star` class; that is, we use the definition shown in Fig. 4.14. We have added to Fig. 4.12 the attribute `birthdate` of type `Date`, which is one of ODL's atomic types. The `birthdate` attribute can be an attribute of the `Star` relation, whose schema now becomes:

> Stars(name, street, city, birthdate)

Let us make another change to the data of Fig. 4.13. Since a set of addresses can be empty, let us assume that Harrison Ford has no address in the database. Then the revised relation is shown in Fig. 4.15. Two bad things have happened:

1. Carrie Fisher's birthdate has been repeated in each tuple, causing redundancy. Note that her name is also repeated, but that repetition is not true redundancy, because without the name appearing in each tuple we could not know that both addresses were associated with Carrie Fisher.

2. Because Harrison Ford has an empty set of addresses, we have lost all information about him. This situation is an example of a deletion anomaly that we discussed in Section 3.6.1.

name	street	city	birthdate
Carrie Fisher	123 Maple St.	Hollywood	9/9/99
Carrie Fisher	5 Locust Ln.	Malibu	9/9/99
Mark Hamill	456 Oak Rd.	Brentwood	8/8/88

Figure 4.15: Adding birthdates

Although `name` is a key for the class `Star`, our need to have several tuples for one star to represent all their addresses means that `name` is *not* a key for the relation `Stars`. In fact, the key for that relation is {`name`, `street`, `city`}. Thus, the functional dependency

$$\texttt{name} \rightarrow \texttt{birthdate}$$

is a BCNF violation. This fact explains why the anomalies mentioned above are able to occur. □

There are several options regarding how to handle set-valued attributes that appear in a class declaration along with other attributes, set-valued or not. First, we may simply place all attributes, set-valued or not, in the schema for the relation, then use the normalization techniques of Sections 3.6 and 3.7 to eliminate the resulting BCNF and 4NF violations. Notice that a set-valued attribute in conjunction with a single-valued attribute leads to a BNCF violation, as in Example 4.19. Two set-valued attributes in the same class declaration will lead to a 4NF violation.

The second approach is to separate out each set-valued attribute as if it were a many-many relationship between the objects of the class and the values that appear in the sets. We shall discuss this approach for relationships in Section 4.4.5.

4.4.4 Representing Other Type Constructors

Besides record structures and sets, an ODL class definition could use `Bag`, `List`, `Array`, or `Dictionary` to construct values. To represent a bag (multiset), in which a single object can be a member of the bag n times, we cannot simply introduce into a relation n identical tuples.[4] Instead, we could add to the relation schema another attribute `count` representing the number of times that each element is a member of the bag. For instance, suppose that `address` in Fig. 4.12 were a bag instead of a set. We could say that 123 Maple St.,

---

[4]To be precise, we cannot introduce identical tuples into relations of the abstract relational model described in Chapter 3. However, SQL-based relational DBMS's *do* allow duplicate tuples; i.e., relations are bags rather than sets in SQL. See Sections 5.3 and 6.4. If queries are likly to ask for tuple counts, we advise using a scheme such as that described here, even if your DBMS allows duplicate tuples.

Hollywood is Carrie Fisher's address twice and 5 Locust Ln., Malibu is her address 3 times (whatever that may mean) by

name	street	city	count
Carrie Fisher	123 Maple St.	Hollywood	2
Carrie Fisher	5 Locust Ln.	Malibu	3

A list of addresses could be represented by a new attribute position, indicating the position in the list. For instance, we could show Carrie Fisher's addresses as a list, with Hollywood first, by:

name	street	city	position
Carrie Fisher	123 Maple St.	Hollywood	1
Carrie Fisher	5 Locust Ln.	Malibu	2

A fixed-length array of addresses could be represented by attributes for each position in the array. For instance, if address were to be an array of two street-city structures, we could represent Star objects as:

name	street1	city1	street2	city2
Carrie Fisher	123 Maple St.	Hollywood	5 Locust Ln.	Malibu

Finally, a dictionary could be represented as a set, but with attributes for both the key-value and range-value components of the pairs that are members of the dictionary. For instance, suppose that instead of star's addresses, we really wanted to keep, for each star, a dictionary giving the mortgage holder for each of their homes. Then the dictionary would have address as the key value and bank name as the range value. A hypothetical rendering of the Carrie-Fisher object with a dictionary attribute is:

name	street	city	mortgage-holder
Carrie Fisher	123 Maple St.	Hollywood	Bank of Burbank
Carrie Fisher	5 Locust Ln.	Malibu	Torrance Trust

Of course attribute types in ODL may involve more than one type constructor. If a type is any collection type besides dictionary applied to a structure (e.g., a set of structs), then we may apply the techniques from Sections 4.4.3 or 4.4.4 as if the struct were an atomic value, and then replace the single attribute representing the atomic value by several attributes, one for each field of the struct. This strategy was used in the examples above, where the address is a struct. The case of a dictionary applied to structs is similar and left as an exercise.

There are many reasons to limit the complexity of attribute types to an optional struct followed by an optional collection type. We mentioned in Section 2.1.1 that some versions of the E/R model allow exactly this much generality in the types of attributes, although we restricted ourselves to atomic

attributes in the E/R model. We recommend that, if you are going to use an
ODL design for the purpose of eventual translation to a relational database
schema, you similarly limit yourself. We take up in the exercises some options
for dealing with more complex types as attributes.

4.4.5   Representing ODL Relationships

Usually, an ODL class definition will contain relationships to other ODL classes.
As in the E/R model, we can create for each relationship a new relation that
connects the keys of the two related classes. However, in ODL, relationships
come in inverse pairs, and we must create only one relation for each pair.

```
class Movie
    (extent Movies key(title, year)
{
    attribute string title;
    attribute integer year;
    attribute integer length;
    attribute enum Film {color,blackAndWhite} filmType;
    relationship Set<Star> stars
                inverse Star::starredIn;
    relationship Studio ownedBy
                inverse Studio::owns;
};

class Studio
    (extent Studios key name)
{
    attribute string name;
    attribute string address;
    relationship Set<Movie> owns
                inverse Movie::ownedBy;
};
```

Figure 4.16: The complete definition of the `Movie` and `Studio` classes

Example 4.20 : Consider the declarations of the classes `Movie` and `Studio`,
which we repeat in Fig. 4.16. We see that `title` and `year` form the key for
`Movie` and `name` is a key for class `Studio`. We may create a relation for the pair
of relationships `owns` and `ownedBy`. The relation needs a name, which can be
arbitrary; we shall pick `StudioOf` as the name. The schema for `StudioOf` has
attributes for the key of `Movie`, that is, `title` and `year`, and an attribute that
we shall call `studioName` for the key of `Studio`. This relation schema is thus:

```
StudioOf(title, year, studioName)
```

Some typical tuples that would be in this relation are:

title	year	studioName
Star Wars	1977	Fox
Mighty Ducks	1991	Disney
Wayne's World	1992	Paramount

□

When a relationship is many-one, we have an option to combine it with the relation that is constructed for the class on the "many" side. Doing so has the effect of combining two relations that have a common key, as we discussed in Section 3.2.3. It therefore does not cause a BCNF violation and is a legitimate and commonly followed option.

Example 4.21: Instead of creating a relation StudioOf for relationship pair owns and ownedBy, as we did in Example 4.20, we may instead modify our relation schema for relation Movies to include an attribute, say studioName to represent the key of Studio. If we do, the schema for Movies becomes

```
Movies(title, year, length, filmType, studioName)
```

and some typical tuples for this relation are:

title	year	length	filmType	studioName
Star Wars	1977	124	color	Fox
Mighty Ducks	1991	104	color	Disney
Wayne's World	1992	95	color	Paramount

Note that title and year, the key for the Movie class, is also a key for relation Movies, since each movie has a unique length, film type, and owning studio. □

We should remember that it is possible but unwise to treat many-many relationships as we did many-one relationships in Example 4.21. In fact, Example 3.6 in Section 3.2.3 was based on what happens if we try to combine the many-many stars relationship between movies and their stars with the other information in the relation Movies to get a relation with schema:

```
Movies(title, year, length, filmType, studioName, starName)
```

There is a resulting BCNF violation, since {title, year, starName} is the key, yet attributes length, filmType, and studioName each are functionally determined by only title and year.

Likewise, if we do combine a many-one relationship with the relation for a class, it must be the class of the "many." For instance, combining owns and its inverse ownedBy with relation Studios will lead to a BCNF violation (see Exercise 4.4.4).

4.4.6   What If There Is No Key?

Since keys are optional in ODL, we may face a situation where the attributes available to us cannot serve to represent objects of a class C uniquely. That situation can be a problem if the class C participates in one or more relationships.

We recommend creating a new attribute or "certificate" that can serve as an identifier for objects of class C in relational designs, much as the hidden object-ID serves to identify those objects in an object-oriented system. The certificate becomes an additional attribute of the relation for the class C, as well as representing objects of class C in each of the relations that come from relationships involving class C. Notice that in practice, many important classes are represented by such certificates: university ID's for students, driver's-license numbers for drivers, and so on.

Example 4.22 : Suppose we accept that names are not a reliable key for movie stars, and we decide instead to adopt a "certificate number" to be assigned to each star as a way of identifying them uniquely. Then the Stars relation would have schema:

        Stars(cert#, name, street, city, birthdate)

If we wish to represent the many-many relationship between movies and their stars by a relation StarsIn, we can use the title and year attributes from Movie and the certificate to represent stars, giving us a relation with schema:

        StarsIn(title, year, cert#)

□

4.4.7   Exercises for Section 4.4

Exercise 4.4.1 : Convert your ODL designs from the following exercises to relational database schemas.

* a) Exercise 4.2.1.

   b) Exercise 4.2.2 (include all four of the modifications specified by that exercise).

   c) Exercise 4.2.3.

* d) Exercise 4.2.4.

   e) Exercise 4.2.5.

Exercise 4.4.2 : Convert the ODL description of Fig. 4.5 to a relational database schema. How does each of the three modifications of Exercise 4.2.6 affect your relational schema?

! **Exercise 4.4.3:** Consider an attribute of type dictionary with key and range types both structs of atomic types. Show how to convert a class with an attribute of this type to a relation.

* **Exercise 4.4.4:** We claimed that if you combine the relation for class `Studio`, as defined in Fig. 4.16, with the relation for the relationship pair `owns` and `ownedBy`, then there is a BCNF violation. Do the combination and show that there is, in fact, a BCNF violation.

Exercise 4.4.5: We mentioned that when attributes are of a type more complex than a collection of structs, it becomes tricky to convert them to relations; in particular, it becomes necessary to create some intermediate concepts and relations for them. The following sequence of questions will examine increasingly more complex types and how to represent them as relations.

* * a) A *card* can be represented as a struct with fields `rank` $(2, 3, \ldots, 10,$ Jack, Queen, King, and Ace) and `suit` (Clubs, Diamonds, Hearts, and Spades). Give a suitable definition of a structured type `Card`. This definition should be independent of any class declarations but available to them all.

* * b) A *hand* is a set of cards. The number of cards may vary. Give a declaration of a class `Hand` whose objects are hands. That is, this class declaration has an attribute `theHand`, whose type is a hand.

* *! c) Convert your class declaration `Hand` from (b) to a relation schema.

* d) A *poker hand* is a set of five cards. Repeat (b) and (c) for poker hands.

* *! e) A *deal* is a set of pairs, each pair consisting of the name of a player and a hand for that player. Declare a class `Deal`, whose objects are deals. That is, this class declaration has an attribute `theDeal`, whose type is a deal.

* f) Repeat (e), but restrict hands of a deal to be hands of exactly five cards.

* g) Repeat (e), using a dictionary for a deal. You may assume the names of players in a deal are unique.

* *!! h) Convert your class declaration from (e) to a relational database schema.

* *! i) Suppose we defined deals to be sets of sets of cards, with no player associated with each hand (set of cards). It is proposed that we represent such deals by a relation schema

    ```
    Deals(dealID, card)
    ```

    meaning that the card was a member of one of the hands in the deal with the given ID. What, if anything, is wrong with this representation? How would you fix the problem?

Exercise 4.4.6: Suppose we have a class C defined by

```
class C (key a) {
    attribute string a;
    attribute T b;
}
```

where T is some type. Give the relation schema for the relation derived from C and indicate its key attributes if T is:

  a) `Set<Struct S {string f, string g}>`

*! b) `Bag<Struct S {string f, string g}>`

 ! c) `List<Struct S {string f, string g}>`

 ! d) `Dictionary<Struct K {string f, string g}, Struct R {string i, string j}>`

4.5   The Object-Relational Model

The relational model and the object-oriented model typified by ODL are two important points in a spectrum of options that could underlie a DBMS. For an extended period, the relational model was dominant in the commercial DBMS world. Object-oriented DBMS's made limited inroads during the 1990's, but have since died off. Instead of a migration from relational to object-oriented systems, as was widely predicted around 1990, the vendors of relational systems have moved to incorporate many of the ideas found in ODL or other object-oriented-database proposals. As a result, many DBMS products that used to be called "relational" are now called "object-relational."

In Chapter 9 we shall meet the new SQL standard for object-relational databases. In this chapter, we cover the topic more abstractly. We introduce the concept of object-relations in Section 4.5.1, then discuss one of its earliest embodiments — nested relations — in Section 4.5.2. ODL-like references for object-relations are discussed in Section 4.5.3, and in Section 4.5.4 we compare the object-relational model against the pure object-oriented approach.

4.5.1   From Relations to Object-Relations

While the relation remains the fundamental concept, the relational model has been extended to the *object-relational model* by incorporation of features such as:

  1. *Structured types for attributes.* Instead of allowing only atomic types for attributes, object-relational systems support a type system like ODL's: types built from atomic types and type constructors for structs, sets, and

bags, for instance. Especially important is a type that is a set[5] of structs, which is essentially a relation. That is, a value of one component of a tuple can be an entire relation.

2. *Methods.* Special operations can be defined for, and applied to, values of a user-defined type. While we haven't yet addressed the question of how values or tuples are manipulated in the relational or object-oriented models, we shall find few surprises when we take up the subject beginning in Chapter 5. For example, values of numeric type are operated on by arithmetic operators such as addition or less-than. However, in the object-relational model, we have the option to define specialized operations for a type, such as those discussed in Example 4.7 on ODL methods for the `Movie` class.

3. *Identifiers for tuples.* In object-relational systems, tuples play the role of objects. It therefore becomes useful in some situations for each tuple to have a unique ID that distinguishes it from other tuples, even from tuples that have the same values in all components. This ID, like the object-identifier assumed in ODL, is generally invisible to the user, although there are even some circumstances where users can see the identifier for a tuple in an object-relational system.

4. *References.* While the pure relational model has no notion of references or pointers to tuples, object-relational systems can use these references in various ways.

In the next sections, we shall elaborate and illustrate each of these additional capabilities of object-relational systems.

4.5.2 Nested Relations

Relations extended by point (1) above are often called "nested relations." In the *nested-relational model*, we allow attributes of relations to have a type that is not atomic; in particular, a type can be a relation schema. As a result, there is a convenient, recursive definition of the types of attributes and the types (schemas) of relations:

BASIS: An atomic type (integer, real, string, etc.) can be the type of an attribute.

INDUCTION: A relation's type can be any *schema* consisting of names for one or more attributes, and any legal type for each attribute. In addition, a schema can also be the type of any attribute.

In our discussion of the relational model, we did not specify the particular atomic type associated with each attribute, because the distinctions among,

---

[5]Strictly speaking, a bag rather than a set, since commercial relational DBMS's prefer to support relations with duplicate tuples, i.e. bags, rather than sets.

integers, reals, strings, and so on had little to do with the issues discussed, such as functional dependencies and normalization. We shall continue to avoid this distinction, but when describing the schema of a nested relation, we must indicate which attributes have relation schemas as types. To do so, we shall treat these attributes as if they were the names of relations and follow them by a parenthesized list of their attributes. Those attributes, in turn, may have associated lists of attributes, down for as many levels as we wish.

Example 4.23 : Let us design a nested relation schema for stars that incorporates within the relation an attribute `movies`, which will be a relation representing all the movies in which the star has appeared. The relation schema for attribute `movies` will include the title, year, and length of the movie. The relation schema for the relation `Stars` will include the name, address, and birthdate, as well as the information found in `movies`. Additionally, the `address` attribute will have a relation type with attributes `street` and `city`. We can record in this relation several addresses for the star. The schema for `Stars` can be written:

```
Stars(name, address(street, city), birthdate,
      movies(title, year, length))
```

An example of a possible relation for nested relation `Stars` is shown in Fig. 4.17. We see in this relation two tuples, one for Carrie Fisher and one for Mark Hamill. The values of components are abbreviated to conserve space, and the dashed lines separating tuples are only for convenience and have no notational significance.

name	address		birthdate	movies		
Fisher	*street*	*city*	9/9/99	*title*	*year*	*length*
	Maple	H'wood		Star Wars	1977	124
	Locust	Malibu		Empire	1980	127
				Return	1983	133
Hamill	*street*	*city*	8/8/88	*title*	*year*	*length*
	Oak	B'wood		Star Wars	1977	124
				Empire	1980	127
				Return	1983	133

Figure 4.17: A nested relation for stars and their movies

In the Carrie Fisher tuple, we see her name, an atomic value, followed by a relation for the value of the address component. That relation has two attributes, `street` and `city`, and there are two tuples, corresponding to her two houses. Next comes the birthdate, another atomic value. Finally, there is a component for the `movies` attribute; this attribute has a relation schema as its type, with components for the title, year, and length of a movie. The relation for the `movies` component of the Carrie Fisher tuple has tuples for her three best-known movies.

The second tuple, for Mark Hamill, has the same components. His relation for `address` has only one tuple, because in our imaginary data, he has only one house. His relation for `movies` looks just like Carrie Fisher's because their best-known movies happen, by coincidence, to be the same. Note that these two relations are two different components of tuples that happen to be the same, just like two components that happened to have the same integer value, like 124. □

4.5.3 References

The fact that movies like *Star Wars* will appear in several relations that are values of the `movies` attribute in the nested relation `Stars` is a cause of redundancy. In effect, the schema of Example 4.23 has the nested-relation analog of not being in BCNF. However, decomposing this `Stars` relation will not eliminate the redundancy. Rather, we need to arrange that among all the tuples of all the `movies` relations, a movie appears only once.

To cure the problem, object-relations need the ability for one tuple t to refer to another tuple s, rather than incorporating s directly in t. We thus add to our model an additional inductive rule: the type of an attribute can also be a reference to a tuple with a given schema.

If an attribute A has a type that is a reference to a single tuple with a relation schema named R, we show the attribute A in a schema as $A(*R)$. Notice that this situation is analogous to an ODL relationship A whose type is R; i.e., it connects to a single object of type R. Similarly, if an attribute A has a type that is a set of references to tuples of schema R, then A will be shown in a schema as $A(\{*R\})$. This situation resembles an ODL relationship A that has type `Set<R>`.

Example 4.24: An appropriate way to fix the redundancy in Fig. 4.17 is to use two relations, one for stars and one for movies. The relation `Movies` will be an ordinary relation with the same schema as the attribute `movies` in Example 4.23. The relation `Stars` will have a schema similar to the nested relation `Stars` of that example, but the movies attribute will have a type that is a set of references to `Movies` tuples. The schemas of the two relations are thus:

```
Movies(title, year, length)
Stars(name, address(street, city), birthdate,
    movies({*Movies}))
```

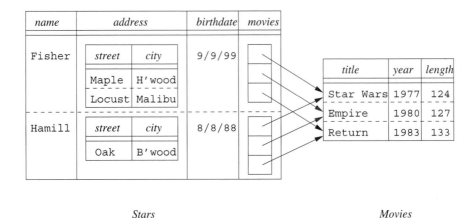

Stars   Movies

Figure 4.18: Sets of references as the value of an attribute

The data of Fig. 4.17, converted to this new schema, is shown in Fig. 4.18. Notice that, because each movie has only one tuple, although it can have many references, we have eliminated the redundancy inherent in the schema of Example 4.23. □

4.5.4 Object-Oriented Versus Object-Relational

The object-oriented data model, as typified by ODL, and the object-relational model discussed here, are remarkably similar. Some of the salient points of comparison follow.

Objects and Tuples

An object's value is really a struct with components for its attributes and relationships. It is not specified in the ODL standard how relationships are to be represented, but we may assume that an object is connected to related objects by some collection of pointers. A tuple is likewise a struct, but in the conventional relational model, it has components for only the attributes. Relationships would be represented by tuples in another relation, as suggested in Section 3.2.2. However the object-relational model, by allowing sets of references to be a component of tuples, also allows relationships to be incorporated directly into the tuples that represent an "object" or entity.

Extents and Relations

ODL treats all objects in a class as living in an "extent" for that class. The object-relational model allows several different relations with identical schemas, so it might appear that there is more opportunity in the object-relational model to distinguish members of the same class. However, ODL allows the definition of interfaces, which are essentially class declarations without an extent (see the box on "Interfaces" in Section 4.3.4). Then, ODL allows you to define any number of classes that inherit this interface, while each class has a distinct extent. In that manner, ODL offers the same opportunity the object-relational approach when it comes to sharing the same declaration among several collections.

Methods

We did not discuss the use of methods as part of an object-relational schema. However, in practice, the SQL-99 standard and all implementations of object-relational ideas allow the same ability as ODL to declare and define methods associated with any class.

Type Systems

The type systems of the object-oriented and object-relational models are quite similar. Each is based on atomic types and construction of new types by struct- and collection-type-constructors. The selection of collection types may vary, but all variants include at least sets and bags. Moreover, the set (or bag) of structs type plays a special role in both models. It is the type of classes in ODL, and the type of relations in the object-relational model.

References and Object-ID's

A pure object-oriented model uses object-ID's that are completely hidden from the user, and thus cannot be seen or queried. The object-relational model allows references to be part of a type, and thus it is possible under some circumstances for the user to see their values and even remember them for future use. You may regard this situation as anything from a serious bug to a stroke of genius, depending on your point of view, but in practice it appears to make little difference.

Backwards Compatibility

With little difference in essential features of the two models, it is interesting to consider why object-relational systems have dominated the pure object-oriented systems in the marketplace. The reason, we believe, is that there was, by the time object-oriented systems were seriously proposed, an enormous number of installations running a relational database system. As relational DBMS's evolved into object-relational DBMS's, the vendors were careful to maintain backwards compatibility. That is, newer versions of the system would still run the old code and accept the same schemas, should the user not care to adopt any of the object-oriented features. On the other hand, migration to a pure object-oriented DBMS would require the installations to rewrite and reorganize extensively. Thus, whatever competitive advantage existed was not enough to convert many databases to a pure object-oriented DBMS.

4.5.5   From ODL Designs to Object-Relational Designs

In Section 4.4 we learned how to convert designs in ODL into schemas of the relational model. Difficulties arose primarily because of the richer modeling constructs of ODL: nonatomic attribute types, relationships, and methods. Some — but not all — of these difficulties are alleviated when we translate an ODL design into an object-relational design. Depending on the specific object-relational model used (we shall consider the concrete SQL-99 model in Chapter 9), we may be able to convert most of the nonatomic types of ODL directly into a corresponding object-relational type; structs, sets, bags, lists, and arrays all fall into this category.

If a type in an ODL design is not available in our object-relational model, we can fall back on the techniques from Sections 4.4.2 through 4.4.4. The representation of relationships in an object-relational model is essentially the same as in the relational model (see Section 4.4.5), although we may prefer to use references in place of keys. Finally, although we were not able to translate ODL designs with methods into the pure relational model, most object-relational models include methods, so this restriction can be lifted.

4.5.6   Exercises for Section 4.5

Exercise 4.5.1: Using the notation developed for nested relations and relations with references, give one or more relation schemas that represent the following information. In each case, you may exercise some discretion regarding what attributes of a relation are included, but try to keep close to the attributes found in our running movie example. Also, indicate whether your schemas exhibit redundancy, and if so, what could be done to avoid it.

* a) Movies, with the usual attributes plus all their stars and the usual information about the stars.

*! b) Studios, all the movies made by that studio, and all the stars of each movie, including all the usual attributes of studios, movies, and stars.

c) Movies with their studio, their stars, and all the usual attributes of these.

* **Exercise 4.5.2:** Represent the banking information of Exercise 2.1.1 in the object-relational model developed in this section. Make sure that it is easy, given the tuple for a customer, to find their account(s) and *also* easy, given the tuple for an account to find the customer(s) that hold that account. Also, try to avoid redundancy.

! **Exercise 4.5.3:** If the data of Exercise 4.5.2 were modified so that an account could be held by only one customer (as in Exercise 2.1.2(a), how could your answer to Exercise 4.5.2 be simplified?

! **Exercise 4.5.4:** Render the players, teams, and fans of Exercise 2.1.3 in the object-relational model.

! **Exercise 4.5.5:** Render the genealogy of Exercise 2.1.6 in the object-relational model.

4.6 Semistructured Data

The *semistructured-data* model plays a special role in database systems:

1. It serves as a model suitable for *integration* of databases, that is, for describing the data contained in two or more databases that contain similar data with different schemas.

2. It serves as a document model in notations such as XML, to be taken up in Section 4.7, that are being used to share information on the Web.

In this section, we shall introduce the basic ideas behind "semistructured data" and how it can represent information more flexibly than the other models we have met previously.

4.6.1 Motivation for the Semistructured-Data Model

Let us begin by recalling the E/R model, and its two fundamental kinds of data — the entity set and the relationship. Remember also that the relational model has only one kind of data — the relation, yet we saw in Section 3.2 how both entity sets and relationships could be represented by relations. There is an advantage to having two concepts: we could tailor an E/R design to the real-world situation we were modeling, using whichever of entity sets or relationships most closely matched the concept being modeled. There is also some advantage to replacing two concepts by one: the notation in which we express schemas is thereby simplified, and implementation techniques that make querying of the database more efficient can be applied to all sorts of data. We shall begin to appreciate these advantages of the relational model when we study implementation of the DBMS, starting in Chapter 11.

Now, let us consider the object-oriented model we introduced in Section 4.2. There are two principal concepts: the class (or its extent) and the relationship. Likewise, the object-relational model of Section 4.5 has two similar concepts: the attribute type (which includes classes) and the relation.

We may see the semistructured-data model as blending the two concepts, class-and-relationship or class-and-relation, much as the relational model blends entity sets and relationships. However, the motivation for the blending appears to be different in each case. While, as we mentioned, the relational model owes some of its success to the fact that it facilitates efficient implementation, interest in the semistructured-data model appears motivated primarily by its flexibility. While the other models seen so far each start from a notion of a schema — E/R diagrams, relation schemas, or ODL declarations, for instance — semistructured data is "schemaless." More properly, the data itself carries information about what its schema is, and that schema can vary arbitrarily, both over time and within a single database.

4.6.2 Semistructured Data Representation

A database of *semistructured data* is a collection of *nodes*. Each node is either a *leaf* or *interior*. Leaf nodes have associated data; the type of this data can be any atomic type, such as numbers and strings. Interior nodes have one or more arcs out. Each arc has a *label*, which indicates how the node at the head of the arc relates to the node at the tail. One interior node, called the *root*, has no arcs entering and represents the entire database. Every node must be reachable from the root, although the graph structure is not necessarily a tree.

Example 4.25 : Figure 4.19 is an example of a semistructured database about stars and movies. We see a node at the top labeled *Root*; this node is the entry point to the data and may be thought of as representing all the information in the database. The central objects or entities — stars and movies in this case — are represented by nodes that are children of the root.

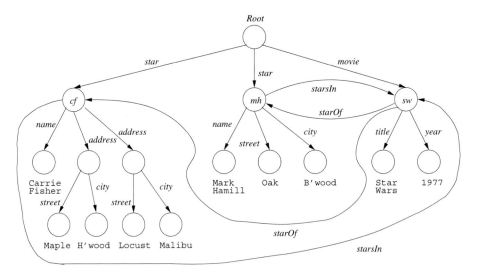

Figure 4.19: Semistructured data representing a movie and stars

We also see many leaf nodes. At the far left is a leaf labeled `Carrie Fisher`, and at the far right is a leaf labeled 1977, for instance. There are also many interior nodes. Three particular nodes we have labeled *cf*, *mh*, and *sw*, standing for "Carrie Fisher," "Mark Hamill," and "Star Wars," respectively. These labels are not part of the model, and we placed them on these nodes only so we would have a way of referring to the nodes, which otherwise would be nameless. We may think of node *sw*, for instance, as representing the concept "Star Wars":

the title and year of this movie, other information not shown, such as its length, and its stars, two of which are shown. □

The labels on arcs play two roles, and thus combine the information contained in class definitions and relationships. Suppose we have an arc labeled L from node N to node M.

1. It may be possible to think of N as representing an object or struct, while M represents one of the attributes of the object or fields of the struct. Then, L represents the name of the attribute or field, respectively.

2. We may be able to think of N and M as objects, and L as the name of a relationship from N to M.

Example 4.26: Consider Fig. 4.19 again. The node indicated by *cf* may be thought of as representing the `Star` object for Carrie Fisher. We see, leaving this node, an arc labeled *name*, which represents the attribute `name` and properly leads to a leaf node holding the correct name. We also see two arcs, each labeled *address*. These arcs lead to unnamed nodes which we may think of as representing the two addresses of Carrie Fisher. Together, these arcs represent the set-valued attribute `address` as in Fig. 4.12.

Each of these addresses is a struct, with fields `street` and `city`. We notice in Fig. 4.19 how both nodes have out-arcs labeled *street* and *city*. Moreover, these arcs each lead to leaf nodes with the appropriate atomic values.

The other kind of arc also appears in Fig. 4.19. For instance, the node *cf* has an out-arc leading to the node *sw* and labeled *starsIn*. The node *mh* (for Mark Hamill) has a similar arc, and the node *sw* has arcs labeled *starOf* to both nodes *cf* and *mh*. These arcs represent the stars-in relationship between stars and movies. □

4.6.3 Information Integration Via Semistructured Data

Unlike the other models we have discussed, data in the semistructured model is *self-describing*; the schema is attached to the data itself. That is, each node (except the root) has an arc or arcs entering it, and the labels on these arcs tell what role the node is playing with respect to the node at the tail of the arc. In all the other models, data has a fixed schema, separate from the data, and the role(s) played by data items is implicit in the schema.

One might naturally wonder whether there is an advantage to creating a database without a schema, where one could enter data at will, and attach to the data whatever schema information you felt was appropriate for that data. There are actually some small-scale information systems such as Lotus Notes that take the self-describing-data approach. However, when people design databases to hold large amounts of data, it is generally accepted that the advantages of fixing the schema far outweigh the flexibility that comes from attaching the schema to the data. For instance, fixing the schema allows the data to be organized with data structures that support efficient answering of queries, as we shall discuss beginning in Chapter 13.

Yet the flexibility of semistructured data has made it important in two applications. We shall discuss its use in documents in Section 4.7, but here we shall consider its use as a tool for information integration. As databases have proliferated, it has become a common requirement that data in two or more of them be accessible as if they were one database. For instance, companies may merge; each has its own personnel database, its own database of sales, inventory, product designs, and perhaps many other matters. If corresponding databases had the same schemas, then combining them would be simple; for instance, we could take the union of the tuples in two relations that had the same schema and played the same roles in the the two databases.

However, life is rarely that simple. Independently developed databases are unlikely to share a schema, even if they talk about the same things, such as personnel. For instance, one employee database may record spouse-name, another not. One may have a way to represent several addresses, phones, or emails for an employee, another database may allow only one of each. One database might be relational, another object-oriented.

To make matters more complex, databases tend over time to be used in so many different applications that it is impossible to shut them down and copy or translate their data into another database, even if we could figure out an efficient way to transform the data from one schema to another. This situation is often referred to as the *legacy-database problem*; once a database has been in existence for a while, it becomes impossible to disentangle it from the applications that grow up around it, so the database can never be decommissioned.

A possible solution to the legacy-database problem is suggested in Fig. 4.20. We show two legacy databases with an interface; there could be many legacy systems involved. The legacy systems are each unchanged, so they can support their usual applications.

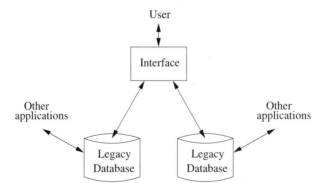

Figure 4.20: Integrating two legacy databases through an interface that supports semistructured data

For flexibility in integration, the interface supports semistructured data, and the user is allowed to query the interface using a query language that is suitable for such data. The semistructured data may be constructed by translating the data at the sources, using components called *wrappers* (or "adapters") that are each designed for the purpose of translating one source to semistructured data.

Alternatively, the semistructured data at the interface may not exist at all. Rather, the user queries the interface as if there were semistructured data, while the interface answers the query by posing queries to the sources, each referring to the schema found at that source.

Example 4.27: We can see in Fig. 4.19 a possible effect of information about stars being gathered from several sources. Notice that the address information for Carrie Fisher has an address concept, and the address is then broken into street and city. That situation corresponds roughly to data that had a nested-relation schema like `Stars(name, address(street, city))`.

On the other hand, the address information for Mark Hamill has no address concept at all, just street and city. This information may have come from a schema such as `Stars(name, street, city)` that only has the ability to represent one address for a star. Some of the other variations in schema that are not reflected in the tiny example of Fig. 4.19, but that could be present if movie information were obtained from several sources, include: optional film-type information, a director, a producer or producers, the owning studio, revenue, and information on where the movie is currently playing. □

4.6.4 Exercises for Section 4.6

Exercise 4.6.1: Since there is no schema to design in the semistructured-data model, we cannot ask you to design schemas to describe different situations. Rather, in the following exercises we shall ask you to suggest how particular data might be organized to reflect certain facts.

* a) Add to Fig. 4.19 the facts that *Star Wars* was directed by George Lucas and produced by Gary Kurtz.

  b) Add to Fig. 4.19 information about *Empire Strikes Back* and *Return of the Jedi*, including the facts that Carrie Fisher and Mark Hamill appeared in these movies.

  c) Add to (b) information about the studio (Fox) for these movies and the address of the studio (Hollywood).

* **Exercise 4.6.2:** Suggest how typical data about banks and customers, as in Exercise 2.1.1, could be represented in the semistructured model.

Exercise 4.6.3: Suggest how typical data about players, teams, and fans, as was described in Exercise 2.1.3, could be represented in the semistructured model.

Exercise 4.6.4: Suggest how typical data about a genealogy, as was described in Exercise 2.1.6, could be represented in the semistructured model.

*! Exercise 4.6.5: The E/R model and the semistructured-data model are both "graphical" in nature, in the sense that they use nodes, labels, and connections among nodes as the medium of expression. Yet there is an essential difference between the two models. What is it?

4.7 XML and Its Data Model

XML (*Extensible Markup Language*) is a tag-based notation for "marking" documents, much like the familiar HTML or less familiar SGML. A *document* is nothing more nor less than a file of characters. However, while HMTL's tags talk about the presentation of the information contained in documents — for instance, which portion is to be displayed in italics or what the entries of a list are — XML tags talk about the meaning of substrings within the document.

In this section we shall introduce the rudiments of XML. We shall see that it captures, in a linear form, the same structure as do the graphs of semistructured data introduced in Section 4.6. In particular, tags play the same role as did the labels on the arcs of a semistructured-data graph. We then introduce the DTD ("document type definition"), which is a flexible form of schema that we can place on certain documents with XML tags.

4.7.1 Semantic Tags

Tags in XML are text surrounded by triangular brackets, i.e., `<...>`, as in HMTL. Also as in HTML, tags generally come in matching pairs, with a beginning tag like `<FOO>` and a matching ending tag that is the same word with a slash, like `</FOO>`. In HTML there is an option to have tags with no matching ender, like `<P>` for paragraphs, but such tags are not permitted in XML. When tags come in matching begin-end pairs, there is a requirement that the pairs be nested. That is, between a matching pair `<FOO>` and `</FOO>`, there can be any number of other matching pairs, but if the beginning of a pair is in this range, then the ending of the pair must also be in the range.

XML is designed to be used in two somewhat different modes:

1. *Well-formed* XML allows you to invent your own tags, much like the arc-labels in semistructured data. This mode corresponds quite closely to semistructured data, in that there is no schema, and each document is free to use whatever tags the author of the document wishes.

2. *Valid* XML involves a Document Type Definition that specifies the allowable tags and gives a grammar for how they may be nested. This form of XML is intermediate between the strict-schema models such as the relational or ODL models, and the completely schemaless world of

semistructured data. As we shall see in Section 4.7.3, DTD's generally allow more flexibility in the data than does a conventional schema; DTD's often allow optional fields or missing fields, for instance.

4.7.2 Well-Formed XML

The minimal requirement for well-formed XML is that the document begin with a declaration that it is XML, and that it have a *root tag* surrounding the entire body of the text. Thus, a well-formed XML document would have an outer structure like:

```
<? XML VERSION = "1.0" STANDALONE = "yes" ?>
<BODY>
    ...
</BODY>
```

The first line indicates that the file is an XML document. The parameter `STANDALONE = "yes"` indicates that there is no DTD for this document; i.e., it is well-formed XML. Notice that this initial declaration is delineated by special markers `<?...?>`.

```
<? XML VERSION = "1.0" STANDALONE = "yes" ?>
<STAR-MOVIE-DATA>
    <STAR><NAME>Carrie Fisher</NAME>
        <ADDRESS><STREET>123 Maple St.</STREET>
            <CITY>Hollywood</CITY></ADDRESS>
        <ADDRESS><STREET>5 Locust Ln.</STREET>
            <CITY>Malibu</CITY></ADDRESS>
    </STAR>
    <STAR><NAME>Mark Hamill</NAME>
        <STREET>456 Oak Rd.</STREET><CITY>Brentwood</CITY>
    </STAR>
    <MOVIE><TITLE>Star Wars</TITLE><YEAR>1977</YEAR>
    </MOVIE>
</STAR-MOVIE-DATA>
```

Figure 4.21: An XML document about stars and movies

Example 4.28 : In Fig. 4.21 is an XML document that corresponds roughly to the data in Fig. 4.19. The root tag is `STAR-MOVIE-DATA`. We see two sections surrounded by the tag `<STAR>` and its matching `</STAR>`. Within each section are subsections giving the name of the star. One, for Carrie Fisher, has two subsections, each giving the address of one of her homes. These sections are surrounded by an `<ADDRESS>` tag and its ender. The section for Mark Hamill has only entries for one street and one city, and does not use an `<ADDRESS>` tag to group these. This distinction appeared as well in Fig. 4.19.

Notice that the document of Fig. 4.21 does not represent the relationship "stars-in" between stars and movies. We could store information about each movie of a star within the section devoted to that star, for instance:

```
<STAR><NAME>Mark Hamill</NAME>
    <STREET>Oak</STREET><CITY>Brentwood</CITY>
    <MOVIE><TITLE>Star Wars</TITLE><YEAR>1977</YEAR></MOVIE>
    <MOVIE><TITLE>Empire</TITLE><YEAR>1980</YEAR></MOVIE>
</STAR>
```

However, that approach leads to redundancy, since all information about the movie is repeated for each of its stars (we have shown no information except a movie's key — title and year — which does not actually represent an instance of redundancy). We shall see in Section 4.7.5 how XML handles the problem that tags inherently form a tree structure.   □

4.7.3   Document Type Definitions

In order for a computer to process XML documents automatically, there needs to be something like a schema for the documents. That is, we need to be told what tags can appear in a collection of documents and how tags can be nested. The description of the schema is given by a grammar-like set of rules, called a *document type definition*, or DTD. It is intended that companies or communities wishing to share data will each create a DTD that describes the form(s) of the documents they share and establishing a shared view of the semantics of their tags. For instance, there could be a DTD for describing protein structures, a DTD for describing the purchase and sale of auto parts, and so on.

The gross structure of a DTD is:

```
<!DOCTYPE root-tag [
    <!ELEMENT element-name (components)>
        more elements
]>
```

The *root-tag* is used (with its matching ender) to surround a document that conforms to the rules of this DTD. An *element* is described by its name, which is the tag used to surround portions of the document that represent that element, and a parenthesized list of components. The latter are tags that may or must appear within the tags for the element being described. The exact requirements on each component are indicated in a manner we shall see shortly.

There is, however, an important special case. (#PCDATA) after an element name means that element has a value that is text, and it has no tags nested within.

Example 4.29 : In Fig. 4.22 we see a DTD for stars.[6] The name and surround-

---

[6]Note that the stars-and-movies data of Fig. 4.21 is not intended to conform to this DTD.

ing tag is STARS (XML, like HTML, is case-insensitive, so STARS is clearly the root-tag). The first element definition says that inside the matching pair of tags `<STARS>...</STARS>` we will find zero or more STAR tags, each representing a single star. It is the * in (STAR*) that says "zero or more," i.e., "any number of."

```
<!DOCTYPE Stars [
    <!ELEMENT STARS (STAR*)>
    <!ELEMENT STAR (NAME, ADDRESS+, MOVIES)>
    <!ELEMENT NAME (#PCDATA)>
    <!ELEMENT ADDRESS (STREET, CITY)>
    <!ELEMENT STREET (#PCDATA)>
    <!ELEMENT CITY (#PCDATA)>
    <!ELEMENT MOVIES (MOVIE*)>
    <!ELEMENT MOVIE (TITLE, YEAR)>
    <!ELEMENT TITLE (#PCDATA)>
    <!ELEMENT YEAR (#PCDATA)>
]>
```

Figure 4.22: A DTD for movie stars

The second element, STAR, is declared to consist of three kinds of subelements: NAME, ADDRESS, and MOVIES. They must appear in this order, and each must be present. However, the + following ADDRESS says "one or more"; that is, there can be any number of addresses listed for a star, but there must be at least one. The NAME element is then defined to be "PCDATA," i.e., simple text. The fourth element says that an address element consists of fields for a street and a city, in that order.

Then, the MOVIES element is defined to have zero or more elements of type MOVIE within it; again, the * says "any number of." A MOVIE element is defined to consist of title and year fields, each of which are simple text. Figure 4.23 is an example of a document that conforms to the DTD of Fig. 4.22. □

The components of an element E are generally other elements. They must appear between the tags $<E>$ and $</E>$ in the order listed. However, there are several operators that control the number of times elements appear.

1. A * following an element means that the element may occur any number of times, including zero times.

2. A + following an element means that the element may occur one or more times.

3. A ? following an element means that the element may occur either zero times or one time, but no more.

```
<STARS>
    <STAR><NAME>Carrie Fisher</NAME>
        <ADDRESS><STREET>123 Maple St.</STREET>
            <CITY>Hollywood</CITY></ADDRESS>
        <ADDRESS><STREET>5 Locust Ln.</STREET>
            <CITY>Malibu</CITY></ADDRESS>
        <MOVIES><MOVIE><TITLE>Star Wars</TITLE>
            <YEAR>1977</YEAR></MOVIE>
            <MOVIE><TITLE>Empire Strikes Back</TITLE>
            <YEAR>1980</YEAR></MOVIE>
            <MOVIE><TITLE>Return of the Jedi</TITLE>
            <YEAR>1983</YEAR></MOVIE>
        </MOVIES>
    </STAR>
    <STAR><NAME>Mark Hamill</NAME>
        <ADDRESS><STREET>456 Oak Rd.<STREET>
            <CITY>Brentwood</CITY></ADDRESS>
        <MOVIES><MOVIE><TITLE>Star Wars</TITLE>
            <YEAR>1977</YEAR></MOVIE>
            <MOVIE><TITLE>Empire Strikes Back</TITLE>
            <YEAR>1980</YEAR></MOVIE>
            <MOVIE><TITLE>Return of the Jedi</TITLE>
            <YEAR>1983</YEAR></MOVIE>
        </MOVIES>
    </STAR>
</STARS>
```

Figure 4.23: Example of a document following the DTD of Fig. 4.22

4. The symbol | may appear between elements, or between parenthesized groups of elements to signify "or"; that is, either the element(s) on the left appear or the element(s) on the right appear, but not both. For example, the expression (#PCDATA | (STREET CITY)) as components for element ADDRESS would mean that an address could be either simple text, or consist of tagged street and city components.

4.7.4 Using a DTD

If a document is intended to conform to a certain DTD, we can either:

a) Include the DTD itself as a preamble to the document, or

b) In the opening line, refer to the DTD, which must be stored separately in the file system accessible to the application that is processing the document.

Example 4.30 : Here is how we might introduce the document of Fig. 4.23 to assert that it is intended to conform to the DTD of Fig. 4.22.

```
<?XML VERSION = "1.0" STANDALONE = "no"?>
<!DOCTYPE Stars SYSTEM "star.dtd">
```

The parameter `STANDALONE = "no"` says that a DTD is being used. Recall we set this parameter to `"yes"` when we did not wish to specify a DTD for the document. The location from which the DTD can be obtained is given in the `!DOCTYPE` clause, where the keyword `SYSTEM` followed by a file name gives this location. □

4.7.5 Attribute Lists

There is a strong relationship between XML documents and semistructured data. Suppose that for some pair of matching tags $<T>$ and $</T>$ in a document we create a node n. Then, if $<S>$ and $</S>$ are matching tags nested directly within the pair $<T>$ and $</T>$ (i.e., there are no matched pairs surrounding the S-pair but surrounded by the T-pair), we draw an arc labeled S from node n to the node for the S-pair. Then the result will be an instance of semistructured data that has essentially the same structure as the document.

Unfortunately, the relationship doesn't go the other way, with the limited subset of XML we have described so far. We need a way to express in XML the idea that an instance of an element might have more than one arc leading to that element. Clearly, we cannot nest a tag-pair directly within more than one tag-pair, so nesting is not sufficient to represent multiple predecessors of a node. The additional features that allow us to represent all semistructured data in XML are attributes within tags, identifiers (ID's), and identifier references (IDREF's).

Opening tags can have *attributes* that appear within the tag, in analogy to constructs like `<A HREF = ...>` in HTML. Keyword `!ATTLIST` introduces a list of attributes and their types for a given element. One common use of attributes is to associate single, labeled values with a tag. This usage is an alternative to subtags that are simple text (i.e., declared as PCDATA).

Another important purpose of such attributes is to represent semistructured data that does not have a tree form. An attribute for elements of type E that is declared to be an *ID* will be given values that uniquely identify each portion of the document that is surrounded by an $<E>$ and matching $</E>$ tag. In terms of semistructured data, an ID provides a unique name for a node.

Other attributes may be declared to be *IDREF's*. Their values are the ID's associated with other tags. By giving one tag instance (i.e., a node in semistructured data) an ID with a value v and another tag instance an IDREF with value v, the latter is effectively given an arc or link to the former. The following example illustrates both the syntax for declaring ID's and IDREF's and the significance of using them in data.

```
<!DOCTYPE Stars-Movies [
    <!ELEMENT STARS-MOVIES (STAR* MOVIE*)>
    <!ELEMENT STAR (NAME, ADDRESS+)>
        <!ATTLIST STAR
            starId ID
            starredIn IDREFS>
    <!ELEMENT NAME (#PCDATA)>
    <!ELEMENT ADDRESS (STREET, CITY)>
    <!ELEMENT STREET (#PCDATA)>
    <!ELEMENT CITY (#PCDATA)>
    <!ELEMENT MOVIE (TITLE, YEAR)>
        <!ATTLIST MOVIE
            movieId ID
            starsOf IDREFS>
    <!ELEMENT TITLE (#PCDATA)>
    <!ELEMENT YEAR (#PCDATA)>
]>
```

Figure 4.24: A DTD for stars and movies, using ID's and IDREF's

Example 4.31 : Figure 4.24 shows a revised DTD, in which stars and movies are given equal status, and ID-IDREF correspondence is used to describe the many-many relationship between movies and stars. Analogously, the arcs between nodes representing stars and movies describe the same many-many relationship in the semistructured data of Fig. 4.19. The name of the root tag for this DTD has been changed to STARS-MOVIES, and its elements are a sequence of stars followed by a sequence of movies.

A star no longer has a set of movies as subelements, as was the case for the DTD of Fig. 4.22. Rather, its only subelements are a name and address, and in the beginning <STAR> tag we shall find an attribute starredIn whose value is a list of ID's for the movies of the star. Note that the attribute starredIn is declared to be of type IDREFS, rather than IDREF. The additional "S" allows the value of starredIn to be a list of ID's for movies, rather than a single movie, as would be the case if the type IDREF were used.

A <STAR> tag also has an attribute starId. Since it is declared to be of type ID, the value of starId may be referenced by <MOVIE> tags to indicate the stars of the movie. That is, when we look at the attribute list for MOVIE in Fig. 4.24, we see that it has an attribute movieId of type ID; these are the ID's that will appear on lists that are the values of starredIn tags. Symmetrically, the attribute starsOf of MOVIE is a list of ID's for stars.

Figure 4.25 is an example of a document that conforms to the DTD of Fig. 4.24. It is quite similar to the semistructured data of Fig. 4.19. It includes more data — three movies instead of only one. However, the only structural difference is that here, all stars have an **ADDRESS** subelement, even if they have only one address, while in Fig. 4.19 we went directly from the Mark-Hamill node to street and city nodes. □

```
<STARS-MOVIES>
    <STAR starId = "cf" starredIn = "sw, esb, rj">
        <NAME>Carrie Fisher</NAME>
        <ADDRESS><STREET>123 Maple St.</STREET>
            <CITY>Hollywood</CITY></ADDRESS>
        <ADDRESS><STREET>5 Locust Ln.</STREET>
            <CITY>Malibu</CITY></ADDRESS>
    </STAR>
    <STAR starId = "mh" starredIn = "sw, esb, rj">
        <NAME>Mark Hamill</NAME>
        <ADDRESS><STREET>456 Oak Rd.<STREET>
            <CITY>Brentwood</CITY></ADDRESS>
    </STAR>
        <MOVIE movieId = "sw" starsOf = "cf, mh">
            <TITLE>Star Wars</TITLE>
            <YEAR>1977</YEAR>
        </MOVIE>
        <MOVIE movieId = "esb" starsOf = "cf, mh">
            <TITLE>Empire Strikes Back</TITLE>
            <YEAR>1980</YEAR>
        </MOVIE>
        <MOVIE movieId = "rj" starsOf = "cf, mh">
            <TITLE>Return of the Jedi</TITLE>
            <YEAR>1983</YEAR>
        </MOVIE>
</STARS-MOVIES>
```

Figure 4.25: Example of a document following the DTD of Fig. 4.24

4.7.6 Exercises for Section 4.7

Exercise 4.7.1: Add to the document of Fig. 4.25 the following facts:

* a) Harrison Ford also starred in the three movies mentioned and the movie *Witness* (1985).

 b) Carrie Fisher also starred in *Hannah and Her Sisters* (1985).

 c) Liam Neeson starred in *The Phantom Menace* (1999).

* Exercise 4.7.2 : Suggest how typical data about banks and customers, as was described in Exercise 2.1.1, could be represented as a DTD.

Exercise 4.7.3 : Suggest how typical data about players, teams, and fans, as was described in Exercise 2.1.3, could be represented as a DTD.

Exercise 4.7.4 : Suggest how typical data about a genealogy, as was described in Exercise 2.1.6, could be represented as a DTD.

4.8   Summary of Chapter 4

◆ *Object Definition Language*: This language is a notation for formally describing the schemas of databases in an object-oriented style. One defines classes, which may have three kinds of properties: attributes, methods, and relationships.

◆ *ODL Relationships*: A relationship in ODL must be binary. It is represented, in the two classes it connects, by names that are declared to be inverses of one another. Relationships can be many-many, many-one, or one-one, depending on whether the types of the pair are declared to be a single object or a set of objects.

◆ *The ODL Type System*: ODL allows types to be constructed, beginning with class names and atomic types such as integer, by applying any of the following type constructors: structure formation, set-of, bag-of, list-of, array-of, and dictionary-of.

◆ *Extents*: A class of objects can have an extent, which is the set of objects of that class currently existing in the database. Thus, the extent corresponds to a relation in the relational model, while the class declaration is like the schema of a relation.

◆ *Keys in ODL*: Keys are optional in ODL. One is allowed to declare one or more keys, but because objects have an object-ID that is not one of its properties, a system implementing ODL can tell the difference between objects, even if they have identical values for all properties.

◆ *Converting ODL Designs to Relations*: If we treat ODL as only a design language, which is then converted to relations, the simplest approach is to create a relation for a the attributes of a class and a relation for each pair of inverse relationships. However, we can combine a many-one relationship with the relation intended for the attributes of the "many" class. It is also necessary to create new attributes to represent the key of a class that has no key.

◆ *The Object-Relational Model*: An alternative to pure object-oriented database models like ODL is to extend the relational model to include the major features of object-orientation. These extensions include nested relations, i.e., complex types for attributes of a relation, including relations as types. Other extensions include methods defined for these types, and the ability of one tuple to refer to another through a reference type.

◆ *Semistructured Data*: In this model, data is represented by a graph. Nodes are like objects or values of their attributes, and labeled arcs connect an object to both the values of its attributes and to other objects to which it is connected by a relationship.

◆ *XML*: The Extensible Markup Language is a World-Wide-Web Consortium standard that implements semistructured data in documents (text files). Nodes correspond to sections of the text, and (some) labeled arcs are represented in XML by pairs of beginning and ending tags.

◆ *Identifiers and References in XML*: To represent graphs that are not trees, XML allows attributes of type `ID` and `IDREF` within the beginning tags. A tag (corresponding to a node of semistructured data) can thus be given an identifier, and that identifier can be referred to by other tags, from which we would like to establish a link (arc in semistructured data).

4.9 References for Chapter 4

The manual defining ODL is [6]. It is the ongoing work of ODMG, the Object Data Management Group. One can also find more about the history of object-oriented database systems from [4], [5], and [8].

Semistructured data as a model developed from the TSIMMIS and LORE projects at Stanford. The original description of the model is in [9]. LORE and its query language are described in [3]. Recent surveys of work on semistructured data include [1], [10], and the book [2]. A bibliography of semistructured data is being compiled on the Web, at [7].

XML is a standard developed by the World-Wide-Web Consortium. The home page for information about XML is [11].

1. S. Abiteboul, "Querying semi-structured data," *Proc. Intl. Conf. on Database Theory* (1997), Lecture Notes in Computer Science 1187 (F. Afrati and P. Kolaitis, eds.), Springer-Verlag, Berlin, pp. 1–18.

2. Abiteboul, S., D. Suciu, and P. Buneman, *Data on the Web: From Relations to Semistructured Data and Xml*, Morgan-Kaufmann, San Francisco, 1999.

3. Abiteboul S., D. Quass, J. McHugh, J. Widom, and J. L. Weiner, "The LOREL query language for semistructured data," In *J. Digital Libraries* **1**:1, 1997.

4. Bancilhon, F., C. Delobel, and P. Kanellakis, *Building an Object-Oriented Database System*, Morgan-Kaufmann, San Francisco, 1992.

5. Cattell, R. G. G., *Object Data Management*, Addison-Wesley, Reading, MA, 1994.

6. Cattell, R. G. G. (ed.), *The Object Database Standard: ODMG–99*, Morgan-Kaufmann, San Francisco, 1999.

7. L. C. Faulstich,

   `http://www.inf.fu-berlin.de/~faulstic/bib/semistruct/`

8. Kim, W. (ed.), *Modern Database Systems: The Object Model, Interoperability, and Beyond*, ACM Press, New York, 1994.

9. Papakonstantinou, Y., H. Garcia-Molina, and J. Widom, "Object exchange across heterogeneous information sources," *IEEE Intl. Conf. on Data Engineering*, pp. 251–260, March 1995.

10. D. Suciu (ed.) Special issue on management of semistructured data, *SIGMOD Record* **26**:4 (1997).

11. World-Wide-Web-Consortium, `http://www.w3.org/XML/`

Chapter 5

Relational Algebra

This chapter begins a study of database programming, that is, how the user can ask queries of the database and can modify the contents of the database. Our focus is on the relational model, and in particular on a notation for describing queries about the content of relations called "relational algebra."

While ODL uses methods that, in principle, can perform any operation on data, and the E/R model does not embrace a specific way of manipulating data, the relational model has a concrete set of "standard" operations on data. Surprisingly, these operations are not "Turing complete" the way ordinary programming languages are. Thus, there are operations we cannot express in relational algebra that could be expressed, for instance, in ODL methods written in C++. This situation is not a defect of the relational model or relational algebra, because the advantage of limiting the scope of operations is that it becomes possible to optimize queries written in a very high level language such as SQL, which we introduce in Chapter 6.

We begin by introducing the operations of relational algebra. This algebra formally applies to sets of tuples, i.e., relations. However, commercial DBMS's use a slightly different model of relations, which are bags, not sets. That is, relations in practice may contain duplicate tuples. While it is often useful to think of relational algebra as a set algebra, we also need to be conscious of the effects of duplicates on the results of the operations in relational algebra. In the final section of this chapter, we consider the matter of how constraints on relations can be expressed.

Later chapters let us see the languages and features that today's commercial DBMS's offer the user. The operations of relational algebra are all implemented by the SQL query language, which we study beginning in Chapter 6. These algebraic operations also appear in the OQL language, an object-oriented query language based on the ODL data model and introduced in Chapter 9.

5.1   An Example Database Schema

As we begin our focus on database programming in the relational model, it is useful to have a specific schema on which to base our examples of queries. Our chosen database schema draws upon the running example of movies, stars, and studios, and it uses normalized relations similar to the ones that we developed in Section 3.6. However, it includes some attributes that we have not used previously in examples, and it includes one relation — `MovieExec` — that has not appeared before. The purpose of these changes is to give us some opportunities to study different data types and different ways of representing information. Figure 5.1 shows the schema.

```
Movie(
     TITLE: string,
     YEAR: integer,
     length: integer,
     inColor: boolean,
     studioName: string,
     producerC#: integer)

StarsIn(
     MOVIETITLE: string,
     MOVIEYEAR: integer,
     STARNAME: string)

MovieStar(
     NAME: string,
     address: string,
     gender: char,
     birthdate: date)

MovieExec(
     name: string,
     address: string,
     CERT#: integer,
     netWorth: integer)

Studio(
     NAME: string,
     address: string,
     presC#: integer)
```

Figure 5.1: Example database schema about movies

Our schema has five relations. The attributes of each relation are listed, along with the intended domain for that attribute. The key attributes for a relation are shown in capitals in Fig. 5.1, although when we refer to them in text, they will be lower-case as they have been heretofore. For instance, all three attributes together form the key for relation `StarsIn`. Relation `Movie` has six attributes; `title` and `year` together constitute the key for `Movie`, as they have previously. Attribute `title` is a string, and `year` is an integer.

The major modifications to the schema compared with what we have seen so far are:

- There is a notion of a *certificate number* for movie executives — studio presidents and movie producers. This certificate is a unique integer that we imagine is maintained by some external authority, perhaps a registry of executives or a "union."

- We use certificate numbers as the key for movie executives, although movie stars do not always have certificates and we shall continue to use `name` as the key for stars. That decision is probably unrealistic, since two stars could have the same name, but we take this road in order to illustrate some different options.

- We introduced the producer as another property of movies. This information is represented by a new attribute, `producerC#`, of relation `Movie`. This attribute is intended to be the certificate number of the producer. Producers are expected to be movie executives, as are studio presidents. There may also be other executives in the `MovieExec` relation.

- Attribute `filmType` of `Movie` has been changed from an enumerated type to a boolean-valued attribute called `inColor`: true if the movie is in color and false if it is in black and white.

- The attribute `gender` has been added for movie stars. Its type is "character," either `M` for male or `F` for female. Attribute `birthdate`, of type "date" (a special type supported by many commercial database systems or just a character string if we prefer) has also been added.

- All addresses have been made strings, rather than pairs consisting of a street and city. The purpose is to make addresses in different relations comparable easily and to simplify operations on addresses.

5.2 An Algebra of Relational Operations

To begin our study of operations on relations, we shall learn about a special algebra, called *relational algebra*, that consists of some simple but powerful ways to construct new relations from given relations. When the given relations are stored data, then the constructed relations can be answers to queries about this data.

Why Bags Can Be More Efficient Than Sets

As a simple example of why bags can lead to implementation efficiency, if you take the union of two relations but do not eliminate duplicates, then you can just copy the relations to the output. If you insist that the result be a set, you have to sort the relations, or do something similar to detect identical tuples that come from the two relations.

The development of an algebra for relations has a history, which we shall follow roughly in our presentation. Initially, relational algebra was proposed by T. Codd as an algebra on sets of tuples (i.e., relations) that could be used to express typical queries about those relations. It consisted of five operations on sets: union, set difference, and Cartesian product, with which you might already be familiar, and two unusual operations — selection and projection. To these, several operations that can be defined in terms of these were added; varieties of "join" are the most important.

When DBMS's that used the relational model were first developed, their query languages largely implemented the relational algebra. However, for efficiency purposes, these systems regarded relations as bags, not sets. That is, unless the user asked explicitly that duplicate tuples be condensed into one (i.e., that "duplicates be eliminated"), relations were allowed to contain duplicates. Thus, in Section 5.3, we shall study the same relational operations on bags and see the changes necessary.

Another change to the algebra that was necessitated by commercial implementations of the relational model is that several other operations are needed. Most important is a way of performing aggregation, e.g., finding the average value of some column of a relation. We shall study these additional operations in Section 5.4.

5.2.1 Basics of Relational Algebra

An algebra, in general, consists of operators and atomic operands. For instance, in the algebra of arithmetic, the atomic operands are variables like x and constants like 15. The operators are the usual arithmetic ones: addition, subtraction, multiplication, and division. Any algebra allows us to build *expressions* by applying operators to atomic operands and/or other expressions of the algebra. Usually, parentheses are needed to group operators and their operands. For instance, in arithmetic we have expressions such as $(x + y) * z$ or $((x + 7)/(y - 3)) + x$.

Relational algebra is another example of an algebra. Its atomic operands are:

1. Variables that stand for relations.

2. Constants, which are finite relations.

As we mentioned, in the classical relational algebra, all operands and the results of expressions are sets. The operations of the traditional relational algebra fall into four broad classes:

a) The usual set operations — union, intersection, and difference — applied to relations.

b) Operations that remove parts of a relation: "selection" eliminates some rows (tuples), and "projection" eliminates some columns.

c) Operations that combine the tuples of two relations, including "Cartesian product," which pairs the tuples of two relations in all possible ways, and various kinds of "join" operations, which selectively pair tuples from two relations.

d) An operation called "renaming" that does not affect the tuples of a relation, but changes the relation schema, i.e., the names of the attributes and/or the name of the relation itself.

We shall generally refer to expressions of relational algebra as *queries*. While we don't yet have the symbols needed to show many of the expressions of relational algebra, you should be familiar with the operations of group (a), and thus recognize $(R \cup S)$ as an example of an expression of relational algebra. R and S are atomic operands standing for relations, whose sets of tuples are unknown. This query asks for the union of whatever tuples are in the relations named R and S.

5.2.2 Set Operations on Relations

The three most common operations on sets are union, intersection, and difference. We assume the reader is familiar with these operations, which are defined as follows on arbitrary sets R and S:

- $R \cup S$, the *union* of R and S, is the set of elements that are in R or S or both. An element appears only once in the union even if it is present in both R and S.

- $R \cap S$, the *intersection* of R and S, is the set of elements that are in both R and S.

- $R - S$, the *difference* of R and S, is the set of elements that are in R but not in S. Note that $R - S$ is different from $S - R$; the latter is the set of elements that are in S but not in R.

When we apply these operations to relations, we need to put some conditions on R and S:

1. R and S must have schemas with identical sets of attributes, and the types (domains) for each attribute must be the same in R and S.

2. Before we compute the set-theoretic union, intersection, or difference of sets of tuples, the columns of R and S must be ordered so that the order of attributes is the same for both relations.

Sometimes we would like to take the union, intersection, or difference of relations that have the same number of attributes, with corresponding domains, but that use different names for their attributes. If so, we may use the renaming operator to be discussed in Section 5.2.9 to change the schema of one or both relations and give them the same set of attributes.

name	address	gender	birthdate
Carrie Fisher	123 Maple St., Hollywood	F	9/9/99
Mark Hamill	456 Oak Rd., Brentwood	M	8/8/88

Relation R

name	address	gender	birthdate
Carrie Fisher	123 Maple St., Hollywood	F	9/9/99
Harrison Ford	789 Palm Dr., Beverly Hills	M	7/7/77

Relation S

Figure 5.2: Two relations

Example 5.1: Suppose we have the two relations R and S, instances of the relation MovieStar of Section 5.1. Current instances of R and S are shown in Fig. 5.2. Then the union $R \cup S$ is

name	address	gender	birthdate
Carrie Fisher	123 Maple St., Hollywood	F	9/9/99
Mark Hamill	456 Oak Rd., Brentwood	M	8/8/88
Harrison Ford	789 Palm Dr., Beverly Hills	M	7/7/77

Note that the two tuples for Carrie Fisher from the two relations appear only once in the result.

The intersection $R \cap S$ is

name	address	gender	birthdate
Carrie Fisher	123 Maple St., Hollywood	F	9/9/99

Now, only the Carrie Fisher tuple appears, because only it is in both relations. The difference $R - S$ is

name	*address*	*gender*	*birthdate*
Mark Hamill	456 Oak Rd., Brentwood	M	8/8/88

That is, the Fisher and Hamill tuples appear in R and thus are candidates for $R - S$. However, the Fisher tuple also appears in S and so is not in $R - S$. □

5.2.3 Projection

The *projection* operator is used to produce from a relation R a new relation that has only some of R's columns. The value of expression $\pi_{A_1, A_2, \ldots, A_n}(R)$ is a relation that has only the columns for attributes $A_1, A_2, \ldots, A_n$ of R. The schema for the resulting value is the set of attributes $\{A_1, A_2, \ldots, A_n\}$, which we conventionally show in the order listed.

title	*year*	*length*	*inColor*	*studioName*	*producerC#*
Star Wars	1977	124	true	Fox	12345
Mighty Ducks	1991	104	true	Disney	67890
Wayne's World	1992	95	true	Paramount	99999

Figure 5.3: The relation `Movie`

Example 5.2: Consider the relation `Movie` with the relation schema described in Section 5.1. An instance of this relation is shown in Fig. 5.3. We can project this relation onto the first three attributes with the expression

$$\pi_{title, year, length}(\texttt{Movie})$$

The resulting relation is

title	*year*	*length*
Star Wars	1977	124
Mighty Ducks	1991	104
Wayne's World	1992	95

As another example, we can project onto the attribute `inColor` with the expression $\pi_{inColor}(\texttt{Movie})$. The result is the single-column relation

inColor
true

Notice that there is only one tuple in the resulting relation, since all three tuples of Fig. 5.3 have the same value in their component for attribute `inColor`, and in the relational algebra of sets, duplicate tuples are always eliminated. □

5.2.4   Selection

The *selection* operator, applied to a relation R, produces a new relation with a subset of R's tuples. The tuples in the resulting relation are those that satisfy some condition C that involves the attributes of R. We denote this operation $\sigma_C(R)$. The schema for the resulting relation is the same as R's schema, and we conventionally show the attributes in the same order as we use for R.

C is a conditional expression of the type with which we are familiar from conventional programming languages; for example, conditional expressions follow the keyword `if` in programming languages such as C or Java. The only difference is that the operands in condition C are either constants or attributes of R. We apply C to each tuple t of R by substituting, for each attribute A appearing in condition C, the component of t for attribute A. If after substituting for each attribute of C the condition C is true, then t is one of the tuples that appear in the result of $\sigma_C(R)$; otherwise t is not in the result.

Example 5.3: Let the relation `Movie` be as in Fig. 5.3. Then the value of expression $\sigma_{length \geq 100}(\text{Movie})$ is

title	year	length	inColor	studioName	producerC#
Star Wars	1977	124	true	Fox	12345
Mighty Ducks	1991	104	true	Disney	67890

The first tuple satisfies the condition $length \geq 100$ because when we substitute for *length* the value 124 found in the component of the first tuple for attribute `length`, the condition becomes $124 \geq 100$. The latter condition is true, so we accept the first tuple. The same argument explains why the second tuple of Fig. 5.3 is in the result.

The third tuple has a `length` component 95. Thus, when we substitute for *length* we get the condition $95 \geq 100$, which is false. Hence the last tuple of Fig. 5.3 is not in the result. □

Example 5.4: Suppose we want the set of tuples in the relation `Movie` that represent Fox movies at least 100 minutes long. We can get these tuples with a more complicated condition, involving the `AND` of two subconditions. The expression is

$$\sigma_{length \geq 100 \text{ AND } studioName = \text{'Fox'}}(\text{Movie})$$

The tuple

title	year	length	inColor	studioName	producerC#
Star Wars	1977	124	true	Fox	12345

is the only one in the resulting relation. □

5.2.5 Cartesian Product

The *Cartesian product* (or *cross-product*, or just *product*) of two sets R and S is the set of pairs that can be formed by choosing the first element of the pair to be any element of R and the second any element of S. This product is denoted $R \times S$. When R and S are relations, the product is essentially the same. However, since the members of R and S are tuples, usually consisting of more than one component, the result of pairing a tuple from R with a tuple from S is a longer tuple, with one component for each of the components of the constituent tuples. By convention, the components from R precede the components from S in the attribute order for the result.

The relation schema for the resulting relation is the union of the schemas for R and S. However, if R and S should happen to have some attributes in common, then we need to invent new names for at least one of each pair of identical attributes. To disambiguate an attribute A that is in the schemas of both R and S, we use $R.A$ for the attribute from R and $S.A$ for the attribute from S.

A	B
1	2
3	4

Relation R

B	C	D
2	5	6
4	7	8
9	10	11

Relation S

A	$R.B$	$S.B$	C	D
1	2	2	5	6
1	2	4	7	8
1	2	9	10	11
3	4	2	5	6
3	4	4	7	8
3	4	9	10	11

Result $R \times S$

Figure 5.4: Two relations and their Cartesian product

Example 5.5 : For conciseness, let us use an abstract example that illustrates the product operation. Let relations R and S have the schemas and tuples shown in Fig. 5.4. Then the product $R \times S$ consists of the six tuples shown in that figure. Note how we have paired each of the two tuples of R with each of the three tuples of S. Since B is an attribute of both schemas, we have used $R.B$ and $S.B$ in the schema for $R \times S$. The other attributes are unambiguous, and their names appear in the resulting schema unchanged.   □

5.2.6   Natural Joins

More often than we want to take the product of two relations, we find a need to *join* them by pairing only those tuples that match in some way. The simplest sort of match is the *natural join* of two relations R and S, denoted $R \bowtie S$, in which we pair only those tuples from R and S that agree in whatever attributes are common to the schemas of R and S. More precisely, let $A_1, A_2, \ldots, A_n$ be all the attributes that are in both the schema of R and the schema of S. Then a tuple r from R and a tuple s from S are successfully paired if and only if r and s agree on each of the attributes $A_1, A_2, \ldots, A_n$.

If the tuples r and s are successfully paired in the join $R \bowtie S$, then the result of the pairing is a tuple, called the *joined tuple*, with one component for each of the attributes in the union of the schemas of R and S. The joined tuple agrees with tuple r in each attribute in the schema of R, and it agrees with s in each attribute in the schema of S. Since r and s are successfully paired, the joined tuple is able to agree with both these tuples on the attributes they have in common. The construction of the joined tuple is suggested by Fig. 5.5.

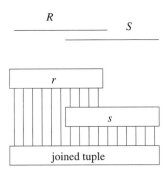

Figure 5.5: Joining tuples

Note also that this join operation is the same one that we used in Section 3.6.5 to recombine relations that had been projected onto two subsets of their attributes. There the motivation was to explain why BCNF decomposition made sense. In Section 5.2.8 we shall see another use for the natural join: combining two relations so that we can write a query that relates attributes of each.

Example 5.6: The natural join of the relations R and S from Fig. 5.4 is

A	B	C	D
1	2	5	6
3	4	7	8

The only attribute common to R and S is B. Thus, to pair successfully, tuples need only to agree in their B components. If so, the resulting tuple has components for attributes A (from R), B (from either R or S), C (from S), and D (from S).

In this example, the first tuple of R successfully pairs with only the first tuple of S; they share the value 2 on their common attribute B. This pairing yields the first tuple of the result: $(1, 2, 5, 6)$. The second tuple of R pairs successfully only with the second tuple of S, and the pairing yields $(3, 4, 7, 8)$. Note that the third tuple of S does not pair with any tuple of R and thus has no effect on the result of $R \bowtie S$. A tuple that fails to pair with any tuple of the other relation in a join is said to be a *dangling tuple*. $\square$

Example 5.7: The previous example does not illustrate all the possibilities inherent in the natural join operator. For example, no tuple paired successfully with more than one tuple, and there was only one attribute in common to the two relation schemas. In Fig. 5.6 we see two other relations, U and V, that share two attributes between their schemas: B and C. We also show an instance in which one tuple joins with several tuples.

For tuples to pair successfully, they must agree in both the B and C components. Thus, the first tuple of U joins with the first two tuples of V, while the second and third tuples of U join with the third tuple of V. The result of these four pairings is shown in Fig. 5.6. $\square$

5.2.7 Theta-Joins

The natural join forces us to pair tuples using one specific condition. While this way, equating shared attributes, is the most common basis on which relations are joined, it is sometimes desirable to pair tuples from two relations on some other basis. For that purpose, we have a related notation called the *theta-join*. Historically, the "theta" refers to an arbitrary condition, which we shall represent by C rather than θ.

The notation for a theta-join of relations R and S based on condition C is $R \underset{C}{\bowtie} S$. The result of this operation is constructed as follows:

1. Take the product of R and S.

2. Select from the product only those tuples that satisfy the condition C.

As with the product operation, the schema for the result is the union of the schemas of R and S, with "R." or "S." prefixed to attributes if necessary to indicate from which schema the attribute came.

A	B	C
1	2	3
6	7	8
9	7	8

Relation U

B	C	D
2	3	4
2	3	5
7	8	10

Relation V

A	B	C	D
1	2	3	4
1	2	3	5
6	7	8	10
9	7	8	10

Result $U \bowtie V$

Figure 5.6: Natural join of relations

Example 5.8 : Consider the operation $U \underset{A<D}{\bowtie} V$, where U and V are the relations from Fig. 5.6. We must consider all nine pairs of tuples, one from each relation, and see whether the A component from the U-tuple is less than the D component of the V-tuple. The first tuple of U, with an A component of 1, successfully pairs with each of the tuples from V. However, the second and third tuples from U, with A components of 6 and 9, respectively, pair successfully with only the last tuple of V. Thus, the result has only five tuples, constructed from the five successful pairings. This relation is shown in Fig. 5.7. □

Notice that the schema for the result in Fig. 5.7 consists of all six attributes, with U and V prefixed to their respective occurrences of attributes B and C to distinguish them. Thus, the theta-join contrasts with natural join, since in the latter common attributes are merged into one copy. Of course it makes sense to do so in the case of the natural join, since tuples don't pair unless they agree in their common attributes. In the case of a theta-join, there is no guarantee that compared attributes will agree in the result, since they may not be compared with =.

A	U.B	U.C	V.B	V.C	D
1	2	3	2	3	4
1	2	3	2	3	5
1	2	3	7	8	10
6	7	8	7	8	10
9	7	8	7	8	10

Figure 5.7: Result of $U \underset{A<D}{\bowtie} V$

Example 5.9: Here is a theta-join on the same relations U and V that has a more complex condition:

$$U \underset{A<D \text{ AND } U.B \neq V.B}{\bowtie} V$$

That is, we require for successful pairing not only that the A component of the U-tuple be less than the D component of the V-tuple, but that the two tuples disagree on their respective B components. The tuple

A	U.B	U.C	V.B	V.C	D
1	2	3	7	8	10

is the only one to satisfy both conditions, so this relation is the result of the theta-join above. □

5.2.8 Combining Operations to Form Queries

If all we could do was to write single operations on one or two relations as queries, then relational algebra would not be as useful as it is. However, relational algebra, like all algebras, allows us to form expressions of arbitrary complexity by applying operators either to given relations or to relations that are the result of applying one or more relational operators to relations.

One can construct expressions of relational algebra by applying operators to subexpressions, using parentheses when necessary to indicate grouping of operands. It is also possible to represent expressions as expression trees; the latter often are easier for us to read, although they are less convenient as a machine-readable notation.

Example 5.10: Let us reconsider the decomposed Movie relation of Example 3.24. Suppose we want to know "What are the titles and years of movies made by Fox that are at least 100 minutes long?" One way to compute the answer to this query is:

1. Select those Movie tuples that have $length \geq 100$.

2. Select those `Movie` tuples that have $studioName =$ 'Fox'.

3. Compute the intersection of (1) and (2).

4. Project the relation from (3) onto attributes `title` and `year`.

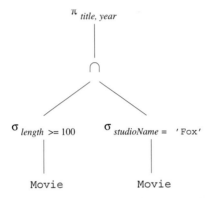

Figure 5.8: Expression tree for a relational algebra expression

In Fig. 5.8 we see the above steps represented as an expression tree. The two selection nodes correspond to steps (1) and (2). The intersection node corresponds to step (3), and the projection node is step (4).

Alternatively, we could represent the same expression in a conventional, linear notation, with parentheses. The formula

$$\pi_{title,year}\Big(\sigma_{length\geq 100}(\text{Movie}) \cap \sigma_{studioName=\text{'Fox'}}(\text{Movie})\Big)$$

represents the same expression.

Incidentally, there is often more than one relational algebra expression that represents the same computation. For instance, the above query could also be written by replacing the intersection by logical `AND` within a single selection operation. That is,

$$\pi_{title,year}\Big(\sigma_{length\geq 100 \text{ AND } studioName=\text{'Fox'}}(\text{Movie})\Big)$$

is an equivalent form of the query.   □

Example 5.11 : One use of the natural join operation is to recombine relations that were decomposed to put them into BCNF. Recall the decomposed relations from Example 3.24:[1]

---

[1]Remember that the relation `Movie` of that example has a somewhat different relation schema from the relation `Movie` that we introduced in Section 5.1 and used in Examples 5.2, 5.3, and 5.4.

Equivalent Expressions and Query Optimization

All database systems have a query-answering system, and many of them are based on a language that is similar in expressive power to relational algebra. Thus, the query asked by a user may have many *equivalent expressions* (expressions that produce the same answer, whenever they are given the same relations as operands), and some of these may be much more quickly evaluated. An important job of the query "optimizer" discussed briefly in Section 1.2.5 is to replace one expression of relational algebra by an equivalent expression that is more efficiently evaluated. Optimization of relational-algebra expressions is covered extensively in Section 16.2.

> Movie1 with schema {title, year, length, filmType, studioName}
> Movie2 with schema {title, year, starName}

Let us write an expression to answer the query "Find the stars of movies that are at least 100 minutes long." This query relates the starName attribute of Movie2 with the length attribute of Movie1. We can connect these attributes by joining the two relations. The natural join successfully pairs only those tuples that agree on title and year; that is, pairs of tuples that refer to the same movie. Thus, Movie1 ⋈ Movie2 is an expression of relational algebra that produces the relation we called Movie in Example 3.24. That relation is the non-BNCF relation whose schema is all six attributes and that contains several tuples for the same movie when that movie has several stars.

To the join of Movie1 and Movie2 we must apply a selection that enforces the condition that the length of the movie is at least 100 minutes. We then project onto the desired attribute: starName. The expression

$$\pi_{starName}\Big(\sigma_{length \geq 100}(\texttt{Movie1} \bowtie \texttt{Movie2})\Big)$$

implements the desired query in relational algebra. □

5.2.9 Renaming

In order to control the names of the attributes used for relations that are constructed by applying relational-algebra operations, it is often convenient to use an operator that explicitly renames relations. We shall use the operator $\rho_{S(A_1, A_2, \ldots, A_n)}(R)$ to rename a relation R. The resulting relation has exactly the same tuples as R, but the name of the relation is S. Moreover, the attributes of the result relation S are named $A_1, A_2, \ldots, A_n$, in order from the left. If we only want to change the name of the relation to S and leave the attributes as they are in R, we can just say $\rho_S(R)$.

Example 5.12 : In Example 5.5 we took the product of two relations R and S from Fig. 5.4 and used the convention that when an attribute appears in both operands, it is renamed by prefixing the relation name to it. These relations R and S are repeated in Fig. 5.9.

Suppose, however, that we do not wish to call the two versions of B by names $R.B$ and $S.B$; rather we want to continue to use the name B for the attribute that comes from R, and we want to use X as the name of the attribute B coming from S. We can rename the attributes of S so the first is called X. The result of the expression $\rho_{S(X,C,D)}(S)$ is a relation named S that looks just like the relation S from Fig. 5.4, but its first column has attribute X instead of B.

A	B
1	2
3	4

Relation R

B	C	D
2	5	6
4	7	8
9	10	11

Relation S

A	B	X	C	D
1	2	2	5	6
1	2	4	7	8
1	2	9	10	11
3	4	2	5	6
3	4	4	7	8
3	4	9	10	11

Result $R \times \rho_{S(X,C,D)}(S)$

Figure 5.9: Renaming before taking a product

When we take the product of R with this new relation, there is no conflict of names among the attributes, so no further renaming is done. That is, the result of the expression $R \times \rho_{S(X,C,D)}(S)$ is the relation $R \times S$ from Fig. 5.4, except that the five columns are labeled A, B, X, C, and D, from the left. This relation is shown in Fig. 5.9.

As an alternative, we could take the product without renaming, as we did in Example 5.5, and then rename the result. The expression $\rho_{RS(A,B,X,C,D)}(R \times S)$ yields the same relation as in Fig. 5.9, with the same set of attributes. But this relation has a name, RS, while the result relation in Fig. 5.9 has no name. $\quad\Box$

5.2.10 Dependent and Independent Operations

Some of the operations that we have described in Section 5.2 can be expressed in terms of other relational-algebra operations. For example, intersection can be expressed in terms of set difference:

$$R \cap S = R - (R - S)$$

That is, if R and S are any two relations with the same schema, the intersection of R and S can be computed by first subtracting S from R to form a relation T consisting of all those tuples in R but not S. We then subtract T from R, leaving only those tuples of R that are also in S.

The two forms of join are also expressible in terms of other operations. Theta-join can be expressed by product and selection:

$$R \underset{C}{\bowtie} S = \sigma_C(R \times S)$$

The natural join of R and S can be expressed by starting with the product $R \times S$. We then apply the selection operator with a condition C of the form

$$R.A_1 = S.A_1 \text{ AND } R.A_2 = S.A_2 \text{ AND} \cdots \text{AND } R.A_n = S.A_n$$

where $A_1, A_2, \ldots, A_n$ are all the attributes appearing in the schemas of both R and S. Finally, we must project out one copy of each of the equated attributes. Let L be the list of attributes in the schema of R followed by those attributes in the schema of S that are not also in the schema of R. Then

$$R \bowtie S = \pi_L\Big(\sigma_C(R \times S)\Big)$$

Example 5.13: The natural join of the relations U and V from Fig. 5.6 can be written in terms of product, selection, and projection as:

$$\pi_{A,U.B,U.C,D}\Big(\sigma_{U.B=V.B \text{ AND } U.C=V.C}(U \times V)\Big)$$

That is, we take the product $U \times V$. Then we select for equality between each pair of attributes with the same name — B and C in this example. Finally, we project onto all the attributes except one of the B's and one of the C's; we have chosen to eliminate the attributes of V whose names also appear in the schema of U.

For another example, the theta-join of Example 5.9 can be written

$$\sigma_{A<D \text{ AND } U.B \neq V.B}(U \times V)$$

That is, we take the product of the relations U and V and then apply the condition that appeared in the theta-join.   □

The rewriting rules mentioned in this section are the only "redundancies" among the operations that we have introduced. The six remaining operations — union, difference, selection, projection, product, and renaming — form an independent set, none of which can be written in terms of the other five.

5.2.11   A Linear Notation for Algebraic Expressions

In Section 5.2.8 we used trees to represent complex expressions of relational algebra. Another alternative is to invent names for the temporary relations that correspond to the interior nodes of the tree and write a sequence of assignments that create a value for each. The order of the assignments is flexible, as long as the children of a node N have had their values created before we attempt to create the value for N itself.

The notation we shall use for assignment statements is:

1. A relation name and parenthesized list of attributes for that relation. The name **Answer** will be used conventionally for the result of the final step; i.e., the name of the relation at the root of the expression tree.

2. The assignment symbol := .

3. Any algebraic expression on the right. We can choose to use only one operator per assignment, in which case each interior node of the tree gets its own assignment statement. However, it is also permissible to combine several algebraic operations in one right side, if it is convenient to do so.

Example 5.14: Consider the tree of Fig. 5.8. One possible sequence of assignments to evaluate this expression is:

$$
\begin{aligned}
&\texttt{R(t,y,l,i,s,p)} \ := \ \sigma_{length \geq 100}(\texttt{Movie}) \\
&\texttt{S(t,y,l,i,s,p)} \ := \ \sigma_{studioName=\texttt{'Fox'}}(\texttt{Movie}) \\
&\texttt{T(t,y,l,i,s,p)} \ := \ \texttt{R} \cap \texttt{S} \\
&\texttt{Answer(title, year)} \ := \ \pi_{t,i}(\texttt{T})
\end{aligned}
$$

The first step computes the relation of the interior node labeled $\sigma_{length \geq 100}$ in Fig. 5.8, and the second step computes the node labeled $\sigma_{studioName=\texttt{'Fox'}}$. Notice that we get renaming "for free," since we can use any attributes and relation name we wish for the left side of an assignment. The last two steps compute the intersection and the projection in the obvious way.

It is also permissible to combine some of the steps. For instance, we could combine the last two steps and write:

$$
\begin{aligned}
&\texttt{R(t,y,l,i,s,p)} \ := \ \sigma_{length \geq 100}(\texttt{Movie}) \\
&\texttt{S(t,y,l,i,s,p)} \ := \ \sigma_{studioName=\texttt{'Fox'}}(\texttt{Movie}) \\
&\texttt{Answer(title, year)} \ := \ \pi_{t,i}(\texttt{R} \cap \texttt{S})
\end{aligned}
$$

□

5.2.12 Exercises for Section 5.2

Exercise 5.2.1: In this exercise we introduce one of our running examples of a relational database schema and some sample data.[2] The database schema consists of four relations, whose schemas are:

```
Product(maker, model, type)
PC(model, speed, ram, hd, rd, price)
Laptop(model, speed, ram, hd, screen, price)
Printer(model, color, type, price)
```

The `Product` relation gives the manufacturer, model number and type (PC, laptop, or printer) of various products. We assume for convenience that model numbers are unique over all manufacturers and product types; that assumption is not realistic, and a real database would include a code for the manufacturer as part of the model number. The `PC` relation gives for each model number that is a PC the speed (of the processor, in megahertz), the amount of RAM (in megabytes), the size of the hard disk (in gigabytes), the speed and type of the removable disk (CD or DVD), and the price. The `Laptop` relation is similar, except that the screen size (in inches) is recorded in place of information about the removable disk. The `Printer` relation records for each printer model whether the printer produces color output (true, if so), the process type (laser, ink-jet, or bubble), and the price.

Some sample data for the relation `Product` is shown in Fig. 5.10. Sample data for the other three relations is shown in Fig. 5.11. Manufacturers and model numbers have been "sanitized," but the data is typical of products on sale at the beginning of 2001.

Write expressions of relational algebra to answer the following queries. You may use the linear notation of Section 5.2.11 if you wish. For the data of Figs. 5.10 and 5.11, show the result of your query. However, your answer should work for arbitrary data, not just the data of these figures.

* a) What PC models have a speed of at least 1000?

b) Which manufacturers make laptops with a hard disk of at least one gigabyte?

c) Find the model number and price of all products (of any type) made by manufacturer B.

d) Find the model numbers of all color laser printers.

e) Find those manufacturers that sell Laptops, but not PC's.

*! f) Find those hard-disk sizes that occur in two or more PC's.

---

[2]Source: manufacturers' Web pages and Amazon.com.

maker	model	type
A	1001	pc
A	1002	pc
A	1003	pc
A	2004	laptop
A	2005	laptop
A	2006	laptop
B	1004	pc
B	1005	pc
B	1006	pc
B	2001	laptop
B	2002	laptop
B	2003	laptop
C	1007	pc
C	1008	pc
C	2008	laptop
C	2009	laptop
C	3002	printer
C	3003	printer
C	3006	printer
D	1009	pc
D	1010	pc
D	1011	pc
D	2007	laptop
E	1012	pc
E	1013	pc
E	2010	laptop
F	3001	printer
F	3004	printer
G	3005	printer
H	3007	printer

Figure 5.10: Sample data for Product

model	speed	ram	hd	rd	price
1001	700	64	10	48xCD	799
1002	1500	128	60	12xDVD	2499
1003	866	128	20	8xDVD	1999
1004	866	64	10	12xDVD	999
1005	1000	128	20	12xDVD	1499
1006	1300	256	40	16xDVD	2119
1007	1400	128	80	12xDVD	2299
1008	700	64	30	24xCD	999
1009	1200	128	80	16xDVD	1699
1010	750	64	30	40xCD	699
1011	1100	128	60	16xDVD	1299
1012	350	64	7	48xCD	799
1013	733	256	60	12xDVD	2499

(a) Sample data for relation PC

model	speed	ram	hd	screen	price
2001	700	64	5	12.1	1448
2002	800	96	10	15.1	2584
2003	850	64	10	15.1	2738
2004	550	32	5	12.1	999
2005	600	64	6	12.1	2399
2006	800	96	20	15.7	2999
2007	850	128	20	15.0	3099
2008	650	64	10	12.1	1249
2009	750	256	20	15.1	2599
2010	366	64	10	12.1	1499

(b) Sample data for relation Laptop

model	color	type	price
3001	true	ink-jet	231
3002	true	ink-jet	267
3003	false	laser	390
3004	true	ink-jet	439
3005	true	bubble	200
3006	true	laser	1999
3007	false	laser	350

(c) Sample data for relation Printer

Figure 5.11: Sample data for relations of Exercise 5.2.1

! g) Find those pairs of PC models that have both the same speed and RAM. A pair should be listed only once; e.g., list (i, j) but not (j, i).

*!! h) Find those manufacturers of at least two different computers (PC's or laptops) with speeds of at least 700.

!! i) Find the manufacturer(s) of the computer (PC or laptop) with the highest available speed.

!! j) Find the manufacturers of PC's with at least three different speeds.

!! k) Find the manufacturers who sell exactly three different models of PC.

Exercise 5.2.2: Draw expression trees for each of your expressions of Exercise 5.2.1.

Exercise 5.2.3: Write each of your expressions from Exercise 5.2.1 in the linear notation of Section 5.2.11.

Exercise 5.2.4: This exercise introduces another running example, concerning World War II capital ships. It involves the following relations:

```
Classes(class, type, country, numGuns, bore, displacement)
Ships(name, class, launched)
Battles(name, date)
Outcomes(ship, battle, result)
```

Ships are built in "classes" from the same design, and the class is usually named for the first ship of that class. The relation `Classes` records the name of the class, the type (`bb` for battleship or `bc` for battlecruiser), the country that built the ship, the number of main guns, the bore (diameter of the gun barrel, in inches) of the main guns, and the displacement (weight, in tons). Relation `Ships` records the name of the ship, the name of its class, and the year in which the ship was launched. Relation `Battles` gives the name and date of battles involving these ships, and relation `Outcomes` gives the result (sunk, damaged, or ok) for each ship in each battle.

Figures 5.12 and 5.13 give some sample data for these four relations.[3] Note that, unlike the data for Exercise 5.2.1, there are some "dangling tuples" in this data, e.g., ships mentioned in `Outcomes` that are not mentioned in `Ships`.

Write expressions of relational algebra to answer the following queries. For the data of Figs. 5.12 and 5.13, show the result of your query. However, your answer should work for arbitrary data, not just the data of these figures.

a) Give the class names and countries of the classes that carried guns of at least 16-inch bore.

---

[3]Source: J. N. Westwood, *Fighting Ships of World War II*, Follett Publishing, Chicago, 1975 and R. C. Stern, *US Battleships in Action*, Squadron/Signal Publications, Carrollton, TX, 1980.

class	type	country	numGuns	bore	displacement
Bismarck	bb	Germany	8	15	42000
Iowa	bb	USA	9	16	46000
Kongo	bc	Japan	8	14	32000
North Carolina	bb	USA	9	16	37000
Renown	bc	Gt. Britain	6	15	32000
Revenge	bb	Gt. Britain	8	15	29000
Tennessee	bb	USA	12	14	32000
Yamato	bb	Japan	9	18	65000

(a) Sample data for relation Classes

name	date
North Atlantic	5/24-27/41
Guadalcanal	11/15/42
North Cape	12/26/43
Surigao Strait	10/25/44

(b) Sample data for relation Battles

ship	battle	result
Bismarck	North Atlantic	sunk
California	Surigao Strait	ok
Duke of York	North Cape	ok
Fuso	Surigao Strait	sunk
Hood	North Atlantic	sunk
King George V	North Atlantic	ok
Kirishima	Guadalcanal	sunk
Prince of Wales	North Atlantic	damaged
Rodney	North Atlantic	ok
Scharnhorst	North Cape	sunk
South Dakota	Guadalcanal	damaged
Tennessee	Surigao Strait	ok
Washington	Guadalcanal	ok
West Virginia	Surigao Strait	ok
Yamashiro	Surigao Strait	sunk

(c) Sample data for relation Outcomes

Figure 5.12: Data for Exercise 5.2.4

name	class	launched
California	Tennessee	1921
Haruna	Kongo	1915
Hiei	Kongo	1914
Iowa	Iowa	1943
Kirishima	Kongo	1915
Kongo	Kongo	1913
Missouri	Iowa	1944
Musashi	Yamato	1942
New Jersey	Iowa	1943
North Carolina	North Carolina	1941
Ramillies	Revenge	1917
Renown	Renown	1916
Repulse	Renown	1916
Resolution	Revenge	1916
Revenge	Revenge	1916
Royal Oak	Revenge	1916
Royal Sovereign	Revenge	1916
Tennessee	Tennessee	1920
Washington	North Carolina	1941
Wisconsin	Iowa	1944
Yamato	Yamato	1941

Figure 5.13: Sample data for relation `Ships`

b) Find the ships launched prior to 1921.

c) Find the ships sunk in the battle of the North Atlantic.

d) The treaty of Washington in 1921 prohibited capital ships heavier than 35,000 tons. List the ships that violated the treaty of Washington.

e) List the name, displacement, and number of guns of the ships engaged in the battle of Guadalcanal.

f) List all the capital ships mentioned in the database. (Remember that all these ships may not appear in the `Ships` relation.)

! g) Find the classes that had only one ship as a member of that class.

! h) Find those countries that had both battleships and battlecruisers.

! i) Find those ships that "lived to fight another day"; they were damaged in one battle, but later fought in another.

Exercise 5.2.5: Draw expression trees for each of your expressions of Exercise 5.2.4.

Exercise 5.2.6: Write each of your expressions from Exercise 5.2.4 in the linear notation of Section 5.2.11.

* **Exercise 5.2.7:** What is the difference between the natural join $R \bowtie S$ and the theta-join $R \underset{C}{\overset{\bowtie}{}} S$ where the condition C is that $R.A = S.A$ for each attribute A appearing in the schemas of both R and S?

! **Exercise 5.2.8:** An operator on relations is said to be *monotone* if whenever we add a tuple to one of its arguments, the result contains all the tuples that it contained before adding the tuple, plus perhaps more tuples. Which of the operators described in this section are monotone? For each, either explain why it is monotone or give an example showing it is not.

! **Exercise 5.2.9:** Suppose relations R and S have n tuples and m tuples, respectively. Give the minimum and maximum numbers of tuples that the results of the following expressions can have.

* a) $R \cup S$.

  b) $R \bowtie S$.

  c) $\sigma_C(R) \times S$, for some condition C.

  d) $\pi_L(R) - S$, for some list of attributes L.

*! **Exercise 5.2.10:** The *semijoin* of relations R and S, written $R \ltimes S$, is the bag of tuples t in R such that there is at least one tuple in S that agrees with t in all attributes that R and S have in common. Give three different expressions of relational algebra that are equivalent to $R \ltimes S$.

! **Exercise 5.2.11:** The *antisemijoin* $R \overline{\ltimes} S$ is the bag of tuples t in R that do *not* agree with any tuple of S in the attributes common to R and S. Give an expression of relational algebra equivalent to $R \overline{\ltimes} S$.

!! **Exercise 5.2.12:** Let R be a relation with schema

$$(A_1, A_2, \ldots, A_n, B_1, B_2, \ldots, B_m)$$

and let S be a relation with schema $(B_1, B_2, \ldots, B_m)$; that is, the attributes of S are a subset of the attributes of R. The *quotient* of R and S, denoted $R \div S$, is the set of tuples t over attributes $A_1, A_2, \ldots, A_n$ (i.e., the attributes of R that are not attributes of S) such that for every tuple s in S, the tuple ts, consisting of the components of t for $A_1, A_2, \ldots, A_n$ and the components of s for $B_1, B_2, \ldots, B_m$, is a member of R. Give an expression of relational algebra, using the operators we have defined previously in this section, that is equivalent to $R \div S$.

5.3   Relational Operations on Bags

While a set of tuples (i.e., a relation) is a simple, natural model of data as it might appear in a database, commercial database systems rarely, if ever, are based purely on sets. In some situations, relations as they appear in database systems are permitted to have duplicate tuples. Recall that if a "set" is allowed to have multiple occurrences of a member, then that set is called a *bag* or *multiset*. In this section, we shall consider relations that are bags rather than sets; that is, we shall allow the same tuple to appear more than once in a relation. When we refer to a "set," we mean a relation without duplicate tuples; a "bag" means a relation that may (or may not) have duplicate tuples.

Example 5.15 : The relation in Fig. 5.14 is a bag of tuples. In it, the tuple $(1, 2)$ appears three times and the tuple $(3, 4)$ appears once. If Fig. 5.14 were a set-valued relation, we would have to eliminate two occurrences of the tuple $(1, 2)$. In a bag-valued relation, we *do* allow multiple occurrences of the same tuple, but like sets, the order of tuples does not matter.   □

A	B
1	2
3	4
1	2
1	2

Figure 5.14: A bag

5.3.1   Why Bags?

When we think about implementing relations efficiently, we can see several ways that allowing relations to be bags rather than sets can speed up operations on relations. We mentioned at the beginning of Section 5.2 how allowing the result to be a bag could speed up the union of two relations. For another example, when we do a projection, allowing the resulting relation to be a bag (even when the original relation is a set) lets us work with each tuple independently. If we want a set as the result, we need to compare each projected tuple with all the other projected tuples, to make sure that each projection appears only once. However, if we can accept a bag as the result, then we simply project each tuple and add it to the result; no comparison with other projected tuples is necessary.

Example 5.16 : The bag of Fig. 5.14 could be the result of projecting the relation shown in Fig. 5.15 onto attributes A and B, provided we allow the result to be a bag and do not eliminate the duplicate occurrences of $(1, 2)$. Had

A	B	C
1	2	5
3	4	6
1	2	7
1	2	8

Figure 5.15: Bag for Example 5.16

we used the ordinary projection operator of relational algebra, and therefore eliminated duplicates, the result would be only:

A	B
1	2
3	4

Note that the bag result, although larger, can be computed more quickly, since there is no need to compare each tuple $(1, 2)$ or $(3, 4)$ with previously generated tuples.

Moreover, if we are projecting a relation in order to take an aggregate (discussed in Section 5.4), such as "Find the average value of A in Fig. 5.15," we could not use the set model to think of the relation projected onto attribute A. As a set, the average value of A is 2, because there are only two values of A — 1 and 3 — in Fig. 5.15, and their average is 2. However, if we treat the A-column in Fig. 5.15 as a bag $\{1, 3, 1, 1\}$, we get the correct average of A, which is 1.5, among the four tuples of Fig. 5.15. □

5.3.2 Union, Intersection, and Difference of Bags

When we take the union of two bags, we add the number of occurrences of each tuple. That is, if R is a bag in which the tuple t appears n times, and S is a bag in which the tuple t appears m times, then in the bag $R \cup S$ tuple t appears $n + m$ times. Note that either n or m (or both) can be 0.

When we intersect two bags R and S, in which tuple t appears n and m times, respectively, in $R \cap S$ tuple t appears $\min(n, m)$ times. When we compute $R - S$, the difference of bags R and S, tuple t appears in $R - S$ $\max(0, n - m)$ times. That is, if t appears in R more times than it appears in S, then in $R - S$ tuple t appears the number of times it appears in R, minus the number of times it appears in S. However, if t appears at least as many times in S as it appears in R, then t does not appear at all in $R - S$. Intuitively, occurrences of t in S each "cancel" one occurrence in R.

Example 5.17: Let R be the relation of Fig. 5.14, that is, a bag in which tuple $(1, 2)$ appears three times and $(3, 4)$ appears once. Let S be the bag

A	B
1	2
3	4
3	4
5	6

Then the bag union $R \cup S$ is the bag in which $(1, 2)$ appears four times (three times for its occurrences in R and once for its occurrence in S); $(3, 4)$ appears three times, and $(5, 6)$ appears once.

The bag intersection $R \cap S$ is the bag

A	B
1	2
3	4

with one occurrence each of $(1, 2)$ and $(3, 4)$. That is, $(1, 2)$ appears three times in R and once in S, and $\min(3, 1) = 1$, so $(1, 2)$ appears once in $R \cap S$. Similarly, $(3, 4)$ appears $\min(1, 2) = 1$ time in $R \cap S$. Tuple $(5, 6)$, which appears once in S but zero times in R appears $\min(0, 1) = 0$ times in $R \cap S$.

The bag difference $R - S$ is the bag

A	B
1	2
1	2

To see why, notice that $(1, 2)$ appears three times in R and once in S, so in $R - S$ it appears $\max(0, 3 - 1) = 2$ times. Tuple $(3, 4)$ appears once in R and twice in S, so in $R - S$ it appears $\max(0, 1 - 2) = 0$ times. No other tuple appears in R, so there can be no other tuples in $R - S$.

As another example, the bag difference $S - R$ is the bag

A	B
3	4
5	6

Tuple $(3, 4)$ appears once because that is the difference in the number of times it appears in S minus the number of times it appears in R. Tuple $(5, 6)$ appears once in $S - R$ for the same reason. The resulting bag happens to be a set in this case. $\square$

5.3.3 Projection of Bags

We have already illustrated the projection of bags. As we saw in Example 5.16, each tuple is processed independently during the projection. If R is the bag of Fig. 5.15 and we compute the bag-projection $\pi_{A,B}(R)$, then we get the bag of Fig. 5.14.

Bag Operations on Sets

Imagine we have two sets R and S. Every set may be thought of as a bag; the bag just happens to have at most one occurrence of any tuple. Suppose we intersect $R \cap S$, but we think of R and S as bags and use the bag intersection rule. Then we get the same result as we would get if we thought of R and S as sets. That is, thinking of R and S as bags, a tuple t is in $R \cap S$ the minimum of the number of times it is in R and S. Since R and S are sets, t can be in each only 0 or 1 times. Whether we use the bag or set intersection rules, we find that t can appear at most once in $R \cap S$, and it appears once exactly when it is in both R and S. Similarly, if we use the bag difference rule to compute $R - S$ or $S - R$ we get exactly the same result as if we used the set rule.

However, union behaves differently, depending on whether we think of R and S as sets or bags. If we use the bag rule to compute $R \cup S$, then the result may not be a set, even if R and S are sets. In particular, if tuple t appears in both R and S, then t appears twice in $R \cup S$ if we use the bag rule for union. But if we use the set rule then t appears only once in $R \cup S$. Thus, when taking unions, we must be especially careful to specify whether we are using the bag or set definition of union.

If the elimination of one or more attributes during the projection causes the same tuple to be created from several tuples, these duplicate tuples are not eliminated from the result of a bag-projection. Thus, the three tuples $(1, 2, 5)$, $(1, 2, 7)$, and $(1, 2, 8)$ of the relation R from Fig. 5.15 each gave rise to the same tuple $(1, 2)$ after projection onto attributes A and B. In the bag result, there are three occurrences of tuple $(1, 2)$, while in the set-projection, this tuple appears only once.

5.3.4 Selection on Bags

To apply a selection to a bag, we apply the selection condition to each tuple independently. As always with bags, we do not eliminate duplicate tuples in the result.

Example 5.18: If R is the bag

A	B	C
1	2	5
3	4	6
1	2	7
1	2	7

then the result of the bag-selection $\sigma_{C \geq 6}(R)$ is

---

Algebraic Laws for Bags

An algebraic law is an equivalence between two expressions of relational algebra whose arguments are variables standing for relations. The equivalence asserts that no matter what relations we substitute for these variables, the two expressions define the same relation. An example of a well-known law is the commutative law for union: $R \cup S = S \cup R$. This law happens to hold whether we regard relation-variables R and S as standing for sets or bags. However, there are a number of other laws that hold when relational algebra is applied to sets but that do not hold when relations are interpreted as bags. A simple example of such a law is the distributive law of set difference over union, $(R \cup S) - T = (R - T) \cup (S - T)$. This law holds for sets but not for bags. To see why it fails for bags, suppose R, S, and T each have one copy of tuple t. Then the expression on the left has one t, while the expression on the right has none. As sets, neither would have t. Some exploration of algebraic laws for bags appears in Exercises 5.3.4 and 5.3.5.

A	B	C
3	4	6
1	2	7
1	2	7

That is, all but the first tuple meets the selection condition. The last two tuples, which are duplicates in R, are each included in the result.   □

5.3.5 Product of Bags

The rule for the Cartesian product of bags is the expected one. Each tuple of one relation is paired with each tuple of the other, regardless of whether it is a duplicate or not. As a result, if a tuple r appears in a relation R m times, and tuple s appears n times in relation S, then in the product $R \times S$, the tuple rs will appear mn times.

Example 5.19: Let R and S be the bags shown in Fig. 5.16. Then the product $R \times S$ consists of six tuples, as shown in Fig. 5.16(c). Note that the usual convention regarding attribute names that we developed for set-relations applies equally well to bags. Thus, the attribute B, which belongs to both relations R and S, appears twice in the product, each time prefixed by one of the relation names.   □

A	B
1	2
1	2

(a) The relation R

B	C
2	3
4	5
4	5

(b) The relation S

A	R.B	S.B	C
1	2	2	3
1	2	2	3
1	2	4	5
1	2	4	5
1	2	4	5
1	2	4	5

(c) The product $R \times S$

Figure 5.16: Computing the product of bags

5.3.6 Joins of Bags

Joining bags also presents no surprises. We compare each tuple of one relation with each tuple of the other, decide whether or not this pair of tuples joins successfully, and if so we put the resulting tuple in the answer. When constructing the answer, we do not eliminate duplicate tuples.

Example 5.20: The natural join $R \bowtie S$ of the relations R and S seen in Fig. 5.16 is

A	B	C
1	2	3
1	2	3

That is, tuple $(1, 2)$ of R joins with $(2, 3)$ of S. Since there are two copies of $(1, 2)$ in R and one copy of $(2, 3)$ in S, there are two pairs of tuples that join to give the tuple $(1, 2, 3)$. No other tuples from R and S join successfully.

As another example on the same relations R and S, the theta-join

$$R \underset{R.B < S.B}{\bowtie} S$$

produces the bag

A	$R.B$	$S.B$	C
1	2	4	5
1	2	4	5
1	2	4	5
1	2	4	5

The computation of the join is as follows. Tuple $(1, 2)$ from R and $(4, 5)$ from S meet the join condition. Since each appears twice in its relation, the number of times the joined tuple appears in the result is 2×2 or 4. The other possible join of tuples — $(1, 2)$ from R with $(2, 3)$ from S — fails to meet the join condition, so this combination does not appear in the result.   □

5.3.7   Exercises for Section 5.3

* **Exercise 5.3.1:** Let PC be the relation of Fig. 5.11(a), and suppose we compute the projection $\pi_{speed}(\text{PC})$. What is the value of this expression as a set? As a bag? What is the average value of tuples in this projection, when treated as a set? As a bag?

Exercise 5.3.2: Repeat Exercise 5.3.1 for the projection $\pi_{hd}(\text{PC})$.

Exercise 5.3.3: This exercise refers to the "battleship" relations of Exercise 5.2.4.

  a) The expression $\pi_{bore}(\text{Classes})$ yields a single-column relation with the bores of the various classes. For the data of Exercise 5.2.4, what is this relation as a set? As a bag?

  ! b) Write an expression of relational algebra to give the bores of the ships (not the classes). Your expression must make sense for bags; that is, the number of times a value b appears must be the number of ships that have bore b.

! **Exercise 5.3.4:** Certain algebraic laws for relations as sets also hold for relations as bags. Explain why each of the laws below hold for bags as well as sets.

  * a) The associative law for union: $(R \cup S) \cup T = R \cup (S \cup T)$.

  b) The associative law for intersection: $(R \cap S) \cap T = R \cap (S \cap T)$.

  c) The associative law for natural join: $(R \bowtie S) \bowtie T = R \bowtie (S \bowtie T)$.

d) The commutative law for union: $(R \cup S) = (S \cup R)$.

e) The commutative law for intersection: $(R \cap S) = (S \cap R)$.

f) The commutative law for natural join: $(R \bowtie S) = (S \bowtie R)$.

g) $\pi_L(R \cup S) = \pi_L(R) \cup \pi_L(S)$. Here, L is an arbitrary list of attributes.

* h) The distributive law of union over intersection: $R \cup (S \cap T) = (R \cup S) \cap (R \cup T)$.

i) $\sigma_{C \text{ AND } D}(R) = \sigma_C(R) \cap \sigma_D(R)$. Here, C and D are arbitrary conditions about the tuples of R.

!! **Exercise 5.3.5 :** The following algebraic laws hold for sets but not for bags. Explain why they hold for sets and give counterexamples to show that they do not hold for bags.

* a) $(R \cap S) - T = R \cap (S - T)$.

b) The distributive law of intersection over union: $R \cap (S \cup T) = (R \cap S) \cup (R \cap T)$.

c) $\sigma_{C \text{ OR } D}(R) = \sigma_C(R) \cup \sigma_D(R)$. Here, C and D are arbitrary conditions about the tuples of R.

5.4 Extended Operators of Relational Algebra

Section 5.2 presented the classical relational algebra, and Section 5.3 introduced the modifications necessary to treat relations as bags of tuples rather than sets. The ideas of these two sections serve as a foundation for most of modern query languages. However, languages such as SQL have several other operations that have proved quite important in applications. Thus, a full treatment of relational operations must include a number of other operators, which we introduce in this section. The additions:

1. The *duplicate-elimination operator* δ turns a bag into a set by eliminating all but one copy of each tuple.

2. *Aggregation operators*, such as sums or averages, are not operations of relational algebra, but are used by the grouping operator (described next). Aggregation operators apply to attributes (columns) of a relation, e.g., the sum of a column produces the one number that is the sum of all the values in that column.

3. *Grouping* of tuples according to their value in one or more attributes has the effect of partitioning the tuples of a relation into "groups." Aggregation can then be applied to columns within each group, giving us the

ability to express a number of queries that are impossible to express in the classical relational algebra. The *grouping operator* γ is an operator that combines the effect of grouping and aggregation.

4. The *sorting operator* τ turns a relation into a list of tuples, sorted according to one or more attributes. This operator should be used judiciously, because other relational-algebra operators apply to sets or bags, but never to lists. Thus, τ only makes sense as the final step of a series of operations.

5. *Extended projection* gives additional power to the operator π. In addition to projecting out some columns, in its generalized form π can perform computations involving the columns of its argument relation to produce new columns.

6. The *outerjoin* operator is a variant of the join that avoids losing dangling tuples. In the result of the outerjoin, dangling tuples are "padded" with the null value, so the dangling tuples can be represented in the output.

5.4.1 Duplicate Elimination

Sometimes, we need an operator that converts a bag to a set. For that purpose, we use $\delta(R)$ to return the set consisting of one copy of every tuple that appears one or more times in relation R.

Example 5.21: If R is the relation

A	B
1	2
3	4
1	2
1	2

from Fig. 5.14, then $\delta(R)$ is

A	B
1	2
3	4

Note that the tuple $(1, 2)$, which appeared three times in R, appears only once in $\delta(R)$. $\Box$

5.4.2 Aggregation Operators

There are several operators that apply to sets or bags of atomic values. These operators are used to summarize or "aggregate" the values in one column of a relation, and thus are referred to as *aggregation* operators. The standard operators of this type are:

1. SUM produces the sum of a column with numerical values.

2. AVG produces the average of a column with numerical values.

3. MIN and MAX, applied to a column with numerical values, produces the smallest or largest value, respectively. When applied to a column with character-string values, they produce the lexicographically (alphabetically) first or last value, respectively.

4. COUNT produces the number of (not necessarily distinct) values in a column. Equivalently, COUNT applied to any attribute of a relation produces the number of tuples of that relation, including duplicates.

Example 5.22: Consider the relation

A	B
1	2
3	4
1	2
1	2

Some examples of aggregations on the attributes of this relation are:

1. $\text{SUM(B)} = 2 + 4 + 2 + 2 = 10$.

2. $\text{AVG(A)} = (1 + 3 + 1 + 1)/4 = 1.5$.

3. $\text{MIN(A)} = 1$.

4. $\text{MAX(B)} = 4$.

5. $\text{COUNT(A)} = 4$.

□

5.4.3 Grouping

Often we do not want simply the average or some other aggregation of an entire column. Rather, we need to consider the tuples of a relation in groups, corresponding to the value of one or more other columns, and we aggregate only within each group. As an example, suppose we wanted to compute the total number of minutes of movies produced by each studio, i.e., a relation such as:

studio	*sumOfLengths*
Disney	12345
MGM	54321
. . .	. . .

Starting with the relation

```
Movie(title, year, length, inColor, studioName, producerC#)
```

from our example database schema of Section 5.1, we must group the tuples according to their value for attribute `studioName`. We must then sum the `length` column within each group. That is, we imagine that the tuples of `Movie` are grouped as suggested in Fig. 5.17, and we apply the aggregation `SUM(length)` to each group independently.

	studioName	
	Disney	
	Disney	
	Disney	
	MGM	
	MGM	
	○	
	○	
	○	

Figure 5.17: A relation with imaginary division into groups

5.4.4   The Grouping Operator

We shall now introduce an operator that allows us to group a relation and/or aggregate some columns. If there is grouping, then the aggregation is within groups.

The subscript used with the γ operator is a list L of elements, each of which is either:

a) An attribute of the relation R to which the γ is applied; this attribute is one of the attributes by which R will be grouped. This element is said to be a *grouping attribute*.

b) An aggregation operator applied to an attribute of the relation. To provide a name for the attribute corresponding to this aggregation in the result, an arrow and new name are appended to the aggregation. The underlying attribute is said to be an *aggregated attribute*.

The relation returned by the expression $\gamma_L(R)$ is constructed as follows:

1. Partition the tuples of R into *groups*. Each group consists of all tuples having one particular assignment of values to the grouping attributes in the list L. If there are no grouping attributes, the entire relation R is one group.

2. For each group, produce one tuple consisting of:

δ is a Special Case of γ

Technically, the δ operator is redundant. If $R(A_1, A_2, \ldots, A_n)$ is a relation, then $\delta(R)$ is equivalent to $\gamma_{A_1, A_2, \ldots, A_n}(R)$. That is, to eliminate duplicates, we group on all the attributes of the relation and do no aggregation. Then each group corresponds to a tuple that is found one or more times in R. Since the result of γ contains exactly one tuple from each group, the effect of this "grouping" is to eliminate duplicates. However, because δ is such a common and important operator, we shall continue to consider it separately when we study algebraic laws and algorithms for implementing the operators.

One can also see γ as an extension of the projection operator on sets. That is, $\gamma_{A_1, A_2, \ldots, A_n}(R)$ is also the same as $\pi_{A_1, A_2, \ldots, A_n}(R)$, if R is a set. However, if R is a bag, then γ eliminates duplicates while π does not. For this reason, γ is often referred to as *generalized projection*.

---

    i. The grouping attributes' values for that group and

    ii. The aggregations, over all tuples of that group, for the aggregated attributes on list L.

Example 5.23 : Suppose we have the relation

    `StarsIn(title, year, starName)`

and we wish to find, for each star who has appeared in at least three movies, the earliest year in which they appeared. The first step is to group, using `starName` as a grouping attribute. We clearly must compute for each group the `MIN(year)` aggregate. However, in order to decide which groups satisfy the condition that the star appears in at least three movies, we must also compute the `COUNT(title)` aggregate for each group.

We begin with the grouping expression

$$\gamma_{starName, \text{MIN}(year) \to minYear, \text{COUNT}(title) \to ctTitle}(\texttt{StarsIn})$$

The first two columns of the result of this expression are needed for the query result. The third column is an auxiliary attribute, which we have named `ctTitle`; it is needed to determine whether a star has appeared in at least three movies. That is, we continue the algebraic expression for the query by selecting for `ctTitle >= 3` and then projecting onto the first two columns. An expression tree for the query is shown in Fig. 5.18. $\square$

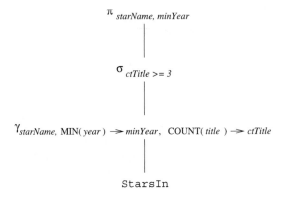

Figure 5.18: Algebraic expression tree for the SQL query of Example 5.23

5.4.5   Extending the Projection Operator

Let us reconsider the projection operator $\pi_L(R)$ introduced in Section 5.2.3. In the classical relational algebra, L is a list of (some of the) attributes of R. We extend the projection operator to allow it to compute with components of tuples as well as choose components. In *extended projection*, also denoted $\pi_L(R)$, projection lists can have the following kinds of elements:

1. A single attribute of R.

2. An expression $x \to y$, where x and y are names for attributes. The element $x \to y$ in the list L asks that we take the attribute x of R and *rename* it y; i.e., the name of this attribute in the schema of the result relation is y.

3. An expression $E \to z$, where E is an expression involving attributes of R, constants, arithmetic operators, and string operators, and z is a new name for the attribute that results from the calculation implied by E. For example, $a+b \to x$ as a list element represents the sum of the attributes a and b, renamed x. Element $c\,|\,|\,d \to e$ means concatenate the (presumably string-valued) attributes c and d and call the result e.

The result of the projection is computed by considering each tuple of R in turn. We evaluate the list L by substituting the tuple's components for the corresponding attributes mentioned in L and applying any operators indicated by L to these values. The result is a relation whose schema is the names of the attributes on list L, with whatever renaming the list specifies. Each tuple of R yields one tuple of the result. Duplicate tuples in R surely yield duplicate tuples in the result, but the result can have duplicates even if R does not.

Example 5.24: Let R be the relation

A	B	C
0	1	2
0	1	2
3	4	5

Then the result of $\pi_{A,B+C\to X}(R)$ is

A	X
0	3
0	3
3	9

The result's schema has two attributes. One is A, the first attribute of R, not renamed. The second is the sum of the second and third attributes of R, with the name X.

For another example, $\pi_{B-A\to X, C-B\to Y}(R)$ is

X	Y
1	1
1	1
1	1

Notice that the calculation required by this projection list happens to turn different tuples $(0,1,2)$ and $(3,4,5)$ into the same tuple $(1,1)$. Thus, the latter tuple appears three times in the result. □

5.4.6 The Sorting Operator

There are several contexts in which we want to sort the tuples of a relation by one or more of its attributes. Often, when querying data, one wants the result relation to be sorted. For instance, in a query about all the movies in which Sean Connery appeared, we might wish to have the list sorted by title, so we could more easily find whether a certain movie was on the list. We shall also see in Section 15.4 how execution of queries by the DBMS is often made more efficient if we sort the relations first.

The expression $\tau_L(R)$, where R is a relation and L a list of some of R's attributes, is the relation R, but with the tuples of R sorted in the order indicated by L. If L is the list $A_1, A_2, \ldots, A_n$, then the tuples of R are sorted first by their value of attribute A_1. Ties are broken according to the value of A_2; tuples that agree on both A_1 and A_2 are ordered according to their value of A_3, and so on. Ties that remain after attribute A_n is considered may be ordered arbitrarily.

Example 5.25: If R is a relation with schema $R(A, B, C)$, then $\tau_{C,B}(R)$ orders the tuples of R by their value of C, and tuples with the same C-value are ordered by their B value. Tuples that agree on both B and C may be ordered arbitrarily. □

The operator τ is anomalous, in that it is the only operator in our relational algebra whose result is a list of tuples, rather than a set. Thus, in terms of expressing queries, it only makes sense to talk about τ as the final operator in an algebraic expression. If another operator of relational algebra is applied after τ, the result of the τ is treated as a set or bag, and no ordering of the tuples is implied.[4]

5.4.7   Outerjoins

A property of the join operator is that it is possible for certain tuples to be "dangling"; that is, they fail to match any tuple of the other relation in the common attributes. Dangling tuples do not have any trace in the result of the join, so the join may not represent the data of the original relations completely. In cases where this behavior is undesirable, a variation on the join, called "outerjoin," has been proposed and appears in various commercial systems.

We shall consider the "natural" case first, where the join is on equated values of all attributes in common to the two relations. The *outerjoin* $R \overset{\circ}{\bowtie} S$ is formed by starting with $R \bowtie S$, and adding any dangling tuples from R or S. The added tuples must be padded with a special *null* symbol, $\perp$, in all the attributes that they do not possess but that appear in the join result.[5]

Example 5.26 : In Fig. 5.19 we see two relations U and V. Tuple $(1, 2, 3)$ of U joins with both $(2, 3, 10)$ and $(2, 3, 11)$ of V, so these three tuples are not dangling. However, the other three tuples — $(4, 5, 6)$ and $(7, 8, 9)$ of U and $(6, 7, 12)$ of V — are dangling. That is, for none of these three tuples is there a tuple of the other relation that agrees with it on both the B and C components. Thus, in $U \overset{\circ}{\bowtie} V$, the three dangling tuples are padded with $\perp$ in the attributes that they do not have: attribute D for the tuples of U and attribute A for the tuple of V. $\square$

There are many variants of the basic (natural) outerjoin idea. The *left outerjoin* $R \overset{\circ}{\bowtie}_L S$ is like the outerjoin, but only dangling tuples of the left argument R are padded with $\perp$ and added to the result. The *right outerjoin* $R \overset{\circ}{\bowtie}_R S$ is like the outerjoin, but only the dangling tuples of the right argument S are padded with $\perp$ and added to the result.

Example 5.27 : If U and V are as in Fig. 5.19, then $U \overset{\circ}{\bowtie}_L V$ is:

A	B	C	D
1	2	3	10
1	2	3	11
4	5	6	$\perp$
7	8	9	$\perp$

---

[4]However, as we shall see in Chapter 15, it sometimes speeds execution of the query if we sort intermediate results.

[5]When we study SQL, we shall find that the null symbol $\perp$ is written out, as NULL. You may use NULL in place of $\perp$ here if you wish.

A	B	C
1	2	3
4	5	6
7	8	9

Relation U

B	C	D
2	3	10
2	3	11
6	7	12

Relation V

A	B	C	D
1	2	3	10
1	2	3	11
4	5	6	$\perp$
7	8	9	$\perp$
$\perp$	6	7	12

Result $U \overset{\circ}{\bowtie} V$

Figure 5.19: Outerjoin of relations

and $U \overset{\circ}{\bowtie}_R V$ is:

A	B	C	D
1	2	3	10
1	2	3	11
$\perp$	6	7	12

$\square$

In addition, all three natural outerjoin operators have theta-join analogs, where first a theta-join is taken and then those tuples that failed to join with any tuple of the other relation, when the condition of the theta-join was applied, are padded with $\perp$ and added to the result. We use $\overset{\circ}{\underset{C}{\bowtie}}$ to denote a theta-outerjoin with condition C. This operator can also be modified with L or R to indicate left- or right-outerjoin.

Example 5.28: Let U and V be the relations of Fig. 5.19, and consider $U \overset{\circ}{\underset{A>V.C}{\bowtie}} V$. Tuples $(4, 5, 6)$ and $(7, 8, 9)$ of U each satisfy the condition with both of the tuples $(2, 3, 10)$ and $(2, 3, 11)$ of V. Thus, none of these four tuples are dangling in this theta-join. However, the two other tuples — $(1, 2, 3)$ of U and $(6, 7, 12)$ of V — are dangling. They thus appear, padded, in the result shown in Fig. 5.20. □

A	$U.B$	$U.C$	$V.B$	$V.C$	D
4	5	6	2	3	10
4	5	6	2	3	11
7	8	9	2	3	10
7	8	9	2	3	11
1	2	3	$\perp$	$\perp$	$\perp$
$\perp$	$\perp$	$\perp$	6	7	12

Figure 5.20: Result of a theta-outerjoin

5.4.8 Exercises for Section 5.4

Exercise 5.4.1: Here are two relations:

$R(A, B)$: $\{(0, 1), (2, 3), (0, 1), (2, 4), (3, 4)\}$

$S(B, C)$: $\{(0, 1), (2, 4), (2, 5), (3, 4), (0, 2), (3, 4)\}$

Compute the following: *a) $\pi_{A+B, A^2, B^2}(R)$; b) $\pi_{B+1, C-1}(S)$; *c) $\tau_{B, A}(R)$; d) $\tau_{B, C}(S)$; *e) $\delta(R)$; f) $\delta(S)$; *g) $\gamma_{A, \text{SUM}(B)}(R)$; h) $\gamma_{B, \text{AVG}(C)}(S)$; ! i) $\gamma_A(R)$; ! j) $\gamma_{A, \text{MAX}(C)}(R \bowtie S)$; *k) $R \underset{L}{\bowtie} S$; l) $R \underset{R}{\bowtie} (S)$; m) $R \overset{\circ}{\bowtie} S$; n) $R \underset{R.B<S.B}{\overset{\circ}{\bowtie}} S$.

! **Exercise 5.4.2:** A unary operator f is said to be *idempotent* if for all relations R, $f(f(R)) = f(R)$. That is, applying f more than once is the same as applying it once. Which of the following operators are idempotent? Either explain why or give a counterexample.

   *a) δ; *b) π_L; c) σ_C; d) γ_L; e) τ.

*! **Exercise 5.4.3:** One thing that can be done with an extended projection, but not with the original version of projection that we defined in Section 5.2.3, is to duplicate columns. For example, if $R(A, B)$ is a relation, then $\pi_{A, A}(R)$ produces the tuple (a, a) for every tuple (a, b) in R. Can this operation be done using only the classical operations of relation algebra from Section 5.2? Explain your reasoning.

5.5 Constraints on Relations

Relational algebra provides a means to express common constraints, such as the referential integrity constraints introduced in Section 2.3. In fact, we shall see that relational algebra offers us convenient ways to express a wide variety of other constraints. Even functional dependencies can be expressed in relational algebra, as we shall see in Example 5.31. Constraints are quite important in database programming, and we shall cover in Chapter 7 how SQL database systems can enforce the same sorts of constraints as we can express in relational algebra.

5.5.1 Relational Algebra as a Constraint Language

There are two ways in which we can use expressions of relational algebra to express constraints.

1. If R is an expression of relational algebra, then $R = \emptyset$ is a constraint that says "The value of R must be empty," or equivalently "There are no tuples in the result of R."

2. If R and S are expressions of relational algebra, then $R \subseteq S$ is a constraint that says "Every tuple in the result of R must also be in the result of S." Of course the result of S may contain additional tuples not produced by R.

These ways of expressing constraints are actually equivalent in what they can express, but sometimes one or the other is clearer or more succinct. That is, the constraint $R \subseteq S$ could just as well have been written $R - S = \emptyset$. To see why, notice that if every tuple in R is also in S, then surely $R - S$ is empty. Conversely, if $R - S$ contains no tuples, then every tuple in R must be in S (or else it would be in $R - S$).

On the other hand, a constraint of the first form, $R = \emptyset$, could just as well have been written $R \subseteq \emptyset$. Technically, $\emptyset$ is not an expression of relational algebra, but since there are expressions that evaluate to $\emptyset$, such as $R - R$, there is no harm in using $\emptyset$ as a relational-algebra expression. Note that these equivalences hold even if R and S are bags, provided we make the conventional interpretation of $R \subseteq S$: each tuple t appears in S at least as many times as it appears in R.

In the following sections, we shall see how to express significant constraints in one of these two styles. As we shall see in Chapter 7, it is the first style — equal-to-the-emptyset — that is most commonly used in SQL programming. However, as shown above, we are free to think in terms of set-containment if we wish and later convert our constraint to the equal-to-the-emptyset style.

5.5.2 Referential Integrity Constraints

A common kind of constraint, called "referential integrity" in Section 2.3, asserts that a value appearing in one context also appears in another, related context. We saw referential integrity as a matter of relationships "making sense." That is, if an object or entity A is related to object or entity B, then B must really exist. For example, in ODL terms, if a relationship in object A is represented physically by a pointer, then referential integrity of this relationship asserts that the pointer must not be null and must point to a genuine object.

In the relational model, referential integrity constraints look somewhat different. If we have a value v in a tuple of one relation R, then because of our design intentions we may expect that v will appear in a particular component of some tuple of another relation S. An example will illustrate how referential integrity in the relational model can be expressed in relational algebra.

Example 5.29: Let us think of our running movie database schema, particularly the two relations

```
Movie(title, year, length, inColor, studioName, producerC#)
MovieExec(name, address, cert#, netWorth)
```

We might reasonably assume that the producer of every movie would have to appear in the `MovieExec` relation. If not, there is something wrong, and we would at least want a system implementing a relational database to inform us that we had a movie with a producer of which the system had no knowledge.

To be more precise, the `producerC#` component of each `Movie` tuple must also appear in the `cert#` component of some `MovieExec` tuple. Since executives are uniquely identified by their certificate numbers, we would thus be assured that the movie's producer is found among the movie executives. We can express this constraint by the set-containment

$$\pi_{producerC\#}(\texttt{Movie}) \subseteq \pi_{cert\#}(\texttt{MovieExec})$$

The value of the expression on the left is the set of all certificate numbers appearing in `producerC#` components of `Movie` tuples. Likewise, the expression on the right's value is the set of all certificates in the `cert#` component of `MovieExec` tuples. Our constraint says that every certificate in the former set must also be in the latter set.

Incidentally, we could express the same constraint as an equality to the emptyset:

$$\pi_{producerC\#}(\texttt{Movie}) - \pi_{cert\#}(\texttt{MovieExec}) = \emptyset$$

□

Example 5.30: We can similarly express a referential integrity constraint where the "value" involved is represented by more than one attribute. For instance, we may want to assert that any movie mentioned in the relation

```
StarsIn(movieTitle, movieYear, starName)
```

also appears in the relation

```
Movie(title, year, length, inColor, studioName, producerC#)
```

Movies are represented in both relations by title-year pairs, because we agreed that one of these attributes alone was not sufficient to identify a movie. The constraint

$$\pi_{movieTitle,\ movieYear}(\texttt{StarsIn}) \subseteq \pi_{title,\ year}(\texttt{Movie})$$

expresses this referential integrity constraint by comparing the title-year pairs produced by projecting both relations onto the appropriate lists of components. □

5.5.3 Additional Constraint Examples

The same constraint notation allows us to express far more than referential integrity. For example, we can express any functional dependency as an algebraic constraint, although the notation is more cumbersome than the FD notation introduced in Section 3.4.

Example 5.31 : Let us express the FD:

$$name \rightarrow address$$

for the relation

```
MovieStar(name, address, gender, birthdate)
```

as an algebraic constraint. The idea is that if we construct all pairs of `MovieStar` tuples (t_1, t_2), we must not find a pair that agree in the **name** component and disagree in the **address** component. To construct the pairs we use a Cartesian product, and to search for pairs that violate the FD we use a selection. We then assert the constraint by equating the result to $\emptyset$.

To begin, since we are taking the product of a relation with itself, we need to rename at least one copy, in order to have names for the attributes of the product. For succinctness, let us use two new names, MS1 and MS2, to refer to the `MovieStar` relation. Then the FD can be expressed by the algebraic constraint:

$$\sigma_{MS1.name=MS2.name\ \texttt{AND}\ MS1.address \neq MS2.address}(\texttt{MS1} \times \texttt{MS2}) = \emptyset$$

In the above, MS1 in the product MS1 × MS2 is shorthand for the renaming:

$$\rho_{MS1(name,address,gender,birthdate)}(\texttt{MovieStar})$$

and MS2 is a similar renaming of MovieStar.   □

Some domain constraints can also be expressed in relational algebra. Often, a domain constraint simply requires that values for an attribute have a specific data type, such as integer or character string of length 30, so we may associate that domain with the attribute. However, often a domain constraint involves specific values that we require for an attribute. If the set of acceptable values can be expressed in the language of selection conditions, then this domain constraint can be expressed in the algebraic constraint language.

Example 5.32 : Suppose we wish to specify that the only legal values for the gender attribute of MovieStar are 'F' and 'M'. We can express this constraint algebraically by:

$$\sigma_{gender\neq 'F' \text{ AND } gender\neq 'M'}(\text{MovieStar}) = \emptyset$$

That is, the set of tuples in MovieStar whose gender component is equal to neither 'F' nor 'M' is empty.   □

Finally, there are some constraints that fall into none of the categories outlined in Section 2.3, nor are they functional or multivalued dependencies. The algebraic constraint language lets us express many new kinds of constraints. We offer one example here.

Example 5.33 : Suppose we wish to require that one must have a net worth of at least \$10,000,000 to be the president of a movie studio. This constraint cannot be classified as a domain, single-value, or referential integrity constraint. Yet we can express it algebraically as follows. First, we need to theta-join the two relations

      MovieExec(name, address, cert#, netWorth)
      Studio(name, address, presC#)

using the condition that presC# from Studio and cert# from MovieExec are equal. That join combines pairs of tuples consisting of a studio and an executive, such that the executive is the president of the studio. If we select from this relation those tuples where the net worth is less than ten million, we have a set that, according to our constraint, must be empty. Thus, we may express the constraint as:

$$\sigma_{netWorth<10000000}(\text{Studio} \underset{presC\#=cert\#}{\bowtie} \text{MovieExec}) = \emptyset$$

An alternative way to express the same constraint is to compare the set of certificates that represent studio presidents with the set of certificates that represent executives with a net worth of at least \$10,000,000; the former must be a subset of the latter. The containment

$$\pi_{presC\#}(\text{Studio}) \subseteq \pi_{cert\#}\left(\sigma_{netWorth\geq 10000000}(\text{MovieExec})\right)$$

expresses the above idea.   □

5.5.4 Exercises for Section 5.5

Exercise 5.5.1: Express the following constraints about the relations of Exercise 5.2.1, reproduced here:

```
Product(maker, model, type)
PC(model, speed, ram, hd, rd, price)
Laptop(model, speed, ram, hd, screen, price)
Printer(model, color, type, price)
```

You may write your constraints either as containments or by equating an expression to the empty set. For the data of Exercise 5.2.1, indicate any violations to your constraints.

* a) A PC with a processor speed less than 1000 must not sell for more than $1500.

  b) A laptop with a screen size less than 14 inches must have at least a 10 gigabyte hard disk or sell for less than $2000.

! c) No manufacturer of PC's may also make laptops.

*!! d) A manufacturer of a PC must also make a laptop with at least as great a processor speed.

! e) If a laptop has a larger main memory than a PC, then the laptop must also have a higher price than the PC.

Exercise 5.5.2: Express the following constraints in relational algebra. The constraints are based on the relations of Exercise 5.2.4:

```
Classes(class, type, country, numGuns, bore)
Ships(name, class, launched)
Battles(name, date)
Outcomes(ship, battle, result)
```

You may write your constraints either as containments or by equating an expression to the empty set. For the data of Exercise 5.2.4, indicate any violations to your constraints.

  a) No class of ships may have guns with larger than 16-inch bore.

  b) If a class of ships has more than 9 guns, then their bore must be no larger than 14 inches.

! c) No class may have more than 2 ships.

! d) No country may have both battleships and battlecruisers.

!! e) No ship with more than 9 guns may be in a battle with a ship having fewer than 9 guns that was sunk.

! Exercise 5.5.3: Suppose R and S are two relations. Let C be the referential integrity constraint that says: whenever R has a tuple with some values $v_1, v_2, \ldots, v_n$ in particular attributes $A_1, A_2, \ldots, A_n$, there must be a tuple of S that has the same values $v_1, v_2, \ldots, v_n$ in particular attributes $B_1, B_2, \ldots, B_n$. Show how to express constraint C in relational algebra.

! Exercise 5.5.4: Let R be a relation, and suppose $A_1 A_2 \cdots A_n \rightarrow B$ is a FD involving the attributes of R. Write in relational algebra the constraint that says this FD must hold in R.

!! Exercise 5.5.5: Let R be a relation, and suppose

$$A_1, A_2, \ldots, A_n \twoheadrightarrow B_1, B_2, \ldots, B_m$$

is a MVD involving the attributes of R. Write in relational algebra the constraint that says this MVD must hold in R.

5.6   Summary of Chapter 5

✦ *Classical Relational Algebra*: This algebra underlies most query languages for the relational model. Its principal operators are union, intersection, difference, selection, projection, Cartesian product, natural join, theta-join, and renaming.

✦ *Selection and Projection*: The selection operator produces a result consisting of all tuples of the argument relation that satisfy the selection condition. Projection removes undesired columns from the argument relation to produce the result.

✦ *Joins*: We join two relations by comparing tuples, one from each relation. In a natural join, we splice together those pairs of tuples that agree on all attributes common to the two relations. In a theta-join, pairs of tuples are concatenated if they meet a selection condition associated with the theta-join.

✦ *Relations as Bags*: In commercial database systems, relations are actually bags, in which the same tuple is allowed to appear several times. The operations of relational algebra on sets can be extended to bags, but there are some algebraic laws that fail to hold.

✦ *Extensions to Relational Algebra*: To match the capabilities of SQL or other query languages, some operators not present in the classical relational algebra are needed. Sorting of a relation is an example, as is an extended projection, where computation on columns of a relation is supported. Grouping, aggregation, and outerjoins are also needed.

✦ *Grouping and Aggregation*: Aggregations summarize a column of a relation. Typical aggregation operators are sum, average, count, minimum, and maximum. The grouping operator allows us to partition the tuples of a relation according to their value(s) in one or more attributes before computing aggregation(s) for each group.

✦ *Outerjoins*: The outerjoin of two relations starts with a join of those relations. Then, dangling tuples (those that failed to join with any tuple) from either relation are padded with null values for the attributes belonging only to the other relation, and the padded tuples are included in the result.

✦ *Constraints in Relational Algebra*: Many common kinds of constraints can be expressed as the containment of one relational algebra expression in another, or as the equality of a relational algebra expression to the empty set. These constraints include functional dependencies and referential-integrity constraints, for example.

5.7 References for Chapter 5

Relational algebra was another contribution of the fundamental paper [1] on the relational model. Extension of projection to include grouping and aggregation are from [2]. The original paper on the use of queries to express constraints is [3].

1. Codd, E. F., "A relational model for large shared data banks," *Comm. ACM* **13**:6, pp. 377–387, 1970.

2. A. Gupta, V. Harinarayan, and D. Quass, "Aggregate-query processing in data warehousing environments," *Proc. Intl. Conf. on Very Large Databases* (1995), pp. 358–369.

3. Nicolas, J.-M., "Logic for improving integrity checking in relational databases," *Acta Informatica* **18**:3, pp. 227–253, 1982.

Chapter 6

The Database Language SQL

The most commonly used relational DBMS's query and modify the database through a language called SQL (sometimes pronounced "sequel"). SQL stands for "Structured Query Language." The portion of SQL that supports queries has capabilities very close to that of relational algebra, as extended in Section 5.4. However, SQL also includes statements for modifying the database (e.g., inserting and deleting tuples from relations) and for declaring a database schema. Thus, SQL serves as both a data-manipulation language and as a data-definition language. SQL also standardizes many other database commands, covered in Chapters 7 and 8.

There are many different dialects of SQL. First, there are three major standards. There is ANSI (American National Standards Institute) SQL and an updated standard adopted in 1992, called SQL-92 or SQL2. The recent SQL-99 (previously referred to as SQL3) standard extends SQL2 with object-relational features and a number of other new capabilities. Then, there are versions of SQL produced by the principal DBMS vendors. These all include the capabilities of the original ANSI standard. They also conform to a large extent to the more recent SQL2, although each has its variations and extensions beyond SQL2, including some of the features in the SQL-99 standard.

In this and the next two chapters we shall emphasize the use of SQL as a query language. This chapter focuses on the generic (or "ad-hoc") query interface for SQL. That is, we consider SQL as a stand-alone query language, where we sit at a terminal and ask queries about a database or request database modifications, such as insertion of new tuples into a relation. Query answers are displayed for us at our terminal.

The next chapter discusses constraints and triggers, as another way of exerting user control over the content of the database. Chapter 8 covers database-related programming in conventional programming languages. Our discussion of SQL in this and the next two chapters will conform to the SQL-99 standard, emphasizing features found in almost all commercial systems as well as the earlier standards.

The intent of this chapter and the following two chapters is to provide the reader with a sense of what SQL is about, more at the level of a "tutorial" than a "manual." Thus, we focus on the most commonly used features only. The references mention places where more of the details of the language and its dialects can be found.

6.1   Simple Queries in SQL

Perhaps the simplest form of query in SQL asks for those tuples of some one relation that satisfy a condition. Such a query is analogous to a selection in relational algebra. This simple query, like almost all SQL queries, uses the three keywords, SELECT, FROM, and WHERE that characterize SQL.

```
Movie(title, year, length, inColor, studioName, producerC#)
StarsIn(movieTitle, movieYear, starName)
MovieStar(name, address, gender, birthdate)
MovieExec(name, address, cert#, netWorth)
Studio(name, address, presC#)
```

Figure 6.1: Example database schema, repeated

Example 6.1 : In this and subsequent examples, we shall use the database schema described in Section 5.1. To review, these relation schemas are the ones shown in Fig. 6.1. We shall see in Section 6.6 how to express schema information in SQL, but for the moment, assume that each of the relations and domains (data types) mentioned in Section 5.1 apply to their SQL counterparts.

As our first query, let us ask about the relation

```
Movie(title, year, length, inColor, studioName, producerC#)
```

for all movies produced by Disney Studios in 1990. In SQL, we say

```
SELECT *
FROM Movie
WHERE studioName = 'Disney' AND year = 1990;
```

This query exhibits the characteristic select-from-where form of most SQL queries.

- The FROM clause gives the relation or relations to which the query refers. In our example, the query is about the relation Movie.

A Trick for Reading and Writing Queries

It is generally easist to examine a select-from-where query by first looking at the FROM clause, to learn which relations are involved in the query. Then, move to the WHERE clause, to learn what it is about tuples that is important to the query. Finally, look at the SELECT clause to see what the output is. The same order — from, then where, then select — is often useful when writing queries of your own, as well.

- The WHERE clause is a condition, much like a selection-condition in relational algebra. Tuples must satisfy the condition in order to match the query. Here, the condition is that the studioName attribute of the tuple has the value 'Disney' and the year attribute of the tuple has the value 1990. All tuples meeting both stipulations satisfy the condition; other tuples do not.

- The SELECT clause tells which attributes of the tuples matching the condition are produced as part of the answer. The * in this example indicates that the entire tuple is produced. The result of the query is the relation consisting of all tuples produced by this process.

One way to interpret this query is to consider each tuple of the relation mentioned in the FROM clause. The condition in the WHERE clause is applied to the tuple. More precisely, any attributes mentioned in the WHERE clause are replaced by the value in the tuple's component for that attribute. The condition is then evaluated, and if true, the components appearing in the SELECT clause are produced as one tuple of the answer. Thus, the result of the query is the Movie tuples for those movies produced by Disney in 1990, for example, *Pretty Woman.*

In detail, when the SQL query processor encounters the Movie tuple

title	*year*	*length*	*inColor*	*studioName*	*producerC#*
Pretty Woman	1990	119	true	Disney	999

(here, 999 is the imaginary certificate number for the producer of the movie), the value 'Disney' is substituted for attribute studioName and value 1990 is substituted for attribute year in the condition of the WHERE clause, because these are the values for those attributes in the tuple in question. The WHERE clause thus becomes

```
WHERE 'Disney' = 'Disney' AND 1990 = 1990
```

Since this condition is evidently true, the tuple for *Pretty Woman* passes the test of the WHERE clause and the tuple becomes part of the result of the query.
□

6.1.1   Projection in SQL

We can, if we wish, eliminate some of the components of the chosen tuples; that is, we can project the relation produced by an SQL query onto some of its attributes. In place of the * of the SELECT clause, we may list some of the attributes of the relation mentioned in the FROM clause. The result will be projected onto the attributes listed.[1]

Example 6.2: Suppose we wish to modify the query of Example 6.1 to produce only the movie title and length. We may write

```
SELECT title, length
FROM Movie
WHERE studioName = 'Disney' AND year = 1990;
```

The result is a table with two columns, headed `title` and `length`. The tuples in this table are pairs, each consisting of a movie title and its length, such that the movie was produced by Disney in 1990. For instance, the relation schema and one of its tuples looks like:

title	length
Pretty Woman	119
. . .	. . .

□

Sometimes, we wish to produce a relation with column headers different from the attributes of the relation mentioned in the FROM clause. We may follow the name of the attribute by the keyword AS and an *alias*, which becomes the header in the result relation. Keyword AS is optional. That is, an alias can immediately follow what it stands for, without any intervening punctuation.

Example 6.3: We can modify Example 6.2 to produce a relation with attributes `name` and `duration` in place of `title` and `length` as follows.

```
SELECT title AS name, length AS duration
FROM Movie
WHERE studioName = 'Disney' AND year = 1990;
```

The result is the same set of tuples as in Example 6.2, but with the columns headed by attributes `name` and `duration`. For example, the result relation might begin:

name	duration
Pretty Woman	119
. . .	. . .

---

[1]Thus, the keyword SELECT in SQL actually corresponds most closely to the projection operator of relational algebra, while the selection operator of the algebra corresponds to the WHERE clause of SQL queries.

□

    Another option in the `SELECT` clause is to use an expression in place of an attribute. Put another way, the `SELECT` list can function like the lists in an extended projection, which we discussed in Section 5.4.5. We shall see in Section 6.4 that the `SELECT` list can also include aggregates as in the γ operator of Section 5.4.4.

Example 6.4 : Suppose we wanted output as in Example 6.3, but with the length in hours. We might replace the `SELECT` clause of that example with

    `SELECT title AS name, length*0.016667 AS lengthInHours`

Then the same movies would be produced, but lengths would be calculated in hours and the second column would be headed by attribute `lengthInHours`, as:

name	lengthInHours
Pretty Woman	1
98334. ...	...

□

Example 6.5 : We can even allow a constant as an expression in the `SELECT` clause. It might seem pointless to do so, but one application is to put some useful words into the output that SQL displays. The following query:

```
SELECT title, length*0.016667 AS length, 'hrs.' AS inHours
FROM Movie
WHERE studioName = 'Disney' AND year = 1990;
```

produces tuples such as

title	length	inHours
Pretty Woman	1.98334	hrs.
...	...	...

We have arranged that the third column is called `inHours`, which fits with the column header `length` in the second column. Every tuple in the answer will have the constant `hrs.` in the third column, which gives the illusion of being the units attached to the value in the second column. □

6.1.2   Selection in SQL

The selection operator of relational algebra, and much more, is available through the `WHERE` clause of SQL. The expressions that may follow `WHERE` include conditional expressions like those found in common languages such as C or Java.

Case Insensitivity

SQL is *case insensitive*, meaning that it treats upper- and lower-case letters as the same letter. For example, although we have chosen to write keywords like FROM in capitals, it is equally proper to write this keyword as From or from, or even FrOm. Names of attributes, relations, aliases, and so on are similarly case insensitive. Only inside quotes does SQL make a distinction between upper- and lower-case letters. Thus, 'FROM' and 'from' are different character strings. Of course, neither is the keyword FROM.

We may build expressions by comparing values using the six common comparison operators: =, <>, <, >, <=, and >=. These operators have the same meanings as in C, but <> is the SQL symbol for "not equal to"; it corresponds to != in C.

The values that may be compared include constants and attributes of the relations mentioned after FROM. We may also apply the usual arithmetic operators, +, *, and so on, to numeric values before we compare them. For instance, $(year - 1930) * (year - 1930) < 100$ is true for those years within 9 of 1930. We may apply the concatenation operator || to strings; for example 'foo' || 'bar' has value 'foobar'.

An example comparison is

```
studioName = 'Disney'
```

in Example 6.1. The attribute studioName of the relation Movie is tested for equality against the constant 'Disney'. This constant is string-valued; strings in SQL are denoted by surrounding them with single quotes. Numeric constants, integers and reals, are also allowed, and SQL uses the common notations for reals such as -12.34 or 1.23E45.

The result of a comparison is a boolean value: either TRUE or FALSE.[2] Boolean values may be combined by the logical operators AND, OR, and NOT, with their expected meanings. For instance, we saw in Example 6.1 how two conditions could be combined by AND. The WHERE clause of this example evaluates to true if and only if both comparisons are satisfied; that is, the studio name is 'Disney' and the year is 1990. Here are some more examples of queries with complex WHERE clauses.

Example 6.6: The following query asks for all the movies made after 1970 that are in black-and-white.

```
SELECT title
```

---

[2]Well there's a bit more to boolean values; see Section 6.1.6.

SQL Queries and Relational Algebra

The simple SQL queries that we have seen so far all have the form:

SELECT L
FROM R
WHERE C

in which L is a list of expressions, R is a relation, and C is a condition. The meaning of any such expression is the same as that of the relational-algebra expression

$$\pi_L\big(\sigma_C(R)\big)$$

That is, we start with the relation in the FROM clause, apply to each tuple whatever condition is indicated in the WHERE clause, and then project onto the list of attributes and/or expressions in the SELECT clause.

```
FROM Movie
WHERE year > 1970 AND NOT inColor;
```

In this condition, we again have the AND of two booleans. The first is an ordinary comparison, but the second is the attribute inColor, negated. The use of this attribute by itself makes sense, because inColor is of type boolean.

Next, consider the query

```
SELECT title
FROM Movie
WHERE (year > 1970 OR length < 90) AND studioName = 'MGM';
```

This query asks for the titles of movies made by MGM Studios that either were made after 1970 or were less than 90 minutes long. Notice that comparisons can be grouped using parentheses. The parentheses are needed here because the precedence of logical operators in SQL is the same as in most other languages: AND takes precedence over OR, and NOT takes precedence over both. □

6.1.3 Comparison of Strings

Two strings are equal if they are the same sequence of characters. SQL allows declarations of different types of strings, for example fixed-length arrays of characters and variable-length lists of characters.[3] If so, we can expect reasonable

---

[3]At least the strings may be thought of as stored as an array or list, respectively. How they are actually stored is an implementation-dependent matter, not specified in any SQL standard.

Representing Bit Strings

A string of bits is represented by B followed by a quoted string of 0's and 1's. Thus, B'011' represents the string of three bits, the first of which is 0 and the other two of which are 1. Hexadecimal notation may also be used, where an X is followed by a quoted string of hexadecimal digits (0 through 9, and a through f, with the latter representing "digits" 10 through 15). For instance, X'7ff' represents a string of twelve bits, a 0 followed by eleven 1's. Note that each hexadecimal digit represents four bits, and leading 0's are not suppressed.

---

coercions among string types. For example, a string like foo might be stored as a fixed-length string of length 10, with 7 "pad" characters, or it could be stored as a variable-length string. We would expect values of both types to be equal to each other and also equal to the constant string 'foo'. More about physical storage of character strings appears in Section 12.1.3.

When we compare strings by one of the "less than" operators, such as < or >=, we are asking whether one precedes the other in lexicographic order (i.e., in dictionary order, or alphabetically). That is, if $a_1 a_2 \cdots a_n$ and $b_1 b_2 \cdots b_m$ are two strings, then the first is "less than" the second if either $a_1 < b_1$, or if $a_1 = b_1$ and $a_2 < b_2$, or if $a_1 = b_1$, $a_2 = b_2$, and $a_3 < b_3$, and so on. We also say $a_1 a_2 \cdots a_n < b_1 b_2 \cdots b_m$ if $n < m$ and $a_1 a_2 \cdots a_n = b_1 b_2 \cdots b_n$; that is, the first string is a proper prefix of the second. For instance, 'fodder' < 'foo', because the first two characters of each string are the same, fo, and the third character of fodder precedes the third character of foo. Also, 'bar' < 'bargain' because the former is a proper prefix of the latter. As with equality, we may expect reasonable coercion among different string types.

SQL also provides the capability to compare strings on the basis of a simple pattern match. An alternative form of comparison expression is

        s LIKE p

where s is a string and p is a *pattern*, that is, a string with the optional use of the two special characters % and _. Ordinary characters in p match only themselves in s. But % in p can match any sequence of 0 or more characters in s, and _ in p matches any one character in s. The value of this expression is true if and only if string s matches pattern p. Similarly, s NOT LIKE p is true if and only if string s does not match pattern p.

Example 6.7: We remember a movie "Star something," and we remember that the something has four letters. What could this movie be? We can retrieve all such names with the query:

        SELECT title

```
FROM Movie
WHERE title LIKE 'Star ____';
```

This query asks if the title attribute of a movie has a value that is nine characters long, the first five characters being `Star` and a blank. The last four characters may be anything, since any sequence of four characters matches the four _ symbols. The result of the query is the set of complete matching titles, such as *Star Wars* and *Star Trek*. □

Example 6.8 : Let us search for all movies with a possessive ('s) in their titles. The desired query is

```
SELECT title
FROM Movie
WHERE title LIKE '%''s%';
```

To understand this pattern, we must first observe that the apostrophe, being the character that surrounds strings in SQL, cannot also represent itself. The convention taken by SQL is that two consecutive apostrophes in a string represent a single apostrophe and do not end the string. Thus, `''s` in a pattern is matched by a single apostrophe followed by an `s`.

The two `%` characters on either side of the `'s` match any strings whatsoever. Thus, any title with `'s` as a substring will match the pattern, and the answer to this query will include films such as *Logan's Run* or *Alice's Restaurant*. □

6.1.4 Dates and Times

Implementations of SQL generally support dates and times as special data types. These values are often representable in a variety of formats such as `5/14/1948` or `14 May 1948`. Here we shall describe only the SQL standard notation, which is very specific about format.

A *date* constant is represented by the keyword `DATE` followed by a quoted string of a special form. For example, `DATE '1948-05-14'` follows the required form. The first four characters are digits representing the year. Then come a hyphen and two digits representing the month. Note that, as in our example, a one-digit month is padded with a leading 0. Finally there is another hyphen and two digits representing the day. As with months, we pad the day with a leading 0 if that is necessary to make a two-digit number.

A *time* constant is represented similarly by the keyword `TIME` and a quoted string. This string has two digits for the hour, on the military (24-hour) clock. Then come a colon, two digits for the minute, another colon, and two digits for the second. If fractions of a second are desired, we may continue with a decimal point and as many significant digits as we like. For instance, `TIME '15:00:02.5'` represents the time at which all students will have left a class that ends at 3 PM: two and a half seconds past three o'clock.

Escape Characters in LIKE expressions

What if the pattern we wish to use in a LIKE expression involves the characters % or _? Instead of having a particular character used as the escape character (e.g., the backslash in most UNIX commands), SQL allows us to specify any one character we like as the escape character for a single pattern. We do so by following the pattern by the keyword ESCAPE and the chosen escape character, in quotes. A character % or _ preceded by the escape character in the pattern is interpreted literally as that character, not as a symbol for any sequence of characters or any one character, respectively. For example,

$$\text{s LIKE 'x\%\%x\%' ESCAPE 'x'}$$

makes x the escape character in the pattern x%%x%. The sequence x% is taken to be a single %. This pattern matches any string that begins and ends with the character %. Note that only the middle % has its "any string" interpretation.

Alternatively, time can be expressed as the number of hours and minutes ahead of (indicated by a plus sign) or behind (indicated by a minus sign) Greenwich Mean Time (GMT). For instance, TIME '12:00:00-8:00' represents noon in Pacific Standard Time, which is eight hours behind GMT.

To combine dates and times we use a value of type TIMESTAMP. These values consist of the keyword TIMESTAMP, a date value, a space, and a time value. Thus, TIMESTAMP '1948-05-14 12:00:00' represents noon on May 14, 1948.

We can compare dates or times using the same comparison operators we use for numbers or strings. That is, < on dates means that the first date is earlier than the second; < on times means that the first is earlier (within the same day) than the second.

6.1.5 Null Values and Comparisons Involving NULL

SQL allows attributes to have a special value NULL, which is called the *null value*. There are many different interpretations that can be put on null values. Here are some of the most common:

1. *Value unknown*: that is, "I know there is some value that belongs here but I don't know what it is." An unknown birthdate is an example.

2. *Value inapplicable*: "There is no value that makes sense here." For example, if we had a spouse attribute for the MovieStar relation, then an unmarried star might have NULL for that attribute, not because we don't know the spouse's name, but because there is none.

3. *Value withheld*: "We are not entitled to know the value that belongs here." For instance, an unlisted phone number might appear as NULL in the component for a `phone` attribute.

We saw in Section 5.4.7 how the use of an outerjoin operator produces null values in some components of tuples; SQL allows outerjoins and also produces NULL's when a query involves outerjoins; see Section 6.3.8. There are other ways SQL produces NULL's as well. For example, certain insertions of tuples create null values, as we shall see in Section 6.5.1.

In WHERE clauses, we must be prepared for the possibility that a component of some tuple we are examining will be NULL. There are two important rules to remember when we operate upon a NULL value.

1. When we operate on a NULL and any value, including another NULL, using an arithmetic operator like × or +, the result is NULL.

2. When we compare a NULL value and any value, including another NULL, using a comparison operator like = or >, the result is UNKNOWN. The value UNKNOWN is another truth-value, like TRUE and FALSE; we shall discuss how to manipulate truth-value UNKNOWN shortly.

However, we must remember that, although NULL is a value that can appear in tuples, it is *not* a constant. Thus, while the above rules apply when we try to operate on an expression whose value is NULL, we cannot use NULL explicitly as an operand.

Example 6.9 : Let x have the value NULL. Then the value of $x + 3$ is also NULL. However, NULL + 3 is not a legal SQL expression. Similarly, the value of $x = 3$ is UNKNOWN, because we cannot tell if the value of x, which is NULL, equals the value 3. However, the comparison NULL = 3 is not correct SQL. □

Incidentally, the correct way to ask if x has the value NULL is with the expression x IS NULL. This expression has the value TRUE if x has the value NULL and it has value FALSE otherwise. Similarly, x IS NOT NULL has the value TRUE unless the value of x is NULL.

6.1.6 The Truth-Value UNKNOWN

In Section 6.1.2 we assumed that the result of a comparison was either TRUE or FALSE, and these truth-values were combined in the obvious way using the logical operators AND, OR, and NOT. We have just seen that when NULL values occur, comparisons can yield a third truth-value: UNKNOWN. We must now learn how the logical operators behave on combinations of all three truth-values.

The rule is easy to remember if we think of TRUE as 1 (i.e., fully true), FALSE as 0 (i.e., not at all true), and UNKNOWN as 1/2 (i.e., somewhere between true and false). Then:

Pitfalls Regarding Nulls

It is tempting to assume that NULL in SQL can always be taken to mean "a value that we don't know but that surely exists." However, there are several ways that intuition is violated. For instance, suppose x is a component of some tuple, and the domain for that component is the integers. We might reason that $0 * x$ surely has the value 0, since no matter what integer x is, its product with 0 is 0. However, if x has the value NULL, rule (1) of Section 6.1.5 applies; the product of 0 and NULL is NULL. Similarly, we might reason that $x - x$ has the value 0, since whatever integer x is, its difference with itself is 0. However, again rule (1) applies and the result is NULL.

---

1. The AND of two truth-values is the minimum of those values. That is, x AND y is FALSE if either x or y is FALSE; it is UNKNOWN if neither is FALSE but at least one is UNKNOWN, and it is TRUE only when both x and y are TRUE.

2. The OR of two truth-values is the maximum of those values. That is, x OR y is TRUE if either x or y is TRUE; it is UNKNOWN if neither is TRUE but at least one is UNKNOWN, and it is FALSE only when both are FALSE.

3. The negation of truth-value v is $1 - v$. That is, NOT x has the value TRUE when x is FALSE, the value FALSE when x is TRUE, and the value UNKNOWN when x has value UNKNOWN.

In Fig. 6.2 is a summary of the result of applying the three logical operators to the nine different combinations of truth-values for operands x and y. The value of the last operator, NOT, depends only on x.

x	y	x AND y	x OR y	NOT x
TRUE	TRUE	TRUE	TRUE	FALSE
TRUE	UNKNOWN	UNKNOWN	TRUE	FALSE
TRUE	FALSE	FALSE	TRUE	FALSE
UNKNOWN	TRUE	UNKNOWN	TRUE	UNKNOWN
UNKNOWN	UNKNOWN	UNKNOWN	UNKNOWN	UNKNOWN
UNKNOWN	FALSE	FALSE	UNKNOWN	UNKNOWN
FALSE	TRUE	FALSE	TRUE	TRUE
FALSE	UNKNOWN	FALSE	UNKNOWN	TRUE
FALSE	FALSE	FALSE	FALSE	TRUE

Figure 6.2: Truth table for three-valued logic

SQL conditions, as appear in WHERE clauses of select-from-where statements, apply to each tuple in some relation, and for each tuple, one of the three truth values, TRUE, FALSE, or UNKNOWN is produced. However, only the tuples for which the condition has the value TRUE become part of the answer; tuples with either UNKNOWN or FALSE as value are excluded from the answer. That situation leads to another surprising behavior similar to that discussed in the box on "Pitfalls Regarding Nulls," as the next example illustrates.

Example 6.10 : Suppose we ask about our running-example relation

```
Movie(title, year, length, inColor, studioName, producerC#)
```

the following query:

```
SELECT *
FROM Movie
WHERE length <= 120 OR length > 120;
```

Intuitively, we would expect to get a copy of the Movie relation, since each movie has a length that is either 120 or less or that is greater than 120.

However, suppose there are Movie tuples with NULL in the length component. Then both comparisons length <= 120 and length > 120 evaluate to UNKNOWN. The OR of two UNKNOWN's is UNKNOWN, by Fig. 6.2. Thus, for any tuple with a NULL in the length component, the WHERE clause evaluates to UNKNOWN. Such a tuple is *not* returned as part of the answer to the query. As a result, the true meaning of the query is "find all the Movie tuples with non-NULL lengths." □

6.1.7 Ordering the Output

We may ask that the tuples produced by a query be presented in sorted order. The order may be based on the value of any attribute, with ties broken by the value of a second attribute, remaining ties broken by a third, and so on, as in the τ operation of Section 5.4.6. To get output in sorted order, we add to the select-from-where statement a clause:

$$\text{ORDER BY } \langle \text{list of attributes} \rangle$$

The order is by default ascending, but we can get the output highest-first by appending the keyword DESC (for "descending") to an attribute. Similarly, we can specify ascending order with the keyword ASC, but that word is unnecessary.

Example 6.11 : The following is a rewrite of our original query of Example 6.1, asking for the Disney movies of 1990 from the relation

```
Movie(title, year, length, inColor, studioName, producerC#)
```

To get the movies listed by length, shortest first, and among movies of equal length, alphabetically, we can say:

```
SELECT *
FROM Movie
WHERE studioName = 'Disney' AND year = 1990
ORDER BY length, title;
```

□

6.1.8   Exercises for Section 6.1

* **Exercise 6.1.1:** If a query has a SELECT clause

```
SELECT A B
```

how do we know whether A and B are two different attributes or B is an alias of A?

Exercise 6.1.2: Write the following queries, based on our running movie database example

```
Movie(title, year, length, inColor, studioName, producerC#)
StarsIn(movieTitle, movieYear, starName)
MovieStar(name, address, gender, birthdate)
MovieExec(name, address, cert#, netWorth)
Studio(name, address, presC#)
```

in SQL.

* a) Find the address of MGM studios.

  b) Find Sandra Bullock's birthdate.

* c) Find all the stars that appeared either in a movie made in 1980 or a movie with "Love" in the title.

  d) Find all executives worth at least $10,000,000.

  e) Find all the stars who either are male or live in Malibu (have string `Malibu` as a part of their address).

Exercise 6.1.3: Write the following queries in SQL. They refer to the database schema of Exercise 5.2.1:

```
Product(maker, model, type)
PC(model, speed, ram, hd, rd, price)
Laptop(model, speed, ram, hd, screen, price)
Printer(model, color, type, price)
```

Show the result of your queries using the data from Exercise 5.2.1.

* a) Find the model number, speed, and hard-disk size for all PC's whose price is under $1200.

* b) Do the same as (a), but rename the `speed` column `megahertz` and the `hd` column `gigabytes`.

c) Find the manufacturers of printers.

d) Find the model number, memory size, and screen size for laptops costing more than $2000.

* e) Find all the tuples in the `Printer` relation for color printers. Remember that `color` is a boolean-valued attribute.

f) Find the model number, speed, and hard-disk size for those PC's that have either a 12x or 16x DVD and a price less than $2000. You may regard the `rd` attribute as having a string type.

Exercise 6.1.4: Write the following queries based on the database schema of Exercise 5.2.4:

```
Classes(class, type, country, numGuns, bore, displacement)
Ships(name, class, launched)
Battles(name, date)
Outcomes(ship, battle, result)
```

and show the result of your query on the data of Exercise 5.2.4.

a) Find the class name and country for all classes with at least 10 guns.

b) Find the names of all ships launched prior to 1918, but call the resulting column `shipName`.

c) Find the names of ships sunk in battle and the name of the battle in which they were sunk.

d) Find all ships that have the same name as their class.

e) Find the names of all ships that begin with the letter "R."

! f) Find the names of all ships whose name consists of three or more words (e.g., King George V).

Exercise 6.1.5: Let a and b be integer-valued attributes that may be NULL in some tuples. For each of the following conditions (as may appear in a WHERE clause), describe exactly the set of (a, b) tuples that satisfy the condition, including the case where a and/or b is NULL.

* a) a = 10 OR b = 20

   b) a = 10 AND b = 20

   c) a < 10 OR a >= 10

*! d) a = b

 ! e) a <= b

! **Exercise 6.1.6:** In Example 6.10 we discussed the query

```
SELECT *
FROM Movie
WHERE length <= 120 OR length > 120;
```

which behaves unintuitively when the length of a movie is NULL. Find a simpler, equivalent query, one with a single condition in the WHERE clause (no AND or OR of conditions).

6.2   Queries Involving More Than One Relation

Much of the power of relational algebra comes from its ability to combine two or more relations through joins, products, unions, intersections, and differences. We get all of these operations in SQL. The set-theoretic operations — union, intersection, and difference — appear directly in SQL, as we shall learn in Section 6.2.5. First, we shall learn how the select-from-where statement of SQL allows us to perform products and joins.

6.2.1   Products and Joins in SQL

SQL has a simple way to couple relations in one query: list each relation in the FROM clause. Then, the SELECT and WHERE clauses can refer to the attributes of any of the relations in the FROM clause.

Example 6.12: Suppose we want to know the name of the producer of *Star Wars*. To answer this question we need the following two relations from our running example:

```
Movie(title, year, length, inColor, studioName, producerC#)
MovieExec(name, address, cert#, netWorth)
```

The producer certificate number is given in the Movie relation, so we can do a simple query on Movie to get this number. We could then do a second query on the relation MovieExec to find the name of the person with that certificate number.

   However, we can phrase both these steps as one query about the pair of relations Movie and MovieExec as follows:

```
SELECT name
FROM Movie, MovieExec
WHERE title = 'Star Wars' AND producerC# = cert#;
```

This query asks us to consider all pairs of tuples, one from `Movie` and the other from `MovieExec`. The conditions on this pair are stated in the `WHERE` clause:

1. The `title` component of the tuple from `Movie` must have value `'Star Wars'`.

2. The `producerC#` attribute of the `Movie` tuple must be the same certificate number as the `cert#` attribute in the `MovieExec` tuple. That is, these two tuples must refer to the same producer.

Whenever we find a pair of tuples satisfying both conditions, we produce the `name` attribute of the tuple from `MovieExec` as part of the answer. If the data is what we expect, the only time both conditions will be met is when the tuple from `Movie` is for *Star Wars*, and the tuple from `MovieExec` is for George Lucas. Then and only then will the title be correct and the certificate numbers agree. Thus, `George Lucas` should be the only value produced. This process is suggested in Fig. 6.3. We take up in more detail how to interpret multirelation queries in Section 6.2.4. □

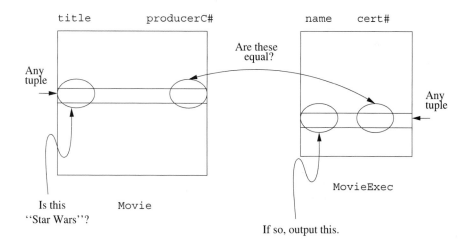

Figure 6.3: The query of Example 6.12 asks us to pair every tuple of `Movie` with every tuple of `MovieExec` and test two conditions

6.2.2 Disambiguating Attributes

Sometimes we ask a query involving several relations, and among these relations are two or more attributes with the same name. If so, we need a way to indicate which of these attributes is meant by a use of their shared name. SQL solves this problem by allowing us to place a relation name and a dot in front of an attribute. Thus $R.A$ refers to the attribute A of relation R.

Example 6.13 : The two relations

```
MovieStar(name, address, gender, birthdate)
MovieExec(name, address, cert#, netWorth)
```

each have attributes **name** and **address**. Suppose we wish to find pairs consisting of a star and an executive with the same address. The following query does the job.

```
SELECT MovieStar.name, MovieExec.name
FROM MovieStar, MovieExec
WHERE MovieStar.address = MovieExec.address;
```

In this query, we look for a pair of tuples, one from **MovieStar** and the other from **MovieExec**, such that their address components agree. The **WHERE** clause enforces the requirement that the **address** attributes from each of the two tuples agree. Then, for each matching pair of tuples, we extract the two **name** attributes, first from the **MovieStar** tuple and then from the other. The result would be a set of pairs such as

MovieStar.name	*MovieExec.name*
Jane Fonda	Ted Turner
. . .	. . .

□

The relation, followed by a dot, is permissible even in situations where there is no ambiguity. For instance, we are free to write the query of Example 6.12 as

```
SELECT MovieExec.name
FROM Movie, MovieExec
WHERE Movie.title = 'Star Wars'
      AND Movie.producerC# = MovieExec.cert#;
```

Alternatively, we may use relation names and dots in front of any subset of the attributes in this query.

6.2.3 Tuple Variables

Disambiguating attributes by prefixing the relation name works as long as the query involves combining several different relations. However, sometimes we need to ask a query that involves two or more tuples from the same relation.

Tuple Variables and Relation Names

Technically, references to attributes in SELECT and WHERE clauses are *always* to a tuple variable. However, if a relation appears only once in the FROM clause, then we can use the relation name as its own tuple variable. Thus, we can see a relation name R in the FROM clause as shorthand for R AS R. Furthermore, as we have seen, when an attribute belongs unambiguously to one relation, the relation name (tuple variable) may be omitted.

We may list a relation R as many times as we need to in the FROM clause, but we need a way to refer to each occurrence of R. SQL allows us to define, for each occurrence of R in the FROM clause, an "alias" which we shall refer to as a *tuple variable*. Each use of R in the FROM clause is followed by the (optional) keyword AS and the name of the tuple variable; we shall generally omit the AS in this context.

In the SELECT and WHERE clauses, we can disambiguate attributes of R by preceding them by the appropriate tuple variable and a dot. Thus, the tuple variable serves as another name for relation R and can be used in its place when we wish.

Example 6.14: While Example 6.13 asked for a star and an executive sharing an address, we might similarly want to know about two stars who share an address. The query is essentially the same, but now we must think of two tuples chosen from relation MovieStar, rather than tuples from each of MovieStar and MovieExec. Using tuple variables as aliases for two uses of MovieStar, we can write the query as

```
SELECT Star1.name, Star2.name
FROM MovieStar Star1, MovieStar Star2
WHERE Star1.address = Star2.address
      AND Star1.name < Star2.name;
```

We see in the FROM clause the declaration of two tuple variables, Star1 and Star2; each is an alias for relation MovieStar. The tuple variables are used in the SELECT clause to refer to the **name** components of the two tuples. These aliases are also used in the WHERE clause to say that the two MovieStar tuples represented by Star1 and Star2 have the same value in their **address** components.

The second condition in the WHERE clause, Star1.name < Star2.name, says that the name of the first star precedes the name of the second star alphabetically. If this condition were omitted, then tuple variables Star1 and Star2 could both refer to the same tuple. We would find that the two tuple variables referred to tuples whose **address** components are equal, of course, and thus produce each star name paired with itself.[4] The second condition also forces us to produce each pair of stars with a common address only once, in alphabetical order. If we used <> (not-equal) as the comparison operator, then we would produce pairs of married stars twice, like

Star1.name	Star2.name
Alec Baldwin	Kim Basinger
Kim Basinger	Alec Baldwin
...	...

□

6.2.4   Interpreting Multirelation Queries

There are several ways to define the meaning of the select-from-where expressions that we have just covered. All are *equivalent*, in the sense that they each give the same answer for each query applied to the same relation instances. We shall consider each in turn.

Nested Loops

The semantics that we have implicitly used in examples so far is that of tuple variables. Recall that a tuple variable ranges over all tuples of the corresponding relation. A relation name that is not aliased is also a tuple variable ranging over the relation itself, as we mentioned in the box on "Tuple Variables and Relation Names." If there are several tuple variables, we may imagine nested loops, one for each tuple variable, in which the variables each range over the tuples of their respective relations. For each assignment of tuples to the tuple variables, we decide whether the WHERE clause is true. If so, we produce a tuple consisting of the values of the expressions following SELECT; note that each term is given a value by the current assignment of tuples to tuple variables. This query-answering algorithm is suggested by Fig. 6.4.

Parallel Assignment

There is an equivalent definition in which we do not explicitly create nested loops ranging over the tuple variables. Rather, we consider in arbitrary order, or in parallel, all possible assignments of tuples from the appropriate relations to the tuple variables. For each such assignment, we consider whether the WHERE clause becomes true. Each assignment that produces a true WHERE clause contributes a tuple to the answer; that tuple is constructed from the attributes of the SELECT clause, evaluated according to that assignment.

---

[4]A similar problem occurs in Example 6.13 when the same individual is both a star and an executive. We could solve that problem by requiring that the two names be unequal.

```
LET the tuple variables in the from-clause range over
        relations R₁, R₂, ..., Rₙ;
FOR each tuple t₁ in relation R₁ DO
    FOR each tuple t₂ in relation R₂ DO
        ...
            FOR each tuple tₙ in relation Rₙ DO
                IF the where-clause is satisfied when the values
                from t₁, t₂, ..., tₙ are substituted for all
                attribute references THEN
                    evaluate the expressions of the select-clause
                    according to t₁, t₂, ..., tₙ and produce the
                    tuple of values that results.
```

Figure 6.4: Answering a simple SQL query

Conversion to Relational Algebra

A third approach is to relate the SQL query to relational algebra. We start with the tuple variables in the FROM clause and take the Cartesian product of their relations. If two tuple variables refer to the same relation, then this relation appears twice in the product, and we rename its attributes so all attributes have unique names. Similarly, attributes of the same name from different relations are renamed to avoid ambiguity.

Having created the product, we apply a selection operator to it by converting the WHERE clause to a selection condition in the obvious way. That is, each attribute reference in the WHERE clause is replaced by the attribute of the product to which it corresponds. Finally, we create from the SELECT clause a list of expressions for a final (extended) projection operation. As we did for the WHERE clause, we interpret each attribute reference in the SELECT clause as the corresponding attribute in the product of relations.

Example 6.15: Let us convert the query of Example 6.14 to relational algebra. First, there are two tuple variables in the FROM clause, both referring to relation MovieStar. Thus, our expression (without the necessary renaming) begins:

$$\text{MovieStar} \times \text{MovieStar}$$

The resulting relation has eight attributes, the first four correspond to attributes name, address, gender, and birthdate from the first copy of relation MovieStar, and the second four correspond to the same attributes from the other copy of MovieStar. We could create names for these attributes with a dot and the aliasing tuple variable — e.g., Star1.gender — but for succinctness, let us invent new symbols and call the attributes simply $A_1, A_2, \ldots, A_8$. Thus, A_1 corresponds to Star1.name, A_5 corresponds to Star2.name, and so on.

An Unintuitive Consequence of SQL Semantics

Suppose R, S, and T are unary (one-component) relations, each having attribute A alone, and we wish to find those elements that are in R and also in either S or T (or both). That is, we want to compute $R \cap (S \cup T)$. We might expect the following SQL query would do the job.

```
SELECT R.A
FROM R, S, T
WHERE R.A = S.A OR R.A = T.A;
```

However, consider the situation in which T is empty. Since then $R.A = T.A$ can never be satisfied, we might expect the query to produce exactly $R \cap S$, based on our intuition about how "OR" operates. Yet whichever of the three equivalent definitions of Section 6.2.4 one prefers, we find that the result is empty, regardless of how many elements R and S have in common. If we use the nested-loop semantics of Figure 6.4, then we see that the loop for tuple variable T iterates 0 times, since there are no tuples in the relation for the tuple variable to range over. Thus, the if-statement inside the for-loops never executes, and nothing can be produced. Similarly, if we look for assignments of tuples to the tuple variables, there is no way to assign a tuple to T, so no assignments exist. Finally, if we use the Cartesian-product approach, we start with $R \times S \times T$, which is empty because T is empty.

Under this naming strategy for attributes, the selection condition obtained from the WHERE clause is $A_2 = A_6$ and $A_1 < A_5$. The projection list is A_1, A_5. Thus,

$$\pi_{A_1,A_5}\left(\sigma_{A_2=A_6 \text{ AND } A_1<A_5}\left(\rho_{M(A_1,A_2,A_3,A_4)}(\texttt{MovieStar}) \times \rho_{N(A_5,A_6,A_7,A_8)}(\texttt{MovieStar})\right)\right)$$

renders the entire query in relational algebra. $\square$

6.2.5 Union, Intersection, and Difference of Queries

Sometimes we wish to combine relations using the set operations of relational algebra: union, intersection, and difference. SQL provides corresponding operators that apply to the results of queries, provided those queries produce relations with the same list of attributes and attribute types. The keywords used are UNION, INTERSECT, and EXCEPT for $\cup$, $\cap$, and $-$, respectively. Words like UNION are used between two queries, and those queries must be parenthesized.

Example 6.16: Suppose we wanted the names and addresses of all female movie stars who are also movie executives with a net worth over $10,000,000. Using the following two relations:

```
MovieStar(name, address, gender, birthdate)
MovieExec(name, address, cert#, netWorth)
```

we can write the query as in Fig. 6.5. Lines (1) through (3) produce a relation whose schema is (name, address) and whose tuples are the names and addresses of all female movie stars.

```
1)   (SELECT name, address
2)    FROM MovieStar
3)    WHERE gender = 'F')
4)        INTERSECT
5)   (SELECT name, address
6)    FROM MovieExec
7)    WHERE netWorth > 10000000);
```

Figure 6.5: Intersecting female movie stars with rich executives

Similarly, lines (5) through (7) produce the set of "rich" executives, those with net worth over $10,000,000. This query also yields a relation whose schema has the attributes name and address only. Since the two schemas are the same, we can intersect them, and we do so with the operator of line (4). □

Example 6.17: In a similar vein, we could take the difference of two sets of persons, each selected from a relation. The query

```
(SELECT name, address FROM MovieStar)
    EXCEPT
(SELECT name, address FROM MovieExec);
```

gives the names and addresses of movie stars who are not also movie executives, regardless of gender or net worth. □

In the two examples above, the attributes of the relations whose intersection or difference we took were conveniently the same. However, if necessary to get a common set of attributes, we can rename attributes as in Example 6.3.

Example 6.18: Suppose we wanted all the titles and years of movies that appeared in either the Movie or StarsIn relation of our running example:

```
Movie(title, year, length, inColor, studioName, producerC#)
StarsIn(movieTitle, movieYear, starName)
```

Readable SQL Queries

Generally, one writes SQL queries so that each important keyword like FROM or WHERE starts a new line. This style offers the reader visual clues to the structure of the query. However, when a query or subquery is short, we shall sometimes write it out on a single line, as we did in Example 6.17. That style, keeping a complete query compact, also offers good readability.

Ideally, these sets of movies would be the same, but in practice it is common for relations to diverge; for instance we might have movies with no listed stars or a StarsIn tuple that mentions a movie not found in the Movie relation.[5] Thus, we might write

```
(SELECT title, year FROM Movie)
    UNION
(SELECT movieTitle AS title, movieYear AS year FROM StarsIn);
```

The result would be all movies mentioned in either relation, with title and year as the attributes of the resulting relation.   □

6.2.6 Exercises for Section 6.2

Exercise 6.2.1: Using the database schema of our running movie example

```
Movie(title, year, length, inColor, studioName, producerC#)
StarsIn(movieTitle, movieYear, starName)
MovieStar(name, address, gender, birthdate)
MovieExec(name, address, cert#, netWorth)
Studio(name, address, presC#)
```

write the following queries in SQL.

* a) Who were the male stars in *Terms of Endearment*?

  b) Which stars appeared in movies produced by MGM in 1995?

  c) Who is the president of MGM studios?

*! d) Which movies are longer than *Gone With the Wind*?

 ! e) Which executives are worth more than Merv Griffin?

Exercise 6.2.2: Write the following queries, based on the database schema

---

[5]There are ways to prevent this divergence; see Section 7.1.4.

```
Product(maker, model, type)
PC(model, speed, ram, hd, rd, price)
Laptop(model, speed, ram, hd, screen, price)
Printer(model, color, type, price)
```

of Exercise 5.2.1, and evaluate your queries using the data of that exercise.

* a) Give the manufacturer and speed of laptops with a hard disk of at least thirty gigabytes.

* b) Find the model number and price of all products (of any type) made by manufacturer B.

  c) Find those manufacturers that sell Laptops, but not PC's.

! d) Find those hard-disk sizes that occur in two or more PC's.

! e) Find those pairs of PC models that have both the same speed and RAM. A pair should be listed only once; e.g., list (i, j) but not (j, i).

!! f) Find those manufacturers of at least two different computers (PC's or laptops) with speeds of at least 1000.

Exercise 6.2.3: Write the following queries, based on the database schema

```
Classes(class, type, country, numGuns, bore, displacement)
Ships(name, class, launched)
Battles(name, date)
Outcomes(ship, battle, result)
```

of Exercise 5.2.4, and evaluate your queries using the data of that exercise.

  a) Find the ships heavier than 35,000 tons.

  b) List the name, displacement, and number of guns of the ships engaged in the battle of Guadalcanal.

  c) List all the ships mentioned in the database. (Remember that all these ships may not appear in the Ships relation.)

! d) Find those countries that have both battleships and battlecruisers.

! e) Find those ships that were damaged in one battle, but later fought in another.

! f) Find those battles with at least three ships of the same country.

*! **Exercise 6.2.4:** A general form of relational-algebra query is

$$\pi_L\Big(\sigma_C(R_1 \times R_2 \times \cdots \times R_n)\Big)$$

Here, L is an arbitrary list of attributes, and C is an arbitrary condition. The list of relations $R_1, R_2, \ldots, R_n$ may include the same relation repeated several times, in which case appropriate renaming may be assumed applied to the R_i's. Show how to express any query of this form in SQL.

! Exercise 6.2.5 : Another general form of relational-algebra query is

$$\pi_L \Big(\sigma_C (R_1 \bowtie R_2 \bowtie \cdots \bowtie R_n) \Big)$$

The same assumptions as in Exercise 6.2.4 apply here; the only difference is that the natural join is used instead of the product. Show how to express any query of this form in SQL.

6.3   Subqueries

In SQL, one query can be used in various ways to help in the evaluation of another. A query that is part of another is called a *subquery*. Subqueries can have subqueries, and so on, down as many levels as we wish. We already saw one example of the use of subqueries; in Section 6.2.5 we built a union, intersection, or difference query by connecting two subqueries to form the whole query. There are a number of other ways that subqueries can be used:

1. Subqueries can return a single constant, and this constant can be compared with another value in a WHERE clause.

2. Subqueries can return relations that can be used in various ways in WHERE clauses.

3. Subqueries can have their relations appear in FROM clauses, just like any stored relation can.

6.3.1   Subqueries that Produce Scalar Values

An atomic value that can appear as one component of a tuple is referred to as a *scalar*. A select-from-where expression can produce a relation with any number of attributes in its schema, and there can be any number of tuples in the relation. However, often we are only interested in values of a single attribute. Furthermore, sometimes we can deduce from information about keys, or from other information, that there will be only a single value produced for that attribute.

If so, we can use this select-from-where expression, surrounded by parentheses, as if it were a constant. In particular, it may appear in a WHERE clause any place we would expect to find a constant or an attribute representing a component of a tuple. For instance, we may compare the result of such a subquery to a constant or attribute.

Example 6.19 : Let us recall Example 6.12, where we asked for the producer of *Star Wars*. We had to query the two relations

```
Movie(title, year, length, inColor, studioName, producerC#)
MovieExec(name, address, cert#, netWorth)
```

because only the former has movie title information and only the latter has producer names. The information is linked by "certificate numbers." These numbers uniquely identify producers. The query we developed is:

```
SELECT name
FROM Movie, MovieExec
WHERE title = 'Star Wars' AND producerC# = cert#;
```

There is another way to look at this query. We need the Movie relation only to get the certificate number for the producer of *Star Wars*. Once we have it, we can query the relation MovieExec to find the name of the person with this certificate. The first problem, getting the certificate number, can be written as a subquery, and the result, which we expect will be a single value, can be used in the "main" query to achieve the same effect as the query above. This query is shown in Fig. 6.6.

```
1)   SELECT name
2)   FROM MovieExec
3)   WHERE cert# =
4)       (SELECT producerC#
5)        FROM Movie
6)        WHERE title = 'Star Wars'
          );
```

Figure 6.6: Finding the producer of *Star Wars* by using a nested subquery

Lines (4) through (6) of Fig. 6.6 are the subquery. Looking only at this simple query by itself, we see that the result will be a unary relation with attribute producerC#, and we expect to find only one tuple in this relation. The tuple will look like (12345), that is, a single component with some integer, perhaps 12345 or whatever George Lucas' certificate number is. If zero tuples or more than one tuple is produced by the subquery of lines (4) through (6), it is a run-time error.

Having executed this subquery, we can then execute lines (1) through (3) of Fig. 6.6, as if the value 12345 replaced the entire subquery. That is, the "main" query is executed as if it were

```
SELECT name
FROM MovieExec
WHERE cert# = 12345;
```

The result of this query should be `George Lucas`.   □

6.3.2   Conditions Involving Relations

There are a number of SQL operators that we can apply to a relation R and produce a boolean result. Typically, the relation R will be the result of a select-from-where subquery. Some of these operators — IN, ALL, and ANY — will be explained first in their simple form where a scalar value s is involved. In this situation, the relation R is required to be a one-column relation. Here are the definitions of the operators:

1. EXISTS R is a condition that is true if and only if R is not empty.

2. s IN R is true if and only if s is equal to one of the values in R. Likewise, s NOT IN R is true if and only if s is equal to no value in R. Here, we assume R is a unary relation. We shall discuss extensions to the IN and NOT IN operators where R has more than one attribute in its schema and s is a tuple in Section 6.3.3.

3. s > ALL R is true if and only if s is greater than every value in unary relation R. Similarly, the > operator could be replaced by any of the other five comparison operators, with the analogous meaning: s stands in the stated relationship to every tuple in R. For instance, s <> ALL R is the same as s NOT IN R.

4. s > ANY R is true if and only if s is greater than at least one value in unary relation R. Similarly, any of the other five comparisons could be used in place of >, with the meaning that s stands in the stated relationship to at least one tuple of R. For instance, s = ANY R is the same as s IN R.

The EXISTS, ALL, and ANY operators can be negated by putting NOT in front of the entire expression, just like any other boolean-valued expression. Thus, NOT EXISTS R is true if and only if R is empty. NOT s > ALL R is true if and only if s is not the maximum value in R, and NOT s > ANY R is true if and only if s is the minimum value in R. We shall see several examples of the use of these operators shortly.

6.3.3   Conditions Involving Tuples

A tuple in SQL is represented by a parenthesized list of scalar values. Examples are (123, 'foo') and (name, address, networth). The first of these has constants as components; the second has attributes as components. Mixing of constants and attributes is permitted.

If a tuple t has the same number of components as a relation R, then it makes sense to compare t and R in expressions of the type listed in Section 6.3.2. Examples are t IN R or t <> ANY R. The latter comparison means that there is some tuple in R other than t. Note that when comparing a tuple with members of a relation R, we must compare components using the assumed standard order for the attributes of R.

```
1)   SELECT name
2)   FROM MovieExec
3)   WHERE cert# IN
4)       (SELECT producerC#
5)        FROM Movie
6)        WHERE (title, year) IN
7)            (SELECT movieTitle, movieYear
8)             FROM StarsIn
9)             WHERE starName = 'Harrison Ford'
             )
         );
```

Figure 6.7: Finding the producers of Harrison Ford's movies

Example 6.20: In Fig. 6.7 is an SQL query on the three relations

```
Movie(title, year, length, inColor, studioName, producerC#)
StarsIn(movieTitle, movieYear, starName)
MovieExec(name, address, cert#, netWorth)
```

asking for all the producers of movies in which Harrison Ford stars. It consists of a "main" query, a query nested within that, and a third query nested within the second.

We should analyze any query with subqueries from the inside out. Thus, let us start with the innermost nested subquery: lines (7) through (9). This query examines the tuples of the relation `StarsIn` and finds all those tuples whose `starName` component is `'Harrison Ford'`. The titles and years of those movies are returned by this subquery. Recall that title and year, not title alone, is the key for movies, so we need to produce tuples with both attributes to identify a movie uniquely. Thus, we would expect the value produced by lines (7) through (9) to look something like Fig. 6.8.

Now, consider the middle subquery, lines (4) through (6). It searches the `Movie` relation for tuples whose title and year are in the relation suggested by Fig. 6.8. For each tuple found, the producer's certificate number is returned, so the result of the middle subquery is the set of certificates of the producers of Harrison Ford's movies.

Finally, consider the "main" query of lines (1) through (3). It examines the tuples of the `MovieExec` relation to find those whose `cert#` component is one of the certificates in the set returned by the middle subquery. For each of these tuples, the name of the producer is returned, giving us the set of producers of Harrison Ford's movies, as desired. □

title	year
Star Wars	1977
Raiders of the Lost Ark	1981
The Fugitive	1993
...	...

Figure 6.8: Title-year pairs returned by inner subquery

Incidentally, the nested query of Fig. 6.7 can, like many nested queries, be written as a single select-from-where expression with relations in the FROM clause for each of the relations mentioned in the main query or a subquery. The IN relationships are replaced by equalities in the WHERE clause. For instance, the query of Fig. 6.9 is essentially that of Fig. 6.7. There is a difference regarding the way duplicate occurrences of a producer — e.g., George Lucas — are handled, as we shall discuss in Section 6.4.1.

```
SELECT name
FROM MovieExec, Movie, StarsIn
WHERE cert# = producerC# AND
      title = movieTitle AND
      year = movieYear AND
      starName = 'Harrison Ford';
```

Figure 6.9: Ford's producers without nested subqueries

6.3.4 Correlated Subqueries

The simplest subqueries can be evaluated once and for all, and the result used in a higher-level query. A more complicated use of nested subqueries requires the subquery to be evaluated many times, once for each assignment of a value to some term in the subquery that comes from a tuple variable outside the subquery. A subquery of this type is called a *correlated* subquery. Let us begin our study with an example.

Example 6.21 : We shall find the titles that have been used for two or more movies. We start with an outer query that looks at all tuples in the relation

```
Movie(title, year, length, inColor, studioName, producerC#)
```

For each such tuple, we ask in a subquery whether there is a movie with the same title and a greater year. The entire query is shown in Fig. 6.10.

As with other nested queries, let us begin at the innermost subquery, lines (4) through (6). If `Old.title` in line (6) were replaced by a constant string such as `'King Kong'`, we would understand it quite easily as a query asking for the year or years in which movies titled *King Kong* were made. The present subquery differs little. The only problem is that we don't know what value `Old.title` has. However, as we range over `Movie` tuples of the outer query of lines (1) through (3), each tuple provides a value of `Old.title`. We then execute the query of lines (4) through (6) with this value for `Old.title` to decide the truth of the `WHERE` clause that extends from lines (3) through (6).

```
1)   SELECT title
2)   FROM Movie Old
3)   WHERE year < ANY
4)       (SELECT year
5)        FROM Movie
6)        WHERE title = Old.title
         );
```

Figure 6.10: Finding movie titles that appear more than once

The condition of line (3) is true if any movie with the same title as `Old.title` has a later year than the movie in the tuple that is the current value of tuple variable `Old`. This condition is true unless the year in the tuple `Old` is the last year in which a movie of that title was made. Consequently, lines (1) through (3) produce a title one fewer times than there are movies with that title. A movie made twice will be listed once, a movie made three times will be listed twice, and so on.[6]   □

When writing a correlated query it is important that we be aware of the *scoping rules* for names. In general, an attribute in a subquery belongs to one of the tuple variables in that subquery's `FROM` clause if some tuple variable's relation has that attribute in its schema. If not, we look at the immediately surrounding subquery, then to the one surrounding that, and so on. Thus, `year` on line (4) and `title` on line (6) of Fig. 6.10 refer to the attributes of the tuple variable that ranges over all the tuples of the copy of relation `Movie` introduced on line (5) — that is, the copy of the `Movie` relation addressed by the subquery of lines (4) through (6).

However, we can arrange for an attribute to belong to another tuple variable if we prefix it by that tuple variable and a dot. That is why we introduced the alias `Old` for the `Movie` relation of the outer query, and why we refer to `Old.title` in line (6). Note that if the two relations in the `FROM` clauses of lines

---

[6]This example is the first occasion on which we've been reminded that relations in SQL are bags, not sets. There are several ways that duplicates may crop up in SQL relations. We shall discuss the matter in detail in Section 6.4.

(2) and (5) were different, we would not need an alias. Rather, in the subquery we could refer directly to attributes of a relation mentioned in line (2).

6.3.5   Subqueries in FROM Clauses

Another use for subqueries is as relations in a FROM clause. In a FROM list, instead of a stored relation, we may use a parenthesized subquery. Since we don't have a name for the result of this subquery, we must give it a tuple-variable alias. We then refer to tuples in the result of the subquery as we would tuples in any relation that appears in the FROM list.

Example 6.22: Let us reconsider the problem of Example 6.20, where we wrote a query that finds the producers of Harrison Ford's movies. Suppose we had a relation that gave the certificates of the producers of those movies. It would then be a simple matter to look up the names of those producers in the relation MovieExec. Figure 6.11 is such a query.

```
1)   SELECT name
2)   FROM MovieExec, (SELECT producerC#
3)                     FROM Movie, StarsIn
4)                     WHERE title = movieTitle AND
5)                         year = movieYear AND
6)                         starname = 'Harrison Ford'
7)                   ) Prod
8)   WHERE cert# = Prod.producerC#;
```

Figure 6.11: Finding the producers of Ford's movies using a subquery in the FROM clause

Lines (2) through (7) are the FROM clause of the outer query. In addition to the relation MovieExec, it has a subquery. That subquery joins Movie and StarsIn on lines (3) through (5), adds the condition that the star is Harrison Ford on line (6), and returns the set of producers of the movies at line (2). This set is given the alias Prod on line (7).

At line (8), the relations MovieExec and the subquery aliased Prod are joined with the requirement that the certificate numbers be the same. The names of the producers from MovieExec that have certificates in the set aliased by Prod is returned at line (1).   □

6.3.6   SQL Join Expressions

We can construct relations by a number of variations on the join operator applied to two relations. These variants include products, natural joins, theta-joins, and outerjoins. The result can stand as a query by itself. Alternatively, all these expressions, since they produce relations, may be used as subqueries in the `FROM` clause of a select-from-where expression.

The simplest form of join expression is a *cross join*; that term is a synonym for what we called a Cartesian product or just "product" in Section 5.2.5. For instance, if we want the product of the two relations

```
Movie(title, year, length, inColor, studioName, producerC#)
StarsIn(movieTitle, movieYear, starName)
```

we can say

```
Movie CROSS JOIN StarsIn;
```

and the result will be a nine-column relation with all the attributes of `Movie` and `StarsIn`. Every pair consisting of one tuple of `Movie` and one tuple of `StarsIn` will be a tuple of the resulting relation.

The attributes in the product relation can be called $R.A$, where R is one of the two joined relations and A is one of its attributes. If only one of the relations has an attribute named A, then the R and dot can be dropped, as usual. In this instance, since `Movie` and `StarsIn` have no common attributes, the nine attribute names suffice in the product.

However, the product by itself is rarely a useful operation. A more conventional theta-join is obtained with the keyword `ON`. We put `JOIN` between two relation names R and S and follow them by `ON` and a condition. The meaning of `JOIN...ON` is that the product of $R \times S$ is followed by a selection for whatever condition follows `ON`.

Example 6.23: Suppose we want to join the relations

```
Movie(title, year, length, inColor, studioName, producerC#)
StarsIn(movieTitle, movieYear, starName)
```

with the condition that the only tuples to be joined are those that refer to the same movie. That is, the titles and years from both relations must be the same. We can ask this query by

```
Movie JOIN StarsIn ON
        title = movieTitle AND year = movieYear;
```

The result is again a nine-column relation with the obvious attribute names. However, now a tuple from `Movie` and one from `StarsIn` combine to form a tuple of the result only if the two tuples agree on both the title and year. As a result, two of the columns are redundant, because every tuple of the result will have the same value in both the `title` and `movieTitle` components and will have the same value in both `year` and `movieYear`.

If we are concerned with the fact that the join above has two redundant components, we can use the whole expression as a subquery in a `FROM` clause and use a `SELECT` clause to remove the undesired attributes. Thus, we could write

```
SELECT title, year, length, inColor, studioName,
       producerC#, starName
FROM Movie JOIN StarsIn ON
       title = movieTitle AND year = movieYear;
```

to get a seven-column relation which is the Movie relation's tuples, each extended in all possible ways with a star of that movie.   □

6.3.7 Natural Joins

As we recall from Section 5.2.6, a natural join differs from a theta-join in that:

1. The join condition is that all pairs of attributes from the two relations having a common name are equated, and there are no other conditions.

2. One of each pair of equated attributes is projected out.

The SQL natural join behaves exactly this way. Keywords NATURAL JOIN appear between the relations to express the ⋈ operator.

Example 6.24 : Suppose we want to compute the natural join of the relations

```
MovieStar(name, address, gender, birthdate)
MovieExec(name, address, cert#, netWorth)
```

The result will be a relation whose schema includes attributes name and address plus all the attributes that appear in one or the other of the two relations. A tuple of the result will represent an individual who is both a star and an executive and will have all the information pertinent to either: a name, address, gender, birthdate, certificate number, and net worth. The expression

```
MovieStar NATURAL JOIN MovieExec;
```

succinctly describes the desired relation.   □

6.3.8 Outerjoins

The outerjoin operator was introduced in Section 5.4.7 as a way to augment the result of a join by the dangling tuples, padded with null values. In SQL, we can specify an outerjoin; NULL is used as the null value.

Example 6.25 : Suppose we wish to take the outerjoin of the two relations

```
MovieStar(name, address, gender, birthdate)
MovieExec(name, address, cert#, netWorth)
```

SQL refers to the standard outerjoin, which pads dangling tuples from both of its arguments, as a *full* outerjoin. The syntax is unsurprising:

```
MovieStar NATURAL FULL OUTER JOIN MovieExec;
```

The result of this operation is a relation with the same six-attribute schema as Example 6.24. The tuples of this relation are of three kinds. Those representing individuals who are both stars and executives have tuples with all six attributes non-NULL. These are the tuples that are also in the result of Example 6.24.

The second kind of tuple is one for an individual who is a star but not an executive. These tuples have values for attributes `name`, `address`, `gender`, and `birthdate` taken from their tuple in `MovieStar`, while the attributes belonging only to `MovieExec`, namely `cert#` and `netWorth`, have NULL values.

The third kind of tuple is for an executive who is not also a star. These tuples have values for the attributes of `MovieExec` taken from their `MovieExec` tuple and NULL's in the attributes `gender` and `birthdate` that come only from `MovieStar`. For instance, the three tuples of the result relation shown in Fig. 6.12 correspond to the three types of individuals, respectively. □

name	address	gender	birthdate	cert#	networth
Mary Tyler Moore	Maple St.	'F'	9/9/99	12345	$100···
Tom Hanks	Cherry Ln.	'M'	8/8/88	NULL	NULL
George Lucas	Oak Rd.	NULL	NULL	23456	$200···

Figure 6.12: Three tuples in the outerjoin of `MovieStar` and `MovieExec`

All the variations on the outerjoin that we mentioned in Section 5.4.7 are also available in SQL. If we want a left- or right-outerjoin, we add the appropriate word LEFT or RIGHT in place of FULL. For instance,

```
MovieStar NATURAL LEFT OUTER JOIN MovieExec;
```

would yield the first two tuples of Fig. 6.12 but not the third. Similarly,

```
MovieStar NATURAL RIGHT OUTER JOIN MovieExec;
```

would yield the first and third tuples of Fig. 6.12 but not the second.

Next, suppose we want a theta-outerjoin instead of a natural outerjoin. Instead of using the keyword NATURAL, we may follow the join by ON and a condition that matching tuples must obey. If we also specify FULL OUTER JOIN, then after matching tuples from the two joined relations, we pad dangling tuples of either relation with NULL's and include the padded tuples in the result.

Example 6.26: Let us reconsider Example 6.23, where we joined the relations `Movie` and `StarsIn` using the conditions that the `title` and `movieTitle` attributes of the two relations agree and that the `year` and `movieYear` attributes of the two relations agree. If we modify that example to call for a full outerjoin:

```
Movie FULL OUTER JOIN StarsIn ON
    title = movieTitle AND year = movieYear;
```

then we shall get not only tuples for movies that have at least one star mentioned in StarsIn, but we shall get tuples for movies with no listed stars, padded with NULL's in attributes movieTitle, movieYear, and starName. Likewise, for stars not appearing in any movie listed in relation Movie we get a tuple with NULL's in the six attributes of Movie.   □

The keyword FULL can be replaced by either LEFT or RIGHT in outerjoins of the type suggested by Example 6.26. For instance,

```
Movie LEFT OUTER JOIN StarsIn ON
    title = movieTitle AND year = movieYear;
```

gives us the Movie tuples with at least one listed star and NULL-padded Movie tuples without a listed star, but will not include stars without a listed movie. Conversely,

```
Movie RIGHT OUTER JOIN StarsIn ON
    title = movieTitle AND year = movieYear;
```

will omit the tuples for movies without a listed star but will include tuples for stars not in any listed movies, padded with NULL's.

6.3.9   Exercises for Section 6.3

Exercise 6.3.1: Write the following queries, based on the database schema

```
Product(maker, model, type)
PC(model, speed, ram, hd, rd, price)
Laptop(model, speed, ram, hd, screen, price)
Printer(model, color, type, price)
```

of Exercise 5.2.1. You should use at least one subquery in each of your answers and write each query in two significantly different ways (e.g., using different sets of the operators EXISTS, IN, ALL, and ANY).

* a) Find the makers of PC's with a speed of at least 1200.

  b) Find the printers with the highest price.

! c) Find the laptops whose speed is slower than that of any PC.

! d) Find the model number of the item (PC, laptop, or printer) with the highest price.

! e) Find the maker of the color printer with the lowest price.

!! f) Find the maker(s) of the PC(s) with the fastest processor among all those PC's that have the smallest amount of RAM.

Exercise 6.3.2: Write the following queries, based on the database schema

```
Classes(class, type, country, numGuns, bore, displacement)
Ships(name, class, launched)
Battles(name, date)
Outcomes(ship, battle, result)
```

of Exercise 5.2.4. You should use at least one subquery in each of your answers and write each query in two significantly different ways (e.g., using different sets of the operators EXISTS, IN, ALL, and ANY).

a) Find the countries whose ships had the largest number of guns.

*! b) Find the classes of ships at least one of which was sunk in a battle.

c) Find the names of the ships with a 16-inch bore.

d) Find the battles in which ships of the Kongo class participated.

!! e) Find the names of the ships whose number of guns was the largest for those ships of the same bore.

! **Exercise 6.3.3:** Write the query of Fig. 6.10 without any subqueries.

! **Exercise 6.3.4:** Consider expression $\pi_L(R_1 \bowtie R_2 \bowtie \cdots \bowtie R_n)$ of relational algebra, where L is a list of attributes all of which belong to R_1. Show that this expression can be written in SQL using subqueries only. More precisely, write an equivalent SQL expression where no FROM clause has more than one relation in its list.

! **Exercise 6.3.5:** Write the following queries without using the intersection or difference operators:

* a) The intersection query of Fig. 6.5.

b) The difference query of Example 6.17.

!! **Exercise 6.3.6:** We have noticed that certain operators of SQL are redundant, in the sense that they always can be replaced by other operators. For example, we saw that s IN R can be replaced by s = ANY R. Show that EXISTS and NOT EXISTS are redundant by explaining how to replace any expression of the form EXISTS R or NOT EXISTS R by an expression that does not involve EXISTS (except perhaps in the expression R itself). *Hint:* Remember that it is permissible to have a constant in the SELECT clause.

Exercise 6.3.7: For these relations from our running movie database schema

```
StarsIn(movieTitle, movieYear, starName)
MovieStar(name, address, gender, birthdate)
MovieExec(name, address, cert#, netWorth)
Studio(name, address, presC#)
```

describe the tuples that would appear in the following SQL expressions:

a) `Studio CROSS JOIN MovieExec;`

b) `StarsIn NATURAL FULL OUTER JOIN MovieStar;`

c) `StarsIn FULL OUTER JOIN MovieStar ON name = starName;`

*! Exercise 6.3.8: Using the database schema

```
Product(maker, model, type)
PC(model, speed, ram, hd, rd, price)
Laptop(model, speed, ram, hd, screen, price)
Printer(model, color, type, price)
```

write an SQL query that will produce information about all products — PC's, laptops, and printers — including their manufacturer if available, and whatever information about that product is relevant (i.e., found in the relation for that type of product).

Exercise 6.3.9: Using the two relations

```
Classes(class, type, country, numGuns, bore, displacement)
Ships(name, class, launched)
```

from our database schema of Exercise 5.2.4, write an SQL query that will produce all available information about ships, including that information available in the `Classes` relation. You need not produce information about classes if there are no ships of that class mentioned in `Ships`.

! Exercise 6.3.10: Repeat Exercise 6.3.9, but also include in the result, for any class C that is not mentioned in `Ships`, information about the ship that has the same name C as its class.

! Exercise 6.3.11: The join operators (other than outerjoin) we learned in this section are redundant, in the sense that they can always be replaced by select-from-where expressions. Explain how to write expressions of the following forms using select-from-where:

* a) `R CROSS JOIN S;`

b) `R NATURAL JOIN S;`

c) `R JOIN S ON C;`, where C is an SQL condition.

6.4 Full-Relation Operations

In this section we shall study some operations that act on relations as a whole, rather than on tuples individually or in small numbers (as do joins of several relations, for instance). First, we deal with the fact that SQL uses relations that are bags rather than sets, and a tuple can appear more than once in a relation. We shall see how to force the result of an operation to be a set in Section 6.4.1, and in Section 6.4.2 we shall see that it is also possible to prevent the elimination of duplicates in circumstances where SQL systems would normally eliminate them.

Then, we discuss how SQL supports the grouping and aggregation operator γ that we introduced in Section 5.4.4. SQL has aggregation operators and a GROUP-BY clause. There is also a "HAVING" clause that allows selection of certain groups in a way that depends on the group as a whole, rather than on individual tuples.

6.4.1 Eliminating Duplicates

As mentioned in Section 6.3.4, SQL's notion of relations differs from the abstract notion of relations presented in Chapter 3. A relation, being a set, cannot have more than one copy of any given tuple. When an SQL query creates a new relation, the SQL system does not ordinarily eliminate duplicates. Thus, the SQL response to a query may list the same tuple several times.

Recall from Section 6.2.4 that one of several equivalent definitions of the meaning of an SQL select-from-where query is that we begin with the Cartesian product of the relations referred to in the FROM clause. Each tuple of the product is tested by the condition in the WHERE clause, and the ones that pass the test are given to the output for projection according to the SELECT clause. This projection may cause the same tuple to result from different tuples of the product, and if so, each copy of the resulting tuple is printed in its turn. Further, since there is nothing wrong with an SQL relation having duplicates, the relations from which the Cartesian product is formed may have duplicates, and each identical copy is paired with the tuples from the other relations, yielding a proliferation of duplicates in the product.

If we do not wish duplicates in the result, then we may follow the keyword SELECT by the keyword DISTINCT. That word tells SQL to produce only one copy of any tuple and is the SQL analog of applying the δ operator of Section 5.4.1 to the result of the query.

Example 6.27: Let us reconsider the query of Fig. 6.9, where we asked for the producers of Harrison Ford's movies using no subqueries. As written, George Lucas will appear many times in the output. If we want only to see each producer once, we may change line (1) of the query to

```
1)   SELECT DISTINCT name
```

The Cost of Duplicate Elimination

One might be tempted to place DISTINCT after every SELECT, on the theory that it is harmless. In fact, it is very expensive to eliminate duplicates from a relation. The relation must be sorted or partitioned so that identical tuples appear next to each other. These algorithms are discussed starting in Section 15.2.2. Only by grouping the tuples in this way can we determine whether or not a given tuple should be eliminated. The time it takes to sort the relation so that duplicates may be eliminated is often greater than the time it takes to execute the query itself. Thus, duplicate elimination should be used judiciously if we want our queries to run fast.

Then, the list of producers will have duplicate occurrences of names eliminated before printing.

Incidentally, the query of Fig. 6.7, where we used subqueries, does not necessarily suffer from the problem of duplicate answers. True, the subquery at line (4) of Fig. 6.7 will produce the certificate number of George Lucas several times. However, in the "main" query of line (1), we examine each tuple of MovieExec once. Presumably, there is only one tuple for George Lucas in that relation, and if so, it is only this tuple that satisfies the WHERE clause of line (3). Thus, George Lucas is printed only once. □

6.4.2   Duplicates in Unions, Intersections, and Differences

Unlike the SELECT statement, which preserves duplicates as a default and only eliminates them when instructed to by the DISTINCT keyword, the union, intersection, and difference operations, which we introduced in Section 6.2.5, normally eliminate duplicates. That is, bags are converted to sets, and the set version of the operation is applied. In order to prevent the elimination of duplicates, we must follow the operator UNION, INTERSECT, or EXCEPT by the keyword ALL. If we do, then we get the bag semantics of these operators as was discussed in Section 5.3.2.

Example 6.28 : Consider again the union expression from Example 6.18, but now add the keyword ALL, as:

```
(SELECT title, year FROM Movie)
    UNION ALL
(SELECT movieTitle AS title, movieYear AS year FROM StarsIn);
```

Now, a title and year will appear as many times in the result as it appears in each of the relations Movie and StarsIn put together. For instance, if a movie appeared once in the Movie relation and there were three stars for that movie listed in `StarsIn` (so the movie appeared in three different tuples of `StarsIn`), then that movie's title and year would appear four times in the result of the union. □

As for union, the operators `INTERSECT ALL` and `EXCEPT ALL` are intersection and difference of bags. Thus, if R and S are relations, then the result of expression

$$R \text{ INTERSECT ALL } S$$

is the relation in which the number of times a tuple t appears is the minimum of the number of times it appears in R and the number of times it appears in S.

The result of expression

$$R \text{ EXCEPT ALL } S$$

has tuple t as many times as the difference of the number of times it appears in R minus the number of times it appears in S, provided the difference is positive. Each of these definitions is what we discussed for bags in Section 5.3.2.

6.4.3 Grouping and Aggregation in SQL

In Section 5.4.4, we introduced the grouping-and-aggregation operator γ for our extended relational algebra. Recall that this operator allows us to partition the tuples of a relation into "groups," based on the values of tuples in one or more attributes, as discussed in Section 5.4.3. We are then able to aggregate certain other columns of the relation by applying "aggregation" operators to those columns. If there are groups, then the aggregation is done separately for each group. SQL provides all the capability of the γ operator through the use of aggregation operators in `SELECT` clauses and a special `GROUP BY` clause.

6.4.4 Aggregation Operators

SQL uses the five aggregation operators `SUM`, `AVG`, `MIN`, `MAX`, and `COUNT` that we met in Section 5.4.2. These operators are used by applying them to a scalar-valued expression, typically a column name, in a `SELECT` clause. One exception is the expression `COUNT(*)`, which counts all the tuples in the relation that is constructed from the `FROM` clause and `WHERE` clause of the query.

In addition, we have the option of eliminating duplicates from the column before applying the aggregation operator by using the keyword `DISTINCT`. That is, an expression such as `COUNT(DISTINCT x)` counts the number of distinct values in column x. We could use any of the other operators in place of `COUNT` here, but expressions such as `SUM(DISTINCT x)` rarely make sense, since it asks us to sum the different values in column x.

Example 6.29: The following query finds the average net worth of all movie executives:

```
SELECT AVG(netWorth)
FROM MovieExec;
```

Note that there is no `WHERE` clause at all, so the keyword `WHERE` is properly omitted. This query examines the `netWorth` column of the relation

```
MovieExec(name, address, cert#, netWorth)
```

sums the values found there, one value for each tuple (even if the tuple is a duplicate of some other tuple), and divides the sum by the number of tuples. If there are no duplicate tuples, then this query gives the average net worth as we expect. If there were duplicate tuples, then a movie executive whose tuple appeared n times would have his or her net worth counted n times in the average. □

Example 6.30: The following query:

```
SELECT COUNT(*)
FROM StarsIn;
```

counts the number of tuples in the `StarsIn` relation. The similar query:

```
SELECT COUNT(starName)
FROM StarsIn;
```

counts the number of values in the `starName` column of the relation. Since duplicate values are not eliminated when we project onto the `starName` column in SQL, this count should be the same as the count produced by the query with `COUNT(*)`.

If we want to be certain that we do not count duplicate values more than once, we can use the keyword `DISTINCT` before the aggregated attribute, as:

```
SELECT COUNT(DISTINCT starName)
FROM StarsIn;
```

Now, each star is counted once, no matter in how many movies they appeared. □

6.4.5 Grouping

To group tuples, we use a `GROUP BY` clause, following the `WHERE` clause. The keywords `GROUP BY` are followed by a list of *grouping* attributes. In the simplest situation, there is only one relation reference in the `FROM` clause, and this relation has its tuples grouped according to their values in the grouping attributes. Whatever aggregation operators are used in the `SELECT` clause are applied only within groups.

Example 6.31: The problem of finding, from the relation

```
Movie(title, year, length, inColor, studioName, producerC#)
```

the sum of the lengths of all movies for each studio is expressed by

```
SELECT studioName, SUM(length)
FROM Movie
GROUP BY studioName;
```

We may imagine that the tuples of relation `Movie` are reorganized and grouped so that all the tuples for Disney studios are together, all those for MGM are together, and so on, as was suggested in Fig. 5.17. The sums of the length components of all the tuples in each group are calculated, and for each group, the studio name is printed along with that sum. □

Observe in Example 6.31 how the `SELECT` clause has two kinds of terms.

1. Aggregations, where an aggregate operator is applied to an attribute or expression involving attributes. As mentioned, these terms are evaluated on a per-group basis.

2. Attributes, such as `studioName` in this example, that appear in the `GROUP BY` clause. In a `SELECT` clause that has aggregations, only those attributes that are mentioned in the `GROUP BY` clause may appear unaggregated in the `SELECT` clause.

While queries involving `GROUP BY` generally have both grouping attributes and aggregations in the `SELECT` clause, it is technically not necessary to have both. For example, we could write

```
SELECT studioName
FROM Movie
GROUP BY studioName;
```

This query would group the tuples of `Movie` according to their studio name and then print the studio name for each group, no matter how many tuples there are with a given studio name. Thus, the above query has the same effect as

```
SELECT DISTINCT studioName
FROM Movie;
```

It is also possible to use a `GROUP BY` clause in a query about several relations. Such a query is interpreted by the following sequence of steps:

1. Evaluate the relation R expressed by the `FROM` and `WHERE` clauses. That is, relation R is the Cartesian product of the relations mentioned in the `FROM` clause, to which the selection of the `WHERE` clause is applied.

2. Group the tuples of R according to the attributes in the `GROUP BY` clause.

3. Produce as a result the attributes and aggregations of the `SELECT` clause, as if the query were about a stored relation R.

Example 6.32: Suppose we wish to print a table listing each producer's total length of film produced. We need to get information from the two relations

```
Movie(title, year, length, inColor, studioName, producerC#)
MovieExec(name, address, cert#, netWorth)
```

so we begin by taking their theta-join, equating the certificate numbers from the two relations. That step gives us a relation in which each `MovieExec` tuple is paired with the `Movie` tuples for all the movies of that producer. Note that an executive who is not a producer will not be paired with any movies, and therefore will not appear in the relation. Now, we can group the selected tuples of this relation according to the name of the producer. Finally, we sum the lengths of the movies in each group. The query is shown in Fig. 6.13. □

```
SELECT name, SUM(length)
FROM MovieExec, Movie
WHERE producerC# = cert#
GROUP BY name;
```

Figure 6.13: Computing the length of movies for each producer

6.4.6   `HAVING` Clauses

Suppose that we did not wish to include all of the producers in our table of Example 6.32. We could restrict the tuples prior to grouping in a way that would make undesired groups empty. For instance, if we only wanted the total length of movies for producers with a net worth of more than $10,000,000, we could change the third line of Fig. 6.13 to

```
WHERE producerC# = cert# AND networth > 10000000
```

However, sometimes we want to choose our groups based on some aggregate property of the group itself. Then we follow the `GROUP BY` clause with a `HAVING` clause. The latter clause consists of the keyword `HAVING` followed by a condition about the group.

Example 6.33: Suppose we want to print the total film length for only those producers who made at least one film prior to 1930. We may append to Fig. 6.13 the clause

---

Grouping, Aggregation, and Nulls

When tuples have nulls, there are a few rules we must remember:

- The value NULL is ignored in any aggregation. It does not contribute to a sum, average, or count, nor can it be the minimum or maximum in its column. For example, COUNT(*) is always a count of the number of tuples in a relation, but COUNT(A) is the number of tuples with non-NULL values for attribute A.

- On the other hand, NULL is treated as an ordinary value in a grouped attribute. For example, SELECT a, AVG(b) FROM R will produce a tuple with NULL for the value of a and the average value of b for the tuples with $a =$ NULL, if there is at least one tuple in R with a component NULL.

```
HAVING MIN(year) < 1930
```

The resulting query, shown in Fig. 6.14, would remove from the grouped relation all those groups in which every tuple had a year component 1930 or higher. □

```
SELECT name, SUM(length)
FROM MovieExec, Movie
WHERE producerC# = cert#
GROUP BY name
HAVING MIN(year) < 1930;
```

Figure 6.14: Computing the total length of film for early producers

There are several rules we must remember about HAVING clauses:

- An aggregation in a HAVING clause applies only to the tuples of the group being tested.

- Any attribute of relations in the FROM clause may be aggregated in the HAVING clause, but only those attributes that are in the GROUP BY list may appear unaggregated in the HAVING clause (the same rule as for the SELECT clause).

Order of Clauses in SQL Queries

We have now met all six clauses that can appear in an SQL "select-from-where" query: SELECT, FROM, WHERE, GROUP BY, HAVING, and ORDER BY. Only the first two are required, but you can't use a HAVING clause without a GROUP BY clause. Whichever additional clauses appear must be in the order listed above.

6.4.7   Exercises for Section 6.4

Exercise 6.4.1: Write each of the queries in Exercise 5.2.1 in SQL, making sure that duplicates are eliminated.

Exercise 6.4.2: Write each of the queries in Exercise 5.2.4 in SQL, making sure that duplicates are eliminated.

! **Exercise 6.4.3:** For each of your answers to Exercise 6.3.1, determine whether or not the result of your query can have duplicates. If so, rewrite the query to eliminate duplicates. If not, write a query without subqueries that has the same, duplicate-free answer.

! **Exercise 6.4.4:** Repeat Exercise 6.4.3 for your answers to Exercise 6.3.2.

*! **Exercise 6.4.5:** In Example 6.27, we mentioned that different versions of the query "find the producers of Harrison Ford's movies" can have different answers as bags, even though they yield the same set of answers. Consider the version of the query in Example 6.22, where we used a subquery in the FROM clause. Does this version produce duplicates, and if so, why?

Exercise 6.4.6: Write the following queries, based on the database schema

```
Product(maker, model, type)
PC(model, speed, ram, hd, rd, price)
Laptop(model, speed, ram, hd, screen, price)
Printer(model, color, type, price)
```

of Exercise 5.2.1, and evaluate your queries using the data of that exercise.

* a) Find the average speed of PC's.

  b) Find the average speed of laptops costing over $2000.

  c) Find the average price of PC's made by manufacturer "A."

! d) Find the average price of PC's and laptops made by manufacturer "D."

  e) Find, for each different speed the average price of a PC.

*! f) Find for each manufacturer, the average screen size of its laptops.

! g) Find the manufacturers that make at least three different models of PC.

! h) Find for each manufacturer who sells PC's the maximum price of a PC.

*! i) Find, for each speed of PC above 800, the average price.

!! j) Find the average hard disk size of a PC for all those manufacturers that make printers.

Exercise 6.4.7: Write the following queries, based on the database schema

```
Classes(class, type, country, numGuns, bore, displacement)
Ships(name, class, launched)
Battles(name, date)
Outcomes(ship, battle, result)
```

of Exercise 5.2.4, and evaluate your queries using the data of that exercise.

a) Find the number of battleship classes.

b) Find the average number of guns of battleship classes.

! c) Find the average number of guns of battleships. Note the difference between (b) and (c); do we weight a class by the number of ships of that class or not?

! d) Find for each class the year in which the first ship of that class was launched.

! e) Find for each class the number of ships of that class sunk in battle.

!! f) Find for each class with at least three ships the number of ships of that class sunk in battle.

!! g) The weight (in pounds) of the shell fired from a naval gun is approximately one half the cube of the bore (in inches). Find the average weight of the shell for each country's ships.

Exercise 6.4.8: In Example 5.23 we gave an example of the query: "find, for each star who has appeared in at least three movies, the earliest year in which they appeared." We wrote this query as a γ operation. Write it in SQL.

*! Exercise 6.4.9: The γ operator of extended relational algebra does not have a feature that corresponds to the HAVING clause of SQL. Is it possible to mimic an SQL query with a HAVING clause in relational algebra? If so, how would we do it in general?

6.5   Database Modifications

To this point, we have focused on the normal SQL query form: the select-from-where statement. There are a number of other statement forms that do not return a result, but rather change the state of the database. In this section, we shall focus on three types of statements that allow us to

1. Insert tuples into a relation.

2. Delete certain tuples from a relation.

3. Update values of certain components of certain existing tuples.

We refer to these three types of operations collectively as *modifications*.

6.5.1   Insertion

The basic form of insertion statement consists of:

1. The keywords `INSERT INTO`,

2. The name of a relation R,

3. A parenthesized list of attributes of the relation R,

4. The keyword `VALUES`, and

5. A tuple expression, that is, a parenthesized list of concrete values, one for each attribute in the list (3).

That is, the basic insertion form is

$$\texttt{INSERT INTO } R(A_1, \ldots, A_n) \texttt{ VALUES } (v_1, \ldots, v_n);$$

A tuple is created using the value v_i for attribute A_i, for $i = 1, 2, \ldots, n$. If the list of attributes does not include all attributes of the relation R, then the tuple created has default values for all missing attributes. The most common default value is `NULL`, the null value, but there are other options to be discussed in Section 6.6.4.

Example 6.34 : Suppose we wish to add Sydney Greenstreet to the list of stars of *The Maltese Falcon*. We say:

```
1) INSERT INTO StarsIn(movieTitle, movieYear, starName)
2) VALUES('The Maltese Falcon', 1942, 'Sydney Greenstreet');
```

The effect of executing this statement is that a tuple with the three components on line (2) is inserted into the relation `StarsIn`. Since all attributes of `StarsIn` are mentioned on line (1), there is no need to add default components. The values on line (2) are matched with the attributes on line (1) in the order given, so `'The Maltese Falcon'` becomes the value of the component for attribute `movieTitle`, and so on.   □

If, as in Example 6.34, we provide values for all attributes of the relation, then we may omit the list of attributes that follows the relation name. That is, we could just say:

```
INSERT INTO StarsIn
VALUES('The Maltese Falcon', 1942, 'Sydney Greenstreet');
```

However, if we take this option, we must be sure that the order of the values is the same as the standard order of attributes for the relation. We shall see in Section 6.6 how relation schemas are declared, and we shall see that as we do so we provide an order for the attributes. This order is assumed when matching values to attributes, if the list of attributes is missing from an INSERT statement.

- If you are not sure of the standard order for the attributes, it is best to list them in the INSERT clause in the order you choose for their values in the VALUES clause.

The simple INSERT described above only puts one tuple into a relation. Instead of using explicit values for one tuple, we can compute a set of tuples to be inserted, using a subquery. This subquery replaces the keyword VALUES and the tuple expression in the INSERT statement form described above.

Example 6.35: Suppose we want to add to the relation

```
Studio(name, address, presC#)
```

all movie studios that are mentioned in the relation

```
Movie(title, year, length, inColor, studioName, producerC#)
```

but do not appear in Studio. Since there is no way to determine an address or a president for such a studio, we shall have to be content with value NULL for attributes address and presC# in the inserted Studio tuples. A way to make this insertion is shown in Fig. 6.15.

```
1)   INSERT INTO Studio(name)
2)       SELECT DISTINCT studioName
3)       FROM Movie
4)       WHERE studioName NOT IN
5)           (SELECT name
6)            FROM Studio);
```

Figure 6.15: Adding new studios

Like most SQL statements with nesting, Fig. 6.15 is easiest to examine from the inside out. Lines (5) and (6) generate all the studio names in the relation

---

The Timing of Insertions

Figure 6.15 illustrates a subtle point about the semantics of SQL statements. In principle, the evaluation of the query of lines (2) through (6) should be accomplished prior to executing the insertion of line (1). Thus, there is no possibility that new tuples added to `Studio` at line (1) will affect the condition on line (4). However, for efficiency purposes, it is possible that an implementation will execute this statement so that changes to `Studio` are made as soon as new studios are found, during the execution of lines (2) through (6).

In this particular example, it does not matter whether or not insertions are delayed until the query is completely evaluated. However, there are other queries where the result can be changed by varying the timing of insertions. For example, suppose `DISTINCT` were removed from line (2) of Fig. 6.15. If we evaluate the query of lines (2) through (6) before doing any insertion, then a new studio name appearing in several `Movie` tuples would appear several times in the result of this query and therefore would be inserted several times into relation `Studio`. However, if we inserted new studios into `Studio` as soon as we found them during the evaluation of the query of lines (2) through (6), then the same new studio would not be inserted twice. Rather, as soon as the new studio was inserted once, its name would no longer satisfy the condition of lines (4) through (6), and it would not appear a second time in the result of the query of lines (2) through (6).

`Studio`. Thus, line (4) tests that a studio name from the `Movie` relation is none of these studios.

Now, we see that lines (2) through (6) produce the set of studio names found in `Movie` but not in `Studio`. The use of `DISTINCT` on line (2) assures that each studio will appear only once in this set, no matter how many movies it owns. Finally, line (1) inserts each of these studios, with `NULL` for the attributes `address` and `presC#`, into relation `Studio`.   □

6.5.2   Deletion

A deletion statement consists of:

1. The keywords `DELETE FROM`,

2. The name of a relation, say R,

3. The keyword `WHERE`, and

4. A condition.

That is, the form of a deletion is

$$\text{DELETE FROM } R \text{ WHERE } <\text{condition}>;$$

The effect of executing this statement is that every tuple satisfying the condition (4) will be deleted from relation R.

Example 6.36: We can delete from relation

```
StarsIn(movieTitle, movieYear, starName)
```

the fact that Sydney Greenstreet was a star in *The Maltese Falcon* by the SQL statement:

```
DELETE FROM StarsIn
WHERE movieTitle = 'The Maltese Falcon' AND
      movieYear = 1942 AND
      starName = 'Sydney Greenstreet';
```

Notice that unlike the insertion statement of Example 6.34, we cannot simply specify a tuple to be deleted. Rather, we must describe the tuple exactly by a WHERE clause. □

Example 6.37: Here is another example of a deletion. This time, we delete from relation

```
MovieExec(name, address, cert#, netWorth)
```

several tuples at once by using a condition that can be satisfied by more than one tuple. The statement

```
DELETE FROM MovieExec
WHERE netWorth < 10000000;
```

deletes all movie executives whose net worth is low — less than ten million dollars. □

6.5.3 Updates

While we might think of both insertions and deletions of tuples as "updates" to the database, an *update* in SQL is a very specific kind of change to the database: one or more tuples that already exist in the database have some of their components changed. The general form of an update statement is:

1. The keyword UPDATE,

2. A relation name, say R,

3. The keyword SET,

4. A list of formulas that each set an attribute of the relation R equal to the value of an expression or constant,

5. The keyword WHERE, and

6. A condition.

That is, the form of an update is

> UPDATE R SET <new-value assignments> WHERE <condition>;

Each new-value assignment (item 4 above) is an attribute, an equal sign, and a formula. If there is more than one assignment, they are separated by commas.

The effect of this statement is to find all the tuples in R that satisfy the condition (6). Each of these tuples are then changed by having the formulas of (4) evaluated and assigned to the components of the tuple for the corresponding attributes of R.

Example 6.38: Let us modify the relation

> MovieExec(name, address, cert#, netWorth)

by attaching the title Pres. in front of the name of every movie executive who is the president of a studio. The condition the desired tuples satisfy is that their certificate numbers appear in the presC# component of some tuple in the Studio relation. We express this update as:

```
1)   UPDATE MovieExec
2)   SET name = 'Pres. ' || name
3)   WHERE cert# IN (SELECT presC# FROM Studio);
```

Line (3) tests whether the certificate number from the MovieExec tuple is one of those that appear as a president's certificate number in Studio.

Line (2) performs the update on the selected tuples. Recall that the operator || denotes concatenation of strings, so the expression following the = sign in line (2) places the characters Pres. and a blank in front of the old value of the name component of this tuple. The new string becomes the value of the name component of this tuple; the effect is that 'Pres. ' has been prepended to the old value of name.   □

6.5.4   Exercises for Section 6.5

Exercise 6.5.1: Write the following database modifications, based on the database schema

```
Product(maker, model, type)
PC(model, speed, ram, hd, rd, price)
Laptop(model, speed, ram, hd, screen, price)
Printer(model, color, type, price)
```

of Exercise 5.2.1. Describe the effect of the modifications on the data of that exercise.

  a) Using two INSERT statements store in the database the fact that PC model 1100 is made by manufacturer C, has speed 1800, RAM 256, hard disk 80, a 20x DVD, and sells for $2499.

! b) Insert the facts that for every PC there is a laptop with the same manufacturer, speed, RAM, and hard disk, a 15-inch screen, a model number 1100 greater, and a price $500 more.

  c) Delete all PC's with less than 20 gigabytes of hard disk.

  d) Delete all Laptops made by a manufacturer that doesn't make printers.

  e) Manufacturer A buys manufacturer B. Change all products made by B so they are now made by A.

  f) For each PC, double the amount of RAM and add 20 gigabytes to the amount of hard disk. (Remember that several attributes can be changed by one UPDATE statement.)

! g) For each laptop made by manufacturer B, add one inch to the screen size and subtract $100 from the price.

Exercise 6.5.2: Write the following database modifications, based on the database schema

```
Classes(class, type, country, numGuns, bore, displacement)
Ships(name, class, launched)
Battles(name, date)
Outcomes(ship, battle, result)
```

of Exercise 5.2.4. Describe the effect of the modifications on the data of that exercise.

* a) The two British battleships of the Nelson class — Nelson and Rodney — were both launched in 1927, had nine 16-inch guns, and a displacement of 34,000 tons. Insert these facts into the database.

  b) Two of the three battleships of the Italian Vittorio Veneto class — Vittorio Veneto and Italia — were launched in 1940; the third ship of that class, Roma, was launched in 1942. Each had nine 15-inch guns and a displacement of 41,000 tons. Insert these facts into the database.

* c) Delete from Ships all ships sunk in battle.

* d) Modify the Classes relation so that gun bores are measured in centimeters (one inch = 2.5 centimeters) and displacements are measured in metric tons (one metric ton = 1.1 tons).

  e) Delete all classes with fewer than three ships.

6.6   Defining a Relation Schema in SQL

In this section we shall begin a discussion of *data definition*, the portions of SQL that involve describing the structure of information in the database. In contrast, the aspects of SQL discussed previously — queries and modifications — are often called *data manipulation*.[7]

The subject of this section is declaration of the schemas of stored relations. We shall see how to describe a new relation or *table* as it is called in SQL. Section 6.7 covers the declaration of "views," which are virtual relations that are not really stored in the database, while some of the more complex issues regarding constraints on relations are deferred to Chapter 7.

6.6.1   Data Types

To begin, let us introduce the principal atomic data types that are supported by SQL systems. All attributes must have a data type.

1. Character strings of fixed or varying length. The type CHAR(n) denotes a fixed-length string of n characters. That is, if an attribute has type CHAR(n), then in any tuple the component for this attribute will be a string of n characters. VARCHAR(n) denotes a string of up to n characters. Components for an attribute of this type will be strings of between 0 and n characters. SQL permits reasonable coercions between values of character-string types. Normally, a string is padded by trailing blanks if it becomes the value of a component that is a fixed-length string of greater length. For example, the string 'foo', if it became the value of a component for an attribute of type CHAR(5), would assume the value 'foo ' (with two blanks following the second o). The padding blanks can then be ignored if the value of this component were compared (see Section 6.1.3) with another string.

2. Bit strings of fixed or varying length. These strings are analogous to fixed and varying-length character strings, but their values are strings of bits rather than characters. The type BIT(n) denotes bit strings of length n, while BIT VARYING(n) denotes bit strings of length up to n.

3. The type BOOLEAN denotes an attribute whose value is logical. The possible values of such an attribute are TRUE, FALSE, and — although it would surprise George Boole — UNKNOWN.

4. The type INT or INTEGER (these names are synonyms) denotes typical integer values. The type SHORTINT also denotes integers, but the number

---

[7]Technically, the material of this section is in the realm of database design, and thus should have been covered earlier in the book, like the analogous ODL for object-oriented databases. However, there are good reasons to group all SQL study together, so we took the liberty of violating our own organization.

of bits permitted may be less, depending on the implementation (as with the types int and short int in C).

5. Floating-point numbers can be represented in a variety of ways. We may use the type FLOAT or REAL (these are synonyms) for typical floating-point numbers. A higher precision can be obtained with the type DOUBLE PRECISION; again the distinction between these types is as in C. SQL also has types that are real numbers with a fixed decimal point. For example, DECIMAL(n,d) allows values that consist of n decimal digits, with the decimal point assumed to be d positions from the right. Thus, 0123.45 is a possible value of type DECIMAL(6,2). NUMERIC is almost a synonym for DECIMAL, although there are possible implementation-dependent differences.

6. Dates and times can be represented by the data types DATE and TIME, respectively. Recall our discussion of date and time values in Section 6.1.4. These values are essentially character strings of a special form. We may, in fact, coerce dates and times to string types, and we may do the reverse if the string "makes sense" as a date or time.

6.6.2 Simple Table Declarations

The simplest form of declaration of a relation schema consists of the keywords CREATE TABLE followed by the name of the relation and a parenthesized list of the attribute names and their types.

Example 6.39 : The relation schema for our example MovieStar relation, which was described informally in Section 5.1, is expressed in SQL as in Fig. 6.16. The first two attributes, name and address, have each been declared to be character strings. However, with the name, we have made the decision to use a fixed-length string of 30 characters, padding a name out with blanks at the end if necessary and truncating a name to 30 characters if it is longer. In contrast, we have declared addresses to be variable-length character strings of up to 255 characters.[8] It is not clear that these two choices are the best possible, but we use them to illustrate two kinds of string data types.

The gender attribute has values that are a single letter, M or F. Thus, we can safely use a single character as the type of this attribute. Finally, the birthdate attribute naturally deserves the data type DATE. If this type were not available in a system that did not conform to the SQL standard, we could use CHAR(10) instead, since all DATE values are actually strings of 10 characters: eight digits and two hyphens. □

---

[8]The number 255 is not the result of some weird notion of what typical addresses look like. A single byte can store integers between 0 and 255, so it is possible to represent a varying-length character string of up to 255 bytes by a single byte for the count of characters plus the bytes to store the string itself. Commercial systems generally support longer varying-length strings, however.

```
1)  CREATE TABLE MovieStar (
2)      name CHAR(30),
3)      address VARCHAR(255),
4)      gender CHAR(1),
5)      birthdate DATE
    );
```

Figure 6.16: Declaring the relation schema for the `MovieStar` relation

6.6.3   Modifying Relation Schemas

We can delete a relation R by the SQL statement:

```
DROP TABLE R;
```

Relation R is no longer part of the database schema, and we can no longer access any of its tuples.

   More frequently than we would drop a relation that is part of a long-lived database, we may need to modify the schema of an existing relation. These modifications are done by a statement that begins with the keywords ALTER TABLE and the name of the relation. We then have several options, the most important of which are

1. ADD followed by a column name and its data type.

2. DROP followed by a column name.

Example 6.40: Thus, for instance, we could modify the `MovieStar` relation by adding an attribute **phone** with

```
ALTER TABLE MovieStar ADD phone CHAR(16);
```

As a result, the `MovieStar` scheme now has five attributes: the four mentioned in Fig. 6.16 and the attribute **phone**, which is a fixed-length string of 16 bytes. In the actual relation, tuples would all have components for **phone**, but we know of no phone numbers to put there. Thus, the value of each of these components would be NULL. In Section 6.6.4, we shall see how it is possible to choose another "default" value to be used instead of NULL for unknown values.

   As another example, we could delete the **birthdate** attribute by

```
ALTER TABLE MovieStar DROP birthdate;
```

□

6.6.4 Default Values

When we create or modify tuples, we sometimes do not have values for all components. For example, we mentioned in Example 6.40 that when we add a column to a relation scheme, the existing tuples do not have a known value, and it was suggested that NULL could be used in place of a "real" value. Or, we suggested in Example 6.35 that we could insert new tuples into the Studio relation knowing only the studio name and not the address or president's certificate number. Again, it would be necessary to use some value that says "I don't know" in place of real values for the latter two attributes.

To address these problems, SQL provides the NULL value, which becomes the value of any component whose value is not specified, with the exception of certain situations where the NULL value is not permitted (see Section 7.1). However, there are times when we would prefer to use another choice of *default* value, the value that appears in a column if no other value is known.

In general, any place we declare an attribute and its data type, we may add the keyword DEFAULT and an appropriate value. That value is either NULL or a constant. Certain other values that are provided by the system, such as the current time, may also be options.

Example 6.41: Let us consider Example 6.39. We might wish to use the character ? as the default for an unknown gender, and we might also wish to use the earliest possible date, DATE '0000-00-00' for an unknown birthdate. We could replace lines (4) and (5) of Fig. 6.16 by:

```
    4)      gender CHAR(1) DEFAULT '?',
    5)      birthdate DATE DEFAULT DATE '0000-00-00'
```

As another example, we could have declared the default value for new attribute phone to be 'unlisted' when we added this attribute in Example 6.40. The alteration statement would then look like:

```
    ALTER TABLE MovieStar ADD phone CHAR(16) DEFAULT 'unlisted';
```

□

6.6.5 Indexes

An *index* on an attribute A of a relation is a data structure that makes it efficient to find those tuples that have a fixed value for attribute A. Indexes usually help with queries in which their attribute A is compared with a constant, for instance $A = 3$, or even $A \leq 3$. The technology of implementing indexes on large relations is of central importance in the implementation of DBMS's. Chapter 13 is devoted to this topic.

When relations are very large, it becomes expensive to scan all the tuples of a relation to find those (perhaps very few) tuples that match a given condition. For example, consider the first query we examined:

```
SELECT *
FROM Movie
WHERE studioName = 'Disney' AND year = 1990;
```

from Example 6.1. There might be 10,000 `Movie` tuples, of which only 200 were made in 1990.

The naive way to implement this query is to get all 10,000 tuples and test the condition of the `WHERE` clause on each. It would be much more efficient if we had some way of getting only the 200 tuples from the year 1990 and testing each of them to see if the studio was Disney. It would be even more efficient if we could obtain directly only the 10 or so tuples that satisfied both the conditions of the `WHERE` clause — that the studio be Disney and the year be 1990; see the discussion of "multiattribute indexes," below.

Although the creation of indexes is not part of any SQL standard up to and including SQL-99, most commercial systems have a way for the database designer to say that the system should create an index on a certain attribute for a certain relation. The following syntax is typical. Suppose we want to have an index on attribute `year` for the relation `Movie`. Then we say:

```
CREATE INDEX YearIndex ON Movie(year);
```

The result will be that an index whose name is `YearIndex` will be created on attribute `year` of the relation `Movie`. Henceforth, SQL queries that specify a year may be executed by the SQL query processor in such a way that only those tuples of `Movie` with the specified year are ever examined; there is a resulting decrease in the time needed to answer the query.

Often, a DBMS allows us to build a single index on multiple attributes. This type of index takes values for several attributes and efficiently finds the tuples with the given values for these attributes.

Example 6.42 : Since `title` and `year` form a key for `Movie`, we might expect it to be common that values for both these attributes will be specified, or neither will. The following is a typical declaration of an index on these two attributes:

```
CREATE INDEX KeyIndex ON Movie(title, year);
```

Since (`title`, `year`) is a key, then when we are given a title and year, we know the index will find only one tuple, and that will be the desired tuple. In contrast, if the query specifies both the title and year, but only `YearIndex` is available, then the best the system can do is retrieve all the movies of that year and check through them for the given title.

If, as is often the case, the key for the multiattribute index is really the concatenation of the attributes in some order, then we can even use this index to find all the tuples with a given value in the first of the the attributes. Thus, part of the design of a multiattribute index is the choice of the order in which the attributes are listed. For instance, if we were more likely to specify a title than a year for a movie, then we would prefer to order the attributes as above; if a year were more likely to be specified, then we would ask for an index on (`year, title`). □

If we wish to delete the index, we simply use its name in a statement like:

```
DROP INDEX YearIndex;
```

6.6.6 Introduction to Selection of Indexes

Selection of indexes requires a trade-off by the database designer, and in practice, this choice is one of the principal factors that influence whether a database design is acceptable. Two important factors to consider are:

- The existence of an index on an attribute greatly speeds up queries in which a value for that attribute is specified, and in some cases can speed up joins involving that attribute as well.

- On the other hand, every index built for an attribute of some relation makes insertions, deletions, and updates to that relation more complex and time-consuming.

Index selection is one of the hardest parts of database design, since it requires estimating what the typical mix of queries and other operations on the database will be. If a relation is queried much more frequently than it is modified, then indexes on the attributes that are most frequently specified in queries make sense. Indexes are useful for attributes that tend to be compared with constants in `WHERE` clauses of queries, but indexes also are useful for attributes that appear frequently in join conditions.

Example 6.43: Recall Figure 6.3, where we suggested an exhaustive pairing of tuples to compute a join. An index on `Movie.title` would help us find the `Movie` tuple for *Star Wars* quickly, and then, after finding its producer-certificate-number, an index on `MovieExec.cert#` would help us quickly find that person in the `MovieExec` relation. □

If modifications are the predominant action, then we should be very conservative about creating indexes. Even then, it may be an efficiency gain to create an index on a frequently used attribute. In fact, since some modification commands involve querying the database (e.g., an `INSERT` with a select-from-where subquery or a `DELETE` with a condition) one must be very careful how one estimates the relative frequency of modifications and queries.

We do not yet have the details — how data is typically stored and how indexes are implemented — that are needed to see the complete picture. However, we can see part of the problem in the following example. We should be aware that the typical relation is stored over many disk blocks, and the principal cost of a query or modification is often the number of disk blocks that need to be brought to main memory (see Section 11.4.1). Thus, indexes that let us find a tuple without examining the entire relation can save a lot of time. However, the indexes themselves have to be stored, at least partially, on disk, so accessing and modifying the indexes themselves cost disk accesses. In fact, modification, since it requires one disk access to read a block and another disk access to write the changed block, is about twice as expensive as accessing the index or the data in a query.

Example 6.44: Let us consider the relation

    StarsIn(movieTitle, movieYear, starName)

Suppose that there are three database operations that we sometimes perform on this relation:

Q_1: We look for the title and year of movies in which a given star appeared. That is, we execute a query of the form:

```
SELECT movieTitle, movieYear
FROM StarsIn
WHERE starName = s;
```

for some constant s.

Q_2: We look for the stars that appeared in a given movie. That is, we execute a query of the form:

```
SELECT starName
FROM StarsIn
WHERE movieTitle = t AND movieYear = y;
```

for constants t and y.

I: We insert a new tuple into StarsIn. That is, we execute an insertion of the form:

```
INSERT INTO StarsIn VALUES(t, y, s);
```

for constants t, y, and s.

Let us make the following assumptions about the data:

1. StarsIn is stored in 10 disk blocks, so if we need to examine the entire relation the cost is 10.

2. On the average, a star has appeared in 3 movies and a movie has 3 stars.

3. Since the tuples for a given star or a given movie are likely to be spread over the 10 disk blocks of StarsIn, even if we have an index on starName or on the combination of movieTitle and movieYear, it will take 3 disk accesses to find the (average of) 3 tuples for a star or movie. If we have no index on the star or movie, respectively, then 10 disk accesses are required.

4. One disk access is needed to read a block of the index every time we use that index to locate tuples with a given value for the indexed attribute(s). If the index block must be modified (in the case of an insertion), then another disk access is needed to write back the modified block.

5. Likewise, in the case of an insertion, one disk access is needed to read a block on which the new tuple will be placed, and another disk access is needed to write back this block. We assume that, even without an index, we can find some block on which an additional tuple will fit, without scanning the entire relation.

Action	No Index	Star Index	Movie Index	Both Indexes
Q_1	10	4	10	4
Q_2	10	10	4	4
I	2	4	4	6
	$2 + 8p_1 + 8p_2$	$4 + 6p_2$	$4 + 6p_1$	$6 - 2p_1 - 2p_2$

Figure 6.17: Costs associated with the three actions, as a function of which indexes are selected

Figure 6.17 gives the costs of each of the three operations; Q_1 (query given a star), Q_2 (query given a movie), and I (insertion). If there is no index, then we must scan the entire relation for Q_1 or Q_2 (cost 10), while an insertion requires merely that we access a block with free space and rewrite it with the new tuple (cost of 2, since we assume that block can be found without an index). These observations explain the column labeled "No Index."

If there is an index on stars only, then Q_2 still requires a scan of the entire relation (cost 10). However, Q_1 can be answered by accessing one index block to find the three tuples for a given star and then making three more accesses to find those tuples. Insertion I requires that we read and write both a disk block for the index and a disk block for the data, for a total of 4 disk accesses.

The case where there is an index on movies only is symmetric to the case for stars only. Finally, if there are indexes on both stars and movies, then it takes 4 disk accesses to answer either Q_1 or Q_2. However, insertion I requires that we read and write two index blocks as well as a data block, for a total of 6 disk accesses. That observation explains the last column in Fig. 6.17.

The final row in Fig. 6.17 gives the average cost of an action, on the assumption that the fraction of the time we do Q_1 is p_1 and the fraction of the time we do Q_2 is p_2; therefore, the fraction of the time we do I is $1 - p_1 - p_2$.

Depending on p_1 and p_2, any of the four choices of index/no index can yield the best average cost for the three actions. For example, if $p_1 = p_2 = 0.1$, then the expression $2 + 8p_1 + 8p_2$ is the smallest, so we would prefer not to create any indexes. That is, if we are doing mostly insertion, and very few queries, then we don't want an index. On the other hand, if $p_1 = p_2 = 0.4$, then the formula $6 - 2p_1 - 2p_2$ turns out to be the smallest, so we would prefer indexes on both `starName` and on the (`movieTitle`, `movieYear`) combination. Intuitively, if we are doing a lot of queries, and the number of queries specifying movies and stars are roughly equally frequent, then both indexes are desired.

If we have $p_1 = 0.5$ and $p_2 = 0.1$, then it turns out that an index on stars only gives the best average value, because $4 + 6p_2$ is the formula with the smallest value. Likewise, $p_1 = 0.1$ and $p_2 = 0.5$ tells us to create an index on only movies. The intuition is that if only one type of query is frequent, create only the index that helps that type of query.   □

6.6.7   Exercises for Section 6.6

* **Exercise 6.6.1:** In this section, we gave a formal declaration for only the relation `MovieStar` among the five relations of our running example. Give suitable declarations for the other four relations:

```
Movie(title, year, length, inColor, studioName, producerC#)
StarsIn(movieTitle, movieYear, starName)
MovieExec(name, address, cert#, netWorth)
Studio(name, address, presC#)
```

Exercise 6.6.2: Below we repeat once again the informal database schema from Exercise 5.2.1.

```
Product(maker, model, type)
PC(model, speed, ram, hd, rd, price)
Laptop(model, speed, ram, hd, screen, price)
Printer(model, color, type, price)
```

Write the following declarations:

   a) A suitable schema for relation `Product`.

   b) A suitable schema for relation `PC`.

 * c) A suitable schema for relation `Laptop`.

   d) A suitable schema for relation `Printer`.

   e) An alteration to your `Printer` schema from (d) to delete the attribute `color`.

* f) An alteration to your Laptop schema from (c) to add the attribute cd. Let the default value for this attribute be 'none' if the laptop does not have a CD reader.

Exercise 6.6.3: Here is the informal schema from Exercise 5.2.4.

```
Classes(class, type, country, numGuns, bore, displacement)
Ships(name, class, launched)
Battles(name, date)
Outcomes(ship, battle, result)
```

Write the following declarations:

a) A suitable schema for relation Classes.

b) A suitable schema for relation Ships.

c) A suitable schema for relation Battles.

d) A suitable schema for relation Outcomes.

e) An alteration to your Classes relation from (a) to delete the attribute bore.

f) An alteration to your Ships relation from (b) to include the attribute yard giving the shipyard where the ship was built.

! **Exercise 6.6.4:** Explain the difference between the statement DROP R and the statement DELETE FROM R.

Exercise 6.6.5: Suppose that the relation StarsIn discussed in Example 6.44 required 100 blocks rather than 10, but all other assumptions of that example continued to hold. Give formulas in terms of p_1 and p_2 to measure the cost of queries Q_1 and Q_2 and insertion I, under the four combinations of index/no index discussed there.

6.7 View Definitions

Relations that are defined with a CREATE TABLE statement actually exist in the database. That is, an SQL system stores tables in some physical organization. They are persistent, in the sense that they can be expected to exist indefinitely and not to change unless they are explicitly told to change by an INSERT or one of the other modification statements we discussed in Section 6.5.

There is another class of SQL relations, called *views*, that do not exist physically. Rather, they are defined by an expression much like a query. Views, in turn, can be queried as if they existed physically, and in some cases, we can even modify views.

6.7.1   Declaring Views

The simplest form of view definition is

1. The keywords CREATE VIEW,

2. The name of the view,

3. The keyword AS, and

4. A query Q. This query is the definition of the view. Any time we query the view, SQL behaves as if Q were executed at that time and the query were applied to the relation produced by Q.

That is, a simple view declaration has the form

$$\text{CREATE VIEW} <\text{view-name}> \text{AS} <\text{view-definition}>;$$

Example 6.45: Suppose we want to have a view that is a part of the

```
Movie(title, year, length, inColor, studioName, producerC#)
```

relation, specifically, the titles and years of the movies made by Paramount Studios. We can define this view by

```
1)   CREATE VIEW ParamountMovie AS
2)       SELECT title, year
3)       FROM Movie
4)       WHERE studioName = 'Paramount';
```

First, the name of the view is ParamountMovie, as we see from line (1). The attributes of the view are those listed in line (2), namely title and year. The definition of the view is the query of lines (2) through (4).   □

6.7.2   Querying Views

Relation ParamountMovie does not contain tuples in the usual sense. Rather, if we query ParamountMovie, the appropriate tuples are obtained from the base table Movie, so the query can be answered. As a result, we can ask the same query about ParamountMovie twice and get different answers. The reason is that, even though we have not changed the definition of view ParamountMovie, the base table Movie may have changed in the interim.

Example 6.46: We may query the view ParamountMovie just as if it were a stored table, for instance:

```
SELECT title
FROM ParamountMovie
WHERE year = 1979;
```

Relations, Tables, and Views

SQL programmers tend to use the term "table" instead of "relation." The reason is that it is important to make a distinction between stored relations, which are "tables," and virtual relations, which are "views." Now that we know the distinction between a table and a view, we shall use "relation" only where either a table or view could be used. When we want to emphasize that a relation is stored, rather than a view, we shall sometimes use the term "base relation" or "base table."

There is also a third kind of relation, one that is neither a view nor stored permanently. These relations are temporary results, as might be constructed for some subquery. Temporaries will also be referred to as "relations" subsequently.

The definition of the view `ParamountMovie` is used to turn the query above into a new query that addresses only the base table `Movie`. We shall illustrate how to convert queries on views to queries on base tables in Section 6.7.5. However, in this simple case it is not hard to deduce what the example query about the view means. We observe that `ParamountMovie` differs from `Movie` in only two ways:

1. Only attributes `title` and `year` are produced by `ParamountMovie`.

2. The condition `studioName = 'Paramount'` is part of any `WHERE` clause about `ParamountMovie`.

Since our query wants only the `title` produced, (1) does not present a problem. For (2), we need only to introduce the condition `studioName = 'Paramount'` into the `WHERE` clause of our query. Then, we can use `Movie` in place of `ParamountMovie` in the `FROM` clause, assured that the meaning of our query is preserved. Thus, the query:

```
SELECT title
FROM Movie
WHERE studioName = 'Paramount' AND year = 1979;
```

is a query about the base table `Movie` that has the same effect as our original query about the view `ParamountMovie`. Note that it is the job of the SQL system to do this translation. We show the reasoning process only to indicate what a query about a view means. □

Example 6.47 : It is also possible to write queries involving both views and base tables. An example is

```
SELECT DISTINCT starName
FROM ParamountMovie, StarsIn
WHERE title = movieTitle AND year = movieYear;
```

This query asks for the name of all stars of movies made by Paramount. Note that the use of DISTINCT assures that stars will be listed only once, even if they appeared in several Paramount movies. □

Example 6.48 : Let us consider a more complicated query used to define a view. Our goal is a relation MovieProd with movie titles and the names of their producers. The query defining the view involves both relation

```
Movie(title, year, length, inColor, studioName, producerC#)
```

from which we get a producer's certificate number, and the relation

```
MovieExec(name, address, cert#, netWorth)
```

where we connect the certificate to the name. We may write:

```
CREATE VIEW MovieProd AS
    SELECT title, name
    FROM Movie, MovieExec
    WHERE producerC# = cert#;
```

We can query this view as if it were a stored relation. For instance, to find the producer of *Gone With the Wind*, ask:

```
SELECT name
FROM MovieProd
WHERE title = 'Gone With the Wind';
```

As with any view, this query is treated as if it were an equivalent query over the base tables alone, such as:

```
SELECT name
FROM Movie, MovieExec
WHERE producerC# = cert# AND title = 'Gone With the Wind';
```

□

6.7.3 Renaming Attributes

Sometimes, we might prefer to give a view's attributes names of our own choosing, rather than use the names that come out of the query defining the view. We may specify the attributes of the view by listing them, surrounded by parentheses, after the name of the view in the CREATE VIEW statement. For instance, we could rewrite the view definition of Example 6.48 as:

```
CREATE VIEW MovieProd(movieTitle, prodName) AS
    SELECT title, name
    FROM Movie, MovieExec
    WHERE producerC# = cert#;
```

The view is the same, but its columns are headed by attributes `movieTitle` and `prodName` instead of `title` and `name`.

6.7.4 Modifying Views

In limited circumstances it is possible to execute an insertion, deletion, or update to a view. At first, this idea makes no sense at all, since the view does not exist the way a base table (stored relation) does. What could it mean, say, to insert a new tuple into a view? Where would the tuple go, and how would the database system remember that it was supposed to be in the view?

For many views, the answer is simply "you can't do that." However, for sufficiently simple views, called *updatable views*, it is possible to translate the modification of the view into an equivalent modification on a base table, and the modification can be done to the base table instead. SQL provides a formal definition of when modifications to a view are permitted. The SQL rules are complex, but roughly, they permit modifications on views that are defined by selecting (using `SELECT`, not `SELECT DISTINCT`) some attributes from one relation R (which may itself be an updatable view). Two important technical points:

- The `WHERE` clause must not involve R in a subquery.

- The list in the `SELECT` clause must include enough attributes that for every tuple inserted into the view, we can fill the other attributes out with `NULL` values or the proper default and have a tuple of the base relation that will yield the inserted tuple of the view.

Example 6.49: Suppose we try to insert into view `ParamountMovie` of Example 6.45 a tuple like:

```
INSERT INTO ParamountMovie
VALUES('Star Trek', 1979);
```

View `ParamountMovie` almost meets the SQL updatability conditions, since the view asks only for some components of some tuples of one base table:

```
Movie(title, year, length, inColor, studioName, producerC#)
```

The only problem is that since attribute `studioName` of `Movie` is not an attribute of the view, the tuple we insert into `Movie` would have `NULL` rather than `'Paramount'` as its value for `studioName`. That tuple does not meet the condition that its studio be Paramount.

Thus, to make the view `ParamountMovie` updatable, we shall add attribute `studioName` to its `SELECT` clause, even though it is obvious to us that the studio name will be Paramount. The revised definition of view `ParamountMovie` is:

```
CREATE VIEW ParamountMovie AS
    SELECT studioName, title, year
    FROM Movie
    WHERE studioName = 'Paramount';
```

Then, we write the insertion into updatable view `ParamountMovie` as:

```
INSERT INTO ParamountMovie
VALUES('Paramount', 'Star Trek', 1979);
```

To effect the insertion, we invent a `Movie` tuple that yields the inserted view tuple when the view definition is applied to `Movie`. For the particular insertion above, the `studioName` component is `'Paramount'`, the `title` component is `'Star Trek'`, and the `year` component is 1979.

The other three attributes that do not appear in the view — `length`, `inColor`, and `producerC#` — surely exist in the inserted `Movie` tuple. However, we cannot deduce their values. As a result, the new `Movie` tuple must have in the components for each of these three attributes the appropriate default value: either `NULL` or some other default that was declared for an attribute. For example, if the default value 0 was declared for attribute `length`, but the other two use `NULL` for the default, then the resulting inserted `Movie` tuple would be:

title	year	length	inColor	studioName	producerC#
'Star Trek'	1979	0	NULL	'Paramount'	NULL

□

We may also delete from an updatable view. The deletion, like the insertion, is passed through to the underlying relation R and causes the deletion of every tuple of R that gives rise to a deleted tuple of the view.

Example 6.50: Suppose we wish to delete from the updatable Paramount-Movie view all movies with "Trek" in their titles. We may issue the deletion statement

```
DELETE FROM ParamountMovie
WHERE title LIKE '%Trek%';
```

This deletion is translated into an equivalent deletion on the `Movie` base table; the only difference is that the condition defining the view `ParamountMovie` is added to the conditions of the `WHERE` clause.

```
DELETE FROM Movie
WHERE title LIKE '%Trek%' AND studioName = 'Paramount';
```

Why Some Views Are Not Updatable

Consider the view `MovieProd` of Example 6.48, which relates movie titles and producers' names. This view is not updatable according to the SQL definition, because there are two relations in the `FROM` clause: `Movie` and `MovieExec`. Suppose we tried to insert a tuple like

('Greatest Show on Earth', 'Cecil B. DeMille')

We would have to insert tuples into both `Movie` and `MovieExec`. We could use the default value for attributes like `length` or `address`, but what could be done for the two equated attributes `producerC#` and `cert#` that both represent the unknown certificate number of DeMille? We could use `NULL` for both of these. However, when joining relations with `NULL`'s, SQL does not recognize two `NULL` values as equal (see Section 6.1.5). Thus, 'Greatest Show on Earth' would not be connected with 'Cecil B. DeMille' in the `MovieProd` view, and our insertion would not have been done correctly.

---

is the resulting delete statement. □

Similarly, an update on an updatable view is passed through to the underlying relation. The view update thus has the effect of updating all tuples of the underlying relation that give rise in the view to updated view tuples.

Example 6.51: The view update

```
UPDATE ParamountMovie
SET year = 1979
WHERE title = 'Star Trek the Movie';
```

is turned into the base-table update

```
UPDATE Movie
SET year = 1979
WHERE title = 'Star Trek the Movie' AND
    studioName = 'Paramount';
```

□

A final kind of modification of a view is to delete it altogether. This modification may be done whether or not the view is updatable. A typical `DROP` statement is

```
DROP VIEW ParamountMovie;
```

Note that this statement deletes the definition of the view, so we may no longer make queries or issue modification commands involving this view. However dropping the view does not affect any tuples of the underlying relation `Movie`. In contrast,

```
DROP TABLE Movie
```

would not only make the `Movie` table go away. It would also make the view `ParamountMovie` unusable, since a query that used it would indirectly refer to the nonexistent relation `Movie`.

6.7.5   Interpreting Queries Involving Views

We can get a good idea of what view queries mean by following the way a query involving a view would be processed. The matter is taken up in more generality in Section 16.2, when we examine query processing in general.

The basic idea is illustrated in Fig. 6.18. A query Q is there represented by its expression tree in relational algebra. This expression tree uses as leaves some relations that are views. We have suggested two such leaves, the views V and W. To interpret Q in terms of base tables, we find the definition of the views V and W. These definitions are also expressed as expression trees of relational algebra.

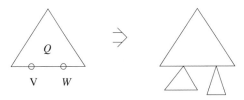

Figure 6.18: Substituting view definitions for view references

To form the query over base tables, we substitute, for each leaf in the tree for Q that is a view, the root of a copy of the tree that defines that view. Thus, in Fig. 6.18 we have shown the leaves labeled V and W replaced by the definitions of these views. The resulting tree is a query over base tables that is equivalent to the original query about views.

Example 6.52: Let us consider the view definition and query of Example 6.46. Recall the definition of view `ParamountMovie` is:

```
CREATE VIEW ParamountMovie AS
    SELECT title, year
    FROM Movie
    WHERE studioName = 'Paramount';
```

An expression tree for the query that defines this view is shown in Fig. 6.19. The query of Example 6.46 is

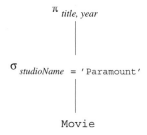

Figure 6.19: Expression tree for view `ParamountMovie`

```
SELECT title
FROM ParamountMovie
WHERE year = 1979;
```

asking for the Paramount movies made in 1979. This query has the expression tree shown in Fig. 6.20. Note that the one leaf of this tree represents the view `ParamountMovie`.

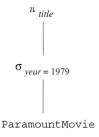

Figure 6.20: Expression tree for the query

We therefore interpret the query by substituting the tree of Fig. 6.19 for the leaf `ParamountMovie` in Fig. 6.20. The resulting tree is shown in Fig. 6.21.

The tree of Fig. 6.21 is an acceptable interpretation of the query. However, it is expressed in an unnecessarily complex way. An SQL system would apply transformations to this tree in order to make it look like the expression tree for the query we suggested in Example 6.46:

```
SELECT title
FROM Movie
WHERE studioName = 'Paramount' AND year = 1979;
```

For example, we can move the projection $\pi_{title,\ year}$ above the selection $\sigma_{year=1979}$. The reason is that delaying a projection until after a selection can never change the result of an expression. Then, we have two projections in a row, first onto `title` and `year` and then onto `title` alone. Clearly the first of these is redundant, and we can eliminate it. Thus, the two projections can be replaced by a single projection onto `title`.

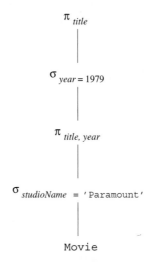

Figure 6.21: Expressing the query in terms of base tables

The two selections can also be combined. In general, two consecutive selections can be replaced by one selection for the AND of their conditions. The resulting expression tree is shown in Fig. 6.22. It is the tree that we would obtain from the query

```
SELECT title
FROM Movie
WHERE studioName = 'Paramount' AND year = 1979;
```

directly. □

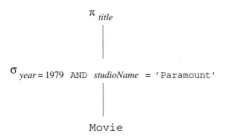

Figure 6.22: Simplifying the query over base tables

6.7.6 Exercises for Section 6.7

Exercise 6.7.1: From the following base tables of our running example

```
MovieStar(name, address, gender, birthdate)
MovieExec(name, address, cert#, netWorth)
Studio(name, address, presC#)
```

Construct the following views:

* a) A view `RichExec` giving the name, address, certificate number and net worth of all executives with a net worth of at least $10,000,000.

  b) A view `StudioPres` giving the name, address, and certificate number of all executives who are studio presidents.

  c) A view `ExecutiveStar` giving the name, address, gender, birth date, certificate number, and net worth of all individuals who are both executives and stars.

Exercise 6.7.2: Which of the views of Exercise 6.7.1 are updatable?

Exercise 6.7.3: Write each of the queries below, using one or more of the views from Exercise 6.7.1 and no base tables.

  a) Find the names of females who are both stars and executives.

* b) Find the names of those executives who are both studio presidents and worth at least $10,000,000.

! c) Find the names of studio presidents who are also stars and are worth at least $50,000,000.

*! **Exercise 6.7.4:** For the view and query of Example 6.48:

  a) Show the expression tree for the view `MovieProd`.

  b) Show the expression tree for the query of that example.

  c) Build from your answers to (a) and (b) an expression for the query in terms of base tables.

  d) Explain how to change your expression from (c) so it is an equivalent expression that matches the suggested solution in Example 6.48.

! **Exercise 6.7.5:** For each of the queries of Exercise 6.7.3, express the query and views as relational-algebra expressions, substitute for the uses of the view in the query expression, and simplify the resulting expressions as best you can. Write SQL queries corresponding to your resulting expressions on the base tables.

Exercise 6.7.6: Using the base tables

```
Classes(class, type, country, numGuns, bore, displacement)
Ships(name, class, launched)
```

from Exercise 5.2.4:

a) Define a view `BritishShips` that gives for each ship of Great Britain its class, type, number of guns, bore, displacement, and year launched.

b) Write a query using your view from (a) asking for the number of guns and displacements of all British battleships launched before 1919.

! c) Express the query of (b) and view of (a) as relational-algebra expressions, substitute for the uses of the view in the query expression, and simplify the resulting expressions as best you can.

! d) Write an SQL query corresponding to your expression from (c) on the base tables `Classes` and `Ships`.

6.8   Summary of Chapter 6

✦ *SQL*: The language SQL is the principal query language for relational database systems. The current standard is called SQL-99 or SQL3. Commercial systems generally vary from this standard.

✦ *Select-From-Where Queries*: The most common form of SQL query has the form select-from-where. It allows us to take the product of several relations (the `FROM` clause), apply a condition to the tuples of the result (the `WHERE` clause), and produce desired components (the `SELECT` clause).

✦ *Subqueries*: Select-from-where queries can also be used as subqueries within a `WHERE` clause or `FROM` clause of another query. The operators `EXISTS`, `IN`, `ALL`, and `ANY` may be used to express boolean-valued conditions about the relations that are the result of a subquery in a `WHERE` clause.

✦ *Set Operations on Relations*: We can take the union, intersection, or difference of relations by connecting the relations, or connecting queries defining the relations, with the keywords `UNION`, `INTERSECT`, and `EXCEPT`, respectively.

✦ *Join Expressions*: SQL has operators such as `NATURAL JOIN` that may be applied to relations, either as queries by themselves or to define relations in a `FROM` clause.

✦ *Null Values*: SQL provides a special value `NULL` that appears in components of tuples for which no concrete value is available. The arithmetic and logic of `NULL` is unusual. Comparison of any value to `NULL`, even another `NULL`, gives the truth value `UNKNOWN`. That truth value, in turn, behaves in boolean-valued expressions as if it were halfway between `TRUE` and `FALSE`.

✦ *Outerjoins*: SQL provides an `OUTER JOIN` operator that joins relations but also includes in the result dangling tuples from one or both relations; the dangling tuples are padded with `NULL`'s in the resulting relation.

✦ *The Bag Model of Relations*: SQL actually regards relations as bags of tuples, not sets of tuples. We can force elimination of duplicate tuples with the keyword `DISTINCT`, while keyword `ALL` allows the result to be a bag in certain circumstances where bags are not the default.

✦ *Aggregations*: The values appearing in one column of a relation can be summarized (aggregated) by using one of the keywords `SUM`, `AVG` (average value), `MIN`, `MAX`, or `COUNT`. Tuples can be partitioned prior to aggregation with the keywords `GROUP BY`. Certain groups can be eliminated with a clause introduced by the keyword `HAVING`.

✦ *Modification Statements*: SQL allows us to change the tuples in a relation. We may `INSERT` (add new tuples), `DELETE` (remove tuples), or `UPDATE` (change some of the existing tuples), by writing SQL statements using one of these three keywords.

✦ *Data Definition*: SQL has statements to declare elements of a database schema. The `CREATE TABLE` statement allows us to declare the schema for stored relations (called tables), specifying the attributes and their types, and default values.

✦ *Altering Schemas*: We can change aspects of the database schema with an `ALTER` statement. These changes include adding and removing attributes from relation schemas and changing the default value associated with an attribute or domain. We may also use a `DROP` statement to completely eliminate relations or other schema elements.

✦ *Indexes*: While not part of the SQL standard, commerical SQL systems allow the declaration of indexes on attributes; these indexes speed up certain queries or modifications that involve specification of a value for the indexed attribute.

✦ *Views*: A view is a definition of how one relation (the view) may be constructed from tables stored in the database. Views may be queried as if they were stored relations, and an SQL system modifies queries about a view so the query is instead about the base tables that are used to define the view.

6.9 References for Chapter 6

The SQL2 and SQL-99 standards are published on-line via anonymous FTP. The primary site is `ftp://jerry.ece.umassd.edu/isowg3`, with mirror sites at `ftp://math0.math.ecu.edu/isowg3` and `ftp://tiu.ac.jp/iso/wg3`. In each case the subdirectory is `dbl/BASEdocs`. As of the time of the printing of this book, not all sites were accepting FTP requests. We shall endeavour to keep the reader up to date on the situation through this book's Web site (see the Preface).

Several books are available that give more details of SQL programming. Some of our favorites are [2], [4], and [6]. [5] is an early exposition of the recent SQL-99 standard.

SQL was first defined in [3]. It was implemented as part of System R [1], one of the first generation of relational database prototypes.

1. Astrahan, M. M. et al., "System R: a relational approach to data management," *ACM Transactions on Database Systems* **1**:2, pp. 97–137, 1976.

2. Celko, J., *SQL for Smarties*, Morgan-Kaufmann, San Francisco, 1999.

3. Chamberlin, D. D., et al., "SEQUEL 2: a unified approach to data definition, manipulation, and control," *IBM Journal of Research and Development* **20**:6, pp. 560–575, 1976.

4. Date, C. J. and H. Darwen, *A Guide to the SQL Standard*, Addison-Wesley, Reading, MA, 1997.

5. Gulutzan, P. and T. Pelzer, *SQL-99 Complete, Really*, R&D Books, Lawrence, KA, 1999.

6. Melton, J. and A. R. Simon, *Understanding the New SQL: A Complete Guide*, Morgan-Kaufmann, San Francisco, 1993.

Chapter 7

Constraints and Triggers

In this chapter we shall cover those aspects of SQL that let us create "active" elements. An *active* element is an expression or statement that we write once, store in the database, and expect the element to execute at appropriate times. The time of action might be when a certain event occurs, such as an insertion into a particular relation, or it might be whenever the database changes so that a certain boolean-valued condition becomes true.

One of the serious problems faced by writers of applications that update the database is that the new information could be wrong in a variety of ways. For example, there are often typographical or transcription errors in manually entered data. The most straightforward way to make sure that database modifications do not allow inappropriate tuples in relations is to write application programs so every insertion, deletion, and update command has associated with it the checks necessary to assure correctness. Unfortunately, the correctness requirements are frequently complex, and they are always repetitive; application programs must make the same tests after every modification.

Fortunately, SQL provides a variety of techniques for expressing *integrity constraints* as part of the database schema. In this chapter we shall study the principal methods. First are key constraints, where an attribute or set of attributes is declared to be a key for a relation. Next, we consider a form of referential integrity, called "foreign-key constraints," which are the requirement that a value in an attribute or attributes of one relation (e.g., a presC# in Studio) must also appear as a value in an attribute or attributes of another relation (e.g., cert# of MovieExec).

Then, we consider constraints on attributes, tuples, and relations as a whole, and we cover interrelation constraints called "assertions." Finally, we discuss "triggers," which are a form of active element that is called into play on certain specified events, such as insertion into a specific relation.

7.1 Keys and Foreign Keys

Perhaps the most important kind of constraint in a database is a declaration that a certain attribute or set of attributes forms a key for a relation. If a set of attributes S is a key for relation R, then any two tuples of R must disagree in at least one attribute in the set S. Note that this rule applies even to duplicate tuples; i.e., if R has a declared key, then R cannot have duplicates.

A key constraint, like many other constraints, is declared within the CREATE TABLE command of SQL. There are two similar ways to declare keys: using the keywords PRIMARY KEY or the keyword UNIQUE. However, a table may have only one primary key but any number of "unique" declarations.

SQL also uses the term "key" in connection with certain referential-integrity constraints. These constraints, called "foreign-key constraints," assert that a value appearing in one relation must also appear in the primary-key component(s) of another relation. We shall take up foreign-key constraints in Section 7.1.4.

7.1.1 Declaring Primary Keys

A relation may have only one primary key. There are two ways to declare a primary key in the CREATE TABLE statement that defines a stored relation.

1. We may declare one attribute to be a primary key when that attribute is listed in the relation schema.

2. We may add to the list of items declared in the schema (which so far have only been attributes) an additional declaration that says a particular attribute or set of attributes forms the primary key.

For method (1), we append the keywords PRIMARY KEY after the attribute and its type. For method (2), we introduce a new element in the list of attributes consisting of the keywords PRIMARY KEY and a parenthesized list of the attribute or attributes that form this key. Note that if the key consists of more than one attribute, we need to use method (2).

The effect of declaring a set of attributes S to be a primary key for relation R is twofold:

1. Two tuples in R cannot agree on all of the attributes in set S. Any attempt to insert or update a tuple that violates this rule causes the DBMS to reject the action that caused the violation.

2. Attributes in S are not allowed to have NULL as a value for their components.

Example 7.1: Let us reconsider the schema for relation MovieStar from Example 6.39. The primary key for this relation is name. Thus, we can add this

```
1)   CREATE TABLE MovieStar (
2)       name CHAR(30) PRIMARY KEY,
3)       address VARCHAR(255),
4)       gender CHAR(1),
5)       birthdate DATE
     );
```

Figure 7.1: Making `name` the primary key

fact to the line declaring `name`. Figure 7.1 is a revision of Fig. 6.16 that reflects this change.

Alternatively, we can use a separate definition of the primary key. After line (5) of Fig. 6.16 we add a declaration of the primary key, and we have no need to declare it in line (2). The resulting schema declaration would look like Fig. 7.2. □

```
1)   CREATE TABLE MovieStar (
2)       name CHAR(30),
3)       address VARCHAR(255),
4)       gender CHAR(1),
5)       birthdate DATE,
6)       PRIMARY KEY (name)
     );
```

Figure 7.2: A separate declaration of the primary key

Note that in Example 7.1, the form of either Fig. 7.1 or Fig. 7.2 is acceptable, because the primary key is a single attribute. However, in a situation where the primary key has more than one attribute, we must use the style of Fig. 7.2. For instance, if we declare the schema for relation `Movie`, whose key is the pair of attributes `title` and `year`, we should add, after the list of attributes, the line

```
PRIMARY KEY (title, year)
```

7.1.2 Keys Declared With `UNIQUE`

Another way to declare a key is to use the keyword `UNIQUE`. This word can appear exactly where `PRIMARY KEY` can appear: either following an attribute and its type or as a separate item within a `CREATE TABLE` statement. The meaning of a `UNIQUE` declaration is almost the same as the meaning of a `PRIMARY KEY` declaration. There are two distinctions, however:

1. We may have any number of UNIQUE declarations for a table, but only one primary key.

2. While PRIMARY KEY forbids NULL's in the attributes of the key, UNIQUE permits them. Moreover, the rule that two tuples may not agree in all of a set of attributes declared UNIQUE may be violated if one or more of the components involved have NULL as a value. In fact, it is even permitted for both tuples to have NULL in all corresponding attributes of the UNIQUE key.

The implementor of a DBMS has the option to make additional distinctions. For instance, a database vendor might always place an index on a key declared to be a primary key (even if that key consisted of more than one attribute), but require the user to call for an index explicitly on other attributes. Alternatively, a table might always be kept sorted on its primary key, if it had one.

Example 7.2: Line (2) of Fig. 7.1 could have been written

```
2)      name CHAR(30) UNIQUE,
```

We could also change line (3) to

```
3)      address VARCHAR(255) UNIQUE,
```

if we felt that two movie stars could not have the same address (a dubious assumption). Similarly, we could change line (6) of Fig. 7.2 to

```
6)      UNIQUE (name)
```

should we choose.   □

7.1.3   Enforcing Key Constraints

Recall our discussion of indexes in Section 6.6.5, where we learned that although they are not part of any SQL standard, each SQL implementation has a way of creating indexes as part of the database schema definition. It is normal to build an index on the primary key, in order to support the common type of query that specifies a value for the primary key. We may also want to build indexes on other attributes declared to be UNIQUE.

Then, when the WHERE clause of the query includes a condition that equates a key to a particular value — for instance name = 'Audrey Hepburn' in the case of the MovieStar relation of Example 7.1 — the matching tuple will be found very quickly, without a search through all the tuples of the relation.

Many SQL implementations offer an index-creation statement using the keyword UNIQUE that declares an attribute to be a key at the same time it creates an index on that attribute. For example, the statement

```
CREATE UNIQUE INDEX YearIndex ON Movie(year);
```

would have the same effect as the example index-creation statement in Section 6.6.5, but it would also declare a uniqueness constraint on attribute `year` of the relation `Movie` (not a reasonable assumption).

Let us consider for a moment how an SQL system would enforce a key constraint. In principle, the constraint must be checked every time we try to change the database. However, it should be clear that the only time a key constraint for a relation R can become violated is when R is modified. In fact, a deletion from R cannot cause a violation; only an insertion or update can. Thus, it is normal practice for the SQL system to check a key constraint only when an insertion or update to that relation occurs.

An index on the attribute(s) declared to be keys is vital if the SQL system is to enforce a key constraint efficiently. If the index is available, then whenever we insert a tuple into the relation or update a key attribute in some tuple, we use the index to check that there is not already a tuple with the same value in the attribute(s) declared to be a key. If so, the system must prevent the modification from taking place.

If there is no index on the key attribute(s), it is still possible to enforce a key constraint. Sorting the relation by key-value helps us search. However, in the absence of any aid to searching, the system must examine the entire relation, looking for a tuple with the given key value. That process is extremely time-consuming and would render database modification of large relations virtually impossible.

7.1.4 Declaring Foreign-Key Constraints

A second important kind of constraint on a database schema is that values for certain attributes must make sense. That is, an attribute like `presC#` of relation `Studio` is expected to refer to a particular movie executive. The implied "referential integrity" constraint is that if a studio's tuple has a certain certificate number c in the `presC#` component, then c is the certificate of a real movie executive. In terms of the database, a "real" executive is one mentioned in the `MovieExec` relation. Thus, there must be some `MovieExec` tuple that has c in the `cert#` attribute.

In SQL we may declare an attribute or attributes of one relation to be a *foreign key*, referencing some attribute(s) of a second relation (possibly the same relation). The implication of this declaration is twofold:

1. The referenced attribute(s) of the second relation must be declared `UNIQUE` or the `PRIMARY KEY` for their relation. Otherwise, we cannot make the foreign-key declaration.

2. Values of the foreign key appearing in the first relation must also appear in the referenced attributes of some tuple. More precisely, let there be a foreign-key F that references set of attributes G of some relation. Suppose a tuple t of the first relation has non-`NULL` values in all the attributes of F; call the list of t's values in these attributes $t[F]$. Then in the referenced

relation there must be some tuple s that agrees with $t[F]$ on the attributes G. That is, $s[G] = t[F]$.

As for primary keys, we have two ways to declare a foreign key.

a) If the foreign key is a single attribute we may follow its name and type by a declaration that it "references" some attribute (which must be a key — primary or unique) of some table. The form of the declaration is

REFERENCES <table>(<attribute>)

b) Alternatively, we may append to the list of attributes in a CREATE TABLE statement one or more declarations stating that a set of attributes is a foreign key. We then give the table and its attributes (which must be a key) to which the foreign key refers. The form of this declaration is:

FOREIGN KEY (<attributes>) REFERENCES <table>(<attributes>)

Example 7.3: Suppose we wish to declare the relation

        Studio(name, address, presC#)

whose primary key is `name` and which has a foreign key `presC#` that references `cert#` of relation

        MovieExec(name, address, cert#, netWorth)

We may declare `presC#` directly to reference `cert#` as follows:

```
CREATE TABLE Studio (
    name CHAR(30) PRIMARY KEY,
    address VARCHAR(255),
    presC# INT REFERENCES MovieExec(cert#)
);
```

An alternative form is to add the foreign key declaration separately, as

```
CREATE TABLE Studio (
    name CHAR(30) PRIMARY KEY,
    address VARCHAR(255),
    presC# INT,
    FOREIGN KEY (presC#) REFERENCES MovieExec(cert#)
);
```

Notice that the referenced attribute, `cert#` in `MovieExec`, is a key of that relation, as it must be. The meaning of either of these two foreign key declarations is that whenever a value appears in the `presC#` component of a `Studio` tuple, that value must also appear in the `cert#` component of some `MovieExec` tuple. The one exception is that, should a particular `Studio` tuple have NULL as the value of its `presC#` component, there is no requirement that NULL appear as the value of a `cert#` component (in fact, `cert#` is a primary key and therefore cannot have NULL's anyway).   □

7.1.5 Maintaining Referential Integrity

We have seen how to declare a foreign key, and we learned that this declaration implies that any set of values for the attributes of the foreign key, none of which are NULL, must also appear in the corresponding attribute(s) of the referenced relation. But how is this constraint to be maintained in the face of modifications to the database? The database implementor may choose from among three alternatives.

The Default Policy: Reject Violating Modifications

SQL has a default policy that any modification violating the referential integrity constraint is rejected by the system. For instance, consider Example 7.3, where it is required that a presC# value in relation Studio also be a cert# value in MovieExec. The following actions will be rejected by the system (i.e., a run-time exception or error will be generated).

1. We try to insert a new Studio tuple whose presC# value is not NULL and is not the cert# component of any MovieExec tuple. The insertion is rejected by the system, and the tuple is never inserted into Studio.

2. We try to update a Studio tuple to change the presC# component to a non-NULL value that is not the cert# component of any MovieExec tuple. The update is rejected, and the tuple is unchanged.

3. We try to delete a MovieExec tuple, and its cert# component appears as the presC# component of one or more Studio tuples. The deletion is rejected, and the tuple remains in MovieExec.

4. We try to update a MovieExec tuple in a way that changes the cert# value, and the old cert# is the value of presC# of some movie studio. The system again rejects the change and leaves MovieExec as it was.

The Cascade Policy

There is another approach to handling deletions or updates to a referenced relation like MovieExec (i.e., the third and fourth types of modifications described above), called the *cascade policy*. Intuitively, changes to the referenced attribute(s) are mimicked at the foreign key.

Under the cascade policy, when we delete the MovieExec tuple for the president of a studio, then to maintain referential integrity the system will delete the referencing tuple(s) from Studio. Updates are handled analogously. If we change the cert# for some movie executive from c_1 to c_2, and there was some Studio tuple with c_1 as the value of its presC# component, then the system will also update this presC# component to have value c_2.

The Set-Null Policy

Yet another approach to handling the problem is to change the `presC#` value from that of the deleted or updated studio president to NULL; this policy is called *set-null*.

These options may be chosen for deletes and updates, independently, and they are stated with the declaration of the foreign key. We declare them with `ON DELETE` or `ON UPDATE` followed by our choice of `SET NULL` or `CASCADE`.

Example 7.4 : Let us see how we might modify the declaration of

        Studio(name, address, presC#)

in Example 7.3 to specify the handling of deletes and updates in the

        MovieExec(name, address, cert#, netWorth)

relation. Figure 7.3 takes the first of the `CREATE TABLE` statements in that example and expands it with `ON DELETE` and `ON UPDATE` clauses. Line (5) says that when we delete a `MovieExec` tuple, we set the `presC#` of any studio of which he or she was the president to NULL. Line (6) says that if we update the `cert#` component of a `MovieExec` tuple, then any tuples in `Studio` with the same value in the `presC#` component are changed similarly.

```
1)   CREATE TABLE Studio (
2)      name CHAR(30) PRIMARY KEY,
3)      address VARCHAR(255),
4)      presC# INT REFERENCES MovieExec(cert#)
5)          ON DELETE SET NULL
6)          ON UPDATE CASCADE
     );
```

Figure 7.3: Choosing policies to preserve referential integrity

Note that in this example, the set-null policy makes more sense for deletes, while the cascade policy seems preferable for updates. We would expect that if, for instance, a studio president retires, the studio will exist with a "null" president for a while. However, an update to the certificate number of a studio president is most likely a clerical change. The person continues to exist and to be the president of the studio, so we would like the `presC#` attribute in `Studio` to follow the change.   □

Dangling Tuples and Modification Policies

A tuple with a foreign key value that does not appear in the referenced relation is said to be a *dangling tuple*. Recall that a tuple which fails to participate in a join is also called "dangling." The two ideas are closely related. If a tuple's foreign-key value is missing from the referenced relation, then the tuple will not participate in a join of its relation with the referenced relation.

The dangling tuples are exactly the tuples that violate referential integrity for this foreign-key constraint.

- The default policy for deletions and updates to the referenced relation is that the action is forbidden if and only if it creates one or more dangling tuples in the referencing relation.

- The cascade policy is to delete or update all dangling tuples created (depending on whether the modification is a delete or update to the referenced relation, respectively).

- The set-null policy is to set the foreign key to NULL in each dangling tuple.

7.1.6 Deferring the Checking of Constraints

Let us assume the situation of Example 7.3, where `presC#` in `Studio` is a foreign key referencing `cert#` of `MovieExec`. Bill Clinton decides, after his national presidency, to found a movie studio, called Redlight Studios, of which he will naturally be the president. If we execute the insertion:

```
INSERT INTO Studio
VALUES('Redlight', 'New York', 23456);
```

we are in trouble. The reason is that there is no tuple of `MovieExec` with certificate number 23456 (the presumed newly issued certificate for Bill Clinton), so there is an obvious violation of the foreign-key constraint.

One possible fix is first to insert the tuple for Redlight without a president's certificate, as:

```
INSERT INTO Studio(name, address)
VALUES('Redlight', 'New York');
```

This change avoids the constraint violation, because the Redlight tuple is inserted with NULL as the value of `presC#`, and NULL in a foreign key does not require that we check for the existence of any value in the referenced column.

However, we must insert a tuple for Bill Clinton into `MovieExec`, with his correct certificate number before we can apply an update statement such as

```
UPDATE Studio
SET presC# = 23456
WHERE name = 'Redlight';
```

If we do not fix `MovieExec` first, then this update statement will also violate the foreign-key constraint.

Of course, inserting Bill Clinton and his certificate number into `MovieExec` before inserting Redlight into `Studio` will surely protect us against a foreign-key violation in this case. However, there are cases of *circular constraints* that cannot be fixed by judiciously ordering the database modification steps we take.

Example 7.5 : If movie executives were limited to studio presidents, then we might want to declare `cert#` to be a foreign key referencing `Studio(presC#)`; we would then have to declare `presC#` to be `UNIQUE`, but that declaration makes sense if you assume a person cannot be the president of two studios at the same time.

Now, it is impossible to insert new studios with new presidents. We can't insert a tuple with a new value of `presC#` into `Studio`, because that tuple would violate the foreign-key constraint from `presC#` to `MovieExec(cert#)`. We can't insert a tuple with a new value of `cert#` into `MovieExec`, because that would violate the foreign-key constraint from `cert#` to `Studio(presC#)`. □

The problem of Example 7.5 has a solution, but it involves several elements of SQL that we have not yet seen.

1. First, we need the ability to group several SQL statements (the two insertions — one into `Studio` and the other into `MovieExec`) into one unit, called a "transaction." We shall meet transactions as an indivisible unit of work in Section 8.6.

2. Then, we need a way to tell the SQL system not to check the constraints until after the whole transaction is finished ("committed" in the terminology of transactions).

We may take point (1) on faith for the moment, but there are two details we must learn to handle point (2):

a) Any constraint — key, foreign-key, or other constraint types we shall meet later in this chapter — may be declared `DEFERRABLE` or `NOT DEFERRABLE`. The latter is the default, and means that every time a database modification occurs, the constraint is checked immediately afterwards, if the modification requires that it be checked at all. However, if we declare a constraint to be `DEFERRABLE`, then we have the option of telling it to wait until a transaction is complete before checking the constraint.

b) If a constraint is deferrable, then we may also declare it to be INITIALLY DEFERRED or INITIALLY IMMEDIATE. In the former case, checking will be deferred to the end of the current transaction, unless we tell the system to stop deferring this constraint. If declared INITIALLY IMMEDIATE, the check will be made before any modification, but because the constraint is deferrable, we have the option of later deciding to defer checking.

Example 7.6: Figure 7.4 shows the declaration of Studio modified to allow the checking of its foreign-key constraint to be deferred until after each transaction. We have also declared presC# to be UNIQUE, in order that it may be referenced by other relations' foreign-key constraints.

```
CREATE TABLE Studio (
    name CHAR(30) PRIMARY KEY,
    address VARCHAR(255),
    presC# INT UNIQUE
        REFERENCES MovieExec(cert#)
        DEFERRABLE INITIALLY DEFERRED
);
```

Figure 7.4: Making presC# unique and deferring the checking of its foreign-key constraint

If we made a similar declaration for the hypothetical foreign-key constraint from MovieExec(cert#) to Studio(presC#) mentioned in Example 7.5, then we could write transactions that inserted two tuples, one into each relation, and the two foreign-key constraints would not be checked until after both insertions had been done. Then, if we insert both a new studio and its new president, and use the same certificate number in each tuple, we would avoid violation of any constraint. □

There are two additional points about deferring constraints that we should bear in mind:

- Constraints of any type can be given names. We shall discuss how to do so in Section 7.3.1.

- If a constraint has a name, say MyConstraint, then we can change a deferrable constraint from immediate to deferred by the SQL statement

```
SET CONSTRAINT MyConstraint DEFERRED;
```

and we can reverse the process by changing DEFERRED in the above to IMMEDIATE.

7.1.7 Exercises for Section 7.1

* Exercise 7.1.1: Our running example movie database of Section 5.1 has keys defined for all its relations.

```
Movie(title, year, length, inColor, studioName, producerC#)
StarsIn(movieTitle, movieYear, starName)
MovieStar(name, address, gender, birthdate)
MovieExec(name, address, cert#, netWorth)
Studio(name, address, presC#)
```

Modify your SQL schema declarations of Exercise 6.6.1 to include declarations of the keys for each of these relations. Recall that all three attributes are the key for StarsIn.

Exercise 7.1.2: Declare the following referential integrity constraints for the movie database as in Exercise 7.1.1.

* *** a)** The producer of a movie must be someone mentioned in MovieExec. Modifications to MovieExec that violate this constraint are rejected.

* b) Repeat (a), but violations result in the producerC# in Movie being set to NULL.

* c) Repeat (a), but violations result in the deletion or update of the offending Movie tuple.

* d) A movie that appears in StarsIn must also appear in Movie. Handle violations by rejecting the modification.

* e) A star appearing in StarsIn must also appear in MovieStar. Handle violations by deleting violating tuples.

*! Exercise 7.1.3: We would like to declare the constraint that every movie in the relation Movie must appear with at least one star in StarsIn. Can we do so with a foreign-key constraint? Why or why not?

Exercise 7.1.4: Suggest suitable keys for the relations of the PC database:

```
Product(maker, model, type)
PC(model, speed, ram, hd, rd, price)
Laptop(model, speed, ram, hd, screen, price)
Printer(model, color, type, price)
```

of Exercise 5.2.1. Modify your SQL schema from Exercise 6.6.2 to include declarations of these keys.

Exercise 7.1.5: Suggest suitable keys for the relations of the battleships database

```
Classes(class, type, country, numGuns, bore, displacement)
Ships(name, class, launched)
Battles(name, date)
Outcomes(ship, battle, result)
```

of Exercise 5.2.4. Modify your SQL schema from Exercise 6.6.3 to include declarations of these keys.

Exercise 7.1.6: Write the following referential integrity constraints for the battleships database as in Exercise 7.1.5. Use your assumptions about keys from that exercise, and handle all violations by setting the referencing attribute value to NULL.

* a) Every class mentioned in Ships must be mentioned in Classes.

  b) Every battle mentioned in Outcomes must be mentioned in Battles.

  c) Every ship mentioned in Outcomes must be mentioned in Ships.

7.2 Constraints on Attributes and Tuples

We have seen key constraints, which force certain attributes to have distinct values among all the tuples of a relation, and we have seen foreign-key constraints, which enforce referential integrity between attributes of two relations. Now, we shall see a third important kind of constraint: one that limits the values that may appear in components for some attributes. These constraints may be expressed as either:

1. A constraint on the attribute in the definition of its relation's schema, or

2. A constraint on a tuple as a whole. This constraint is part of the relation's schema, not associated with any of its attributes.

In Section 7.2.1 we shall introduce a simple type of constraint on an attribute's value: the constraint that the attribute not have a NULL value. Then in Section 7.2.2 we cover the principal form of constraints of type (1): *attribute-based* CHECK *constraints*. The second type, the tuple-based constraints, are covered in Section 7.2.3.

There are other, more general kinds of constraints that we shall meet in Section 7.4. These constraints can be used to restrict changes to whole relations or even several relations, as well as to constrain the value of a single attribute or tuple.

7.2.1   Not-Null Constraints

One simple constraint to associate with an attribute is NOT NULL. The effect is to disallow tuples in which this attribute is NULL. The constraint is declared by the keywords NOT NULL following the declaration of the attribute in a CREATE TABLE statement.

Example 7.7: Suppose relation Studio required presC# not to be NULL, perhaps by changing line (4) of Fig. 7.3 to:

```
    4)    presC# INT REFERENCES MovieExec(cert#) NOT NULL
```

This change has several consequences. For instance:

- We could not insert a tuple into Studio by specifying only the name and address, because the inserted tuple would have NULL in the presC# component.

- We could not use the set-null policy in situations like line (5) of Fig. 7.3, which tells the system to fix foreign-key violations by making presC# be NULL.

□

7.2.2   Attribute-Based CHECK Constraints

More complex constraints can be attached to an attribute declaration by the keyword CHECK, followed by a parenthesized condition that must hold for every value of this attribute. In practice, an attribute-based CHECK constraint is likely to be a simple limit on values, such as an enumeration of legal values or an arithmetic inequality. However, in principle the condition can be anything that could follow WHERE in an SQL query. This condition may refer to the attribute being constrained, by using the name of that attribute in its expression. However, if the condition refers to any other relations or attributes of relations, then the relation must be introduced in the FROM clause of a subquery (even if the relation referred to is the one to which the checked attribute belongs).

An attribute-based CHECK constraint is checked whenever any tuple gets a new value for this attribute. The new value could be introduced by an update for the tuple, or it could be part of an inserted tuple. If the constraint is violated by the new value, then the modification is rejected. As we shall see in Example 7.9, the attribute-based CHECK constraint is not checked if a database modification does not change a value of the attribute with which the constraint is associated, and this limitation can result in the constraint becoming violated. First, let us consider a simple example of an attribute-based check.

Example 7.8: Suppose we want to require that certificate numbers be at least six digits. We could modify line (4) of Fig. 7.3, a declaration of the schema for relation

```
    Studio(name, address, presC#)
```

to be

```
4)      presC# INT REFERENCES MovieExec(cert#)
                CHECK (presC# >= 100000)
```

For another example, the attribute **gender** of relation

```
    MovieStar(name, address, gender, birthdate)
```

was declared in Fig. 6.16 to be of data type `CHAR(1)` — that is, a single character. However, we really expect that the only characters that will appear there are 'F' and 'M'. The following substitute for line (4) of Fig. 6.16 enforces the rule:

```
4) gender CHAR(1) CHECK (gender IN ('F', 'M')),
```

The above condition uses an explicit relation with two tuples, and says that the value of any **gender** component must be in this set. □

It is permitted for the condition being checked to mention other attributes or tuples of the relation, or even to mention other relations, but doing so requires a subquery in the condition. As we said, the condition can be anything that could follow `WHERE` in a select-from-where SQL statement. However, we should be aware that the checking of the constraint is associated with the attribute in question only, not with every relation or attribute mentioned by the constraint. As a result, a complex condition can become false if some element other than the checked attribute changes.

Example 7.9: We might suppose that we could simulate a referential integrity constraint by an attribute-based `CHECK` constraint that requires the existence of the referred-to value. The following is an *erroneous* attempt to simulate the requirement that the **presC#** value in a

```
    Studio(name, address, presC#)
```

tuple must appear in the **cert#** component of some

```
    MovieExec(name, address, cert#, netWorth)
```

tuple. Suppose line (4) of Fig. 7.3 were replaced by

```
4)      presC# INT CHECK
            (presC# IN (SELECT cert# FROM MovieExec))
```

This statement is a legal attribute-based `CHECK` constraint, but let us look at its effect.

- If we attempt to insert a new tuple into `Studio`, and that tuple has a `presC#` value that is not the certificate of any movie executive, then the insertion is rejected.

- If we attempt to update the `presC#` component of a `Studio` tuple, and the new value is not the `cert#` of a movie executive, the update is rejected.

- However, if we change the `MovieExec` relation, say by deleting the tuple for the president of a studio, this change is invisible to the above `CHECK` constraint. Thus, the deletion is permitted, even though the attribute-based `CHECK` constraint on `presC#` is now violated.

We shall see in Section 7.4.1 how more powerful constraint forms can correctly express this condition.   □

7.2.3   Tuple-Based `CHECK` Constraints

To declare a constraint on the tuples of a single table R, when we define that table with a `CREATE TABLE` statement we may add to the list of attributes and key or foreign-key declarations the keyword `CHECK` followed by a parenthesized condition. This condition can be anything that could appear in a `WHERE` clause. It is interpreted as a condition about a tuple in the table R, and the attributes of R may be referred to by name in this expression. However, as for attribute-based `CHECK` constraints, the condition may also mention, in subqueries, other relations or other tuples of the same relation R.

The condition of a tuple-based `CHECK` constraint is checked every time a tuple is inserted into R and every time a tuple of R is updated, and is evaluated for the new or updated tuple. If the condition is false for that tuple, then the constraint is violated and the insertion or update statement that caused the violation is rejected. However, if the condition mentions some relation (even R itself) in a subquery, and a change to that relation causes the condition to become false for some tuple of R, the check does not inhibit this change. That is, like an attribute-based `CHECK`, a tuple-based `CHECK` is invisible to other relations.

Although tuple-based checks can involve some very complex conditions, it is often best to leave complex checks to SQL's "assertions," which we discuss in Section 7.4.1. The reason is that, as discussed above, tuple-based checks can be violated under certain conditions. However, if the tuple-based check involves only attributes of the tuple being checked and has no subqueries, then its constraint will always hold. Here is one example of a simple tuple-based `CHECK` constraint that involves several attributes of one tuple.

Example 7.10: Recall Example 6.39, where we declared the schema of table `MovieStar`. Figure 7.5 repeats the `CREATE TABLE` statement with the addition of a primary-key declaration and one other constraint, which is one of several possible "consistency conditions" that we might wish to check. This constraint says that if the star's gender is male, then his name must not begin with 'Ms.'.

```
1)  CREATE TABLE MovieStar (
2)      name CHAR(30) PRIMARY KEY,
3)      address VARCHAR(255),
4)      gender CHAR(1),
5)      birthdate DATE,
6)      CHECK (gender = 'F' OR name NOT LIKE 'Ms.%')
    );
```

Figure 7.5: A constraint on the table `MovieStar`

Writing Constraints Correctly

Many constraints are like Example 7.10, where we want to forbid tuples that satisfy two or more conditions. The expression that should follow the check is the `OR` of the negations, or opposites, of each condition; this transformation is one of "DeMorgan's laws": the negation of the `AND` of terms is the `OR` of the negations of the same terms. Thus, in Example 7.10 the first condition was that the star is male, and we used `gender = 'F'` as a suitable negation (although perhaps `gender <> 'M'` would be the more normal way to phrase the negation). The second condition is that the `name` begins with `'Ms.'`, and for this negation we used the `NOT LIKE` comparison. This comparison negates the condition itself, which would be `name LIKE 'Ms.%'` in SQL.

In line (2), `name` is declared the primary key for the relation. Then line (6) declares a constraint. The condition of this constraint is true for every female movie star and for every star whose name does not begin with `'Ms.'`. The only tuples for which it is *not* true are those where the gender is male and the name *does* begin with `'Ms.'`. Those are exactly the tuples we wish to exclude from `MovieStar`. □

7.2.4 Exercises for Section 7.2

Exercise 7.2.1: Write the following constraints for attributes of the relation

    Movie(title, year, length, inColor, studioName, producerC#)

* a) The year cannot be before 1895.

  b) The length cannot be less than 60 nor more than 250.

* c) The studio name can only be Disney, Fox, MGM, or Paramount.

Limited Constraint Checking: Bug or Feature?

One might wonder why attribute- and tuple-based checks are allowed to be violated if they refer to other relations or other tuples of the same relation. The reason is that such constraints can be implemented more efficiently than more general constraints such as assertions (see Section 7.4.1) can. With attribute- or tuple-based checks, we only have to evaluate that constraint for the tuple(s) that are inserted or updated. On the other hand, assertions must be evaluated every time any one of the relations they mention is changed. The careful database designer will use attribute- and tuple-based checks only when there is no possibility that they will be violated, and will use another mechanism, such as assertions or triggers (Section 7.4.2) otherwise.

Exercise 7.2.2: Write the following constraints on attributes from our example schema

```
Product(maker, model, type)
PC(model, speed, ram, hd, rd, price)
Laptop(model, speed, ram, hd, screen, price)
Printer(model, color, type, price)
```

of Exercise 5.2.1.

a) The speed of a laptop must be at least 800.

b) A removable disk can only be a 32x or 40x CD, or a 12x or 16x DVD.

c) The only types of printers are laser, ink-jet, and bubble.

d) The only types of products are PC's, laptops, and printers.

! e) A model of a product must also be the model of a PC, a laptop, or a printer.

Exercise 7.2.3: We mentioned in Example 7.13 that the tuple-based CHECK constraint of Fig. 7.7 does only half the job of the assertion of Fig. 7.6. Write the CHECK constraint on MovieExec that is necessary to complete the job.

Exercise 7.2.4: Write the following constraints as tuple-based CHECK constraints on one of the relations of our running movies example:

```
Movie(title, year, length, inColor, studioName, producerC#)
StarsIn(movieTitle, movieYear, starName)
MovieStar(name, address, gender, birthdate)
MovieExec(name, address, cert#, netWorth)
Studio(name, address, presC#)
```

If the constraint actually involves two relations, then you should put constraints in both relations so that whichever relation changes, the constraint will be checked on insertions and updates. Assume no deletions; it is not possible to maintain tuple-based constraints in the face of deletions.

* a) A movie may not be in color if it was made before 1939.

  b) A star may not appear in a movie made before they were born.

  ! c) No two studios may have the same address.

*! d) A name that appears in `MovieStar` must not also appear in `MovieExec`.

  ! e) A studio name that appears in `Studio` must also appear in at least one `Movie` tuple.

  !! f) If a producer of a movie is also the president of a studio, then they must be the president of the studio that made the movie.

Exercise 7.2.5: Write the following as tuple-based `CHECK` constraints about our "PC" schema.

  a) A PC with a processor speed less than 1200 must not sell for more than $1500.

  b) A laptop with a screen size less than 15 inches must have at least a 20 gigabyte hard disk or sell for less than $2000.

Exercise 7.2.6: Write the following as tuple-based `CHECK` constraints about our "battleships" schema Exercise 5.2.4:

```
Classes(class, type, country, numGuns, bore, displacement)
Ships(name, class, launched)
Battles(name, date)
Outcomes(ship, battle, result)
```

  a) No class of ships may have guns with larger than 16-inch bore.

  b) If a class of ships has more than 9 guns, then their bore must be no larger than 14 inches.

  ! c) No ship can be in battle before it is launched.

7.3 Modification of Constraints

It is possible to add, modify, or delete constraints at any time. The way to express such modifications depends on whether the constraint involved is associated with an attribute, a table, or (as in Section 7.4.1) a database schema.

7.3.1   Giving Names to Constraints

In order to modify or delete an existing constraint, it is necessary that the constraint have a name. To do so, we precede the constraint by the keyword CONSTRAINT and a name for the constraint.

Example 7.11 : We could rewrite line (2) of Fig. 7.1 to name the constraint that says attribute name is a primary key, as

```
    2)    name CHAR(30) CONSTRAINT NameIsKey PRIMARY KEY,
```

Similarly, we could name the attribute-based CHECK constraint that appeared in Example 7.8 by:

```
    4) gender CHAR(1) CONSTRAINT NoAndro
                    CHECK (gender IN ('F', 'M')),
```

Finally, the following constraint:

```
    6)    CONSTRAINT RightTitle
              CHECK (gender = 'F' OR name NOT LIKE 'Ms.%');
```

is a rewriting of the tuple-based CHECK constraint in line (6) of Fig. 7.5 to give that constraint a name.   □

7.3.2   Altering Constraints on Tables

We mentioned in Section 7.1.6 that we can switch the checking of a constraint from immediate to deferred or vice-versa with a SET CONSTRAINT statement. Other changes to constraints are effected with an ALTER TABLE statement. We previously discussed some uses of the ALTER TABLE statement in Section 6.6.3, where we used it to add and delete attributes.

These statements can also be used to alter constraints; ALTER TABLE is used for both attribute-based and tuple-based checks. We may drop a constraint with keyword DROP and the name of the constraint to be dropped. We may also add a constraint with the keyword ADD, followed by the constraint to be added. Note, however, that you cannot add a constraint to a table unless it holds for the current instance of that table.

Example 7.12 : Let us see how we would drop and add the constraints of Example 7.11 on relation MovieStar. The following sequence of three statements drops them:

```
    ALTER TABLE MovieStar DROP CONSTRAINT NameIsKey;
    ALTER TABLE MovieStar DROP CONSTRAINT NoAndro;
    ALTER TABLE MovieStar DROP CONSTRAINT RightTitle;
```

Should we wish to reinstate these constraints, we would alter the schema for relation MovieStar by adding the same constraints, for example:

Name Your Constraints

Remember, it is a good idea to give each of your constraints a name, even if you do not believe you will ever need to refer to it. Once the constraint is created without a name, it is too late to give it one later, should you wish to alter it. However, should you be faced with a situation of having to alter a nameless constraint, you will find that your DBMS probably has a way for you to query it for a list of all your constraints, and that it has given your unnamed constraint an internal name of its own, which you may use to refer to the constraint.

```
ALTER TABLE MovieStar ADD CONSTRAINT NameIsKey
    PRIMARY KEY (name);
ALTER TABLE MovieStar ADD CONSTRAINT NoAndro
    CHECK (gender IN ('F', 'M'));
ALTER TABLE MovieStar ADD CONSTRAINT RightTitle
    CHECK (gender = 'F' OR name NOT LIKE 'Ms.%');
```

These constraints are now tuple-based, rather than attribute-based checks. We could not bring them back as attribute-based constraints.

The name is optional for these reintroduced constraints. However, we cannot rely on SQL remembering the dropped constraints. Thus, when we add a former constraint we need to write the constraint again; we cannot refer to it by its former name. □

7.3.3 Exercises for Section 7.3

Exercise 7.3.1: Show how to alter your relation schemas for the movie example:

```
Movie(title, year, length, inColor, studioName, producerC#)
StarsIn(movieTitle, movieYear, starName)
MovieStar(name, address, gender, birthdate)
MovieExec(name, address, cert#, netWorth)
Studio(name, address, presC#)
```

in the following ways.

* a) Make `title` and `year` the key for `Movie`.

  b) Require the referential integrity constraint that the producer of every movie appear in `MovieExec`.

  c) Require that no movie length be less than 60 nor greater than 250.

*! d) Require that no name appear as both a movie star and movie executive (this constraint need not be maintained in the face of deletions).

! e) Require that no two studios have the same address.

Exercise 7.3.2 : Show how to alter the schemas of the "battleships" database:

```
Classes(class, type, country, numGuns, bore, displacement)
Ships(name, class, launched)
Battles(name, date)
Outcomes(ship, battle, result)
```

to have the following tuple-based constraints.

a) `Class` and `country` form a key for relation `Classes`.

b) Require the referential integrity constraint that every ship appearing in `Battles` also appears in `Ships`.

c) Require the referential integrity constraint that every ship appearing in `Outcomes` appears in `Ships`.

d) Require that no ship has more than 14 guns.

! e) Disallow a ship being in battle before it is launched.

7.4 Schema-Level Constraints and Triggers

The most powerful forms of active elements in SQL are not associated with particular tuples or components of tuples. These elements, called "triggers" and "assertions," are part of the database schema, on a par with the relations and views themselves.

- An assertion is a boolean-valued SQL expression that must be true at all times.

- A trigger is a series of actions that are associated with certain events, such as insertions into a particular relation, and that are performed whenever these events arise.

While assertions are easier for the programmer to use, since they merely require the programmer to state what must be true, triggers are the feature DBMS's typically provide as general-purpose, active elements. The reason is that it is very hard to implement assertions efficiently. The DBMS must deduce whether any given database modification could affect the truth of an assertion. Triggers, on the other hand, tell exactly when the DBMS needs to deal with them.

7.4.1 Assertions

The SQL standard proposes a simple form of *assertion* (also called a "general constraint") that allows us to enforce any condition (expression that can follow WHERE). Like other schema elements, we declare an assertion with a CREATE statement. The form of an assertion is:

1. The keywords CREATE ASSERTION,

2. The name of the assertion,

3. The keyword CHECK, and

4. A parenthesized condition.

That is, the form of this statement is

CREATE ASSERTION <name> CHECK (<condition>)

The condition in an assertion must be true when the assertion is created and must always remain true; any database modification whatsoever that causes it to become false will be rejected. Recall that the other types of CHECK constraints we have covered can be violated under certain conditions, if they involve subqueries.

There is a difference between the way we write tuple-based CHECK constraints and the way we write assertions. Tuple-based checks can refer to the attributes of that relation in whose declaration they appear. For instance, in line (6) of Fig. 7.5 we used attributes gender and name without saying where they came from. They refer to components of a tuple being inserted or updated in the table MovieStar, because that table is the one being declared in the CREATE TABLE statement.

The condition of an assertion has no such privilege. Any attributes referred to in the condition must be introduced in the assertion, typically by mentioning their relation in a select-from-where expression. Since the condition must have a boolean value, it is normal to aggregate the results of the condition in some way to make a single true/false choice. For example, we might write the condition as an expression producing a relation, to which NOT EXISTS is applied; that is, the constraint is that this relation is always empty. Alternatively, we might apply an aggregate operator like SUM to a column of a relation and compare it to a constant. For instance, this way we could require that a sum always be less than some limiting value.

Example 7.13 : Suppose we wish to require that no one can become the president of a studio unless their net worth is at least $10,000,000. We declare an assertion to the effect that the set of movie studios with presidents having a net worth less than $10,000,000 is empty. This assertion involves the two relations

```
MovieExec(name, address, cert#, netWorth)
Studio(name, address, presC#)
```

```
CREATE ASSERTION RichPres CHECK
    (NOT EXISTS
        (SELECT *
         FROM Studio, MovieExec
         WHERE presC# = cert# AND netWorth < 10000000
        )
    );
```

Figure 7.6: Assertion guaranteeing rich studio presidents

The assertion is shown in Fig. 7.6.

Incidentally, it is worth noting that even though this constraint involves two relations, we could write it as tuple-based CHECK constraints on the two relations rather than as a single assertion. For instance, we can add to the CREATE TABLE statement of Example 7.3 a constraint on Studio as shown in Fig. 7.7.

```
CREATE TABLE Studio (
    name CHAR(30) PRIMARY KEY,
    address VARCHAR(255),
    presC# INT REFERENCES MovieExec(cert#),
    CHECK (presC# NOT IN
        (SELECT cert# FROM MovieExec
         WHERE netWorth < 10000000)
    )
);
```

Figure 7.7: A constraint on Studio mirroring an assertion

Note, however, that the constraint of Fig. 7.7 will only be checked when a change to its relation, Studio occurs. It would not catch a situation where the net worth of some studio president, as recorded in relation MovieExec, dropped below $10,000,000. To get the full effect of the assertion, we would have to add another constraint to the declaration of the table MovieExec, requiring that the net worth be at least $10,000,000 if that executive is the president of a studio. □

Example 7.14: Here is another example of an assertion. It involves the relation

```
Movie(title, year, length, inColor, studioName, producerC#)
```

Comparison of Constraints

The following table lists the principal differences among attribute-based checks, tuple-based checks, and assertions.

Type of Constraint	Where Declared	When Activated	Guaranteed to Hold?
Attribute-based CHECK	With attribute	On insertion to relation or attribute update	Not if subqueries
Tuple-based CHECK	Element of relation schema	On insertion to relation or tuple update	Not if subqueries
Assertion	Element of database schema	On any change to any mentioned relation	Yes

---

and says the total length of all movies by a given studio shall not exceed 10,000 minutes.

```
CREATE ASSERTION SumLength CHECK (10000 >= ALL
    (SELECT SUM(length) FROM Movie GROUP BY studioName)
);
```

As this constraint involves only the relation `Movie`, it could have been expressed as a tuple-based `CHECK` constraint in the schema for `Movie` rather than as an assertion. That is, we could add to the definition of table `Movie` the tuple-based `CHECK` constraint

```
CHECK (10000 >= ALL
    (SELECT SUM(length) FROM Movie GROUP BY studioName));
```

Notice that in principle this condition applies to every tuple of table `Movie`. However, it does not mention any attributes of the tuple explicitly, and all the work is done in the subquery.

Also observe that if implemented as a tuple-based constraint, the check would not be made on deletion of a tuple from the relation `Movie`. In this example, that difference causes no harm, since if the constraint was satisfied before the deletion, then it is surely satisfied after the deletion. However, if the constraint were a lower bound on total length, rather than an upper bound as in this example, then we could find the constraint violated had we written it as a tuple-based check rather than an assertion. □

As a final point, it is possible to drop an assertion. The statement to do so follows the pattern for any database schema element:

```
DROP ASSERTION <assertion name>
```

7.4.2 Event-Condition-Action Rules

Triggers, sometimes called *event-condition-action rules* or *ECA rules*, differ from the kinds of constraints discussed previously in three ways.

1. Triggers are only awakened when certain *events*, specified by the database programmer, occur. The sorts of events allowed are usually insert, delete, or update to a particular relation. Another kind of event allowed in many SQL systems is a transaction end (we mentioned transactions briefly in Section 7.1.6 and cover them with more detail in Section 8.6).

2. Instead of immediately preventing the event that awakened it, a trigger tests a *condition*. If the condition does not hold, then nothing else associated with the trigger happens in response to this event.

3. If the condition of the trigger is satisfied, the *action* associated with the trigger is performed by the DBMS. The action may then prevent the event from taking place, or it could undo the event (e.g., delete the tuple inserted). In fact, the action could be any sequence of database operations, perhaps even operations not connected in any way to the triggering event.

7.4.3 Triggers in SQL

The SQL trigger statement gives the user a number of different options in the event, condition, and action parts. Here are the principal features.

1. The action may be executed either before or after the triggering event.

2. The action can refer to both old and/or new values of tuples that were inserted, deleted, or updated in the event that triggered the action.

3. Update events may be limited to a particular attribute or set of attributes.

4. A condition may be specified by a WHEN clause; the action is executed only if the rule is triggered *and* the condition holds when the triggering event occurs.

5. The programmer has an option of specifying that the action is performed either:

    (a) Once for each modified tuple, or

    (b) Once for all the tuples that are changed in one database operation.

Before giving the details of the syntax for triggers, let us consider an example that will illustrate the most important syntactic as well as semantic points. In this example, the trigger executes once for each tuple that is updated.

Example 7.15: We shall write an SQL trigger that applies to the

```
MovieExec(name, address, cert#, netWorth)
```

table. It is triggered by updates to the `netWorth` attribute. The effect of this trigger is to foil any attempt to lower the net worth of a movie executive. The trigger declaration appears in Fig. 7.8.

```
1)   CREATE TRIGGER NetWorthTrigger
2)   AFTER UPDATE OF netWorth ON MovieExec
3)   REFERENCING
4)       OLD ROW AS OldTuple,
5)       NEW ROW AS NewTuple
6)   FOR EACH ROW
7)   WHEN (OldTuple.netWorth > NewTuple.netWorth)
8)       UPDATE MovieExec
9)       SET netWorth = OldTuple.netWorth
10)      WHERE cert# = NewTuple.cert#;
```

Figure 7.8: An SQL trigger

Line (1) introduces the declaration with the keywords `CREATE TRIGGER` and the name of the trigger. Line (2) then gives the triggering event, namely the update of the `netWorth` attribute of the `MovieExec` relation. Lines (3) through (5) set up a way for the condition and action portions of this trigger to talk about both the old tuple (the tuple before the update) and the new tuple (the tuple after the update). These tuples will be referred to as `OldTuple` and `NewTuple`, according to the declarations in lines (4) and (5), respectively. In the condition and action, these names can be used as if they were tuple variables declared in the `FROM` clause of an ordinary SQL query.

Line (6), the phrase `FOR EACH ROW`, expresses the requirement that this trigger is executed once for each updated tuple. If this phrase is missing or it is replaced by the default `FOR EACH STATEMENT`, then the triggering would occur once for an SQL statement, no matter how many triggering-event changes to tuples it made. We would not then declare alias for old and new rows, but we might use `OLD TABLE` and `NEW TABLE`, introduced below.

Line (7) is the condition part of the trigger. It says that we only perform the action when the new net worth is lower than the old net worth; i.e., the net worth of an executive has shrunk.

Lines (8) through (10) form the action portion. This action is an ordinary SQL update statement that has the effect of restoring the net worth of the

executive to what it was before the update. Note that in principle, every tuple of
`MovieExec` is considered for update, but the `WHERE`-clause of line (10) guarantees
that only the updated tuple (the one with the proper `cert#`) will be affected.
□

Of course Example 7.15 illustrates only some of the features of SQL triggers.
In the points that follow, we shall outline the options that are offered by triggers
and how to express these options.

- Line (2) of Fig. 7.8 says that the action of the rule is executed after the
  triggering event, as indicated by the keyword `AFTER`. We may replace
  `AFTER` by `BEFORE`, in which case the `WHEN` condition is tested before the
  triggering event, that is, before the modification that awakened the trigger
  has been made to the database. If the condition is true, then the action
  of the trigger is executed. Then, the event that awakened the trigger is
  executed, regardless of whether the condition is true.

- Besides `UPDATE`, other possible triggering events are `INSERT` and `DELETE`.
  The `OF netWorth` clause in line (2) of Fig. 7.8 is optional for `UPDATE`
  events, and if present defines the event to be only an update of the at-
  tribute(s) listed after the keyword `OF`. An `OF` clause is not permitted for
  `INSERT` or `DELETE` events; these events make sense for entire tuples only.

- The `WHEN` clause is optional. If it is missing, then the action is executed
  whenever the trigger is awakened.

- While we showed a single SQL statement as an action, there can be any
  number of such statements, separated by semicolons and surrounded by
  `BEGIN...END`.

- When the triggering event is an update, then there will be old and new tuples, which are the tuple before the update and after, respectively. We give
  these tuples names by the `OLD ROW AS` and `NEW ROW AS` clauses seen in
  lines (4) and (5). If the triggering event is an insertion, then we may use a
  `NEW ROW AS` clause to give a name for the inserted tuple, and `OLD ROW AS`
  is disallowed. Conversely, on a deletion `OLD ROW AS` is used to name the
  deleted tuple and `NEW ROW AS` is disallowed.

- If we omit the `FOR EACH ROW` on line (6), then a *row-level trigger* such
  as Fig. 7.8 becomes a *statement-level trigger*. A statement-level trigger is
  executed once whenever a statment of the appropriate type is executed,
  no matter how many rows — zero, one, or many — it actually affects.
  For instance, if we update an entire table with an SQL update statement,
  a statement-level update trigger would execute only once, while a tuple-
  level trigger would execute once for each tuple to which an update is
  applied. In a statement-level trigger, we cannot refer to old and new tuples
  directly, as we did in lines (4) and (5). However, any trigger — whether

row- or statement-level — can refer to the relation of *old tuples* (deleted tuples or old versions of updated tuples) and the relation of *new tuples* (inserted tuples or new versions of updated tuples), using declarations such as `OLD TABLE AS OldStuff` and `NEW TABLE AS NewStuff`.

Example 7.16 : Suppose we want to prevent the average net worth of movie executives from dropping below $500,000. This constraint could be violated by an insertion, a deletion, or an update to the `netWorth` column of

```
MovieExec(name, address, cert#, netWorth)
```

The subtle point is that we might, in one `INSERT` or `UPDATE` statement insert or change many tuples of `MovieExec`, and during the modification, the average net worth might temporarily dip below $500,000 and then rise above it by the time all the modifications are made. We only want to reject the entire set of modifications if the net worth is below $500,000 at the end of the statement.

It is necessary to write one trigger for each of these three events: insert, delete, and update of relation `MovieExec`. Figure 7.9 shows the trigger for the update event. The triggers for the insertion and deletion of tuples are similar but slightly simpler.

```
1)   CREATE TRIGGER AvgNetWorthTrigger
2)   AFTER UPDATE OF netWorth ON MovieExec
3)   REFERENCING
4)       OLD TABLE AS OldStuff,
5)       NEW TABLE AS NewStuff
6)   FOR EACH STATEMENT
7)   WHEN (500000 > (SELECT AVG(netWorth) FROM MovieExec))
8)   BEGIN
9)       DELETE FROM MovieExec
10)      WHERE (name, address, cert#, netWorth) IN NewStuff;
11)      INSERT INTO MovieExec
12)          (SELECT * FROM OldStuff);
13)  END;
```

Figure 7.9: Constraining the average net worth

Lines (3) through (5) declare that `NewStuff` and `OldStuff` are the names of relations containing the new tuples and old tuples that are involved in the database operation that awakened our trigger. Note that one database statement can modify many tuples of a relation, and if such a statement executes, there can be many tuples in `NewStuff` and `OldStuff`.

If the operation is an update, then `NewStuff` and `OldStuff` are the new and old versions of the updated tuples, respectively. If an analogous trigger were written for deletions, then the deleted tuples would be in `OldStuff`, and there would be no declaration of a relation name like `NewStuff` for `NEW TABLE` in this trigger. Likewise, in the analogous trigger for insertions, the new tuples would be in `NewStuff`, and there would be no declaration of `OldStuff`.

Line (6) tells us that this trigger is executed once for a statement, regardless of how many tuples are modified. Line (7) is the condition. This condition is satisfied if the average net worth *after* the update is less than $500,000.

The action of lines (8) through (13) consists of two statements that restore the old relation `MovieExec` if the condition of the `WHEN` clause is satisfied; i.e., the new average net worth is too low. Lines (9) and (10) remove all the new tuples, i.e., the updated versions of the tuples, while lines (11) and (12) restore the tuples as they were before the update.   □

7.4.4 Instead-Of Triggers

There is a useful feature of triggers that did not make the SQL-99 standard, but figured into the discussion of the standard and is supported by some commercial systems. This extension allows `BEFORE` or `AFTER` to be replaced by `INSTEAD OF`; the meaning is that when an event awakens a trigger, the action of the trigger is done instead of the event itself.

This capability offers little when the trigger is on a stored table, but it is very powerful when used on a view. The reason is that we cannot really modify a view (see Section 6.7.4). An instead-of trigger intercepts attempts to modify the view and in its place performs whatever action the database designer deems appropriate. The following is a typical example.

Example 7.17: Let us recall the definition of the view of all movies owned by Paramount:

```
CREATE VIEW ParamountMovie AS
    SELECT title, year
    FROM Movie
    WHERE studioName = 'Paramount';
```

from Example 6.45. As we discussed in Example 6.49, this view is updatable, but it has the unexpected flaw that when you insert a tuple into `Paramount-Movie`, the system cannot deduce that the `studioName` attribute is surely Paramount, so that attribute is `NULL` in the inserted `Movie` tuple.

A better result can be obtained if we create an instead-of trigger on this view, as shown in Fig. 7.10. Much of the trigger is unsurprising. We see the keyword `INSTEAD OF` on line (2), establishing that an attempt to insert into `ParamountMovie` will never take place.

Rather, we see in lines (5) and (6) the action that replaces the attempted insertion. There is an insertion into `Movie`, and it specifies the three attributes that we know about. Attributes `title` and `year` come from the tuple we tried to insert into the view; we refer to these values by the tuple variable `NewRow` that was declared in line (3) to represent the tuple we are trying to insert. The

```
1)  CREATE TRIGGER ParamountInsert
2)  INSTEAD OF INSERT ON ParamountMovie
3)  REFERENCING NEW ROW AS NewRow
4)  FOR EACH ROW
5)  INSERT INTO Movie(title, year, studioName)
6)  VALUES(NewRow.title, NewRow.year, 'Paramount');
```

Figure 7.10: Trigger to replace an insertion on a view by an insertion on the underlying base table

value of attribute `studioName` is the constant `'Paramount'`. This value is not part of the inserted tuple. Rather, we assume it is the correct studio for the inserted movie, because the insertion came through the view `ParamountMovie`. □

7.4.5 Exercises for Section 7.4

Exercise 7.4.1: Write the triggers analogous to Fig. 7.9 for the insertion and deletion events on `MovieExec`.

Exercise 7.4.2: Write the following as triggers or assertions. In each case, disallow or undo the modification if it does not satisfy the stated constraint. The database schema is from the "PC" example of Exercise 5.2.1:

```
Product(maker, model, type)
PC(model, speed, ram, hd, rd, price)
Laptop(model, speed, ram, hd, screen, price)
Printer(model, color, type, price)
```

* a) When updating the price of a PC, check that there is no lower priced PC with the same speed.

* b) No manufacturer of PC's may also make laptops.

*! c) A manufacturer of a PC must also make a laptop with at least as great a processor speed.

   d) When inserting a new printer, check that the model number exists in `Product`.

! e) When making any modification to the `Laptop` relation, check that the average price of laptops for each manufacturer is at least $2000.

! f) When updating the RAM or hard disk of any PC, check that the updated PC has at least 100 times as much hard disk as RAM.

! g) If a laptop has a larger main memory than a PC, then the laptop must also have a higher price than the PC.

! h) When inserting a new PC, laptop, or printer, make sure that the model number did not previously appear in any of PC, Laptop, or Printer.

! i) If the relation Product mentions a model and its type, then this model must appear in the relation appropriate to that type.

Exercise 7.4.3: Write the following as triggers or assertions. In each case, disallow or undo the modification if it does not satisfy the stated constraint. The database schema is from the battleships example of Exercise 5.2.4.

```
Classes(class, type, country, numGuns, bore, displacement)
Ships(name, class, launched)
Battles(name, date)
Outcomes(ship, battle, result)
```

* a) When a new class is inserted into Classes, also insert a ship with the name of that class and a NULL launch date.

 b) When a new class is inserted with a displacement greater than 35,000 tons, allow the insertion, but change the displacement to 35,000.

 c) No class may have more than 2 ships.

! d) No country may have both battleships and battlecruisers.

! e) No ship with more than 9 guns may be in a battle with a ship having fewer than 9 guns that was sunk.

! f) If a tuple is inserted into Outcomes, check that the ship and battle are listed in Ships and Battles, respectively, and if not, insert tuples into one or both of these relations, with NULL components where necessary.

! g) When there is an insertion into Ships or an update of the class attribute of Ships, check that no country has more than 20 ships.

! h) No ship may be launched before the ship that bears the name of the first ship's class.

! i) For every class, there is a ship with the name of that class.

!! j) Check, under all circumstances that could cause a violation, that no ship fought in a battle that was at a later date than another battle in which that ship was sunk.

! **Exercise 7.4.4:** Write the following as triggers or assertions. In each case, disallow or undo the modification if it does not satisfy the stated constraint. The problems are based on our running movie example:

```
Movie(title, year, length, inColor, studioName, producerC#)
StarsIn(movieTitle, movieYear, starName)
MovieStar(name, address, gender, birthdate)
MovieExec(name, address, cert#, netWorth)
Studio(name, address, presC#)
```

You may assume that the desired condition holds before any change to the database is attempted. Also, prefer to modify the database, even if it means inserting tuples with NULL or default values, rather than rejecting the attempted modification.

a) Assure that at all times, any star appearing in StarsIn also appears in MovieStar.

b) Assure that at all times every movie executive appears as either a studio president, a producer of a movie, or both.

c) Assure that every movie has at least one male and one female star.

d) Assure that the number of movies made by any studio in any year is no more than 100.

e) Assure that the average length of all movies made in any year is no more than 120.

7.5 Summary of Chapter 7

✦ *Key Constraints*: We can declare an attribute or set of attributes to be a key with a UNIQUE or PRIMARY KEY declaration in a relation schema.

✦ *Referential Integrity Constraints*: We can declare that a value appearing in some attribute or set of attributes must also appear in the corresponding attributes of some tuple of another relation with a REFERENCES or FOREIGN KEY declaration in a relation schema.

✦ *Attribute-Based Check Constraints*: We can place a constraint on the value of an attribute by adding the keyword CHECK and the condition to be checked after the declaration of that attribute in its relation schema.

✦ *Tuple-Based Check Constraints*: We can place a constraint on the tuples of a relation by adding the keyword CHECK and the condition to be checked to the declaration of the relation itself.

✦ *Modifying Constraints*: A tuple-based check can be added or deleted with an ALTER statement for the appropriate table.

✦ *Assertions*: We can declare an assertion as an element of a database schema with the keyword CHECK and the condition to be checked. This condition may involve one or more relations of the database schema, and may involve the relation as a whole, e.g., with aggregation, as well as conditions about individual tuples.

✦ *Invoking the Checks*: Assertions are checked whenever there is a change to one of the relations involved. Attribute- and tuple-based checks are only checked when the attribute or relation to which they apply changes by insertion or update. Thus, these constraints can be violated if they have subqueries.

✦ *Triggers*: The SQL standard includes triggers that specify certain events (e.g., insertion, deletion, or update to a particular relation) that awaken them. Once awakened, a condition can be checked, and if true, a specified sequence of actions (SQL statements such as queries and database modifications) will be executed.

7.6 References for Chapter 7

The reader should go to the bibliographic notes for Chapter 6 for information about how to get the SQL2 or SQL-99 standards documents. References [5] and [4] survey all aspects of active elements in database systems. [1] discusses recent thinking regarding active elements in SQL-99 and future standards. References [2] and [3] discuss HiPAC, an early prototype system that offered active database elements.

1. Cochrane, R. J., H. Pirahesh, and N. Mattos, "Integrating triggers and declarative constraints in SQL database systems," *Intl. Conf. on Very Large Database Systems*, pp. 567–579, 1996.

2. Dayal, U., et al., "The HiPAC project: combining active databases and timing constraints," *SIGMOD Record* **17**:1, pp. 51–70, 1988.

3. McCarthy, D. R., and U. Dayal, "The architecture of an active database management system," *Proc. ACM SIGMOD Intl. Conf. on Management of Data*, pp. 215–224, 1989.

4. N. W. Paton and O. Diaz, "Active database systems," *Computing Surveys* **31**:1 (March, 1999), pp. 63–103.

5. Widom, J. and S. Ceri, *Active Database Systems*, Morgan-Kaufmann, San Francisco, 1996.

Chapter 8

System Aspects of SQL

We now turn to the question of how SQL fits into a complete programming environment. In Section 8.1 we see how to embed SQL in programs that are written in an ordinary programming language, such as C. A critical issue is how we move data between SQL relations and the variables of the surrounding, or "host," language.

Section 8.2 considers another way to combine SQL with general-purpose programming: persistent stored modules, which are pieces of code stored as part of a database schema and executable on command from the user. Section 8.3 covers additional system issues, such as support for a client-server model of computing.

A third programming approach is a "call-level interface," where we program in some conventional language and use a library of functions to access the database. In Section 8.4 we discuss the SQL-standard library called SQL/CLI, for making calls from C programs. Then, in Section 8.5 we meet Java's JDBC (database connectivity), which is an alternative call-level interface.

Then, Section 8.6 introduces us to the "transaction," an atomic unit of work. Many database applications, such as banking, require that operations on the data appear atomic, or indivisible, even though a large number of concurrent operations may be in progress at once. SQL provides features to allow us to specify transactions, and SQL systems have mechanisms to make sure that what we call a transaction is indeed executed atomically. Finally, Section 8.7 discusses how SQL controls unauthorized access to data, and how we can tell the SQL system what accesses are authorized.

8.1 SQL in a Programming Environment

To this point, we have used the *generic SQL interface* in our examples. That is, we have assumed there is an SQL interpreter, which accepts and executes the sorts of SQL queries and commands that we have learned. Although provided as an option by almost all DBMS's, this mode of operation is actually rare. In

---

The Languages of the SQL Standard

Implementations conforming to the SQL standard are required to support at least one of the following seven host languages: ADA, C, Cobol, Fortran, M (formerly called Mumps), Pascal, and PL/I. Each of these should be familiar to the student of computer science, with the possible exception of M or Mumps, which is a language used primarily in the medical community. We shall use C in our examples.

---

practice, most SQL statements are part of some larger piece of software. A more realistic view is that there is a program in some conventional *host* language such as C, but some of the steps in this program are actually SQL statements. In this section we shall describe one way SQL can be made to operate within a conventional program.

A sketch of a typical programming system that involves SQL statements is in Fig. 8.1. There, we see the programmer writing programs in a host language, but with some special "embedded" SQL statements that are not part of the host language. The entire program is sent to a preprocessor, which changes the embedded SQL statements into something that makes sense in the host language. The representation of the SQL could be as simple as a call to a function that takes the SQL statement as a character-string argument and executes that SQL statement.

The preprocessed host-language program is then compiled in the usual manner. The DBMS vendor normally provides a library that supplies the necessary function definitions. Thus, the functions that implement SQL can be executed, and the whole program behaves as one unit. We also show in Fig. 8.1 the possibility that the programmer writes code directly in the host language, using these function calls as needed. This approach, often referred to as a *call-level interface* or CLI, will be discussed in Section 8.4.

8.1.1 The Impedance Mismatch Problem

The basic problem of connecting SQL statements with those of a conventional programming language is *impedance mismatch*, the fact that the data model of SQL differs so much from the models of other languages. As we know, SQL uses the relational data model at its core. However, C and other common programming languages use a data model with integers, reals, arithmetic, characters, pointers, record structures, arrays, and so on. Sets are not represented directly in C or these other languages, while SQL does not use pointers, loops and branches, or many other common programming-language constructs. As a result, jumping or passing data between SQL and other languages is not straightforward, and a mechanism must be devised to allow the development of programs that use both SQL and another language.

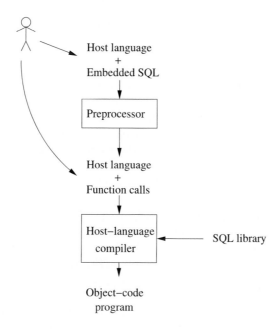

Figure 8.1: Processing programs with SQL statements embedded

One might first suppose that it is preferable to use a single language; either do all computation in SQL or forget SQL and do all computation in a conventional language. However, we can quickly dispense with the idea of omitting SQL when there are database operations involved. SQL systems greatly aid the programmer in writing database operations that can be executed efficiently, yet that can be expressed at a very high level. SQL takes from the programmer's shoulders the need to understand how data is organized in storage or how to exploit that storage structure to operate efficiently on the database.

On the other hand, there are many important things that SQL cannot do at all. For example, one cannot write an SQL query to compute the factorial of a number n [$n! = n \times (n-1) \times \cdots \times 2 \times 1$], something that is an easy exercise in C or similar languages.[1] As another example, SQL cannot format its output directly into a convenient form such as a graphic. Thus, real database programming requires both SQL and a conventional language; the latter is often referred to as the *host language*.

---

[1] We should be careful here. There are extensions to the basic SQL language, such as recursive SQL discussed in Section 10.4 or the SQL/PSM discussed in Section 8.2, that do offer "Turing completeness," i.e., the ability to compute anything that can be computed in any other programming language. However, these extensions were never intended for general purpose calculation, and we do not regard them as general-purpose languages.

8.1.2   The SQL/Host Language Interface

The transfer of information between the database, which is accessed only by SQL statements, and the host-language program is through variables of the host language that can be read or written by SQL statements. All such *shared variables* are prefixed by a colon when they are referred to within an SQL statement, but they appear without the colon in host-language statements.

When we wish to use an SQL statement within a host-language program, we warn that SQL code is coming with the keywords `EXEC SQL` in front of the statement. A typical system will preprocess those statements and replace them by suitable function calls in the host language, making use of an SQL-related library of functions.

A special variable, called `SQLSTATE` in the SQL standard, serves to connect the host-language program with the SQL execution system. The type of `SQLSTATE` is an array of five characters. Each time a function of the SQL library is called, a code is put in the variable `SQLSTATE` that indicates any problems found during that call. The SQL standard also specifies a large number of five-character codes and their meanings.

For example, '00000' (five zeroes) indicates that no error condition occurred, and '02000' indicates that a tuple requested as part of the answer to an SQL query could not be found. We shall see that the latter code is very important, since it allows us to create a loop in the host-language program that examines tuples from some relation one-at-a-time and to break the loop after the last tuple has been examined. The value of `SQLSTATE` can be read by the host-language program and a decision made on the basis of the value found there.

8.1.3   The `DECLARE` Section

To declare shared variables, we place their declarations between two embedded SQL statements:

```
EXEC SQL BEGIN DECLARE SECTION;
    ...
EXEC SQL END DECLARE SECTION;
```

What appears between them is called the *declare section*. The form of variable declarations in the declare section is whatever the host language requires. Moreover, it only makes sense to declare variables to have types that both the host language and SQL can deal with, such as integers, reals, and character strings or arrays.

Example 8.1: The following statements might appear in a C function that updates the `Studio` relation:

```
EXEC SQL BEGIN DECLARE SECTION;
    char studioName[50], studioAddr[256];
    char SQLSTATE[6];
EXEC SQL END DECLARE SECTION;
```

The first and last statements are the required beginning and end of the declare section. In the middle is a statement declaring two variables `studioName` and `studioAddr`. These are both character arrays and, as we shall see, they can be used to hold a name and address of a studio that are made into a tuple and inserted into the `Studio` relation. The third statement declares `SQLSTATE` to be a six-character array.[2] □

8.1.4 Using Shared Variables

A shared variable can be used in SQL statements in places where we expect or allow a constant. Recall that shared variables are preceded by a colon when so used. Here is an example in which we use the variables of Example 8.1 as components of a tuple to be inserted into relation `Studio`.

Example 8.2: In Fig. 8.2 is a sketch of a C function `getStudio` that prompts the user for the name and address of a studio, reads the responses, and inserts the appropriate tuple into `Studio`. Lines (1) through (4) are the declarations we learned about in Example 8.1. We omit the C code that prints requests and scans entered text to fill the two arrays `studioName` and `studioAddr`.

Then, in lines (5) and (6) is an embedded SQL statement that is a conventional `INSERT` statement. This statement is preceded by the keywords `EXEC SQL` to indicate that it is indeed an embedded SQL statement rather than ungrammatical C code. The preprocessor suggested in Fig. 8.1 will look for `EXEC SQL` to detect statements that must be preprocessed.

The values inserted by lines (5) and (6) are not explicit constants, as they were in previous examples such as in Example 6.34. Rather, the values appearing in line (6) are shared variables whose current values become components of the inserted tuple. □

There are many kinds of SQL statements besides an `INSERT` statement that can be embedded into a host language, using shared variables as an interface. Each embedded SQL statement is preceded by `EXEC SQL` in the host-language program and may refer to shared variables in place of constants. Any SQL statement that does not return a result (i.e., is not a query) can be embedded. Examples of embeddable SQL statements include delete- and update-statements and those statements that create, modify, or drop schema elements such as tables and views.

---

[2]We shall use six characters for the five-character value of `SQLSTATE` because in programs to follow we want to use the C function `strcmp` to test whether `SQLSTATE` has a certain value. Since `strcmp` expects strings to be terminated by '\0', we need a sixth character for this endmarker. The sixth character must be set initially to '\0', but we shall not show this assignment in programs to follow.

```
      void getStudio() {

1)        EXEC SQL BEGIN DECLARE SECTION;
2)            char studioName[50], studioAddr[256];
3)            char SQLSTATE[6];
4)        EXEC SQL END DECLARE SECTION;

          /* print request that studio name and address
             be entered and read response into variables
             studioName and studioAddr */

5)        EXEC SQL INSERT INTO Studio(name, address)
6)                VALUES (:studioName, :studioAddr);
      }
```

Figure 8.2: Using shared variables to insert a new studio

However, select-from-where queries are not embeddable directly into a host language, because of the "impedance mismatch." Queries produce sets of tuples as a result, while none of the major host languages supports a set data type directly. Thus, embedded SQL must use one of two mechanisms for connecting the result of queries with a host-language program.

1. A query that produces a single tuple can have that tuple stored in shared variables, one variable for each component of the tuple. To do so, we use a modified form of select-from-where statement called a *single-row select*.

2. Queries producing more than one tuple can be executed if we declare a *cursor* for the query. The cursor ranges over all tuples in the answer relation, and each tuple in turn can be fetched into shared variables and processed by the host-language program.

We shall consider each of these mechanisms in turn.

8.1.5 Single-Row Select Statements

The form of a single-row select is the same as an ordinary select-from-where statement, except that following the SELECT clause is the keyword INTO and a list of shared variables. These shared variables are preceded by colons, as is the case for all shared variables within an SQL statement. If the result of the query is a single tuple, this tuple's components become the values of these variables. If the result is either no tuple or more than one tuple, then no assignment to the shared variables are made, and an appropriate error code is written in the variable SQLSTATE.

Example 8.3: We shall write a C function to read the name of a studio and print the net worth of the studio's president. A sketch of this function is shown in Fig. 8.3. It begins with a declare section, lines (1) through (5), for the variables we shall need. Next, C statements that we do not show explicitly obtain a studio name from the standard input.

Lines (6) through (9) are the single-row select statement. It is quite similar to queries we have already seen. The two differences are that the value of variable `studioName` is used in place of a constant string in the condition of line (9), and there is an `INTO` clause at line (7) that tells us where to put the result of the query. In this case, we expect a single tuple, and tuples have only one component, that for attribute `netWorth`. The value of this one component of one tuple is stored in the shared variable `presNetWorth`. □

```
          void printNetWorth() {

1)            EXEC SQL BEGIN DECLARE SECTION;
2)                char studioName[50];
3)                int presNetWorth;
4)                char SQLSTATE[6];
5)            EXEC SQL END DECLARE SECTION;

              /* print request that studio name be entered.
                 read response into studioName */

6)            EXEC SQL SELECT netWorth
7)                    INTO :presNetWorth
8)                    FROM Studio, MovieExec
9)                    WHERE presC# = cert# AND
                          Studio.name = :studioName;

              /* check that SQLSTATE has all 0's and if so, print
                 the value of presNetWorth */
          }
```

Figure 8.3: A single-row select embedded in a C function

8.1.6 Cursors

The most versatile way to connect SQL queries to a host language is with a cursor that runs through the tuples of a relation. This relation can be a stored table, or it can be something that is generated by a query. To create and use a cursor, we need the following statements:

1. A cursor declaration. The simplest form of a cursor declaration consists of:

   (a) An introductory EXEC SQL, like all embedded SQL statements.

   (b) The keyword DECLARE.

   (c) The name of the cursor.

   (d) The keywords CURSOR FOR.

   (e) An expression such as a relation name or a select-from-where expression, whose value is a relation. The declared cursor *ranges* over the tuples of this relation; that is, the cursor refers to each tuple of this relation, in turn, as we "fetch" tuples using the cursor.

   In summary, the form of a cursor declaration is

   EXEC SQL DECLARE <cursor> CURSOR FOR <query>

2. A statement EXEC SQL OPEN, followed by the cursor name. This statement initializes the cursor to a position where it is ready to retrieve the first tuple of the relation over which the cursor ranges.

3. One or more uses of a *fetch statement*. The purpose of a fetch statement is to get the next tuple of the relation over which the cursor ranges. If the tuples have been exhausted, then no tuple is returned, and the value of SQLSTATE is set to '02000', a code that means "no tuple found." The fetch statement consists of the following components:

   (a) The keywords EXEC SQL FETCH FROM.

   (b) The name of the cursor.

   (c) The keyword INTO.

   (d) A list of shared variables, separated by commas. If there is a tuple to fetch, then the components of this tuple are placed in these variables, in order.

   That is, the form of a fetch statement is:

   EXEC SQL FETCH FROM <cursor> INTO <list of variables>

4. The statement EXEC SQL CLOSE followed by the name of the cursor. This statement closes the cursor, which now no longer ranges over tuples of the relation. It can, however, be reinitialized by another OPEN statement, in which case it ranges anew over the tuples of this relation.

Example 8.4: Suppose we wish to determine the number of movie executives whose net worths fall into a sequence of bands of exponentially growing size, each band corresponding to a number of digits in the net worth. We shall design a query that retrieves the netWorth field of all the MovieExec tuples into a shared variable called worth. A cursor called execCursor will range over all these one-component tuples. Each time a tuple is fetched, we compute the number of digits in the integer worth and increment the appropriate element of an array counts.

The C function worthRanges begins in line (1) of Fig. 8.4. Line (2) declares some variables used only by the C function, not by the embedded SQL. The array counts holds the counts of executives in the various bands, digits counts the number of digits in a net worth, and i is an index ranging over the elements of array counts.

```
1)   void worthRanges() {

2)       int i, digits, counts[15];
3)       EXEC SQL BEGIN DECLARE SECTION;
4)           int worth;
5)           char SQLSTATE[6];
6)       EXEC SQL END DECLARE SECTION;
7)       EXEC SQL DECLARE execCursor CURSOR FOR
8)           SELECT netWorth FROM MovieExec;

9)       EXEC SQL OPEN execCursor;
10)      for(i=0; i<15; i++) counts[i] = 0;
11)      while(1) {
12)          EXEC SQL FETCH FROM execCursor INTO :worth;
13)          if(NO_MORE_TUPLES) break;
14)          digits = 1;
15)          while((worth /= 10) > 0) digits++;
16)          if(digits <= 14) counts[digits]++;
         }
17)      EXEC SQL CLOSE execCursor;
18)      for(i=0; i<15; i++)
19)          printf("digits = %d: number of execs = %d\n",
                 i, counts[i]);
     }
```

Figure 8.4: Grouping executive net worths into exponential bands

Lines (3) through (6) are an SQL declare section in which shared variable worth and the usual SQLSTATE are declared. Lines (7) and (8) declare execCursor to be a cursor that ranges over the values produced by the query

on line (8). This query simply asks for the `netWorth` components of all the tuples in `MovieExec`. This cursor is then opened at line (9). Line (10) completes
the initialization by zeroing the elements of array `counts`.

The main work is done by the loop of lines (11) through (16). At line (12)
a tuple is fetched into shared variable `worth`. Since tuples produced by the
query of line (8) have only one component, we need only one shared variable,
although in general there would be as many variables as there are components
of the retrieved tuples. Line (13) tests whether the fetch has been successful.
Here, we use a macro `NO_MORE_TUPLES`, which we may suppose is defined by

```
#define NO_MORE_TUPLES !(strcmp(SQLSTATE,"02000"))
```

Recall that "02000" is the `SQLSTATE` code that means no tuple was found.
Thus, line (13) tests if all the tuples returned by the query had previously been
found and there was no "next" tuple to be obtained. If so, we break out of the
loop and go to line (17).

If a tuple has been fetched, then at line (14) we initialize the number of digits
in the net worth to 1. Line (15) is a loop that repeatedly divides the net worth
by 10 and increments `digits` by 1. When the net worth reaches 0 after division
by 10, `digits` holds the correct number of digits in the value of `worth` that was
originally retrieved. Finally, line (16) increments the appropriate element of the
array `counts` by 1. We assume that the number of digits is no more than 14.
However, should there be a net worth with 15 or more digits, line (16) will not
increment any element of the `counts` array, since there is no appropriate range;
i.e., enormous net worths are thrown away and do not affect the statistics.

Line (17) begins the wrap-up of the function. The cursor is closed, and lines
(18) and (19) print the values in the `counts` array.   □

8.1.7 Modifications by Cursor

When a cursor ranges over the tuples of a base table (i.e., a relation that is stored
in the database, rather than a view or a relation constructed by a query), then
one can not only read and process the value of each tuple, but one can update or
delete tuples. The syntax of these `UPDATE` and `DELETE` statements are the same
as we encountered in Section 6.5, with the exception of the `WHERE` clause. That
clause may only be `WHERE CURRENT OF` followed by the name of the cursor. Of
course it is possible for the host-language program reading the tuple to apply
whatever condition it likes to the tuple before deciding whether or not to delete
or update it.

Example 8.5: In Fig. 8.5 we see a C function that looks at each tuple of
`MovieExec` and decides either to delete the tuple or to double the net worth. In
lines (3) and (4) we declare variables that correspond to the four attributes of
`MovieExec`, as well as the necessary `SQLSTATE`. Then, at line (6), `execCursor` is
declared to range over the stored relation `MovieExec` itself. Note that, while we
could try to modify tuples through a cursor that ranged over some temporary

relation that was the result of some query, we can only have a lasting effect on the database if the cursor ranges over a stored relation such as `MovieExec`.

```
1)  void changeWorth() {

2)      EXEC SQL BEGIN DECLARE SECTION;
3)          int certNo, worth;
4)          char execName[30], execAddr[256], SQLSTATE[6];
5)      EXEC SQL END DECLARE SECTION;
6)      EXEC SQL DECLARE execCursor CURSOR FOR MovieExec;

7)      EXEC SQL OPEN execCursor;
8)      while(1) {
9)          EXEC SQL FETCH FROM execCursor INTO :execName,
                :execAddr, :certNo, :worth;
10)         if(NO_MORE_TUPLES) break;
11)         if (worth < 1000)
12)             EXEC SQL DELETE FROM MovieExec
                        WHERE CURRENT OF execCursor;
13)         else
14)             EXEC SQL UPDATE MovieExec
                        SET netWorth = 2 * netWorth
                        WHERE CURRENT OF execCursor;
        }
15)     EXEC SQL CLOSE execCursor;
    }
```

Figure 8.5: Modifying executive net worths

Lines (8) through (14) are the loop, in which the cursor `execCursor` refers to each tuple of `MovieExec`, in turn. Line (9) fetches the current tuple into the four variables used for this purpose; note that only `worth` is actually used. Line (10) tests whether we have exhausted the tuples of `MovieExec`. We have again used the macro `NO_MORE_TUPLES` for the condition that variable `SQLSTATE` has the "no more tuples" code `"02000"`.

In the test of line (11) we ask if the net worth is under $1000. If so, the tuple is deleted by the `DELETE` statement of line (12). Note that the `WHERE` clause refers to the cursor, so the current tuple of `MovieExec`, the one we just fetched, is deleted from `MovieExec`. If the net worth is at least $1000, then at line (14), the net worth in the same tuple is doubled, instead. □

8.1.8   Protecting Against Concurrent Updates

Suppose that as we examine the net worths of movie executives using the function `worthRanges` of Fig. 8.4, some other process is modifying the underlying `MovieExec` relation. We shall have more to say about several processes accessing a single database simultaneously when we discuss transactions in Section 8.6. However, for the moment, let us simply accept the possibility that there are other processes that could modify a relation as we use it.

What should we do about this possibility? Perhaps nothing. We might be happy with approximate statistics, and we don't care whether or not we count an executive who was in the process of being deleted, for example. Then, we simply accept what tuples we get through the cursor.

However, we may not wish to allow concurrent changes to affect the tuples we see through this cursor. Rather, we may insist on the statistics being taken on the relation as it exists at some point in time. We cannot control exactly which modifications to `MovieExec` occur before our gathering of statistics, but we can expect that all modification statements appear either to have occurred completely before or completely after the function `worthRanges` ran, regardless of how many executives were affected by one modification statement. To obtain this guarantee, we may declare the cursor *insensitive* to concurrent changes.

Example 8.6: We could modify lines (7) and (8) of Fig. 8.4 to be:

```
7)      EXEC SQL DECLARE execCursor INSENSITIVE CURSOR FOR
8)          SELECT netWorth FROM MovieExec;
```

If `execCursor` is so declared, then the SQL system will guarantee that changes to relation `MovieExec` made between one opening and closing of `execCursor` will not affect the set of tuples fetched.   □

An insensitive cursor could be expensive, in the sense that the SQL system might spend a lot of time managing data accesses to assure that the cursor is insensitive. Again, a discussion of managing concurrent operations on the database is deferred to Section 8.6. However, one simple way to support an insensitive cursor is for the SQL system to hold up any process that could access relations that our insensitive cursor's query uses.

There are certain cursors ranging over a relation R about which we may say with certainty that they will not change R. Such a cursor can run simultaneously with an insensitive cursor for R, without risk of changing the relation R that the insensitive cursor sees. If we declare a cursor `FOR READ ONLY`, then the database system can be sure that the underlying relation will not be modified because of access to the relation through this cursor.

Example 8.7: We could append after line (8) of Fig. 8.4 a line

```
FOR READ ONLY;
```

If so, then any attempt to execute a modification through cursor `execCursor` would cause an error.   □

8.1.9 Scrolling Cursors

Cursors give us a choice of how we move through the tuples of the relation. The default, and most common choice is to start at the beginning and fetch the tuples in order, until the end. However, there are other orders in which tuples may be fetched, and tuples could be scanned several times before the cursor is closed. To take advantage of these options, we need to do two things.

1. When declaring the cursor, put the keyword SCROLL before the keyword CURSOR. This change tells the SQL system that the cursor may be used in a manner other than moving forward in the order of tuples.

2. In a FETCH statement, follow the keyword FETCH by one of several options that tell where to find the desired tuple. These options are:

   (a) NEXT or PRIOR to get the next or previous tuple in the order. Recall that these tuples are relative to the current position of the cursor. NEXT is the default if no option is specified, and is the usual choice.

   (b) FIRST or LAST to get the first or last tuple in the order.

   (c) RELATIVE followed by a positive or negative integer, which indicates how many tuples to move forward (if the integer is positive) or backward (if negative) in the order. For instance, RELATIVE 1 is a synonym for NEXT, and RELATIVE -1 is a synonym for PRIOR.

   (d) ABSOLUTE followed by a positive or negative integer, which indicates the position of the desired tuple counting from the front (if positive) or back (if negative). For instance, ABSOLUTE 1 is a synonym for FIRST and ABSOLUTE -1 is a synonym for LAST.

Example 8.8: Let us rewrite the function of Fig. 8.5 to begin at the last tuple and move backward through the list of tuples. First, we need to declare cursor `execCursor` to be scrollable, which we do by adding the keyword SCROLL in line (6), as:

```
6) EXEC SQL DECLARE execCursor SCROLL CURSOR FOR MovieExec;
```

Also, we need to initialize the fetching of tuples with a FETCH LAST statement, and in the loop we use FETCH PRIOR. The loop that was lines (8) through (14) in Fig. 8.5 is rewritten in Fig. 8.6. The reader should not assume that there is any advantage to reading tuples in the reverse of the order in which they are stored in `MovieExec`. □

8.1.10 Dynamic SQL

Our model of SQL embedded in a host language has been that of specific SQL queries and commands within a host-language program. An alternative style

```
EXEC SQL FETCH LAST FROM execCursor INTO :execName,
    :execAddr, :certNo, :worth;
while(1) {
    /* same as lines (10) through (14) */
    EXEC SQL FETCH PRIOR FROM execCursor INTO :worth;
}
```

Figure 8.6: Reading `MovieExec` tuples backwards

of embedded SQL has the statements themselves be computed by the host language. Such statements are not known at compile time, and thus cannot be handled by an SQL preprocessor or a host-language compiler.

An example of such a situation is a program that prompts the user for an SQL query, reads the query, and then executes that query. The generic interface for ad-hoc SQL queries that we assumed in Chapter 6 is an example of just such a program; every commercial SQL system provides this type of generic SQL interface. If queries are read and executed at run-time, there is nothing that can be done at compile-time. The query has to be parsed and a suitable way to execute the query found by the SQL system, immediately after the query is read.

The host-language program must instruct the SQL system to take the character string just read, to turn it into an executable SQL statement, and finally to execute that statement. There are two *dynamic SQL* statements that perform these two steps.

1. `EXEC SQL PREPARE`, followed by an SQL variable V, the keyword `FROM`, and a host-language variable or expression of character-string type. This statement causes the string to be treated as an SQL statement. Presumably, the SQL statement is parsed and a good way to execute it is found by the SQL system, but the statement is not executed. Rather, the plan for executing the SQL statement becomes the value of V.

2. `EXEC SQL EXECUTE` followed by an SQL variable such as V in (1). This statement causes the SQL statement denoted by V to be executed.

Both steps can be combined into one, with the statement:

```
EXEC SQL EXECUTE IMMEDIATE
```

followed by a string-valued shared variable or a string-valued expression. The disadvantage of combining these two parts is seen if we prepare a statement once and then execute it many times. With `EXECUTE IMMEDIATE` the cost of preparing the statement is borne each time the statement is executed, rather than borne only once, when we prepare it.

Example 8.9: In Fig. 8.7 is a sketch of a C program that reads text from standard input into a variable `query`, prepares it, and executes it. The SQL variable `SQLquery` holds the prepared query. Since the query is only executed once, the line:

```
EXEC SQL EXECUTE IMMEDIATE :query;
```

could replace lines (6) and (7) of Fig. 8.7. □

```
1)   void readQuery() {

2)       EXEC SQL BEGIN DECLARE SECTION;
3)           char *query;
4)       EXEC SQL END DECLARE SECTION;

5)       /* prompt user for a query, allocate space (e.g.,
              use malloc) and make shared variable :query point
              to the first character of the query */
6)       EXEC SQL PREPARE SQLquery FROM :query;
7)       EXEC SQL EXECUTE SQLquery;
     }
```

Figure 8.7: Preparing and executing a dynamic SQL query

8.1.11 Exercises for Section 8.1

Exercise 8.1.1: Write the following embedded SQL queries, based on the database schema

```
Product(maker, model, type)
PC(model, speed, ram, hd, rd, price)
Laptop(model, speed, ram, hd, screen, price)
Printer(model, color, type, price)
```

of Exercise 5.2.1. You may use any host language with which you are familiar, and details of host-language programming may be replaced by clear comments if you wish.

* a) Ask the user for a price and find the PC whose price is closest to the desired price. Print the maker, model number, and speed of the PC.

  b) Ask the user for minimum values of the speed, RAM, hard-disk size, and screen size that they will accept. Find all the laptops that satisfy these requirements. Print their specifications (all attributes of `laptop`) and their manufacturer.

! c) Ask the user for a manufacturer. Print the specifications of all products by that manufacturer. That is, print the model number, product-type, and all the attributes of whichever relation is appropriate for that type.

!! d) Ask the user for a "budget" (total price of a PC and printer), and a minimum speed of the PC. Find the cheapest "system" (PC plus printer) that is within the budget and minimum speed, but make the printer a color printer if possible. Print the model numbers for the chosen system.

e) Ask the user for a manufacturer, model number, speed, RAM, hard-disk size, speed and kind or the removable disk, and price of a new PC. Check that there is no PC with that model number. Print a warning if so, and otherwise insert the information into tables `Product` and PC.

*! f) Lower the price of all "old" PC's by $100. Make sure that any "new" PC inserted during the time that your program is running does not have its price lowered.

Exercise 8.1.2: Write the following embedded SQL queries, based on the database schema

```
Classes(class, type, country, numGuns, bore, displacement)
Ships(name, class, launched)
Battles(name, date)
Outcomes(ship, battle, result)
```

of Exercise 5.2.4.

a) The firepower of a ship is roughly proportional to the number of guns times the cube of the bore of the guns. Find the class with the largest firepower.

! b) Ask the user for the name of a battle. Find the countries of the ships involved in the battle. Print the country with the most ships sunk and the country with the most ships damaged.

c) Ask the user for the name of a class and the other information required for a tuple of table `Classes`. Then ask for a list of the names of the ships of that class and their dates launched. However, the user need not give the first name, which will be the name of the class. Insert the information gathered into `Classes` and `Ships`.

! d) Examine the `Battles`, `Outcomes`, and `Ships` relations for ships that were in battle before they were launched. Prompt the user when there is an error found, offering the option to change the date of launch or the date of the battle. Make whichever change is requested.

*! **Exercise 8.1.3:** In this exercise, our goal is to find all PC's in the relation

```
PC(model, speed, ram, hd, rd, price)
```

for which there are at least two more expensive PC's of the same speed. While there are many ways we could approach the problem, you should use a scrolling cursor in this exercise. Read the tuples of `PC` ordered first by `speed` and then by `price`. *Hint*: For each tuple read, skip ahead two tuples to see if the speed has not changed.

8.2   Procedures Stored in the Schema

In this section, we introduce you to a recent SQL standard called *Persistent, Stored Modules* (SQL/PSM, or just PSM, or PSM-96). Each commercial DBMS offers a way for the user to store with a database schema some functions or procedures that can be used in SQL queries or other SQL statements. These pieces of code are written in a simple, general-purpose language, and allow us to perform, within the database itself, computations that cannot be expressed in the SQL query language. In this book, we shall describe the SQL/PSM standard, which captures the major ideas of these facilities, and which should help you understand the language associated with any particular system.

In PSM, you define *modules*, which are collections of function and procedure definitions, temporary relation declarations, and several other optional declarations. We discuss modules further in Section 8.3.7; here we shall discuss only the functions and procedures of PSM.

8.2.1   Creating PSM Functions and Procedures

The major elements of a procedure declaration are

```
CREATE PROCEDURE <name> (<parameters>)
    local declarations
    procedure body;
```

This form should be familiar from a number of programming languages; it consists of a procedure name, a parenthesized list of parameters, some optional local-variable declarations, and the executable body of code that defines the procedure. A function is defined in almost the same way, except that the keyword `FUNCTION` is used and there is a return-value type that must be specified. That is, the elements of a function definition are:

```
CREATE FUNCTION <name> (<parameters>) RETURNS <type>
    local declarations
    function body;
```

The parameters of a procedure are triples of mode-name-type, much like the parameters of ODL methods, which we discussed in Section 4.2.7. That is, the parameter name is not only followed by its declared type, as usual in programming languages, but it is preceded by a "mode," which is either IN, OUT, or INOUT. These three keywords indicate that the parameter is input-only, output-only, or both input and output, respectively. IN is the default, and can be omitted.

Function parameters, on the other hand, may only be of mode IN. That is, PSM forbids side-effects in functions, so the only way to obtain information from a function is through its return-value. We shall not specify the IN mode for function parameters, although we do so in procedure definitions.

Example 8.10: While we have not yet learned the variety of statements that can appear in procedure and function bodies, one kind should not surprise us: an SQL statement. The limitation on these statements is the same as for embedded SQL, as we introduced in Section 8.1.4: only single-row-select statements and cursor-based accesses are permitted as queries. In Fig. 8.8 is a PSM procedure that takes two addresses — an old address and a new address — and changes to the new address the **address** attribute of every star who lived at the old address.

```
1)   CREATE PROCEDURE Move(
2)       IN oldAddr VARCHAR[255],
3)       IN newAddr VARCHAR[255]
     )
4)   UPDATE MovieStar
5)   SET address = newAddr
6)   WHERE address = oldAddr;
```

Figure 8.8: A procedure to change addresses

Line (1) introduces the procedure and its name, Move. Lines (2) and (3) contain the two parameters, both of which are input parameters whose type is variable-length character strings of length 255. Note that this type is consistent with the type we declared for the attribute **address** of **MovieStar** in Fig. 6.16. Lines (4) through (6) are a conventional UPDATE statement. However, notice that the parameter names can be used as if they were constants. Unlike host-language variables, which require a colon prefix when used in SQL (see Section 8.1.2), parameters and other local variables of PSM procedures and functions require no colon. □

8.2.2 Some Simple Statement Forms in PSM

Let us begin with a potpourri of statement forms that are easy to master.

1. *The call-statement*: The form of a procedure call is:

```
CALL <procedure name> (<argument list>);
```

That is, the keyword `CALL` is followed by the name of the procedure and a parenthesized list of arguments, as in most any language. This call can, however, be made from a variety of places:

i. From a host-language program, in which it might appear as

```
EXEC SQL CALL Foo(:x, 3);
```

for instance.

ii. As a statement of another PSM function or procedure.

iii. As an SQL command issued to the generic SQL interface. For example, we can issue a statement such as

```
CALL Foo(1, 3);
```

to such an interface, and have stored procedure `Foo` executed with its two parameters set equal to 1 and 3, respectively.

Note that it is not permitted to call a function. You invoke functions in PSM as you do in C: use the function name and suitable arguments as part of an expression.

2. *The return-statement*: Its form is

```
RETURN <expression>;
```

This statement can only appear in a function. It evaluates the expression and sets the return-value of the function equal to that result. However, at variance with common programming languages, the return-statement of PSM does *not* terminate the function. Rather, control continues with the following statement, and it is possible that the return-value will be changed before the function completes.

3. *Declarations of local variables*: The statement form

```
DECLARE <name> <type>;
```

declares a variable with the given name to have the given type. This variable is local, and its value is not preserved by the DBMS after a running of the function or procedure. Declarations must precede executable statements in the function or procedure body.

4. *Assignment Statements*: The form of an assignment is:

```
SET <variable> = <expression>;
```

Except for the introductory keyword `SET`, assignment in PSM is quite like assignment in other languages. The expression on the right of the equal-sign is evaluated, and its value becomes the value of the variable on the left. `NULL` is a permissible expression. The expression may even be a query, as long as it returns a single value.

5. *Statement groups*: We can form a list of statements ended by semicolons and surrounded by keywords `BEGIN` and `END`. This construct is treated as a single statement and can appear anywhere a single statement can. In particular, since a procedure or function body is expected to be a single statement, we can put any sequence of statements in the body by surrounding them by `BEGIN...END`.

6. *Statement labels*: We shall see in Section 8.2.5 one reason why certain statements need a label. We label a statement by prefixing it with a name (the label) and a colon.

8.2.3 Branching Statements

For our first complex PSM statement type, let us consider the if-statement. The form is only a little strange; it differs from C or similar languages in that:

1. The statement ends with keywords `END IF`.

2. If-statements nested within the else-clause are introduced with the single word `ELSEIF`.

Thus, the general form of an if-statement is as suggested by Fig. 8.9. The condition is any boolean-valued expression, as can appear in the `WHERE` clause of SQL statements. Each statement list consists of statements ended by semicolons, but does not need a surrounding `BEGIN...END`. The final `ELSE` and its statement(s) are optional; i.e., `IF...THEN...END IF` alone or with `ELSEIF`'s is acceptable.

```
IF <condition> THEN
    <statement list>
ELSEIF <condition> THEN
    <statement list>
ELSEIF
    ...
ELSE <statement list>
END IF;
```

Figure 8.9: The form of an if-statement

Example 8.11: Let us write a function to take a year y and a studio s, and return a boolean that is TRUE if and only if studio s produced at least one black-and-white movie in year y or did not produce any movies at all in that year. The code appears in Fig. 8.10.

```
1)  CREATE FUNCTION BandW(y INT, s CHAR[15]) RETURNS BOOLEAN

2)  IF NOT EXISTS(
3)      SELECT * FROM Movie WHERE year = y AND
            studioName = s)
4)  THEN RETURN TRUE;
5)  ELSEIF 1 <=
6)      (SELECT COUNT(*) FROM Movie WHERE year = y AND
            studioName = s AND NOT inColor)
7)  THEN RETURN TRUE;
8)  ELSE RETURN FALSE;
9)  END IF;
```

Figure 8.10: If there are any movies at all, then at least one has to be in black-and-white

Line (1) introduces the function and includes its arguments. We do not need to specify a mode for the arguments, since that can only be IN for a function. Lines (2) and (3) test for the case where there are no movies at all by studio s in year y, in which case we set the return-value to TRUE at line (4). Note that line (4) does not cause the function to return. Technically, it is the flow of control dictated by the if-statements that causes control to jump from line (4) to line (9), where the function completes and returns.

If studio s made movies in year y, then lines (5) and (6) test if at least one of them was not in color. If so, the return-value is again set to true, this time at line (7). In the remaining case, studio s made movies but only in color, so we set the return-value to FALSE at line (8). □

8.2.4 Queries in PSM

There are several ways that select-from-where queries are used in PSM.

1. Subqueries can be used in conditions, or in general, any place a subquery is legal in SQL. We saw two examples of subqueries in lines (3) and (6) of Fig. 8.10, for instance.

2. Queries that return a single value can be used as the right sides of assignment statements.

3. A single-row select statement is a legal statement in PSM. Recall this statement has an INTO clause that specifies variables into which the components of the single returned tuple are placed. These variables could be local variables or parameters of a PSM procedure. The general form was discussed in the context of embedded SQL in Section 8.1.5.

4. We can declare and use a cursor, essentially as it was described in Section 8.1.6 for embedded SQL. The declaration of the cursor, OPEN, FETCH, and CLOSE statements are all as described there, with the exceptions that:

   (a) No EXEC SQL appears in the statements, and

   (b) The variables, being local, do not use a colon prefix.

```
CREATE PROCEDURE SomeProc(IN studioName CHAR[15])

DECLARE presNetWorth INTEGER;

SELECT netWorth
INTO presNetWorth
FROM Studio, MovieExec
WHERE presC# = cert# AND Studio.name = studioName;
    ...
```

Figure 8.11: A single-row select in PSM

Example 8.12: In Fig. 8.11 is the single-row select of Fig. 8.3, redone for PSM and placed in the context of a hypothetical procedure definition. Note that, because the single-row select returns a one-component tuple, we could also get the same effect from an assignment statement, as:

```
SET presNetWorth = (SELECT netWorth
    FROM Studio, MovieExec
    WHERE presC# = cert# AND Studio.name = studioName);
```

We shall defer examples of cursor use until we learn the PSM loop statements in the next section. □

8.2.5 Loops in PSM

The basic loop construct in PSM is:

```
LOOP
    <statement list>
END LOOP;
```

One often labels the LOOP statement, so it is possible to break out of the loop, using a statement:

    LEAVE <loop label>;

In the common case that the loop involves the fetching of tuples via a cursor, we often wish to leave the loop when there are no more tuples. It is useful to declare a *condition* name for the SQLSTATE value that indicates no tuple found ('02000', recall); we do so with:

    DECLARE Not_Found CONDITION FOR SQLSTATE '02000';

More generally, we can declare a condition with any desired name corresponding to any SQLSTATE value by

    DECLARE <name> CONDITION FOR SQLSTATE <value>;

We are now ready to take up an example that ties together cursor operations and loops in PSM.

Example 8.13 : Figure 8.12 shows a PSM procedure that takes a studio name *s* as an input argument and produces in output arguments mean and variance the mean and variance of the lengths of all the movies owned by studio *s*. Lines (1) through (4) declare the procedure and its parameters.

Lines (5) through (8) are local declarations. We define Not_Found to be the name of the condition that means a FETCH failed to return a tuple at line (5). Then, at line (6), the cursor MovieCursor is defined to return the set of the lengths of the movies by studio *s*. Lines (7) and (8) declare two local variables that we'll need. Integer newLength holds the result of a FETCH, while movieCount counts the number of movies by studio *s*. We need movieCount so that, at the end, we can convert a sum of lengths into an average (mean) of lengths and a sum of squares of the lengths into a variance.

The rest of the lines are the body of the procedure. We shall use mean and variance as temporary variables, as well as for "returning" the results at the end. In the major loop, mean actually holds the sum of the lengths, and variance actually holds the sum of the squares of the lengths. Thus, lines (9) through (11) initialize these variables and the count of the movies to 0. Line (12) opens the cursor, and lines (13) through (19) form the loop labeled movieLoop.

Line (14) performs a fetch, and at line (15) we check that another tuple was found. If not, we leave the loop. Lines (15) through (18) accumulate values; we add 1 to movieCount, add the length to mean (which, recall, is really computing the sum of lengths), and we add the square of the length to variance.

When all movies by studio *s* have been seen, we leave the loop, and control passes to line (20). At that line, we turn mean into its correct value by dividing the sum of lengths by the count of movies. At line (21), we make variance truly hold the variance by dividing the sum of squares of the lengths by the

```
 1)   CREATE PROCEDURE MeanVar(
 2)       IN s CHAR[15],
 3)       OUT mean REAL,
 4)       OUT variance REAL
      )
 5)   DECLARE Not_Found CONDITION FOR SQLSTATE '02000';
 6)   DECLARE MovieCursor CURSOR FOR
          SELECT length FROM Movie WHERE studioName = s;
 7)   DECLARE newLength INTEGER;
 8)   DECLARE movieCount INTEGER;

      BEGIN
 9)       SET mean = 0.0;
10)       SET variance = 0.0;
11)       SET movieCount = 0;
12)       OPEN MovieCursor;
13)       movieLoop: LOOP
14)           FETCH MovieCursor INTO newLength;
15)           IF Not_Found THEN LEAVE movieLoop END IF;
16)           SET movieCount = movieCount + 1;
17)           SET mean = mean + newLength;
18)           SET variance = variance + newLength * newLength;
19)       END LOOP;
20)       SET mean = mean/movieCount;
21)       SET variance = variance/movieCount - mean * mean;
22)       CLOSE MovieCursor;
      END;
```

Figure 8.12: Computing the mean and variance of lengths of movies by one studio

number of movies and subtracting the square of the mean. See Exercise 8.2.4 for a discussion of why this calculation is correct. Line (22) closes the cursor, and we are done. □

8.2.6 For-Loops

There is also in PSM a for-loop construct, but it is used for only one, important purpose: to iterate over a cursor. The form of the statement is:

```
FOR <loop name> AS <cursor name> CURSOR FOR
    <query>
DO
```

Other Loop Constructs

PSM also allows while- and repeat-loops, which have the expected meaning, as in C. That is, we can create a loop of the form

```
WHILE <condition> DO
    <statement list>
END WHILE;
```

or a loop of the form

```
REPEAT
    <statement list>
UNTIL <condition>
END REPEAT;
```

Incidentally, if we label these loops, or the loop formed by a loop-statement or for-statement, then we can place the label as well after the END LOOP or other ender. The advantage of doing so is that it makes clearer where each loop ends, and it allows the PSM interpreter to catch some syntactic errors involving the omission of an END.

```
        <statement list>
    END FOR;
```

This statement not only declares a cursor, but it handles for us a number of "grubby details": the opening and closing of the cursor, the fetching, and the checking whether there are no more tuples to be fetched. However, since we are not fetching tuples for ourselves, we can not specify the variable(s) into which component(s) of a tuple are placed. Thus, the names used for the attributes in the result of the query are also treated by PSM as local variables of the same type.

Example 8.14: Let us redo the procedure of Fig. 8.12 using a for-loop. The code is shown in Fig. 8.13. Many things have not changed. The declaration of the procedure in lines (1) through (4) of Fig. 8.13 are the same, as is the declaration of local variable movieCount at line (5).

However, we no longer need to declare a cursor in the declaration portion of the procedure, and we do not need to define the condition Not_Found. Lines (6) through (8) initialize the variables, as before. Then, in line (9) we see the for-loop, which also defines the cursor MovieCursor. Lines (11) through (13) are the body of the loop. Notice that in lines (12) and (13), we refer to the length retrieved via the cursor by the attribute name length, rather than by the local variable name newLength, which does not exist in this version of the procedure.

```
1)  CREATE PROCEDURE MeanVar(
2)      IN s CHAR[15],
3)      OUT mean REAL,
4)      OUT variance REAL
    )
5)  DECLARE movieCount INTEGER;

    BEGIN
6)      SET mean = 0.0;
7)      SET variance = 0.0;
8)      SET movieCount = 0;
9)      FOR movieLoop AS MovieCursor CURSOR FOR
            SELECT length FROM Movie WHERE studioName = s;
10)     DO
11)         SET movieCount = movieCount + 1;
12)         SET mean = mean + length;
13)         SET variance = variance + length * length;
14)     END FOR;
15)     SET mean = mean/movieCount;
16)     SET variance = variance/movieCount - mean * mean;
    END;
```

Figure 8.13: Computing the mean and variance of lengths using a for-loop

Lines (15) and (16) compute the correct values for the output variables, exactly as in the earlier version of this procedure.   □

8.2.7   Exceptions in PSM

An SQL system indicates error conditions by setting a nonzero sequence of digits in the five-character string SQLSTATE. We have seen one example of these codes: '02000' for "no tuple found." For another example, '21000' indicates that a single-row select has returned more than one row.

PSM allows us to declare a piece of code, called an *exception handler*, that is invoked whenever one of a list of these error codes appears in SQLSTATE during the execution of a statement or list of statements. Each exception handler is associated with a block of code, delineated by BEGIN...END. The handler appears within this block, and it applies only to statements within the block.

The components of the handler are:

1. A list of exception conditions that invoke the handler when raised.

2. Code to be executed when one of the associated exceptions is raised.

Why Do We Need Names in For-Loops?

Notice that `movieLoop` and `MovieCursor`, although declared at line (9) of Fig. 8.13, are never used in that procedure. Nonetheless, we have to invent names, both for the for-loop itself and for the cursor over which it iterates. The reason is that the PSM interpreter will translate the for-loop into a conventional loop, much like the code of Fig. 8.12, and in this code, there is a need for both names.

---

3. An indication of where to go after the handler has finished its work.

The form of a handler declaration is:

```
DECLARE <where to go> HANDLER FOR <condition list>
    <statement>
```

The choices for "where to go" are:

a) `CONTINUE`, which means that after executing the statement in the handler declaration, we execute the statement after the one that raised the exception.

b) `EXIT`, which means that after executing the handler's statement, control leaves the `BEGIN...END` block in which the handler is declared. The statement after this block is executed next.

c) `UNDO`, which is the same as `EXIT`, except that any changes to the database or local variables that were made by the statements of the block executed so far are "undone." That is, their effects are canceled, and it is as if those statements had not executed.

The "condition list" is a comma-separated list of conditions, which are either declared conditions, like `Not_Found` in line (5) of Fig. 8.12, or expressions of the form `SQLSTATE` and a five-character string.

Example 8.15: Let us write a PSM function that takes a movie title as argument and returns the year of the movie. If there is no movie of that title or more than one movie of that title, then `NULL` must be returned. The code is shown in Fig. 8.14.

Lines (2) and (3) declare symbolic conditions; we do not have to make these definitions, and could as well have used the SQL states for which they stand in line (4). Lines (4), (5), and (6) are a block, in which we first declare a handler for the two conditions in which either zero tuples are returned, or more than one tuple is returned. The action of the handler, on line (5), is simply to set the return-value to `NULL`.

```
1)   CREATE FUNCTION GetYear(t VARCHAR[255]) RETURNS INTEGER

2)   DECLARE Not_Found CONDITION FOR SQLSTATE '02000';
3)   DECLARE Too_Many CONDITION FOR SQLSTATE '21000';

     BEGIN
4)       DECLARE EXIT HANDLER FOR Not_Found, Too_Many
5)           RETURN NULL;
6)       RETURN (SELECT year FROM Movie WHERE title = t);
     END;
```

Figure 8.14: Handling exceptions in which a single-row select returns other than one tuple

Line (6) is the statement that does the work of the function GetYear. It is a SELECT statement that is expected to return exactly one integer, since that is what the function GetYear returns. If there is exactly one movie with title t (the input parameter of the function), then this value will be returned. However, if an exception is raised at line (6), either because there is no movie with title t or several movies with that title, then the handler is invoked, and NULL instead becomes the return-value. Also, since the handler is an EXIT handler, control next passes to the point after the END. Since that point is the end of the function, GetYear returns at that time, with the return-value NULL.   □

8.2.8   Using PSM Functions and Procedures

As we mentioned in Section 8.2.2, we can call a PSM function or procedure from a program with embedded SQL, from PSM code itself, or from ordinary SQL commands issued to the generic interface. The use of these procedures and functions is the same as in most programming languages, with procedures invoked by CALL, and functions appearing as part of an expression. We shall give one example of how a function can be called from the generic interface.

Example 8.16: Suppose that our schema includes a module with the function GetYear of Fig. 8.14. Imagine that we are sitting at the generic interface, and we want to enter the fact that Denzel Washington was a star of *Remember the Titans*. However, we forget the year in which that movie was made. As long as there was only one movie of that name, and it is in the Movie relation, we don't have to look it up in a preliminary query. Rather, we can issue to the generic SQL interface the following insertion:

```
INSERT INTO StarsIn(movieTitle, movieYear, starName)
VALUES('Remember the Titans', GetYear('Remember the Titans'),
    'Denzel Washington');
```

Since `GetYear` returns `NULL` if there is not a unique movie by the name of *Remember the Titans*, it is possible that this insertion will have `NULL` in the middle component. □

8.2.9 Exercises for Section 8.2

Exercise 8.2.1: Using our running movie database:

```
Movie(title, year, length, inColor, studioName, producerC#)
StarsIn(movieTitle, movieYear, starName)
MovieStar(name, address, gender, birthdate)
MovieExec(name, address, cert#, netWorth)
Studio(name, address, presC#)
```

write PSM procedures or functions to perform the following tasks:

* a) Given the name of a movie studio, produce the net worth of its president.

* b) Given a name and address, return 1 if the person is a movie star but not an executive, 2 if the person is an executive but not a star, 3 if both, and 4 if neither.

*! c) Given a studio name, assign to output parameters the titles of the two longest movies by that studio. Assign `NULL` to one or both parameters if there is no such movie (e.g., if there is only one movie by a studio, there is no "second-longest").

! d) Given a star name, find the earliest (lowest year) movie of more than 120 minutes length in which they appeared. If there is no such movie, return the year 0.

e) Given an address, find the name of the unique star with that address if there is exactly one, and return `NULL` if there is none or more than one.

f) Given the name of a star, delete them from `MovieStar` and delete all their movies from `StarsIn` and `Movie`.

Exercise 8.2.2: Write the following PSM functions or procedures, based on the database schema

```
Product(maker, model, type)
PC(model, speed, ram, hd, rd, price)
Laptop(model, speed, ram, hd, screen, price)
Printer(model, color, type, price)
```

of Exercise 5.2.1.

* a) Take a price as argument and return the model number of the PC whose price is closest.

b) Take a maker, model, and price as arguments, and return the price of whatever type of product that model is.

! c) Take model, speed, ram, hard-disk, removable-disk, and price information as arguments, and insert this information into the relation PC. However, if there is already a PC with that model number (tell by assuming that violation of a key constraint on insertion will raise an exception with SQLSTATE equal to '23000'), then keep adding 1 to the model number until you find a model number that is not already a PC model number.

! d) Given a price, produce the number of PC's the number of laptops, and the number of printers selling for more than that price.

Exercise 8.2.3: Write the following PSM functions or procedures, based on the database schema

```
Classes(class, type, country, numGuns, bore, displacement)
Ships(name, class, launched)
Battles(name, date)
Outcomes(ship, battle, result)
```

of Exercise 5.2.4.

a) The firepower of a ship is roughly proportional to the number of guns times the cube of the bore. Given a class, find its firepower.

! b) Given the name of a battle, produce the two countries whose ships were involved in the battle. If there are more or fewer than two countries involved, produce NULL for both countries.

c) Take as arguments a new class name, type, country, number of guns, bore, and displacement. Add this information to Classes and also add the ship with the class name to Ships.

! d) Given a ship name, determine if the ship was in a battle with a date before the ship was launched. If so, set the date of the battle and the date the ship was launched to 0.

! **Exercise 8.2.4:** In Fig. 8.12, we used a tricky formula for computing the variance of a sequence of numbers $x_1, x_2, \ldots, x_n$. Recall that the variance is the average square of the deviation of these numbers from their mean. That is, the variance is $\left(\sum_{i=1}^{n}(x_i - \bar{x})^2\right)/n$, where the mean $\bar{x}$ is $\left(\sum_{i=1}^{n} x_i\right)/n$. Prove that the formula for the variance used in Fig. 8.12, which is

$$\left(\sum_{i=1}^{n}(x_i)^2\right)/n - \left(\left(\sum_{i=1}^{n} x_i\right)/n\right)^2$$

yields the same value.

8.3 The SQL Environment

In this section we shall take the broadest possible view of a DBMS and the databases and programs it supports. We shall see how databases are defined and organized into clusters, catalogs, and schemas. We shall also see how programs are linked with the data they need to manipulate. Many of the details depend on the particular implementation, so we shall concentrate on the general ideas that are contained in the SQL standard. Sections 8.4 and 8.5 illustrate how these high-level concepts appear in a "call-level interface," which requires the programmer to make explicit connections to databases.

8.3.1 Environments

An *SQL environment* is the framework under which data may exist and SQL operations on data may be executed. In practice, we should think of an SQL environment as a DBMS running at some installation. For example, ABC company buys a license for the Megatron 2002 DBMS to run on a collection of ABC's machines. The system running on these machines constitutes an SQL environment.

All the database elements we have discussed — tables, views, triggers, stored procedures, and so on — are defined within an SQL environment. These elements are organized into a hierarchy of structures, each of which plays a distinct role in the organization. The structures defined by the SQL standard are indicated in Fig. 8.15.

Briefly, the organization consists of the following structures:

1. *Schemas.*[3] These are collections of tables, views, assertions, triggers, PSM modules, and some other types of information that we do not discuss in this book (but see the box on "More Schema Elements" in Section 8.3.2). Schemas are the basic units of organization, close to what we might think of as a "database," but in fact somewhat less than a database as we shall see in point (3) below.

2. *Catalogs.* These are collections of schemas. They are the basic unit for supporting unique, accessible terminology. Each catalog has one or more schemas; the names of schemas within a catalog must be unique, and each catalog contains a special schema called INFORMATION_SCHEMA that contains information about all the schemas in the catalog.

3. *Clusters.* These are collections of catalogs. Each user has an associated cluster: the set of all catalogs accessible to the user (see Section 8.7 for an explanation of how access to catalogs and other elements is controlled). SQL is not very precise about what a cluster is, e.g., whether clusters for various users can overlap without being identical. A cluster is the

---

[3]Note that the term "schema" in this context refers to a database schema, not a relation schema.

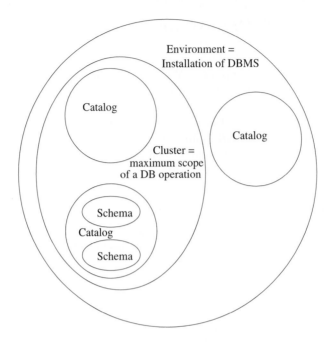

Figure 8.15: Organization of database elements within the environment

maximum scope over which a query can be issued, so in a sense, a cluster is "the database" as seen by a particular user.

8.3.2 Schemas

The simplest form of schema declaration consists of:

1. The keywords `CREATE SCHEMA`.

2. The name of the schema.

3. A list of declarations for schema elements such as base tables, views, and assertions.

That is, a schema may be declared by:

         `CREATE SCHEMA` <schema name> <element declarations>

The element declarations are of the forms discussed in various places, such as Sections 6.6, 6.7.1, 7.4.3, and 8.2.1.

Example 8.17: We could declare a schema that includes the five relations about movies that we have been using in our running example, plus some of the other elements we have introduced, such as views. Figure 8.16 sketches the form of such a declaration.   □

```
CREATE SCHEMA MovieSchema
    CREATE TABLE MovieStar ... as in Fig. 7.5
        Create-table statements for the four other tables
    CREATE VIEW MovieProd ... as in Example 6.48
        Other view declarations
    CREATE ASSERTION RichPres ... as in Example 7.13
```

Figure 8.16: Declaring a schema

It is not necessary to declare the schema all at once. One can modify or add to a schema using the appropriate CREATE, DROP, or ALTER statement, e.g., CREATE TABLE followed by the declaration of a new table for the schema. One problem is that the SQL system needs to know in which schema the new table belongs. If we alter or drop a table or other schema element, we may also need to disambiguate the name of the element, since two or more schemas may have distinct elements of the same name.

We change the "current" schema with a SET SCHEMA statement. For example,

```
SET SCHEMA MovieSchema;
```

makes the schema described in Fig. 8.16 the current schema. Then, any declarations of schema elements are added to that schema, and any DROP or ALTER statements refer to elements already in that schema.

8.3.3 Catalogs

Just as schema elements like tables are created within a schema, schemas are created and modified within a catalog. In principle, we would expect the process of creating and populating catalogs to be analogous to the process of creating and populating schemas. Unfortunately, SQL does not define a standard way to do so, such as a statement

```
CREATE CATALOG <catalog name>
```

followed by a list of schemas belonging to that catalog and the declarations of those schemas.

However, SQL does stipulate a statement

```
SET CATALOG <catalog name>
```

This statement allows us to set the "current" catalog, so new schemas will go into that catalog and schema modifications will refer to schemas in that catalog should there be a name ambiguity.

More Schema Elements

Some schema elements that we have not already mentioned, but that occasionally are useful are:

- *Domains*: These are sets of values or simple data types. They are little used today, because object-relational DBMS's provide more powerful type-creation mechanisms; see Section 9.4.

- *Character sets*: These are sets of symbols and methods for encoding them. ASCII is the best known character set, but an SQL implementation may support many others, such as sets for various foreign languages.

- *Collations*: Recall from Section 6.1.3 that character strings are compared lexicographically, assuming that any two characters can be compared by a "less than" relation we denoted <. A collation specifies which characters are "less than" which others. For example, we might use the ordering implied by the ASCII code, or we might treat lower-case and capital letters the same and not compare anything that isn't a letter.

- *Grant statements*: These concern who has access to schema elements. We shall discuss the granting of privileges in Section 8.7.

8.3.4   Clients and Servers in the SQL Environment

An SQL environment is more than a collection of catalogs and schemas. It contains elements whose purpose is to support operations on the database or databases represented by those catalogs and schemas. Within an SQL environment are two special kinds of processes: SQL clients and SQL servers. A server supports operations on the database elements, and a client allows a user to connect to a server and operate on the database. It is envisioned that the server runs on a large host that stores the database and the client runs on another host, perhaps a personal workstation remote from the server. However, it is also possible that both client and server run on the same host.

8.3.5   Connections

If we wish to run some program involving SQL at a host where an SQL client exists, then we may open a connection between the client and server by executing an SQL statement

---

Complete Names for Schema Elements

Formally, the name for a schema element such as a table is its catalog name, its schema name, and its own name, connected by dots in that order. Thus, the table `Movie` in the schema `MovieSchema` in the catalog `MovieCatalog` can be referred to as

$$\texttt{MovieCatalog.MovieSchema.Movie}$$

If the catalog is the default or current catalog, then we can omit that component of the name. If the schema is also the default or current schema, then that part too can be omitted, and we are left with the element's own name, as is usual. However, we have the option to use the full name if we need to access something outside the current schema or catalog.

```
CONNECT TO <server name> AS <connection name>
        AUTHORIZATION <name and password>
```

The server name is something that depends on the installation. The word `DEFAULT` can substitute for a name and will connect the user to whatever SQL server the installation treats as the "default server." We have shown an authorization clause followed by the user's name and password. The latter is the typical method by which a user would be identified to the server, although other strings following `AUTHORIZATION` might be used.

The connection name can be used to refer to the connection later on. The reason we might have to refer to the connection is that SQL allows several connections to be opened by the user, but only one can be active at any time. To switch among connections, we can make `conn1` become the active connection by the statement:

```
SET CONNECTION conn1;
```

Whatever connection was currently active becomes *dormant* until it is reactivated with another `SET CONNECTION` statement that mentions it explicitly.

We also use the name when we drop the connection. We can drop connection `conn1` by

```
DISCONNECT conn1;
```

Now, `conn1` is terminated; it is not dormant and cannot be reactivated.

However, if we shall never need to refer to the connection being created, then `AS` and the connection name may be omitted from the `CONNECT TO` statement. It is also permitted to skip the connection statements altogether. If we simply execute SQL statements at a host with an SQL client, then a default connection will be established on our behalf.

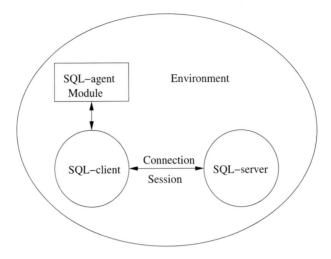

Figure 8.17: The SQL client-server interactions

8.3.6 Sessions

The SQL operations that are performed while a connection is active form a
session. The session is coextensive with the connection that created it. For
example, when a connection is made dormant, its session also becomes dormant,
and reactivation of the connection by a `SET CONNECTION` statement also makes
the session active. Thus, we have shown the session and connection as two
aspects of the link between client and server in Fig. 8.17.

Each session has a current catalog and a current schema within that catalog.
These may be set with statements `SET SCHEMA` and `SET CATALOG`, as discussed
in Sections 8.3.2 and 8.3.3. There is also an authorized user for every session,
as we shall discuss in Section 8.7.

8.3.7 Modules

A *module* is the SQL term for an application program. The SQL standard
suggests that there are three kinds of modules, but insists only that an SQL
implementation offer the user at least one of these types.

1. *Generic SQL Interface.* The user may type SQL statements that are
   executed by an SQL server. In this mode, each query or other statement
   is a module by itself. It is this mode that we imagined for most of our
   examples in this book, although in practice it is rarely used.

2. *Embedded SQL*. This style was discussed in Section 8.1, where SQL statements appear within host-language programs and are introduced by `EXEC`
   `SQL`. Presumably, a preprocessor turns the embedded SQL statements into

suitable function or procedure calls to the SQL system. The compiled host-language program, including these function calls, is a module.

3. *True Modules.* The most general style of modules envisioned by SQL is one in which there are a collection of stored functions or procedures, some of which are host-language code and some of which are SQL statements. They communicate among themselves by passing parameters and perhaps via shared variables. PSM modules (Section 8.2) are an example of this type of module.

An execution of a module is called an *SQL agent.* In Fig. 8.17 we have shown both a module and an SQL agent, as one unit, calling upon an SQL client to establish a connection. However, we should remember that the distinction between a module and an SQL agent is analogous to the distinction between a program and a process; the first is code, the second is an execution of that code.

8.4 Using a Call-Level Interface

In this section we return to the matter of coordinating SQL operations and host-language programs. We saw embedded SQL in Section 8.1 and we covered procedures stored in the schema (Section 8.2). In this section, we take up a third approach. When using a *call-level interface* (CLI), we write ordinary host-language code, and we use a library of functions that allow us to connect to and access a database, passing SQL statements to that database.

The differences between this approach and embedded SQL programming are, in one sense, cosmetic. If we observed what the preprocessor does with embedded SQL statements, we would find that they were replaced by calls to library functions much like the functions in the standard SQL/CLI. However, when SQL is passed by CLI functions directly to the database server, there is a certain level of system independence gained. That is, in principle, we could run the same host-language program at several sites that used different DBMS's. As long as those DBMS's accepted standard SQL (which unfortunately is not always the case), then the same code could run at all these sites, without a specially designed preprocessor.

We shall give two examples of call-level interfaces. In this section, we cover the standard SQL/CLI, which is an adaptation of ODBC (Open Database Connectivity). In Section 8.5, we consider JDBC (Java Database Connectivity), a similar standard that links Java programs to databases in an object-oriented style. In neither case do we cover the standard exhaustively, preferring to show the flavor only.

8.4.1 Introduction to SQL/CLI

A program written in C and using SQL/CLI (hereafter, just CLI) will include the header file `sqlcli.h`, from which it gets a large number of functions, type definitions, structures, and symbolic constants. The program is then able to create and deal with four kinds of records (structs, in C):

1. *Environments.* A record of this type is created by the application (client) program in preparation for one or more connections to the database server.

2. *Connections.* One of these records is created to connect the application program to the database. Each connection exists within some environment.

3. *Statements.* An application program can create one or more statement records. Each holds information about a single SQL statement, including an implied cursor if the statement is a query. At different times, the same CLI statement can represent different SQL statements. Every CLI statement exists within some connection.

4. *Descriptions.* These records hold information about either tuples or parameters. The application program or the database server, as appropriate, sets components of description records to indicate the names and types of attributes and/or their values. Each statement has several of these created implicitly, and the user can create more if needed. In our presentation of CLI, description records will generally be invisible.

Each of these records is represented in the application program by a *handle*, which is a pointer to the record.[4] The header file `sqlcli.h` provides types for the handles of environments, connections, statements, and descriptions: `SQLHENV`, `SQLHDBC`, `SQLHSTMT`, and `SQLHDESC`, respectively, although we may think of them as pointers or integers. We shall use these types and also some other defined types with obvious interpretations, such as `SQLCHAR` and `SQLINTEGER`, that are provided in `sqlcli.h`.

We shall not go into detail about how descriptions are set and used. However, (handles for) the other three types of records are created by the use of a function

$$\text{SQLAllocHandle}(hType, hIn, hOut)$$

Here, the three arguments are:

1. *hType* is the type of handle desired. Use `SQL_HANDLE_ENV` for a new environment, `SQL_HANDLE_DBC` for a new connection, or `SQL_HANDLE_STMT` for a new statement.

2. *hIn* is the handle of the higher-level element in which the newly allocated element lives. This parameter is `SQL_NULL_HANDLE` if you want an environment; the latter name is a defined constant telling `SQLAllocHandle`

---

[4]Do not confuse this use of the term "handle" with the handlers for exceptions that were discussed in Section 8.2.7.

that there is no relevant value here. If you want a connection handle, then *hIn* is the handle of the environment within which the connection will exist, and if you want a statement handle, then *hIn* is the handle of the connection within which the statement will exist.

3. *hOut* is the address of the handle that is created by `SQLAllocHandle`.

`SQLAllocHandle` also returns a value of type `SQLRETURN` (an integer). This value is 0 if no errors occurred, and there are certain nonzero values returned in the case of errors.

Example 8.18 : Let us see how the function `worthRanges` of Fig. 8.4, which we used as an example of embedded SQL, would begin in CLI. Recall this function examines all the tuples of `MovieExec` and breaks their net worths into ranges. The initial steps are shown in Fig. 8.18.

```
1)   #include sqlcli.h
2)   SQLHENV myEnv;
3)   SQLHDBC myCon;
4)   SQLHSTMT execStat;
5)   SQLRETURN errorCode1, errorCode2, errorCode3;

6)   errorCode1 = SQLAllocHandle(SQL_HANDLE_ENV,
          SQL_NULL_HANDLE, &myEnv);
7)   if(!errorCode1)
8)       errorCode2 = SQLAllocHandle(SQL_HANDLE_DBC,
             myEnv, &myCon);
9)   if(!errorCode2)
10)      errorCode3 = SQLAllocHandle(SQL_HANDLE_STMT,
             myCon, &execStat);
```

Figure 8.18: Declaring and creating an environment, a connection, and a statement

Lines (2) through (4) declare handles for an environment, connection, and statement, respectively; their names are `myEnv`, `myCon`, and `execStat`, respectively. We plan that `execStat` will represent the SQL statement

```
SELECT netWorth FROM MovieExec;
```

much as did the cursor `execCursor` in Fig. 8.4, but as yet there is no SQL statement associated with `execStat`. Line (5) declares three variables into which function calls can place their response and indicate an error. A value of 0 indicates no error occurred in the call, and we are counting on that being the case.

What is in Environments and Connections?

We shall not examine the contents of the records that represent environments and connections. However, there may be useful information contained in fields of these records. This information is generally not part of the standard, and may depend on the implementation. However, as an example, the environment record is required to indicate how character strings are represented, e.g., terminated by '\0' as in C, or fixed-length.

Line (6) calls `SQLAllocHandle`, asking for an environment handle (the first argument), providing a null handle in the second argument (because none is needed when we are requesting an environment handle), and providing the address of `myEnv` as the third argument; the generated handle will be placed there. If line (6) is successful, lines (7) and (8) use the environment handle to get a connection handle in `myCon`. Assuming that call is also successful, lines (9) and (10) get a statement handle for `execStat`. □

8.4.2 Processing Statements

At the end of Fig. 8.18, a statement record whose handle is `execStat`, has been created. However, there is as yet no SQL statement with which that record is associated. The process of associating and executing SQL statements with statement handles is analogous to the dynamic SQL described in Section 8.1.10. There, we associated the text of an SQL statement with what we called an "SQL variable," using `PREPARE`, and then executed it using `EXECUTE`.

The situation in CLI is quite analogous, if we think of the "SQL variable" as a statement handle. There is a function

$$\texttt{SQLPrepare}(\textit{sh, st, sl})$$

that takes:

1. A statement handle *sh*,

2. A pointer to an SQL statement *st*, and

3. A length *sl* for the character string pointed to by *st*. If we don't know the length, a defined constant `SQL_NTS` tells `SQLPrepare` to figure it out from the string itself. Presumably, the string is a "null-terminated string," and it is sufficient for `SQLPrepare` to scan it until encountering the endmarker '\0'.

The effect of this function is to arrange that the statement referred to by the handle *sh* now represents the particular SQL statement *st*.

Another function

SQLExecute(*sh*)

causes the statement to which handle *sh* refers to be executed. For many forms of SQL statement, such as insertions or deletions, the effect of executing this statement on the database is obvious. Less obvious is what happens when the SQL statement referred to by *sh* is a query. As we shall see in Section 8.4.3, there is an implicit cursor for this statement that is part of the statement record itself. The statement is in principle executed, so we can imagine that all the answer tuples are sitting somewhere, ready to be accessed. We can fetch tuples one at a time, using the implicit cursor, much as we did with real cursors in Sections 8.1 and 8.2.

Example 8.19: Let us continue with the function `worthRanges` that we began in Fig. 8.18. The following two function calls associate the query

```
SELECT netWorth FROM MovieExec;
```

with the statement referred to by handle `execStat`:

```
11)  SQLPrepare(execStat, "SELECT netWorth FROM MovieExec",
         SQL_NTS);
12)  SQLExecute(execStat);
```

They could appear right after line (10) of Fig. 8.18. Remember that SQL_NTS tells `SQLPrepare` to determine the length of the null-terminated string to which its second argument refers. □

As with dynamic SQL, the prepare and execute steps can be combined into one if we use the function `SQLExecDirect`. An example that combines lines (11) and (12) above is:

```
SQLExecDirect(execStat, "SELECT netWorth FROM MovieExec",
    SQL_NTS);
```

8.4.3 Fetching Data From a Query Result

The function that corresponds to a FETCH command in embedded SQL or PSM is

SQLFetch(*sh*)

where *sh* is a statement handle. We presume the statement referred to by *sh* has been executed already, or the fetch will cause an error. `SQLFetch`, like all CLI functions, returns a value of type SQLRETURN that indicates either success or an error. We should be especially aware of the return value represented by the symbolic constant SQL_NO_DATA, which indicates that no more tuples were left in the query result. As in our previous examples of fetching, this value will

be used to get us out of a loop in which we repeatedly fetch new tuples from
the result.

However, if we follow the SQLExecute of Example 8.19 by one or more
SQLFetch calls, where does the tuple appear? The answer is that its components
go into one of the description records associated with the statement whose
handle appears in the SQLFetch call. We can extract the same component at
each fetch by binding the component to a host-language variable, before we
begin fetching. The function that does this job is:

$$SQLBindCol(sh, colNo, colType, pVar, varSize, varInfo)$$

The meanings of these six arguments are:

1. *sh* is the handle of the statement involved.

2. *colNo* is the number of the component (within the tuple) whose value we
    obtain.

3. *colType* is a code for the type of the variable into which the value of the
    component is to be placed. Examples of codes provided by sqlcli.h are
    SQL_CHAR for character arrays and strings, and SQL_INTEGER for integers.

4. *pVar* is a pointer to the variable into which the value is to be placed.

5. *varSize* is the length in bytes of the value of the variable pointed to by
    pVar.

6. *varInfo* is a pointer to an integer that can be used by SQLBindCol to
    provide additional information about the value produced.

Example 8.20 : Let us redo the entire function worthRanges from Fig. 8.4,
using CLI calls instead of embedded SQL. We begin as in Fig. 8.18, but for
the sake of succinctness, we skip all error checking except for the test whether
SQLFetch indicates that no more tuples are present. The code is shown in
Fig. 8.19.

Line (3) declares the same local variables that the embedded-SQL version
of the function uses, and lines (4) through (7) declare additional local variables
using the types provided in sqlcli.h; these are variables that involve SQL in
some way. Lines (4) through (6) are as in Fig. 8.18. New are the declarations
on line (7) of worth (which corresponds to the shared variable of that name in
Fig. 8.4) and worthInfo, which is required by SQLBindCol, but not used.

Lines (8) through (10) allocate the needed handles, as in Fig. 8.18, and
lines (11) and (12) prepare and execute the SQL statement, as discussed in
Example 8.19. In line (13), we see the binding of the first (and only) column of
the result of this query to the variable worth. The first argument is the handle
for the statement involved, and the second argument is the column involved,
1 in this case. The third argument is the type of the column, and the fourth
argument is a pointer to the place where the value will be placed: the variable

```
1)   #include sqlcli.h
2)   void worthRanges() {

3)       int i, digits, counts[15];
4)       SQLHENV myEnv;
5)       SQLHDBC myCon;
6)       SQLHSTMT execStat;
7)       SQLINTEGER worth, worthInfo;

8)       SQLAllocHandle(SQL_HANDLE_ENV,
                 SQL_NULL_HANDLE, &myEnv);
9)       SQLAllocHandle(SQL_HANDLE_DBC, myEnv, &myCon);
10)      SQLAllocHandle(SQL_HANDLE_STMT, myCon, &execStat);
11)      SQLPrepare(execStat,
                 "SELECT netWorth FROM MovieExec", SQL_NTS);
12)      SQLExecute(execStat);
13)      SQLBindCol(execStat, 1, SQL_INTEGER, &worth,
                 size(worth), &worthInfo);
14)      while(SQLFetch(execStat != SQL_NO_DATA) {
15)          digits = 1;
16)          while((worth /= 10) > 0) digits++;
17)          if(digits <= 14) counts[digits]++;
         }
18)      for(i=0; i<15; i++)
19)          printf("digits = %d: number of execs = %d\n",
                 i, counts[i]);
     }
```

Figure 8.19: Grouping executive net worths: CLI version

worth. The fifth argument is the size of that variable, and the final argument points to worthInfo, a place for SQLBindCol to put additional information (which we do not use here).

The balance of the function resembles closely lines (11) through (19) of Fig. 8.4. The while-loop begins at line (14) of Fig. 8.19. Notice that we fetch a tuple and check that we are not out of tuples, all within the condition of the while-loop, on line (14). If there is a tuple, then in lines (15) through (17) we determine the number of digits the integer (which is bound to worth) has and increment the appropriate count. After the loop finishes, i.e., all tuples returned by the statement execution of line (12) have been examined, the resulting counts are printed out at lines (18) and (19). □

Extracting Components with `SQLGetData`

An alternative to binding a program variable to an output of a query's result relation is to fetch tuples without any binding and then transfer components to program variables as needed. The function to use is `SQLGetData`, and it takes the same arguments as `SQLBindCol`. However, it only copies data once, and it must be used after each fetch in order to have the same effect as initially binding the column to a variable.

8.4.4 Passing Parameters to Queries

Embedded SQL gives us the ability to execute an SQL statement, part of which consists of values determined by the current contents of shared variables. There is a similar capability in CLI, but it is rather more complicated. The steps needed are:

1. Use `SQLPrepare` to prepare a statement in which some portions, called *parameters*, are replaced by a question-mark. The ith question-mark represents the ith parameter.

2. Use function `SQLBindParameter` to bind values to the places where the question-marks are found. This function has ten arguments, of which we shall explain only the essentials.

3. Execute the query with these bindings, by calling `SQLExecute`. Note that if we change the values of one or more parameters, we need to call `SQLExecute` again.

The following example will illustrate the process, as well as indicate the important arguments needed by `SQLBindParameter`.

Example 8.21 : Let us reconsider the embedded SQL code of Fig. 8.2, where we obtained values for two variables `studioName` and `studioAddr` and used them as the components of a tuple, which we inserted into `Studio`. Figure 8.20 sketches how this process would work in CLI. It assumes that we have a statement handle `myStat` to use for the insertion statement.

The code begins with steps (not shown) to give `studioName` and `studioAddr` values. Line (1) shows statement `myStat` being prepared to be an insertion statement with two parameters (the question-marks) in the `VALUE` clause. Then, lines (2) and (3) bind the first and second question-marks, to the current contents of `studioName` and `studioAddr`, respectively. Finally, line (4) executes the insertion. If the entire sequence of steps in Fig. 8.20, including the unseen work to obtain new values for `studioName` and `studioAddr`, are placed in a loop, then each time around the loop, a new tuple, with a new name and address for a studio, is inserted into `Studio`. □

```
    /* get values for studioName and studioAddr */

1)  SQLPrepare(myStat,
        "INSERT INTO Studio(name, address) VALUES(?, ?)",
        SQL_NTS);
2)  SQLBindParameter(myStat, 1,..., studioName,...);
3)  SQLBindParameter(myStat, 2,..., studioAddr,...);
4)  SQLExecute(myStat);
```

Figure 8.20: Inserting a new studio by binding parameters to values

8.4.5 Exercises for Section 8.4

Exercise 8.4.1: Repeat the problems of Exercise 8.1.1, but write the code in C with CLI calls.

Exercise 8.4.2: Repeat the problems of Exercise 8.1.2, but write the code in C with CLI calls.

8.5 Java Database Connectivity

JDBC, which stands for "Java Database Connectivity," is a facility similar to CLI for allowing Java programs to access SQL databases. The concepts are quite similar to those of CLI, although Java's object-oriented flavor is evident in JDBC.

8.5.1 Introduction to JDBC

The first steps we must take to use JDBC are:

1. Load a "driver" for the database system we shall use. This step may be installation- and implementation-dependent. The effect, however, is that an object called `DriverManager` is created. This object is analogous in many ways to the environment whose handle we get as the first step in using CLI.

2. Establish a connection to the database. A variable of type `Connection` is created if we apply the method `getConnection` to `DriverManager`.

The Java statement to establish a connection looks like:

```
Connection myCon = DriverManager.getConnection(<URL>,
    <name>, <password>);
```

That is, the method `getConnection` takes as arguments the URL for the database to which you wish to connect, your user name, and your password. It returns an object of type `Connection`, which we have chosen to call `myCon`. Note that in the Java style, `myCon` is given its type and value in one statement.

This connection is quite analogous to a CLI connection, and it serves the same purpose. By applying the appropriate methods to a connection like `myCon`, we can create statement objects, place SQL statements "in" those objects, bind values to SQL statement parameters, execute the SQL statements, and examine results a tuple at a time. Since the differences between JDBC and CLI are often more syntactic than semantic, we shall go only briefly through these steps.

8.5.2 Creating Statements in JDBC

There are two methods we can apply to a connection in order to create statements. They have the same name, but differ in the number of their arguments:

1. `createStatement()` returns an object of type `Statement`. This object has no associated SQL statement yet, so method `createStatement()` may be thought of as analogous to the CLI call to `SQLAllocHandle` that takes a connection handle and returns a statement handle.

2. `createStatement(Q)`, where Q is an SQL query passed as a string argument, returns an object of type `PreparedStatement`. Thus, we may draw an analogy between executing `createStatement(Q)` in JDBC with the two CLI steps in which we get a statement handle with `SQLAllocHandle` and then apply `SQLPrepare` to that handle and the query Q.

There are four different methods that execute SQL statements. Like the methods above, they differ in whether or not they take a statement as an argument. However, these methods also distinguish between SQL statements that are queries and other statements, which are collectively called "updates." Note that the SQL `UPDATE` statement is only one small example of what JDBC terms an "update." The latter include all modification statements, such as inserts, and all schema-related statements such as `CREATE TABLE`. The four "execute" methods are:

a) `executeQuery(Q)` takes a statement Q, which must be a query, and is applied to a `Statement` object. This method returns an object of type `ResultSet`, which is the set (bag, to be precise) of tuples produced by the query Q. We shall see how to access these tuples in Section 8.5.3.

b) `executeQuery()` is applied to a `PreparedStatement` object. Since a prepared statement already has an associated query, there is no argument. This method also returns an object of type `ResultSet`.

c) `executeUpdate(U)` takes a nonquery statement U and, when applied to a `Statement` object, executes U. The effect is felt on the database only; no result set is returned.

d) executeUpdate(), with no argument, is applied to a PreparedStatement. In that case, the SQL statement associated with the prepared statement is executed. This SQL statement must not be a query, of course.

Example 8.22: Suppose we have a connection object myCon, and we wish to execute the query

```
SELECT netWorth FROM MovieExec;
```

One way to do so is to create a statement object execStat, and then use it to execute the query directly. The result set will be placed in an object Worths of type ResultSet; we'll see in Section 8.5.3 how to extract the net worths and process them. The Java code to accomplish this task is:

```
Statement execStat = myCon.createStatement();
ResultSet Worths = execStat.executeQuery(
    "SELECT netWorth FROM MovieExec");
```

An alternative is to prepare the query immediately and later execute it. This approach would be preferable, as in the analogous CLI situation, should we want to execute the same query repeatedly. Then, it makes sense to prepare it once and execute it many times, rather than having the DBMS prepare the same query repeatedly. The JDBC steps needed to follow this approach are:

```
PreparedStatement execStat = myCon.createStatement(
    "SELECT netWorth FROM MovieExec");
ResultSet Worths = execStat.executeQuery();
```

☐

Example 8.23: If we want to execute a parameterless nonquery, we can perform analogous steps in both styles. There is no result set, however. For instance, suppose we want to insert into StarsIn the fact that Denzel Washington starred in *Remember the Titans* in the year 2000. We may create and use a statement starStat in either of the following ways:

```
Statement starStat = myCon.createStatement();
starStat.executeUpdate("INSERT INTO StarsIn VALUES(" +
    "'Remember the Titans', 2000, 'Denzel Washington')");
```

or

```
PreparedStatement starStat = myCon.createStatement(
    "INSERT INTO StarsIn VALUES('Remember the Titans'," +
    "2000, 'Denzel Washington')");
starStat.executeUpdate();
```

Notice that each of these sequences of Java statements takes advantage of the fact that + is a Java operator that concatenates strings. Thus, we are able to extend SQL statements over several lines of Java, as needed.   ☐

8.5.3 Cursor Operations in JDBC

When we execute a query and obtain a result-set object, we may, in effect, run a cursor through the tuples of the result set. To do so, the `ResultSet` class provides the following useful methods:

1. `next()`, when applied to a result-set object, causes an implicit cursor to move to the next tuple (to the first tuple the first time it is applied). This method returns `FALSE` if there is no next tuple.

2. `getString(`i`)`, `getInt(`i`)`, `getFloat(`i`)`, and analogous methods for the other types that SQL values can take, each return the ith component of the tuple currently indicated by the cursor. The method appropriate to the type of the ith component must be used.

Example 8.24: Having obtained the result set `Worths` as in Example 8.22, we may access its tuples one at a time. Recall that these tuples have only one component, of type integer. The form of the loop is:

```
while(Worths.next()) {
    worth = Worths.getInt(1);
    /* process this net worth */
}
```

□

8.5.4 Parameter Passing

As in CLI, we can use a question-mark in place of a portion of a query, then bind values to those *parameters*. To do so in JDBC, we need to create a prepared statement, and we need to apply to that statement object methods such as `setString(`i`, `v`)` or `setInt(`i`, `v`)` that bind the value v, which must be of the appropriate type for the method, to the ith parameter in the query.

Example 8.25: Let us mimic the CLI code in Example 8.21, where we prepared a statement to insert a new studio into relation `Studio`, with parameters for the value of the name and address of that studio. The Java code to prepare this statement, set its parameters, and execute it is shown in Fig. 8.21. We continue to assume that connection object `myCon` is available to us.

In lines (1) and (2), we create and prepare the insertion statement. It has parameters for each of the values to be inserted. After line (2), we could begin a loop in which we repeatedly ask the user for a studio name and address, and place these strings in the variables `studioName` and `studioAddr`. This assignment is not shown, but represented by a comment. Lines (3) and (4) set the first and second parameters to the strings that are the current values of `studioName` and `studioAddr`, respectively. Finally, at line (5), we execute the insertion statement with the current values of its parameters. After line (5), we could go around the loop again, beginning with the steps represented by the comment.   □

```
1)  PreparedStatement studioStat = myCon.createStatement(
2)      "INSERT INTO Studio(name, address) VALUES(?, ?)");
    /* get values for variables studioName and studioAddr
       from the user */
3)  studioStat.setString(1, studioName);
4)  studioStat.setString(2, studioAddr);
5)  studioStat.executeUpdate();
```

Figure 8.21: Setting and using parameters in JDBC

8.5.5 Exercises for Section 8.5

Exercise 8.5.1: Repeat Exercise 8.1.1, but write the code in Java using JDBC.

Exercise 8.5.2: Repeat Exercise 8.1.2, but write the code in Java using JDBC.

8.6 Transactions in SQL

To this point, our model of operations on the database has been that of one user querying or modifying the database. Thus, operations on the database are executed one at a time, and the database state left by one operation is the state upon which the next operation acts. Moreover, we imagine that operations are carried out in their entirety ("atomically"). That is, we assumed it is impossible for the hardware or software to fail in the middle of an operation, leaving the database in a state that cannot be explained as the result of the operations performed on it.

Real life is often considerably more complicated. We shall first consider what can happen to leave the database in a state that doesn't reflect the operations performed on it, and then we shall consider the tools SQL gives the user to assure that these problems do not occur.

8.6.1 Serializability

In applications like banking or airline reservations, hundreds of operations per second may be performed on the database. The operations initiate at any of hundreds or thousands of sites, such as automatic teller machines or machines on the desks of travel agents, airline employees, or airline customers themselves. It is entirely possible that we could have two operations affecting the same account or flight, and for those operations to overlap in time. If so, they might interact in strange ways. Here is an example of what could go wrong if the DBMS were completely unconstrained as to the order in which it operated upon the database. We emphasize that database systems do not normally behave in this manner, and that one has to go out of one's way to make these sorts of errors occur when using a commercial DBMS.

```
1)  EXEC SQL BEGIN DECLARE SECTION;
2)      int flight; /* flight number */
3)      char date[10]; /* flight date in SQL format */
4)      char seat[3]; /* two digits and a letter represents
                          a seat */
5)      int occ; /* boolean to tell if seat is occupied */
6)  EXEC SQL END DECLARE SECTION;

7)  void chooseSeat() {
8)      /* C code to prompt the user to enter a flight,
           date, and seat and store these in the three
           variables with those names */
9)      EXEC SQL SELECT occupied INTO :occ
10)             FROM Flights
11)             WHERE fltNum = :flight AND fltDate = :date
                      AND fltSeat = :seat;
12)     if (!occ) {
13)         EXEC SQL UPDATE Flights
14)                 SET occupied = TRUE
15)                 WHERE fltNum = :flight
                        AND fltDate = :date
                        AND fltSeat = :seat;
16)         /* C and SQL code to record the seat assignment
               and inform the user of the assignment */
        }
17)     else /* C code to notify user of unavailability and
               ask for another seat selection */
    }
```

Figure 8.22: Choosing a seat

Example 8.26 : Suppose that we write a function chooseSeat(), in C with embedded SQL, to read a relation about flights and the seats available, find if a particular seat is available, and make it occupied if so. The relation upon which we operate will be called Flights, and it has attributes fltNum, fltDate, fltSeat, and occ with the obvious meanings. The seat-choosing program is sketched in Fig. 8.22.

Lines (9) through (11) of Fig. 8.22 are a single-row select that sets shared variable occ to true or false (1 or 0) depending on whether the specified seat is or is not occupied. Line (12) tests whether that seat is occupied, and if not, the tuple for that seat is updated to make it occupied. The update is done by lines (13) through (15), and at line (16) the seat is assigned to the customer who requested it. In practice, we would probably store seat-assignment information in another relation. Finally, at line (17), if the seat is occupied the customer is told that.

Now, remember that the function `chooseSeat()` may be executed simultaneously by two or more customers. Suppose by coincidence that two agents are trying to book the same seat for the same flight and date at approximately the same time, as suggested by Fig. 8.23. They both get to line (9) at the same time, and their copies of local variable `occ` both get value 0; that is, the seat is currently unassigned. At line (12), each execution of `chooseSeat()` decides to update `occ` to `TRUE`, that is, to make the seat occupied. These updates execute, perhaps one after the other, and each execution tells its customer at line (16) that the seat belongs to them. □

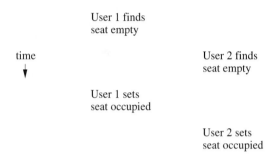

Figure 8.23: Two customers trying to book the same seat simultaneously

As we see from Example 8.26, it is conceivable that two operations could each be performed correctly, and yet the global result not be correct: both customers believe they have been granted the seat in question. The problem can be solved by several SQL mechanisms that serve to *serialize* the execution of the two function executions. We say an execution of functions operating on the same database is *serial* if one function executes completely before any other function begins. We say the execution is *serializable* if they behave as if they were run serially, even though their executions may overlap in time.

Clearly, if the two invocations of `chooseSeat()` are run serially (or serializably), then the error we saw cannot occur. One customer's invocation occurs first. This customer sees an empty seat and books it. The other customer's invocation then begins and sees that the seat is already occupied. It may matter to the customers who gets the seat, but to the database all that is important is that a seat is assigned only once.

8.6.2 Atomicity

In addition to nonserialized behavior that can occur if two or more database operations are performed about the same time, it is possible for a single operation to put the database in an unacceptable state if there is a hardware or software "crash" while the operation is executing. Here is another example suggesting

---

Assuring Serializable Behavior

In practice it is often impossible to require that operations run serially; there are just too many of them and some parallelism is required. Thus, DBMS's adopt a mechanism for assuring serializable behavior; even if the execution is not serial, the result looks to users as if operations were executed serially.

One common approach is for the DBMS to *lock* elements of the database so that two functions cannot access them at the same time. We mentioned locking in Section 1.2.4, and the idea will be covered extensively, starting in Section 18.3. For example, if the function `chooseSeat()` of Example 8.26 were written to lock other operations out of the `Flights` relation, then operations that did not access `Flights` could run in parallel with this invocation of `chooseSeat()`, but no other invocation of `chooseSeat()` could run.

---

what might occur. As in Example 8.26, we should remember that real database systems do not allow this sort of error to occur in properly designed application programs.

Example 8.27: Let us picture another common sort of database: a bank's account records. We can represent the situation by a relation `Accounts` with attributes `acctNo` and `balance`. Pairs in this relation are an account number and the balance in that account.

We wish to write a function `transfer()` that reads two accounts and an amount of money, checks that the first account has at least that much money, and if so moves the money from the first account to the second. Figure 8.24 is a sketch of the function `transfer()`.

The working of Fig. 8.24 is straightforward. Lines (8) through (10) retrieve the balance of the first account. At line (11), it is determined whether this balance is sufficient to allow the desired amount to be subtracted from it. If so, then lines (12) through (14) add the amount to the second account, and lines (15) through (17) subtract the amount from the first account. If the amount in the first account is insufficient, then no transfer is made, and a warning is printed at line (18).

Now, consider what happens if there is a failure after line (14); perhaps the computer fails or the network connecting the database to the processor that is actually performing the transfer fails. Then the database is left in a state where money has been transferred into the second account, but the money has not been taken out of the first account. The bank has in effect given away the amount of money that was to be transferred. □

The problem illustrated by Example 8.27 is that certain combinations of database operations, like the two updates of Fig. 8.24, need to be done *atomi-*

```
1)    EXEC SQL BEGIN DECLARE SECTION;
2)        int acct1, acct2; /* the two accounts */
3)        int balance1; /* the amount of money in the
                            first account */
4)        int amount; /* the amount of money to transfer */
5)    EXEC SQL END DECLARE SECTION;

6)    void transfer() {
7)        /* C code to prompt the user to enter accounts
              1 and 2 and an amount of money to transfer,
              in variables acct1, acct2, and amount */
8)        EXEC SQL SELECT balance INTO :balance1
9)                 FROM Accounts
10)                WHERE acctNo = :acct1;
11)        if (balance1 >= amount) {
12)           EXEC SQL UPDATE Accounts
13)                    SET balance = balance + :amount
14)                    WHERE acctNo = :acct2;
15)           EXEC SQL UPDATE Accounts
16)                    SET balance = balance - :amount
17)                    WHERE acctNo = :acct1;
           }
18)        else /* C code to print a message that there were
                   insufficient funds to make the transfer */
       }
```

Figure 8.24: Transferring money from one account to another

cally; that is, either they are both done or neither is done. For example, a simple solution is to have all changes to the database done in a local workspace, and only after all work is done do we *commit* the changes to the database, whereupon all changes become part of the database and visible to other operations.

8.6.3 Transactions

The solution to the problems of serialization and atomicity posed in Sections 8.6.1 and 8.6.2 is to group database operations into *transactions*. A transaction is a collection of one or more operations on the database that must be executed atomically; that is, either all operations are performed or none are. In addition, SQL requires that, as a default, transactions are executed in a serializable manner. A DBMS may allow the user to specify a less stringent constraint on the interleaving of operations from two or more transactions. We shall discuss these modifications to the serializability condition in later sections.

When using the generic SQL interface, each statement is normally a transaction by itself.[5] However, when writing code with embedded SQL or code that uses the SQL/CLI or JDBC, we usually want to control transactions explicitly. Transactions begin automatically, when any SQL statement that queries or manipulates either the database or the schema begins. The SQL command START TRANSACTION may be used if we wish.

In the generic interface, unless started with a START TRANSACTION command, the transaction ends with the statement. In all other cases, there are two ways to end a transaction:

1. The SQL statement COMMIT causes the transaction to end successfully. Whatever changes to the database were caused by the SQL statement or statements since the current transaction began are installed permanently in the database (i.e., they are *committed*). Before the COMMIT statement is executed, changes are tentative and may or may not be visible to other transactions.

2. The SQL statement ROLLBACK causes the transaction to *abort*, or terminate unsuccessfully. Any changes made in response to the SQL statements of the transaction are undone (i.e., they are *rolled back*), so they no longer appear in the database.

There is one exception to the above points. If we attempt to commit a transaction, but there are deferred constraints (see Section 7.1.6) that need to be checked, and these constraints are now violated, then the transaction is *not* committed, even if we tell it to with a COMMIT statement. Rather, the transaction is rolled back, and an indication in **SQLSTATE** tells the application that the transaction was aborted for this reason.

Example 8.28: Suppose we want an execution of function transfer() of Fig. 8.24 to be a single transaction. The transaction begins at line (8) when we read the balance of the first account. If the test of line (11) is true, and we perform the transfer of funds, then we would like to commit the changes made. Thus, we put at the end of the if-block of lines (12) through (17) the additional SQL statement

        EXEC SQL COMMIT;

If the test of line (11) is false — that is, there are insufficient funds to make the transfer — then we might prefer to abort the transaction. We can do so by placing

        EXEC SQL ROLLBACK;

---

[5]However, any triggers awakened by the statement are also part of this same transaction. Some systems even allow triggers to awaken other triggers, and if so, all these actions form part of the transaction as well.

How the Database Changes During Transactions

Different systems may do different things to implement transactions. It is possible that as a transaction executes, it makes changes to the database. If the transaction aborts, then (without precautions) it is possible that these changes were seen by some other transaction. The most common solution is for the database system to lock the changed items until `COMMIT` or `ROLLBACK` is chosen, thus preventing other transactions from seeing the tentative change. Locks or an equivalent would surely be used if the user wants the transactions to run in a serializable fashion.

However, as we shall see starting in Section 8.6.4, SQL offers us several options regarding the treatment of tentative database changes. It is possible that the changed data is not locked and becomes visible even though a subsequent rollback makes the change disappear. It is up to the author of the transactions to decide whether visibility of tentative changes needs to be avoided. If so, all SQL implementations provide a method, such as locking, to keep changes invisible before commitment.

---

at the end of the else-block suggested by line (18). Actually, since in this branch there were no database modification statements executed, it doesn't matter whether we commit or abort, since there are no changes to be committed. □

8.6.4 Read-Only Transactions

Examples 8.26 and 8.27 each involved a transaction that read and then (possibly) wrote some data into the database. This sort of transaction is prone to serialization problems. Thus we saw in Example 8.26 what could happen if two executions of the function tried to book the same seat at the same time, and we saw in Example 8.27 what could happen if there was a crash in the middle of function execution. However, when a transaction only reads data and does not write data, we have more freedom to let the transaction execute in parallel with other transactions.[6]

Example 8.29: Suppose we wrote a function that read data to determine whether a certain seat was available; this function would behave like lines (1) through (11) of Fig. 8.22. We could execute many invocations of this function at once, without risk of permanent harm to the database. The worst that could happen is that while we were reading the availability of a certain seat, that

---

[6]There is a comparison to be made between transactions on one hand and the management of cursors on the other. For example, we noted in Section 8.1.8 that more parallelism was possible with read-only cursors than with general cursors. Similarly, read-only transactions enable parallelism; read/write transactions inhibit it.

Application- Versus System-Generated Rollbacks

In our discussion of transactions, we have presumed that the decision whether a transaction is committed or rolled back is made as part of the application issuing the transaction. That is, as in Examples 8.30 and 8.28, a transaction may perform a number of database operations, then decide whether to make any changes permanent by issuing COMMIT, or to return to the original state by issuing ROLLBACK. However, the system may also perform transaction rollbacks, to ensure that transactions are executed atomically and conform to their specified isolation level in the presence of other concurrent transactions or system crashes. Typically, if the system aborts a transaction then a special error code or exception is generated. If an application wishes to guarantee that its transactions are executed successfully, it must catch such conditions (e.g., through the SQLSTATE value) and reissue the transaction in question.

---

seat was being booked or was being released by the execution of some other function. Thus, we might get the answer "available" or "occupied," depending on microscopic differences in the time at which we executed the query, but the answer would make sense at some time. □

If we tell the SQL execution system that our current transaction is *read-only*, that is, it will never change the database, then it is quite possible that the SQL system will be able to take advantage of that knowledge. Generally it will be possible for many read-only transactions accessing the same data to run in parallel, while they would not be allowed to run in parallel with a transaction that wrote the same data.

We tell the SQL system that the next transaction is read-only by:

```
SET TRANSACTION READ ONLY;
```

This statement must be executed before the transaction begins. For example, if we had a function consisting of lines (1) through (11) of Fig. 8.22, we could declare it read-only by placing

```
EXEC SQL SET TRANSACTION READ ONLY;
```

just prior to line (9), which begins the transaction. It would be too late to make the read-only declaration after line (9).

We can also inform SQL that the coming transaction may write data by the statement

```
SET TRANSACTION READ WRITE;
```

However, this option is the default and thus is unnecessary.

8.6.5 Dirty Reads

Dirty data is a common term for data written by a transaction that has not yet committed. A *dirty read* is a read of dirty data. The risk in reading dirty data is that the transaction that wrote it may eventually abort. If so, then the dirty data will be removed from the database, and the world is supposed to behave as if that data never existed. If some other transaction has read the dirty data, then that transaction might commit or take some other action that reflects its knowledge of the dirty data.

Sometimes the dirty read matters, and sometimes it doesn't. Other times it matters little enough that it makes sense to risk an occasional dirty read and thus avoid:

1. The time-consuming work by the DBMS that is needed to prevent dirty reads, and

2. The loss of parallelism that results from waiting until there is no possibility of a dirty read.

Here are some examples of what might happen when dirty reads are allowed.

Example 8.30: Let us reconsider the account transfer of Example 8.27. However, suppose that transfers are implemented by a program P that executes the following sequence of steps:

1. Add money to account 2.

2. Test if account 1 has enough money.

   (a) If there is not enough money, remove the money from account 2 and end.[7]

   (b) If there is enough money, subtract the money from account 1 and end.

If program P is executed serializably, then it doesn't matter that we have put money temporarily into account 2. No one will see that money, and it gets removed if the transfer can't be made.

However, suppose dirty reads are possible. Imagine there are three accounts: $A1$, $A2$, and $A3$, with $100, $200, and $300, respectively. Suppose transaction T_1 executes program P to transfer $150 from $A1$ to $A2$. At roughly the same time, transaction T_2 runs program P to transfer $250 from $A2$ to $A3$. Here is a possible sequence of events:

1. T_2 executes step 1 and adds $250 to $A3$, which now has $550.

---

[7]You should be aware that the program P is trying to perform functions that would more typically be done by the DBMS. In particular, when P decides, as it has done at this step, that it must not complete the transaction, it would issue a rollback (abort) command to the DBMS and have the DBMS reverse the effects of this execution of P.

2. T_1 executes step 1 and adds \$150 to $A2$, which now has \$350.

3. T_2 executes the test of step 2 and finds that $A2$ has enough funds (\$350) to allow the transfer of \$250 from $A2$ to $A3$.

4. T_1 executes the test of step 2 and finds that $A1$ does not have enough funds (\$100) to allow the transfer of \$150 from $A1$ to $A2$.

5. T_2 executes step 2b. It subtracts \$250 from $A2$, which now has \$100, and ends.

6. T_1 executes step 2a. It subtracts \$150 from $A2$, which now has $-$\$50, and ends.

The total amount of money has not changed; there is still \$600 among the three accounts. But because T_2 read dirty data at the third of the six steps above, we have not protected against an account going negative, which supposedly was the purpose of testing the first account to see if it had adequate funds. □

Example 8.31: Let us imagine a variation on the seat-choosing function of Example 8.26. In the new approach:

1. We find an available seat and reserve it by setting occ to TRUE for that seat. If there is none, abort.

2. We ask the customer for approval of the seat. If so, we commit. If not, we release the seat by setting occ to FALSE and repeat step 1 to get another seat.

If two transactions are executing this algorithm at about the same time, one might reserve a seat S, which later is rejected by the customer. If the second transaction executes step 1 at a time when seat S is marked occupied, the customer for that transaction is not given the option to take seat S.

As in Example 8.30, the problem is that a dirty read has occurred. The second transaction saw a tuple (with S marked occupied) that was written by the first transaction and later modified by the first transaction. □

How important is the fact that a read was dirty? In Example 8.30 it was very important; it caused an account to go negative despite apparent safeguards against that happening. In Example 8.31, the problem does not look too serious. Indeed, the second traveler might not get their favorite seat, or even be told that no seats existed. However, in the latter case, running the transaction again will almost certainly reveal the availability of seat S. It might well make sense to implement this seat-choosing function in a way that allowed dirty reads, in order to speed up the average processing time for booking requests.

SQL allows us to specify that dirty reads are acceptable for a given transaction. We use the SET TRANSACTION statement that we discussed in Section 8.6.4. The appropriate form for a transaction like that described in Example 8.31 is:

```
1)  SET TRANSACTION READ WRITE
2)      ISOLATION LEVEL READ UNCOMMITTED;
```

The statement above does two things:

1. Line (1) declares that the transaction may write data.

2. Line (2) declares that the transaction may run with the "isolation level" *read-uncommitted*. That is, the transaction is allowed to read dirty data. We shall discuss the four isolation levels in Section 8.6.6. So far, we have seen two of them: serializable and read-uncommitted.

Note that if the transaction is not read-only (i.e., it may modify the database), and we specify isolation level `READ UNCOMMITTED`, then we must also specify `READ WRITE`. Recall from Section 8.6.4 that the default assumption is that transactions are read-write. However, SQL makes an exception for the case where dirty reads are allowed. Then, the default assumption is that the transaction is read-only, because read-write transactions with dirty reads entail significant risks, as we saw. If we want a read-write transaction to run with read-uncommitted as the isolation level, then we need to specify `READ WRITE` explicitly, as above.

8.6.6 Other Isolation Levels

SQL provides a total of four *isolation levels*. Two of them we have already seen: serializable and read-uncommitted (dirty reads allowed). The other two are *read-committed* and *repeatable-read*. They can be specified for a given transaction by

```
SET TRANSACTION ISOLATION LEVEL READ COMMITTED;
```

or

```
SET TRANSACTION ISOLATION LEVEL REPEATABLE READ;
```

respectively. For each, the default is that transactions are read-write, so we can add `READ ONLY` to either statement, if appropriate. Incidentally, we also have the option of specifying

```
SET TRANSACTION ISOLATION LEVEL SERIALIZABLE;
```

However, that is the SQL default and need not be stated explicitly.

The read-committed isolation level, as its name implies, forbids the reading of dirty (uncommitted) data. However, it does allow one transaction to issue the same query several times and get different answers, as long as the answers reflect data that has been written by transactions that already committed.

Interactions Among Transactions Running at Different Isolation Levels

A subtle point is that the isolation level of a transaction affects only what data *that* transaction may see; it does not affect what any other transaction sees. As a case in point, if a transaction T is running at level serializable, then the execution of T must appear as if all other transactions run either entirely before or entirely after T. However, if some of those transactions are running at another isolation level, then *they* may see the data written by T as T writes it. They may even see dirty data from T if they are running at isolation level read-uncommitted, and T aborts.

Example 8.32: Let us reconsider the seat-choosing function of Example 8.31, but suppose we declare it to run with isolation level read-committed. Then when it searches for a seat at step 1, it will not see seats as booked if some other transaction is reserving them but not committed.[8] However, if the traveler rejects seats, and one execution of the function queries for available seats many times, it may see a different set of available seats each time it queries, as other transactions successfully book seats or cancel seats in parallel with our transaction. □

Now, let us consider isolation level repeatable-read. The term is something of a misnomer, since the same query issued more than once is not quite guaranteed to get the same answer. Under repeatable-read isolation, if a tuple is retrieved the first time, then we can be sure that the identical tuple will be retrieved again if the query is repeated. However, it is also possible that a second or subsequent execution of the same query will retrieve *phantom* tuples. The latter are tuples that are the result of insertions into the database while our transaction is executing.

Example 8.33: Let us continue with the seat-choosing problem of Examples 8.31 and 8.32. If we execute this function under isolation level repeatable-read, then a seat that is available on the first query at step 1 will remain available at subsequent queries.

However, suppose some new tuples enter the relation `Flights`. For example, the airline may have switched the flight to a larger plane, creating some new tuples that weren't there before. Then under repeatable-read isolation, a subsequent query for available seats may also retrieve the new seats. □

---

[8] What actually happens may seem mysterious, since we have not addressed the algorithms for enforcing the various isolation levels. Possibly, should two transactions both see a seat as available and try to book it, one will be forced by the system to roll back in order to break the deadlock (see the box on 'Application- Versus System-Generated Rollbacks" in Section 8.6.3.

8.6.7 Exercises for Section 8.6

Exercise 8.6.1: This and the next exercises involve certain programs that operate on the two relations

```
Product(maker, model, type)
PC(model, speed, ram, hd, rd, price)
```

from our running PC exercise. Sketch the following programs, using embedded SQL and an appropriate host language. Do not forget to issue COMMIT and ROLLBACK statements at the proper times and to tell the system your transactions are read-only if they are.

  a) Given a speed and amount of RAM (as arguments of the function), look up the PC's with that speed and RAM, printing the model number and price of each.

 * b) Given a model number, delete the tuple for that model from both PC and Product.

  c) Given a model number, decrease the price of that model PC by $100.

  d) Given a maker, model number, processor speed, RAM size, hard-disk size, removable-disk type, and price, check that there is no product with that model. If there is such a model, print an error message for the user. If no such model existed, enter the information about that model into the PC and Product tables.

 ! **Exercise 8.6.2:** For each of the programs of Exercise 8.6.1, discuss the atomicity problems, if any, that could occur should the system crash in the middle of an execution of the program.

 ! **Exercise 8.6.3:** Suppose we execute as a transaction T one of the four programs of Exercise 8.6.1, while other transactions that are executions of the same or a different one of the four programs may also be executing at about the same time. What behaviors of transaction T may be observed if all the transactions run with isolation level READ UNCOMMITTED that would not be possible if they all ran with isolation level SERIALIZABLE? Consider separately the case that T is any of the programs (a) through (d) of Exercise 8.6.1.

*!! **Exercise 8.6.4:** Suppose we have a transaction T that is a function which runs "forever," and at each hour checks whether there is a PC that has a speed of 1500 or more and sells for under $1000. If it finds one, it prints the information and terminates. During this time, other transactions that are executions of one of the four programs described in Exercise 8.6.1 may run. For each of the four isolation levels — serializable, repeatable read, read committed, and read uncommitted — tell what the effect on T of running at this isolation level is.

8.7   Security and User Authorization in SQL

SQL postulates the existence of *authorization ID's*, which are essentially user
names. SQL also has a special authorization ID, PUBLIC, which includes any
user. Authorization ID's may be granted privileges, much as they would be in
the file system environment maintained by an operating system. For example,
a UNIX system generally controls three kinds of privileges: read, write, and
execute. That list of privileges makes sense, because the protected objects of a
UNIX system are files, and these three operations characterize well the things
one typically does with files. However, databases are much more complex than
file systems, and the kinds of privileges used in SQL are correspondingly more
complex.

In this section, we shall first learn what privileges SQL allows on database
elements. We shall then see how privileges may be acquired by users (by authorization ID's, that is). Finally, we shall see how privileges may be taken
away.

8.7.1   Privileges

SQL defines nine types of privileges: SELECT, INSERT, DELETE, UPDATE, REF-
ERENCES, USAGE, TRIGGER, EXECUTE, and UNDER. The first four of these apply
to a relation, which may be either a base table or a view. As their names
imply, they give the holder of the privilege the right to query (select from) the
relation, insert into the relation, delete from the relation, and update tuples of
the relation, respectively.

A module containing an SQL statement cannot be executed without the
privilege appropriate to that statement; e.g., a select-from-where statement
requires the SELECT privilege on every table it accesses. We shall see how the
module can get those privileges shortly. SELECT, INSERT, and UPDATE may also
have an associated list of attributes, for instance, SELECT(name, addr). If so,
then it is only those attributes that may be seen in a selection, specified in an
insertion, or changed in an update. Note that, when granted, privileges such
as these will be associated with a particular relation, so it will be clear at that
time to what relation attributes name and addr belong.

The REFERENCES privilege on a relation is the right to refer to that relation in
an integrity constraint. These constraints may take any of the forms mentioned
in Chapter 7, such as assertions, attribute- or tuple-based checks, or referential
integrity constraints. The REFERENCES privilege may also have an attached
list of attributes, in which case only those attributes may be referenced in a
constraint. A constraint cannot be checked unless the owner of the schema in
which the constraint appears has the REFERENCES privilege on all data involved
in the constraint.

USAGE is a privilege that applies to several kinds of schema elements other
than relations and assertions (see Section 8.3.2); it is the right to use that
element in one's own declarations. The TRIGGER privilege on a relation is the

---

Triggers and Privileges

It is a bit subtle how privileges are handled for triggers. First, if you have the `TRIGGER` privilege for a relation, you can attempt to create any trigger you like on that relation. However, since the condition and action portions of the trigger are likely to query and/or modify portions of the database, the trigger creator must have the necessary privileges for those actions. When someone performs an activity that awakens the trigger, they do not need the privileges that the trigger condition and action require; the trigger is executed under the privileges of its creator.

---

right to define triggers on that relation. `EXECUTE` is the right to execute a piece of code, such as a PSM procedure or function. Finally, `UNDER` is the right to create subtypes of a given type. This matter has been deferred until Chapter 9, when we take up object-oriented features of SQL.

Example 8.34: Let us consider what privileges are needed to execute the insertion statement of Fig. 6.15, which we reproduce here as Fig. 8.25. First, it is an insertion into the relation `Studio`, so we require an `INSERT` privilege on `Studio`. However, since the insertion specifies only the component for attribute `name`, it is acceptable to have either the privilege `INSERT` or the privilege `INSERT(name)` on relation `Studio`. The latter privilege allows us to insert `Studio` tuples that specify only the `name` component and leave other components to take their default value or `NULL`, which is what Fig. 8.25 does.

```
1) INSERT INTO Studio(name)
2)     SELECT DISTINCT studioName
3)     FROM Movie
4)     WHERE studioName NOT IN
5)         (SELECT name
6)          FROM Studio);
```

Figure 8.25: Adding new studios

However, notice that the insertion statement of Fig. 8.25 involves two subqueries, starting at lines (2) and (5). To carry out these selections we require the privileges needed for the subqueries. Thus, we need the `SELECT` privilege on both relations involved in `FROM` clauses: `Movie` and `Studio`. Note that just because we have the `INSERT` privilege on `Studio` doesn't mean we have the `SELECT` privilege on `Studio`, or vice versa. Since it is only particular attributes of `Movie` and `Studio` that get selected, it is sufficient to have the privilege

SELECT(studioName) on Movie and the privilege SELECT(name) on Studio, or privileges that included these attributes within a list of attributes. □

8.7.2 Creating Privileges

We have seen what the SQL privileges are and observed that they are required to perform SQL operations. Now we must learn how one obtains the privileges needed to perform an operation. There are two aspects to the awarding of privileges: how they are created initially, and how they are passed from user to user. We shall discuss initialization here and the transmission of privileges in Section 8.7.4.

First, SQL elements such as schemas or modules have an owner. The owner of something has all privileges associated with that thing. There are three points at which ownership is established in SQL.

1. When a schema is created, it and all the tables and other schema elements in it are assumed owned by the user who created it. This user thus has all possible privileges on elements of the schema.

2. When a session is initiated by a CONNECT statement, there is an opportunity to indicate the user with an AUTHORIZATION clause. For instance, the connection statement

   ```
   CONNECT TO Starfleet-sql-server AS conn1
       AUTHORIZATION kirk;
   ```

   would create a connection called conn1 to an SQL server whose name is Starfleet-sql-server, on behalf of a user kirk. Presumably, the SQL implementation would verify that the user name is valid, for example by asking for a password. It is also possible to include the password in the AUTHORIZATION clause, as we discussed in Section 8.3.5. That approach is somewhat insecure, since passwords are then visible to someone looking over Kirk's shoulder.

3. When a module is created, there is an option to give it an owner by using an AUTHORIZATION clause. For instance, a clause

   ```
   AUTHORIZATION picard;
   ```

   in a module-creation statement would make user picard the owner of the module. It is also acceptable to specify no owner for a module, in which case the module is publicly executable, but the privileges necessary for executing any operations in the module must come from some other source, such as the user associated with the connection and session during which the module is executed.

8.7.3 The Privilege-Checking Process

As we saw above, each module, schema, and session has an associated user; in SQL terms, there is an associated authorization ID for each. Any SQL operation has two parties:

1. The database elements upon which the operation is performed and

2. The agent that causes the operation.

The privileges available to the agent derive from a particular authorization ID called the *current authorization ID*. That ID is either

a) The module authorization ID, if the module that the agent is executing has an authorization ID, or

b) The session authorization ID if not.

We may execute the SQL operation only if the current authorization ID possesses all the privileges needed to carry out the operation on the database elements involved.

Example 8.35 : To see the mechanics of checking privileges, let us reconsider Example 8.34. We might suppose that the referenced tables — `Movie` and `Studio` — are part of a schema called `MovieSchema` that was created by, and owned by, user `janeway`. At this point, user `janeway` has all privileges on these tables and any other elements of the schema `MovieSchema`. She may choose to grant some privileges to others by the mechanism to be described in Section 8.7.4, but let us assume none have been granted yet. There are several ways that the insertion of Example 8.34 can be executed.

1. The insertion could be executed as part of a module created by user `janeway` and containing an `AUTHORIZATION janeway` clause. The module authorization ID, if there is one, always becomes the current authorization ID. Then, the module and its SQL insertion statement have exactly the same privileges user `janeway` has, which includes all privileges on the tables `Movie` and `Studio`.

2. The insertion could be part of a module that has no owner. User `janeway` opens a connection with an `AUTHORIZATION janeway` clause in the `CONNECT` statement. Now, `janeway` is again the current authorization ID, so the insertion statement has all the privileges needed.

3. User `janeway` grants all privileges on tables `Movie` and `Studio` to user `sisko`, or perhaps to the special user `PUBLIC`, which stands for "all users." The insertion statement is in a module with the clause

```
AUTHORIZATION sisko
```

Since the current authorization ID is now `sisko`, and this user has the needed privileges, the insertion is again permitted.

4. As in (3), user `janeway` has given user `sisko` the needed privileges. The insertion statement is in a module without an owner; it is executed in a session whose authorization ID was set by an `AUTHORIZATION sisko` clause. The current authorization ID is thus `sisko`, and that ID has the needed privileges.

☐

There are several principles that are illustrated by Example 8.35. We shall summarize them below.

- The needed privileges are always available if the data is owned by the same user as the user whose ID is the current authorization ID. Scenarios (1) and (2) above illustrate this point.

- The needed privileges are available if the user whose ID is the current authorization ID has been granted those privileges by the owner of the data, or if the privileges have been granted to user `PUBLIC`. Scenarios (3) and (4) illustrate this point.

- Executing a module owned by the owner of the data, or by someone who has been granted privileges on the data, makes the needed privileges available. Of course, one needs the `EXECUTE` privilege on the module itself. Scenarios (1) and (3) illustrate this point.

- Executing a publicly available module during a session whose authorization ID is that of a user with the needed privileges is another way to execute the operation legally. Scenarios (2) and (4) illustrate this point.

8.7.4 Granting Privileges

We saw in Example 8.35 the importance to a user (i.e., an authorization ID) of having the needed privileges. But so far, the only way we have seen to have privileges on a database element is to be the creator and owner of that element. SQL provides a `GRANT` statement to allow one user to give a privilege to another. The first user retains the privilege granted, as well; thus `GRANT` can be thought of as "copy a privilege."

There is one important difference between granting privileges and copying. Each privilege has an associated *grant option*. That is, one user may have a privilege like `SELECT` on table `Movie` "with grant option," while a second user may have the same privilege, but without the grant option. Then the first user may grant the privilege `SELECT` on `Movie` to a third user, and moreover that grant may be with or without the grant option. However, the second user, who does not have the grant option, may not grant the privilege `SELECT` on `Movie` to anyone else. If the third user later gets this same privilege with the grant option, then that user may grant the privilege to a fourth user, again with or without the grant option, and so on.

A *grant statement* consists of the following elements:

1. The keyword `GRANT`.

2. A list of one or more privileges, e.g., `SELECT` or `INSERT(name)`. Optionally, the keywords `ALL PRIVILEGES` may appear here, as a shorthand for all the privileges that the grantor may legally grant on the database element in question (the element mentioned in item 4 below).

3. The keyword `ON`.

4. A database element. This element is typically a relation, either a base table or a view. It may also be a domain or other element we have not discussed (see the box "More Schema Elements" in Section 8.3.2), but in these cases the element name must be preceded by the keyword `DOMAIN` or another appropriate keyword.

5. The keyword `TO`.

6. A list of one or more users (authorization ID's).

7. Optionally, the keywords `WITH GRANT OPTION`

That is, the form of a grant statement is:

GRANT <privilege list> ON <database element> TO <user list>

possibly followed by `WITH GRANT OPTION`.

In order to execute this grant statement legally, the user executing it must possess the privileges granted, and these privileges must be held with the grant option. However, the grantor may hold a more general privilege (with the grant option) than the privilege granted. For instance, the privilege `INSERT(name)` on table `Studio` might be granted, while the grantor holds the more general privilege `INSERT` on `Studio`, with grant option.

Example 8.36: User `janeway`, who is the owner of the `MovieSchema` schema that contains tables

```
Movie(title, year, length, inColor, studioName, producerC#)
Studio(name, address, presC#)
```

grants the `INSERT` and `SELECT` privileges on table `Studio` and privilege `SELECT` on `Movie` to users `kirk` and `picard`. Moreover, she includes the grant option with these privileges. The grant statements are:

```
    GRANT SELECT, INSERT ON Studio TO kirk, picard
        WITH GRANT OPTION;
    GRANT SELECT ON Movie TO kirk, picard
        WITH GRANT OPTION;
```

Now, `picard` grants to user `sisko` the same privileges, but without the grant option. The statements executed by `picard` are:

```
    GRANT SELECT, INSERT ON Studio TO sisko;
    GRANT SELECT ON Movie TO sisko;
```

Also, `kirk` grants to `sisko` the minimal privileges needed for the insertion of Fig. 8.25, namely SELECT and INSERT(name) on Studio and SELECT on Movie. The statements are:

```
    GRANT SELECT, INSERT(name) ON Studio TO sisko;
    GRANT SELECT ON Movie TO sisko;
```

Note that `sisko` has received the SELECT privilege on Movie and Studio from two different users. He has also received the INSERT(name) privilege on Studio twice: directly from `kirk` and via the generalized privilege INSERT from `picard`. □

8.7.5   Grant Diagrams

Because of the complex web of grants and overlapping privileges that may result from a sequence of grants, it is useful to represent grants by a graph called a *grant diagram*. An SQL system maintains a representation of this diagram to keep track of both privileges and their origins (in case a privilege is revoked; see Section 8.7.6).

   The nodes of a grant diagram correspond to a user and a privilege. Note that a privilege with and without the grant option must be represented by two different nodes. If user U grants privilege P to user V, and this grant was based on the fact that U holds privilege Q (Q could be P with the grant option, or it could be some generalization of P, again with the grant option), then we draw an arc from the node for U/Q to the node for V/P.

Example 8.37 : Figure 8.26 shows the grant diagram that results from the sequence of grant statements of Example 8.36. We use the convention that a * after a user-privilege combination indicates that the privilege includes the grant option. Also, ** after a user-privilege combination indicates that the privilege derives from ownership of the database element in question and was not due to a grant of the privilege from elsewhere. This distinction will prove important when we discuss revoking privileges in Section 8.7.6. A doubly starred privilege automatically includes the grant option.   □

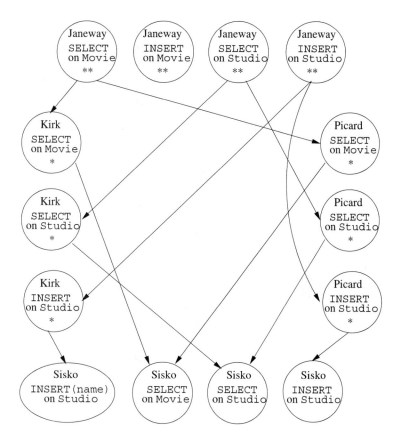

Figure 8.26: A grant diagram

8.7.6 Revoking Privileges

A granted privilege can be revoked at any time. In fact, the revoking of privileges may be required to *cascade*, in the sense that revoking a privilege with the grant option that has been passed on to other users may require those privileges to be revoked too. The simple form of a *revoke statement* is:

1. The keyword REVOKE.

2. A list of one or more privileges.

3. The keyword ON.

4. A database element, as discussed in item (4) in the description of a grant statement.

5. The keyword FROM.

6. A list of one or more users (authorization ID's).

That is, the following is the form of a revoke statement:

    REVOKE <privilege list> ON <database element> FROM <user list>

However, one of the following items must also be included in the statement:

1. The statement can end with the word `CASCADE`. If so, then when the specified privileges are revoked, we also revoke any privileges that were granted *only* because of the revoked privileges. More precisely, if user U has revoked privilege P from user V, based on privilege Q belonging to U, then we delete the arc in the grant diagram from U/Q to V/P. Now, any node that is not accessible from some ownership node (doubly starred node) is also deleted.

2. The statement can instead end with `RESTRICT`, which means that the revoke statement cannot be executed if the cascading rule described in the previous item would result in the revoking of any privileges due to the revoked privileges having been passed on to others.

   It is permissible to replace `REVOKE` by `REVOKE GRANT OPTION FOR`, in which case the core privileges themselves remain, but the option to grant them to others is removed. We may have to modify a node, redirect arcs, or create a new node to reflect the changes for the affected users. This form of `REVOKE` also must be made in combination with either `CASCADE` or `RESTRICT`.

Example 8.38: Continuing with Example 8.36, suppose that `janeway` revokes the privileges she granted to `picard` with the statements:

    REVOKE SELECT, INSERT ON Studio FROM picard CASCADE;
    REVOKE SELECT ON Movie FROM picard CASCADE;

   We delete the arcs of Fig. 8.26 from these `janeway` privileges to the corresponding `picard` privileges. Since `CASCADE` was stipulated, we also have to see if there are any privileges that are not reachable in the graph from a doubly starred (ownership-based) privilege. Examining Fig. 8.26, we see that `picard`'s privileges are no longer reachable from a doubly starred node (they might have been, had there been another path to a `picard` node). Also, `sisko`'s privilege to `INSERT` into `Studio` is no longer reachable. We thus delete not only `picard`'s privileges from the grant diagram, but we delete `sisko`'s `INSERT` privilege.

   Note that we do not delete `sisko`'s `SELECT` privileges on `Movie` and `Studio` or his `INSERT(name)` privilege on `Studio`, because these are all reachable from `janeway`'s ownership-based privileges via `kirk`'s privileges. The resulting grant diagram is shown in Fig. 8.27. □

Example 8.39: There are a few subtleties that we shall illustrate with abstract examples. First, when we revoke a general privilege p, we do not also revoke a privilege that is a special case of p. For instance, consider the following sequence

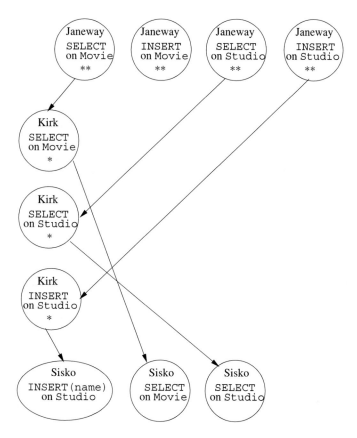

Figure 8.27: Grant diagram after revocation of `picard`'s privileges

of steps, whereby user U, the owner of relation R, grants the INSERT privilege on relation R to user V, and also grants the INSERT(A) privilege on the same relation.

Step	By	Action
1	U	GRANT INSERT ON R TO V
2	U	GRANT INSERT(A) ON R TO V
3	U	REVOKE INSERT ON R FROM V RESTRICT

When U revokes INSERT from V, the INSERT(A) privilege remains. The grant diagrams after steps (2) and (3) are shown in Fig. 8.28.

Notice that after step (2) there are two separate nodes for the two similar but distinct privileges that user V has. Also observe that the RESTRICT option in step (3) does not prevent the revocation, because V had not granted the option to any other user. In fact, V could not have granted either privilege, because V obtained them without grant option. □

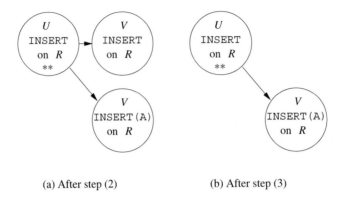

(a) After step (2)   (b) After step (3)

Figure 8.28: Revoking a general privilege leaves a more specific privilege

Example 8.40: Now, let us consider a similar example where U grants V a privilege p with the grant option and then revokes only the grant option. In this case, we must change V's node to reflect the loss of the grant option, and any grants of p made by V must be cancelled by eliminating arcs out of the V/p node. The sequence of steps is as follows:

Step	By	Action
1	U	GRANT p TO V WITH GRANT OPTION
2	V	GRANT p TO W
3	U	REVOKE GRANT OPTION FOR p FROM V CASCADE

In step (1), U grants the privilege p to V with the grant option. In step (2), V uses the grant option to grant p to W. The diagram is then as shown in Fig. 8.29(a).

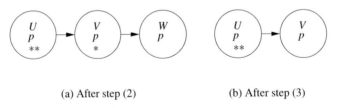

(a) After step (2)   (b) After step (3)

Figure 8.29: Revoking a grant option leaves the underlying privilege

Then in step (3), U revokes the grant option for privilege p from V, but does not revoke the privilege itself. Thus, the star is removed from the node for V and p. However, a node without a * may not have an arc out, because such a node cannot be the source of the granting of a privilege. Thus, we must also remove the arc out of the node V/p that goes to the node for W/p.

Now, the node W/p has no path to it from a ** node that represents the origin of privilege p. As a result, node W/p is deleted from the diagram. However, node V/p remains; it is just modified by removing the $*$ that represents the grant option. The resulting grant diagram is shown in Fig. 8.29(b). □

8.7.7 Exercises for Section 8.7

Exercise 8.7.1: Indicate what privileges are needed to execute the following queries. In each case, mention the most specific privileges as well as general privileges that are sufficient.

a) The query of Fig. 6.5.

b) The query of Fig. 6.7.

* c) The insertion of Fig. 6.15.

d) The deletion of Example 6.36.

e) The update of Example 6.38.

f) The tuple-based check of Fig. 7.5.

g) The assertion of Example 7.13.

* **Exercise 8.7.2:** Show the grant diagrams after steps (4) through (6) of the sequence of actions listed in Fig. 8.30. Assume A is the owner of the relation to which privilege p refers.

Step	By	Action
1	A	GRANT p TO B WITH GRANT OPTION
2	A	GRANT p TO C
3	B	GRANT p TO D WITH GRANT OPTION
4	D	GRANT p TO B, C, E WITH GRANT OPTION
5	B	REVOKE p FROM D CASCADE
6	A	REVOKE p FROM C CASCADE

Figure 8.30: Sequence of actions for Exercise 8.7.2

Exercise 8.7.3: Show the grant diagrams after steps (5) and (6) of the sequence of actions listed in Fig. 8.31. Assume A is the owner of the relation to which privilege p refers.

! **Exercise 8.7.4:** Show the final grant diagram after the following steps, assuming A is the owner of the relation to which privilege p refers.

Step	By	Action
1	A	GRANT p TO B WITH GRANT OPTION
2	B	GRANT p TO B WITH GRANT OPTION
3	A	REVOKE p FROM B CASCADE

Step	By	Action
1	A	GRANT p TO B, E WITH GRANT OPTION
2	B	GRANT p TO C WITH GRANT OPTION
3	C	GRANT p TO D WITH GRANT OPTION
4	E	GRANT p TO C
5	E	GRANT p TO D WITH GRANT OPTION
6	A	REVOKE GRANT OPTION FOR p FROM B CASCADE

Figure 8.31: Sequence of actions for Exercise 8.7.3

8.8   Summary of Chapter 8

✦ *Embedded SQL*: Instead of using a generic query interface to express SQL queries and modifications, it is often more effective to write programs that embed SQL queries in a conventional host language. A preprocessor converts the embedded SQL statements into suitable function calls of the host language.

✦ *Impedance Mismatch*: The data model of SQL is quite different from the data models of conventional host languages. Thus, information passes between SQL and the host language through shared variables that can represent components of tuples in the SQL portion of the program.

✦ *Cursors*: A cursor is an SQL variable that indicates one of the tuples of a relation. Connection between the host language and SQL is facilitated by having the cursor range over each tuple of the relation, while the components of the current tuple are retrieved into shared variables and processed using the host language.

✦ *Dynamic SQL*: Instead of embedding particular SQL statements in a host-language program, the host program may create character strings that are interpreted by the SQL system as SQL statements and executed.

✦ *Persistent Stored Modules*: We may create collections of procedures and functions as part of a database schema. These are written in a special language that has all the familiar control primitives, as well as SQL statements. They may be invoked from either embedded SQL or through a generic query interface.

✦ *The Database Environment*: An installation using an SQL DBMS creates an SQL environment. Within the environment, database elements such as relations are grouped into (database) schemas, catalogs, and clusters. A catalog is a collection of schemas, and a cluster is the largest collection of elements that one user may see.

✦ *Client/Server Systems*: An SQL client connects to an SQL server, creating a connection (link between the two processes) and a session (sequence of operations). The code executed during the session comes from a module, and the execution of the module is called an SQL agent.

● *The Call-Level Interface*: There is a standard library of functions called SQL/CLI or ODBC, which can be linked into any C program. These allow capabilities similar to embedded SQL, but without the need for a preprocessor.

✦ *JDBC*: Java Database Connectivity is a system similar to CLI, but using the Java, object-oriented style.

✦ *Concurrency Control*: SQL provides two mechanisms to prevent concurrent operations from interfering with one another: transactions and restrictions on cursors. Restrictions on cursors include the ability to declare a cursor to be "insensitive," in which case no changes to its relation will be seen by the cursor.

✦ *Transactions*: SQL allows the programmer to group SQL statements into transactions, which may be committed or rolled back (aborted). Transactions may be rolled back by the application in order to undo changes, or by the system in order to guarantee atomicity and isolation.

✦ *Isolation Levels*: SQL allows transactions to run with four isolation levels called, from most stringent to least stringent: "serializable" (the transaction must appear to run either completely before or completely after each other transaction), "repeatable-read" (every tuple read in response to a query will reappear if the query is repeated), "read-committed" (only tuples written by transactions that have already committed may be seen by this transaction), and "read-uncommitted" (no constraint on what the transaction may see).

✦ *Read-Only Cursors and Transactions*: Either a cursor or a transaction may be declared read-only. This declaration is a guarantee that the cursor or transaction will not change the database, thus informing the SQL system that it will not affect other transactions or cursors in ways that may violate insensitivity, serializability, or other requirements.

✦ *Privileges*: For security purposes, SQL systems allow many different kinds of privileges to be obtained on database elements. These privileges include the right to select (read), insert, delete, or update relations, the right to reference relations (refer to them in a constraint), and the right to create triggers.

✦ *Grant Diagrams*: Privileges may be granted by owners to other users or to the general user PUBLIC. If granted with the grant option, then these privileges may be passed on to others. Privileges may also be revoked.

The grant diagram is a useful way to remember enough about the history of grants and revocations to keep track of who has what privilege and from whom they obtained those privileges.

8.9   References for Chapter 8

Again, the reader is referred to the bibliographic notes of Chapter 6 for information on obtaining the SQL standards. The PSM standard is [4], and [5] is a comprehensive book on the subject. [6] is a popular reference on JDBC.

There is a discussion of problems with this standard in the area of transactions and cursors in [1]. More about transactions and how they are implemented can be found in the bibliographic notes to Chapter 18.

The ideas behind the SQL authorization mechanism originated in [3] and [2].

1. Berenson, H., P. A. Bernstein, J. N. Gray, J. Melton, E. O'Neil, and P. O'Neil, "A critique of ANSI SQL isolation levels," *Proceedings of ACM SIGMOD Intl. Conf. on Management of Data*, pp. 1–10, 1995.

2. Fagin, R., "On an authorization mechanism," *ACM Transactions on Database Systems* **3**:3, pp. 310–319, 1978.

3. Griffiths, P. P. and B. W. Wade, "An authorization mechanism for a relational database system," *ACM Transactions on Database Systems* **1**:3, pp. 242–255, 1976.

4. ISO/IEC Report 9075-4, 1996.

5. Melton, J., *Understanding SQL's Stored Peocedures: A Complete Guide to SQL/PSM*, Morgan-Kaufmann, San Francisco.

6. White, S., M. Fisher, R. Cattell, G. Hamilton, and M. Hapner, *JDBC API Tutorial and Reference*, Addison-Wesley, Boston, 1999.

Chapter 9

Object-Orientation in Query Languages

In this chapter, we shall discuss two ways in which object-oriented programming enters the world of query languages. OQL, or *Object Query Language*, is a standardized query language for object-oriented databases. It combines the high-level, declarative programming of SQL with the object-oriented programming paradigm. OQL is designed to operate on data described in ODL, the object-oriented data-description language that we introduced in Section 4.2.

If OQL is an attempt to bring the best of SQL into the object-oriented world, then the relatively new, object-relational features of the SQL-99 standard can be characterized as bringing the best of object-orientation into the relational world. In some senses, the two languages "meet in the middle," but there are differences in approach that make certain things easier in one language than the other.

In essence, the two approaches to object-orientation differ in their answer to the question: "how important is the relation?" For the object-oriented community centered around ODL and OQL, the answer is "not very." Thus, in OQL we find objects of all types, some of which are sets or bags of structures (i.e., relations). For the SQL community, the answer is that relations are still the fundamental data-structuring concept. In the object-relational approach that we introduced in Section 4.5, the relational model is extended by allowing more complex types for the tuples of relations and for attributes. Thus, objects and classes are introduced into the relational model, but always in the context of relations.

9.1 Introduction to OQL

OQL, the *Object Query Language*, gives us an SQL-like notation for expressing queries. It is intended that OQL will be used as an extension to some object-oriented *host* language, such as C++, Smalltalk, or Java. Objects will be manipulated both by OQL queries and by the conventional statements of the host language. The ability to mix host-language statements and OQL queries without explicitly transferring values between the two languages is an advance over the way SQL is embedded into a host language, as was discussed in Section 8.1.

9.1.1 An Object-Oriented Movie Example

In order to illustrate the dictions of OQL, we need a running example. It will involve the familiar classes `Movie`, `Star`, and `Studio`. We shall use the definitions of `Movie`, `Star`, and `Studio` from Fig. 4.3, augmenting them with key and extent declarations. Only `Movie` has methods, gathered from Fig. 4.4. The complete example schema is in Fig. 9.1.

9.1.2 Path Expressions

We access components of objects and structures using a dot notation that is similar to the dot used in C and also related to the dot used in SQL. The general rule is as follows. If a denotes an object belonging to class C, and p is some property of the class — either an attribute, relationship, or method of the class — then $a.p$ denotes the result of "applying" p to a. That is:

1. If p is an attribute, then $a.p$ is the value of that attribute in object a.

2. If p is a relationship, then $a.p$ is the object or collection of objects related to a by relationship p.

3. If p is a method (perhaps with parameters), then $a.p(\cdots)$ is the result of applying p to a.

Example 9.1: Let `myMovie` denote an object of type `Movie`. Then:

- The value of `myMovie.length` is the length of the movie, that is, the value of the `length` attribute for the `Movie` object denoted by `myMovie`.

- The value of `myMovie.lengthInHours()` is a real number, the length of the movie in hours, computed by applying the method `lengthInHours` to object `myMovie`.

- The value of `myMovie.stars` is the set of `Star` objects related to the movie `myMovie` by the relationship `stars`.

- Expression `myMovie.starNames(myStars)` returns no value (i.e., in C++ the type of this expression is `void`). As a side effect, however, it sets the value of the output variable `myStars` of the method `starNames` to be a set of strings; those strings are the names of the stars of the movie.

```
class Movie
    (extent Movies key (title, year))
{
   attribute string title;
   attribute integer year;
   attribute integer length;
   attribute enum Film {color,blackAndWhite} filmType;
   relationship Set<Star> stars
               inverse Star::starredIn;
   relationship Studio ownedBy
               inverse Studio::owns;
   float lengthInHours() raises(noLengthFound);
   void starNames(out Set<String>);
   void otherMovies(in Star, out Set<Movie>)
               raises(noSuchStar);
};


class Star
    (extent Stars key name)
{
   attribute string name;
   attribute Struct Addr
       {string street, string city} address;
   relationship Set<Movie> starredIn
               inverse Movie::stars;
};


class Studio
    (extent Studios key name)
{
   attribute string name;
   attribute string address;
   relationship Set<Movie> owns
               inverse Movie::ownedBy;
};
```

Figure 9.1: Part of an object-oriented movie database

Arrows and Dots

OQL allows the arrow -> as a synonym for the dot. This convention is partly in the spirit of C, where the dot and arrow both obtain components of a structure. However, in C, the arrow and dot operators have slightly different meanings; in OQL they are the same. In C, expression a.f expects a to be a structure, while p->f expects p to be a pointer to a structure. Both produce the value of the field f of that structure.

□

   If it makes sense, we can form expressions with several dots. For example, if myMovie denotes a movie object, then myMovie.ownedBy denotes the Studio object that owns the movie, and myMovie.ownedBy.name denotes the string that is the name of that studio.

9.1.3   Select-From-Where Expressions in OQL

OQL permits us to write expressions using a select-from-where syntax similar to SQL's familiar query form. Here is an example asking for the year of the movie *Gone With the Wind.*

```
SELECT m.year
FROM Movies m
WHERE m.title = "Gone With the Wind"
```

Notice that, except for the double-quotes around the string constant, this query could be SQL rather than OQL.

   In general, the OQL select-from-where expression consists of:

1. The keyword SELECT followed by a list of expressions.

2. The keyword FROM followed by a list of one or more variable declarations. A variable is declared by giving

   (a) An expression whose value has a collection type, e.g. a set or bag.

   (b) The optional keyword AS, and

   (c) The name of the variable.

   Typically, the expression of (a) is the extent of some class, such as the extent Movies for class Movie in the example above. An extent is the analog of a relation in an SQL FROM clause. However, it is possible to use in a variable declaration any collection-producing expression, such as another select-from-where expression.

3. The keyword WHERE and a boolean-valued expression. This expression, like the expression following the SELECT, may only use as operands constants and those variables declared in the FROM clause. The comparison operators are like SQL's, except that !=, rather than <>, is used for "not equal to." The logical operators are AND, OR, and NOT, like SQL's.

The query produces a bag of objects. We compute this bag by considering all possible values of the variables in the FROM clause, in nested loops. If any combination of values for these variables satisfies the condition of the WHERE clause, then the object described by the SELECT clause is added to the bag that is the result of the select-from-where statement.

Example 9.2: Here is a more complex OQL query:

```
SELECT s.name
FROM Movies m, m.stars s
WHERE m.title = "Casablanca"
```

This query asks for the names of the stars of *Casablanca*. Notice the sequence of terms in the FROM clause. First we define m to be an arbitrary object in the class Movie, by saying m is in the extent of that class, which is Movies. Then, for each value of m we let s be a Star object in the set m.stars of stars of movie m. That is, we consider in two nested loops all pairs (m, s) such that m is a movie and s a star of that movie. The evaluation can be sketched as:

```
FOR each m in Movies DO
    FOR each s in m.stars DO
        IF m.title = "Casablanca" THEN
            add s.name to the output bag
```

The WHERE clause restricts our consideration to those pairs that have m equal to the Movie object whose title is *Casablanca*. Then, the SELECT clause produces the bag (which should be a set in this case) of all the name attributes of star objects s in the (m, s) pairs that satisfy the WHERE clause. These names are the names of the stars in the set m_c.stars, where m_c is the *Casablanca* movie object.   □

9.1.4 Modifying the Type of the Result

A query like Example 9.2 produces a bag of strings as a result. That is, OQL follows the SQL default of not eliminating duplicates in its answer unless directed to do so. However, we can force the result to be a set or a list if we wish.

- To make the result a set, use the keyword DISTINCT after SELECT, as in SQL.

Alternative Form of `FROM` Lists

In addition to the SQL-style elements of `FROM` clauses, where the collection is followed by a name for a typical element, OQL allows a completely equivalent, more logical, yet less SQL-ish form. We can give the typical element name, then the keyword `IN`, and finally the name of the collection. For instance,

```
FROM m IN Movies, s IN m.stars
```

is an equivalent `FROM` clause for the query in Example 9.2.

- To make the result a list, add an `ORDER BY` clause at the end of the query, again as in SQL.

The following examples will illustrate the correct syntax.

Example 9.3: Let us ask for the names of the stars of Disney movies. The following query does the job, eliminating duplicate names in the situation where a star appeared in several Disney movies.

```
SELECT DISTINCT s.name
FROM Movies m, m.stars s
WHERE m.ownedBy.name = "Disney"
```

The strategy of this query is similar to that of Example 9.2. We again consider all pairs of a movie and a star of that movie in two nested loops as in Example 9.2. But now, the condition on that pair (m, s) is that "Disney" is the name of the studio whose `Studio` object is `m.ownedBy`. □

The `ORDER BY` clause in OQL is quite similar to the same clause in SQL. Keywords `ORDER BY` are followed by a list of expressions. The first of these expressions is evaluated for each object in the result of the query, and objects are ordered by this value. Ties, if any, are broken by the value of the second expression, then the third, and so on. By default, the order is ascending, but a choice of ascending or descending order can be indicated by the keyword `ASC` or `DESC`, respectively, following an attribute, as in SQL.

Example 9.4: Let us find the set of Disney movies, but let the result be a list of movies, ordered by length. If there are ties, let the movies of equal length be ordered alphabetically. The query is:

```
SELECT m
FROM Movies m
WHERE m.ownedBy.name = "Disney"
ORDER BY m.length, m.title
```

In the first three lines, we consider each `Movie` object m. If the name of the studio that owns this movie is "Disney," then the complete object m becomes a member of the output bag. The fourth line specifies that the objects m produced by the select-from-where query are to be ordered first by the value of `m.length` (i.e., the length of the movie) and then, if there are ties, by the value of `m.title` (i.e., the title of the movie). The value produced by this query is thus a list of `Movie` objects. □

9.1.5 Complex Output Types

The elements in the `SELECT` clause need not be simple variables. They can be any expression, including expressions built using type constructors. For example, we can apply the `Struct` type constructor to several expressions and get a select-from-where query that produces a set or bag of structures.

Example 9.5: Suppose we want the set of pairs of stars living at the same address. We can get this set with the query:

```
SELECT DISTINCT Struct(star1: s1, star2: s2)
FROM Stars s1, Stars s2
WHERE s1.address = s2.address AND s1.name < s2.name
```

That is, we consider all pairs of stars, `s1` and `s2`. The `WHERE` clause checks that they have the same address. It also checks that the name of the first star precedes the name of the second in alphabetic order, so we don't produce pairs consisting of the same star twice and we don't produce the same pair of stars in two different orders.

For every pair that passes the two tests, we produce a record structure. The type of this structure is a record with two fields, named `star1` and `star2`. The type of each field is the class `Star`, since that is the type of the variables `s1` and `s2` that provide values for the two fields. That is, formally, the type of the structure is

```
Struct{star1: Star, star2: Star}
```

The type of the result of the query is a set of these structures, that is:

```
Set<Struct{star1: Star, star2: Star}>
```

□

9.1.6 Subqueries

We can use a select-from-where expression anywhere a collection is appropriate. We shall give one example: in the `FROM` clause. Several other examples of subquery use appear in Section 9.2.

SELECT **Lists of Length One Are Special**

Notice that when a SELECT list has only a single expression, the type of the result is a collection of values of the type of that expression. However, if we have more than one expression in the SELECT list, there is an implicit stucture formed with components for each expression. Thus, even had we started the query of Example 9.5 with

$$\text{SELECT DISTINCT star1: s1, star2: s2}$$

the type of the result would be

$$\text{Set<Struct\{star1: Star, star2: Star\}>}$$

However, in Example 9.3, the type of the result is Set<String>, not Set<Struct{name: String}>.

In the FROM clause, we may use a subquery to form a collection. We then allow a variable representing a typical element of that collection to range over each member of the collection.

Example 9.6 : Let us redo the query of Example 9.3, which asked for the stars of the movies made by Disney. First, the set of Disney movies could be obtained by the query, as was used in Example 9.4.

```
SELECT m
FROM Movies m
WHERE m.ownedBy.name = "Disney"
```

We can now use this query as a subquery to define the set over which a variable d, representing the Disney movies, can range.

```
SELECT DISTINCT s.name
FROM (SELECT m
      FROM Movies m
      WHERE m.ownedBy.name = "Disney") d,
     d.stars s
```

This expression of the query "Find the stars of Disney movies" is no more succinct than that of Example 9.3, and perhaps less so. However, it does illustrate a new form of building queries available in OQL. In the query above, the FROM clause has two nested loops. In the first, the variable d ranges over all Disney movies, the result of the subquery in the FROM clause. In the second loop, nested within the first, the variable s ranges over all stars of the Disney movie d. Notice that no WHERE clause is needed in the outer query. □

9.1.7 Exercises for Section 9.1

Exercise 9.1.1: In Fig. 9.2 is an ODL description of our running products exercise. We have made each of the three types of products subclasses of the main `Product` class. The reader should observe that a type of a product can be obtained either from the attribute `type` or from the subclass to which it belongs. This arrangement is not an excellent design, since it allows for the possibility that, say, a PC object will have its `type` attribute equal to "laptop" or "printer". However, the arrangement gives you some interesting options regarding how one expresses queries.

Because `type` is inherited by `Printer` from the superclass `Product`, we have had to rename the `type` attribute of `Printer` to be `printerType`. The latter attribute gives the process used by the printer (e.g., laser or inkjet), while `type` of `Product` will have values such as PC, laptop, or printer.

Add to the ODL code of Fig. 9.2 method signatures (see Section 4.2.7) appropriate for functions that do the following:

* a) Subtract x from the price of a product. Assume x is provided as an input parameter of the function.

* b) Return the speed of a product if the product is a PC or laptop and raise the exception `notComputer` if not.

  c) Set the screen size of a laptop to a specified input value x.

! d) Given an input product p, determine whether the product q to which the method is applied has a higher speed and a lower price than p. Raise the exception `badInput` if p is not a product with a speed (i.e., neither a PC nor laptop) and the exception `noSpeed` if q is not a product with a speed.

Exercise 9.1.2: Using the ODL schema of Exercise 9.1.1 and Fig. 9.2, write the following queries in OQL:

* a) Find the model numbers of all products that are PC's with a price under $2000.

  b) Find the model numbers of all the PC's with at least 128 megabytes of RAM.

*! c) Find the manufacturers that make at least two different models of laser printer.

  d) Find the set of pairs (r, h) such that some PC or laptop has r megabytes of RAM and h gigabytes of hard disk.

  e) Create a list of the PC's (objects, not model numbers) in ascending order of processor speed.

! f) Create a list of the model numbers of the laptops with at least 64 megabytes of RAM, in descending order of screen size.

```
class Product
    (extent Products
     key model)
 {
    attribute integer model;
    attribute string manufacturer;
    attribute string type;
    attribute real price;
 };


class PC extends Product
    (extent PCs)
 {
    attribute integer speed;
    attribute integer ram;
    attribute integer hd;
    attribute string rd;
 };


class Laptop extends Product
    (extent Laptops)
 {
    attribute integer speed;
    attribute integer ram;
    attribute integer hd;
    attribute real screen;
 };


class Printer extends Product
    (extent Printers)
 {
    attribute boolean color;
    attribute string printerType;
 };
```

Figure 9.2: Product schema in ODL

```
class Class
    (extent Classes
     key name)
 {
    attribute string name;
    attribute string country;
    attribute integer numGuns;
    attribute integer bore;
    attribute integer displacement;
    relationship Set<Ship> ships inverse Ship::classOf;
 };

class Ship
    (extent Ships
     key name)
 {
    attribute string name;
    attribute integer launched;
    relationship Class classOf inverse Class::ships;
    relationship Set<Outcome> inBattles
                inverse Outcome::theShip;
 };

class Battle
    (extent Battles
     key name)
 {
    attribute name;
    attribute Date dateFought;
    relationship Set<Outcome> results
                inverse Outcome::theBattle;
 };

class Outcome
    (extent Outcomes)
 {
    attribute enum Stat {ok,sunk,damaged} status;
    relationship Ship theShip inverse Ship::inBattles;
    relationship Battle theBattle inverse Battle::results;
 };
```

Figure 9.3: Battleships database in ODL

Exercise 9.1.3 : In Fig. 9.3 is an ODL description of our running "battleships" database. Add the following method signatures:

a) Compute the firepower of a ship, that is, the number of guns times the cube of the bore.

b) Find the sister ships of a ship. Raise the exception `noSisters` if the ship is the only one of its class.

c) Given a battle *b* as a parameter, and applying the method to a ship *s*, find the ships sunk in the battle *b*, provided *s* participated in that battle. Raise the exception `didNotParticipate` if ship *s* did not fight in battle *b*.

d) Given a name and a year launched as parameters, add a ship of this name and year to the class to which the method is applied.

! Exercise 9.1.4 : Repeat each part of Exercise 9.1.2 using at least one subquery in each of your queries.

Exercise 9.1.5 : Using the ODL schema of Exercise 9.1.3 and Fig. 9.3, write the following queries in OQL:

a) Find the names of the classes of ships with at least nine guns.

b) Find the ships (objects, not ship names) with at least nine guns.

c) Find the names of the ships with a displacement under 30,000 tons. Make the result a list, ordered by earliest launch year first, and if there are ties, alphabetically by ship name.

d) Find the pairs of objects that are sister ships (i.e., ships of the same class). Note that the objects themselves are wanted, not the names of the ships.

! e) Find the names of the battles in which ships of at least two different countries were sunk.

!! f) Find the names of the battles in which no ship was listed as damaged.

9.2   Additional Forms of OQL Expressions

In this section we shall see some of the other operators, besides select-from-where, that OQL provides to help us build expressions. These operators include logical quantifiers — for-all and there-exists — aggregation operators, the group-by operator, and set operators — union, intersection, and difference.

9.2.1 Quantifier Expressions

We can test whether all members of a collection satisfy some condition, and we can test whether at least one member of a collection satisfies a condition. To test whether all members x of a collection S satisfy condition $C(x)$, we use the OQL expression:

$$\text{FOR ALL } x \text{ IN } S : C(x)$$

The result of this expression is TRUE if every x in S satisfies $C(x)$ and is FALSE otherwise. Similarly, the expression

$$\text{EXISTS } x \text{ IN } S : C(x)$$

has value TRUE if there is at least one x in S such that $C(x)$ is TRUE and it has value FALSE otherwise.

Example 9.7: Another way to express the query "find all the stars of Disney movies" is shown in Fig. 9.4. Here, we focus on a star s and ask if they are the star of some movie m that is a Disney movie. Line (3) tells us to consider all movies m in the set of movies s.starredIn, which is the set of movies in which star s appeared. Line (4) then asks whether movie m is a Disney movie. If we find even one such movie m, the value of the EXISTS expression in lines (3) and (4) is TRUE; otherwise it is FALSE. □

```
1)   SELECT s
2)   FROM Stars s
3)   WHERE EXISTS m IN s.starredIn :
4)       m.ownedBy.name = "Disney"
```

Figure 9.4: Using an existential subquery

Example 9.8: Let us use the for-all operator to write a query asking for the stars that have appeared only in Disney movies. Technically, that set includes "stars" who appear in no movies at all (as far as we can tell from our database). It is possible to add another condition to our query, requiring that the star appear in at least one movie, but we leave that improvement as an exercise. Figure 9.5 shows the query. □

9.2.2 Aggregation Expressions

OQL uses the same five aggregation operators that SQL does: AVG, COUNT, SUM, MIN, and MAX. However, while these operators in SQL may be thought of as

```
SELECT s
FROM Stars s
WHERE FOR ALL m IN s.starredIn :
    m.ownedBy.name = "Disney"
```

Figure 9.5: Using a subquery with universal quantification

applying to a designated column of a table, the same operators in OQL apply to all collections whose members are of a suitable type. That is, COUNT can apply to any collection; SUM and AVG can be applied to collections of arithmetic types such as integers, and MIN and MAX can be applied to collections of any type that can be compared, e.g., arithmetic values or strings.

Example 9.9 : To compute the average length of all movies, we need to create a bag of all movie lengths. Note that we don't want the *set* of movie lengths, because then two movies that had the same length would count as one. The query is:

```
AVG(SELECT m.length FROM Movies m)
```

That is, we use a subquery to extract the length components from movies. Its result is the bag of lengths of movies, and we apply the AVG operator to this bag, giving the desired answer.   □

9.2.3   Group-By Expressions

The GROUP BY clause of SQL carries over to OQL, but with an interesting twist in perspective. The form of a GROUP BY clause in OQL is:

1. The keywords GROUP BY.

2. A comma-separated list of one or more *partition attributes*. Each of these consists of

   (a) A field name,
   (b) A colon, and
   (c) An expression.

That is, the form of a GROUP BY clause is:

$$\text{GROUP BY } f_1{:}e_1, \ f_2{:}e_2, \ldots, f_n{:}e_n$$

Each GROUP BY clause follows a select-from-where query. The expressions $e_1, e_2, \ldots, e_n$ may refer to variables mentioned in the FROM clause. To facilitate the explanation of how GROUP BY works, let us restrict ourselves to the common case where there is only one variable x in the from clause. The value of x ranges over some collection, C. For each member of C, say i, that satisfies the condition of the WHERE clause, we evaluate all the expressions that follow the GROUP BY, to obtain values $e_1(i), e_2(i), \ldots, e_n(i)$. This list of values is the group to which value i belongs.

The Intermediate Collection

The actual value returned by the GROUP BY is a set of structures, which we shall call the *intermediate collection*. The members of the intermediate collection have the form

$$\texttt{Struct}(f_1{:}v_1, \ f_2{:}v_2, \ldots, f_n{:}v_n, \ \texttt{partition}{:}P)$$

The first n fields indicate the group. That is, $(v_1, v_2, \ldots, v_n)$ must be the list of values $\big(e_1(i), e_2(i), \ldots, e_n(i)\big)$ for at least one value of i in the collection C that meets the condition of the WHERE clause.

The last field has the special name partition. Its value P is, intuitively, the values i that belong in this group. More precisely, P is a bag consisting of structures of the form Struct(x:i), where x is the variable of the FROM clause.

The Output Collection

The SELECT clause of a select-from-where expression that has a GROUP BY clause may refer only to the fields in the structures of the intermediate collection, namely $f_1, f_2, \ldots, f_n$ and partition. Through partition, we may refer to the field x that is present in the structures that are members of the bag P that forms the value of partition. Thus, we may refer to the variable x that appears in the FROM clause, but we may only do so within an aggregation operator that aggregates over all the members of a bag P. The result of the SELECT clause will be referred to as the *output collection*.

Example 9.10: Let us build a table of the total length of movies for each studio and for each year. In OQL, what we actually construct is a bag of structures, each with three components — a studio, a year, and the total length of movies for that studio and year. The query is shown in Fig. 9.6.

```
SELECT stdo, yr, sumLength: SUM(SELECT p.m.length
                                FROM partition p)
FROM Movies m
GROUP BY stdo: m.ownedBy.name, yr: m.year
```

Figure 9.6: Grouping movies by studio and year

To understand this query, let us start at the FROM clause. There, we find that variable m ranges over all Movie objects. Thus, m here plays the role of x

in our general discussion. In the `GROUP BY` clause are two fields `stdo` and `yr`, corresponding to the expressions `m.ownedBy.name` and `m.year`, respectively.

For instance, *Pretty Woman* is a movie made by Disney in 1990. When m is the object for this movie, the value of `m.ownedBy.name` is `"Disney"` and the value of `m.year` is 1990. As a result, the intermediate collection has, as one member, the structure:

$$\text{Struct(stdo:"Disney", yr:1990, partition:}P)$$

Here, P is a set of structures. It contains, for example,

$$\text{Struct(m:}m_{pw})$$

where m_{pw} is the `Movie` object for *Pretty Woman*. Also in P are one-component structures with field name m for every other Disney movie of 1990.

Now, let us examine the `SELECT` clause. For each structure in the intermediate collection, we build one structure that is in the output collection. The first component of each output structure is `stdo`. That is, the field name is `stdo` and its value is the value of the `stdo` field of the corresponding structure in the intermediate collection. Similarly, the second component of the result has field name `yr` and a value equal to the `yr` component of the intermediate collection.

The third component of each structure in the output is

```
SUM(SELECT p.m.length FROM partition p)
```

To understand this select-from expression we first realize that variable p ranges over the members of the `partition` field of the structure in the `GROUP BY` result. Each value of p, recall, is a structure of the form `Struct(m:o)`, where o is a movie object. The expression `p.m` therefore refers to this object o. Thus, `p.m.length` refers to the length component of this `Movie` object.

As a result, the select-from query produces the bag of lengths of the movies in a particular group. For instance, if `stdo` has the value `"Disney"` and `yr` has the value 1990, then the result of the select-from is the bag of the lengths of the movies made by Disney in 1990. When we apply the `SUM` operator to this bag we get the sum of the lengths of the movies in the group. Thus, one member of the output collection might be

$$\text{Struct(stdo:"Disney", yr:1990, sumLength:1234)}$$

if 1234 is the correct total length of all the Disney movies of 1990. $\square$

Grouping When the `FROM` Clause has Multiple Collections

In the event that there is more than one variable in the `FROM` clause, a few changes to the interpretation of the query are necessary, but the principles remain the same as in the one-variable case above. Suppose that the variables appearing in the `FROM` clause are $x_1, x_2, \ldots, x_k$. Then:

1. All variables $x_1, x_2, \ldots, x_k$ may be used in the expressions $e_1, e_2, \ldots, e_n$ of the GROUP BY clause.

2. Structures in the bag that is the value of the **partition** field have fields named $x_1, x_2, \ldots, x_k$.

3. Suppose $i_1, i_2, \ldots, i_k$ are values for variables $x_1, x_2, \ldots, x_k$, respectively, that make the WHERE clause true. Then there is a structure in the intermediate collection of the form

$$\texttt{Struct}(f_1{:}e_1(i_1, \ldots, i_k), \ldots, f_n{:}e_n(i_1, \ldots, i_k), \ \texttt{partition:P})$$

and in bag P is the structure:

$$\texttt{Struct}(x_1{:}i_1, \ x_2{:}i_2, \ldots, x_k{:}i_k)$$

9.2.4 HAVING Clauses

A GROUP BY clause of OQL may be followed by a HAVING clause, with a meaning like that of SQL's HAVING clause. That is, a clause of the form

HAVING <condition>

serves to eliminate some of the groups created by the GROUP BY. The condition applies to the value of the **partition** field of each structure in the intermediate collection. If true, then this structure is processed as in Section 9.2.3, to form a structure of the output collection. If false, then this structure does not contribute to the output collection.

Example 9.11 : Let us repeat Example 9.10, but ask for the sum of the lengths of movies for only those studios and years such that the studio produced at least one movie of over 120 minutes. The query of Fig. 9.7 does the job. Notice that in the HAVING clause we used the same query as in the SELECT clause to obtain the bag of lengths of movies for a given studio and year. In the HAVING clause, we take the maximum of those lengths and compare it to 120. □

```
SELECT stdo, yr, sumLength: SUM(SELECT p.m.length
                                FROM partition p)
FROM Movies m
GROUP BY stdo: m.ownedBy.name, yr: m.year
HAVING MAX(SELECT p.m.length FROM partition p) > 120
```

Figure 9.7: Restricting the groups considered

9.2.5 Union, Intersection, and Difference

We may apply the union, intersection, and difference operators to two objects of set or bag type. These three operators are represented, as in SQL, by the keywords UNION, INTERSECT, and EXCEPT, respectively.

```
1)      (SELECT DISTINCT m
2)       FROM Movies m, m.stars s
3)       WHERE s.name = "Harrison Ford")
4)  EXCEPT
5)      (SELECT DISTINCT m
6)       FROM Movies m
7)       WHERE m.ownedBy.name = "Disney")
```

Figure 9.8: Query using the difference of two sets

Example 9.12: We can find the set of movies starring Harrison Ford that were not made by Disney with the difference of two select-from-where queries shown in Fig. 9.8. Lines (1) through (3) find the set of movies starring Ford, and lines (5) through (7) find the set of movies made by Disney. The EXCEPT at line (4) takes their difference. □

We should notice the DISTINCT keywords in lines (1) and (5) of Fig. 9.8. This keyword forces the results of the two queries to be of set type; without DISTINCT, the result would be of bag (multiset) type. In OQL, the operators UNION, INTERSECT, and EXCEPT operate on either sets or bags. When both arguments are sets, then the operators have their usual set meaning.

However, when both arguments are of bag type, or one is a bag and one is a set, then the bag meaning of the operators is used. Recall Section 5.3.2, where the definitions of union, intersection, and difference for bags was explained.

For the particular query of Fig. 9.8, the number of times a movie appears in the result of either subquery is zero or one, so the result is the same regardless of whether DISTINCT is used. However, the *type* of the result differs. If DISTINCT is used, then the type of the result is Set<Movie>, while if DISTINCT is omitted in one or both places, then the result is of type Bag<Movie>.

9.2.6 Exercises for Section 9.2

Exercise 9.2.1: Using the ODL schema of Exercise 9.1.1 and Fig. 9.2, write the following queries in OQL:

* a) Find the manufacturers that make both PC's and printers.

* b) Find the manufacturers of PC's, all of whose PC's have at least 20 gigabytes of hard disk.

    c) Find the manufacturers that make PC's but not laptops.

* d) Find the average speed of PC's.

* e) For each CD or DVD speed, find the average amount of RAM on a PC.

! f) Find the manufacturers that make some product with at least 64 megabytes of RAM and also make a product costing under $1000.

!! g) For each manufacturer that makes PC's with an average speed of at least 1200, find the maximum amount of RAM that they offer on a PC.

Exercise 9.2.2: Using the ODL schema of Exercise 9.1.3 and Fig. 9.3, write the following queries in OQL:

    a) Find those classes of ship all of whose ships were launched prior to 1919.

    b) Find the maximum displacement of any class.

! c) For each gun bore, find the earliest year in which any ship with that bore was launched.

*!! d) For each class of ships at least one of which was launched prior to 1919, find the number of ships of that class sunk in battle.

! e) Find the average number of ships in a class.

! f) Find the average displacement of a ship.

!! g) Find the battles (objects, not names) in which at least one ship from Great Britain took part and in which at least two ships were sunk.

! **Exercise 9.2.3:** We mentioned in Example 9.8 that the OQL query of Fig. 9.5 would return stars who starred in no movies at all, and therefore, technically appeared "only in Disney movies." Rewrite the query to return only those stars who have appeared in at least one movie and all movies in which they appeared where Disney movies.

! **Exercise 9.2.4:** Is it ever possible for FOR ALL x IN S : $C(x)$ to be true, while EXISTS x IN S : $C(x)$ is false? Explain your reasoning.

9.3 Object Assignment and Creation in OQL

In this section we shall consider how OQL connects to its host language, which we shall take to be C++ in examples, although another object-oriented, general-purpose programming language (e.g. Java) might be the host language in some systems.

9.3.1   Assigning Values to Host-Language Variables

Unlike SQL, which needs to move data between components of tuples and host-language variables, OQL fits naturally into its host language. That is, the expressions of OQL that we have learned, such as select-from-where, produce objects as values. It is possible to assign to any host-language variable of the proper type a value that is the result of one of these OQL expressions.

Example 9.13: The OQL expression

```
SELECT DISTINCT m
FROM Movies m
WHERE m.year < 1920
```

produces the set of all those movies made before 1920. Its type is `Set<Movie>`. If `oldMovies` is a host-language variable of the same type, then we may write (in C++ extended with OQL):

```
oldMovies = SELECT DISTINCT m
            FROM Movies m
            WHERE m.year < 1920;
```

and the value of `oldMovies` will become the set of these `Movie` objects.   □

9.3.2   Extracting Elements of Collections

Since the select-from-where and group-by expressions each produce collections — either sets, bags, or lists — we must do something extra if we want a single element of that collection. This statement is true even if we have a collection that we are sure contains only one element. OQL provides the operator `ELEMENT` to turn a singleton collection into its lone member. This operator can be applied, for instance, to the result of a query that is known to return a singleton.

Example 9.14: Suppose we would like to assign to the variable `gwtw`, of type `Movie` (i.e., the `Movie` class is its type) the object representing the movie *Gone With the Wind*. The result of the query

```
SELECT m
FROM Movies m
WHERE m.title = "Gone With the Wind"
```

is the bag containing just this one object. We cannot assign this bag to variable `gwtw` directly, because we would get a type error. However, if we apply the `ELEMENT` operator first,

```
gwtw = ELEMENT(SELECT m
               FROM Movies m
               WHERE m.title = "Gone With the Wind"
        );
```

then the type of the variable and the expression match, and the assignment is legal. □

9.3.3 Obtaining Each Member of a Collection

Obtaining each member of a set or bag is more complex, but still simpler than the cursor-based algorithms we needed in SQL. First, we need to turn our set or bag into a list. We do so with a select-from-where expression that uses ORDER BY. Recall from Section 9.1.4 that the result of such an expression is a list of the selected objects or values.

Example 9.15: Suppose we want a list of all the movie objects in the class Movie. We can use the title and (to break ties) the year of the movie, since (title, year) is a key for Movie. The statement

```
movieList = SELECT m
            FROM Movies m
            ORDER BY m.title, m.year;
```

assigns to host-language variable movieList a list of all the Movie objects, sorted by title and year. □

Once we have a list, sorted or not, we can access each element by number; the ith element of the list L is obtained by $L[i-1]$. Note that lists and arrays are assumed numbered starting at 0, as in C or C++.

Example 9.16: Suppose we want to write a C++ function that prints the title, year, and length of each movie. A sketch of the function is shown in Fig. 9.9.

```
1)   movieList = SELECT m
                 FROM Movies m
                 ORDER BY m.title, m.year;
2)   numberOfMovies = COUNT(Movies);
3)   for(i=0; i<numberOfMovies; i++) {
4)       movie = movieList[i];
5)       cout << movie.title << " " << movie.year << " "
6)            << movie.length << "\n";
     }
```

Figure 9.9: Examining and printing each movie

Line (1) sorts the Movie class, placing the result into variable movieList, whose type is List<Movie>. Line (2) computes the number of movies, using the OQL operator COUNT. Lines (3) through (6) are a for-loop in which integer variable i ranges over each position of the list. For convenience, the ith element of the list is assigned to variable `movie`. Then, at lines (5) and (6) the relevant attributes of the movie are printed.   □

9.3.4 Constants in OQL

Constants in OQL (sometimes referred to as *immutable objects*) are constructed from a basis and recursive constructors, in a manner analogous to the way ODL types are constructed.

1. *Basic values*, which are either

   (a) *Atomic values*: integers, floats, characters, strings, and booleans. These are represented as in SQL, with the exception that double-quotes are used to surround strings.

   (b) *Enumerations*. The values in an enumeration are actually declared in ODL. Any one of these values may be used as a constant.

2. *Complex values* built using the following type constructors:

   (a) `Set(...)`.
   (b) `Bag(...)`.
   (c) `List(...)`.
   (d) `Array(...)`.
   (e) `Struct(...)`.

   The first four of these are called *collection types*. The collection types and `Struct` may be applied at will to any values of the appropriate type(s), basic or complex. However, when applying the `Struct` operator, one needs to specify the field names and their corresponding values. Each field name is followed by a colon and the value, and field-value pairs are separated by commas. Note that the same type constructors are used in ODL, but here we use round, rather than triangular, brackets.

Example 9.17: The expression `bag(2,1,2)` denotes the bag in which integer 2 appears twice and integer 1 appears once. The expression

```
Struct(foo: bag(2,1,2), bar: "baz")
```

denotes a structure with two fields. Field `foo`, has the bag described above as its value, and `bar`, has the string `"baz"` for its value.   □

9.3.5 Creating New Objects

We have seen that OQL expressions such as select-from-where allow us to create new objects. It is also possible to create objects by assembling constants or other expressions into structures and collections explicitly. We saw an example of this convention in Example 9.5, where the line

```
SELECT DISTINCT Struct(star1: s1, star2: s2)
```

was used to specify that the result of the query is a set of objects whose type is `Struct{star1: Star, star2: Star}`. We gave the field names `star1` and `star2` to specify the structure, while the types of these fields could be deduced from the types of the variables `s1` and `s2`.

Example 9.18: The construction of constants that we saw in Section 9.3.4 can be used with assignments to variables, in a manner similar to that of other programming languages. For instance, consider the following sequence of assignments:

```
x = Struct(a:1, b:2);
y = Bag(x, x, Struct(a:3, b:4));
```

The first line gives variable `x` a value of type

```
Struct(a:integer, b:integer)
```

a structure with two integer-valued fields named `a` and `b`. We may represent values of this type as pairs, with just the integers as components and not the field names `a` and `b`. Thus, the value of x may be represented by $(1, 2)$. The second line defines `y` to be a bag whose members are structures of the same type as x, above. The pair $(1, 2)$ appears twice in this bag, and $(3, 4)$ appears once. □

Classes or other defined types can have instances created by *constructor functions*. Classes typically have several different forms of constructor functions, depending on which properties are initialized explicitly and which are given some default value. For example, methods are not initialized, most attributes will get initial values, and relationships might be initialized to the empty set and augmented later. The name for each of these constructor functions is the name of the class, and they are distinguished by the field names mentioned in their arguments. The details of how these constructor functions are defined depend on the host language.

Example 9.19: Let us consider a possible constructor function for `Movie` objects. This function, we suppose, takes values for the attributes `title`, `year`, `length`, and `ownedBy`, producing an object that has these values in the listed fields and an empty set of stars. Then, if `mgm` is a variable whose value is the MGM `Studio` object, we might create a *Gone With the Wind* object by:

```
gwtw = Movie(title: "Gone With the Wind",
             year: 1939,
             length: 239,
             ownedBy: mgm);
```

This statement has two effects:

1. It creates a new `Movie` object, which becomes part of the extent `Movies`.

2. It makes this object the value of host-language variable `gwtw`.

□

9.3.6   Exercises for Section 9.3

Exercise 9.3.1: Assign to a host-language variable x the following constants:

* a) The set $\{1, 2, 3\}$.

  b) The bag $\{1, 2, 3, 1\}$.

  c) The list $(1, 2, 3, 1)$.

  d) The structure whose first component, named a, is the set $\{1, 2\}$ and whose second component, named b, is the bag $\{1, 1\}$.

  e) The bag of structures, each with two fields named a and b. The respective pairs of values for the three structures in the bag are $(1, 2)$, $(2, 1)$, and $(1, 2)$.

Exercise 9.3.2: Using the ODL schema of Exercise 9.1.1 and Fig. 9.2, write statements of C++ (or an object-oriented host language of your choice) extended with OQL to do the following:

* a) Assign to host-language variable x the object for the PC with model number 1000.

  b) Assign to host-language variable y the set of all laptop objects with at least 64 megabytes of RAM.

  c) Assign to host-language variable z the average speed of PC's selling for less than $1500.

! d) Find all the laser printers, print a list of their model numbers and prices, and follow it by a message indicating the model number with the lowest price.

!! e) Print a table giving, for each manufacturer of PC's, the minimum and maximum price.

Exercise 9.3.3 : In this exercise, we shall use the ODL schema of Exercise 9.1.3 and Fig. 9.3. We shall assume that for each of the four classes of that schema, there is a constructor function of the same name that takes values for each of the attributes and single-valued relationships, but not the multivalued relationships, which are initialized to be empty. For the single-valued relationships to other classes, you may postulate a host-language variable whose current value is the related object. Create the following objects and assign the object to be the value of a host-language variable in each case.

* a) The battleship Colorado of the Maryland class, launched in 1923.

  b) The battleship Graf Spee of the Lützow class, launched in 1936.

  c) An outcome of the battle of Malaya was that the battleship Prince of Wales was sunk.

  d) The battle of Malaya was fought Dec. 10, 1941.

  e) The Hood class of British battlecruisers had eight 15-inch guns and a displacement of 41,000 tons.

9.4 User-Defined Types in SQL

We now turn to the way SQL-99 incorporates many of the object-oriented features that we have seen in ODL and OQL. Because of these recent extensions to SQL, a DBMS that follows this standard is often referred to as "object-relational." We met many of the object-relational concepts abstractly in Section 4.5. Now, it is time for us to study the details of the standard.

OQL has no specific notion of a relation; it is just a set (or bag) of structures. However, the relation is so central to SQL that objects in SQL keep relations as the core concept. The classes of ODL are transmogrified into *user-defined types*, or UDT's, in SQL. We find UDT's used in two distinct ways:

1. A UDT can be the type of a table.

2. A UDT can be the type of an attribute belonging to some table.

9.4.1 Defining Types in SQL

A user-defined type declaration in SQL can be thought of as roughly analogous to a class declaration in ODL, with some distinctions. First, key declarations for a relation with a user-defined type are part of the table definition, not the type definition; that is, many SQL relations can be declared to have the same (user-defined) type but different keys and other constraints. Second, in SQL we do not treat relationships as properties. A relationship must be represented by a separate relation, as was discussed in Section 4.4.5. A simple form of UDT definition is:

1. The keywords `CREATE TYPE`,

2. A name for the type,

3. The keyword `AS`,

4. A parenthesized, comma-separated list of attributes and their types.

5. A comma-separated list of methods, including their argument type(s), and return type.

That is, the definition of a type T has the form

$$\text{CREATE TYPE } T \text{ AS } <\text{attribute and method declarations}> ;$$

Example 9.20: We can create a type representing movie stars, analogous to the class `Star` found in the OQL example of Fig. 9.1. However, we cannot represent directly a set of movies as a field within `Star` tuples. Thus, we shall start with only the `name` and `address` components of `Star` tuples.

To begin, note that the type of an address in Fig. 9.1 is itself a tuple, with components `street` and `city`. Thus, we need two type definitions, one for addresses and the other for stars. The necessary definitions are shown in Fig. 9.10.

```
CREATE TYPE AddressType AS (
    street  CHAR(50),
    city    CHAR(20)
);

CREATE TYPE StarType AS (
    name    CHAR(30),
    address AddressType
);
```

Figure 9.10: Two type definitions

A tuple of type `AddressType` has two components, whose attributes are `street` and `city`. The types of these components are character strings of length 50 and 20, respectively. A tuple of type `StarType` also has two components. The first is attribute `name`, whose type is a 30-character string, and the second is `address`, whose type is itself a UDT `AddressType`, that is, a tuple with `street` and `city` components.   □

9.4.2 Methods in User-Defined Types

The declaration of a method resembles the way a function in PSM is introduced; see Section 8.2.1. There is no analog of PSM procedures as methods. That is, every method returns a value of some type. While function declarations and definitions in PSM are combined, a method needs both a declaration, within the definition of its type, and a separate definition, in a `CREATE METHOD` statement.

A method declaration looks like a PSM function declaration, with the keyword `METHOD` replacing `CREATE FUNCTION`. However, SQL methods typically have no arguments; they are applied to rows, just as ODL methods are applied to objects. In the definition of the method, `SELF` refers to this tuple, if necessary.

Example 9.21: Let us extend the definition of the type `AddressType` of Fig. 9.10 with a method `houseNumber` that extracts from the `street` component the portion devoted to the house address. For instance, if the `street` component were `'123 Maple St.'`, then `houseNumber` should return `'123'`. The revised type definition is thus:

```
CREATE TYPE AddressType AS (
    street  CHAR(50),
    city    CHAR(20)
    )
    METHOD houseNumber() RETURNS CHAR(10);
```

We see the keyword `METHOD`, followed by the name of the method and a parenthesized list of its arguments and their types. In this case, there are no arguments, but the parentheses are still needed. Had there been arguments, they would have appeared, followed by their types, such as `(a INT, b CHAR(5))`. □

Separately, we need to define the method. A simple form of method definition consists of:

1. The keywords `CREATE METHOD`.

2. The method name, arguments and their types, and the return clause, as in the declaration of the method.

3. The keyword `FOR` and the name of the UDT in which the method is declared.

4. The body of the method, which is written in the same language as the bodies of PSM functions.

For instance, we could define the method `houseNumber` from Example 9.21 as:

```
CREATE METHOD houseNumber() RETURNS CHAR(10)
FOR AddressType
```

```
BEGIN
    ...
END;
```

We have omitted the body of the method because accomplishing the intended separation of the string `address` as intended is nontrivial, even in PSM.

9.4.3   Declaring Relations with a UDT

Having declared a type, we may declare one or more relations whose tuples are of that type. The form of relation declarations is like that of Section 6.6.2, but we use

$$\text{OF <type name>}$$

in place of the list of attribute declarations in a normal SQL table declaration. Other elements of a table declaration, such as keys, foreign keys, and tuple-based constraints, may be added to the table declaration if desired, and apply only to this table, not to the UDT itself.

Example 9.22: We could declare `MovieStar` to be a relation whose tuples were of type `StarType` by

```
CREATE TABLE MovieStar OF StarType;
```

As a result, table `MovieStar` has two attributes, `name` and `address`. The first attribute, `name`, is an ordinary character string, but the second, `address`, has a type that is itself a UDT, namely the type `AddressType`.   □

It is common to have one relation for each type, and to think of that relation as the extent (in the sense of Section 4.3.4) of the class corresponding to that type. However, it is permissible to have many relations or none of a given type.

9.4.4   References

The effect of object identity in object-oriented languages is obtained in SQL through the notion of a *reference*. Tables whose type is a UDT may have a *reference column* that serves as its "identity." This column could be the primary key of the table, if there is one, or it could be a column whose values are generated and maintained unique by the DBMS, for example. We shall defer the matter of defining reference columns until we first see how reference types are used.

To refer to the tuples of a table with a reference column, an attribute may have as its type a reference to another type. If T is a UDT, then $\text{REF}(T)$ is the type of a reference to a tuple of type T. Further, the reference may be given a *scope*, which is the name of the relation whose tuples are referred to. Thus, an attribute A whose values are references to tuples in relation R, where R is a table whose type is the UDT T, would be declared by:

A REF(T) SCOPE R

If no scope is specified, the reference can go to any relation of type T.

Example 9.23: Reference attributes are not sufficient to record in `MovieStar` the set of all movies they starred in, but they let us record the best movie for each star. Assume that we have declared a relation `Movie`, and that the type of this relation is the UDT `MovieType`; we shall define both `MovieType` and `Movie` later, in Fig. 9.11. The following is a new definition of `StarType` that includes an attribute `bestMovie` that is a reference to a movie.

```
CREATE TYPE StarType AS (
    name      CHAR(30),
    address   AddressType,
    bestMovie REF(MovieType) SCOPE Movie
);
```

Now, if relation `MovieStar` is defined to have the UDT above, then each star tuple will have a component that refers to a `Movie` tuple — the star's best movie. □

Next, we must arrange that a table such as `Movie` in Example 9.23 will have a reference column. Such a table is said to be *referenceable*. In a `CREATE TABLE` statement where the type of the table is a UDT (as in Section 9.4.3), we may append a clause of the form:

REF IS <attribute name> <how generated>

The attribute name is a name given to the column that will serve as an "object identifier" for tuples. The "how generated" clause is typically either:

1. `SYSTEM GENERATED`, meaning that the DBMS is responsible for maintaining a unique value in this column of each tuple, or

2. `DERIVED`, meaning that the DBMS will use the primary key of the relation to produce unique values for this column.

Example 9.24: Figure 9.11 shows how the UDT `MovieType` and relation `Movie` could be declared so that `Movie` is referenceable. The UDT is declared in lines (1) through (4). Then the relation `Movie` is defined to have this type in lines (5) through (7). Notice that we have declared `title` and `year`, together, to be the key for relation `Movie` in line (7).

We see in line (6) that the name of the "identity" column for `Movie` is `movieID`. This attribute, which automatically becomes a fourth attribute of `Movie`, along with `title`, `year`, and `inColor`, may be used in queries like any other attribute of `Movie`.

Line (6) also says that the DBMS is responsible for generating the value of `movieID` each time a new tuple is inserted into `Movie`. Had we replaced "SYSTEM

```
1)  CREATE TYPE MovieType AS (
2)      title   CHAR(30),
3)      year    INTEGER,
4)      inColor BOOLEAN,
    );

5)  CREATE TABLE Movie OF MovieType (
6)      REF IS movieID SYSTEM GENERATED,
7)      PRIMARY KEY (title, year)
    );
```

Figure 9.11: Creating a referenceable table

GENERATED" by "DERIVED," then new tuples would get their value of `movieID` by some calculation, performed by the system, on the values of the primary-key attributes `title` and `year` from the same tuple.   □

Example 9.25 : Now, let us see how to represent the many-many relationship between movies and stars using references. Previously, we represented this relationship by a relation like `StarsIn` that contains tuples with the keys of `Movie` and `MovieStar`. As an alternative, we may define `StarsIn` to have references to tuples from these two relations.

First, we need to redefine `MovieStar` so it is a referenceable table, thusly:

```
CREATE TABLE MovieStar OF StarType (
    REF IS starID SYSTEM GENERATED;
)
```

Then, we may declare the relation `StarsIn` to have two attributes, which are references, one to a movie tuple and one to a star tuple. Here is a direct definition of this relation:

```
CREATE TABLE StarsIn (
    star    REF(StarType) SCOPE MovieStar,
    movie   REF(MovieType) SCOPE Movie
);
```

Optionally, we could have defined a UDT as above, and then declared `StarsIn` to be a table of that type.   □

9.4.5   Exercises for Section 9.4

Exercise 9.4.1 : Write type declarations for the following types:

a) `NameType`, with components for first, middle, and last names and a title.

* b) `PersonType`, with a name of the person and references to the persons that are their mother and father. You must use the type from part (a) in your declaration.

   c) `MarriageType`, with the date of the marriage and references to the husband and wife.

Exercise 9.4.2: Redesign our running products database schema of Exercise 5.2.1 to use type declarations and reference attributes where appropriate. In particular, in the relations `PC`, `Laptop`, and `Printer` make the `model` attribute be a reference to the `Product` tuple for that model.

! **Exercise 9.4.3:** In Exercise 9.4.2 we suggested that model numbers in the tables `PC`, `Laptop`, and `Printer` could be references to tuples of the `Product` table. Is it also possible to make the `model` attribute in `Product` a reference to the tuple in the relation for that type of product? Why or why not?

* **Exercise 9.4.4:** Redesign our running battleships database schema of Exercise 5.2.4 to use type declarations and reference attributes where appropriate. The schema from Exercise 9.1.3 should suggest where reference attributes are useful. Look for many-one relationships and try to represent them using an attribute with a reference type.

9.5 Operations on Object-Relational Data

All appropriate SQL operations from previous chapters apply to tables that are declared with a UDT or that have attributes whose type is a UDT. There are also some entirely new operations we can use, such as reference-following. However, some familiar operations, especially those that access or modify columns whose type is a UDT, involve new syntax.

9.5.1 Following References

Suppose x is a value of type REF(T). Then x refers to some tuple t of type T. We can obtain tuple t itself, or components of t, by two means:

1. Operator `->` has essentially the same meaning as this operator does in C. That is, if x is a reference to a tuple t, and a is an attribute of t, then `x->a` is the value of the attribute a in tuple t.

2. The `DEREF` operator applies to a reference and produces the tuple referenced.

Example 9.26: Let us use the relation `StarsIn` from Example 9.25 to find the movies in which Mel Gibson starred. Recall that the schema is

```
StarsIn(star, movie)
```

where `star` and `movie` are references to tuples of `MovieStar` and `Movie`, respectively. A possible query is:

```
1)   SELECT DEREF(movie)
2)   FROM StarsIn
3)   WHERE star->name = 'Mel Gibson';
```

In line (3), the expression `star->name` produces the value of the `name` component of the `MovieStar` tuple referred to by the `star` component of any given `StarsIn` tuple. Thus, the `WHERE` clause identifies those `StarsIn` tuples whose `star` component are references to the Mel-Gibson `MovieStar` tuple. Line (1) then produces the movie tuple referred to by the `movie` component of those tuples. All three attributes — `title`, `year`, and `inColor` — will appear in the printed result.

Note that we could have replaced line (1) by:

```
1)   SELECT  movie
```

However, had we done so, we would have gotten a list of system-generated gibberish that serves as the internal unique identifiers for those tuples. We would not see the information in the referenced tuples.   □

9.5.2   Accessing Attributes of Tuples with a UDT

When we define a relation to have a UDT, the tuples must be thought of as single objects, rather than lists with components corresponding to the attributes of the UDT. As a case in point, consider the relation `Movie` declared in Fig. 9.11. This relation has UDT `MovieType`, which has three attributes: `title`, `year`, and `inColor`. However, a tuple t in `Movie` has only *one* component, not three. That component is the object itself.

If we "drill down" into the object, we can extract the values of the three attributes in the type `MovieType`, as well as use any methods defined for that type. However, we have to access these attributes properly, since they are not attributes of the tuple itself. Rather, every UDT has an implicitly defined *observer method* for each attribute of that UDT. The name of the observer method for an attribute x is $x()$. We apply this method as we would any other method for this UDT; we attach it with a dot to an expression that evaluates to an object of this type. Thus, if t is a variable whose value is of type T, and x is an attribute of T, then $t.x()$ is the value of x in the tuple (object) denoted by t.

Example 9.27 : Let us find, from the relation `Movie` of Fig. 9.11 the year(s) of movies with title *King Kong*. Here is one way to do so:

```
SELECT m.year()
FROM Movie m
WHERE m.title() = 'King Kong';
```

Even though the tuple variable m would appear not to be needed here, we need a variable whose value is an object of type `MovieType` — the UDT for relation `Movie`. The condition of the `WHERE` clause compares the constant `'King Kong'` to the value of `m.title()`. The latter is the observer method for attribute `title` of type `MovieType`. Similarly, the value in the `SELECT` clause is expressed `m.year()`; this expression applies the observer method for `year` to the object m. $\square$

9.5.3 Generator and Mutator Functions

In order to create data that conforms to a UDT, or to change components of objects with a UDT, we can use two kinds of methods that are created automatically, along with the observer methods, whenever a UDT is defined. These are:

1. A *generator method*. This method has the name of the type and no argument. It also has the unusual property that it may be invoked without being applied to any object. That is, if T is a UDT, then $T()$ returns an object of type T, with no values in its various components.

2. *Mutator methods*. For each attribute x of UDT T, there is a mutator method $x(v)$. When applied to an object of type T, it changes the x attribute of that object to have value v. Notice that the mutator and observer method for an attribute each have the name of the attribute, but differ in that the mutator has an argument.

Example 9.28: We shall write a PSM procedure that takes as arguments a street, a city, and a name, and inserts into the relation `MovieStar` (of type `StarType` according to Example 9.22) an object constructed from these values, using calls to the proper generator and mutator functions. Recall from Example 9.20 that objects of `StarType` have a `name` component that is a character string, but an `address` component that is itself an object of type `AddressType`. The procedure `InsertStar` is shown in Fig. 9.12.

Lines (2) through (4) introduce the arguments s, c, and n, which will provide values for a street, city, and star name, respectively. Lines (5) and (6) declare two local variables. Each is of one of the UDT's involved in the type for objects that exist in the relation `MovieStar`. At lines (7) and (8) we create empty objects of each of these two types.

Lines (9) and (10) put real values in the object `newAddr`; these values are taken from the procedure arguments that provide a street and a city. Line (11) similarly installs the argument n as the value of the `name` component in the object `newStar`. Then line (12) takes the entire `newAddr` object and makes it the value of the `address` component in `newStar`. Finally, line (13) inserts the constructed object into relation `MovieStar`. Notice that, as always, a relation that has a UDT as its type has but a single component, even if that component has several attributes, such as `name` and `address` in this example.

```
1)   CREATE PROCEDURE InsertStar(
2)       IN s CHAR(50),
3)       IN c CHAR(20),
4)       IN n CHAR(30)
     )
5)   DECLARE newAddr AddressType;
6)   DECLARE newStar StarType;

     BEGIN
7)       SET newAddr = AddressType();
8)       SET newStar = StarType();
9)       newAddr.street(s);
10)      newAddr.city(c);
11)      newStar.name(n);
12)      newStar.address(newAddr);
13)      INSERT INTO MovieStar VALUES(newStar);
     END;
```

Figure 9.12: Creating and storing a StarType object

To insert a star into MovieStar, we can call procedure InsertStar.

```
InsertStar('345 Spruce St.', 'Glendale', 'Gwyneth Paltrow');
```

is an example. □

It is much simpler to insert objects into a relation with a UDT if your DBMS provides, or if you create, a generator function that takes values for the attributes of the UDT and returns a suitable object. For example, if we have functions AddressType(s,c) and StarType(n,a) that return objects of the indicated types, then we can make the insertion at the end of Example 9.28 with an INSERT statement of a familiar form:

```
INSERT INTO MovieStar VALUES(
    StarType('Gwyneth Paltrow',
        AddressType('345 Spruce St.', 'Glendale')));
```

9.5.4 Ordering Relationships on UDT's

Objects that are of some UDT are inherently abstract, in the sense that there is no way to compare two objects of the same UDT, either to test whether they are "equal" or whether one is less than another. Even two objects that have all components identical will not be considered equal unless we tell the system to regard them as equal. Similarly, there is no obvious way to sort the tuples of a relation that has a UDT unless we define a function that tells which of two objects of that UDT precedes the other.

Yet there are many SQL operations that require either an equality test or both an equality and a "less than" test. For instance, we cannot eliminate duplicates if we can't tell whether two tuples are equal. We cannot group by an attribute whose type is a UDT unless there is an equality test for that UDT. We cannot use an `ORDER BY` clause or a comparison like < in a `WHERE` clause unless we can compare any two elements.

To specify an ordering or comparison, SQL allows us to issue a `CREATE ORDERING` statement for any UDT. There are a number of forms this statement may take, and we shall only consider the two simplest options:

1. The statement

   CREATE ORDERING FOR T EQUALS ONLY BY STATE;

   says that two members of UDT T are considered equal if all of their corresponding components are equal. There is no < defined on objects of UDT T.

2. The following statement

   CREATE ORDERING FOR T
   ORDERING FULL BY RELATIVE WITH F

   says that any of the six comparisons (<, <=, >, >=, =, and <>) may be performed on objects of UDT T. To tell how objects x_1 and x_2 compare, we apply the function F to these objects. This function must be written so that $F(x_1, x_2) < 0$ whenever we want to conclude that $x_1 < x_2$; $F(x_1, x_2) = 0$ means that $x_1 = x_2$, and $F(x_1, x_2) > 0$ means that $x_1 > x_2$. If we replace "ORDERING FULL" with "EQUALS ONLY," then $F(x_1, x_2) = 0$ indicates that $x_1 = x_2$, while any other value of $F(x_1, x_2)$ means that $x_1 \neq x_2$. Comparison by < is impossible in this case.

Example 9.29: Let us consider a possible ordering on the UDT `StarType` from Example 9.20. If we want only an equality on objects of this UDT, we could declare:

CREATE ORDERING FOR StarType EQUALS ONLY BY STATE;

That statement says that two objects of `StarType` are equal if and only if their names are the same as character strings, and their addresses are the same as objects of UDT `AddressType`.

The problem is that, unless we define an ordering for `AddressType`, an object of that type is not even equal to itself. Thus, we also need to create at least an equality test for `AddressType`. A simple way to do so is to declare that two `AddressType` objects are equal if and only if their streets and cities are each the same. We could do so by:

CREATE ORDERING FOR AddressType EQUALS ONLY BY STATE;

Alternatively, we could define a complete ordering of AddressType objects. One reasonable ordering is to order addresses first by cities, alphabetically, and among addresses in the same city, by street address, alphabetically. To do so, we have to define a function, say AddrLEG, that takes two AddressType arguments and returns a negative, zero, or positive value to indicate that the first is less than, equal to, or greater than the second. We declare:

CREATE ORDERING FOR AddressType
ORDER FULL BY RELATIVE WITH AddrLEG

The function AddrLEG is shown in Fig. 9.13. Notice that if we reach line (7), it must be that the two city components are the same, so we compare the street components. Likewise, if we reach line (9), the only remaining possibility is that the cities are the same and the first street precedes the second alphabetically. □

```
1)   CREATE FUNCTION AddrLEG(
2)       x1 AddressType,
3)       x2 AddressType
4)   ) RETURNS INTEGER

5)   IF x1.city() < x2.city() THEN RETURN(-1)
6)   ELSEIF x1.city() > x2.city() THEN RETURN(1)
7)   ELSEIF x1.street() < x2.street() THEN RETURN(-1)
8)   ELSEIF x1.street() = x2.street() THEN RETURN(0)
9)   ELSE RETURN(1)
     END IF;
```

Figure 9.13: A comparison function for address objects

9.5.5 Exercises for Section 9.5

Exercise 9.5.1: Using the StarsIn relation of Example 9.25, and the Movie and MovieStar relations accessible through StarsIn, write the following queries:

   * a) Find the names of the stars of *Ishtar*.

 *! b) Find the titles and years of all movies in which at least one star lives in Malibu.

    c) Find all the movies (objects of type MovieType that starred Melanie Griffith.

! d) Find the movies (title and year) with at least five stars.

Exercise 9.5.2: Using your schema from Exercise 9.4.2, write the following queries. Don't forget to use references whenever appropriate.

a) Find the manufacturers of PC's with a hard disk larger than 60 gigabytes.

b) Find the manufacturers of laser printers.

! c) Produce a table giving for each model of laptop, the model of the laptop having the highest processor speed of any laptop made by the same manufacturer.

Exercise 9.5.3: Using your schema from Exercise 9.4.4, write the following queries. Don't forget to use references whenever appropriate and avoid joins (i.e., subqueries or more than one tuple variable in the FROM clause).

* a) Find the ships with a displacement of more than 35,000 tons.

b) Find the battles in which at least one ship was sunk.

! c) Find the classes that had ships launched after 1930.

!! d) Find the battles in which at least one US ship was damaged.

Exercise 9.5.4: Assuming the function AddrLEG of Fig. 9.13 is available, write a suitable function to compare objects of type StarType, and declare your function to be the basis of the ordering of StarType objects.

*! Exercise 9.5.5: Write a procedure to take a star name as argument and delete from StarsIn and MovieStar all tuples involving that star.

9.6 Summary of Chapter 9

◆ *Select-From-Where Statements in OQL*: OQL offers a select-from-where expression that resembles SQL's. In the FROM clause, we can declare variables that range over any collection, including both extents of classes (analogous to relations) and collections that are the values of attributes in objects.

◆ *Common OQL Operators*: OQL offers for-all, there-exists, IN, union, intersection, difference, and aggregation operators that are similar in spirit to SQL's. However, aggregation is always over a collection, not a column of a relation.

◆ *OQL Group-By*: OQL also offers a GROUP BY clause in select-from-where statements that is similar to SQL's. However, in OQL, the collection of objects in each group is explicitly accessible through a field name called partition.

✦ *Extracting Elements From OQL Collections*: We can obtain the lone member of a collection that is a singleton by applying the ELEMENT operator. The elements of a collection with more than one member can be accessed by first turning the collection into a list, using an ORDER BY clause in a select-from-where statement, and then using a loop in the surrounding host-language program to visit each element of the list in turn.

✦ *User-Defined Types in SQL*: Object-relational capabilities of SQL are centered around the UDT, or user-defined type. These types may be declared by listing their attributes and other information, as in table declarations. In addition, methods may be declared for UDT's.

✦ *Relations With a UDT as Type*: Instead of declaring the attributes of a relation, we may declare that relation to have a UDT. If we do so, then its tuples have one component, and this component is an object of the UDT.

✦ *Reference Types*: A type of an attribute can be a reference to a UDT. Such attributes essentially are pointers to objects of that UDT.

✦ *Object Identity for UDT's*: When we create a relation whose type is a UDT, we declare an attribute to serve as the "object-ID" of each tuple. This component is a reference to the tuple itself. Unlike in object-oriented systems, this "OID" column may be accessed by the user, although it is rarely meaningful.

✦ *Accessing components of a UDT*: SQL provides observer and mutator functions for each attribute of a UDT. These functions, respectively, return and change the value of that attribute when applied to any object of that UDT.

9.7   References for Chapter 9

The reference for OQL is the same as for ODL: [1]. Material on Object-relational features of SQL can be obtained as described in the bibliographic notes to Chapter 6.

1. Cattell, R. G. G. (ed.), *The Object Database Standard: ODMG–99*, Morgan-Kaufmann, San Francisco, 1999.

Chapter 10

Logical Query Languages

Some query languages for the relational model resemble a logic more than they do the algebra that we introduced in Section 5.2. However, logic-based languages appear to be difficult for many programmers to grasp. Thus, we have delayed our coverage of logic until the end of our study of query languages.

We shall introduce Datalog, which is the simplest form of logic devised for the relational model. In its nonrecursive form, Datalog has the same power as the classical relational algebra. However, by allowing recursion, we can express queries in Datalog that cannot be expressed in SQL2 (except by adding procedural programming such as PSM). We discuss the complexities that come up when we allow recursive negation, and finally, we see how the solution provided by Datalog has been used to provide a way to allow meaningful recursion in the most recent SQL-99 standard.

10.1 A Logic for Relations

As an alternative to abstract query languages based on algebra, one can use a form of logic to express queries. The logical query language *Datalog* ("database logic") consists of if-then rules. Each of these rules expresses the idea that from certain combinations of tuples in certain relations we may infer that some other tuple is in some other relation, or in the answer to a query.

10.1.1 Predicates and Atoms

Relations are represented in Datalog by *predicates*. Each predicate takes a fixed number of arguments, and a predicate followed by its arguments is called an *atom*. The syntax of atoms is just like that of function calls in conventional programming languages; for example $P(x_1, x_2, \ldots, x_n)$ is an atom consisting of the predicate P with arguments $x_1, x_2, \ldots, x_n$.

In essence, a predicate is the name of a function that returns a boolean value. If R is a relation with n attributes in some fixed order, then we shall also use R as the name of a predicate corresponding to this relation. The atom $R(a_1, a_2, \ldots, a_n)$ has value TRUE if $(a_1, a_2, \ldots, a_n)$ is a tuple of R; the atom has value FALSE otherwise.

Example 10.1 : Let R be the relation

A	B
1	2
3	4

Then $R(1, 2)$ is true and so is $R(3, 4)$. However, for any other values x and y, $R(x, y)$ is false.   □

A predicate can take variables as well as constants as arguments. If an atom has variables for one or more of its arguments, then it is a boolean-valued function that takes values for these variables and returns TRUE or FALSE.

Example 10.2 : If R is the predicate from Example 10.1, then $R(x, y)$ is the function that tells, for any x and y, whether the tuple (x, y) is in relation R. For the particular instance of R mentioned in Example 10.1, $R(x, y)$ returns TRUE when either

1. $x = 1$ and $y = 2$, or

2. $x = 3$ and $y = 4$

and FALSE otherwise. As another example, the atom $R(1, z)$ returns TRUE if $z = 2$ and returns FALSE otherwise.   □

10.1.2   Arithmetic Atoms

There is another kind of atom that is important in Datalog: an *arithmetic atom*. This kind of atom is a comparison between two arithmetic expressions, for example $x < y$ or $x + 1 \geq y + 4 \times z$. For contrast, we shall call the atoms introduced in Section 10.1.1 *relational atoms*; both are "atoms."

Note that arithmetic and relational atoms each take as arguments the values of any variables that appear in the atom, and they return a boolean value. In effect, arithmetic comparisons like $<$ or $\geq$ are like the names of relations that contain all the true pairs. Thus, we can visualize the relation "$<$" as containing all the tuples, such as $(1, 2)$ or $(-1.5, 65.4)$, that have a first component less than their second component. Remember, however, that database relations are always finite, and usually change from time to time. In contrast, arithmetic-comparison relations such as $<$ are both infinite and unchanging.

10.1.3 Datalog Rules and Queries

Operations similar to those of the classical relational algebra of Section 5.2 are described in Datalog by *rules*, which consist of

1. A relational atom called the *head*, followed by

2. The symbol ←, which we often read "if," followed by

3. A *body* consisting of one or more atoms, called *subgoals*, which may be either relational or arithmetic. Subgoals are connected by AND, and any subgoal may optionally be preceded by the logical operator NOT.

Example 10.3 : The Datalog rule

$$\text{LongMovie(t,y)} \leftarrow \text{Movie(t,y,l,c,s,p) AND } l \geq 100$$

defines the set of "long" movies, those at least 100 minutes long. It refers to our standard relation Movie with schema

    Movie(title, year, length, inColor, studioName, producerC#)

The head of the rule is the atom *LongMovie*(t, y). The body of the rule consists of two subgoals:

1. The first subgoal has predicate *Movie* and six arguments, corresponding to the six attributes of the Movie relation. Each of these arguments has a different variable: t for the title component, y for the year component, l for the length component, and so on. We can see this subgoal as saying: "Let (t, y, l, c, s, p) be a tuple in the current instance of relation Movie." More precisely, *Movie*(t, y, l, c, s, p) is true whenever the six variables have values that are the six components of some one Movie tuple.

2. The second subgoal, $l \geq 100$, is true whenever the length component of a Movie tuple is at least 100.

The rule as a whole can be thought of as saying: *LongMovie*(t, y) is true whenever we can find a tuple in Movie with:

a) t and y as the first two components (for title and year),

b) A third component l (for length) that is at least 100, and

c) Any values in components 4 through 6.

Notice that this rule is thus equivalent to the "assignment statement" in relational algebra:

$$\text{LongMovie} := \pi_{title,year}\left(\sigma_{length \geq 100}(\text{Movie})\right)$$

Anonymous Variables

Frequently, Datalog rules have some variables that appear only once. The names used for these variables are irrelevant. Only when a variable appears more than once do we care about its name, so we can see it is the same variable in its second and subsequent appearances. Thus, we shall allow the common convention that an underscore, _, as an argument of an atom, stands for a variable that appears only there. Multiple occurrences of _ stand for different variables, never the same variable. For instance, the rule of Example 10.3 could be written

$$\texttt{LongMovie(t,y)} \leftarrow \texttt{Movie(t,y,l,\_,\_,\_)} \texttt{ AND } \texttt{l} \geq 100$$

The three variables c, s, and p that appear only once have each been replaced by underscores. We cannot replace any of the other variables, since each appears twice in the rule.

---

whose right side is a relational-algebra expression.   □

A *query* in Datalog is a collection of one or more rules. If there is only one relation that appears in the rule heads, then the value of this relation is taken to be the answer to the query. Thus, in Example 10.3, LongMovie is the answer to the query. If there is more than one relation among the rule heads, then one of these relations is the answer to the query, while the others assist in the definition of the answer. We must designate which relation is the intended answer to the query, perhaps by giving it a name such as Answer.

10.1.4   Meaning of Datalog Rules

Example 10.3 gave us a hint of the meaning of a Datalog rule. More precisely, imagine the variables of the rule ranging over all possible values. Whenever these variables all have values that make all the subgoals true, then we see what the value of the head is for those variables, and we add the resulting tuple to the relation whose predicate is in the head.

For instance, we can imagine the six variables of Example 10.3 ranging over all possible values. The only combinations of values that can make all the subgoals true are when the values of (t, y, l, c, s, p) in that order form a tuple of Movie. Moreover, since the $l \geq 100$ subgoal must also be true, this tuple must be one where l, the value of the length component, is at least 100. When we find such a combination of values, we put the tuple (t, y) in the head's relation LongMovie.

There are, however, restrictions that we must place on the way variables are used in rules, so that the result of a rule is a finite relation and so that rules with arithmetic subgoals or with *negated* subgoals (those with NOT in front of them) make intuitive sense. This condition, which we call the *safety* condition, is:

- Every variable that appears anywhere in the rule must appear in some nonnegated, relational subgoal.

In particular, any variable that appears in the head, in a negated relational subgoal, or in any arithmetic subgoal, must also appear in a nonnegated, relational subgoal.

Example 10.4 : Consider the rule

$$\text{LongMovie(t,y)} \leftarrow \text{Movie(t,y,l,\_,\_,\_) AND } l \geq 100$$

from Example 10.3. The first subgoal is a nonnegated, relational subgoal, and it contains all the variables that appear anywhere in the rule. In particular, the two variables t and y that appear in the head also appear in the first subgoal of the body. Likewise, variable l appears in an arithmetic subgoal, but it also appears in the first subgoal. □

Example 10.5 : The following rule has three safety violations:

$$\text{P(x,y)} \leftarrow \text{Q(x,z) AND NOT R(w,x,z) AND x} < \text{y}$$

1. The variable y appears in the head but not in any nonnegated, relational subgoal. Notice the fact that y appears in the arithmetic subgoal $x < y$ does not help to limit the possible values of y to a finite set. As soon as we find values a, b, and c for w, x, and z respectively that satisfy the first two subgoals, the infinite number of tuples (b, d) such that $d > b$ wind up in the head's relation P.

2. Variable w appears in a negated, relational subgoal but not in a nonnegated, relational subgoal.

3. Variable y appears in an arithmetic subgoal, but not in a nonnegated, relational subgoal.

Thus, it is not a safe rule and cannot be used in Datalog. □

There is another way to define the meaning of rules. Instead of considering all of the possible assignments of values to variables, we consider the sets of tuples in the relations corresponding to each of the nonnegated, relational subgoals. If some assignment of tuples for each nonnegated, relational subgoal is *consistent*, in the sense that it assigns the same value to each occurrence of a variable, then consider the resulting assignment of values to all the variables of the rule. Notice that because the rule is safe, every variable is assigned a value.

For each consistent assignment, we consider the negated, relational subgoals and the arithmetic subgoals, to see if the assignment of values to variables makes them all true. Remember that a negated subgoal is true if its atom is false. If all the subgoals are true, then we see what tuple the head becomes under this assignment of values to variables. This tuple is added to the relation whose predicate is the head.

Example 10.6 : Consider the Datalog rule

$$\text{P(x,y)} \leftarrow \text{Q(x,z) AND R(z,y) AND NOT Q(x,y)}$$

Let relation Q contain the two tuples $(1, 2)$ and $(1, 3)$. Let relation R contain tuples $(2, 3)$ and $(3, 1)$. There are two nonnegated, relational subgoals, $Q(x, z)$ and $R(z, y)$, so we must consider all combinations of assignments of tuples from relations Q and R, respectively, to these subgoals. The table of Fig. 10.1 considers all four combinations.

	Tuple for Q(x,z)	Tuple for R(z,y)	Consistent Assignment?	NOT Q(x,y) True?	Resulting Head
1)	$(1, 2)$	$(2, 3)$	Yes	No	—
2)	$(1, 2)$	$(3, 1)$	No; $z = 2, 3$	Irrelevant	—
3)	$(1, 3)$	$(2, 3)$	No; $z = 3, 2$	Irrelevant	—
4)	$(1, 3)$	$(3, 1)$	Yes	Yes	$P(1, 1)$

Figure 10.1: All possible assignments of tuples to $Q(x, z)$ and $R(z, y)$

The second and third options in Fig. 10.1 are not consistent. Each assigns two different values to the variable z. Thus, we do not consider these tuple-assignments further.

The first option, where subgoal $Q(x, z)$ is assigned the tuple $(1, 2)$ and subgoal $R(z, y)$ is assigned tuple $(2, 3)$, yields a consistent assignment, with x, y, and z given the values 1, 3, and 2, respectively. We thus proceed to the test of the other subgoals, those that are not nonnegated, relational subgoals. There is only one: NOT Q(x,y). For this assignment of values to the variables, this subgoal becomes NOT Q(1,3). Since $(1, 3)$ is a tuple of Q, this subgoal is false, and no head tuple is produced for the tuple-assignment (1).

The final option is (4). Here, the assignment is consistent; x, y, and z are assigned the values 1, 1, and 3, respectively. The subgoal NOT Q(x,y) takes on the value NOT Q(1,1). Since $(1, 1)$ is not a tuple of Q, this subgoal is true. We thus evaluate the head $P(x, y)$ for this assignment of values to variables and find it is $P(1, 1)$. Thus the tuple $(1, 1)$ is in the relation P. Since we have exhausted all tuple-assignments, this is the only tuple in P. □

10.1.5 Extensional and Intensional Predicates

It is useful to make the distinction between

- *Extensional* predicates, which are predicates whose relations are stored in a database, and

- *Intensional* predicates, whose relations are computed by applying one or more Datalog rules.

The difference is the same as that between the operands of a relational-algebra expression, which are "extensional" (i.e., defined by their *extension,* which is another name for the "current instance of a relation") and the relations computed by a relational-algebra expression, either as the final result or as an intermediate result corresponding to some subexpression; these relations are "intensional" (i.e., defined by the programmer's "intent").

When talking of Datalog rules, we shall refer to the relation corresponding to a predicate as "intensional" or "extensional," if the predicate is intensional or extensional, respectively. We shall also use the abbreviation *IDB* for "intensional database" to refer to either an intensional predicate or its corresponding relation. Similarly, we use abbreviation *EDB*, standing for "extensional database," for extensional predicates or relations.

Thus, in Example 10.3, `Movie` is an EDB relation, defined by its extension. The predicate *Movie* is likewise an EDB predicate. Relation and predicate `LongMovie` are both intensional.

An EDB predicate can never appear in the head of a rule, although it can appear in the body of a rule. IDB predicates can appear in either the head or the body of rules, or both. It is also common to construct a single relation by using several rules with the same predicate in the head. We shall see an illustration of this idea in Example 10.10, regarding the union of two relations.

By using a series of intensional predicates, we can build progressively more complicated functions of the EDB relations. The process is similar to the building of relational-algebra expressions using several operators.

10.1.6 Datalog Rules Applied to Bags

Datalog is inherently a logic of sets. However, as long as there are no negated, relational subgoals, the ideas for evaluating Datalog rules when relations are sets apply to bags as well. When relations are bags, it is conceptually simpler to use the second approach for evaluating Datalog rules that we gave in Section 10.1.4. Recall this technique involves looking at each of the nonnegated, relational subgoals and substituting for it all tuples of the relation for the predicate of that subgoal. If a selection of tuples for each subgoal gives a consistent value to each variable, and the arithmetic subgoals all become true,[1] then we see what

---

[1] Note that there must not be any negated relational subgoals in the rule. There is not a clearly defined meaning of arbitrary Datalog rules with negated, relational subgoals under the bag model.

the head becomes with this assignment of values to variables. The resulting tuple is put in the head relation.

Since we are now dealing with bags, we do not eliminate duplicates from the head. Moreover, as we consider all combinations of tuples for the subgoals, a tuple appearing n times in the relation for a subgoal gets considered n times as the tuple for that subgoal, in conjunction with all combinations of tuples for the other subgoals.

Example 10.7: Consider the rule

$$H(x,z) \leftarrow R(x,y) \text{ AND } S(y,z)$$

where relation $R(A, B)$ has the tuples:

A	B
1	2
1	2

and $S(B, C)$ has tuples:

B	C
2	3
4	5
4	5

The only time we get a consistent assignment of tuples to the subgoals (i.e., an assignment where the value of y from each subgoal is the same) is when the first subgoal is assigned the tuple $(1, 2)$ from R and the second subgoal is assigned tuple $(2, 3)$ from S. Since $(1, 2)$ appears twice in R, and $(2, 3)$ appears once in S, there will be two assignments of tuples that give the variable assignments $x = 1$, $y = 2$, and $z = 3$. The tuple of the head, which is (x, z), is for each of these assignments $(1, 3)$. Thus the tuple $(1, 3)$ appears twice in the head relation H, and no other tuple appears there. That is, the relation

1	3
1	3

is the head relation defined by this rule. More generally, had tuple $(1, 2)$ appeared n times in R and tuple $(2, 3)$ appeared m times in S, then tuple $(1, 3)$ would appear nm times in H. □

If a relation is defined by several rules, then the result is the bag-union of whatever tuples are produced by each rule.

Example 10.8: Consider a relation H defined by the two rules

```
H(x,y) ← S(x,y) AND x>1
H(x,y) ← S(x,y) AND y<5
```

where relation $S(B, C)$ is as in Example 10.7; that is, $S = \{(2,3), (4,5), (4,5)\}$. The first rule puts each of the three tuples of S into H, since they each have a first component greater than 1. The second rule puts only the tuple $(2,3)$ into H, since $(4,5)$ does not satisfy the condition $y < 5$. Thus, the resulting relation H has two copies of the tuple $(2,3)$ and two copies of the tuple $(4,5)$. □

10.1.7 Exercises for Section 10.1

Exercise 10.1.1: Write each of the queries of Exercise 5.2.1 in Datalog. You should use only safe rules, but you may wish to use several IDB predicates corresponding to subexpressions of complicated relational-algebra expressions.

Exercise 10.1.2: Write each of the queries of Exercise 5.2.4 in Datalog. Again, use only safe rules, but you may use several IDB predicates if you like.

!! **Exercise 10.1.3:** The requirement we gave for safety of Datalog rules is sufficient to guarantee that the head predicate has a finite relation if the predicates of the relational subgoals have finite relations. However, this requirement is too strong. Give an example of a Datalog rule that violates the condition, yet whatever finite relations we assign to the relational predicates, the head relation will be finite.

10.2 From Relational Algebra to Datalog

Each of the relational-algebra operators of Section 5.2 can be mimicked by one or several Datalog rules. In this section we shall consider each operator in turn. We shall then consider how to combine Datalog rules to mimic complex algebraic expressions.

10.2.1 Intersection

The set intersection of two relations is expressed by a rule that has subgoals for both relations, with the same variables in corresponding arguments.

Example 10.9: Let us use the relations R:

name	*address*	*gender*	*birthdate*
Carrie Fisher	123 Maple St., Hollywood	F	9/9/99
Mark Hamill	456 Oak Rd., Brentwood	M	8/8/88

and S:

name	address	gender	birthdate
Carrie Fisher	123 Maple St., Hollywood	F	9/9/99
Harrison Ford	789 Palm Dr., Beverly Hills	M	7/7/77

as an example. Their intersection is computed by the Datalog rule

$$\texttt{I(n,a,g,b)} \leftarrow \texttt{R(n,a,g,b) AND S(n,a,g,b)}$$

Here, I is an IDB predicate, whose relation becomes $R \cap S$ when we apply this rule. That is, in order for a tuple (n, a, g, b) to make both subgoals true, that tuple must be in both R and S.   □

10.2.2   Union

The union of two relations is constructed by two rules. Each has an atom corresponding to one of the relations as its sole subgoal, and the heads of both rules have the same IDB predicate in the head. The arguments in each head are exactly the same as in the subgoal of its rule.

Example 10.10 : To take the union of the relations R and S from Example 10.9 we use two rules

$$\text{1. } \texttt{U(n,a,g,b)} \leftarrow \texttt{R(n,a,g,b)}$$
$$\text{2. } \texttt{U(n,a,g,b)} \leftarrow \texttt{S(n,a,g,b)}$$

Rule (1) says that every tuple in R is a tuple in the IDB relation U. Rule (2) similarly says that every tuple in S is in U. Thus, the two rules together imply that every tuple in $R \cup S$ is in U. If we write no more rules with U in the head, then there is no way any other tuples can get into the relation U, in which case we can conclude that U is exactly $R \cup S$.[2] Note that, unlike the construction for intersection, which works only for sets, this pair of rules takes either the set- or bag-union, depending on how we interpret the union of the results of the two rules. We shall assume the "set" interpretation unless we say otherwise.   □

10.2.3   Difference

The set difference of relations R and S is computed by a single rule with a negated subgoal. That is, the nonnegated subgoal has predicate R and the negated subgoal has predicate S. These subgoals and the head all have the same variables for corresponding arguments.

Example 10.11 : If R and S are the relations from Example 10.9 then the rule

$$\texttt{D(n,a,g,b)} \leftarrow \texttt{R(n,a,g,b) AND NOT S(n,a,g,b)}$$

defines D to be the relation $R - S$.   □

---

[2]In fact, we should assume in each of the examples of this section that there are no other rules for an IDB predicate besides those that we show explicitly. If there are other rules, then we cannot rule out the existence of other tuples in the relation for that predicate.

Variables Are Local to a Rule

Notice that the names we choose for variables in a rule are arbitrary and have no connection to the variables used in any other rule. The reason there is no connection is that each rule is evaluated alone and contributes tuples to its head's relation independent of other rules. Thus, for instance, we could replace the second rule of Example 10.10 by

$$U(w,x,y,z) \leftarrow S(w,x,y,z)$$

while leaving the first rule unchanged, and the two rules would still compute the union of R and S. Note, however, that when substituting one variable a for another variable b within a rule, we must substitute a for all occurrences of b within the rule. Moreover, the substituting variable a that we choose must not be a variable that already appears in the rule.

10.2.4 Projection

To compute a projection of a relation R, we use one rule with a single subgoal with predicate R. The arguments of this subgoal are distinct variables, one for each attribute of the relation. The head has an atom with arguments that are the variables corresponding to the attributes in the projection list, in the desired order.

Example 10.12: Suppose we want to project the relation

        Movie(title, year, length, inColor, studioName, producerC#)

onto its first three attributes — title, year, and length. The rule

$$P(t,y,l) \leftarrow Movie(t,y,l,c,s,p)$$

serves, defining a relation called P to be the result of the projection. □

10.2.5 Selection

Selections can be somewhat more difficult to express in Datalog. The simple case is when the selection condition is the AND of one or more arithmetic comparisons. In that case, we create a rule with

  1. One relational subgoal for the relation upon which we are performing the selection. This atom has distinct variables for each component, one for each attribute of the relation.

2. For each comparison in the selection condition, an arithmetic subgoal that is identical to this comparison. However, while in the selection condition an attribute name was used, in the arithmetic subgoal we use the corresponding variable, following the correspondence established by the relational subgoal.

Example 10.13: The selection

$$\sigma_{length \geq 100 \text{ AND } studioName=\text{'Fox'}}(\text{Movie})$$

from Example 5.4 can be written as a Datalog rule

```
S(t,y,l,c,s,p) ← Movie(t,y,l,c,s,p) AND l ≥ 100 AND s = 'Fox'
```

The result is the relation S. Note that l and s are the variables corresponding to attributes `length` and `studioName` in the standard order we have used for the attributes of `Movie`. □

Now, let us consider selections that involve the OR of conditions. We cannot necessarily replace such selections by single Datalog rules. However, selection for the OR of two conditions is equivalent to selecting for each condition separately and then taking the union of the results. Thus, the OR of n conditions can be expressed by n rules, each of which defines the same head predicate. The ith rule performs the selection for the ith of the n conditions.

Example 10.14: Let us modify the selection of Example 10.13 by replacing the AND by an OR to get the selection:

$$\sigma_{length \geq 100 \text{ OR } studioName=\text{'Fox'}}(\text{Movie})$$

That is, find all those movies that are either long or by Fox. We can write two rules, one for each of the two conditions:

```
1. S(t,y,l,c,s,p) ← Movie(t,y,l,c,s,p) AND l ≥ 100
2. S(t,y,l,c,s,p) ← Movie(t,y,l,c,s,p) AND s = 'Fox'
```

Rule (1) produces movies at least 100 minutes long, and rule (2) produces movies by Fox. □

Even more complex selection conditions can be formed by several applications, in any order, of the logical operators AND, OR, and NOT. However, there is a widely known technique, which we shall not present here, for rearranging any such logical expression into "disjunctive normal form," where the expression is the disjunction (OR) of "conjuncts." A *conjunct*, in turn, is the AND of "literals," and a *literal* is either a comparison or a negated comparison.[3]

---

[3]See, e.g., A. V. Aho and J. D. Ullman, *Foundations of Computer Science*, Computer Science Press, New York, 1992.

We can represent any literal by a subgoal, perhaps with a NOT in front of it. If the subgoal is arithmetic, the NOT can be incorporated into the comparison operator. For example, NOT x $\geq$ 100 can be written as x < 100. Then, any conjunct can be represented by a single Datalog rule, with one subgoal for each comparison. Finally, every disjunctive-normal-form expression can be written by several Datalog rules, one rule for each conjunct. These rules take the union, or OR, of the results from each of the conjuncts.

Example 10.15: We gave a simple instance of this algorithm in Example 10.14. A more difficult example can be formed by negating the condition of that example. We then have the expression:

$$\sigma_{\text{NOT }(length \geq 100 \text{ OR } studioName='\text{Fox'})}(\text{Movie})$$

That is, find all those movies that are neither long nor by Fox.

Here, a NOT is applied to an expression that is itself not a simple comparison. Thus, we must push the NOT down the expression, using one form of *DeMorgan's law*, which says that the negation of an OR is the AND of the negations. That is, the selection can be rewritten:

$$\sigma_{(\text{NOT }(length \geq 100)) \text{ AND }(\text{NOT }(studioName='\text{Fox'}))}(\text{Movie})$$

Now, we can take the NOT's inside the comparisons to get the expression:

$$\sigma_{length < 100 \text{ AND } studioName \neq '\text{Fox'}}(\text{Movie})$$

This expression can be converted into the Datalog rule

```
S(t,y,l,c,s,p) ← Movie(t,y,l,c,s,p) AND l < 100 AND s ≠ 'Fox'
```

□

Example 10.16: Let us consider a similar example where we have the negation of an AND in the selection. Now, we use the second form of DeMorgan's law, which says that the negation of an AND is the OR of the negations. We begin with the algebraic expression

$$\sigma_{\text{NOT }(length \geq 100 \text{ AND } studioName='\text{Fox'})}(\text{Movie})$$

That is, find all those movies that are not both long and by Fox.

We apply DeMorgan's law to push the NOT below the AND, to get:

$$\sigma_{(\text{NOT }(length \geq 100)) \text{ OR }(\text{NOT }(studioName='\text{Fox'}))}(\text{Movie})$$

Again we take the NOT's inside the comparisons to get:

$$\sigma_{length < 100 \text{ OR } studioName \neq '\text{Fox'}}(\text{Movie})$$

Finally, we write two rules, one for each part of the OR. The resulting Datalog rules are:

```
1. S(t,y,l,c,s,p) ← Movie(t,y,l,c,s,p) AND l < 100
2. S(t,y,l,c,s,p) ← Movie(t,y,l,c,s,p) AND s ≠ 'Fox'
```

□

10.2.6   Product

The product of two relations $R \times S$ can be expressed by a single Datalog rule. This rule has two subgoals, one for R and one for S. Each of these subgoals has distinct variables, one for each attribute of R or S. The IDB predicate in the head has as arguments all the variables that appear in either subgoal, with the variables appearing in the R-subgoal listed before those of the S-subgoal.

Example 10.17 : Let us consider the two four-attribute relations R and S from Example 10.9. The rule

$$P(a,b,c,d,w,x,y,z) \leftarrow R(a,b,c,d) \text{ AND } S(w,x,y,z)$$

defines P to be $R \times S$. We have arbitrarily used variables at the beginning of the alphabet for the arguments of R and variables at the end of the alphabet for S. These variables all appear in the rule head.   □

10.2.7   Joins

We can take the natural join of two relations by a Datalog rule that looks much like the rule for a product. The difference is that if we want $R \bowtie S$, then we must be careful to use the same variable for attributes of R and S that have the same name and to use different variables otherwise. For instance, we can use the attribute names themselves as the variables. The head is an IDB predicate that has each variable appearing once.

Example 10.18 : Consider relations with schemas $R(A, B)$ and $S(B, C, D)$. Their natural join may be defined by the rule

$$J(a,b,c,d) \leftarrow R(a,b) \text{ AND } S(b,c,d)$$

Notice how the variables used in the subgoals correspond in an obvious way to the attributes of the relations R and S.   □

We also can convert theta-joins to Datalog. Recall from Section 5.2.10 how a theta-join can be expressed as a product followed by a selection. If the selection condition is a conjunct, that is, the AND of comparisons, then we may simply start with the Datalog rule for the product and add additional, arithmetic subgoals, one for each of the comparisons.

Example 10.19 : Let us consider the relations $U(A, B, C)$ and $V(B, C, D)$ from Example 5.9, where we applied the theta-join

$$U \underset{A<D \text{ AND } U.B \neq V.B}{\bowtie} V$$

We can construct the Datalog rule

$$J(a,ub,uc,vb,vc,d) \leftarrow U(a,ub,uc) \text{ AND } V(vb,vc,d) \text{ AND}$$
$$a < d \text{ AND } ub \neq vb$$

to perform the same operation. We have used ub as the variable corresponding to attribute B of U, and similarly used vb, uc, and vc, although any six distinct variables for the six attributes of the two relations would be fine. The first two subgoals introduce the two relations, and the second two subgoals enforce the two comparisons that appear in the condition of the theta-join. □

If the condition of the theta-join is not a conjunction, then we convert it to disjunctive normal form, as discussed in Section 10.2.5. We then create one rule for each conjunct. In this rule, we begin with the subgoals for the product and then add subgoals for each literal in the conjunct. The heads of all the rules are identical and have one argument for each attribute of the two relations being theta-joined.

Example 10.20 : In this example, we shall make a simple modification to the algebraic expression of Example 10.19. The AND will be replaced by an OR. There are no negations in this expression, so it is already in disjunctive normal form. There are two conjuncts, each with a single literal. The expression is:

$$U \underset{A<D \text{ OR } U.B \neq V.B}{\bowtie} V$$

Using the same variable-naming scheme as in Example 10.19, we obtain the two rules

1. J(a,ub,uc,vb,vc,d) ← U(a,ub,uc) AND V(vb,vc,d) AND a < d
2. J(a,ub,uc,vb,vc,d) ← U(a,ub,uc) AND V(vb,vc,d) AND ub ≠ vb

Each rule has subgoals for the two relations involved plus a subgoal for one of the two conditions $A < D$ or $U.B \neq V.B$. □

10.2.8 Simulating Multiple Operations with Datalog

Datalog rules are not only capable of mimicking a single operation of relational algebra. We can in fact mimic any algebraic expression. The trick is to look at the expression tree for the relational-algebra expression and create one IDB predicate for each interior node of the tree. The rule or rules for each IDB predicate is whatever we need to apply the operator at the corresponding node of the tree. Those operands of the tree that are extensional (i.e., they are relations of the database) are represented by the corresponding predicate. Operands that are themselves interior nodes are represented by the corresponding IDB predicate.

Example 10.21 : Consider the algebraic expression

$$\pi_{title,year}\Big(\sigma_{length \geq 100}(\text{Movie}) \cap \sigma_{studioName=\text{'Fox'}}(\text{Movie})\Big)$$

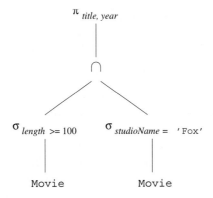

Figure 10.2: Expression tree

```
1. W(t,y,l,c,s,p) ← Movie(t,y,l,c,s,p) AND l ≥ 100
2. X(t,y,l,c,s,p) ← Movie(t,y,l,c,s,p) AND s = 'Fox'
3. Y(t,y,l,c,s,p) ← W(t,y,l,c,s,p) AND X(t,y,l,c,s,p)
4. Z(t,y) ← Y(t,y,l,c,s,p)
```

Figure 10.3: Datalog rules to perform several algebraic operations

from Example 5.10, whose expression tree appeared in Fig. 5.8. We repeat this tree as Fig. 10.2. There are four interior nodes, so we need to create four IDB predicates. Each of these predicates has a single Datalog rule, and we summarize all the rules in Fig. 10.3.

The lowest two interior nodes perform simple selections on the EDB relation Movie, so we can create the IDB predicates W and X to represent these selections. Rules (1) and (2) of Fig. 10.3 describe these selections. For example, rule (1) defines W to be those tuples of Movie that have a length at least 100.

Then rule (3) defines predicate Y to be the intersection of W and X, using the form of rule we learned for an intersection in Section 10.2.1. Finally, rule (4) defines predicate Z to be the projection of Y onto the title and year attributes. We here use the technique for simulating a projection that we learned in Section 10.2.4. The predicate Z is the "answer" predicate; that is, regardless of the value of relation Movie, the relation defined by Z is the same as the result of the algebraic expression with which we began this example.

Note that, because Y is defined by a single rule, we can substitute for the Y subgoal in rule (4) of Fig. 10.3, replacing it with the body of rule (3). Then, we can substitute for the W and X subgoals, using the bodies of rules (1) and (2). Since the Movie subgoal appears in both of these bodies, we can eliminate one copy. As a result, Z can be defined by the single rule:

```
Z(t,y) ← Movie(t,y,l,c,s,p) AND l ≥ 100 AND s = 'Fox'
```

However, it is not common that a complex expression of relational algebra is equivalent to a single Datalog rule. $\square$

10.2.9 Exercises for Section 10.2

Exercise 10.2.1: Let $R(a, b, c)$, $S(a, b, c)$, and $T(a, b, c)$ be three relations. Write one or more Datalog rules that define the result of each of the following expressions of relational algebra:

  a) $R \cup S$.

  b) $R \cap S$.

  c) $R - S$.

* d) $(R \cup S) - T$.

! e) $(R - S) \cap (R - T)$.

  f) $\pi_{a,b}(R)$.

*! g) $\pi_{a,b}(R) \cap \rho_{U(a,b)}(\pi_{b,c}(S))$.

Exercise 10.2.2: Let $R(x, y, z)$ be a relation. Write one or more Datalog rules that define $\sigma_C(R)$, where C stands for each of the following conditions:

  a) $x = y$.

* b) $x < y$ AND $y < z$.

  c) $x < y$ OR $y < z$.

  d) NOT $(x < y$ OR $x > y)$.

*! e) NOT $\big((x < y$ OR $x > y)$ AND $y < z\big)$.

! f) NOT $\big((x < y$ OR $x < z)$ AND $y < z\big)$.

Exercise 10.2.3: Let $R(a, b, c)$, $S(b, c, d)$, and $T(d, e)$ be three relations. Write single Datalog rules for each of the natural joins:

  a) $R \bowtie S$.

  b) $S \bowtie T$.

  c) $(R \bowtie S) \bowtie T$. (*Note:* since the natural join is associative and commutative, the order of the join of these three relations is irrelevant.)

Exercise 10.2.4: Let $R(x, y, z)$ and $S(x, y, z)$ be two relations. Write one or more Datalog rules to define each of the theta-joins $R \overset{\bowtie}{_C} S$, where C is one of the conditions of Exercise 10.2.2. For each of these conditions, interpret each arithmetic comparison as comparing an attribute of R on the left with an attribute of S on the right. For instance, $x < y$ stands for $R.x < S.y$.

! **Exercise 10.2.5:** It is also possible to convert Datalog rules into equivalent relational-algebra expressions. While we have not discussed the method of doing so in general, it is possible to work out many simple examples. For each of the Datalog rules below, write an expression of relational algebra that defines the same relation as the head of the rule.

* a) P(x,y) ← Q(x,z) AND R(z,y)

  b) P(x,y) ← Q(x,z) AND Q(z,y)

  c) P(x,y) ← Q(x,z) AND R(z,y) AND x < y

10.3   Recursive Programming in Datalog

While relational algebra can express many useful operations on relations, there are some computations that cannot be written as an expression of relational algebra. A common kind of operation on data that we cannot express in relational algebra involves an infinite, recursively defined sequence of similar expressions.

Example 10.22: Often, a successful movie is followed by a sequel; if the sequel does well, then the sequel has a sequel, and so on. Thus, a movie may be ancestral to a long sequence of other movies. Suppose we have a relation `SequelOf(movie, sequel)` containing pairs consisting of a movie and its immediate sequel. Examples of tuples in this relation are:

movie	sequel
Naked Gun	Naked Gun $2_{1/2}$
Naked Gun $2_{1/2}$	Naked Gun $33_{1/3}$

We might also have a more general notion of a *follow-on* to a movie, which is a sequel, a sequel of a sequel, and so on. In the relation above, *Naked Gun $33_{1/3}$* is a follow-on to *Naked Gun*, but not a sequel in the strict sense we are using the term "sequel" here. It saves space if we store only the immediate sequels in the relation and construct the follow-ons if we need them. In the above example, we store only one fewer pair, but for the five *Rocky* movies we store six fewer pairs, and for the 18 *Friday the 13th* movies we store 136 fewer pairs.

However, it is not immediately obvious how we construct the relation of follow-ons from the relation `SequelOf`. We can construct the sequels of sequels by joining `SequelOf` with itself once. An example of such an expression in relational algebra, using renaming so that the join becomes a natural join, is:

$$\pi_{first,third}\big(\rho_{R(first,second)}(\text{SequelOf}) \bowtie \rho_{S(second,third)}(\text{SequelOf})\big)$$

In this expression, `SequelOf` is renamed twice, once so its attributes are called `first` and `second`, and again so its attributes are called `second` and `third`.

Thus, the natural join asks for tuples (m_1, m_2) and (m_3, m_4) in `SequelOf` such that $m_2 = m_3$. We then produce the pair (m_1, m_4). Note that m_4 is the sequel of the sequel of m_1.

Similarly, we could join three copies of `SequelOf` to get the sequels of sequels of sequels (e.g., *Rocky* and *Rocky IV*). We could in fact produce the ith sequels for any fixed value of i by joining `SequelOf` with itself $i - 1$ times. We could then take the union of `SequelOf` and a finite sequence of these joins to get all the sequels up to some fixed limit.

What we cannot do in relational algebra is ask for the "infinite union" of the infinite sequence of expressions that give the ith sequels for $i = 1, 2, \ldots$. Note that relational algebra's union allows us only to take the union of two relations, not an infinite number. By applying the union operator any finite number of times in an algebraic expression, we can take the union of any finite number of relations, but we cannot take the union of an unlimited number of relations in an algebraic expression. $\square$

10.3.1 Recursive Rules

By using an IDB predicate both in the head and the body of rules, we can express an infinite union in Datalog. We shall first see some examples of how to express recursions in Datalog. In Section 10.3.2 we shall examine the *least fixedpoint* computation of the relations for the IDB predicates of these rules. A new approach to rule-evaluation is needed for recursive rules, since the straightforward rule-evaluation approach of Section 10.1.4 assumes all the predicates in the body of rules have fixed relations.

Example 10.23 : We can define the IDB relation `FollowOn` by the following two Datalog rules:

1. `FollowOn(x,y) ← SequelOf(x,y)`
2. `FollowOn(x,y) ← SequelOf(x,z) AND FollowOn(z,y)`

The first rule is the basis; it tells us that every sequel is a follow-on. The second rule says that every follow-on of a sequel of movie x is also a follow-on of x. More precisely: if z is a sequel of x, and we have found that y is a follow-on of z, then y is a follow-on of x. $\square$

10.3.2 Evaluating Recursive Datalog Rules

To evaluate the IDB predicates of recursive Datalog rules, we follow the principle that we never want to conclude that a tuple is in an IDB relation unless we are forced to do so by applying the rules as in Section 10.1.4. Thus, we:

1. Begin by assuming all IDB predicates have empty relations.

2. Perform a number of *rounds*, in which progressively larger relations are constructed for the IDB predicates. In the bodies of the rules, use the

IDB relations constructed on the previous round. Apply the rules to get new estimates for all the IDB predicates.

3. If the rules are safe, no IDB tuple can have a component value that does not also appear in some EDB relation. Thus, there are a finite number of possible tuples for all IDB relations, and eventually there will be a round on which no new tuples are added to any IDB relation. At this point, we can terminate our computation with the answer; no new IDB tuples will ever be constructed.

This set of IDB tuples is called the *least fixedpoint* of the rules.

Example 10.24 : Let us show the computation of the least fixedpoint for relation `FollowOn` when the relation `SequelOf` consists of the following three tuples:

movie	sequel
Rocky	Rocky II
Rocky II	Rocky III
Rocky III	Rocky IV

At the first round of computation, `FollowOn` is assumed empty. Thus, rule (2) cannot yield any `FollowOn` tuples. However, rule (1) says that every `SequelOf` tuple is a `FollowOn` tuple. Thus, after the first round, the value of `FollowOn` is identical to the `SequelOf` relation above. The situation after round 1 is shown in Fig. 10.4(a).

In the second round, we use the relation from Fig. 10.4(a) as `FollowOn` and apply the two rules to this relation and the given `SequelOf` relation. The first rule gives us the three tuples that we already have, and in fact it is easy to see that rule (1) will never yield any tuples for `FollowOn` other than these three. For rule (2), we look for a tuple from `SequelOf` whose second component equals the first component of a tuple from `FollowOn`.

Thus, we can take the tuple (Rocky, Rocky II) from `SequelOf` and pair it with the tuple (Rocky II, Rocky III) from `FollowOn` to get the new tuple (Rocky, Rocky III) for `FollowOn`. Similarly, we can take the tuple

(Rocky II, Rocky III)

from `SequelOf` and tuple (Rocky III, Rocky IV) from `FollowOn` to get new tuple (Rocky II, Rocky IV) for `FollowOn`. However, no other pairs of tuples from `SequelOf` and `FollowOn` join. Thus, after the second round, `FollowOn` has the five tuples shown in Fig. 10.4(b). Intuitively, just as Fig. 10.4(a) contained only those follow-on facts that are based on a single sequel, Fig. 10.4(b) contains those follow-on facts based on one or two sequels.

In the third round, we use the relation from Fig. 10.4(b) for `FollowOn` and again evaluate the body of rule (2). We get all the tuples we already had, of course, and one more tuple. When we join the tuple (Rocky, Rocky II)

x	y
Rocky	Rocky II
Rocky II	Rocky III
Rocky III	Rocky IV

(a) After round 1

x	y
Rocky	Rocky II
Rocky II	Rocky III
Rocky III	Rocky IV
Rocky	Rocky III
Rocky II	Rocky IV

(b) After round 2

x	y
Rocky	Rocky II
Rocky II	Rocky III
Rocky III	Rocky IV
Rocky	Rocky III
Rocky II	Rocky IV
Rocky	Rocky IV

(c) After round 3 and subsequently

Figure 10.4: Recursive computation of relation `FollowOn`

from `SequelOf` with the tuple (`Rocky II`, `Rocky IV`) from the current value of
`FollowOn`, we get the new tuple (`Rocky`, `Rocky IV`). Thus, after round 3, the
value of `FollowOn` is as shown in Fig. 10.4(c).

When we proceed to round 4, we get no new tuples, so we stop. The true
relation `FollowOn` is as shown in Fig. 10.4(c). □

There is an important trick that simplifies all recursive Datalog evaluations,
such as the one above:

- At any round, the only new tuples added to any IDB relation will come
  from applications of rules in which at least one IDB subgoal is matched
  to a tuple that was added to its relation at the previous round.

Other Forms of Recursion

In Example 10.23 we used a *right-recursive* form for the recursion, where the use of the recursive relation `FollowOn` appears after the EDB relation `SequelOf`. We could also write similar *left-recursive* rules by putting the recursive relation first. These rules are:

    1. `FollowOn(x,y) ← SequelOf(x,y)`
    2. `FollowOn(x,y) ← FollowOn(x,z) AND SequelOf(z,y)`

Informally, y is a follow-on of x if it is either a sequel of x or a sequel of a follow-on of x.

We could even use the recursive relation twice, as in the *nonlinear* recursion:

    1. `FollowOn(x,y) ← SequelOf(x,y)`
    2. `FollowOn(x,y) ← FollowOn(x,z) AND FollowOn(z,y)`

Informally, y is a follow-on of x if it is either a sequel of x or a follow-on of a follow-on of x. All three of these forms give the same value for relation `FollowOn`: the set of pairs (x,y) such that y is a sequel of a sequel of $\cdots$ (some number of times) of x.

The justification for this rule is that should all subgoals be matched to "old" tuples, the tuple of the head would already have been added on the previous round. The next two examples illustrate this strategy and also show us more complex examples of recursion.

Example 10.25 : Many examples of the use of recursion can be found in a study of paths in a graph. Figure 10.5 shows a graph representing some flights of two hypothetical airlines — *Untried Airlines* (UA), and *Arcane Airlines* (AA) — among the cities San Francisco, Denver, Dallas, Chicago, and New York.

We may imagine that the flights are represented by an EDB relation:

$$\text{Flights(airline, from, to, departs, arrives)}$$

The tuples in this relation for the data of Fig. 10.5 are shown in Fig. 10.6.

The simplest recursive question we can ask is "For what pairs of cities (x, y) is it possible to get from city x to city y by taking one or more flights?" The following two rules describe a relation `Reaches(x,y)` that contains exactly these pairs of cities.

    1. `Reaches(x,y) ← Flights(a,x,y,d,r)`
    2. `Reaches(x,y) ← Reaches(x,z) AND Reaches(z,y)`

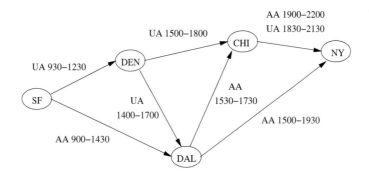

Figure 10.5: A map of some airline flights

airline	from	to	departs	arrives
UA	SF	DEN	930	1230
AA	SF	DAL	900	1430
UA	DEN	CHI	1500	1800
UA	DEN	DAL	1400	1700
AA	DAL	CHI	1530	1730
AA	DAL	NY	1500	1930
AA	CHI	NY	1900	2200
UA	CHI	NY	1830	2130

Figure 10.6: Tuples in the relation `Flights`

The first rule says that `Reaches` contains those pairs of cities for which there is a direct flight from the first to the second; the airline a, departure time d, and arrival time r are arbitrary in this rule. The second rule says that if you can reach from city x to city z and you can reach from z to y, then you can reach from x to y. Notice that we have used the nonlinear form of recursion here, as was described in the box on "Other Forms of Recursion." This form is slightly more convenient here, because another use of `Flights` in the recursive rule would involve three more variables for the unused components of `Flights`.

To evaluate the relation `Reaches`, we follow the same iterative process introduced in Example 10.24. We begin by using Rule (1) to get the following pairs in `Reaches`: (SF, DEN), (SF, DAL), (DEN, CHI), (DEN, DAL), (DAL, CHI), (DAL, NY), and (CHI, NY). These are the seven pairs represented by arcs in Fig. 10.5.

In the next round, we apply the recursive Rule (2) to put together pairs of arcs such that the head of one is the tail of the next. That gives us the additional pairs (SF, CHI), (DEN, NY), and (SF, NY). The third round combines all one- and two-arc pairs together to form paths of length up to four arcs. In this particular diagram, we get no new pairs. The relation `Reaches` thus consists of the ten pairs (x, y) such that y is reachable from x in the diagram of Fig. 10.5. Because of the way we drew the diagram, these pairs happen to be exactly those (x, y) such that y is to the right of x in Fig 10.5.   □

Example 10.26 : A more complicated definition of when two flights can be combined into a longer sequence of flights is to require that the second leaves an airport at least an hour after the first arrives at that airport. Now, we use an IDB predicate, which we shall call `Connects(x,y,d,r)`, that says we can take one or more flights, starting at city x at time d and arriving at city y at time r. If there are any connections, then there is at least an hour to make the connection.

The rules for `Connects` are:[4]

```
    1.  Connects(x,y,d,r)   ←   Flights(a,x,y,d,r)
    2.  Connects(x,y,d,r)   ←   Connects(x,z,d,t1) AND
                                Connects(z,y,t2,r) AND
                                t1 <= t2 - 100
```

In the first round, rule (1) gives us the eight `Connects` facts shown above the first line in Fig. 10.7 (the line is not part of the relation). Each corresponds to one of the flights indicated in the diagram of Fig. 10.5; note that one of the seven arcs of that figure represents two flights at different times.

We now try to combine these tuples using Rule (2). For example, the second and fifth of these tuples combine to give the tuple (SF, CHI, 900, 1730). However, the second and sixth tuples do not combine because the arrival time in Dallas is 1430, and the departure time from Dallas, 1500, is only half an hour later. The `Connects` relation after the second round consists of all those tuples above the first or second line in Fig. 10.7. Above the top line are the original tuples from round 1, and the six tuples added on round 2 are shown between the first and second lines.

In the third round, we must in principle consider all pairs of tuples above one of the two lines in Fig. 10.7 as candidates for the two `Connects` tuples in the body of rule (2). However, if both tuples are above the first line, then they would have been considered during round 2 and therefore will not yield a `Connects` tuple we have not seen before. The only way to get a new tuple is if at least one of the two `Connects` tuple used in the body of rule (2) were added at the previous round; i.e., it is between the lines in Fig. 10.7.

The third round only gives us three new tuples. These are shown at the bottom of Fig. 10.7. There are no new tuples in the fourth round, so our computation is complete. Thus, the entire relation `Connects` is Fig. 10.7.   □

10.3.3   Negation in Recursive Rules

Sometimes it is necessary to use negation in rules that also involve recursion. There is a safe way and an unsafe way to mix recursion and negation. Generally, it is considered appropriate to use negation only in situations where the negation does not appear inside the fixedpoint operation. To see the difference, we shall

---

[4]These rules only work on the assumption that there are no connections spanning midnight.

x	y	d	r
SF	DEN	930	1230
SF	DAL	900	1430
DEN	CHI	1500	1800
DEN	DAL	1400	1700
DAL	CHI	1530	1730
DAL	NY	1500	1930
CHI	NY	1900	2200
CHI	NY	1830	2130
SF	CHI	900	1730
SF	CHI	930	1800
SF	DAL	930	1700
DEN	NY	1500	2200
DAL	NY	1530	2130
DAL	NY	1530	2200
SF	NY	900	2130
SF	NY	900	2200
SF	NY	930	2200

Figure 10.7: Relation `Connects` after third round

consider two examples of recursion and negation, one appropriate and the other paradoxical. We shall see that only "stratified" negation is useful when there is recursion; the term "stratified" will be defined precisely after the examples.

Example 10.27: Suppose we want to find those pairs of cities (x, y) in the map of Fig. 10.5 such that UA flies from x to y (perhaps through several other cities), but AA does not. We can recursively define a predicate `UAreaches` as we defined `Reaches` in Example 10.25, but restricting ourselves only to UA flights, as follows:

```
1. UAreaches(x,y) ← Flights(UA,x,y,d,r)
2. UAreaches(x,y) ← UAreaches(x,z) AND UAreaches(z,y)
```

Similarly, we can recursively define the predicate `AAreaches` to be those pairs of cities (x, y) such that one can travel from x to y using only AA flights, by:

```
1. AAreaches(x,y) ← Flights(AA,x,y,d,r)
2. AAreaches(x,y) ← AAreaches(x,z) AND AAreaches(z,y)
```

Now, it is a simple matter to compute the `UAonly` predicate consisting of those pairs of cities (x, y) such that one can get from x to y on UA flights but not on AA flights, with the nonrecursive rule:

```
UAonly(x,y) ← UAreaches(x,y) AND NOT AAreaches(x,y)
```

This rule computes the set difference of UAreaches and AAreaches.

For the data of Fig. 10.5, UAreaches is seen to consist of the following pairs: (SF, DEN), (SF, DAL), (SF, CHI), (SF, NY), (DEN, DAL), (DEN, CHI), (DEN, NY), and (CHI, NY). This set is computed by the iterative fixedpoint process outlined in Section 10.3.2. Similarly, we can compute the value of AAreaches for this data; it is: (SF, DAL), (SF, CHI), (SF, NY), (DAL, CHI), (DAL, NY), and (CHI, NY). When we take the difference of these sets of pairs we get: (SF, DEN), (DEN, DAL), (DEN, CHI), and (DEN, NY). This set of four pairs is the relation UAonly. □

Example 10.28 : Now, let us consider an abstract example where things don't work as well. Suppose we have a single EDB predicate R. This predicate is unary (one-argument), and it has a single tuple, (0). There are two IDB predicates, P and Q, also unary. They are defined by the two rules

> 1. P(x) ← R(x) AND NOT Q(x)
> 2. Q(x) ← R(x) AND NOT P(x)

Informally, the two rules tell us that an element x in R is either in P or in Q but not both. Notice that P and Q are defined recursively in terms of each other.

When we defined what recursive rules meant in Section 10.3.2, we said we want the least fixedpoint, that is, the smallest IDB relations that contain all tuples that the rules require us to allow. Rule (1), since it is the only rule for P, says that as relations, $P = R - Q$, and rule (2) likewise says that $Q = R - P$. Since R contains only the tuple (0), we know that only (0) can be in either P or Q. But where is (0)? It cannot be in neither, since then the equations are not satisfied; for instance $P = R - Q$ would imply that $\emptyset = \{(0)\} - \emptyset$, which is false.

If we let $P = \{(0)\}$ while $Q = \emptyset$, then we do get a solution to both equations. $P = R - Q$ becomes $\{(0)\} = \{(0)\} - \emptyset$, which is true, and $Q = R - P$ becomes $\emptyset = \{(0)\} - \{(0)\}$, which is also true.

However, we can also let $P = \emptyset$ and $Q = \{(0)\}$. This choice too satisfies both rules. We thus have two solutions:

> a) $P = \{(0)\}$ $Q = \emptyset$
> b) $P = \emptyset$ $Q = \{(0)\}$

Both are minimal, in the sense that if we throw any tuple out of any relation, the resulting relations no longer satisfy the rules. We cannot, therefore, decide between the two least fixedpoints (a) and (b), so we cannot answer a simple question such as "Is $P(0)$ true?" □

In Example 10.28, we saw that our idea of defining the meaning of recursive rules by finding the least fixedpoint no longer works when recursion and negation are tangled up too intimately. There can be more than one least fixedpoint, and these fixedpoints can contradict each other. It would be good if some other approach to defining the meaning of recursive negation would work better, but unfortunately, there is no general agreement about what such rules should mean.

Thus, it is conventional to restrict ourselves to recursions in which negation is *stratified*. For instance, the SQL-99 standard for recursion discussed in Section 10.4 makes this restriction. As we shall see, when negation is stratified there is an algorithm to compute one particular least fixedpoint (perhaps out of many such fixedpoints) that matches our intuition about what the rules mean. We define the property of being stratified as follows.

1. Draw a graph whose nodes correspond to the IDB predicates.

2. Draw an arc from node A to node B if a rule with predicate A in the head has a negated subgoal with predicate B. Label this arc with a $-$ sign to indicate it is a *negative* arc.

3. Draw an arc from node A to node B if a rule with head predicate A has a non-negated subgoal with predicate B. This arc does not have a minus-sign as label.

If this graph has a cycle containing one or more negative arcs, then the recursion is not stratified. Otherwise, the recursion is stratified. We can group the IDB predicates of a stratified graph into *strata*. The stratum of a predicate A is the largest number of negative arcs on a path beginning from A.

If the recursion is stratified, then we may evaluate the IDB predicates in the order of their strata, lowest first. This strategy produces one of the least fixedpoints of the rules. More importantly, computing the IDB predicates in the order implied by their strata appears always to make sense and give us the "right" fixedpoint. In contrast, as we have seen in Example 10.28, unstratified recursions may leave us with no "right" fixedpoint at all, even if there are many to choose from.

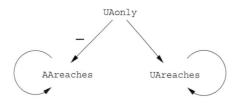

Figure 10.8: Graph constructed from a stratified recursion

Example 10.29 : The graph for the predicates of Example 10.27 is shown in Fig. 10.8. `AAreaches` and `UAreaches` are in stratum 0, because none of the paths beginning at their nodes involves a negative arc. `UAonly` has stratum 1, because there are paths with one negative arc leading from that node, but no paths with more than one negative arc. Thus, we must completely evaluate `AAreaches` and `UAreaches` before we start evaluating `UAonly`.

Compare the situation when we construct the graph for the IDB predicates of Example 10.28. This graph is shown in Fig. 10.9. Since rule (1) has head P with negated subgoal Q, there is a negative arc from P to Q. Since rule (2) has head Q with negated subgoal P, there is also a negative arc in the opposite direction. There is thus a negative cycle, and the rules are not stratified.   □

P Q

Figure 10.9: Graph constructed from an unstratified recursion

10.3.4 Exercises for Section 10.3

Exercise 10.3.1: If we add or delete arcs to the diagram of Fig. 10.5, we may change the value of the relation Reaches of Example 10.25, the relation Connects of Example 10.26, or the relations UAreaches and AAreaches of Example 10.27. Give the new values of these relations if we:

* a) Add an arc from CHI to SF labeled AA, 1900-2100.

  b) Add an arc from NY to DEN labeled UA, 900-1100.

  c) Add both arcs from (a) and (b).

  d) Delete the arc from DEN to DAL.

Exercise 10.3.2: Write Datalog rules (using stratified negation, if negation is necessary) to describe the following modifications to the notion of "follow-on" from Example 10.22. You may use EDB relation SequelOf and the IDB relation FollowOn defined in Example 10.23.

* a) P(x,y) meaning that movie y is a follow-on to movie x, but not a sequel of x (as defined by the EDB relation SequelOf).

  b) Q(x,y) meaning that y is a follow-on of x, but neither a sequel nor a sequel of a sequel.

! c) R(x) meaning that movie x has at least two follow-ons. Note that both could be sequels, rather than one being a sequel and the other a sequel of a sequel.

!! d) S(x,y), meaning that y is a follow-on of x but y has at most one follow-on.

Exercise 10.3.3: ODL classes and their relationships can be described by a relation `Rel(class, rclass, mult)`. Here, `mult` gives the multiplicity of a relationship, either `multi` for a multivalued relationship, or `single` for a single-valued relationship. The first two attributes are the related classes; the relationship goes from `class` to `rclass` (related class). For example, the relation `Rel` representing the three ODL classes of our running movie example from Fig. 4.3 is shown in Fig. 10.10.

class	rclass	mult
Star	Movie	multi
Movie	Star	multi
Movie	Studio	single
Studio	Movie	multi

Figure 10.10: Representing ODL relationships by relational data

We can also see this data as a graph, in which the nodes are classes and the arcs go from a class to a related class, with label `multi` or `single`, as appropriate. Figure 10.11 illustrates this graph for the data of Fig. 10.10.

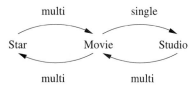

Figure 10.11: Representing relationships by a graph

For each of the following, write Datalog rules, using stratified negation if negation is necessary, to express the described predicate(s). You may use `Rel` as an EDB relation. Show the result of evaluating your rules, round-by-round, on the data from Fig. 10.10.

a) Predicate `P(class, eclass)`, meaning that there is a path[5] in the graph of classes that goes from `class` to `eclass`. The latter class can be thought of as "embedded" in `class`, since it is in a sense part of a part of an $\cdots$ object of the first class.

*! b) Predicates `S(class, eclass)` and `M(class, eclass)`. The first means that there is a "single-valued embedding" of `eclass` in `class`, that is, a path from `class` to `eclass` along which every arc is labeled `single`. The second, M, means that there is a "multivalued embedding" of `eclass` in `class`, i.e., a path from `class` to `eclass` with at least one arc labeled `multi`.

---

[5] We shall not consider empty paths to be "paths" in this exercise.

c) Predicate Q(class, eclass) that says there is a path from class to eclass but no single-valued path. You may use IDB predicates defined previously in this exercise.

10.4 Recursion in SQL

The SQL-99 standard includes provision for recursive rules, based on the recursive Datalog described in Section 10.3. Although this feature is not part of the "core" SQL-99 standard that every DBMS is expected to implement, at least one major system — IBM's DB2 — does implement the SQL-99 proposal. This proposal differs from our description in two ways:

1. Only *linear* recursion, that is, rules with at most one recursive subgoal, is mandatory. In what follows, we shall ignore this restriction; you should remember that there could be an implementation of standard SQL that prohibits nonlinear recursion but allows linear recursion.

2. The requirement of stratification, which we discussed for the negation operator in Section 10.3.3, applies also to other operators of SQL that can cause similar problems, such as aggregations.

10.4.1 Defining IDB Relations in SQL

The WITH statement allows us to define the SQL equivalent of IDB relations. These definitions can then be used within the WITH statement itself. A simple form of the WITH statement is:

WITH R AS <definition of R> <query involving R>

That is, one defines a temporary relation named R, and then uses R in some query. More generally, one can define several relations after the WITH, separating their definitions by commas. Any of these definitions may be recursive. Several defined relations may be mutually recursive; that is, each may be defined in terms of some of the other relations, optionally including itself. However, any relation that is involved in a recursion must be preceded by the keyword RECURSIVE. Thus, a WITH statement has the form:

1. The keyword WITH.

2. One or more definitions. Definitions are separated by commas, and each definition consists of

   (a) An optional keyword RECURSIVE, which is required if the relation being defined is recursive.

   (b) The name of the relation being defined.

   (c) The keyword AS.

(d) The query that defines the relation.

3. A query, which may refer to any of the prior definitions, and forms the result of the WITH statement.

It is important to note that, unlike other definitions of relations, the definitions inside a WITH statement are only available within that statement and cannot be used elsewhere. If one wants a persistent relation, one should define that relation in the database schema, outside any WITH statement.

Example 10.30: Let us reconsider the airline flights information that we used as an example in Section 10.3. The data about flights is in a relation[6]

        Flights(airline, frm, to, departs, arrives)

The actual data for our example was given in Fig. 10.5.

In Example 10.25, we computed the IDB relation Reaches to be the pairs of cities such that it is possible to fly from the first to the second using the flights represented by the EDB relation Flights. The two rules for Reaches are:

> 1. Reaches(x,y) ← Flights(a,x,y,d,r)
> 2. Reaches(x,y) ← Reaches(x,z) AND Reaches(z,y)

From these rules, we can develop an SQL query that produces the relation Reaches. This SQL query places the rules for Reaches in a WITH statement, and follows it by a query. In Example 10.25, the desired result was the entire Reaches relation, but we could also ask some query about Reaches, for instance the set of cities reachable from Denver.

```
1)   WITH RECURSIVE Reaches(frm, to) AS
2)          (SELECT frm, to FROM Flights)
3)       UNION
4)          (SELECT R1.frm, R2.to
5)           FROM Reaches R1, Reaches R2
6)           WHERE R1.to = R2.frm)
7)   SELECT * FROM Reaches;
```

Figure 10.12: Recursive SQL query for pairs of reachable cities

Figure 10.12 shows how to compute Reaches as an SQL query. Line (1) introduces the definition of Reaches, while the actual definition of this relation is in lines (2) through (6).

That definition is a union of two queries, corresponding to the two rules by which Reaches was defined in Example 10.25. Line (2) is the first term

---

[6]We changed the name of the second attribute to frm, since from in SQL is a keyword.

Mutual Recursion

There is a graph-theoretic way to check whether two relations or predicates are mutually recursive. Construct a *dependency graph* whose nodes correspond to the relations (or predicates if we are using Datalog rules). Draw an arc from relation A to relation B if the definition of B depends directly on the definition of A. That is, if Datalog is being used, then A appears in the body of a rule with B at the head. In SQL, A would appear somewhere in the definition of B, normally in a FROM clause, but possibly as a term in a union, intersection, or difference.

If there is a cycle involving nodes R and S, then R and S are *mutually recursive*. The most common case will be a loop from R to R, indicating that R depends recursively upon itself.

Note that the dependency graph is similar to the graph we introduced in Section 10.3.3 to define stratified negation. However, there we had to distinguish between positive and negative dependence, while here we do not make that distinction.

---

of the union and corresponds to the first, or basis rule. It says that for every tuple in the Flights relation, the second and third components (the frm and to components) are a tuple in Reaches.

Lines (4) through (6) correspond to the second, or inductive, rule in the definition of Reaches. The two Reaches subgoals are represented in the FROM clause by two aliases R1 and R2 for Reaches. The first component of R1 corresponds to x in Rule (2), and the second component of R2 corresponds to y. Variable z is represented by both the second component of R1 and the first component of R2; note that these components are equated in line (6).

Finally, line (7) describes the relation produced by the entire query. It is a copy of the Reaches relation. As an alternative, we could replace line (7) by a more complex query. For instance,

```
7)  SELECT to FROM Reaches WHERE frm = 'DEN';
```

would produce all those cities reachable from Denver.   □

10.4.2 Stratified Negation

The queries that can appear as the definition of a recursive relation are not arbitrary SQL queries. Rather, they must be restricted in certain ways; one of the most important requirements is that negation of mutually recursive relations be stratified, as discussed in Section 10.3.3. In Section 10.4.3, we shall see how the principle of stratification extends to other constructs that we find in SQL but not in Datalog, such as aggregation.

Example 10.31: Let us re-examine Example 10.27, where we asked for those pairs of cities (x, y) such that it is possible to travel from x to y on the airline UA, but not on AA. We need recursion to express the idea of traveling on one airline through an indefinite sequence of hops. However, the negation aspect appears in a stratified way: after using recursion to compute the two relations UAreaches and AAreaches in Example 10.27, we took their difference.

We could adopt the same strategy to write the query in SQL. However, to illustrate a different way of proceeding, we shall instead define recursively a single relation Reaches(airline, frm, to), whose triples (a, f, t) mean that one can fly from city f to city t, perhaps using several hops but using only flights of airline a. We shall also use a nonrecursive relation Triples(airline, frm, to) that is the projection of Flights onto the three relevant components. The query is shown in Fig. 10.13.

The definition of relation Reaches in lines (3) through (9) is the union of two terms. The basis term is the relation Triples at line (4). The inductive term is the query of lines (6) through (9) that produces the join of Triples with Reaches itself. The effect of these two terms is to put into Reaches all tuples (a, f, t) such that one can travel from city f to city t using one or more hops, but with all hops on airline a.

The query itself appears in lines (10) through (12). Line (10) gives the city pairs reachable via UA, and line (12) gives the city pairs reachable via AA. The result of the query is the difference of these two relations.   □

```
1) WITH
2)      Triples AS SELECT airline, frm, to FROM Flights,

3)      RECURSIVE Reaches(airline, frm, to) AS
4)            (SELECT * FROM Triples)
5)          UNION
6)            (SELECT Triples.airline, Triples.frm, Reaches.to
7)             FROM Triples, Reaches
8)             WHERE Triples.to = Reaches.frm AND
9)                   Triples.airline = Reaches.airline)

10)     (SELECT frm, to FROM Reaches WHERE airline = 'UA')
11) EXCEPT
12)     (SELECT frm, to FROM Reaches WHERE airline = 'AA');
```

Figure 10.13: Stratified query for cities reachable by one of two airlines

Example 10.32: In Fig. 10.13, the negation represented by EXCEPT in line (11) is clearly stratified, since it applies only after the recursion of lines (3) through

(9) has been completed. On the other hand, the use of negation in Example 10.28, which we observed was unstratified, must be translated into a use of EXCEPT within the definition of mutually recursive relations. The straightforward translation of that example into SQL is shown in Fig. 10.14. This query asks only for the value of P, although we could have asked for Q, or some function of P and Q.

```
1)   WITH
2)       RECURSIVE P(x) AS
3)               (SELECT * FROM R)
4)           EXCEPT
5)               (SELECT * FROM Q),

6)       RECURSIVE Q(x) AS
7)               (SELECT * FROM R)
8)           EXCEPT
9)               (SELECT * FROM P)

10)  SELECT * FROM P;
```

Figure 10.14: Unstratified query, illegal in SQL

The two uses of EXCEPT, in lines (4) and (8) of Fig. 10.14 are illegal in SQL, since in each case the second argument is a relation that is mutually recursive with the relation being defined. Thus, these uses of negation are not stratified negation and therefore not permitted. In fact, there is no work-around for this problem in SQL, nor should there be, since the recursion of Fig. 10.14 does not define unique values for relations P and Q.   □

10.4.3   Problematic Expressions in Recursive SQL

We have seen in Example 10.32 that the use of EXCEPT to help define a recursive relation can violate SQL's requirement that negation be stratified. However, there are other unacceptable forms of query that do not use EXCEPT. For instance, negation of a relation can also be expressed by the use of NOT IN. Thus, lines (2) through (5) of Fig. 10.14 could also have been written

```
RECURSIVE P(x) AS
    SELECT x FROM R WHERE x NOT IN Q
```

This rewriting still leaves the recursion unstratified and therefore illegal.

On the other hand, simply using NOT in a WHERE clause, such as NOT x=y (which could be written x<>y anyway) does not automatically violate the condition that negation be stratified. What then is the general rule about what sorts of SQL queries can be used to define recursive relations in SQL?

The principle is that to be a legal SQL recursion, the definition of a recursive relation R may only involve the use of a mutually recursive relation S (S can be R itself) if that use is *monotone* in S. A use of S is monotone if adding an arbitrary tuple to S might add one or more tuples to R, or it might leave R unchanged, but it can never cause any tuple to be deleted from R.

This rule makes sense when one considers the least-fixedpoint computation outlined in Section 10.3.2. We start with our recursively defined IDB relations empty, and we repeatedly add tuples to them in successive rounds. If adding a tuple in one round could cause us to have to delete a tuple at the next round, then there is the risk of oscillation, and the fixedpoint computation might never converge. In the following examples, we shall see some constructs that are nonmonotone and therefore are outlawed in SQL recursion.

Example 10.33: Figure 10.14 is an implementation of the Datalog rules for the unstratified negation of Example 10.28. There, the rules allowed two different minimal fixedpoints. As expected, the definitions of P and Q in Fig. 10.14 are not monotone. Look at the definition of P in lines (2) through (5) for instance. P depends on Q, with which it is mutually recursive, but adding a tuple to Q can delete a tuple from P. To see why, suppose that R consists of the two tuples (a) and (b), and Q consists of the tuples (a) and (c). Then $P = \{(b)\}$. However, if we add (b) to Q, then P becomes empty. Addition of a tuple to Q has caused the deletion of a tuple from P, so we have a nonmonotone, illegal construct.

This lack of monotonicity leads directly to an oscillating behavior when we try to evaluate the relations P and Q by computing a minimal fixedpoint.[7] For instance, suppose that R has the two tuples $\{(a), (b)\}$. Initially, both P and Q are empty. Thus, in the first round, lines (3) through (5) of Fig. 10.14 compute P to have value $\{(a), (b)\}$. Lines (7) through (9) compute Q to have the same value, since the old, empty value of P is used at line (9).

Now, both R, P, and Q have the value $\{(a), (b)\}$. Thus, on the next round, P and Q are each computed to be empty at lines (3) through (5) and (7) through (9), respectively. On the third round, both would therefore get the value $\{(a), (b)\}$. This process continues forever, with both relations empty on even rounds and $\{(a), (b)\}$ on odd rounds. Therefore, we never obtain clear values for the two relations P and Q from their "definitions" in Fig. 10.14. □

Example 10.34: Aggregation can also lead to nonmonotonicity, although the connection may not be obvious at first. Suppose we have unary (one-attribute) relations P and Q defined by the following two conditions:

1. P is the union of Q and an EDB relation R.

---

[7]When the recursion is not monotone, then the order in which we evaluate the relations in a WITH clause can affect the final answer, although when the recursion is monotone, the result is independent of order. In this and the next example, we shall assume that on each round, P and Q are evaluated "in parallel." That is, the old value of each relation is used to compute the other at each round. See the box on "Using New Values in Fixedpoint Calculations."

2. Q has one tuple that is the sum of the members of P.

We can express these conditions by a WITH statement, although this statement violates the monotonicity requirement of SQL. The query shown in Fig. 10.15 asks for the value of P.

```
1)  WITH
2)      RECURSIVE P(x) AS
3)              (SELECT * FROM R)
4)          UNION
5)              (SELECT * FROM Q),

6)      RECURSIVE Q(x) AS
7)              SELECT SUM(x) FROM P

8)  SELECT * FROM P;
```

Figure 10.15: Nonmonotone query involving aggregation, illegal in SQL

Suppose that R consists of the tuples (12) and (34), and initially P and Q are both empty, as they must be at the beginning of the fixedpoint computation. Figure 10.16 summarizes the values computed in the first six rounds. Recall that we have adopted the strategy that all relations are computed in one round from the values at the previous round. Thus, P is computed in the first round to be the same as R, and Q is empty, since the old, empty value of P is used in line (7).

At the second round, the union of lines (3) through (5) is the set $R = \{(12), (34)\}$, so that becomes the new value of P. The old value of P was the same as the new value, so on the second round $Q = \{(46)\}$. That is, 46 is the sum of 12 and 34.

At the third round, we get $P = \{(12), (34), (46)\}$ at lines (2) through (5). Using the old value of P, $\{(12), (34)\}$, Q is defined by lines (6) and (7) to be

Round	P	Q
1)	$\{(12), (34)\}$	$\emptyset$
2)	$\{(12), (34)\}$	$\{(46)\}$
3)	$\{(12), (34), (46)\}$	$\{(46)\}$
4)	$\{(12), (34), (46)\}$	$\{(92)\}$
5)	$\{(12), (34), (92)\}$	$\{(92)\}$
6)	$\{(12), (34), (92)\}$	$\{(138)\}$

Figure 10.16: Iterative calculation of fixedpoint for a nonmonotone aggregation

Using New Values in Fixedpoint Calculations

One might wonder why we used the old values of P to compute Q in Examples 10.33 and 10.34, rather than the new values of P. If these queries were legal, and we used new values in each round, then the query results might depend on the order in which we listed the definitions of the recursive predicates in the WITH clause. In Example 10.33, P and Q would converge to one of the two possible fixedpoints, depending on the order of evaluation. In Example 10.34, P and Q would still not converge, and in fact they would change at every round, rather than every other round.

$\{(46)\}$ again.

At the fourth round, P has the same value, $\{(12), (34), (46)\}$, but Q gets the value $\{(92)\}$, since 12+34+46=92. Notice that Q has lost the tuple (46), although it gained the tuple (92). That is, adding the tuple (46) to P has caused a tuple (by coincidence the same tuple) to be deleted from Q. That behavior is the nonmonotonicity that SQL prohibits in recursive definitions, confirming that the query of Fig. 10.15 is illegal. In general, at the $2i$th round, P will consist of the tuples (12), (34), and $(46i - 46)$, while Q consists only of the tuple $(46i)$. □

10.4.4 Exercises for Section 10.4

Exercise 10.4.1: In Example 10.23 we discussed a relation

```
SequelOf(movie, sequel)
```

that gives the immediate sequels of a movie. We also defined an IDB relation FollowOn whose pairs (x, y) were movies such that y was either a sequel of x, a sequel of a sequel, or so on.

a) Write the definition of FollowOn as an SQL recursion.

b) Write a recursive SQL query that returns the set of pairs (x, y) such that movie y is a follow-on to movie x, but not a sequel of x.

c) Write a recursive SQL query that returns the set of pairs (x, y) meaning that y is a follow-on of x, but neither a sequel nor a sequel of a sequel.

! d) Write a recursive SQL query that returns the set of movies x that have at least two follow-ons. Note that both could be sequels, rather than one being a sequel and the other a sequel of a sequel.

! e) Write a recursive SQL query that returns the set of pairs (x, y) such that movie y is a follow-on of x but y has at most one follow-on.

Exercise 10.4.2 : In Exercise 10.3.3, we introduced a relation

```
Rel(class, eclass, mult)
```

that describes how one ODL class is related to other classes. Specifically, this relation has tuple (c, d, m) if there is a relation from class c to class d. This relation is multivalued if $m = $ 'multi' and it is single-valued if $m = $ 'single'. We also suggested in Exercise 10.3.3 that it is possible to view Rel as defining a graph whose nodes are classes and in which there is an arc from c to d labeled m if and only if (c, d, m) is a tuple of Rel. Write a recursive SQL query that produces the set of pairs (c, d) such that:

a) There is a path from class c to class d in the graph described above.

* b) There is a path from c to d along which every arc is labeled single.

*! c) There is a path from c to d along which at least one arc is labeled multi.

d) There is a path from c to d but no path along which all arcs are labeled single.

! e) There is a path from c to d along which arc labels alternate single and multi.

f) There are paths from c to d and from d to c along which every arc is labeled single.

10.5   Summary of Chapter 10

✦ *Datalog*: This form of logic allows us to write queries in the relational model. In Datalog, one writes rules in which a head predicate or relation is defined in terms of a body, consisting of subgoals.

✦ *Atoms*: The head and subgoals are each atoms, and an atom consists of an (optionally negated) predicate applied to some number of arguments. Predicates may represent relations or arithmetic comparisons such as $<$.

✦ *IDB and EDB Predicates*: Some predicates correspond to stored relations, and are called EDB (extensional database) predicates or relations. Other predicates, called IDB (intensional database), are defined by the rules. EDB predicates may not appear in rule heads.

✦ *Safe Rules*: We generally restrict Datalog rules to be safe, meaning that every variable in the rule appears in some nonnegated, relational subgoal of the body. Safe rules guarantee that if the EDB relations are finite, then the IDB relations will be finite.

✦ *Relational Algebra and Datalog*: All queries that can be expressed in relational algebra can also be expressed in Datalog. If the rules are safe and nonrecursive, then they define exactly the same set of queries as relational algebra.

✦ *Recursive Datalog*: Datalog rules can be recursive, allowing a relation to be defined in terms of itself. The meaning of recursive Datalog rules without negation is the least fixedpoint: the smallest set of tuples for the IDB relations that makes the heads of the rules exactly equal to what their bodies collectively imply.

✦ *Stratified Negation*: When a recursion involves negation, the least fixedpoint may not be unique, and in some cases there is no acceptable meaning to the Datalog rules. Therefore, uses of negation inside a recursion must be forbidden, leading to a requirement for stratified negation. For rules of this type, there is one (of perhaps several) least fixedpoint that is the generally accepted meaning of the rules.

✦ *SQL Recursive Queries*: In SQL, one can define temporary relations to be used in a manner similar to IDB relations in Datalog. These temporary relations may be used to construct answers to queries recursively.

✦ *Stratification in SQL*: Negations and aggregations involved in an SQL recursion must be monotone, a generalization of the requirement for stratified negation in Datalog. Intuitively, a relation may not be defined, directly or indirectly, in terms of a negation or aggregation of itself.

10.6 References for Chapter 10

Codd introduced a form of first-order logic called *relational calculus* in one of his early papers on the relational model [4]. Relational calculus is an expression language, much like relational algebra, and is in fact equivalent in expressive power to relational algebra, a fact proved in [4].

Datalog, looking more like logical rules, was inspired by the programming language Prolog. Because it allows recursion, it is more expressive than relational calculus. The book [6] originated much of the development of logic as a query language, while [2] placed the ideas in the context of database systems.

The idea that the stratified approach gives the correct choice of fixedpoint comes from [3], although using this approach to evaluating Datalog rules was the independent idea of [1], [8], and [10]. More on stratified negation, on the relationship between relational algebra, Datalog, and relational calculus, and on the evaluation of Datalog rules, with or without negation, can be found in [9].

[7] surveys logic-based query languages. The source of the SQL-99 proposal for recursion is [5].

1. Apt, K. R., H. Blair, and A. Walker, "Towards a theory of declarative knowledge," in *Foundations of Deductive Databases and Logic Programming* (J. Minker, ed.), pp. 89–148, Morgan-Kaufmann, San Francisco, 1988.

2. Bancilhon, F. and R. Ramakrishnan, "An amateur's introduction to recursive query-processing strategies," *ACM SIGMOD Intl. Conf. on Management of Data*, pp. 16–52, 1986.

3. Chandra, A. K. and D. Harel, "Structure and complexity of relational queries," *J. Computer and System Sciences* **25**:1, pp. 99–128.

4. Codd, E. F., "Relational completeness of database sublanguages," in *Database Systems* (R. Rustin, ed.), Prentice Hall, Engelwood Cliffs, NJ, 1972.

5. Finkelstein, S. J., N. Mattos, I. S. Mumick, and H. Pirahesh, "Expressing recursive queries in SQL," ISO WG3 report X3H2–96–075, March, 1996.

6. Gallaire, H. and J. Minker, *Logic and Databases*, Plenum Press, New York, 1978.

7. M. Liu, "Deductive database languages: problems and solutions," *Computing Surveys* **31**:1 (March, 1999), pp. 27–62.

8. Naqvi, S., "Negation as failure for first-order queries," *Proc. Fifth ACM Symp. on Principles of Database Systems*, pp. 114–122, 1986.

9. Ullman, J. D., *Principles of Database and Knowledge-Base Systems, Volume I*, Computer Science Press, New York, 1988.

10. Van Gelder, A., "Negation as failure using tight derivations for general logic programs," in *Foundations of Deductive Databases and Logic Programming* (J. Minker, ed.), pp. 149–176, Morgan-Kaufmann, San Francisco, 1988.

Index